West To Far Michigan

West To Far Michigan

Settling the Lower Peninsula, 1815–1860

Kenneth E. Lewis

Michigan State University Press

East Lansing

∞The paper used in this publication meets the minimum requirements of ANSI/NISO Z39.48–1992 (R 1997) (Permanence of Paper).

Michigan State University Press
East Lansing, Michigan 48823–5202
Printed and bound in the United States of America.

08 07 06 05 04 03 02   1 2 3 4 5 6 7 8 9 10

LIBRARY OF CONGRESS CATALOGING-IN-PUBLICATION DATA

Lewis, Kenneth E.
    West to far Michigan : settling the Lower Peninsula, 1815–1860 /
Kenneth E. Lewis.
        p. cm.
Includes bibliographical references and index.
    ISBN 0–87013–551–1 (cloth : alk. paper)
    1. Land tenure—Michigan—Lower Peninsula—History—19th century. 2. Land settlement—Michigan—
Lower Peninsula—History—19th century. 3.Land settlement patterns—Michigan—Lower Peninsula—
History—19th century. 4. Agricultural colonies—Michigan—Lower Peninsula—History—19th century.
5. Indians of North America—Land tenure—Michigan—Lower Peninsula—History—19th century.
6. Lower Peninsula (Mich.) —History—19th century. 7. Michigan—History—19th century.   I. Title.
    HD211.M5 L49 2002
    333.3'09774—dc21

                                                                                        2001003823

Cover design by Sharp Des!gn
Book design by Michael Brooks

Visit Michigan State University Press on the World Wide Web at:
www.msupress.msu.edu

*For Carolyn, without whose encouragement
this work would not have been possible*

Contents

   Landscapes, Settlement Patterning, and Frontiers

   Processes of Frontier Colonization

   Settlement Patterning on the Michigan Frontier

       Production and Spatial Organization

       Transportation and Spatial Patterning

       Settlement Patterning and Organization

   The Distinctness of Colonization in Southern Michigan

   The European Presence

   The Aboriginal Response

   Political Change in the Old Northwest

   The Pacification of Aboriginal Peoples

   A Knowledge of the Regional Landscape

   The Entrepôt of Detroit

   Routes of Access to the Michigan Frontier

   The Rise of the Northeast and Western Expansion

   The Orientation of Frontier Perspective

   The Physical Landscape

Figures

CHAPTER 7

CHAPTER 9

Tables

Abbreviations

AFC	Allcott Family Correspondence
AP	Alphadelphia Papers
ASP/IA	American State Papers, Indian Affairs
ASP/MA	American State Papers, Military Affairs
ASP/M	American State Papers, Miscellaneous
ASP/PL	American State Papers, Public Lands
BHP	Bela Hubbard Papers
CFL	Clover Flanders Letters
CFP	Chamberlain Family Papers
CHL	Clark Historical Library, Mt. Pleasant, Michigan
DFC	Dibble Family Correspondence
DLPP	David L. Porter Papers
DMP	Denison-McOmber Papers
DWC	Dorothy Waage Collection
EHC	Mr. and Mrs. Emor Hice Collection
EMCP	Elizabeth Margaret Chandler Papers
ETBC	Edwin T. Brown Collection
FFC	Fay Family Correspondence
FLPP	Franklin Leonidas Parker Papers
GNSP	George Nelson Smith Papers
GSML	General Sanford Memorial Library, Sanford, Florida
HD	U.S. House of Representatives, Documents
HED	U.S. House of Representatives, Executive Documents
HFL	Hall Family Letters
HFP	Halbert Family Papers
HHCP	Henry Howland Crapo Papers

HHL	Hannah Hinckley Letters
HPSP	Henry Parker Smith Papers
HR	U.S. House of Representatives, Reports
HSC	Harris Seymour Correspondence
HSSP	Henry Shelton Sanford Papers
HWFP	Hall and Wilcox Family Papers
HWP	Henry Waldron Papers
JCGD	Joshua C. Goodrich Diary
JCL	Jane Comstock Letter
JFFC	Joshua Fay Family Correspondence
JGP	Jacob Gerrish Papers
JRL	James Rogers Letter
JSP	Jonathan Searles Papers
KFP	Kenny Family Papers
LACC	L. A. Chase Collection
LHL	Lovira Hart Letters
LSCC	Lutheria Stoner Crandell Collection
MAL/L	*Michigan, Acts of the Legislature, Acts*
MAL/R	*Michigan, Acts of the Legislature, Resolutions*
MCC	Michigan, Cass Code
MDNRIILC	Michigan, Department of Natural Resources, Internal Improvement Land Certificates
MEA	Michigan, Executive Acts
MHC	Michigan Historical Collections, University of Michigan, Ann Arbor
MPHC	*Michigan Pioneer and Historical Collections*
MJC	Mildred Jones Collection
MLCLB	Michigan, Laws Compiled by the Legislative Board
MLCLC	Michigan, Laws Compiled by the Legislative Council
MLSL	Mrs. M. L. Sanford Letters
MREOCAONMS	Michigan, Records of the Executive Office, Correspondence, Affairs Outside, National, Michigan Senators

MSASR	Michigan, State Agricultural Society Records
MSBA	Michigan, State Board of Agriculture
MSUAHC	Michigan State University Archives and History Collections, East Lansing
MTL	Michigan, Territorial Laws
NMTAB	N. M. Thomas Account Book
NTP	Nathan Thomas Papers
OWD	O'Shea Wilder Diary
ORN	Obadiah Rogers Notebook
PaFP	Parsons Family Papers
PFP	Powell Family Papers
PSC	Pierpont Smith Correspondence
SAM	State Archives of Michigan, Lansing
SBSFC	Stanley-Barney-Smith Family Correspondence
SED	U.S. Senate, Executive Documents
SFP	Stebbins Family Papers
SHFP	Samuel H. Fulton Papers
SLUS	*Statutes at Large of the United States*
SMD	U.S. Senate, Miscellaneous Documents
SR	U.S. Senate, Reports
SRes	U.S. Senate, Resolutions
TAL	Thomas Andrews Letters
TPUS/MT	Territorial Papers of the United States, Territory of Michigan
TPUS/NWT	Territorial Papers of the United States, Territory Northwest of the Ohio River
TWD	Thomas Wright Diary
WMUARHC	Western Michigan University Archives and Regional History Collections, Kalamazoo

Acknowledgments

I undertook this study of agricultural colonization in southern Michigan because the story of this process, so critical to understanding the region's history, had not been adequately told. Although many factors influenced the course of Michigan's past, the spread of agricultural settlement and the changes it introduced during the first half of the nineteenth century played a singular role in shaping the modern state. As perhaps the most significant component of the antebellum American economy, agricultural production underwrote western expansion and transformed an aboriginal landscape into one harnessed to the needs of the larger society that directed its growth. The task of describing and analyzing so broad a process posed many questions that led in numerous directions and required the assistance of people in many fields. At long last I am now able to acknowledge their contributions to my efforts.

Central to historical research are the repositories of documents, both official and private, that chronicled the spread of American settlement in antebellum Michigan and the development of colonial economy and society. I wish to thank the staff members of the State Archives of Michigan, the Library of Michigan, the Bentley Historical Library of the University of Michigan, the Clark Historical Library of Central Michigan University, the Western Michigan University Archives and Regional History Collections, the Michigan State University Archives and History Collections, and the General Sanford Memorial Library. I am particularly indebted to LeRoy Barnett, Dorothy Frye, Richard Hathaway, William Mulligan, Wayne Mann, and Frederick L. Honhart for their interest and assistance with the material in their collections.

My research also benefited from discussions with colleagues, whose ideas and information contributed to my understanding of this multifaceted topic, and whose reading of portions of the manuscript helped clarify its content. I wish to thank LeRoy Barnett, Thomas Beauvais, Elton Bruins, Jay Climo, Margaret Holman, Victor Howard, John Houdek, Iwao Ishino, Carolyn B. Lewis, Michael J. Lipsey, Fred V. Nurnberger, Terry Shafer, Susan Sleeper-Smith, Joseph Spielberg, and Paul Trap for their help over the years. Research always draws from previous scholarship, and I am indebted to David M. Ellis for permission to use data from his *Michigan Postal History* to construct maps of antebellum settlement flow. Graydon Meints's unpublished manuscript on Michigan railroad construction helped greatly in tracing the growth of transportation networks in the state.

Support for beginning this study was provided by an All University Research Initiation Grant from Michigan State University, and a College of Social Science, Faculty Initiatives Fund Grant from the same institution provided funding for the illustrations to accompany the text. Frank J.

Krist employed a geographic information system to analyze the spatial variables used to estimate settlement spread in chapter 9. Leslie Riegler and he produced the maps and other graphics appearing throughout the book. The Department of Anthropology at Michigan State University provided me with assistance in carrying out documentary research, and I thank Rene Somora for his diligence in carrying out this work.

Although crucial to preparing a manuscript for publication, the task of editing rarely receives due credit. I owe a great debt to Keith Widder of the MSU Press for his tireless efforts in helping me transform my original study into its present form. LeRoy Barnett graciously agreed to read the manuscript, and its final version benefited greatly from his broad knowledge of Michigan's history as well as his cartographic expertise.

Finally, my deepest thanks are due my wife Carolyn for the support she has given me throughout the preparation of this work. I appreciate her assistance in collecting archival information as well as her sharing of material acquired for her own research. Our many discussions of substantive issues and her critique of my writing almost always improved both my arguments and their presentation. In spite of setbacks and many personal tragedies that occurred during this time, she never let me lose faith in the feasibility of its completion. I dedicate this book to her.

1

Frontier Studies
An Approach to Michigan's Past

Traveling across the southern portion of Michigan's Lower Peninsula, one encounters a largely rural landscape. Farms and small- to medium-sized towns lie scattered over a gently rolling to occasionally hilly countryside intersected by meandering rivers leading to the shores of surrounding lakes. Only where recent urban and suburban growth has overtaken agriculture is this pattern obscured. The roads, highways, and railway network that link Michigan's towns and cities are also part of the cultural landscape, binding settlements inextricably together in a manner that suggests both historical continuity and change.

Much of Michigan's past is preserved in the form of material objects; the buildings, fields, transportation routes, industrial sites, and other artifacts created by people who once lived and worked on the land. Many structures, like the well-preserved courthouses at Berrien Springs and Lapeer, may be placed in a specific historical context. On the other hand, the domestic buildings of so many villages, hiding under later additions and encrusted with worn layers of siding, provide the untrained eye with few clues about their past. Road patterns often prompt questions with no immediate answers. Why does U.S. 12 meander across the southern part of the state, missing many of its prominent communities, while I-94 connects Detroit with a line of major cities? Why do many section roads seem to lead nowhere? All of these elements are part of Michigan's cultural landscape, yet our inability to always comprehend them suggests that their roles and meanings have changed despite their continued use.

The present differs from the past but grew out of it, and the modern landscape is shaped by the nature and arrangement of activities over time, especially those associated with the dominant features of a region's economy. Commercial agriculture shaped contemporary southern Michigan. Its landscape is tangible evidence of the process by which American immigrants occupied the region and converted its land to farms. This experience took place between 1815 and 1860 and witnessed the dispersal of aboriginal peoples, the influx of a diverse new population, and the creation of an export-oriented agricultural economy that formed the basis of the state's economy. The landscape created by colonization is a cumulative record of its development and holds the key to understanding Michigan's past, as well as its impact on the present.[1]

This study reconstructs the history of southern Lower Michigan by investigating how frontier settlement created its historical landscape. Agricultural colonization is a process of change common to many regions, although always influenced by conditions more or less distinct to its time and place. An examination of Michigan's development as a consequence of this process differs from traditional approaches to Michigan's formative history that have focused on the uniqueness of events without regard to causes that underlay their occurrence and which may hold the key to their explanation. Because agricultural settlement lacks the romance of the fur trade, the drama of the Indian wars, or the excitement of modern industrial development, it has often been treated as little more than a transition between these larger, more important things. Despite its significance in shaping the destiny of the region, Michigan's agricultural frontier and the process that created it remain largely ignored.

More than eighty years ago, George N. Fuller, one of Michigan's preeminent historians, argued persuasively that the key to comprehending Michigan's modern history lies in the nature of agricultural colonization. He based his conclusions on an examination of the territorial period, from 1815 to 1837, a time that witnessed the spread of American settlement across southern Lower Michigan and the creation of a pioneer economy. Fuller wove a story that demonstrated the link between such diverse factors as the environment, the historical relationships with native peoples, the development of technology, and the direction and nature of Michigan's colonization. His work emphasized the importance of an integrated approach to understanding this crucial phase of the state's history and the need to employ it in examining the relationship between a historical process and the landscapes it creates.[2]

Although Fuller's work is largely forgotten, his assertions remain valid. This study will build upon them, using additional evidence and new methodologies to demonstrate how colonization produced patterns of settlement that influenced the form of pioneer Michigan. It will carry the story forward into the early years of statehood, during which time economic and social forces transformed the frontier to create the new landscape in which the modern state arose. This transition, as profound as that which preceded it, completed the process of colonization and played a crucial role in Michigan's genesis.

Because Michigan's colonization paralleled that of other agricultural regions, its landscape shared characteristics deriving from the common process that underlay their development. Particular historical factors, however, also played a significant role in its settlement. Establishing a colony and securing its survival depended on attracting potential settlers, effectively evaluating the potential of land and resources, transferring their control to immigrant farmers, and developing strategies for successful colonization. These variables influenced the colonization process to create a frontier economy that set the stage for subsequent change. Integration within the national economy required that frontier institutions be altered to accommodate a more complex marketing system. Changes in the technology of transportation, agriculture, and the structure of finance and marketing worked to create a new infrastructure of production and trade. Crucial to the consolidation of the Michigan frontier, these factors helped direct its emergence as a commercial producer for national markets.

LANDSCAPES, SETTLEMENT PATTERNING, AND FRONTIERS

The study of landscape as a product of human activities is an important key to the past. Being the arrangement of things on a portion of the earth's surface, cultural landscapes are a spatial manifestation of the relations between a human population and its environment, and contain concrete elements of both natural and human origin. Although the form, composition, and distribution of landscape elements are clearly a result of utilitarian adaptations, they are also influenced by social organization and its ideology. A cultural landscape is an expression of multiple facets of the society responsible for its creation. Because of this quality and its regional scope, such a landscape is a vast, sweeping medium in which to examine the role and significance of settlements within their larger milieu. Its elements do not remain static, and a landscape is continually evolving. Its form reveals its current content as well as a record of what has gone before. The cultural landscape is a material legacy of a region's history, composed of material traces in space that form a repository of information about development and the forces that propelled change.[3]

Central to the discussion of landscape is the concept of region. As a portion of space defined on the basis of its characteristics, the size and boundaries of a region are determined arbitrarily and vary with the nature and scale of the phenomena under study. A frontier region encompasses the area in which pioneer settlement is contemplated or under way, and this characteristic sets it apart from surrounding regions. Southern Lower Michigan's regional boundaries were delineated by environmental, social, and political variables that limited agricultural colonization and defined it as a distinct area. Regions defined on other criteria differ in size and extent. Within Lower Michigan, an examination of smaller-scale processes occurring in circumscribed space dictates the use of more restricted regions. The economic sphere of a town, the customer base of a mill, or the extent of a crop's cultivation encompass only parts of an area of colonization. Similarly, regions based on organization of the antebellum American economy might include all frontiers collectively as components of this larger system. In this study, the definition of a region is based on the context in which the term is used.[4]

The dominant aspect of a landscape is the patterning of its settlement. This refers not only to its distribution but also to the functions of settlements and their relationships with one another. Because such patterning is a result of the spatial organization of human activities and the manner in which they are integrated, its form can reveal economic, social, and political interaction within a region as well as an explanation of its organization. Settlement patterning is also a product of earlier occupations, and its form and content reflect a region's historical development. Just as factors of the physical environment influence where people live, work, travel, and engage in all of the other endeavors that constitute human activities, so do the previous distribution of settlements and the layout of networks of trade and communication that link them together. We must delineate and explain the historical development of its patterns of settlement over time to understand the present landscape.[5]

Because changing settlement patterns are expressed through the evolving distribution of various spatial phenomena, this study must rely heavily on graphic evidence to examine Michigan's development. A substantial number of maps will be employed to analyze the spread of population, the growth of transportation networks, and the development of settlement hierarchies in antebellum Michigan. These maps provide a visual statement of colonization in regional context, as well as a spatial perspective by which to analyze those factors that have shaped Michigan's historical landscape.

The process responsible for the development of settlement patterning in Lower Michigan is one associated with agricultural settlement in regions undergoing colonial expansion. Such regions, known as frontiers, represent areas of recent occupation wherethe outer edge of an expanding society adapts to the conditions of attenuated contact with the homeland, the physical conditions of a new environment, the response of indigenous peoples to their presence, and the influence of competing colonial nations. Because of the nature of expansion, the frontier is both spatially and temporally impermanent. It is a zone of transition in which the "wilderness" is occupied and "civilized." Because colonists must repeat their adaptation as the frontier incorporates new lands, the process of colonization follows an evolutionary sequence in the sense that the pattern of change that once occurred at the center of a newly settled area is later repeated along its periphery. A frontier is the region where settlement occurs as well as the adaptive process by which colonists establish themselves. Although all frontiers follow a common pattern of change, distinctive physical and social factors make the form and extent of each frontier unique and influence the rate by which it is transformed into an integral part of the larger economy.[6]

The frontier process also recognizes changes in the form and organization of the colony as it expands in area and achieves greater levels of economic complexity. Growth and development alter patterns of settlement, causing individual settlements to be founded, to grow, and to change. Many decline and some are abandoned as their roles become obsolete or are taken over by others more auspiciously situated. The location, function, and interconnectedness of settlements reflect the organization of the frontier region and its change over time. These three aspects of patterning are related directly to the process of agricultural colonization and can reveal its role in the development of Lower Michigan.

PROCESSES OF FRONTIER COLONIZATION

An understanding of agricultural colonization as a general phenomenon is central to this study because it provides a context in which to examine and evaluate the colonization of Michigan. In its broadest sense, this process played an integral part in the expansion of Europe that began in the fifteenth century, and the westward growth of the United States manifested its significance three hundred years later. Agricultural colonization in Lower Michigan was not an isolated episode in history, and it exhibited characteristics comparable to those found in instances of expansion elsewhere. The Michigan frontier was an integrated regional system linked to an external economy, and the patterning of its settlement was affected by the conditions encountered in newly settled areas. Within the broader context of this system, regional conditions distinctive to the time and place of its occupation required further adaptations. Although Michigan's frontier development was similar to that of other areas undergoing agricultural colonization, its historical uniqueness must also be considered.[7]

Michigan's colonization, which occurred between 1815 and 1860, arose from the economic milieu created by the integration of the New World into a capitalist world economy, whose structure was defined by the linkages and exchanges that bound its geographic components together on a global scale. The economy's size prevented domination by a single nation and created an inherent instability that encouraged competition and fostered continual expansion. Because the success of the world economy depended on growth, settlement processes played a significant role in its development.[8]

The core states of Europe dominated the world economy, the hierarchical organization of which was based on a geographical division of the labor involved in production. This structure situated lower-ranking economies in peripheral areas, closer to the system's boundaries. Here less well rewarded labor worked to furnish necessary raw commodities, which could then be exchanged for finished goods. Although the peripheral position of British North America determined the nature of colonial production, its geographical isolation also gave rise to a semiperipheral area on the northern Atlantic Seaboard in the eighteenth century. Lying between periphery and core, this region played the role of a commercial intermediary and political buffer, which permitted it to develop as the focus of the early American economy.[9]

The growth of the European world economy hinged on the development of a capitalist mode of production. Capitalism attempted to increase productivity through the reorganization of labor under increasingly unified management and the introduction of more efficient manufacturing technology. Growing production required the development of new markets, the acquisition of which encouraged the expansion of European trade and the domination of foreign networks of exchange. The flexibility of capitalist production also permitted exchange with noncapitalist economies, such as those of native North America. The unequal power relationship, however, created working arrangements that insured the siphoning off of wealth and people for the benefit of the core.[10]

Economic interests in the core states found it advantageous to expand the limits of the global economy to encompass new resources and develop the means to produce them. Exploitation of resources on the periphery, coupled with continual improvement in the organization and technology of production, increased both productivity and the accumulation of capital. Expansion into new regions, such as the North American interior, helped avoid crises of overproduction and the decline of investment opportunities. It also opened or enlarged markets for core-produced goods and provided opportunities for capital investment in undeveloped areas.[11]

The successful operation of the world economy relied on the establishment of political domination over foreign territories as well as routes of trade and communication, and Great Britain's substantial investment in its American provinces, backed by naval and military power, provided the stability required to protect settlers and nurture colonial economic development. British authority underwrote production and insured the availability of commodities crucial to the operation of its far-flung economy. State political influence made possible the settlement expansion that accompanied the economic penetration of the American interior, and its presence became integral to the colonization of the Great Lakes region.[12]

The economic emphasis of colonization shaped the form of settlement on the frontier because variation in the nature of production encouraged the development of distinctive settlement systems. Production requirements affected the number of interacting links connecting the colony and homeland and determined the "insularity" between the two regions. Insularity, in turn, governed the degree of change experienced by a colonial society. Fewer and more tenuous

links increased the insularity of the colony and required more profound adaptations in its economic structure and organization. Two types of frontiers emerged as a result of differences in
insularity.

"Cosmopolitan" frontiers shared the least insularity, because the success of their specialized economies tied them closely to the policies of the parent state. Direct manipulation of the
colony's activities left few opportunities for indigenous development and resulted in little alteration of economic, political, or social forms. These frontiers changed only in response to the
development of more efficient production technologies or shifts in market demand for
exports, and their existence could be cut short if production costs exceeded their products'
value. Cosmopolitan frontiers often involved extensive activities such as lumbering, mining,
cattle ranching, and trading.[13]

Although the establishment of a cosmopolitan frontier involved economic, social, and
political processes distinct from those of agricultural settlement, it provided a secure base for
intensive economic development when favorable conditions arose. A cosmopolitan frontier
brought about regular contact and trade between the parent state and the colony, created a permanent entrepôt in the region, amassed knowledge of resources and geography in the new
country, and resulted in the pacification or displacement of its aboriginal inhabitants.
Although these conditions, in themselves, did not bring about intensive frontier colonization,
they nevertheless shaped the landscape in which it developed and must be taken into consideration when modeling this process. In examining colonization in Lower Michigan we must
consider the nature of preceding cosmopolitan frontier activities that established the initial
base for settlement.

Colonization usually passed through a series of progressively more intensive phases ranging from intermittent contact and low investment to permanent settlement and finally incorporation within the homeland economy. As colonization progressed, commercial investment
increased, supported by military and missionary activities to pacify the region and establish a
dominant intrusive presence. Core states incorporated aboriginal production into colonial
economic networks and usually disrupted or decimated local populations. These events set the
stage for the fundamental economic changes associated with more intensive settlement.
Because the greater intensity of agricultural production offered strong economic incentives for
adoption, compared to more extensive and specialized strategies, a shift to farming became
almost inevitable if conditions permitted. Permanent settlement, accompanied by economic
diversification, indigenous institutional development and reinvestment, and expansion into
new territories, brought a shift of social, economic, and political interests from the homeland
to the colony and fostered the region's potential for independent development.[14]

The resulting "insular" frontiers possessed more diverse economies and depended less on
specialized production for export. Their success rested on extensive adaptations to local conditions and relied less on links to homeland markets. Consequently, such ties became fewer and
more indirect. Insular frontier residents turned to developing indigenous resources and reinvested surpluses locally, reducing their dependence on outside support. These practices led to
pervasive political and social changes, and sometimes brought colonists into competition with

producers in the parent state. Colonists' reliance on regional adaptations also introduced a certain amount of variation in the insular frontier process, and environmental, economic, technological, political, and social factors often influenced the use of land and the form settlement. The economies of insular frontiers generally rested on agricultural production by farmers and managers of settlement plantations and attracted immigrants seeking permanent residence in the colony.[15]

Insular frontier colonization brought about the settlement of Lower Michigan in the first half of the nineteenth century. Like other regions unsuitable for the production of specialized commodities with ready export markets, it did not attract the large-scale investment of capital and industrialized production technology. Instead, agricultural commodities capable of being grown efficiently on a small scale dominated production, and the family-sized farm was the primary unit of production. Lower requirements of capital outlay and managerial expertise served as powerful inducements for immigration. Resident settlers engaged in diversified agricultural production that reduced expenditures for imports to the mother country and reinvested funds in the real assets of the colony. These trends encouraged internal economic diversification and the rapid spread of production, altering Michigan's colonial economy and creating a new cultural landscape.[16]

SETTLEMENT PATTERNING ON THE MICHIGAN FRONTIER

Michigan's colonization witnessed the process of insular frontier change played out in the context of a particular time and place. To understand the landscape it produced, we must first examine the nature of this process. Michigan's peripheral economic position influenced the nature of production, limited the capacity of its transportation system, and affected the organization of its regional economy. These factors, in turn, determined the layout and nature of activities and settlements, which constituted the central elements of this landscape. The distribution, interconnectedness, and function of its settlements produced a patterning that grew out of Michigan's role as an agricultural frontier.

Production and Spatial Organization

In frontier Michigan, as in other peripheral regions of the world economy, the expense of transportation to eastern markets determined the relative value of land, resources, and labor, and limited production to lower-cost, raw commodities. As the cost of transport increased with the distance from the market, the profitability of economic activities declined and affected land value and use. Economic distance concentrated the highest rent-yielding activities around the market and placed those of increasingly lesser value increasingly farther away from it. Consequently, the production of grain and other extensively grown crops came to characterize agriculture in Michigan and other frontiers of the Old Northwest.[17]

Agriculture in frontier Michigan developed as conditions altered the economic distance to outside markets. Increasing demand and accompanying rises in price extended the distance at which crops could be profitably grown, and the growth of transport capacity through advances in technology lowered the rate at which shipping income decreased by distance. These factors became mutually reinforcing. Greater market demand provided capital and incentive to invest in expansion and technological improvement in transportation. Similarly, cheaper transport led to a growing need for consumer goods on the frontier, which increased urban employment, raised wages, and brought about greater market demand for agricultural products. Increased consumption encouraged the expansion of frontier agriculture to enlarge supplies, resulting in continuous pressure to expand production. Over time, Michigan's production grew and changed in response to the region's role in the national economy.[18]

Transportation and Spatial Patterning

As a crucial variable in insular frontier expansion, Michigan's transportation network provided an evolving spatial framework for production. Its ability to accommodate shipment influenced the nature of commodities, but the need to adjust to increased traffic in the face of rising demand promoted expansion and the adoption of more efficient methods and technologies. Improvements in transportation helped overcome the fluctuations of rapid and uneven frontier growth.[19]

A network of roads and water routes, and later railroads, bound together frontier settlements and tied Michigan with the Eastern Seaboard. By assuming a dendritic form centered on the entrepôt of Detroit, this network provided access to all parts of the expanding colonial area, using the fewest routes to cover the least total distance and facilitate the most direct movement of trade. Ann Arbor, Jackson, Kalamazoo, and other key centers of colonial production and trade arose along the transportation network. These settlements served as internal markets, whose functions reflected the structure of the transportation and changed in response to alterations in its network over time.[20]

Michigan's transportation network and the settlement system it served evolved as the frontier expanded. Dependence on Detroit as an entrepôt conditioned early growth and created a geographical insularity that initially discouraged external connections and focused trade inward. Interior transportation routes dominated exchange, terminating at secondary settlements that become centers of feeder networks. The penetration of commercial trade in the 1840s and the growing importance of export markets altered the nature of transportation on the frontier. An emphasis on external commerce encouraged innovations in transportation with direct links between Detroit and regional centers such as Adrian, Pontiac, and Grand Rapids to accommodate the disproportionately greater traffic between these major points. The new network of trade and communications underwrote changes in production and land use to accommodate increasing demand from commercial markets, and marked the closing of the frontier.[21]

Settlement Patterning and Organization

In Michigan and other frontier regions, people attempted to organize settlements and activities to achieve the most efficient use of available resources. The resulting patterning is evidenced by the distribution of settlements, their functions, and the structure of the transportation system that connected them. Settlement patterning was conditioned by the need to occupy an extensive, largely undeveloped area; establish an economic base capable of growing, processing, shipping, and marketing agricultural products; and implement social and political structures capable of supporting the frontier economy. Such patterning encompassed consisted of a hierarchy of functionally different settlements that formed a "colonization gradient," observable in the distinctive roles of individual places or in the changing function of individual settlements over time.[22]

The nature of Michigan's frontier settlements arose from the low density of the colonial population. A few urban places combined the economic, political, and social functions normally distributed among many lower-level settlements. The entrepôt stood at the apex of the settlement hierarchy. Detroit was the central market, the terminus of the regional transportation network, the principal link to the eastern states, and the major port of entry. It contained the central political, social, and religious institutions and served as the colonial capital.[23]

Frontier towns, such as Howell, Marshall, and Grand Rapids, became centers of internal trade and communications and provided links to interior settlements. These towns occupied central locations in the dendritic transportation network, and immigrants passed through them on their way from the entrepôt. As principal collection, processing, and redistribution centers, frontier towns dominated the colonial economy and were the region's largest settlements. They often possessed some form of municipal government and housed vital social and political functions. Many served as regional administrative centers and housed branches of wider institutions, including courts, jails, churches, banks, land offices, fairs, markets, and entertainment facilities.[24]

Nucleated settlements were smaller secondary marketing and administrative centers situated at key points along routes emanating from frontier towns. Some, such as Dexter, Albion, Schoolcraft, and Bellevue, served as smaller markets and often possessed centralizing institutions, such as churches and schools. Others, like Hillsdale, Charlotte, and Hastings, also played a political role as court seats. Smaller, more geographically dispersed, seminucleated settlements served as minor points of exchange and occasionally contained social or political activities normally centered in nearby nucleated settlements. Because settlements such as Hudson, DeWitt, and Yankee Springs possessed no permanent integrating institutions, they carried out these functions only irregularly.[25]

Dispersed farms were the smallest and most numerous form of frontier habitation, constituting the source of the colony's production as well as the initial form of frontier land occupancy. The web of roads and trails that formed the transportation network linked them to seminucleated settlements, nucleated settlements, and frontier towns, making farms an integral component of the frontier economy. Lacking political and social functions beyond the household, they remained the least thoroughly integrated with larger colonial institutions.[26]

The need to organize settlement components around the production of wheat and other grains shaped settlement patterning in Michigan and other insular frontier regions. Marketing agricultural commodities required a hierarchically arranged network connecting individual settlements in which produce from a wide hinterland could be collected, processed centrally, and redistributed. The nature and technology of grain production had to accommodate a bulky, weighty, and perishable commodity that required complex processing. As a frontier devoted to grain farming, Michigan contained a large number of nucleated and seminucleated settlements, relatively evenly distributed and connected by a complex transportation network.[27]

Michigan experienced a change in settlement distribution in response to population growth and increased interaction. Initially a small number of pioneers had access to a large area of land and situated themselves to take advantage of environmental variation and access to markets. By the mid-1820s, widely dispersed settlements lay across the peninsula. Continued immigration resulted in an increase in overall settlement density, but left many areas, such as Michigan's central forest lands, vacant as immigrants sought areas they perceived better-suited to the production and shipment of crops. As agricultural population density approached its limits in the 1850s, competition for remaining vacant areas created a more even distribution of settlement. At the same time, increased competition among settlements for a share in the growing internal market promoted the success of Grand Rapids, Kalamazoo, and others advantageously situated and forced less efficient producers and poorly placed economic centers into decline.[28]

A growing population, an expanding production base, a developing hierarchy of marketing centers connected by an expanding network of roads and rail routes, and an increasingly complex administrative structure brought about changes that marked Michigan's emergence from its peripheral status in the world economy. This transformation was accompanied by the growing complexity and increasing interdependence of many settlements as a result of changing regional economic organization. Grand Rapids, Jackson, Kalamazoo, and others acquired new economic functions and differed markedly in size and demography from their colonial counterparts. Some older frontier centers, such as Adrian and Ann Arbor, retained their earlier importance in the transitional period, while Ionia, Niles and others, assumed lesser roles. Detroit continued as the region's central settlement and entrepôt, but a restructuring of trade and communications networks altered its relationship to interior settlements and permitted Lansing to usurp its political role. Although a level of regional organization comparable to that of older agricultural regions emerged by 1860, Michigan's settlement patterning had been shaped by its frontier development. In this sense, the colonial experience continued to influence the region's future.[29]

THE DISTINCTNESS OF COLONIZATION IN SOUTHERN MICHIGAN

Because the insular frontier process deals with patterning and change cross-culturally to account for regularities in the evolution of large regional landscapes, it provides a means of explaining the structure of agricultural colonization in southern Michigan, as well as a framework within which to investigate distinctive aspects of its development. Historical circumstances particular to the time and place of Michigan's colonization also influenced the creation of the frontier landscape. We must examine specific factors that affected settlement patterning to explain its specific form.[30]

Although nineteenth-century economic growth and political expansion clearly produced the agricultural frontier in southern Lower Michigan, it occurred in a region already modified by earlier colonization. A century-and-a-half of European competition to gain strategic influence and acquire resources, the adaptations by native peoples to the shifting economic and political milieu created by the newcomers' presence, and the accommodation of both groups to one another's interests had created a distinctive landscape by the beginning of the nineteenth century. These conditions established parameters for the American entry into Lower Michigan and influenced both the form and direction of settlement after 1815. Michigan's pioneer economy developed in the wake of cosmopolitan frontier activity in the Great Lakes, and its history cannot be divorced from the landscape created by this earlier interaction.

The time and circumstances of Michigan's settlement helped shape the insular frontier process and influence the patterning of settlement. The environment and its perception by pioneers helped determine assessments of land suitability and use and affected the direction and extent of colonization. Aboriginal peoples initially controlled all territory occupied, and the manner in which the United States acquired it from them and subsequently transferred it to immigrants also shaped the form of settlement. Although production and marketing in a peripheral region affected the nature of the frontier economy, rapid and profound innovations in antebellum technology and transportation worked to alter the regional economic structure and promote change. Diverse motivations for colonization brought immigrants to Michigan and, together with various strategies they devised to insure success, further influenced the direction and rate of settlement in the new country. Between 1815 and 1860, the operation of all of these particular factors helped produce southern Michigan's distinctive landscape.

2

Michigan before 1815
Prelude to American Settlement

The year 1815 marked a watershed in Michigan's history, as it brought to a close the War of 1812 and the British threat to American immigration in the Old Northwest. These events precipitated a rapid transition of the region's economy from the specialized fur trade with native peoples for natural resources to the production of agricultural staples by resident colonists. These two forms of colonization differed markedly, and the transformation from one to the other occasioned a discontinuity in the region's development. American settlement, however, was not unaffected by the region's past. Previous European colonial activity left its mark on the Great Lakes area, affecting its inhabitants and resources profoundly and creating a landscape that influenced subsequent development. This landscape reflected the struggle by the core states of Europe for hegemony and control of regional resources, as well as the responses of indigenous peoples to the European presence.

The European Presence

The economic strategies of the European states that sought political hegemony in North America shaped Michigan's early colonial history, and the manner of their overseas expansion reflected the position of each in the European world economy. The Spanish voyages to the New World in the closing years of the fifteenth century marked the beginning of transatlantic exploration and brought the northern coast of North America under the scrutiny of the Netherlands, England, and France, all of which had developed strong maritime economies and possessed centers of fishing and coastal trade. The fishing grounds in the North Atlantic offered both wealth and vast territories whose resources might be exploited.[1]

The defeat of the Spanish Armada by England in 1588 opened the Atlantic trade to northern European nations and marked the emergence of England as a sea power. England's dominant role in the expansion of northern Europe had strong implications for the direction of North American colonization. In England, a sharp population increase during the sixteenth century, brought about by natural increase and in-migration of skilled European labor and made acute by the dislocation and impoverishment of rural populations and a massive increase in urban unemployment, also affected the nature of colonization. Overseas resettlement provided a fortuitous means of alleviating an unwanted consequence of economic growth, and distinguished England's colonies from those of other core nations in the European world economy.[2]

France also emerged as a contender in the expanding world economy, but its failure to develop an integrated national economy prevented it from rivaling its northern European neighbors in the seventeenth century. A centralized political organization instead provided the structure for overseas expansion and affected both the form and nature of colonization in North America. France did not actively promote settlement colonization, and emigration remained an unorganized and haphazard affair that never came close to the levels experienced by the English.[3]

The economic impetus for colonization along the northern Atlantic Seaboard grew out of the fur trade. Furs attracted the attention of French, English, and Dutch interests and brought together conflicting forces that shaped the development of the Great Lakes region. By the sixteenth century the fur-bearing animal populations in Europe and Russia had declined, but the increased prices of furs maintained by high demand rewarded those who brought new sources of furs into market. Early European explorations in North America revealed the presence of fur-bearing animals as well as aboriginal peoples with whom a lucrative trade in furs might be established. Demand for furs made North America a region of potential colonization for Europeans capable of assembling and organizing the economic resources necessary for such an undertaking.[4]

French explorations along the coast and into the interior along the St. Lawrence River made the Europeans aware of the region's potential as a source of furs and established a precedent for acquiring furs through trade with aboriginal peoples who possessed the knowledge and skills to collect and process fur pelts to exchange for European finished goods. The Indians' central role in the fur trade characterized this cosmopolitan frontier activity throughout its history and enmeshed Native American societies with the European world economy and with the political designs of its participant states.[5]

French procurement of furs for the luxury trade in Europe established a pattern for colonization in Canada that persisted for a century and a half. Chartered companies with monopoly rights to trade initiated colonization. They acquired and stored furs for overseas shipment, which resulted in the establishment of settlements distributed along key transportation routes linking aboriginal peoples, who supplied the furs, and the home country. The French built trading centers at Quebec and Montreal on the St. Lawrence River, which stretched inland from the Atlantic to the Great Lakes. Although a focus on fur trading limited the nature of the French presence in Canada, limited resettlement occurred in the second half of the seventeenth century. The French monarchy created a modified feudal system that placed the burden and expense of settlement on a seigniorial administration, while at the same time limiting its independence, power, and wealth. This system, however, failed to provide the opportunities for economic gain and social mobility necessary to attract or maintain substantial immigration. In the early eighteenth century, high-density French settlement in Canada was limited to a corridor along the St. Lawrence Valley between Quebec and Montreal.[6]

The French trade continued to expand until 1760, but not without problems. Because internal trade was a spatially dispersed activity, it became more difficult to manage as it grew. The role of native people was integral to the production of furs, and they became involved in the trade as trappers, processors, middlemen, and marriage partners. Increased European demand for furs led to the expansion of and competition for hunting territories, altering drastically the relationships among native peoples. As rival European nations competed in the trade, they exacerbated tension among the Indians and laid seeds of economic and political conflict that affected the Great Lakes region profoundly.[7]

By 1760 French settlement extended into the Great Lakes and beyond. One line of outposts ranged westerly from the St. Lawrence Valley to Michilimackinac at the straits between Lakes Michigan and Huron, from which point routes diverged north to Lake Winnipeg and the Saskatchewan River and south through Lake Michigan to the Illinois country and the upper Mississippi drainage. Fort Frontenac, Fort Niagara, and Detroit established a presence on the lower lakes. These western settlements did not comprise the contiguous communities of a permanently settled region, but instead were relatively isolated, specialized enclaves whose presence characterized the nature of initial frontier occupation of the Great Lakes region.[8]

England colonized North America to resettle segments of its population as well as to secure the region as its economic domain. Religious dissenters and those adversely affected by economic changes formed a large wave of emigration to North America in the seventeenth and eighteenth centuries. English emigrants established agricultural colonies in New England and occupied much of the region by the mid-seventeenth century.[9] The presence of growing permanent settlements in North America gave the English a great advantage in gaining control of the North Atlantic fishery as well as in making inroads into the fur trade. The seizure of the Dutch colony of New Netherland in 1664 permitted English fur traders to expand their activities westward and absorb the lucrative Hudson Valley trade; however, as they pushed farther into the interior of the continent, they competed with the French for the cooperation and loyalty of the native peoples who controlled the production of furs.[10]

The land-extensive nature of the fur trade and the absence of control over production also put this colonial activity at an economic disadvantage to agriculture. The intensive nature of farming permitted a higher rate of return from a given amount of land and eliminated the uncertainty associated with the fur trade, which depended on the cooperation of those on the fringes of the world economy. Colonial agriculture thus possessed a competitive advantage that allowed it to prevail over trading as a frontier economic strategy, an advantage great enough to justify the costs of gaining control over new lands for agricultural expansion.

Agricultural expansion in English North America was shaped by the relative abundance of available land, which encouraged a dispersed settlement pattern of small, nucleated centers amid individual farmsteads distributed over the landscape. The extensive nature of frontier agricultural settlement facilitated rapid westward expansion into upstate New York during the eighteenth century, when the development of markets and a phenomenal growth of population, largely through natural increase, provided the incentive and capability for such areal growth. By 1770 agricultural settlement in the English colonies of the Atlantic Seaboard had reached, and even extended beyond, the Appalachian Mountains. Despite attempts by the Crown to restrict further growth, American independence thwarted English efforts to limit the spread of agricultural settlement. By the close of the eighteenth century, expansion was beginning to engulf the Great Lakes.[11]

THE ABORIGINAL RESPONSE

The participation of Native peoples in the fur trade and the international conflicts for control the Old Northwest were a second major factor in the creation of the regional landscape of southern lower Michigan. The French fur trade depended upon Indians as sources of furs and as "middlemen" who carried out exchange with more distant groups. A need for access to peoples displaced by the Iroquois Wars of the seventeenth century forced the French to extend their settlements into the Great Lakes, where they established an outpost at Michilimackinac at the Straits of Mackinac in the 1670s and at Detroit in 1701. These settlements marked the beginning of a European presence in Michigan.[12]

By the early eighteenth century the cessation of the Iroquois Wars allowed the displaced peoples of the Great Lakes to reoccupy Michigan's Lower Peninsula. Several of them occupied territories that allowed them to play important roles in the colonization of the area a century later.[13] They included the Ottawas, who earlier had played a key role in the long-distance trade of the Hurons. Following the destruction of the latter in the middle of the seventeenth century, the Ottawas assumed the position of middlemen and expanded their trading networks and political influence throughout the northern lakes. By 1670 they occupied a strategic position at the Straits of Mackinac and later moved southward to take advantage of the post at Detroit. Subsequently, the Ottawas expanded their domain to include most of western Michigan north of the Kalamazoo River.[14]

The traditional territory of the Ojibwas, or Chippewas, stretched northward from the eastern shore of Georgian Bay. Displaced by the Iroquois Wars, many moved their settlements closer to those of the French on the St. Lawrence, spreading northwestward along the northern shores of Lakes Huron and Superior. From here they migrated into eastern Michigan, where most settled in the area around Detroit and Saginaw Bay, occupying lands as far west as the upper Grand drainage.[15]

The movement of displaced aboriginal peoples from the West brought the return of the Potawatomis to western Michigan, to reoccupy lands along the southern Lake Michigan shoreline as far north as the Kalamazoo River. Later they expanded their territory eastward across the peninsula to Lake Erie to gain access to Detroit. Within the next decade other groups were drawn to Detroit, including the Sauks and the Mascoutens from Green Bay and the Miamis from the southwest. Disharmony among so many diverse groups led to hostilities that drove out the Sauks, the Mascoutens, and the recently arrived Foxes. The Miamis moved south to the Maumee River, leaving the region around Detroit in the possession of the Ottawas, Potawatomis, and Hurons. These larger groups retained close ties to the European enclave at Detroit throughout the eighteenth century and maintained a permanent residence in the Lower Peninsula. Their presence in the region, together with their continued participation in the fur trade, was an important aspect of Lower Michigan's cosmopolitan frontier landscape in 1815.[16]

The establishment of a permanent European presence in the Great Lakes drew the region and its inhabitants into global strategic conflicts between France and Great Britain, a process that disrupted Native societies and saw control of the fur trade slip increasingly out of the hands of indigenous middlemen and into those of European traders. The eighteenth century brought a succession of colonial conflicts that removed France as a political presence in the Great Lakes region after 1760, established at least nominal British "sovereignty" over Indian lands, and opened western lands to agricultural settlement by Europeans.[17]

An expansion of the fur trade drew Native peoples increasingly further into the European world economy and saw a decline in their role as middlemen. Although the procurement of furs remained in the hands of aboriginal peoples, the control of production was passing to European entrepreneurs whose access to individual Indian trappers offered them incentives of lower cost and convenience.[18] Exchange was now carried out by an occupational class of the voyageur-traders, who dealt directly with Native peoples. The regular interaction led to inter-marriages between French traders and Indian women, a phenomenon that resulted in a grow-ing population of mixed-bloods, or Métis, a group whose social position, bridging two cultures, permitted its members to assume an increasingly important role in the fur trade. Employing kinship ties to create networks of exchange with producers, Métis built an ever-enlarging sphere of contacts that extended the trade to ever more distant sources. Métis com-munities became key elements in the procurement of furs in the Great Lakes region, and their social and economic links to the principal trading centers provided a flexible framework that contributed to the success of the trade.[19]

The increased volume of trade and the changing nature of the exchange relationship fos-tered Indian economic dependency and enhanced the political role of Europeans in Indian affairs. Incomplete dominance by Europeans fostered an accommodation to one anothers' interests in order to achieve their separate ends. In such a "middle ground," alliances were formed and maintained on the basis of conventions arrived at by mutual agreement between the parties involved. The growing interdependence of Indian and European political and eco-nomic interests grew in response to these arrangements and increasingly allied Native peoples with European interests.[20]

POLITICAL CHANGE IN THE OLD NORTHWEST

British hegemony in the Old Northwest brought with it the seeds of political destruction for many aboriginal societies in the Great Lakes region. The incompatible purposes of agricultural settlement and the fur trade created an irresolvable paradox that led to a failed pan-Indian rebellion and official attempts to prevent agricultural settlement west of the Appalachians.[21] The Peace of Paris that ended the American Revolution in 1783 transferred sovereignty over all lands north of the Ohio River to the newly independent United States, which began persistent attempts to secure these lands. A series of Indian treaties concluded in the 1780s and 1790s gradually established claims to lands north of the Ohio River and resulted in several military conflicts with alliances of Native peoples. The last of these ended with the decisive defeat of a large Indian force at Fallen Timbers in 1794. The following year, various Indian peoples were forced to cede much of southern and eastern Ohio and a number of strategic points in the

Great Lakes. A six-mile-wide strip of land stretching from the River Raisin northward to the St. Clair River was the first American claim to Indian lands in Michigan and laid the groundwork for the permanent settlement of the region.[22]

The last decade of the eighteenth century witnessed the establishment of an American military presence in southern Lower Michigan and the organization of the area as a region for settlement. Under the Northwest Ordinance of 1787, Congress created a framework for administering the territory northwest of the Ohio River and a procedure for creating states that would eventually join those in the federal union. Still consisting almost entirely of unceded Indian lands, Michigan Territory was established in 1805 with Detroit as its capital. Although its organization as a territory did not bring about the immediate commencement of settlement, it provided the institutional basis for later growth.[23]

Prior to the War of 1812 the United States government increased the amount of land available for settlement through two treaties. The Treaty of Detroit, concluded with Ottawa, Ojibwa, Potawatomi, and Wyandot representatives in 1807, ceded a large portion of Indian land in the eastern half of the southern Lower Peninsula, leaving only scattered reserves for resident aboriginal groups. A second treaty, negotiated at Brownstown a year later, provided overland access to Michigan by ceding a right-of-way through Indian lands in western Ohio. Although neither the western lands nor the roadway were developed until after the War of 1812, they provided a precedent for expansion and lay the groundwork for a series of later treaties that would within thirty years establish claim over the remainder of southern Lower Michigan and dispossess its former inhabitants of the lands they occupied.[24]

The American Revolution and subsequent American expansion into the Ohio country and the Great Lakes marked another reorientation of the fur trade. Control was monopolized by British interests in Montreal and was further enhanced by a consolidation of trading companies whose trading rights with Indians living in U.S. territory were guaranteed by international agreement. Large British companies dominated the fur trade in Michigan, and their free navigation of the interior waterways allowed them to import goods from Europe and the Eastern Seaboard much more cheaply and efficiently than could their American counterparts, who were obliged to travel overland.[25]

American trading interests finally gained a foothold in the fur trade after the War of 1812, and the trade continued unabated well into the settlement period. Fur exports remained high throughout the 1820s and into the 1830s. Extensive trapping and habitat destruction resulting from the conversion of the land to agricultural purposes led to the rapid depletion of fur bearing animal populations and the decline of the trade in the following decade, forcing its participants into an increasingly marginal economic position.[26]

The War of 1812 marked the close of overt international rivalry in the Great Lakes region and reduced British influence over its aboriginal inhabitants. The Treaty of Ghent, formally ending the war, restored the prewar boundary between the United States and British Canada, but curtailed British influence among and support of indigenous peoples within the territories of the United States, leaving them at the mercy of their former enemies, who were anxious to usurp their lands. The Indian presence in Lower Michigan and Americans' negative perceptions of

them shaped the nature of ethnic relations during the subsequent period and exerted a potentially powerful influence on the region's settlement.[27]

The end of the war in 1815 removed the last political obstacle to agricultural settlement in
Michigan. Previous European colonial activity had left a profound mark on the Great Lakes
area and its inhabitants, and had created a landscape that would influence the region's subsequent development. In order to exploit this landscape, however, Americans had first to accomplish four tasks: pacifying resident indigenous groups, acquiring a knowledge of the region and
the use of its resources, establishing an entrepôt linking the region with the outside world, and
developing routes of access to and within the region.

THE PACIFICATION OF ABORIGINAL PEOPLES

Agricultural expansion in southern Michigan could occur only after permanent and unimpeded access to the area had been insured and American immigrants were protected from the
competitive claims of Native peoples who lived in the region. In 1815 a number of Indian societies resided on traditional territories in Lower Michigan (fig 2.1). Although they did not pose
a formal threat to the United States, Americans viewed their presence as an obstacle to agricultural expansion, and implemented various strategies designed to acquire their estates.

By the second decade of the nineteenth century, Michigan's indigenous peoples had suffered not only from the effects of incessant warfare but also from introduced diseases.
Beginning in the mid-eighteenth century, several epidemics struck aboriginal peoples in the
region. Although the extent of their impact on Michigan Indians is unknown, European diseases were usually devastating to aboriginal peoples, who lacked any resistance to them. The
decimation of populations by widespread epidemic diseases left resident Native societies in dis-
array, weakening them and making them even more susceptible to social and political manipulation by the Americans.[28]

A key element in pacification was the treaty process that governed the relationship
between the U.S. government and Indian societies. Treaties normally acknowledged a dependence on the government by aboriginal peoples, a condition that restricted their sovereignty,
managed their affairs, and oversaw their relations with outsiders. The Treaty of Springwells,
negotiated in 1815, marked the first step in the pacification of Michigan's Native peoples. By
requiring its Ottawa, Chippewa, and Potawatomi representatives to pledge their loyalty to the
United States, it effectively reduced their political autonomy and established a precedent for
their future relationship with the government. As a restatement of federal authority, the 1815
treaty reaffirmed the land cessions of the 1795 and 1807 treaties.[29]

Treaties also gave the government the right to preempt ownership of Indian lands, subject
to the Indians' willingness to sell. Although Indians retained a right of occupancy to their estates
after ceding them, they lost the right of ultimate ownership. Preemption of these lands did not
bring about their immediate acquisition, but it did establish an avenue to facilitate their transfer. Agricultural colonization required that the Native peoples be denied the use of their land as
a resource, and the most effective way of restricting their access to it was through containment

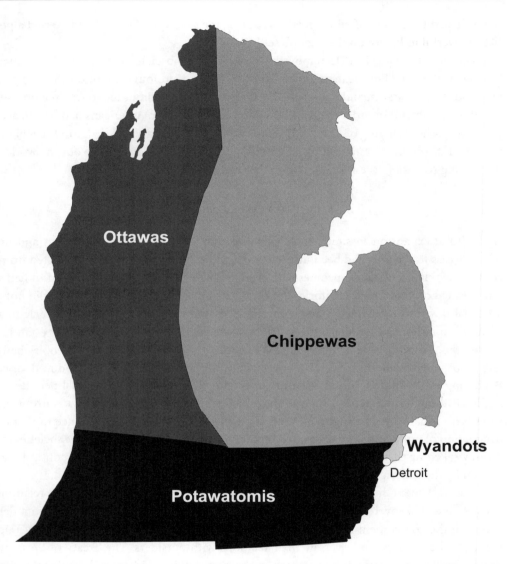

FIGURE 2.1 *DISTRIBUTION OF NATIVE GROUPS IN SOUTHERN MICHIGAN IN 1812.* (Source: Tanner, *Atlas*, 58–59, 98–99).

or removal. Containment on reservations provided the initial solution to accommodating Native peoples displaced by land cessions in Michigan, and the region's early landscape was characterized by scattered enclaves of Indians. In the 1807 treaty, reservations had been set aside for the Wyandots, Chippewas, and Potawatomis in eastern Michigan, and in subsequent treaties, concluded in 1819 at Saginaw and 1821 at Chicago, additional reserves were established for the Chippewas around Saginaw Bay and the Potawatomis in southwestern Michigan.[30]

Confinement to reservations was underlain by the erroneous philosophical belief that it would lead to acculturation and solve the dilemma posed by Native peoples on the agricultural frontier. Reservations maintained Indians as peaceful wards of the government while simulta-neously preparing to integrate them into larger American society. Although this facilitated gov-ernment-sponsored attempts at forced acculturation, centered around education, agricultural training, and religious instruction, it failed to destroy tribal identity and instead encouraged Native peoples to adapt in creative ways to their distinctive status on the frontier. After 1815, Indians developed an economic niche in which their annuity payments made them a financial asset and their traditional subsistence practices permitted them to become important suppli-ers of foodstuffs and other goods to immigrants. Their indispensable role, together with a growing knowledge of American culture arising from the reservation experience, allowed abo-riginal peoples to effectively resist the efforts of teachers, farmers, and missionaries to alter their way of life, as they devised and employed effective strategies to maintain their identity as Americans began to settle around them.[31]

In the early years of settlement the participation of Native peoples in a more diversified economy grew, and with it the complexity of their linkages and their dependency on the Americans. This trend is illustrated by the rising intensity of the fur trade in Michigan. Competing American fur trading interests, seeking to increase profits, abandoned the tradi-tional practice of dealing with Native trappers on the periphery of their territories and estab-lished interior posts. This move reduced the role of Indians in the procurement and exchange of furs and linked them directly to trading companies as raw commodity producers in the larger market economy.[32]

A KNOWLEDGE OF THE REGIONAL LANDSCAPE

Although Europeans had been acquainted with Michigan for more than 150 years, its physical landscape was still imperfectly understood in the first decades of the nineteenth century. The nature of contact limited geographical knowledge of the region, and during the period of initial colonization most Europeans confined their activities to the lakeshores, where their settlements lay close to water routes connecting Michigan with the eastern Great Lakes and the St. Lawrence Valley. A better knowledge of the region's geography was needed for colonization to proceed.

Early mapping of Michigan did not proceed in a systematic manner, yet generated useful car-tographic images of the area. Portions of the region were recorded by the Jesuits in the seven-teenth century, and throughout the following century French and British cartographers produced increasingly more accurate maps of Michigan's extensive shoreline. Europeans participating in the wars of the second half of the eighteenth century and the War of 1812 generated additional geographic information. One important map published during the American Revolution by Captain Thomas Hutchins, a British military engineer, revealed variations in soils and their fer-tility inland of Lakes Michigan and Huron. By the time of the American occupation in 1796, the external geography of Michigan was well known, although the precise shapes of the lakes and that of the Lower Peninsula itself were not recorded accurately for another half century. In contrast, nearly two centuries of European contact accumulated relatively little knowledge of the region's interior. The nature of inland Michigan remained largely a mystery in 1815.[33]

Ignorance of Michigan's geography helped create several misperceptions regarding the region's amenability for settlement. The first of these was that a physical barrier in the form of a high ridge, occasionally portrayed as a mountain range, extended from north to south through the center of the Lower Peninsula. It first appeared on maps in 1718 and may have been imagined to account for the topographic divide separating the rivers flowing into the surrounding lakes. Whatever its origin, this potential obstacle to travel and settlement was not removed from maps until actual surveys in the 1820s demonstrated its nonexistence.[34]

A second misperception was that of an interminably swampy interior. It seems to have resulted from observations by residents and travelers of swampy lands inland of the Lake Erie shore. The uncertain extent of such lands apparently influenced the perceptions of the first American surveyors sent there to examine ceded Indian lands in eastern Michigan. A tract, intended for distribution as bounty lands for War of 1812 veterans, was described as low and wet ground, containing marshes, swamps, and lakes interspersed with barren, sandy hills. The land was described as nearly impassable, and the report by Surveyor General Edward Tiffin estimated that "there would not be an acre out of one hundred, if there would be one out of one thousand, that would, of any case, admit of cultivation."[35]

These errors, however, were not universally accepted, and other contemporary writers found a region with very different qualities. As early as 1797 Jedidiah Morse's *Gazetteer* described Michigan as a "fruitful" country of fertile soil. United States Indian Agent Charles Jouett's 1803 report of his survey of the eastern shore lands indicated that most were of good agricultural quality. Judge Augustus Woodward estimated two years later that Michigan's Lower Peninsula must contain at least eighteen to twenty million acres of good land. John Melish's geographical works of 1813 and 1816 also described the soil generally as rich and fertile.[36]

Indeed, the conclusions of Tiffin's surveyors were immediately challenged by Lewis Cass, Michigan's territorial governor, who criticized both the seasonal timing and the limited extent of the survey and presented contrasting testimony from a more recent survey still in progress.[37] The bounty land survey was followed almost immediately by others preceding sales of land. Reports of these surveys corrected earlier misperceptions and led to the accumulation of accurate information prior to the actual distribution of lands for settlement. By the fall of 1816 the fallacy of an interminable swamp had been officially laid to rest, although it persisted in literature long after the frontier period. Overall, early visitors to the peninsula saw its environment as amenable to agricultural colonization.[38]

THE ENTREPÔT OF DETROIT

Detroit played the role of entrepôt for southern Michigan after 1815. It linked the region with the economy, government, and society of the eastern states and served as a point of ingress for immigrants and supplies, a shipping point to outside markets, and an administrative center for the region.

Like other urban centers that spearheaded frontier expansion south of the Great Lakes, Detroit lay on a major transportation route. Yet, unlike most settlements west of the

Appalachians, Detroit had been settled for more than a century before the arrival of American settlers. The French established a post there in 1701 to facilitate trade with the western Indians and serve as a center for military and missionary activities. Linked by water with the colonial centers of Montreal and Quebec on the St. Lawrence, Detroit became an important focus of French influence as well as a supplier of agricultural foodstuffs for French residents and traders in the region.[39]

Detroit's role as an agricultural supply depot introduced a rural European population to southern Lower Michigan. Immigrant farmers, known as habitants, came primarily from western France. They were settled along the eastern shore on long, narrow tracts of land stretching inland from streams that emptied into the straits. The narrow stream frontage permitted farms to be arranged in closely spaced linear settlements, or *côtes,* in which all habitants had access to the waterways that served as the avenues of transportation. This pattern of settlement, sometimes called a "line village," offers the advantage of placing farmers on their land without isolating them from their neighbors, and is easily adaptable to the topographic variation encountered in settling a riverine environment. Linear riverine settlement had precedents in western Europe, particularly in France, and was employed successfully in the St. Lawrence Valley and other French colonial areas in North America. It was a familiar pattern, adaptive to conditions on the frontier.[40]

The purpose of French colonization initially limited the extent and nature of farming in Michigan. Farming was not carried out with the intent of producing a marketable surplus, and land was not seen as a commodity to be acquired for profitable speculation. Controls on land, production, and the processing and sale of agricultural commodities discouraged expansion of production, and the poor market conditions resulting from the colony's isolation favored a level of production barely above that of subsistence. These conditions exerted a conservative influence that worked to preserve the original pattern of land ownership and occupancy. This lack of entrepreneurial effort, which later baffled American observers, was clearly a successful adaptation by French settlers to an insecure, isolated, and economically specialized frontier that was chronically beset by unrest and warfare conditions that favored the flexibility offered by unspecialized farming combined with other subsistence activities.[41]

The thirty-year British occupation of Michigan witnessed only a small increase in the amount of land settled by Europeans. Although a number of large tracts along the eastern shore were acquired by British inhabitants, only a few were actually settled, most notably at Grosse Isle and along the St. Clair River. At the time of the American occupation the rural population of the region still consisted primarily of French subsistence farmers living in scattered riverine settlements stretching from the St. Clair River south to Lake Erie.[42]

Detroit itself remained a fairly small settlement because its relatively specialized function did not require a large supporting population. Indeed, many of its inhabitants who were involved in the fur trade were absent much of the year. Its population grew slowly during the eighteenth century, from an estimated 270 persons in 1707 to about 600 in 1760, at the close of the French and Indian War. A decade later the population had doubled. During the years of the American Revolution an influx of Loyalist refugees increased the number of persons in

Detroit to over 2,000, but by the first decade of the nineteenth century its population had dropped to less than 1,000.[43]

From its earliest days, the form and content of Detroit reflected its role as a supply center and military strongpoint. Forts, or palisaded enclosures, characterized the settlement well into the American period, by which time they had become surrounded by the houses, stores, warehouses, taverns, hotels, and other buildings that comprised the town. Detroit grew largely as a consequence of its increasing importance in trade and defense rather than as a result of natural increase. Before 1760 the French organized military expeditions there to challenge British incursions into the Ohio country, and subsequently the British used it as a base from which to launch forays against American frontier settlements.[44]

At the beginning of the nineteenth century Detroit remained small, but it grew substantially over the next several decades. When the town burned in June 1805, newly arrived American administrators rebuilt the settlement and redesigned it to fit its new role as the seat of government for Michigan Territory and the gateway to the region's interior. Augustus Woodward, one of three judges appointed to administer the new territory, proposed an ambitious plan in which the streets would form a series of right triangles arranged so as to provide major thoroughfares running at right angles as well as diagonally across the town. Clearly Woodward's design proposed a metropolis for a settled region with a growing population, the central location of which facilitated its role as an entry point for settlers moving into southern Michigan. Yet Detroit did not immediately relinquish its roles as a fur trading mart or military supply base, for the trade continued well into the 1830s, and Michigan's position on an international boundary dictated that an armed presence be maintained there.[45]

ROUTES OF ACCESS TO THE MICHIGAN FRONTIER

Routes of transportation to Michigan were reasonably well established by 1815. The accessibility of so much of its territory by water, however, discouraged exploration of the interior and the development of internal routes of communication. Despite this handicap, Detroit's establishment as the focus of the fur trade provided the means to tie internal networks of trade and communication with water routes linking the region to older settled areas.

Detroit's central position arose as a result of the growing role of the Great Lakes as an avenue of commerce and the expansion of American settlement along Lake Erie (fig. 2.2). The occupation of the southern shoreline began in 1796, and within two decades a number of settlements served as ports of call between Michigan and the eastern United States. Buffalo and Black Rock, located at the edge of newly settled lands in western New York, served as the terminus of the overland road system from the eastern part of that state. Buffalo thrived as a point of departure for passengers coming from throughout the Northeast. Between Buffalo and Detroit were the settlements of Erie (Presque Isle), Pennsylvania and Cleveland, Lorain, Vermilion, Huron, and Sandusky, in Ohio. Travel on Lake Erie could be hazardous in bad weather and impossible when the lake froze over during the winter months, but it was rapid and efficient. It took sailing craft from four to nine days to cross from Buffalo to Detroit. The introduction of steamboats in 1818 reduced this time to as little as two and a half days. The termination of the War of 1812 brought the expansion of settlement and shipping in the Lake Erie region, as well as the beginning of European settlement along its Canadian shore.[46]

Rivers were important in the fur trade, linking the interior of the Midwest with the Great Lakes and the Mississippi-Ohio River drainage (fig. 2.2). The Maumee River stretched from Lake Erie westward into Ohio and Indiana, approaching the headwaters of the Illinois, St. Joseph, and Miami Rivers that flowed, respectively, into the Mississippi River, Lake Michigan, and the Ohio River. So important were these watercourses that free access over them by the United States was mentioned explicitly in the cessions granted in the 1795 Treaty of Greenville. The use of the Maumee for immigration was, however, curtailed by its limited navigability.[47]

In Michigan, several eastward-flowing rivers offered limited passage inland along the peninsula's eastern shore (fig. 2.2). These included the Raisin, with its natural harbor at Monroe, the Rouge, the St. Clair, the Clinton, and the Huron. Although the peninsula's westward flowing rivers and those of the Saginaw Bay drainage presented greater potential as routes of riverine immigration, distance to their mouths from Detroit and the delay in the initial availability of lands in their drainages effectively prevented them from developing as early routes of entry.[48]

Overland routes south of Lake Erie were an alternative to lake and river transportation (fig 2.2). In 1811 Congress authorized the construction of a road through a 120-foot-wide corridor connecting the Western Reserve in northeastern Ohio with Michigan Territory, but the road was not opened until after the War of 1812. The chief obstacle to its completion was the Black Swamp, south of the Maumee River, a thirty-mile-wide irregular strip of standing water and saturated soils that served as a barrier to movement during all seasons. Although the federal government opened a track through the swamp in 1812 and a postal route was established in 1804, its usefulness for general transport was limited. By 1817 improvements allowed mail to be delivered to Michigan on a weekly basis, but the road was not completed until 1827. In the meantime the Black Swamp remained an impediment to travel and a detriment to settlement in Michigan's southern counties.[49]

In the early nineteenth century a road network served as the primary link between the eastern shore settlements (fig 2.2). The principal road ran parallel to the lake shore and straits from Lake St. Clair south to the River Raisin. Some parts of this road north of Detroit were cleared as early as 1785, and by 1812 Detroit was linked with the Clinton River. When the War of 1812 broke out, roads with bridges at the major river crossings extended south to the Huron River. Within a year of the war's end a permanent road was completed as far south as the River Raisin, and bridges were in place over this river. By 1818 the road extended to within eight miles of the Maumee River.[50]

In 1815 most interior routes converged on Detroit, and its role in the fur trade placed it at the center of a trail network that reached all portions of southern Lower Michigan. Detroit continued to be a destination of Michigan Indians after the War of 1812 because it lay just across the river from Fort Malden. Until 1842 this British post was the site of annual disbursements of presents in recognition for the Natives' wartime service. Americans were aware that

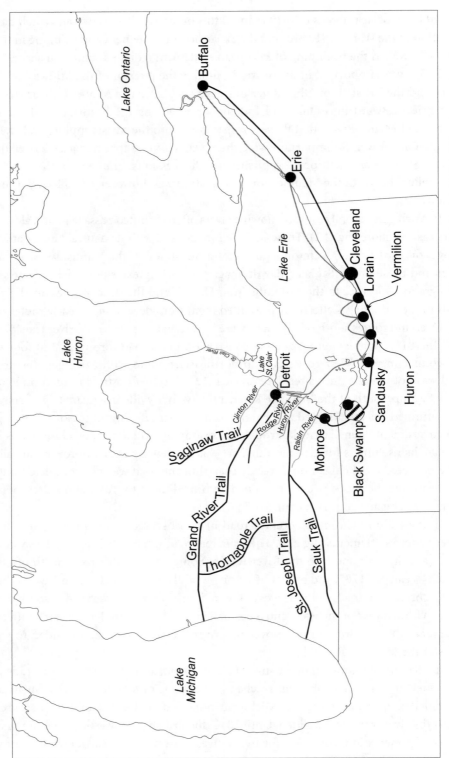

FIGURE 2.2. *EARLY ROUTES OF ACCESS TO AND WITHIN SOUTHERN MICHIGAN.* (Source: see text).

this system of trails linked Detroit to all parts of the interior, and improved them to facilitate the movement of immigrants into the interior.[51]

Five trails used in the fur trade were of particular importance for subsequent settlement (fig. 2.2). The first followed roughly the drainages of the Huron and St. Joseph Rivers, terminating near the mouth of the latter on Lake Michigan. The Sauk Trail was surmised to have great antiquity, although it was associated most closely with the Potawatomis who had reoccupied southern Michigan after the Iroquois Wars. This trail was used by Indians traveling to Fort Malden to receive annuity payments after 1815 and was the route of the first road constructed across the Lower Peninsula.[52]

The St. Joseph Trail stretched westward to the upper drainage of the Kalamazoo River and turned southward to intersect the lower St. Joseph River drainage. Used by the Potawatomis and other Michigan Indians in the period following the War of 1812, this trail became a territorial road. The Thornapple, or Potawatomi, Trail branched northwestward from the St. Joseph Trail and proceeded into the upper drainages of the Grand and Thornapple Rivers. The Saginaw Trail emanated from Detroit in a northwestward direction to the Saginaw Bay region. The Saginaw-Chippewas took this route on their annual visits to Fort Malden. Shortly after the War of 1812 the Americans built a cleared road along its path, and it became the earliest route of agricultural expansion in Michigan. The fifth route, called the Grand River Trail, branched from the Saginaw Trail at the future site of Pontiac and passed westward into the Grand Valley. It linked the lower Grand River Valley as well as the upper Shiawassee River drainage with Detroit and is thought to have been the principal thoroughfare used by the Ottawas in crossing the peninsula. This trail also became a major route of American immigration into the interior.[53]

The country into which the stream of American immigration began to flow following the War of 1812 was not an unoccupied wilderness waiting to be settled. A century and a half of European presence in Michigan had altered both the land and its inhabitants to create a landscape that facilitated the development of an agricultural colony. Activities associated with trading and warfare established political control over the region, ascertained its suitability for agriculture, created a central entrepôt, and laid the groundwork for an internal communications network. These developments provided a basis for successful settlement and the eventual incorporation of the region within the larger national economy. The results of initial colonization encouraged Michigan's growth as an insular frontier, and that process shaped the subsequent history of the region.

THE RISE OF THE NORTHEAST AND WESTERN EXPANSION

Although conditions in Michigan made it amenable to agricultural settlement, successful colonization depended on the ability of the American economy to support a marked growth in farming. Conditions favoring agricultural expansion came about following independence as a result of the evolving position of the United States in the world economy and the increasingly central role of the Northeast in American development. The movement by Britain's former Eastern Seaboard colonies away from their peripheral position brought structural changes to the American economy that altered the nature of regional production and created new markets for farm products. Economic change in the East provided the impetus for western expansion.

The economic position of the United States in the 1790s derived from its former colonial status. It developed in response to British mercantilist policy that enmeshed the Eastern Seaboard colonies in a complex system of global trade that involved transferring cheaply acquired colonial products to a variety of destinations in North America, the Caribbean, Africa, and Asia in exchange for other commodities that were shipped directly or indirectly to England for consumption or re-export to Europe. Situated in the center of this network, England paid for imports with manufactured goods and accumulated the surplus of this trade. Participation in global trade profoundly affected regional production in British North America. The northeastern colonies occupied an important position in the organization of Atlantic trade because their merchants supplied both provisions and labor for sugar production in the West Indies. Participation in this lucrative trade generated enormous profits and established mercantile capitalism as a fundamental part of the regional economy of the Northeast before independence.[54]

Because colonial rule left the American economy heavily reliant on export trade, the new nation relied heavily on an expansion of overseas commerce. The abrupt growth of postrevolutionary external commerce created distinctive regional patterns of production and reinvestment in the United States. The economy of the southern states adjusted to an enlarged export market by expanding specialized commercial agricultural production of cotton and rice. The growth of plantation agriculture required a heavy investment in slave labor. Profits, though substantial, were consumed by purchasing imports or enlarging the production base. In the South, commodity-dispersed production shaped transportation networks, and the marketing requirements of plantation crops affected settlement patterning. Such an economy lacked internal integration and provided little impetus for urbanization or an industrial manufacturing base.[55]

In the northern states an economy centered around income from trade and regional production responded very differently to expanding trade in the 1790s. As merchants in the major ports of the Northeast reinvested profits, they promoted the region's rise as the axis of the emerging American economy. Merchants in Boston, New York, Philadelphia, and Baltimore channeled earnings into domestic investments which propelled development in the region. A diversified economy permitted a wider segment of the population to accumulate savings, and provided wide opportunities for reinvestment, encouraging the growth of internal markets and manufacturing activities. The seasonal nature of northern agriculture, which created periodic unemployment and low incomes from farm work, helped provide the needed labor force by encouraging migration to urban areas.[56]

Internal markets supported the rise of commercial urban centers in the Northeast. By the late eighteenth century, integrated markets for farm products existed in eastern Massachusetts together with a regional capital market that allowed farmers to rechannel savings into other forms of investment. In Philadelphia, regional internal markets also encouraged the expansion of home industries, the products of which began to supplant imports. Overland transport routes linking the coastal urban centers with their agricultural hinterlands and more distant points facilitated intraregional integration. By the time of the War of 1812 a network of roads connected the chief commercial centers of the Northeast.[57]

Early government financial policies also contributed to the growth of the northeastern economy. Federalist efforts to fund federal and state debts established a sound basis for credit, and the creation of a national bank provided the foundation for a national credit market. These initiatives furnished investment capital that underwrote the growth of trade, shipping, and warehousing, which in turn helped create a manufacturing base and the transportation infrastructure necessary for regional integration.[58]

International events hastened the industrial development of the Northeast. Increasing tensions between the belligerent nations of Europe led to an embargo of foreign goods in 1808 and war with Great Britain four years later. American external trade declined suddenly and severely, forcing producers to seek internal markets and consumers to depend upon home industries. A shift in investment from shipping to domestic manufacturing provided capital to underwrite technical innovation and increase the scale of production. The expansion of northeastern industry also cushioned the loss of foreign outlets in the agricultural South by offering a domestic market for its cotton crop. Changes brought by war helped coalesce the economic base of the Northeast and permitted the region to assume a central role in national development.[59]

The central role of the Northeast in American manufacturing and internal commerce became increasingly tied to cotton production after 1815. Growing postwar demand by British textile industries resulted in a rise in cotton prices and a boom in production. As a consequence, the region's economy was increasingly devoted to this crop, and its cultivation expanded into western lands east of the Mississippi. Cotton became America's most valuable export commodity, and its importance accentuated the differences between North and South and shaped the future development of both regions. Falling cotton prices in the 1820s, coupled with improved modes of transportation, led to the growth of textile mills in the Northeast. This, in turn, encouraged the industrial manufacture of other products, including furniture, clothing, soap, and boots and shoes. Textile-making led the way for urban industrialization to dominate the region's economy.[60]

Cotton exportation to Europe promoted a concentration of commercial marketing services in the Northeast. Although cotton was shipped directly from southern ports to Europe, the actual management of the trade came under the control of New York concerns that provided the financing, accounting, insurance, storage, shipping, and other services not available in the cotton ports of Charleston, Savannah, Mobile, and New Orleans. Soon New York-based packet lines, carrying American cotton outboard and European imports on their return journeys, controlled trade. The substantial income derived from managing the Atlantic cotton trade was reinvested in commercial marketing services in the Northeast.[61]

The role of the Northeast in the cotton trade established the region as a center of national exchange, and its dominance of interregional trade became a prominent feature of the antebellum American economy. Northeastern merchants shipped imported and domestic goods to southern ports, from which they found their way into the interior through the Mississippi and

Ohio River drainages. The Great Lakes provided a another route to western markets, and expanding settlement opened an extensive economic hinterland for growing northern industries and other interests anxious to tap the vast agricultural resources of the American interior.[62]

Industrialization and urbanization dramatically affected the geographical distribution of production in the antebellum Northeast. Large-scale industrial manufacturing of durable goods introduced economies of scale and innovations in technology that resulted in cheaper, better-made, and more diversified products for general consumption. American consumer demand responded to the availability of these products and hastened their rapid dissemination to all areas accessible to eastern markets. The demands of growing industries increased the proportion of the nonagricultural population, substantially increasing consumer demand for foodstuffs and creating an enlarged market for agricultural products. These changes dramatically altered rural production. In Massachusetts' Connecticut River Valley, for example, the orientation of agriculture changed from the production of export staples, such as wheat, to truck crops, dairy products, and other specialized commodities for regional urban markets.[63]

Urban demand for agricultural products created an enormous market for farmers. In areas closest to cities, producers specialized in high-demand foodstuffs such as dairy products, eggs, vegetables, beef, pork, and mutton. Farmers also raised horses for transportation and grain and hay to feed farm and work animals. Successful specialized producers often found their business lucrative enough for them to forgo raising subsistence crops. Market-oriented agriculture depended on adequate intraregional transportation, and by 1825 networks of turnpikes and canals formed a well-integrated system in the Northeast. Their existence made the exchange of goods easier and greatly expanded markets available for interior settlements.[64]

The production of specialized commodities for urban markets changed the composition of regional agriculture and encouraged the westward expansion of commercial production. By dramatically increasing the value of lands closest to markets, specialized farming forced the growing of less profitable crops further into the interior. On cheaper lands that lay beyond the transportation limits of specialized agriculture, crops requiring large amounts of land could be grown efficiently, and thus grain production migrated to more peripheral zones. While wheat cultivation declined in New England after 1820, its production increased farther west, in upstate New York, where large tracts of inexpensive and easily cleared open lands in the Genesee Valley provided farmers with adequate space for growing it. Grain producers willing to relocate to the West gained a competitive advantage over smaller farmers in New England. Growing market demand for western grain promoted the construction of long-distance transportation links to facilitate interregional trade with the West and to open Michigan and other lands bordering the Great Lakes to agricultural development.[65]

3

The Environmental Context
of Colonization

Nineteenth-century observers created an image of Michigan that was based on their interpretation of climate, soils, topography, vegetation, and other factors. They did not draw upon a common source, but rather upon contemporary values and interests that attached great importance to some environmental attributes while excluding others deemed less significant. As a result, conflicting perceptions were often drawn from the same observations.

Two early perspectives are useful in assessing pioneer interpretations of the West and explaining the origins of frontier images. Each reflects distinct but not mutually exclusive viewpoints regarding the relationship between humans and the physical landscape and embodies elements of both academic and popular culture whose acceptance was broad enough to have produced widely shared perceptions of the environment. Because pioneer attitudes toward the environment affected the way it was generally understood and exploited, these perceptions influenced developing patterns of settlement on the Michigan frontier.[1]

The Utilitarian approach viewed the landscape as a source of wealth and placed the highest value on tangible resources that could be exploited by existing production and marketing technologies. This attitude toward the environment reflected a trend in western European thought that separated people from the natural world by making them master over it. Western Christianity, abetted by industrial technology, supported this view by placing nature at the disposal of humanity, to be exploited for purposes of accumulating wealth and creating a higher standard of living. The availability of cheap and abundant resources in the West made a utilitarian perspective appealing to antebellum American interests seeking to promote the growth of a national economy.[2]

The Utilitarian approach set wilderness apart from the human-created order of agricultural lands, villages, and towns. It reflected a view of the natural world in which disorder and chaos reigned in forests, mountains, heaths, swamps, and fens. Wild animals, dangerous mythological creatures, and even Satan himself could be found in the wilderness. The image of America as wilderness encouraged its exploitation by those who believed that controlling the new land and developing its resources modified it for the benefit of humankind.[3]

Americans had little trouble fitting the conversion of wilderness to useful purposes into contemporary notions of the world that emphasized material improvement. Alexis de Tocqueville, commenting on contemporary Americans' obsession with "improvement," wrote:

As they are always dissatisfied with the position that they occupy and are always free to leave it, they think of nothing but the means of changing their fortune or increasing it. To minds thus predisposed, every new method that leads by a shorter road to wealth, every machine that spares labor, every instrument that diminishes the cost of production, every discovery that facilitates pleasures or augments them, seems to be the grandest effort of the human intellect.[4]

Americans assigned monetary value to objects and relationships and commodified all that was nonhuman (and some that was). They encouraged the conspicuous accumulation of wealth, saw nature as a storehouse of raw materials, and valued the earth largely for its capacity to furnish usable resources. Consequently, natural landscapes were ranked according to their ability to supply the wants of production.[5]

In the first part of the nineteenth century the expansion of the United States increased the geographical range of commercial agriculture. Visitors to the West often wrote of the region's potential as farmland and of its abundant forests and minerals. Many wished to promote immigration by appealing to the desires of Americans seeking economic gain. The promotional literature, travelers' guides, gazetteers, official reports, and travelers' and settlers' accounts portrayed southern Michigan as having great potential for agriculture, which was the economic basis for settlement in the Old Northwest. It was only after this base was established that mining and forestry developed in the Lower Peninsula.[6]

In contrast to a Utilitarian orientation, the Romantic perspective saw the natural world as a series of images whose significance derived from the human intuitive response to them. This movement had its roots in late-eighteenth-century European Romanticism, from which it drew assumptions about the nature of humankind and the world it occupied. Romanticism marked an intellectual shift in Western thought by emphasizing the role of the senses in discovery and interpretation. Emotion, not logical analysis, held the key to the ultimate comprehension of the universe. The Romantic movement accepted the notion of nature as a distinct entity and emphasized that the environment was a separate physical world, apart from humanity and its achievements. Nature represented the work of the Creator unspoiled by human interference. The Romantic view of wilderness replaced its image as the domain of chaos, mystery, and evil with that of the perfection of God's handiwork. Scenery exhibited a divine beauty and grandeur that could be experienced by the senses, rejuvenating and purifying the individual.[7]

The American West, with an abundance of wild places in a land undergoing rapid change, offered an ideal setting for the revitalization of people. The frontier was a Romantic environment. It was a new land settled by a transitory people who had broken with their own past. The colonists' encounter with this new environment was seen as an emotional experience with nature that produced a self-reliant individualism and a faith in continual progress.[8]

At its heart, Romanticism was a human-centered approach concerned with the impact of the environmental experience on the human condition. It did not necessarily advocate conservation of the wilderness; the natural landscape was intended for human use and its resources were available for expropriation.[9] An awareness of nature's role in shaping the human character, however, made the composition of frontier environments a factor that affected settlement.

Romantic perceptions of the physical landscape proved powerful inducements in the evaluation and occupation of frontier lands.

The Romantic's characterization of the West as a vast land of bountiful natural resources, alien aboriginal peoples, and colorful frontiersmen greatly influenced its settlement. The recent past had witnessed epic struggles between Europeans and Indians, and the emergence of the post-revolutionary United States as a principal player in a struggle of mythic proportions. The West lent itself to those moved by Romantic notions and became the setting for a body of popular fictional literature that focused on specific themes distilled from the previous frontier experience. The effect of these literary themes was pervasive, and created an image of the frontier that influenced the manner in which subsequent pioneers perceived new lands.[10]

Two general themes emerged from the early literature of the West. One, rooted in the Indian wars and colonial struggles of the fur trade period, is that of the West as a "dark and bloody ground." The other, arising from the experiences of trappers, traders, travelers, riverboat men, and other early visitors, was that of "western humor." While the former featured the heroic backwoodsman who was a part of nature, the latter offered the loquacious and often eccentric frontiersman who lived off of its resources. Both of these fictional themes placed their characters in an environment often more idealized than real. Because the frontier represented a land of hope and promise, whatever the current adversity, it was always presented in a favorable light. The Romantic model became a popular element in American fiction, and even authors who had lived and traveled on the frontier appear to have often forsaken accuracy to write for the contemporary public taste.[11]

Authors of travel accounts and semi-autobiographical fiction portrayed the Michigan landscape in a Romantic perspective. All presented an optimistic image of the West, a theme prevalent in nineteenth-century American literature, to a popular audience. Charles Fenno Hoffman's *Winter in the West* (1835) was a typical travel account, in which he waxed poetic at the beauty of prairie scenery and made extravagant claims regarding the ease of farming in this "garden of the Union."[12] Hoffman and others stressed the ideal and dismissed the detrimental aspects of the new country, creating exaggerated perceptions that shaped the perspective of immigrants and influenced the nature of their settlement.

Fictional accounts, published during the settlement period, also created images of southern Michigan. James Fenimore Cooper used information gathered during his short visit to the Kalamazoo area in *Oak-Openings* (1848). Semi-autobiographical works by actual Michigan settlers include Caroline Kirkland's *A New Home—Who'll Follow?* (1839), Henry H. Riley's *Knickerbocker Magazine* articles later published as the *Puddleford Papers* (1857), Benjamin Taylor's *Theophilus Trent, Old Times in the Oak Openings* (1887), Orlando B. Willcox's *Shoepac Recollections* (1856), and Jerome J. Wood's *The Wilderness and the Rose* (1890). The first four novels described, respectively, conditions around Pinckney in Livingston County, in the vicinity of Constantine in St. Joseph County, at an unnamed location in southern Michigan, and at Hudson and Keene in Lenawee County. Written in the theme of western humor, they were largely satires of the harsh conditions encountered on the frontier, and portrayed the environment as a noble, tolerant, and beneficent backdrop to the foibles of the pioneer characters. The

Eastern Lowlands environment was a positive influence in the struggle of Willcox's poor but resourceful protagonist to overcome the machinations of enemies and the adversity of human institutions to find success in the new land.[13]

Romantic fictional works of Michigan presented an environment distinct from that found in Utilitarian literature. Ever optimists, the Romantics saw the physical world as separate but not alien, comforting rather than hostile to the pioneer, available but not commodified, and while presenting difficulties to settlement, it also provided the inspiration to overcome them. Subjective and selective, the Romantics relished nature more for its beauty than for potential monetary profit, although they recognized that settlers needed to use the environment to survive. Romantic literature and fiction, popular during and after Michigan's colonization, created pervasive images that influenced the perceptions of immigrants upon coming to Michigan and colored their recollections of those experiences in later years.

Public and private accounts of the Michigan frontier added to popular perceptions of its environment. Immigrant and travelers' guides, newspaper articles, histories, and promotional literature stressed the natural beauty, grandeur, and even the mystery of the region's wild landscapes. Aimed at a general audience, these works sought to mold public images of the new land and to encourage colonization. Romantic perceptions and the role they played in evaluation of the environment also influenced the writing of travelers and immigrants, whose diaries, journals, and letters were intended for a more limited audience.

The extent to which Utilitarian and Romantic writers influenced pioneer images must be considered in evaluating pioneer perceptions of Lower Michigan. Although advocates of both approaches sought to identify landscapes suitable for agricultural settlement, the criteria by which each recognized and compared the quality of landscapes varied. Because the relationship between landscape characteristics and the nature of resources was poorly understood, it is difficult to judge the effectiveness of either approach on settlement. How accurately, for example, could the quality of the soil for agriculture be evaluated by observing the type or extent of native vegetation, or the physical attractiveness of the topography? The establishment of settlement and the success of agriculture depended on a reasonably accurate appraisal of new lands. Traditional environmental concepts possessed by American farmers in the early nineteenth century provided a body of knowledge capable of guiding the selection of land based on familiar environmental criteria, but Utilitarian and Romantic perspectives affected the perception of those criteria in the choice of farmland as well as the patterning of settlement in frontier Michigan.

During the first thirty-five years of settlement in southern Michigan, colonists' awareness of the environment changed as they became more familiar with the land. At the close of the War of 1812, knowledge of Michigan's interior was not only incomplete but also often erroneous and contradictory. Soon, however, explorers, surveyors, and other reliable observers began to produce reliable accounts of the interior which made settlement possible. This growing body of information about topography, soils, vegetation, and climate flowed out of the territory as public officials and private interests enticed people to immigrate to Michigan.

Lewis Cass, territorial governor for nearly twenty years, actively promoted Michigan by leading an expedition along its coastline and through its interior in 1820. His widely circulated published account of his findings publicized the region and its natural resources. Others also penetrated the interior to obtain information about the physical environment. Their reports appeared in periodical literature, particularly the *Detroit Gazette,* as well as in the form of travel accounts and travelers' guides.[14] Increasingly more detailed and comprehensive immigration literature, including journal accounts, guides, directories, gazetteers, and statistical accounts followed, and their contents reveal the changing knowledge of the landscape and perceptions of Michigan's environment before 1860.[15]

Maps supplied an additional source of environmental information on Lower Michigan. Because of its location amid the navigable waterways of the Great Lakes and its proximity to international boundaries, Michigan had long been of interest to cartographers. Until the 1820s, maps of Michigan emphasized the form of its shoreline and its proximity to other territories bordering the lakes. Indeed, one of the earliest American cartographic projects was a federal survey to determine the location of the border through the lakes and rivers that divided the United States and British Canada. The distribution of land and construction of interior roads, however, required maps of the interior, and those produced illustrated both cultural and natural features of Michigan's landscape. Perhaps the most significant were those of John Farmer. Beginning in 1826, he published accurate, small-scale maps of Michigan, based on survey data and other reports. Printed in large numbers, updated frequently, and distributed widely as immigrant guides throughout the settlement period, his maps provide a nearly continuous graphic image of current landscape knowledge of Lower Michigan.[16]

The economic relationship of the Old Northwest to the states of the Eastern Seaboard altered perceptions of the frontier environment in the first half of the nineteenth century. A Utilitarian response to expansion, technological innovation, industrialization, the development of more efficient transportation, and the exploitation of western resources dramatically reshaped both the physical environment and the way people in both the East and the West viewed newly opened lands.

The Utilitarian perspective of the western landscape evolved in response to changes in the economic role of the northeastern United States as it assumed a more central position in the world economy. The West, as a peripheral area to this growing center of manufacturing and trade, supplied increasingly larger quantities of agricultural produce for outside markets, which affected how environmental resources were valued. The expansion of production of grain and other extensive agricultural commodities required frontier growers to continually reevaluate land in terms of its capacity to yield maximum returns in an expanding and increasingly competitive market situation. As a result, American views of open and forested environments underwent a transformation in the first half of the nineteenth century.

Eastern Seaboard farmers found themselves largely in forested environments, similar to those for which previous technological adaptations in Europe had prepared them. Inherent in their preference for forestlands was an assumed association between vegetation and soil quality. They saw the humus created by forest growth as crucial for good farmland. By the beginning of the nineteenth century, American pioneers had encountered new physical landscapes as they moved west of the Appalachian Mountains. In the "Genesee country" of western New

York, for example, they found thinly timbered oak woodlands, called "openings." The need to expand the area of extensive grain agriculture beyond the limits of a rapidly industrializing Eastern Seaboard encouraged farmers to cultivate lands originally thought infertile. Experimentation revealed otherwise and resulted in the subsequent rapid cultivation of these lands. The success of agriculture on such lands, in New York and elsewhere in the trans-Appalachian West, altered American notions of land use. Because of the ease with which such lands could be prepared for production, open lands became desired as farm locations, leading pioneers to prefer openings, barrens, and prairies over once-coveted woodlands.[17]

Changing land use resulted in a similar shift in the Romantic perception of forested and open frontier environments in the first four decades of the nineteenth century. The image of the forest evolved from one that welcomed settlement to one that frustrated it. Rather than a refuge, the forest was seen as an environment difficult to master, the home of hostile Indians, dangerous animals, and dissipating diseases. Open lands, on the other hand, offered a vastness and beauty that increasingly enchanted easterners and Europeans alike, with an immaculate landscape, the scale of which reflected humanity's place in the larger divine order.[18]

Marked changes in perception of environment affected the colonization of Lower Michigan. Americans examining the peninsula's landforms and vegetation zones faced numerous choices in locating settlements. Their decisions, based on changing perceptions, influenced the direction and form of settlement over time. Frontier settlement patterning reflected contemporary perceptions of environment throughout the period of colonization.

THE PHYSICAL LANDSCAPE

Immigrants to Michigan formed perceptions of the region based on its perceived suitability for settlement and agricultural production. Knowledge of landforms, soils, climate, and vegetation all shaped the image of Michigan as a potential area for colonization, because these variables were crucial to its success. This analysis will assess the implications that Michigan's landforms, soils, climate, and vegetation had for the type of farming practiced by immigrant agriculturists. Michigan's geologic history produced a complex physical landscape that provided dissimilar opportunities for agricultural exploitation. Understanding the physiographic structure of this region is crucial in evaluating its potential for colonization as well as in assessing the effect of pioneer perceptions on settlement.

Environmental variables combined to create a physical landscape characterized by the latitudinal division of Michigan's Lower Peninsula into two broad regions. Its physiography is a result of geological forces that shaped the Great Lakes region during the Pleistocene epoch, when continental glaciation scoured the region's surface and depressed the earth's crust. The retreat of the last glacial advance brought differential rebounding of depressed surfaces as well as deposition of material carried in the ice. Much of the region's current topographic variation reflects the action of these processes to produce distinctive landforms.[19]

The surface topography of Lower Michigan varies across the peninsula (fig. 3.1). The northern portion is characterized by higher elevations that descend relatively sharply toward the

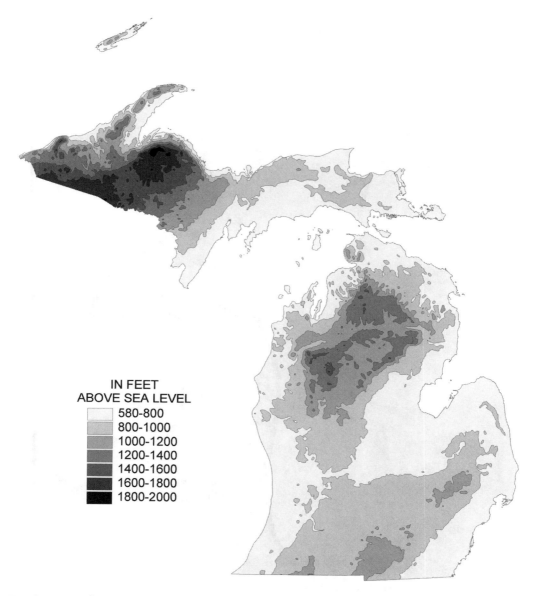

FIGURE 3.1. *TOPOGRAPHY OF MICHIGAN.* (Source: Leverett, *Surface Geology,* 108).

lakeshores and to a less marked degree toward the south. In general, the topography of southern Lower Michigan is more uniform and the surface is less uneven in appearance, although areas of higher elevation are located in Hillsdale and Oakland Counties. Broad relief features have been used as the basis for defining the character of the landforms found in the Lower Peninsula.[20]

Lower Michigan possesses four distinctive landform types (fig. 3.2). Hilly Moraines encompass much of the region's interior and are characterized by low ridges, or moraines, formed by the

FIGURE 3.2. *LANDFORMS OF MICHIGAN.* (Source: Sommers, *Michigan: A Geography*, 61).

extensive deposition of till at the slowly melting edge of glaciers. Between moraines lie till plains, which accumulated where ice fronts made a rapid recession, and outwash plains, deposited by flowing water from rapidly melting glaciers. The topography of the Hilly Moraines region is gently rolling to hilly, with large amounts of relatively level land. To the north a high sandy plain marks the southern boundary of the High Plains and Moraines, an interior landform characterized by higher elevations, more massive moraines, and a varied and uneven topography.[21]

Michigan's shorelines are characterized by two distinctive landforms. The very flat Eastern Lowlands occupy the eastern shoreline of the Lower Peninsula. A lake bottom at the end of the Pleistocene epoch, this region emerged as dry land when the earth's crust rebounded following the retreat of the glaciers. The Eastern Lowlands reach their broadest extent in the area surrounding Saginaw Bay and bordering Lakes St. Clair and Erie. Along the western shoreline, bordering Lake Michigan, wind and water have produced Beaches and Dunes that contrast markedly with landforms lying immediately inland. Both are a product of wind and wave action and have been subject to cyclical building and erosion. The dunes are often glacial ridges, the size of which has been accentuated by blowing beach sand carried inland by the prevailing westerly winds. Vegetation covers those farthest inland to produce relatively stable landscape features.[22]

The drainage patterns of the Lower Peninsula are closely linked to its landforms. The region's river systems flow westward into Lake Michigan, southeastward into Lakes Erie and St. Clair, northeastward into Saginaw Bay, or eastward into Lake Huron. Their headwaters flow outward from a divide that bisects the peninsula in a north-south direction following the highest altitudes of the Hilly Moraines and High Plains and Moraines regions. Midway along the peninsula's length, however, the divide extends westward abruptly, skirting the western boundary of the Eastern Lowlands. The great variation in the size of the watersheds of the area's major stream drainages is immediately apparent (fig. 3.3). The longest and broadest streams occupy the southern and western portions of the region, while the smaller stream systems are found further to the north and in the narrow portions of the Eastern Lowlands, through which inland streams descend relatively rapidly from the higher altitudes immediately to the west.[23]

Drainage patterns, which reflect the degree to which a stream has evolved an adequate system of tributaries, are also a product of topography (fig. 3.4). In Lower Michigan, much of the high, uneven portion of the peninsula exhibits a mature stream pattern characterized by rivers with well-developed tributary networks. A mature drainage pattern characterizes much of the northern Lower Peninsula, the Eastern Lowlands around Saginaw Bay, and the higher elevations of the eastern shore. The Beach and Dune region along Lake Michigan also exhibits a well-developed stream system. In contrast, much of the eastern shoreline exhibits a youthful stream pattern. Characterized by the presence of many parallel stream channels and intermediate areas of poor drainage, this pattern permitted the aggregation of the early French colonial population in linear riverine villages with direct access to Detroit. The region's poor drainage also fostered early perceptions of a swampy interior. Much of the southern interior exhibits an incomplete drainage pattern, characterized by small lakes, swamps, and bogs with dry land in between. Lakes are especially numerous in some areas of incomplete drainage. Oakland County, lying in the eastern part of this hydrographic region, contains 447 lakes within its boundaries.[24]

Michigan's potential as an agricultural region was also dependent on the nature of its soils, developed largely from material deposited by glaciers. The distribution of two predominant soil types divides the Lower Peninsula roughly into northern and southern sections (fig 3.5). Those in the north are called Spodosols, generally well-drained soils with low moisture-holding

FIGURE 3.3. *PATTERNING OF RIVER DRAINAGES IN MICHIGAN.* (Sources: Hudgins, *Michigan*, 4; Sommers, *Michigan: A Geography*, 43).

capacity that are subject to wind erosion. A short growing season and a predominant coniferous forest cover inhibits the accumulation of organic materials in these soils, and they possess a low natural fertility. Topography and hydrology affect the character of these sandy northern soils and result in a transition to the more fertile loams in the southern portion of the region. In southern Lower Michigan, Alfisols are the dominant soils. These fertile, well-drained soils are

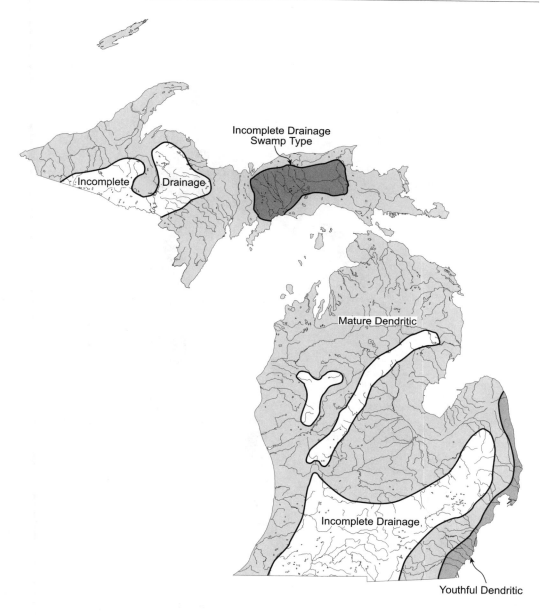

FIGURE 3.4. *HYDROGRAPHIC REGIONS OF MICHIGAN.* (Source: Davis, "Hydrographic Regions," 214).

the product of a longer growing season and the presence of deciduous vegetation that encourages the formation of humus. Their character also varies in response to topography and hydrology. For example, along the eastern shore region, level, poorly-drained land is wet and swampy in its natural state. Further inland, soils are drier because they occur on rolling to hilly terrain that provides more complete drainage.[25]

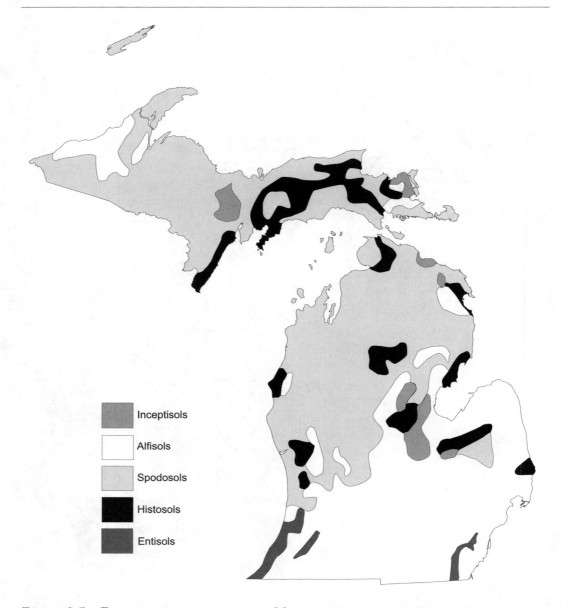

FIGURE 3.5. *DISTRIBUTION OF SOIL TYPES IN MICHIGAN.* (Source: Hill and Mawby, *Types of Farming*, 69).

Three other, minor soil types found in the region are poorly suited for agriculture in their natural state. These are alluvial Entisols, dry, infertile soils concentrated along the southern Lake Michigan shoreline. Moderately rich but poorly drained Histosols, composed of unde-cayed vegetable matter and peat, are found in pockets along the western shore, in the vicinity of Saginaw Bay, and in the northern part of the Lower Peninsula. Although the area around

Saginaw Bay also contains areas of richer Inceptisols, they are waterlogged in their natural state.[26]

Climatic variables also shape the environment of Michigan's Lower Peninsula. The region's latitudinal position, about midway between the equator and the pole, produces a region with moderate temperatures and strongly differentiated seasons. Michigan's continental position in the center of the North American landmass also creates a more seasonally extreme climate and subjects it to the influence of continental air masses which can change weather rapidly as they pass over the area. Its distance from the source of tropical moisture-laden air masses gives Michigan a drier climate than regions to the east and south.[27]

The changeability of Michigan's weather is accentuated by the region's location along the path of westerly air flows in the upper atmosphere. Deviations in the direction of the westerlies permit the invasion of Pacific, tropical, or polar air masses, resulting in rapid, short-term variations in weather as the region comes under their influence. Seasonal fluctuations in the configuration and intensity of the jet stream, which comprises the core of the strongest westerly winds in the upper atmosphere, produce spells of abnormally cold or warm weather.[28]

The Great Lakes surrounding the Lower Peninsula influence its weather on a smaller scale. Differences in surface temperatures of land and adjacent large bodies of water create lake effects. During warmer weather the lakes remove heat from the atmosphere, lowering average maximum temperatures along the Michigan shoreline. In the winter, when water temperatures are higher than those of the land, the lakes tend to warm the atmosphere passing overhead, forming cumulus clouds that drift inland to produce lake effect snow along the western shoreline. The cloudiness also serves to moderate winter temperatures by slowing nighttime reradiation in lakeshore areas, permitting these areas to enjoy higher minimal temperatures than at inland locations.[29]

Terrain and elevation have little affect on climate in the relatively level southern portion of the peninsula; however, in the northern Lower Peninsula, hilly terrain encourages the drainage of cold air formations and the formation of frost pockets in low-lying areas. Portions of this region commonly experience earlier fall and later spring frosts then would otherwise occur at comparable latitudes.

These variables combine to form two climatic provinces in the Lower Peninsula (fig. 3.6). In the south, the Transitional Province exhibits a warmer climate with a greater degree of variability. It has a higher average mean temperature and is milder in winter and warmer in summer than the northern part of the peninsula. All of the Transitional Province has a frost-free period of at least 140 days, and the seasonal pattern of precipitation produces a wet spring and a dry fall. Snowfall is relatively light, with heaviest accumulations in the west. Severe weather occurs with greater frequency in this region, however, and can include hailstorms, freezing rain, thunderstorms, and tornadoes.[30]

The Lacustrine Province in the northern Lower Peninsula exhibits a more stable climate. This province is colder and has a shorter growing season, which ranges from 120 to 140 frost-free days on the lake periphery to between 80 and 120 days in the uplands of the interior. Precipitation varies across the province and is seasonal, with the heaviest amounts occurring in the fall. Although winter snowfall is heavier, especially in the western and northern parts of the region, the Lacustrine Province experiences fewer forms of severe weather than does the Transitional Province.[31]

Although climate is generally stable and predictable, it is also subject to change over long periods of time and fluctuations over the short term. During the last thousand years, climates in Europe and North America have undergone several major fluctuations. Between A.D. 900 and 1300, a period of extremely mild weather prevailed, followed by a period of progressively colder climate, known as the "Little Ice Age." Because this cold period did not abate until the second half of the nineteenth century, Michigan's colonization occurred during the shift toward a warmer and drier climate more typical of recent years.[32] Although this recent climatic fluctuation did not alter natural vegetation patterns or the overall habitability of Lower Michigan, this trend may have affected perceptions of the region as an area of potential agricultural settlement. The occupation of Michigan occurred at a time when the warming of northern climates was of especial interest to those concerned with determining the course of agricultural expansion in the Old Northwest.

Variation in landforms, soils, and climate all affected the nature of the biotic communities in Michigan's Lower Peninsula at the time of colonization. The region lies on the boundary of two of the major biotic provinces of North America and is transected by a zone of transition (fig. 3.7). To the north, the Canadian Province was characterized by hardwood climax forest, although the prevalent sandy soils of the northern Lower Peninsula resulted in extensive growth of subclimax pine forest. The Carolinian Province immediately to the south was characterized by a hardwood climax forest dominated by hard maple and beech on heavier soils or oak and hickory on sandier soils. A subclimax forest of elm and ash occurred in wetter locations surrounding Saginaw Bay and along the eastern lowlands. In southwestern Michigan large areas were covered by tall grass prairies. This subclimax community appears to have been a vestige of earlier prairie intrusions and a result of its nearly level topography, which exposed the areas to high wind and fire risks. Pine communities, so prevalent to the north, occurred only in the dune areas bordering Lake Michigan. The boundary between the two biotic provinces forms a tension zone containing a mixture of species from both. This zone approximates the transition from finer to coarser-textured soils and extends about thirty-one miles on either side of a line drawn from Saginaw to Muskegon.[33]

In the early nineteenth century, the forests of both biotic provinces dominated the landscape of the Lower Peninsula. These plant communities are thought to have been relatively stable at a macro-environmental level, although disturbances by natural and aboriginal human agents had impacts on a smaller scale.[34] For example, the use of fire by Native peoples seems to have played an active role in maintaining both prairies and associated open woodlands in southwestern Lower Michigan. Land clearing by aboriginal agriculturists also resulted in the destruction of forests along river bottoms and upland areas. Many of these clearings were extensive, containing up to several hundred acres. Both of these modifications affected American perceptions of Michigan and helped shape assessments of its potential for agricultural production.[35]

FIGURE 3.6. *MICHIGAN'S CLIMATIC PROVINCES.* (Source: Niedringhaus, *Climatology of Michigan,* 182).

Although viewed through the lens of antebellum perceptions, the agricultural capacity of Michigan's aboriginal environment was tied to physical factors crucial to raising pioneer crops. Michigan lands have been classified in terms of their potential to support modern farming on the basis of climate, soils, and topography. Because these aspects of the environment have not changed substantially since the time of colonization, such a classification is useful as a means of determining the land's capacity for sustaining past agriculture as well.

FIGURE 3.7. *VEGETATION ZONES IN MICHIGAN*. (Source: Medley and Harman, "Vegetation Tension Zone," 79).

The climate of the Lower Peninsula is amenable to the production of a wide variety of commercial cultigens and does not, if all other things are equal, preclude any area from potential production. Both average mean temperature and length of growing season decrease as one proceeds northward and inland from the lakeshores (fig. 3.8). Because these variables are critical to the raising of crops, the distribution of temperatures tends to restrict the nature of crops grown as well as the geographical range of their production. Lower Michigan's climate is amenable to

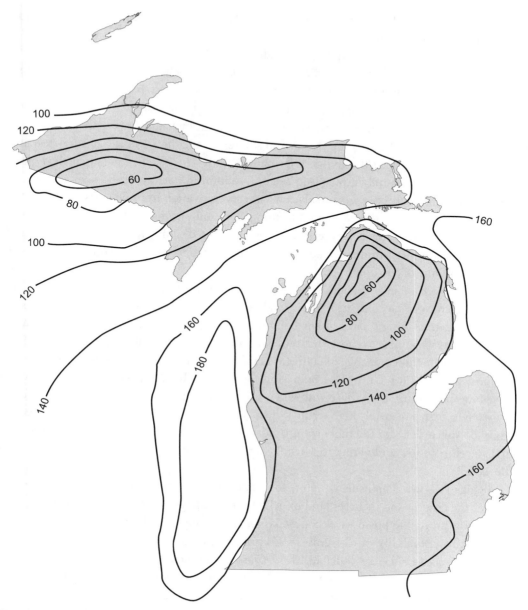

FIGURE 3.8. *LENGTH OF GROWING SEASON IN MICHIGAN, AS MEASURED BY THE MEAN ANNUAL NUMBER OF FROST-FREE DAYS.* (Source: Eichenlaub, *Weather and Climate,* 206).

the production of cultigens commonly found in northern latitudes, such as corn, wheat, oats, barley, and rye, as well as potatoes, vegetables, fruits, and hay. Length of growing season limits the range of corn to the southern half of the peninsula. Wheat and rye, on the other hand, can be grown over a much wider area, and oats and barley can be cultivated under all the climate conditions experienced in the Lower Peninsula. Fruit production is also possible in the climatic zone along the Lake Michigan shore, where long, cool springs, mild summers, and late fall frosts provide ideal conditions for the cultivation of fruit trees.[36]

Successful agriculture also requires adequate soils and topography. In the northern part of the region, sandier soils of lower organic content possess generally lower fertility and moisture-holding capacity. This limits the cultivation of grains in the northern half of the peninsula, and restricts the growing of most crops to the lakeshores. Topography also helps to determine agricultural capability. Extreme elevations in the north influence climate, which markedly decreases the length of the growing season and severely limits the area's agricultural potential. The slope of the land affects the ability of farmers to cultivate the soil and restricts the types of crops that can be successfully grown. Although the southern portion of the peninsula is relatively level, rough and rolling terrain adversely affects cultivation in some areas. Extreme conditions of drainage and erosion also limit farming. For example, the level, poorly drained lands around Saginaw Bay, although very fertile, require artificial draining to make them productive. On the other hand, well-drained sandier soils in more rolling areas are subject to droughty conditions and topsoil erosion.[37]

An assessment of the agricultural potential of land must consider the growing requirements of the crops to be cultivated. Michigan lands may be assessed with regard to their suitability for mixed farming typical of antebellum northern agriculture to create a classification employing criteria similar to those that pioneer farmers found useful in selecting lands. Such general farming included a range of cultigens consisting of cash crops as well as forage for livestock and products for family use, and lands suitable only for specialty crop production received lower rankings than those with wider capability. The ideal land type for mixed farming possesses, first, a relatively high fertility of soil and durability of yields; second, relative uniformity of soil over a considerable area; third, a physical character favorable for good tilth; fourth, level or gently undulating topography; and finally, intermediate amounts of moisture in the soil.[38]

Michigan's Lower Peninsula contains four categories of farmland. First-Class Land satisfies all of the criteria and includes land on which well-managed mixed agriculture can be carried on as a profitable business. Second-Class Land is only slightly inferior on the basis of natural fertility, durability, or topography. It is considered usable, but might represent a second choice if first-class land were available. Third-Class Land is generally arable, but exhibits some characteristic or combination of characteristics that makes its potential for agricultural use remote. Such lands might provide a base for limited subsistence farming or intensive farming for specialty crops on small tracts, but are marginal for mixed agriculture. Finally, Fourth-Class Lands are unsuitable for farming. They consist of sandy soils of lowest fertility and durability, peat swamps, and steep and rocky lands.[39]

Because mixed farming will most likely be successful on First- and Second-Class lands, their relative distribution should indicate those areas where agricultural colonization could have been most efficiently carried out. Table 3.1 reveals that these lands are most prevalent in the southern half of the peninsula and constitute more than 90 percent of the total area in some counties. In contrast, they generally constitute less than 50 percent of the territory in

TABLE 3.1. *PERCENTAGE OF LAND CLASSES BY COUNTY IN MICHIGAN'S LOWER PENINSULA*

County	1st Class	2d Class	3rd Class	4th Class
Alcona	8	26	31	35
Allegan	25	38	10	18
Alpena	26	22	31	21
Antrim	16	36	32	16
Arenac	28	25	16	31
Barry	28	48	15	9
Bay	50	35	11	4
Benzie	5	31	44	20
Berrien	39	39	16	6
Branch	46	43	8	3
Calhoun	43	38	15	4
Cass	26	35	27	12
Charlevoix	15	31	35	19
Cheboygan	9	30	28	33
Clare	11	22	27	40
Clinton	70	26	3	1
Crawford	2	5	20	73
Eaton	69	27	4	1
Emmet	8	19	42	31
Genesee	67	23	9	1
Gladwin	10	32	22	36
Grand Traverse	10	31	26	33
Gratiot	65	25	7	3
Hillsdale	62	28	5	5
Huron	71	27	1	1
Ingham	38	47	13	2
Ionia	60	33	5	2
Iosco	7	20	16	57
Isabella	37	33	15	15
Jackson	36	42	14	8
Kalamazoo	44	34	13	9
Kalkaska	4	23	29	44
Kent	43	38	11	8
Lake	1	11	16	72
Lapeer	54	35	9	2

TABLE 3.1. (*CONTINUED*)

County	1st Class	2d Class	3rd Class	4th Class
Leelanau	7	57	24	12
Lenawee	68	28	3	1
Livingston	33	47	15	5
Macomb	60	22	15	3
Manistee	4	29	26	41
Mason	13	25	21	41
Mecosta	13	31	26	30
Midland	16	30	22	32
Missaukee	7	28	39	26
Monroe	58	17	23	2
Montcalm	25	47	21	7
Montmorency	5	17	24	54
Muskegon	12	12	24	52
Newaygo	9	19	29	43
Oakland	32	46	16	6
Oceana	10	37	29	24
Ogemaw	13	22	25	40
Osceola	5	50	34	11
Oscoda	3	11	19	67
Otsego	6	17	28	49
Ottawa	32	33	27	8
Presque Isle	19	24	21	36
Roscommon	2	10	21	67
Saginaw	48	37	12	3
St. Clair	52	31	9	8
St. Joseph	15	58	22	5
Sanilac	68	28	3	1
Shiawassee	60	37	2	1
Tuscola	46	36	13	5
Van Buren	22	42	27	9
Washtenaw	45	40	10	5
Wayne	31	35	33	1
Wexford	3	30	42	25

Source: Veatch, *Soils and Land of Michigan*, 63-65.

counties to the north. Figure 3.9 reveals that First- and Second-Class lands comprise from 61 to 97 percent of the land in all of the counties south of Saginaw Bay. The occurrence of these land classes drops sharply north of the tension zone between the major biotic communities, and this line seems to define a northern limit for antebellum mixed farming. Even today, it delineates the most intensively cultivated portion of Michigan.[40]

IMAGES OF THE LAND: PIONEER EVALUATIONS OF MICHIGAN'S ENVIRONMENT

Although the interior of Michigan's Lower Peninsula was still largely unknown to Americans in 1815, within a decade explorers and settlers had collected information sufficient to create images of the new land. Early image-makers tended to describe Michigan's environment broadly, ignoring diversity, to create pictures of the region as a whole. By the 1820s two broad but contrasting images of Michigan had appeared, portraying it in both a positive and a negative light.[41]

The first of these grew out of efforts to encourage immigration. Both the territorial government and private interests sought to promote settlement in Michigan, and each sponsored expeditions into the interior for the purpose of gathering favorable information about the area and its resources. As early as 1818 a party of Detroit citizens explored newly ceded lands northwest of the entrepôt. The 1820 Cass expedition traversed the Lower Peninsula from west to east, and in the following year the Sciawassa Company examined portions of the upper Saginaw drainage. Americans penetrated the lower Saginaw and River Raisin drainages in 1822 and explored beyond the headwaters of the latter the following year. Before the close of the decade much of the southern portion of the peninsula had been examined and described.[42]

These explorations produced favorable reports, which contrasted with earlier accounts of a low, wet, swampy interior. The editor of a White Pigeon newspaper confidently challenged earlier perceptions, proclaiming that

> The character of the interior of Michigan is much misunderstood. Instead of being a cold wet region, there is no country more dry, rolling, and pleasant, after you get 15 or 20 miles from the Lakes and their connecting rivers. The innumerable little lakes dispersed through the country serve to drain it perfectly; and one can scarce encounter a more pleasing sight than the gently rolling hills, covered with the orchard-like woods, which constitute the oak openings, surrounding one of those deep, clean and crystal like pools, abounding in fish.[43]

Favorable representations appealed to observers with both Romantic and Utilitarian perspectives and projected a positive image of the region without having to deal with specific environmental details. Writers of fictional literature drew upon contemporary attitudes regarding frontier Michigan. In Orlando B. Willcox's *Shoepac Recollections,* for example, a pioneer legislator extolled the virtues of the regional landscape to his peers: "Her oak openings are like the garden of Eden. Her forests are boundless. The scope of her prairies is unlimited." Stressing the potential of the region in its pre-settlement form, Jerome Wood in *The Wilderness and the Rose*

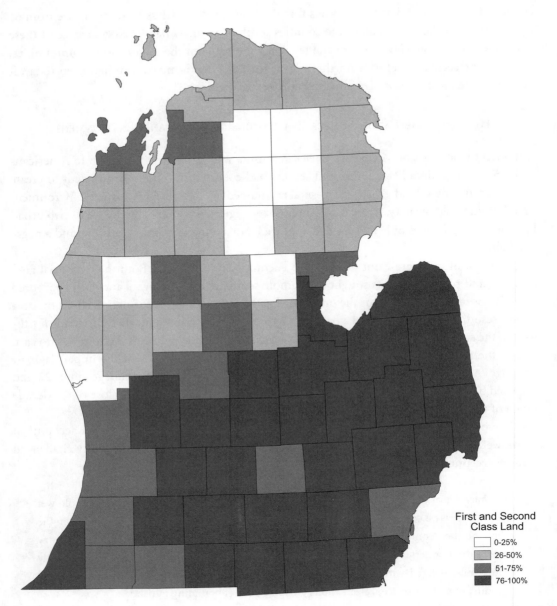

FIGURE 3.9. *DISTRIBUTION OF AGRICULTURAL LAND IN MICHIGAN BY CLASS.* (Source: Veatch, *Soils and Land*, 63–65).

envisioned the flower of productive agriculture, disguised by the cover of the natural vegetation, awaiting only the presence of "sturdy pioneers" to reveal its promise.[44]

In spite of overwhelmingly positive images that encouraged immigration to Michigan, an opposite view of an unfriendly environment also emerged that reflected Michigan's peripheral geographical position relative to settled portions of the United States and its vulnerability to invasion by its recently hostile neighbor, British Upper Canada. As a consequence, many Americans expressed uncertainty as to the nature of this frontier area. Estwick Evans, writing shortly after the War of 1812, observed that Michigan had "until lately been viewed as scarcely within the jurisdiction of the United States." Ignorance of the territory's geography was not uncommon among prospective immigrants. Thaddeus Smith, who later settled in Schoolcraft, admitted that on his arrival he "had no more idea of Michigan than I have of the most distant country in Europe."[45]

Unfamiliarity with the new country heightened newcomers' sense of isolation and fostered perceptions of a potentially hostile environment. Settling in unfamiliar landscapes in the absence of a dense, settled population and its associated institutions caused many to form impressions similar to those of Henry Little of Kalamazoo, who recalled that in the 1820s,

> Ann Arbor was the extreme west end of the habitable world, beyond which the sun went down into a bottomless morass; where the frightful sounds of yelling Indians, howling wolves, rattling massasaugas, and buzzing mosquitoes added to the horrors of that awful place.[46]

The editor of a Marshall newspaper reported that, to many, "the country west of Jackson is considered the *ultima Thule* of western population, and that beyond this point . . . is a barren waste." These generalizations were echoed on an individual level by immigrants such as Edward Parsons, who settled in Grand Blanc Township in 1835. Sitting "alone and forlorn" in his log house shortly after arriving, he confided in his diary that, "It seemed as though I had commenced farming in a boundless wilderness."[47]

Failed colonists spread stories of a poor and inhospitable environment, and speculators and others attempting to direct western settlement elsewhere added their accounts of how difficult life was in Michigan. Their descriptions emphasized the personal dangers and deprivations of the frontier and repeated earlier erroneous reports of a wet and foreboding land unfit for agriculture. Despite the generally positive image Michigan enjoyed in the eastern press, contradictory views persisted well into the settlement period. As late as 1837, a friend in Albany, New York, could still chide a recent immigrant to Monroe by inquiring, "What made you go to Michigan, that country of swamps, bogs, and fever ague?"[48]

Michigan interests, sensitive to slander, combated unfavorable publicity by publishing detailed information about the territory in works such as Blois's *Gazetteer* of 1838, and by sending official agents to the East to promote immigration. In addition, settlers' and travelers' experiences, disseminated through private correspondence and the popular press, helped counter negative images by providing eastern readers with glowing reports of the agricultural potential of the newly opened country. For example a former Ohio colonist arriving in DuPlain Township in Clinton County, proclaimed, "Michigan is an excellent country of land, far superior to Ohio," and a previously unsuccessful land-seeker from Ohio "felt [so] pleased when I saw that country that I laid my money in Michigan." The increasing flow of information helped expand immigrants' knowledge of Michigan's landscape and changed the territory's image from that of a wilderness to that of a settled agricultural region.[49]

Understandably, early observers of the Michigan environment looked carefully at variables most crucial to the development of agriculture. Their evaluations depended heavily on perceptions of soil fertility, composition, and drainage, characteristics that were thought to be reflected in the natural vegetative cover. The use of vegetation as a guide to the usefulness of soil for agriculture derived from the colonial experience in America, but limited contemporary understanding of the links between vegetation and fertility, coupled with changing general perceptions of grassland and forest soils, served to confuse the assessment of Michigan's varied physical landscape.

Initial explorations of the interior examined and systematically evaluated newly ceded lands for their potential to support commercial agriculture. They revealed distinct regional environments, many of which compared favorably with familiar types in the eastern United States. They were "properly adapted to the various purposes of agriculture, and inferior to no inland country." An early visitor from Connecticut compared the open forests of Oakland and Macomb counties to those of "Ontario county, (N.Y.) in its early state." Contemporary guidebooks recognized variation in the environments of the interior, but noted that an absence of steep or broken topography and the generally good quality of its soils indicated that Michigan possessed great potential as a region for grain agriculture. The familiarity of these environments led observers to describe the country in Romantic terms. One immigrant noted that it had "no appearance of a wilderness or new country, only the lack of inhabitants. It resembles more what we imagine to be the *Fairy* or *enchanted land* . . . and . . . more beautiful than art can make any park." Even those with scientific training often chose to characterize the interior landscape in terms of its picturesque nature rather than its utilitarian content.[50]

Although pioneers disagreed as to which frontier lands were best for farming, their increasing familiarity with Michigan's countryside resulted in the recognition of several land types. Each was perceived to possess particular advantages or disadvantages that affected its potential agricultural value and could be identified on the basis of distinctive vegetational characteristics. What were the principal land types recognized by immigrants to Lower Michigan, and how did the newcomers' images of them affect their settlement of the new country?

Heavy Timbered Lands

Pioneer farmers encountered heavy timbered lands in many areas across the Lower Peninsula. Drainage patterns, however, distinguished the forests of the Lake Erie shoreline from the interior forests. Wet conditions inland from the Lake Erie shoreline generated negative assessments that described the area as a "flat, wet country . . . much of it heavy timbered,—the streams muddy and sluggish . . . ," or a land "clothed with a dark, thick forest, and deficient in running water, [that] presents a rather forbidding appearance." On the other hand, the well-drained interior forests exhibited "rolling, heavy timbered land, of the first quality, interspersed with oak openings, plains, and occasionally prairies," or "dense and lofty forests and scattered groves, interspersed with timber of the largest size."[51]

The soils of timbered lands attracted immigrant farmers who associated "dense and luxuriant vegetation" with fertility and believed that woodland soils, composed of clays, wet mucks, and dry black sandy loams, were enriched by the "deep vegetable mold" that accumulated on the forest floor. Settlers presumed that oats, buckwheat, rye, potatoes, and hay could be grown on these heavy soils, but that they were not as amenable to wheat. Forest soils produced good crops of corn only when sufficiently "dry and warm."[52]

Colonizers had to expend tremendous effort to prepare timbered lands for agriculture. In 1836, James Hall summed up the difficulties.

> The labor of clearing a woodland is the most arduous task to which the western farmer is subjected, and has constituted in itself, the greatest draw back to the continued growth of the new states, where the soil is rich and the timber is generally heavy; . . . a lifetime is consumed in opening a farm.[53]

First, farmers cut and burned the smaller trees and brush, and girdled the larger trees to kill them and to remove the overhead canopy of leaves. In this "deadening," some crops could be planted by hoe or harrow amidst the dead trees; however, the threat of falling limbs and branches made cultivating especially hazardous. Sometimes the larger trees were also cut, piled into large heaps, and burned prior to breaking the ground with a harrow. Even this more thorough destruction left the cleared ground filled with stumps and roots whose slow rate of decay prevented the use of the plow for several more years. On the whole, timbered land was the most expensive to make ready for cultivation. James Lanman's estimate of $15.00 per acre exceeded that of all other land types in Michigan.[54]

In spite of these disadvantages, New England emigrants sought out forestlands that were familiar to them. Pioneers such as Eugene Davenport's family found security and abundance in the timbered lands of the Grand River Valley. To these people the forest provided not only farmland but building materials, edible wild plants and animals, and a physiographic setting with which they, through previous experience, were well acquainted. Difficulties in preparing heavily timbered lands did not present a practical barrier to the settlement of forested areas in Michigan.[55]

To nineteenth-century Americans the western forest symbolized not only the crucible that had produced the frontiersman, but also a land of opportunity in which the Transcendental individualist might find the resources to achieve success in the new country.[56] In addition, the familiarity of the forest presented a noble and reassuring image to the immigrant assessing the character of the frontier landscape. Henry S. Sanford, exploring lands he had purchased in Kalamazoo County, left his impressions of the native forest:

> I love to go through our forests, and surely there can be no grander ones in America. Here were trees running up straight as an arrow 40 to 80 feet without throwing out a limb of all kinds, and noble trees they were . . . their trunks forming fluted columns whose shafts ran up beautifully to support the living canopy above and whose capitols were models formed by the Great Architect, . . . All around the view was enclosed by those living columns seen nearby,

towering up till man standing beneath feels diminutive & . . . and seeks to measure himself by them.[57]

Romantic perceptions of contemporary observers such as Sanford reflected many Americans' comfort and familiarity with the forest as well as its symbolic presence as a manifestation of humankind's place in the larger order. Timbered lands, however, were only one among several land types in frontier Michigan, each of which was perceived to possess distinct advantages for settlement and agriculture.

Oak Openings

Settlers moving inland from Detroit first encountered oak openings. In 1831, a resident of Tecumseh described the romantic grandeur of the countryside:

> These oak lands generally appear at the distance of ten to fifteen miles from the lakes. Here the surface of the country assumes the shape of a vast ocean, subsiding into its original tranquility when the fury of the tempest is assuaged, the land gradually rising and declining in regular and gentle swells for many hundred rods . . . these openings . . . are from twenty to thirty miles broad in some places, . . . As the emigrant proceeds west, . . . at a distance of fifty miles from Lake Erie, he finds himself in the region of the heavy oak openings and prairies.[58]

The openness, gently rolling character, and adequate drainage of this land type contrasted markedly with the wet forests and swamplands of the eastern shore. "I have now got among the rolling land, in a region full of lakes and oak openings," a relieved Charles Fenno Hoffman wrote in his journal. "I need hardly say how much more grateful such a country is to my eye than the level thickly-timbered lands about Detroit and Monroe." Contemporary sources reported that oak openings covered two-thirds of the surface in many interior counties.[59]

Pioneers recognized two types of openings, on the basis of topographic variation. Those on rolling terrain were called oak openings, while those on level land were called burr oak openings, burr oak plains, or simply plains. The openings impressed observers with their parklike appearance. Here trees generally of uniform size, about four to five feet tall, were distributed evenly over the surface of the land, like trees in an orchard, or sometimes clustered in groups. To James Fenimore Cooper, the vacant spaces bore "no small affinity to artificial lawns, being covered with verdure."[60]

Clearing oak opening lands was less laborious than preparing those covered by dense forest. It usually involved girdling the trees, removing those necessary for fencing, burning the debris and brush, and plowing. According to one pioneer, "the farmer has nothing to do but to girdle his trees & plow his ground." Because of the tightly matted grass and grub roots lying just below the surface, a team of three to six yoke of oxen was usually required to break the soil initially; however, subsequent cultivation was accomplished without such an extraordinary effort. The cost of preparing oak openings for cultivation was less than that for heavy timbered lands, averaging $8.00 to $12.00 an acre in 1839.[61]

The ease of clearing such lands led one farmer to estimate that he could "seed down forty acres the first year." The rate at which openings could be placed in production was a compelling reason for their settlement. The *Jackson Michigan State Gazette* cited the success of later immigrants who were forced to occupy the "neglected barrens" overlooked by earlier pioneers who had taken up all the wooded lands. Because of the lower labor requirement involved in clearing the openings, " . . . these settlers opened farms and enriched themselves . . . while those who preceded them were yet struggling for existence among the sullen forests. . . ."[62]

Immigrants wishing to engage in commercial agriculture recognized the potential of oak openings as a familiar natural landscape amenable to growing familiar crops, especially wheat. To many they resembled the lands lying west of the Genesee River in New York. These oak woodlands, first colonized in the late eighteenth century, proved to be extremely productive lands for wheat. The success of wheat farming in the Genesee country precipitated the shift in the perception of open landscapes discussed earlier and facilitated the settlement of oak openings in Michigan by northern colonists familiar with their agricultural potential. Immigrants from the southern Atlantic Seaboard who colonized Kentucky and Tennessee during the same period, and later portions of Indiana and Ohio, also recognized the advantages of farming oak woodlands. Pioneers who had initially settled further south often migrated to southwestern Michigan because they found the openings a familiar land type.[63]

Prairies

Michigan settlers' changing perception of open and treeless lands from wastes to potential gardens hastened the acceptance of prairies as a destination for agricultural colonists. Michigan prairies, generally much smaller in size than those in nearby Indiana and Illinois, did not present the eastern immigrant with the harsh winter winds, lack of wood and water, and isolation associated with these lands elsewhere. Combining the advantages of familiar environments with those of an open landscape, prairies became the land type desired most by immigrants from New York and the upland South.[64]

Early observers recognized treeless landscapes as a distinctive land type. Major John Biddle, who traversed the Lower Peninsula from west to east in 1819, reported that beyond the "thick woods" around Detroit, "the country is either prairie, or covered with wood thinly dispersed." Later writers recognized that prairies, characterized as "destitute of timber" and covered with a "heavy growth of grass," were confined "mostly to the southern or southwestern portion of the Peninsula." This land type appeared picturesque to the eye of the Romantic observer, and its vastness often overwhelmed those accustomed to living in forested environments. "I can compare these prairies to nothing better than an immense lake of land extending as far as the eye can reach," wrote Lansing B. Swan of Rochester, New York, in 1841. "They meet the traveler at any point, . . . seeming like so many lakes, being often studded with wooded islands, and surrounded by forests," echoed James Lanman. Harriet Martineau described prairies as "a wilderness of flowers," and concluded that "Milton must have traveled in Michigan before he wrote the garden parts of 'Paradise Lost.'"[65]

Contemporary writers spoke of dry and wet prairies, the former being distinguished by a slightly undulating topography that allowed natural drainage. Wet prairies, on the other hand, occurred on level ground and were poorly drained. To a contributor to the *Calhoun County Patriot*, they had the "appearance of submerged land. In them grass is often six or seven feet high. They are the retreat of waterfowl, muskrats, pike and pickerel." Because of the similarity of the descriptions of wet prairies and marshlands, the two terms are likely often to have been used interchangeably.[66]

The distinction between wet and dry prairies gave rise to two alternate explanations for the creation of grasslands. The first contended that prairies were beds of evaporated lakes over which subsequent deposits had accumulated. Support for this idea was based on the presence of existing ponds overlain by deposits of vegetable matter which were assumed to be vestiges of such bodies of water. Opponents of this explanation, including the majority of settlers in prairie areas, countered that prairies had been created by periodic ground fires, presumably set by aboriginal peoples for hunting purposes. Colonists believed that these fires, which occurred well into the early years of settlement, destroyed all trees and undergrowth and permitted grass to remain as the dominant vegetation.[67]

The advantages of cultivating dry prairies derived from the nature of their soils and the relative ease with which these lands could be cleared. Prairie soils, believed to be four to six feet deep, consisted of "a black vegetable mould intermixed in small measure with clay, sand, or gravel." Many considered these soils to be the most fertile in Michigan, as well as extremely durable. Farmers produced yields of thirty to eighty bushels of corn and twenty-five to forty bushels of wheat per acre on the prairies, in addition to good crops of oats and potatoes. Prairie soils were seen as particularly well adapted for wheat. Wet prairies, on the other hand, served as a source of hay or for winter pasture.[68]

Although prairies possessed no forest cover to clear, the tough grass sod required at least three yoke of oxen to break the soil. The heavy soil was difficult to work, but required no hoeing between seeding and harvest. Wood for construction and fuel was supplied by adjacent timbered lands or islands of forest. The cost of clearing and fencing prairies was about $10.00 an acre.[69]

Marsh and Swamplands

Antebellum observers recognized two categories of wetlands: marshes, which were intermittently wet, and swamps, whose surfaces lay submerged the entire year. Marshes were scattered over much of Lower Michigan and were generally believed to be remnants of older shallow lakes or a result of streams impounded by beavers. Marsh vegetation consisted of scattered trees or small groves of tamarack, and tall grass.[70]

Although marshlands were undesirable areas for human settlement, farmers harvested grass from these lands for hay and seasonally grazed their livestock on these wetlands.[71] M. Shoemaker, who settled in Jackson County in 1830, later recounted that

> For hay [early immigrants] found a ready, abundant and excellent supply in the grasses on the marshes, which were on the borders of all the streams and lakes in the county. This was a most favorable circumstance for the pioneer, as it enabled him to feed his teams and winter his stock . . . at an expense much less than he could otherwise have done.[72]

While traveling in Allegan County, Bela Hubbard inquired into the worth of a particular wetland, only to be informed that an estimated three thousand sheep were regularly wintered on marsh hay there.[73]

The permanently inundated swamps of the Eastern Lowlands assumed a more pessimistic image. Here the relatively level terrain produced slow-moving streams and a great deal of standing water. Passing up the River Rouge in 1828, Munnis Kenny entered in his diary that he traveled along "a sluggish nasty stream full of logs, and weeds, no current, can hardly tell which way it runs, the land's a dead level, and everything looks unhealthy and poisonous."[74] Large swamps were also a hindrance to travel. In the mid-1830s, an early resident recalled that

> Southern Michigan was considered one of the most difficult regions to settle, mostly on account of the great cottonwood swamp, which emigrants encountered shortly after entering the state. This swamp was about twenty miles across and in the spring time it was almost a complete barrier to emigration.[75]

Although these swamplands were seen as "poor country," their elevation was great enough to allow them to be drained for agricultural purposes. The absence of adequate technology and effective political coordination, however, delayed large-scale drainage of the eastern swamplands, and much of this area remained unsettled until the second half of the nineteenth century. The avoidance of swamplands had profound implications for settlement patterning in southeastern Michigan.[76]

Pine Lands

To the north of the deciduous forest region of Michigan lay the pine lands that marked the transition to the coniferous forests of the northern Lower Peninsula. Although this area was opened to settlement shortly after its cession to the United States in 1836, it was not rapidly occupied. Immigrants generally avoided the pinelands because of their reputation for having mediocre agricultural soil. Soil quality and an association with swamps and lowlands, coupled with the notion that pine lands were most valuable for their timber, caused this land type to rank below prairies, oak openings, and timbered lands.

Perceptions that pinelands were less than satisfactory for agriculture impeded settlement in the north. Contemporary authors characterized the region as one of softwood forests with soils of uncertain quality. John Blois expressed its ambiguous image when he observed in 1838 that

> On the north-eastern border, the evergreens seem to predominate, as pine, spruce, hemlock &c. and in the northern part, . . . large forests of pine . . . The sandy soil of the pine lands . . . is generally well known, though it is stronger and more productive than it is commonly believed to be, by those unacquainted with it. . . . [77]

James Lanman, writing a year later, was also guardedly optimistic about pinelands. Such areas, he reported, "contain extensive groves of pine; and the land, although broken by small hillocks and swamps, is in many parts favorable for agriculture." Others countered these perceptions, emphasizing that the "dark forests of pine" were inaccessible and were filled with swamps and other uninhabitable landforms. Faced with alternatives, farmers avoided pinelands, even when offered at minimum prices.[78]

The value of pinelands rested on their potential as a source of lumber and other forest products. Although the development of large-scale industrial lumbering did not occur until the second half of the nineteenth century, a regional market for lumber developed early, and specialized mills were in operation by the 1830s, primarily in the Saginaw Bay area. Here land values were based on the quality of timber as well as access to navigable water routes by which it could be removed.[79]

PERCEPTIONS OF MICHIGAN'S CLIMATE

Next to the land itself, climate determined the success or failure of commercial and subsistence agriculture. "Every other advantage of a settlement is secondary to that of climate," proclaimed Sidney Smith to the readers of his guidebook published in 1849. Climate dictated the range of crops to be grown and helped to form the perceptions of immigrant farmers regarding the suitability of Lower Michigan for agriculture as they practiced it. Settlers found the region amenable to the cultivation of crops grown in the northeastern United States; however, their understanding of its climate was influenced by a limited knowledge of contemporary weather, particularly in the West, as well as by myths that arose in an effort to explain it. Both affected evaluations of the peninsula's potential for commercial production.[80]

Michigan was colonized at the close of the "Little Ice Age," a period when temperatures over much of the earth remained relatively cool. The climate, however, fluctuated considerably during this period. Although weather statistics for the first half of the nineteenth century are incomplete, contemporary records from the eastern United States and Europe present a reasonably complete picture of climatic trends.[81]

Perhaps the most noticeable factor in climatic fluctuation is temperature. Temperature distribution is crucial to agriculture because it determines the length of the growing season, and temperature extremes can affect transportation and communications as well as an area's

perceived habitability. Average annual mean temperatures in the northern hemisphere fluctuated before 1860, with markedly cold periods in the closing years of the eighteenth century
and the first decade of the nineteenth century (fig. 3.10). Mean winter temperatures followed
a similar trend, and the very cold decade of the 1810s laid the basis for the advance of
European glaciers in the 1820s. In the northern United States, the "cold year" of 1816 brought
frosts in June and August as well as two June snowstorms that produced a disastrous harvest
in New England and jeopardized agricultural production. The mid-1820s brought significantly milder weather; though, the following three decades saw fluctuating average temperatures punctuated by extremely cold episodes in 1831, 1835–36, and 1842–43.[82]

Weather statistics for Lower Michigan are available only after 1840, but they mirror the
patterning observed elsewhere. The distribution of mean winter temperature averages at
Detroit (fig. 3.11) clearly reveals cold winters in 1843, 1847, 1849, and 1855–57, as well as warm
winters in 1842, 1844, 1845, 1851, and 1853.[83]

Although the antebellum climate did not preclude western colonization, its extreme fluctuations affected immigration by creating two important weather myths. The first centered on
a dangerously unpredictable New England climate so severe that it played an important role in
encouraging the abandonment of eastern agricultural lands in favor of those in the West. The
devastating hurricane of 1815, followed by cold and drought the following year, resulted in
agricultural failures. Coupled with the industrial downturn following the War of 1812, these
agricultural failures produced a severe economic depression that encouraged thousands to
emigrate to western New York and Ohio. When temperatures once more plummeted in the
1830s, New England farmers again became concerned about a regional climate many perceived
as too erratic to support a wide range of crops. This image, reinforced by the cold winters of
the 1830s and 1840s, caused a second migration of New England farmers to places believed to
have a less hostile climate.[84]

The second myth arose from an erroneous romantic perception that the land west of the
Appalachian Mountains was inherently warmer than that found in similar latitudes on the
Atlantic Seaboard. This myth was reinforced by subjective observations of a mild climate and
the presence of warm weather flora in northerly latitudes along the Ohio and Mississippi Rivers
and over time gained a general acceptance. Despite conflicting evidence, the myth remained in
popular literature until disproved by scientific observation and the weight of pioneer experience. The myth of a warmer West undoubtedly played an important role in attracting farmers
to Michigan and to other newly opened regions, especially those who had endured the uncertainty of cold and variable climates in Europe and the northern Atlantic Seaboard.[85]

The nature of Michigan's climate was of concern throughout the settlement period. Early
observers found its climate comparable to that of the northeastern states, and the author of one
account described it as "delightful . . . a good medium between our extreme northern and
southern latitudes." Advocates of immigration portrayed the climate as ideal for raising grain
and livestock on the newly opened lands and argued that it, like the West generally, "is several
degrees *milder* than in the same parallels of latitudes in the eastern states." Warden's statistical
account echoed the myth of a warmer West by comparing southern Michigan with southern

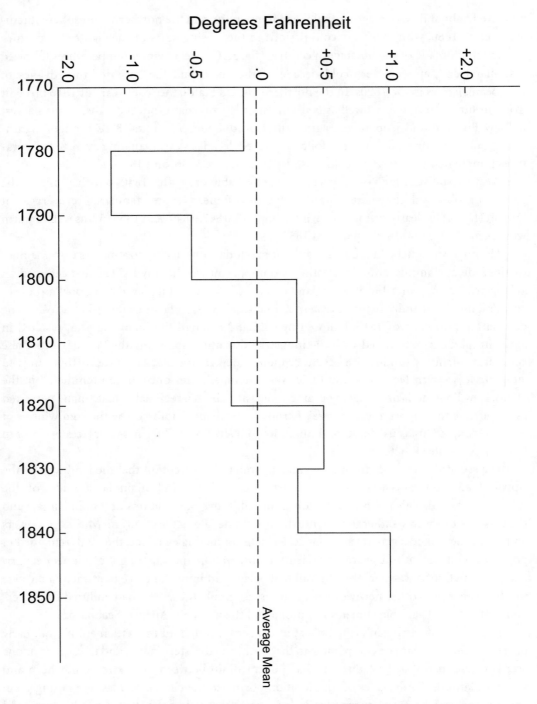

FIGURE 3.10. *GENERAL TEMPERATURE TRENDS BY DECADE IN THE NORTHERN HEMISPHERE FROM 1770 TO 1850, AS MEASURED BY THE DIFFERENCE FROM THE MEAN TEMPERATURE OF THE ENTIRE PERIOD.* (Source: Bloget, *Climatology of the United States,* 490).

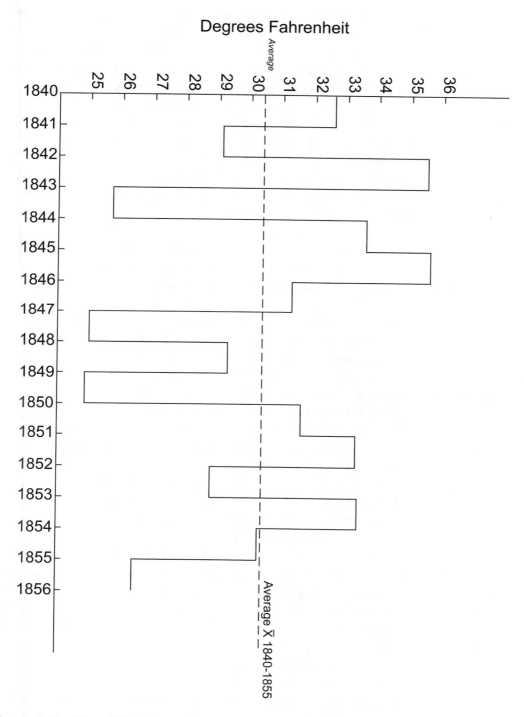

FIGURE 3.11. *MEAN WINTER TEMPERATURES AT DETROIT FROM 1840 TO 1856.* (Source: Harrington, "Climate of Detroit," 318).

and western New York, Pennsylvania, New Jersey, Delaware, Maryland, and the northern extremes of Ohio, Indiana, and Illinois. Its author emphasized that the winter season was shorter in Lower Michigan than those of the East and was characterized by a relative absence of snow. In contrast, he characterized that part of the peninsula north of the southern extreme of Lake Huron as having a more forbidding climate, with short summers and long winters resembling those of Canada and New England. Pioneer observers saw southern Lower Michigan's climate as generally uniform, although slightly milder near the Lake Erie shore, and without the temperature extremes experienced in parts of the Northeast. In addition, they believed that the region was not prone to violent weather.[86]

Short winters and an early transition to summer in southern Lower Michigan insured a lengthy growing season amenable to the cultivation of crops normally grown in temperate latitudes. The editors of *Atkinson's Casket* reported that,

> wheat, Indian corn, oats, barley, buckwheat, potatoes, turnips, peas, apples, pears, plums, cherries, and peaches are raised easily and in abundance. It is more favorable to cultivated grasses than the western country generally, and in short, is in every way adapted to northern farmers.[87]

Others observed that latitudinal differences had a marked effect on the nature and scheduling of agriculture. The editor of the *Michigan Farmer* was careful to inform his readers that the wheat harvest took place progressively later, the farther north one traveled, and emphasized that corn cultivation possessed geographical limits in southern Michigan.[88]

Antebellum writers attributed the climate of Lower Michigan to factors both real and imaginary. Michigan's situation amid the Great Lakes was believed to subject it to their "tempering" or "softening" effect on climatic extremes and ameliorating effect on winter storms. Southwesterly winds, emanating from the hot western plains, were seen to produce a warmer climate than at comparable latitudes in the East, and their continental origin was believed responsible for a drier climate with less snow in the winter. The presumed burning of large tracts of western prairie lands by Indians in the early fall was believed to have had a transient warming effect. The fires, and the smoky atmosphere they produced, created the "Indian Summer" weather characteristic of the northeastern United States.[89]

Many felt that human modification of the environment also modified the climate. Advocates assumed that the clearing of lands for agricultural settlement resulted in a perceptible lowering of winter temperatures. Francis R. Stebbins, a longtime resident of Adrian, recalled that although mild winters had prevailed in the 1830s, "Twenty years of settlement and clearing up of the timberlands so changed the climate that . . . the springs [in the later part of the century occurred] fully thirty days later than before 1854." He attributed the abandonment of peach production in southeastern Michigan largely to this climatic shift. Although dramatic, the perceived cooling trend and the persistence of Indian summer were more likely a result of climatic fluctuations in the closing part of the Little Ice Age than a consequence of human activity.[90]

Climatic variation and its dramatic effect on weather, especially in winter, was not immediately apparent to early Michigan pioneers. Although occasionally severe, winters of the 1820s were often warm. That of 1822–23 was long remembered for its deep snows and terrible cold temperatures that were especially devastating to wildlife. So mild was the weather the following year, however, that cattle fared well outside all winter and residents of Tecumseh commenced planting in February.[91] The *Detroit Gazette* proclaimed:

> The calendar tells us we have winter, and that it is nearly passed. We have had very little cold weather; almost no snow; . . . such a season, even in this comparatively mild climate, has not been seen within the recollection of the oldest inhabitant.[92]

Indeed, many winters of the 1820s were so moderate in Michigan that some new residents were caught unprepared for more severe winters. Those of 1830–31 and 1831–32 were accompanied by heavy snows and cold temperatures. In 1830, storms set in by early November and continued through the end of the year. Even Deputy Surveyor Lucius Lyon, accustomed to the region's winters, was surprised by this sudden fluctuation in climate. Throughout December 1831, temperatures remained below freezing, and "old inhabitants" as well as new immigrants found it "uncommonly" cold. Thomas Wright wrote in his diary one cold January day, "I had expected to find mild winters here, but I find I was deceived." New settlers in Jackson County were similarly unprepared and survived only with the help of local Indians.[93]

Although mild winters from 1832 through 1835 and a particularly hot summer in 1834 presented the image of a relatively warmer climate to the immigrants who flooded into Michigan, two disastrous winters finally demolished this notion. The long winter of 1835–36, known as the "Starving Time," was characterized by the persistence of very cold weather and heavy snows from early November through March, eliminating winter grazing and exhausting provisions. Edward Parsons noted in his diary, "Such a winter has never been known here . . . May we all learn our dependence." The cold weather adversely affected wildlife in Michigan as well, causing predators to migrate well south of their normal ranges.[94]

The losses of livestock and near famine conditions experienced in parts of Michigan in 1836 increased awareness of extreme winter weather; however, the isolated appearance of disastrous seasons made its occurrence unpredictable. Many assumed that the sudden return of a warmer winter in 1836–37 indicated that the previous cold winter had been only an anomaly, a conclusion that seemed to be borne out by a series of three warm winters. Edward W. Barber, an early settler in Vermontville in Eaton County, remarked that the seasons, "caused much favorable comment when comparing them with the severer winters of New England."[95]

The "Long Winter" of 1842–43 finally destroyed the perception of a warm West in Michigan. Like the winter of 1935–36, it brought severe cold of long duration and lasted nearly five months. The early onset of winter caught settlers unprepared and abruptly ended the shipping season on the lakes. Conditions were especially hard for farmers. Wells dried up and hay and fodder became scarce by late winter. The *Livingston Courier* commented, "the few who have any to spare command any price that their consciences will allow them, or their cupidity prompt them to ask." In the midst of the season, one resident of New Buffalo compared it to "a New Hampshire winter."

Starvation again took a heavy toll on livestock, and many new residents survived the winter on less than adequate supplies.[96]

The experience of two severe and long-lasting winters changed the image of Michigan's climate. Bitter experience and systematically collected weather data brought about a realization that the area's weather was subject to the same cold extremes encountered at similar latitudes in the East and that prudent frontier farmers had to anticipate them. This realization did not dismiss Michigan's great agricultural potential; however, it made its residents aware that the regional physiography placed limits on settlement and agricultural production in the new country.[97]

HEALTH AND DISEASE IN MICHIGAN

In frontier regions, low population density and a poorly developed economic infrastructure placed a premium on a pioneer's ability to complete the extraordinary labor of farm-making, and made good health important to settlers' success. Pioneers generally perceived Michigan to be a healthy destination, because of the absence of many diseases endemic to older settled areas of the Eastern Seaboard. Nevertheless, travelers and immigrants continually introduced illnesses from other parts of the United States, and the region was not immune to such diseases as malaria, which plagued other frontiers of the upper Mississippi and Ohio Valleys.

Developing practical perceptions about the nature and causes of diseases and an understanding of their association with the frontier landscape became crucial to immigrants' success in this new country. Pioneer anxiety regarding health was apparent to eastern visitors like Henry Sanford, who remarked on "the interest manifested here . . . in inquiries about health. It shows," he remarked, "much more than the ordinary feeling which we show at home in our casual inquiries."[98]

Malaria, often referred to as the "ague" or "bilious fevers" in contemporary accounts, was perhaps the most widespread disease in the Old Northwest. Malaria is caused by several species of protozoa, spread from an infected to a noninfected host by the anopheles mosquito. Although not indigenous to Michigan, infected human hosts brought the disease into the Great Lakes area, where its vector spread malaria widely among the human inhabitants. Bilious fevers became endemic in Michigan by the early nineteenth century and occurred so regularly that the absence of malaria was sometimes a newsworthy event.[99]

So prevalent was malaria that many immigrants saw it as an unavoidable part of the pioneering experience. The disease was perceived to have only a temporarily disabling effect. Although victims experienced severe symptoms, they were usually fatigued but otherwise healthy between attacks. Indeed, exposure to malaria was believed to produce a "seasoning" that insured . . . against all further liability." The remitting nature of the disease led many to dismiss its seriousness. In nineteenth-century fictional literature, malaria was treated lightly and even humorously. Others, however, recognized the aftereffects of the disease on its victims, one of whom remembered that the "feeling of languor, stupidity, and soreness took possession of the body. . . . You felt as if you were . . . not killed outright, but so demoralized that life seemed a burden."[100] Although an obnoxious and debilitating ailment that interrupted or delayed the crucial work of farm-making and other frontier activities, pioneers recognized that malaria produced fewer hardships than other epidemic diseases. Henry Chamberlain, of New Buffalo, commented that it was "nothing to compare with consumption and typhus fever of the East." Malaria's peculiar nature thus reduced its perceived threat, and may have mitigated attempts to treat the disease medically.[101]

Even though pioneers did not see malaria as life threatening, they attempted to avoid its adverse effects by settling in areas where they believed it unlikely to occur. Immigrants based their decisions on the perceived causes of malaria and the existence of environmental conditions thought to be associated with the disease. Generally malaria was believed to be a result of exposure to "miasmas" that arose from decaying vegetation encountered in undeveloped lands, particularly in marshes and river bottoms, or where initial cultivation had destroyed the natural ground cover. Drinking tainted water from springs or rivers was also believed to bring on malaria or related complaints. Although pioneers often remarked on the "great number of . . . musketoes [sic]" that caused such a "great annoyance in warm weather," antebellum Americans generally did not associate these insects with the ague.[102]

During the period of initial settlement, most immigrants sought to prevent the ague by avoiding environmental conditions believed to produce miasmas. An Oakland County pioneer attributed the area's unhealthiness to the presence of standing water in the lakes, and Blois recommended areas possessing rapidly flowing water that prevented the formation of swamps and marshes. Pioneers often saw that altering the environment led to the disappearance of the disease. They perceived that damming rivers, draining marshes, and maintaining land permanently in cultivation brought about healthier conditions, which decreased the incidence of the disease and curtailed other offensive miasmas. Indeed, the residents of Marshall attributed the disappearance of malaria in 1841 to the draining of marshes, which increased the "purity of the atmosphere." Perceptions linking the incidence of malaria with wet conditions, decaying vegetation, and associated miasmas affected colonists' understanding of the Michigan environment and influenced their choice of lands for settlement.[103]

The periodic occurrence of epidemic diseases in Michigan affected perceptions of regional health differently than did malaria. Many of these, variously described as catarrh, erysipelas, scarlet fever, measles, smallpox, lake fever, diphtheria, typhoid fever, pneumonia, diarrhea, cutaneous disease, and influenza were common to other parts of the United States and occurred with some degree of regularity. Their impact varied in severity, but could be quite devastating to frontier communities. In 1832 Thomas Wright of Tecumseh wrote, "The influenza this winter has spread throughout the country and myself as well as most everyone else here have got it." Twelve years later an epidemic of "mortal distemper" brought "a good deal of sickness [and] quite a number of deaths of late at Michigan City." A similar distemper ravaged Shiawassee County, and particularly the settlements of Owosso and Corunna, in 1844. Such epidemics often nearly overwhelmed newcomers, who were still attempting to establish themselves in the new country and had few resources to fall back upon. Outbreaks of epidemic diseases were only sporadic, however, and their occurrence failed to alter perceptions of health in the region. Correspondents to Michigan newspapers regularly proclaimed that Michigan was as healthy as their previous homes had been, and saw proportionately lower death rates in Michigan as evidence of the region's healthy environment.[104]

In one dramatic instance, however, the occurrence of epidemic disease did slow colonization. The disease was Asiatic cholera, an extremely contagious and dangerous illness that spread rapidly westward from Europe to the Eastern Seaboard of North America. Unlike other diseases, cholera ran its course quickly and was often fatal. It appeared in Detroit in July 1832 and spread rapidly across the territory. Widespread fear of the disease, together with its high death toll, disrupted trade and immigration. "Business everywhere gives way to the excitement," proclaimed a Detroit newspaper, "and the cholera will have a great effect upon the commerce of western Michigan." Cholera's reappearance in 1834 brought a shorter but more serious epidemic which took an even higher toll of lives, and Detroit is reported to have lost a seventh of its population.[105]

The disruption caused by the cholera and other epidemics temporarily slowed western immigration and was felt most strongly in those parts of Michigan coming open to settlement. These outbreaks were considered anomalous occurrences of ubiquitous diseases of short duration that did not affect the region's healthiness. Consequently, they did not alter the positive image of Michigan's environment or permanently deter immigration to this agricultural frontier.[106]

THE IMPORTANCE OF THE ABORIGINAL LANDSCAPE

As American immigrants entered Lower Michigan after 1815, they encountered a landscape created by its previous inhabitants. Although pioneers viewed the region as a bountiful untapped wilderness, they were also aware of aboriginal modifications, many of which could be helpful in exploiting the new land.

Physical alterations to the land revealed evidence of previous occupants. Pioneers recognized human modifications and employed them in assessing the usefulness of the environment for agricultural production. Prairies and oak openings were seen as the result of the annual burning of grasslands and open forest by Indians to clear it of undergrowth.. Burning remained so prevalent in the late 1820s that the territorial government passed legislation to protect settlers' property threatened by those burning woods or prairies owned by others.[107]

Settlement sites, many of which predated the American occupation, comprised further direct evidence of aboriginal land use. Early explorers mentioned villages, some of which were still occupied and others only recently abandoned. Penetrating the Saginaw Bay region in 1821, the Sciawassa Company exploring party carefully noted the locations of villages and the agricultural potential of surrounding lands on the drainages of the Flint, Shiawassee, and Tittabawassee Rivers. Travelers' guides often listed village sites, describing their characteristics and potential for agriculture, and John Farmer's detailed immigrant maps provided a graphic portrayal of these potentially valuable landscape features as early as 1826.[108]

Immigrant farmers valued village sites because of their assumed association with fertile land as well as for their proximity to existing routes of access. Such trails influenced the placement of principal thoroughfares leading into the interior and shaped the transportation network linking individual frontier settlements. At the time of their arrival in 1829, pioneers saw the site of Jackson as highly desirable because it was situated at "a concentration of all the leading trails of the Peninsula," a situation they believed would make it "a central and important place of business."[109]

Indian agricultural fields, either abandoned or still in use for corn and other crops cultivated with the hoe, attracted the attention of American settlers. Old fields represented cleared land and, even if abandoned and overgrown, could rapidly be put into production using plow technology. American colonists were well aware of these advantages, and the presence of old fields had influenced the placement of earlier settlements on the Eastern Seaboard. Their presence along major rivers marked areas of previous cultivation, and immigrants recognized old fields easily from the surrounding groundcover. Mary Overton, who settled in the vicinity of Owosso in 1834, recalled how "an old Indian clearing of many acres" stood out clearly from the native forest vegetation. Elsewhere fields were smaller, but still clearly discernible to the immigrant farmers. In Walton Township in Eaton County, for example, early settlers found hundreds of acres among the oak openings cleared in small fields. Here, as elsewhere, these were easily identified, even when abandoned, by the presence of raised "corn hills," a distinctive feature in fields cultivated with the hoe.[110]

Often the presence of aboriginal fields drew settlement, and these were among the first lands farmed by Americans. W. R. McCormick, whose family settled in Bridgeport Township in Genesee County in 1832, for example, related that not long after their arrival, "My father took a great fancy to this old Indian field, which contained about one hundred and fifty acres without a stump or stone, and [was] ready for the plough." Daniel Harrington remembered clearly that his father, for example, sought out "Indian fields" on Black River in St. Clair County as early as 1819. Similarly, an "old Indian cornfield" attracted Sherman Stevens's family to the vicinity of Grand Blanc six years later. The earliest American settlement in Ingham County was made by Hiram Putnam on an "Indian planting ground" on the banks of the Red Cedar River. In the spring of 1837, Steven Davis, the first American settler on Charlotte Prairie in Eaton County, recalled that he "turned the first furrows with a civilized plow on land which heretofore had been cultivated only by Indians." Many nucleated settlements of the interior grew up on the sites of aboriginal occupations, including Jackson, Ionia, Charlotte, Bellevue, Ada, and Lowell. Clearly the aboriginal landscape was a factor that influenced frontier settlement patterning.[111]

Settlers observed aboriginal earthworks, including mounds, embankments, and ditches, and discovered habitation and burial sites on cleared land associated with old fields. Their association with earlier residents became clear as farmers unearthed artifacts as well as human bones in the course of preparing land for cultivation. In Michigan, as elsewhere, Americans attributed prehistoric remains to ancient peoples with no connection to the region's contemporary inhabitants. Because Michigan Indians were said to claim no knowledge of them, these relics were generally assigned to lost races without descendants. Pioneers treated evidence of prehistoric occupations with curiosity, but the study of the past was seldom reason to avoid developing land for agriculture or settlement. As a consequence, most aboveground prehistoric landscape features did not survive the period of agricultural colonization. Immigrants, however, often distinguished recently used burial grounds from ancient sites, and many were left undisturbed. Some were even incorporated into pioneer cemeteries.[112]

Pioneers used their knowledge of earlier land use to evaluate land for settlement. Because most immigrants to Michigan were primarily concerned with farm-making, Indian fields, villages, and earthworks were of special interest. Settlers often recognized aboriginal landscape features as improvements, whose presence identified the high agricultural potential of surrounding lands and increased their value. Many echoed the words of a chronicler of Ionia County who commented that early settlers near Lyons and Muir recognized that the "favorite abiding place for a race for whom we have . . . but little knowledge . . . [was] the most suitable and attractive situation," for their farms.[113]

4

The Impact of Perception on Settlement

The arrangement of overland routes leading into Michigan's interior encouraged the movement of settlement from the eastern lakeshore westward and northward parallel to the major stream drainages leading toward Lake Michigan and Saginaw Bay. Although expansion generally followed this pattern, perceptions of the environment affected the distribution of settlement and helped shape the form of frontier expansion. Michigan's pioneers developed clear images about the relationship of the region's physical environment to the potential success of settlement and agricultural production, and these images affected both the direction and order of colonization.

Pioneer perceptions of Michigan reflected both Utilitarian concerns of subsistence and commercial production and Romantic ideals about the natural world and contemporary myths regarding the American West. By the mid–1820s, Americans had explored the region's interior and found that it reflected the "unspoiled" natural beauty of the wilderness, while also possessing a climate and resources suitable for agriculture. It was not, however, regarded as uniformly desirable for cultivation. Based on the nature and distribution of vegetation, together with varying topographic and hydrographic conditions, colonists developed distinctive images of the interior as a series of environmental zones, or land types, of varying quality.

Settlers to Lower Michigan recognized six broad subregions, and believed each possessed a distinctive combination of general physical characteristics that affected its agricultural and settlement potential (fig. 4.1). Although they lacked precise boundaries and uniform environments, each became a distinctive zone, the form of which guided the placement of corridors of access as well as the movement of immigration into the interior. Pioneer images of subregional environments provide the key to assessing the role of environmental perception in Michigan's colonization.

THE EASTERN SHORE

The first American settlement in Michigan occurred along Lakes Erie and St. Clair and the Straits of Detroit and followed inland immigration routes into the upper drainages of the eastward-flowing rivers. Not far inland lay some of the highest elevations in Lower Michigan, and the resulting combination of topography, drainage patterns, and vegetation forms exposed colonists to a variety of environments. Experience gained on the Eastern Shore altered perceptions of Michigan's potential for agriculture by the 1820s and provided an impetus for inland settlement.

71

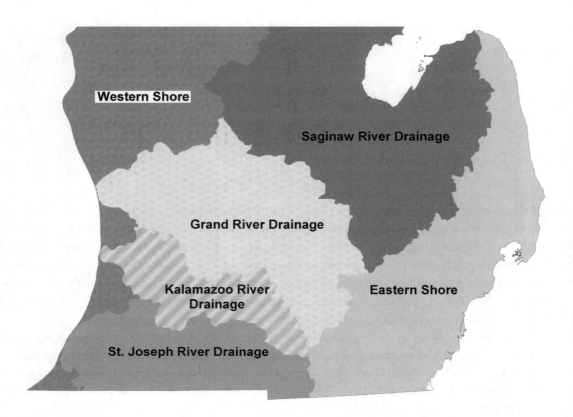

FIGURE 4.1. *DISTRIBUTION OF PERCEIVED ENVIRONMENTS IN ANTEBELLUM MICHIGAN.* (Sources: see text).

During the summer and fall of 1818, D. C. M'Kinstry organized a group of Detroit citizens to explore territory inland from the entrepôt and assess its capacity for settlement. They penetrated the interior as far as the center of present-day Oakland County and found openings containing "good soil," that would "do well for wheat." Furthermore, they believed that the undulating, heavily timbered lands nearer Detroit also were capable of supporting "excellent farms." The expedition's report also noted the ease with which the openings could be cleared and placed in cultivation.[1]

The positive report of this early exploration provided an encouraging image of the interior and established a precedent for the direction of settlement. The oak openings, in particular, became a magnet of settlement, and promoters of Oakland County stressed its similarity to the well-known wheat lands of western New York, as well as its prospects for waterpower. Accounts also appealed to those with other than utilitarian interests, referring to portions of this area as "a romantic and delightful country, abounding in rich and lofty hills, fertile vales, and numerous pleasant lakes."[2]

Although observers recognized the fertility of the timbered lands of the Eastern Shore, river bottoms and poorly drained intervening areas made the forests appear wet and conducive to disease. Traveling through Wayne County in 1831, O'Shea Wilder confided in his diary that the "timber & bottom lands [are] very sickly—none but Frenchmen can live in this region." Farmers who preferred woodland soils occupied only the higher elevations and used low-lying lands for grazing. Generally bypassed in search of open lands, the eastern forests remained initially sparsely settled.[3]

The impetus of settlement inland from Detroit carried exploration toward the Saginaw Valley and northward along Lake St. Clair and the St. Clair River. As early as 1822, observers described lands in present Oakland and Genesee Counties as "elevated and . . . gracefully uneven," and noted that the oak openings possessed rich soil. Level timbered lands farther north were "particularly adapted to the growth of Indian corn." Reports from Macomb County described a variety of deciduous timber, and soils comparable to those of central New York. One correspondent to the *Macomb Statesman* even claimed the soil there was superior to that on his previous farm in Lancaster County, Pennsylvania, a region highly regarded for its productive agricultural lands.[4]

In contrast, settlers perceived the low-lying Lake Erie shoreline to be much less suitable for settlement. Its lands were divided by numerous river channels and the swamplands of the lower Maumee River impeded access by land from both Detroit and Toledo. Existing French settlements near the mouth of the River Raisin at Monroe and other shoreline streams could be reached only by water, and the area's inaccessibility discouraged American immigration until the 1820s.[5]

Although initial impressions of the River Raisin led American observers to characterize the surrounding area as largely impassible, wet timbered lands, unfit for settlement, the discovery of oak openings soon changed the region's image and increased its appeal to immigrants. In 1820 the editor of the *Detroit Gazette* proclaimed, "The superiority of the soil, the salubrity of the climate, and the comparative ease with which the laboring man can acquire an easy independence render it an object worthy of the attention of immigrants." Subsequent observers favorably compared the soils of these uplands to those of the famed Genesee country. Changing environmental perceptions provided an impetus for inland settlement, and by the early 1820s southeastern Michigan had become a second focus for immigration.[6]

Pioneer accounts of the southern interior stressed the utilitarian advantage of the oak openings in their evaluation of the new country. Settlers in the Tecumseh area of Lenawee County, for example, clearly noted these "extensive tracts . . . where there is not a tree to obstruct the use of the plough, and where all varieties of grain can be produced plentifully, and in no country is there a more luxuriant growth of grass." The productivity of the openings soils impressed immigrants. Elizabeth M. Chandler, who with her brother and aunt settled near Tecumseh in 1830, wrote enthusiastically of the yields of corn and wheat, as well as the size of the vegetables produced. Comparing the openings' soils to those of her native Pennsylvania, she concluded that the former "will bear crops year after year without exhaustion. . . . It will even bear being served or planted with the same crop for several years in succession." The physical attractiveness of the openings further contributed to their image as a "pleasant" landscape, in contrast to the heavily timbered woodlands. Although both openings and interior timbered lands were successfully cultivated and proved equally productive, the low, wet, forested lands closer to the Lake Erie shore remained largely unsettled and unused even after the interior was developed as a stable agricultural region.[7]

Immigrants to the open, rolling countryside of Washtenaw County found a healthy climate, a well-watered surface, and soils "well adapted to the culture of all kinds of grains and vegetables."[8] The Romantic image of the area also appealed to newcomers such as Thomas Andrews, who wrote to his mother,

> No country ever possessed such advantages as this. It is filled with beautiful rivers and lakes of clear and transparent water . . . and the wide extended prairie where no shrubs or trees is [sic] visible to the eye. All covered with luxuriant grass, and the most delicate and beautiful flowers. I never saw a flower garden that looked gayer or richer than does [sic] the uncultivated lands of this country.[9]

Toward the western part of Washtenaw and Lenawee Counties, travelers encountered uneven terrain that marked the hydrological divide separating rivers running east and west on the peninsula. Characterized by hills and lakes, many of which could often be seen at one time, this "uneven and rough" land possessed the charm of mountainous countryside and appealed to the Romantic eye, but was perceived as a "poor country" for agriculture.[10]

This high ground formed a line from which inland migration diverged to follow distinct routes along the drainages of the principal river systems flowing westward to Lake Michigan and northward into Saginaw Bay. The earliest substantial inland settlements, Pontiac, Ann Arbor, and Tecumseh, arose along these routes near the inland periphery of the Eastern Peninsula Drainage as foci for expansion into distinct settlement regions. As Michigan's inland settlement continued, images of these regions formed as a consequence of the time and circumstances of their occupations.

THE SAGINAW RIVER DRAINAGE

Settlement in Oakland County led to the exploration of much of the area lying northwest of the Eastern Shore and helped establish a perceptual settlement boundary in Lower Michigan. Frontier images of the Saginaw Drainage were not uniform, and the contrasting views that emerged reflect the region's varied environments. Initial impressions of the region were very favorable. In 1821 the Sciawassa Company exploring party surveyed portions of the Flint and Shiawassee river drainages and predicted that they were capable of being transformed from a wilderness into productive farmland. An expedition from Detroit the following year intended to establish a "correct view" of the land between the entrepôt and Saginaw Bay. Traveling north along the Saginaw Trail beyond Pontiac, its members traversed elevated level to rolling terrain covered with oak openings and some timbered lands. They found the soils rich and well watered and very amenable to agriculture. Rivers here, as in Oakland County, were noted to have "many mill privileges" for agricultural processing and industrial activities.[11]

Subsequent experience of pioneer farmers supported initial perceptions of the lands in the upper Saginaw drainage. An immigrant to Lapeer County in the 1830s described his farm there as "first rate land . . . and a great wheat country." The openings that dominated the landscape provided adequate timber, yet required little effort to bring under cultivation. The timbered lands and openings drained by the Shiawassee River were recognized by many as the best in the region, comparing favorably "with any part of the territory for natural advantages."[12]

Very different impressions, however, soon developed for the lower Saginaw drainage. Explorers noted extensive flatlands along the river, below the confluence of the Flint and Saginaw Rivers, but believed them to be sufficiently elevated to permit settlement and cultivation. Their accounts, however, could not ignore the presence of low, wetlands in the vicinity of Saginaw Bay. The prevailing view of such terrain as unhealthy, coupled with the experience of the first permanent American settlement on the Saginaw River, created a far bleaker image for the lower Saginaw drainage than that envisioned by the first American visitors. In 1822 the United States built a fort at present-day Saginaw. Its garrison suffered the misfortunes of a cold winter in 1822–23, followed by a rapid spring thaw that flooded low-lying lands and created conditions conducive to malaria the following summer. So prevalent were the "intermittent fevers" that nearly all of Fort Saginaw's inhabitants became ill, leading to several deaths. As a result, the army abandoned the post in August 1823, but the experience of its short occupation created a lingering image of the lower Saginaw as an unhealthy country, unfit for settlement.[13]

Surveys of the region prior to settlement reinforced negative perceptions. In the mid-1820s an observer characterized the lower Saginaw as a "wet and swampy district," that "on account of the tamarack swamps, cranberry marshes, and low and level surface, can never be settled." Government surveyors presented similar evaluations of the region as one offering little or no inducement to immigrants, and helped establish the region as a northern boundary for settlement. Together with the Fort Saginaw experience, the surveys produced a singularly negative perception of the area surrounding Saginaw Bay, and retarded settlement there for years. The unhealthy image associated with low, wetlands on the lower Saginaw was also transferred to those along the Tittibawassee River, where the increasing occurrence of coniferous forests reinforced its reputation as an area unfavorable for agricultural settlement.[14]

Perceptions of the Saginaw Bay lands changed slowly as the region gained more favorable publicity in the press, and settlers began to understand the nature of the land and to modify its topography. Newcomers recognized the fertility of the alluvial soils and the necessity of confining settlement to the higher elevations, while cultivating the lowlands or using them for grazing. Even the threat of disease eventually came to be seen as no worse here than in other newly settled regions. Although a substantial change in the image of the lower Saginaw Drainage occurred by the late 1830s, its earlier reputation persisted, impeding settlement south of Saginaw Bay and fixing the region as the northern boundary for agriculture in Michigan.[15]

THE ST. JOSEPH RIVER DRAINAGE

The earliest thrust of settlement across the Lower Peninsula occurred in the south, along the overland route that traversed the drainage of the St. Joseph River. This territory came into market in the 1820s, following the cession of Indian lands in southwestern Michigan. Unlike the Eastern Shore and the Saginaw drainage, this region contained little land that was not considered habitable or potentially productive. These favorable perceptions spread rapidly as the reports of surveyors, land seekers, and promoters became public knowledge. In contrast to the low, wet lands encountered elsewhere, the St. Joseph Drainage presented an environment both aesthetically pleasing and amenable to commercial agriculture.[16]

Passing through Hillsdale County in the late 1830s, Joshua C. Goodrich noted in his diary the relief he felt at leaving the "poor country" of the hills and lakes. Farther west he observed a landscape of mixed hardwood forest, oak openings, and prairies, one that was well watered and possessed fertile soils and a salubrious climate.[17] Two land office officials remarked that "the country bordering on the St. Joseph & Kalamazoo [Rivers] is (with few exceptions) very beautiful and inviting." The prairies, in particular, impressed travelers such as Goodrich, who on viewing White Pigeon Prairie in St. Joseph County remarked, "To one who has lived as long as I have between the hills of Naples [New York], the view of a prairie is delightful and leads one to imagine whence the origin and why such bodies of land so much different from the rest of creation [exist]."[18]

Evaluations of heavily timbered lands in the St. Joseph drainage reflected earlier notions of land types and topography. These lands lay mainly in the eastern portion of the subregion, and farther west in portions of Berrien and Cass Counties. Surveyors and immigrants normally rated these lands highly if situated on a level to rolling surface; however, hilly or broken terrain made them less desirable. Forests located on wetlands adjacent to streams were seen to have limited agricultural potential, despite the assumed richness of their soils.[19]

Oak openings dominated the landscape of the St. Joseph drainage in southern Calhoun and Kalamazoo Counties, much of Cass County, and nearly all of St. Joseph County. Although surveyors did not rank the soils in openings as highly as they did those on prairies or some timbered lands, openings were viewed as good agricultural lands. The ease with which they could be placed in production permitted openings to be turned into "good and convenient farms, [that] produce excellent wheat." The soil quality, drainage, and access to water found in the oak openings led a Detroit editor to declare St. Joseph County one of the best locations for settlement in the territory.[20]

The prairies of southwestern Michigan captured the imagination of American pioneers. Although prairies occurred along much of the St. Joseph drainage, they were most prevalent in St. Joseph, Cass, and southern Kalamazoo Counties. Surveyors rated the prairie soils as particularly favorable for agriculture and compared them favorably to the best farmlands in the East. Their richness and the short time needed to place them in cultivation made prairie lands the most highly desirable landforms in the region. Because they did not need to clear forests, settlers chronically short of labor could place larger tracts of prairie in cultivation more rapidly than in other areas of Lower Michigan.[21]

THE KALAMAZOO RIVER DRAINAGE

The lands drained by the Kalamazoo River lay directly north and parallel to those of the St. Joseph Valley and were opened to settlement by the 1830s. Although this open landscape had many environmental characteristics similar to those of the subregion immediately to the south, significant differences gave the Kalamazoo River drainage an image distinct from that of its southern neighbor.[22]

The Kalamazoo River drainage passed through expansive oak openings, extending from Jackson County as far west as northwestern Kalamazoo County. Wet timbered lands were confined largely to the river valleys, with some prairies interspersed throughout the subregion. Mixed forest that included substantial areas of swamp forest characterized extensive areas at the western end of the drainage.[23]

The oak opening landscape of the Kalamazoo River drainage was reported as "second to no section of the country . . . for general farming purposes" by the *Jackson Sentinel.* "The land is generally a rich, sandy loam, freely interspersed with small pebbles of limestone, gently undulating and sufficiently elevated to admit of the healthful drainage of . . . streams." Overall, immigrants perceived the country very positively, characterized its soils as "rich, mellow and fertile," and compared them favorably with those of western New York. Here, as in the St. Joseph Valley, the oak openings were considered excellent farmlands, but prairie soils were seen as the most fertile.[24]

The labor needed to prepare timbered lands of the eastern Kalamazoo drainage for cultivation made them less desirable to immigrants than oak openings. In addition, the forests of the lower Kalamazoo Valley possessed a distinctive environment that often contained floodplains, swamps, or other extensive wetlands. Pioneers considered these timberlands to be of varied suitability for settlement and agriculture and generally superior to those of the Eastern Shore.[25] The western forests also included small, scattered concentrations of pinelands. Initially, Americans thought them useful only for pine lumber, a valuable commodity for construction on the treeless prairie settlements to the south. Experience eventually demonstrated that western pinelands possessed the capacity to produce crops such as corn and rye, although their sandier soils did not yield the same quantities of wheat per acre as did deciduous forest soils. They were never considered good agricultural lands.[26]

THE GRAND RIVER DRAINAGE

This vast river system drained the northwestern portion of southern Lower Michigan, encompassing the lands north of the Kalamazoo and east of the Saginaw River drainages. The southern portion of this region was opened to settlement in the 1830s, but western lands north of Grand River remained unavailable for another decade. Consequently, perceptions of the region as a whole developed slowly and unsystematically, and created diverse images of the Grand River drainage.

The Grand River drainage was in large part heavily timbered. Its hardwood forests, dominated by beech and sugar maple, were similar to those in the upper Saginaw drainage, and Americans living along the region's eastern periphery recognized them early on as good agricultural land. Immigrants judged the country between the Saginaw and Grand River systems to be a "fertile agricultural district." John Biddle, clerk of the Detroit Land Office, believed that the area's physical character was "better calculated to attract purchasers than the lands embraced in the late surveys to the north [around Saginaw Bay] . . . where the country is said to be very uninviting."[27]

Exploration of the Grand River Valley proceeded largely from two sources. In the north it pushed westward from the upper Saginaw drainage, following the oak openings along the headwaters of the Maple and Looking Glass Rivers in Shiawassee and Clinton Counties. Pioneers saw these lands as desirable because of soil fertility and the reduced cost of land clearing. As they encountered forested lands farther west, the general absence of marshes, ponds, swamps, and wastelands produced an image of great agricultural potential as well as "unsurpassed beauty." Harriet Munro Longyear, whose parents immigrated to Clinton County in 1836, remembered that, "They liked the beautiful forests with their magnificent trees. My father was captivated at first sight, arguing that land which supported such a growth of trees would raise anything planted." In addition to its agricultural potential, the region also impressed visitors with other natural resources of commercial value, including stone, coal, iron, plaster, salt springs, and stands of pine timber along its northern margin.[28]

A second direction of exploration proceeded up the Thornapple River Valley in Barry County. Here, too, pioneers followed a wedge of openings that led into heavily timbered lands. These were an extension of the broad area of openings and prairies in southwestern Michigan and were attractive to immigrant agriculturists. In the summer of 1834, John T. Hayt described the open landscape of the Thornapple Valley in southern Eaton County as the most beautiful spot he had ever seen. Others recognized these openings as "good wheat lands." Further north, the lower Thornapple Valley penetrated the timbered lands of the lower Grand River and these forests continued through Kent and eastern Ottawa Counties. Here the well-drained nature of these western forests and the quality of their soils bespoke their agricultural potential.[29]

Both the lower Thornapple Valley route and that following the Maple drainage farther north penetrated the timbered lands of the Grand River drainage, directing exploration westward toward Lake Michigan. As a result, the exploration of much of the interior upper Grand River drainage was delayed. Munnis Kenny, a visitor from Vermont who traveled into portions of Livingston and Ingham Counties in 1826, remarked, "no one had explored that part of the country." A decade later, J. Seymour, a land speculator in Marshall, could still write that "the country about Ingham is still a wilderness."[30]

THE WESTERN SHORE

Europeans had frequented the Lake Michigan shoreline since the seventeenth century. Both the French and the British placed posts at strategic locations in order to establish a presence, and the U.S. government explored and mapped the region and its major rivers before 1820. Concern with the region's strategic significance rather than its potential for settlement, however, led explorers to ignore environmental variables crucial to its development for farming and knowledge of its agricultural resources remained limited until the middle of the nineteenth century. The task of evaluating these westerly lands began only when these lands were surveyed for settlement in the 1820s.[31]

Contemporary notions of vegetation and soils often produced negative evaluations of the area's suitability for agriculture. As an 1830 traveler entered the region from the interior, he noted the presence of dense forestland that he deemed to be of "inferior quality" because of its low, wet condition. As he came within three to four miles of the lake, the occurrence of oak and pine indicated "very poor" land. Finally, the shore itself, "composed of hills, white sand, [had] a most sterile appearance, affording neither a good harbor nor site for a town or farm." The lake beaches and associated dunes were "so swept by the bleak gales of the lake as not to promise much to the cultivator."[32]

The image of the forested lands inland from the lake changed slowly over time. Varied soils of the Western Shore supported mixed forests and extensive areas of pine. The perception of pinelands as "worthless for settlement" discouraged immigrant farmers from settling on them. Large stands of conifers and other timber attracted lumbering interests, whose clearing activities delayed the availability of timbered lands for settlement. By the 1840s, following the removal of the forest, farmers found the land to be of better agricultural quality than previously imagined, capable of producing field crops as well as fruit. Although immigrants still ranked the agricultural potential of the Western Shore below that of the interior, land modification and changing perceptions of pineland fertility at last opened the region to colonization.[33]

The proximity of Michigan's Western Shore to the Lake Michigan produced unique physiographic conditions that set this region apart from the remainder of the Lower Peninsula. A combination of sandy, droughty soils, persistent westerly winds, and the ameliorating effect of the lake created a distinctive environment. Believing that the proximity of Lake Michigan protected lakeside lands from severe frosts, settlers cultivated climate-sensitive crops and extended general agriculture farther north along the Western Shore than elsewhere in the territory. By the 1840s, Americans had concluded that the boundary of agriculture in this region lay farther north than elsewhere in Lower Michigan, which, in turn, increased its settlement potential. The mixed-forest lands in Muskegon, Oceana, and southern Mason Counties, and around Grand Traverse Bay, possessed rich, sandy soils capable of producing corn and oats, as well as tree fruit, including apples and peaches. The discovery of a narrow northern mircoclimatic zone distinguished this region further and affected the direction of settlement in the western Lower Peninsula.[34]

PERCEPTIONS AND SETTLEMENT

The strong perceived correlation between land cover and quality influenced the direction and sequence of settlement of southern Lower Michigan. Although immigrants concluded that the greater part of Lower Michigan possessed fertile soils well suited for agriculture, they found some land types more attractive than others. Images of land quality affected pioneer decisions as to where to locate, and the distribution of open lands, dry forests, wet forests, and pinelands played an important role in shaping the frontier landscape.

Although several land types were considered arable, the ease of preparation of open lands offered an economic advantage that led to their selection over others. As a result, early settlement spread westward along the upper Saginaw drainage in the north and along a wide corridor further south paralleling the valleys of the St. Joseph and Kalamazoo Rivers. The distribution of oak openings and prairies fostered rapid population movement across the Lower Peninsula.

The preference for open lands also affected the order of settlement of deciduous forest-lands. Rather than moving uniformly from east to west, immigrants entered forested areas along their boundaries with prairies and oak openings. The large timbered region encompass-ing much of the Grand River drainage was occupied in this manner, with settlement taking place along its entire southern periphery, especially along the wedge created by the Thornapple River Valley in the West. A similar extension of openings along the streams in the north offered an entrance to the timbered lands in the central Grand River Valley. The occupation of forest-lands in the Saginaw River drainage occurred northward along a line stretching from Shiawassee to Lapeer Counties, and pioneers entered the Western Shore forests at many points along their eastern margin.

Extensive wet forests, perceived as less desirable land, lay nearer the lakeshores. Immigrants saw those on the Eastern Shore as difficult to improve and prone to disease in their natural, undrained state. This area remained sparsely and unevenly settled, as settlement bypassed it for open lands farther west. A similar belt of low, wet forests around the lower portion of Saginaw Bay deterred settlement there, and the wet forests on the Western Shore were also avoided as poor agricultural land.

Pioneers associated pinelands with agriculturally marginal soils, and initially avoided them. Only as the forest cover was removed for lumber did immigrants find the dry portions more attractive and begin to settle them. The occurrence of pinelands also marked the per-ceived northern boundary of agriculture in Lower Michigan. A line stretching roughly west-ward from Saginaw Bay to the mouth of the Muskegon River became a barrier that slowed the northward spread of settlement. The discovery of the distinctively warm climate of the Western Shore, however, drew agriculturists much farther northward along a narrow strip of pineland paralleling Lake Michigan.

Antebellum perceptions of the Michigan environment influenced the direction, sequence, and distribution of agricultural settlement in Lower Michigan. The geographical distribution of land types prevented colonization from progressing uniformly across the peninsula. Instead, perceptions of land quality encouraged initial thrusts into the open lands, followed by expan-sion into adjacent forested areas, and finally the occupation of less desirable environments on the region's northern, eastern, and western peripheries. As such, environmental perceptions became a powerfully compelling force in determining the course of pioneer settlement.

5

The Transfer of Land

The order in which lands were occupied affected the movement of immigration and shaped the patterning of settlement in Lower Michigan. American agriculturists acquired land in a two-phase process. The U.S. government first negotiated treaties to gain legal possession of lands inhabited by Native peoples and then transferred control over such lands and their resources by grant or sale to newcomers. Procedures for taking control of Indian lands in Michigan and assigning them to others evolved over nearly forty years as the parties involved gained experience and federal policy changed. This two-part transfer process limited and encouraged pioneer migration on the Michigan frontier.

Obtaining Government Possession: The Treaty Process

Although the United States and several European powers had claimed sovereignty over Lower Michigan by right of discovery, conquest, or negotiation, none had actually exercised complete control over the region or incorporated the area's aboriginal inhabitants within its larger social and political milieu. Until the latter part of the eighteenth century, Native peoples maintained control over the territory they occupied in Michigan. As masters of their traditional estates, they retained their traditional subsistence base and social and political institutions in spite of European expansion and the penetration of the world economy into the interior of North America. The American Revolution, however, changed the relationship between Indians and Europeans in the Old Northwest, creating irreversible conditions that imperiled the aboriginal way of life and changed forever the use and control of land in Michigan.

The closing decades of the eighteenth century brought the expansion of American agricultural populations west of the Appalachians into the territory south of the Great Lakes. This migration was accompanied by the extension of commercial agricultural production into western lands, a development that resulted in a very different relationship between the resources of these territories and the colonial government that claimed them. American settlers now sought access to the land itself as an agricultural resource rather than to specific resources, such as fur-bearing animals. To achieve this, the United States was compelled to dispossess Native peoples who occupied the arable portions of Lower Michigan. The government gained control over Indian-occupied territories through negotiations that led to the formal ceding of land ownership to the young republic. The evolution of federal Indian policy from restriction to removal influenced the manner in which Indian lands in

Michigan were acquired and provided the basis for land acquisition in this frontier region, a process that affected the order and direction of subsequent agricultural expansion.

Between 1795 and 1855 the federal government and resident Indian groups negotiated a number of written agreements affecting rights to lands within Michigan. United States policy recognized the transfer of ultimate domain over Native territories to a colonizing state by virtue of discovery. The latter gained sole authority to grant tracts to others, subject only to the Native people's right of occupancy, a right that could be terminated under certain conditions, such as negotiations or "just" wars of conquest. American territorial claims in the region north of the Ohio River derived from Jay's Treaty of 1795, which relinquished Great Britain's claim to this territory to the new federal government. The United States consolidated its authority over frontier lands by assuming all state claims in the West and asserting congressional control over all dealings involving the acquisition and distribution of Indian lands.[1]

The consolidation of former British territories, together with the Louisiana Purchase in 1803, created an immense American territory in the West that could easily absorb agricultural expansion, if only its current inhabitants could be induced to cede their lands. The military defeat of the Indians east of the Mississippi in the first two decades of the nineteenth century set the stage for negotiated settlements preempting their use rights to the lands they occupied. Initially these treaties sought to solve the problems resulting from the occupation of frontier lands by both Native and colonial populations by restricting Native peoples to portions of their former territories. Soon, however, the perceived incompatibility of reservations amid developing agricultural regions brought demands for the removal of eastern Indians to more distant locations.[2] Henry Schoolcraft, one-time superintendent of Indian affairs in Michigan, summarized this shift in policy when he concluded:

> Two diverse states of society . . . cannot prosperously exist together; the stronger type must inevitably absorb the weaker. As the States increased in population and emigration progressed westward, it became evident that the Indians could not sustain themselves amid a society whose every custom, maxim, and opinion, directly controverted their preconceived ideas. . . . [T]he mass of aborigines continued to live on . . . without deriving any profit from contact with their civilized neighbors. Whatever may have been the sentiments and views of humanitarians, . . . no practicable prospect of their reclamation and restoration to society was presented, . . . except in their total separation from the evils surrounding them . . . on the territory specially appropriated for their use, where, under the operation of their own laws and institutions, their better qualities might develop themselves.[3]

Federal legislation supporting the removal of eastern Indians to the West was enacted in 1825 and pursued with increasing vigor, including the use of force, through the 1830s, during the administrations of Andrew Jackson and Martin Van Buren. By 1840 relocation of the majority of these Native peoples had been completed, opening much of the territory east of the Mississippi to colonial settlement.[4]

MICHIGAN INDIANS AND THE CESSION OF LANDS

At the time the United States established a presence in Lower Michigan, the disposition of the region's Native peoples reflected recent historical developments (fig. 2.1). As we have seen, they consisted of three larger groups, the Potawatomis, who occupied the southern portion of the peninsula; the Ottawas, concentrated mainly in the west, north of the Kalamazoo River; and the Saginaw-Chippewas, an Ojibwa people who lived in the area south of Saginaw Bay. The Saginaw-Chippewa settlements extended westward, mixing with those of the Ottawas on the upper Grand River drainage. In addition, several settlements of Hurons, called Wyandots, were situated south of Detroit. Although these groups occupied generally separate areas, geographical boundaries between them were not rigid and often overlapped, particularly in the Grand River drainage. The traditional estates of the Indian societies in Lower Michigan represented the spatial distributions of peoples who lived by hunting, gathering, and to some extent agriculture, and the nature of these territories was linked to the requirements of these forms of subsistence.[5]

Although European and American observers chose to perceive the region's inhabitants as members of "tribes" or "nations," Native societies actually comprised acephalous groups of varying levels of complexity. Because of the dispersed nature of the natural resources on which their subsistence depended, the Ottawas and Saginaw-Chippewas were relatively decentralized. Their social and political organization was based largely on extended family units that provided the flexibility necessary to successfully exploit a variety of seasonal resources and establish and maintain trading relationships in the shifting economic context created by the European and American presence. Leadership in such societies was achieved through success in trade, war, and production; however, a leader's power was not absolute or immutable, and rested on consensus. Likewise, political alliances were impermanent, and dependent upon the continual maintenance of ties between separate kin groups. The Potawatomis, who traditionally relied more heavily on agriculture and followed a more sedentary way of life, developed more complex political institutions, in which leaders occupied more clearly defined roles, and more permanent linkages existed between social units. Nevertheless, leadership remained associated with specific purposes and rested with individuals at different levels in the society. Here again, the acephalous nature of political organization prevented individuals from representing the group as a whole. The nonhierarchical organization characteristic of aboriginal societies in Lower Michigan effectively dispersed authority and power within these groups and affected the manner in which the control of land, the basis of their subsistence, was transferred to outsiders.[6]

Michigan's Native peoples did not consider land a resource in and of itself. Although individuals possessed rights to use particular resources within delimited areas, the notion of land itself as a commodity of value, capable of being used as a medium of exchange and investment, was an alien concept to them, yet one that had to be dealt with in the face of American expansion. Ownership of lands occupied by Native peoples consequently remained unclear in the European sense, and this uncertainty, together with the decentralized authority over natural resources in general, facilitated the quest by American officials to gain possession of tribal estates in Lower Michigan.[7]

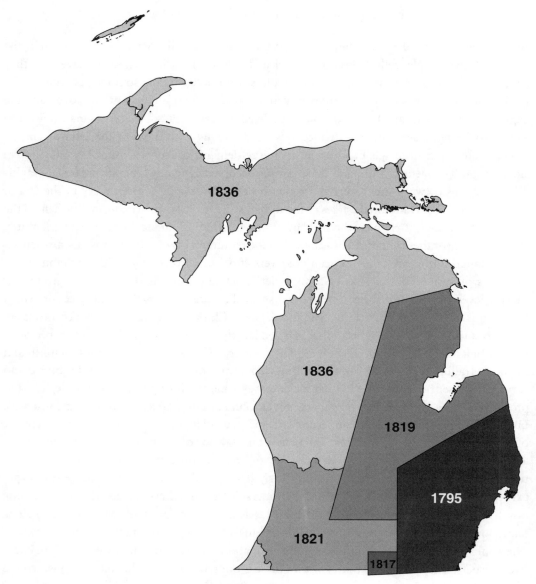

FIGURE 5.1 *INDIAN LAND CESSIONS IN MICHIGAN FROM 1795 THROUGH 1836.* (Sources: see text).

By the close of the eighteenth century, aboriginal peoples had been forced to accept U.S. authority and acknowledge its sovereignty. The Treaty of Greenville, signed in the summer of 1795, formally proclaimed the right of the United States to acquire Indian lands in Michigan through treaty and marked the first cessions of lands at Detroit and Michilimackinac (fig. 5.1). The treaty also claimed American rights to other resources, namely the use of harbors, rivers, and portages in Ohio and Indiana, to serve as gateways to the interior. In addition, it established authority to acquire Indian lands and provided a framework for accomplishing this.[8]

Because the notion of land as a commodity was alien to the Native peoples of Michigan, the process of transferring ownership of land and the question of who had the right to do so became unclear. The aboriginal peoples who took part in treaty negotiations regarding the ceding of land were generally not persons delegated to transact such an agreement, but rather a collection of Indian leaders representing the "tribes" whose lands were in question. The aboriginal participants usually expressed the interests of their own constituencies, and many leaders attended treaty negotiations primarily for the prestige that could be gained through the distribution of treaty gifts. American negotiators took advantage of potential disunity by seeking cessions from agreeable claimants to Indian territory, while ignoring other, less compliant parties. They exploited intergroup animosities to weaken overall resistance and offered gifts, liquor, promises of annuities, and other incentives to persuade reluctant Indian participants to agree to land cessions. On the surface, the results of the treaty negotiations seem a foregone conclusion, and Michigan Indians appear helpless victims in a process whose end was never in doubt. Certainly the traditional estates of Native peoples in Lower Michigan were transferred to the United States government and the aboriginal populations relocated. As the treaty process expanded across the peninsula, however, Michigan Indians responded adaptively to threats of resource loss and displacement and, with varying success, imposed conditions on the cession of their lands. Consequently, the results of the treaty process were not always predictable, and this uncertainty had implications for subsequent frontier settlement patterning.[9]

THE EASTERN PENINSULA GROUPS AND THE SAGINAW-CHIPPEWAS

Although the 1795 Treaty of Greenville established an American presence in Lower Michigan, the Treaty of Detroit, signed twelve years later, marked the first attempt to expropriate a large tract of Indian land (Fig. 5.1). Territorial governor William Hull concluded the treaty in November 1807 with Ottawa, Potawatomi, Chippewa, and Wyandot representatives. Most Saginaw-Chippewas strongly opposed the treaty, but the United States recognized only those representatives who supported the cession. The treaty provided annuities and reserved lands for affected Indians, and permitted the use of unsold lands for hunting. Although the treaty formally ceded lands, it would be another decade before American settlement began.[10]

Even before American immigration posed a serious threat to the people of the eastern peninsula, however, the Saginaw-Chippewas let it be known that new settlers were unwelcome. Similarly, the Wyandots protested the size of their reservations at Brownstown and Maguagon along the Detroit River-Lake Erie shore and challenged the illegal settlement of Americans in the area. The outbreak of general hostilities in the West in 1811 gave tangible form to Indian frustration with the American presence in Michigan, but the outcome of the War of 1812 marked the end of warfare as a viable response to American colonization and altered the context in which all future negotiations for land took place.[11]

Wartime experience caused Americans to view eastern Michigan as a "dark and bloody ground" and to characterize its Indian inhabitants as defiant, potentially hostile, and opposed to the occupation of their lands. In addition, Americans feared continued British influence among the Indians who received the annual distribution of gifts at Malden, located on the opposite side of the Detroit River, just above the head of Lake Erie. These feelings fostered an atmosphere of mistrust and fear that came to characterize the American image of the Wyandots and Saginaw-Chippewas as vigorous opponents of settlement and a threat to colonization.[12]

American officials feared that the continued presence of the Saginaw-Chippewas would turn away potential immigrants. Consequently, the U.S. government negotiated the Treaty of Saginaw in 1819 to purchase additional Indian lands, establish a federal military presence, and restrict Native inhabitants to defined reservations. This instrument extended the U.S. domain to include all of the Saginaw River drainage, the upper drainage of the Grand River, portions of the Kalamazoo River drainage, and the northeastern part of the Lower Peninsula (fig. 5.1). The ceded tract included all of the lands occupied by the Saginaw-Chippewas, as well as the eastern portion of the territory inhabited by the Grand River Ottawas. Gaining title to the former group's traditional estate gave the United States direct control over the region, its people, and its resources.[13]

The federal government built Fort Saginaw in 1822 to insure the safety of the region for surveyors and settlers. During the fort's eighteen-month existence, surveys of the surrounding area were completed and immigration to the Saginaw valley commenced, events that sealed forever the future of the region. The site of the fort became the center of the American Fur Company's operations in 1824, and the settlement of Saginaw served as an early focus for American activity.[14]

The Treaty of 1819 dramatically changed the economy of the Michigan interior. American fur traders arrived in large numbers and increased the competitive nature of the trade, which resulted in an intensification of fur gathering. As the fur-bearing animal populations declined in the 1820s, the trade shifted to supplying provisions to American immigrants. This had additional ecological consequences, in that it further strained traditional Indian food supplies while contributing to the expansion of American settlement, which directly competed with Native peoples for the region's resources.[15]

The creation of reservations contributed to the social and political disruption as well as the physical dispersal of the Saginaw-Chippewas. Reservations were established along the Saginaw River and its tributaries, to restrict the movement of the Native peoples and acculturate them through agricultural training and missionizing. Resistance to these poorly conceived and half-heartedly implemented government programs led to their failure as a tool of directed culture change. In the face of American expansion, the position of the Saginaw-Chippewas on their traditional estate rapidly became untenable. Competition with immigrants, who often selected the better agricultural lands, made life on ceded lands less certain.[16]

As a result, the Saginaw-Chippewas dispersed. Those not granted reserves in their traditional areas moved to other communities or occupied lands off the reservations, and many bands continued to share villages with the Ottawas in the upper Grand River drainage. Those who continued to reside in the Saginaw Valley faced pressures that decimated their numbers and fragmented their cultural integrity. European diseases, particularly epidemics of cholera in 1834 and smallpox in 1837, exacerbated the disintegration of Saginaw-Chippewa communities. Aboriginal populations in the Saginaw drainage were reduced to a third of their original size, and survivors scattered to Canada and elsewhere in Michigan. Those who lived along Lake St. Clair and the St. Clair River ceded their reservation lands in 1836 and relinquished their Saginaw valley reserves the following year. In return, they received lands on the west side of Saginaw Bay for five years in anticipation of their removal to Kansas. They avoided deportation, however, by occupying large new reservations in northern Michigan that were set aside by treaty in 1836.[17]

The cession of other reservation lands in eastern Michigan followed a similar pattern. The original Wyandot reserves at Brownstown and Maguagon were given up in 1818 for a single tract on the Huron River in Wayne County. The Wyandots subsequently abandoned the Michigan lands for a larger reserve in Ohio. In 1842 they relinquished these claims and moved to Kansas and later the Indian Territory. The smaller reserves allotted to Potawatomi bands in eastern Michigan were exchanged by treaty in 1827 for lands located elsewhere in the peninsula.[18]

With the acquisition of the Saginaw Valley reserves, the federal government finally gained domain over the north-central portion of Lower Michigan, nearly two decades after it was originally transferred by treaty. Although much of the territory was surveyed preparatory to sale, however, the long-term presence of reservations occupied by Indians who were perceived to be potentially hostile to American settlers remained a detriment to colonization. By creating these reserves in an area it wished to settle, the government actually deterred immigration and, in effect, compromised growth during the initial period of inland agricultural expansion.

THE POTAWATOMIS IN THE SOUTHWEST

The two decades following the War of 1812 witnessed the cession of the entire Potawatomi estate in Michigan, followed by its occupation by American immigrants. Conditions surrounding the treaty process were different from those that had prevailed earlier in eastern Michigan, and permitted the Potawatomis to respond more knowledgeably to the treaty's consequences than had their eastern neighbors. The nature of their response affected both the Potawatomis' presence in Lower Michigan and the manner in which their lands passed into federal control.

Because the Potawatomis had sided with the British during the War of 1812, American authorities initially viewed them with suspicion and judged them a potential threat to settlement between Detroit and Lake Michigan. Settlers who interacted directly with the Potawatomis, however, soon painted a far different picture of them. Pioneer accounts characterized them as "peaceful and inoffensive," and "not warlike to the white man." Even during the uncertain days of the Black Hawk War in 1832, amicable relationships were maintained between pioneers and resident Potawatomis in southern Michigan. In contrast to the Saginaw-Chippewas, the Potawatomis were not considered threatening by immigrants, and their presence was, in fact, seen as an asset to the success of many pioneers.[19]

Pioneers and Indians established a strong economic link as the Potawatomis adapted to the American presence by becoming suppliers of game and gathered food products. Potawatomi traders regularly visited individual homesteads and larger settlements to exchange berries, venison, fish, maple sugar, and furs for salt pork, corn meal, wheat flour, dry goods, and whiskey. Rather than avoiding contact, many Potawatomis were, as recalled by Melville McGee of Concord Township in Jackson County, "not backward in making the acquaintances of the early settlers" and establishing long-term relationships with American immigrants.[20]

By 1832, the Potawatomi bands, collectively or singly, had ceded nearly all their lands to the United States. The 1817 Treaty of Fort Meigs acquired an area corresponding roughly to the southern half of Hillsdale County in exchange for annual payments. Four years later, the Treaty of Chicago extended this cession to include all territory south of Grand River with the exception of the southwestern tip of Berrien County (fig. 5.1). In addition to a further annuity, the Potawatomis received four reserves in southwestern Michigan and continued to use ceded lands until their sale. The Potawatomi estate was reduced further by the Treaty of 1827, which took most of the reserves, and another, signed the following year, that ceded the Berrien County lands.[21]

The acquisition of remaining Potawatomi lands reflected the shift in federal Indian policy from restriction to removal, and two subsequent treaties intended to evict the Potawatomis from southern Michigan. The Tippecanoe Treaty of 1832 ceded all lands in Michigan south of Grand River to the United States in return for an annuity. The two reserves exempted from this session were given up in the 1833 Treaty of Washington. Although the treaties set the stage for the removal of most of the Michigan Potawatomis, some bands employed a stipulation in the Removal Act forbidding forced cessions to successfully oppose this process.[22]

Perhaps the most successful in avoiding removal were those Potawatomis under the leadership of Leopold Pokagon, who drew on their previous experience with Americans to devise and implement maneuvers to retain portions of their traditional estate in Michigan. By adopting an assimilation strategy that involved espousing Catholicism, purchasing and owning real estate, and becoming agriculturalists, the Pokagons established their legal right to remain in Michigan and successfully resisted removal efforts that forcibly transplanted the bulk of the Potawatomis to Kansas in 1839 and 1840. Other Potawatomis avoided removal by fleeing to northern Michigan or Canada. At least some returned in later years, including those who settled on a state reserve south of Battle Creek purchased for them by sympathetic American neighbors.[23]

American Indian policy forced the Potawatomis to adapt in order to maintain their cultural identity as their lands were occupied by American agriculturists. With the exception of a few bands, the Potawatomis did not adapt to the rapidly changing context of colonization and were removed from their traditional estate. Those who remained adopted a strategy of assimilation that permitted them to purchase lands and become settlers in their own territory. Invisibility insured the survival of Potawatomi identity in the face of American colonization. Their success represented a marked change in the aboriginal response to the treaty process and had implications for other Native peoples of Michigan who would soon face the threat posed by agricultural expansion.[24]

THE OTTAWAS ON GRAND RIVER

After the 1833 cessions, the lower Grand River Valley remained the only portion of Lower Michigan lying outside federal jurisdiction. This region was occupied by Ottawa bands whose territory extended from the Muskegon River south to the Kalamazoo. Although Ottawas had participated in earlier treaty cessions and had relinquished some of the lands they had occupied, the geographical distance between the core of their territory and the eastern source of American expansion insulated them from the effects of immediate confrontation. Residing on what remained of their territorial estate in western Michigan, the Ottawas retained access to the natural resources upon which their economy was based. At the same time, their proximity to the settlement frontier and their participation in previous treaties provided them with economic assets that could be exploited to thwart federal Indian policy. Ottawa social and political institutions also remained intact, providing a basis for dealing with the American government and its agents.

By the time colonial expansion reached the Ottawa homeland, federal policy had turned fully toward removal. Unlike their neighbors to the east and south, the Ottawas faced the threat of removal immediately upon ceding their lands. This condition influenced the treaty process leading up to Ottawa cession and shaped the nature of their response to colonization in western Michigan. The treaties of 1819 and 1821 placed the Ottawa at the edge of the frontier and exposed them to the impact of settlement expansion. They soon became active suppliers of subsistence goods to immigrants, and pioneer perceptions of the Ottawas characterized them as hospitable and ready to assist new settlers in need. Thaddeus O. Brownell of Kent County recalled that their interaction with individual pioneers was commonplace: "Indians were by no means curiosities." As active participants in trade, the Ottawas avoided the image of hostile enemies, being seen as helpful, yet distant, neighbors, "always sober and peaceable."[25]

Pressure to extend U.S. domain into the Ottawa homeland resulted in the cession of all remaining Indian-held territory in the Lower Peninsula (fig 5.1). The 1836 Treaty of Washington included a compromise, however, that permitted the Ottawas to remain in Michigan, if only temporarily, and retain access to their traditional resource base. By the terms of the treaty, the Ottawas received reservations in the northern Lower Peninsula for an uncertain period. In the time thus gained, the Ottawas employed several strategies to avoid removal. They used funds received as treaty annuities and through other economic ventures to purchase land in their traditional estate, thereby demonstrating their desire to become agriculturists. In addition, the Ottawas set out to convince missionaries and authorities of their intent to become assimilated. Through networks of friends and allies they petitioned the United States for citizenship and supported the work of traders, missionaries, and others with an interest in their continued presence. By cultivating such contacts and establishing personal links through marriage and friendship, the Ottawas acquired influential advocates for their cause.[26]

The economic position of the Ottawas also strengthened their case to remain in Lower Michigan. Established as participants in the fur trade on the lower Grand River and as suppliers of provisions to American immigrants to western Michigan, the Ottawas participated actively in the expanding economy at the time of the treaty cession. The terms of the treaty injected cash into the regional economy through annuity payments. Traders, not wishing to lose the substantial profits gained from continued credit sales to Indians, retained a clear interest in keeping the Ottawas, who had money to pay their debts, where they were.[27]

Ottawa political organization also worked to thwart removal. Composed of small, kin-related groups and lineages of shallow time depth, the Ottawas consisted of a number of politically autonomous units whose leaders held uncertain power and could make agreements only with the consent of their followers. Because decisions regarding the Ottawas as a whole required consensus among these units, federal agents faced the daunting task of negotiating with people who held numerous interests. Ottawa leaders could unite when common interests were at stake, however, and did so to oppose removal. Their decentralized political organization also permitted a scattered distribution of settlement that did not present the specter of a large resident Native population threatening pioneer settlement in western Michigan. As small, autonomous groups residing in small clusters, the Ottawas, too, became invisible, and immigrants exerted little pressure for their removal.[28]

Although the Ottawas ceded their territories in Lower Michigan, they ultimately avoided dispersal and removal. In 1850 the Ottawas were offered Michigan citizenship, and a year later the Michigan legislature petitioned the U.S. government to grant them permanent residency in Michigan. Congress supported this position, and the subsequent Treaty of Washington provided the Ottawas with communal reservations in western Michigan, north of the Muskegon River. The northern reserves were more extensive than those set aside in the 1836 treaty and provided a focus for a continued Ottawa presence in Michigan.[29]

The sequence of land cessions just described opened territory for pioneer settlement, and perceptions of resident Native peoples clearly played an important role in immigrants' success on the Michigan frontier. Settlers could legally occupy land only after they purchased it from the United States, and its transfer depended on the order in which the federal government surveyed ceded tracts and offered them for sale. The manner in which this process occurred grew out of the milieu of evolving federal land policy in the first half of the nineteenth century.

THE LEGAL FRAMEWORK OF LAND DISTRIBUTION

Pioneer settlement of Michigan involved far more than the simple transferal of ceded territories to available immigrants. The alienation of western lands by the U.S. government followed procedures set forth in a series of congressional acts passed into law between 1784 and 1862. These laws established conditions for land sales during a period of extraordinary expansion and represented federal efforts to increasingly facilitate the transfer of the public domain into private hands. This legislation also attempted to manage expansion into newly acquired territory by regulating the availability of land as well as the nature of its transfer. The manner in which it did so dramatically affected the form of settlement in this frontier region.

American land policy in the late eighteenth century grew out of precedents established in Great Britain's Eastern Seaboard colonies, where the experience of a century and a half had produced types of land occupancy that formed the basis for settlement in the West. Colonial land policy reflected the political and economic diversity of its separate provinces, each of which controlled the distribution of inhabited and unoccupied lands within its boundaries. Out of this experience, two distinct methods of alienating new territory emerged.

Pennsylvania and the southern colonies often distributed interior lands by granting large tracts to proprietors, who, in turn, sold them directly to individuals in smaller units. Although proprietors found such sales to be profitable, colonial governments had to create an administrative system capable of facilitating the transfer of land in what was usually unexplored territory. These colonies established land offices to oversee sales and the appointment of a surveyor general and a land commission to manage and adjudicate land acquisition.[30] The selection of claims, however, was loosely controlled. Immigrants moved onto land that they perceived to possess useful resources, and avoided locations deemed undesirable, resulting in an uneven distribution of settlement that often left large areas unoccupied. Because lands were surveyed only after they were selected, property boundaries relied upon metes and bounds recording based on rivers, trees, rocks, ridgetops, and other natural, though not necessarily permanent, landscape features. The confusion over property ownership engendered by the inaccuracies of such a survey system, together with the continuous litigation it created, was a serious shortcoming of land policy in these colonies. Yet the administrative system devised to implement land transfer there contributed substantially to national land policy.[31]

In the North, colonial legislatures distributed land in large tracts to organizations such as church congregations, town proprietors, land jobbers, and land companies, who would, in turn, transfer the land to individual immigrants. Under this system land was conveyed in units, called townships, that were generally contiguous with areas already occupied. This sequential method of opening up land produced a much more even occupation of new territories, with pioneers being obliged to take up all types of lands before new townships were opened. This system permitted much more accurate surveying of the land prior to settlement. Contiguous expansion and survey of land before settlement systematized the occupation of new lands and afforded the government a greater measure of control over the direction of settlement.[32]

At the close of the American Revolution the individual states gained title to all provincial and Crown-held lands. These included a vast uncolonized territory subject to state claims west of the Appalachians. The new national government struggled to gain control of these claims, and by the 1790s the greater part of them were extinguished and their distribution placed in the hands of a central federal authority. The manner in which the federal government dealt with this newly acquired public domain set a precedent for the transfer of western lands and provided the basis for federal land policy in next century.[33]

Demands for land in the public domain led the Confederation Congress to develop a system of land distribution that combined the useful precedents of colonial practice. The Ordinance of 1785 and the Land Act of 1796 introduced the use of systematic surveys as well as an administrative arrangement for alienating the public lands. This legislation provided that such lands be divided into townships six miles square. Each of these, in turn, was subdivided into thirty-six consecutively numbered sections, each of which was one square mile in size. The locations of individual townships were fixed in space through reference to a larger grid system, the axes of which were formed by an east-west oriented base line and, later, a meridian line running north and south. The location of a township was indicated by its relative distance north or south of the base line and east or west of the meridian, expressed respectively in ranges and townships. As federal authority expanded, new base lines and meridians were established to permit new territories to be incorporated by a consolidated network of survey lines. By superimposing an arbitrary grid on the frontier, this method of survey systematized its structure and shaped the character of the new country.[34]

The relative ease with which the design and operation of the township system could be understood proved advantageous to those administrating and occupying new lands. It described precisely the location of any tract of land and thus obviated the costly litigation often required to establish property boundaries. The square shape of the townships also imposed a sense of orderliness and stability, providing a frame of reference and orientation for the newcomer. Furthermore, townships were easy to subdivide into units of comparable size. Altogether, the township system was a very practical method of land division, which facilitated the incorporation of large uncharted territories within the administrative jurisdiction of the United States.[35]

Despite its advantages, however, the township system often presented immigrants from the East with a visual perspective that was outside their experience. Henry S. Sanford, for example, observed that, "One can scarce find a field in all Michigan where the fences do not terminate at right angles, quite different from what one sees in Connecticut." On concluding business at the Kalamazoo Land Office the following day, he complained of the "confusion it puts my head in to talk of Towns, Sections & Ranges by numbers so." The utility of the system, however, soon became evident as he observed the ease with which residents could establish the locations and boundaries of tracts based on surveyors' marks and the regularity of the fields produced by the survey grid, and he concluded that, "There is much good arising from this means of dividing land here."[36]

The Ordinance of 1785 established an administrative organization to oversee both the survey and sale of lands. The first of these duties was charged to a geographer of the United States, appointed by the president, who supervised surveyors from each state who were tasked with laying out the townships. Land plats prepared by the geographer were submitted to the board of the treasury, to be employed as the basis for allotment to the states for sale to the public. Although ownership of land remained in the hands of the central government, this act delegated its survey and sale to each state or territory.[37]

Subsequent legislation refined the procedures and organizational structure established in this act. The Land Act of 1800 placed land offices directly in the western districts, each with a register and receiver who would, respectively, record and collect payment for lands purchased. It also appointed a surveyor general to oversee the work of deputy surveyors and provide survey plats for the registers. Twelve years later, Congress created a General Land Office (GLO) to consolidate all activities relating to public lands within a single agency of the Treasury Department. By the beginning of the War of 1812, an administrative structure was in place to oversee the alienation of federally controlled lands in the West. This framework provided both stability and continuity for the transfer of land in Lower Michigan.[38]

In spite of the fact that the legal structure for land transfer remained unchanged, the process itself evolved in response to changing perceptions regarding the role of public lands in the development of the nation. These arose from a debate centered round the extent to which the sale of such lands should constitute a source of revenue for the federal treasury. In its early years the United States was heavily indebted to European creditors, and lacked a substantial tax base upon which to derive an income. Sale of the public lands offered an opportunity to generate substantial funds, and the Federalist administrations saw this as a means of providing the capital to establish the new nation's credit. Other interests, represented by the Jeffersonian Republicans who came to power in 1801, felt that the importance of the settling of western lands lay in expanding the agricultural production base that was necessary to promote the democratic ideals of the agrarian republic. An increasing emphasis on land distribution as a means of increasing national wealth and security, rather than as a source of revenue, was reflected in a federal land policy that gradually altered the terms of sale of public lands from one that favored large, well capitalized, speculative interests toward one amenable to purchasers of more modest means.[39]

When Michigan lands were first placed in market, the early Federalist policy of selling land in large blocks at higher prices had already begun to change. In 1796 the minimum price of federal land was $2.00 per acre and sales were in tracts no smaller than a section (640 acres). Subsequent land acts in 1800 and 1804 altered these conditions by instituting credit payments, reducing the size of minimum purchase to a quarter section (160 acres), and offering discounts for cash purchases. This legislation facilitated purchase by settlers of modest means, but its credit provisions also encouraged speculation by others who acquired large tracts in hopes of selling them at profit in smaller parcels before their payments came due. Although many speculators profited, the western agricultural economy suffered from overexpansion of production and underdevelopment of transportation linkages with the East, conditions that lowered prices for western produce and undermined the expansion of production based on credit sales of land. The inflationary spiral of western lands collapsed with the Panic of 1819, a nationwide economic depression. The role played by the credit system of land purchase in creating this disaster resulted in a restructuring of land laws that produced the legal context under which the bulk of Michigan lands were transferred to private ownership.[40]

The Land Act of 1820 was the principal piece of legislation affecting the manner of land transfer in Lower Michigan. This law abolished the credit provisions of earlier acts and placed land sales on a cash basis. Its major provisions favored small settlers by lowering the price of land to $1.25 per acre and permitting purchases as small as eighty acres. Indebted landowners were not neglected in this new era of cash sales, and during the 1820s several relief bills were passed to aid those faced with forfeiture of their lands. In addition, Congress passed legislation over the next decade recognizing the rights of squatters to preempt lands. The federal government facilitated the distribution of the public domain as broadly, cheaply, and rapidly as possible.[41]

The fact that nearly all of Michigan's settlement occurred after 1820 spared it from the impact of large-scale speculation and absentee ownership found in other parts of the country. The editor of the *Detroit Gazette,* commenting on the territory's growth, observed that since the alteration of the land laws, in 1820, . . . there was a marked *increase in the amount of receipts* for land. . . . In all the purchases which have been made under the new system, not one, that we have heard of, has been made for purposes of *"speculation,"* as it is called—no one has purchased, we believe, merely for the purpose of letting land lie unimproved and making money by selling it again when it shall increase in value. On the contrary, nearly every quarter section has been taken up & by practical farmers, and most of them have already received an astonishing degree of improvement.[42]

While this observer might have been unrealistically optimistic about the absence of speculation in Michigan lands, his statement regarding the predominant role of small landowners was correct. He and other writers like "Z" of Ann Arbor, attributed the influx of so many farmer-settlers to changes in the method of land distribution.[43]

THE SURVEY AND DISTRIBUTION OF MICHIGAN LANDS

The United States surveyed Michigan lands using a township system that allowed individual tracts to be located precisely relative to two fixed axes which were tied to an existing survey grid in Ohio. All of the Lower Peninsula was to be subdivided into the townships and sections specified in the Ordinance of 1785 and the Land Act of 1796, with the exception of tracts granted prior to American rule, which retained their original boundaries.

Because of the importance of the central axes of the survey grid, meridian and base lines were established prior to the actual delineation of townships. In the fall of 1815 coordinated expeditions began laying the Michigan meridian along the western boundary of the lands ceded in the 1807 treaty and the base line westward from a point on Lake St. Clair north of Detroit. Despite difficulties presented by the poorly drained lands of the Eastern Shore, surveyors had laid out all lands east of the meridian and south of Township 7 North by 1820.[44] Although perceived environmental barriers slowed the completion of the meridian northward into the Saginaw drainage, the survey of Michigan lands proceeded rapidly in the southwest. Following the completion of the base line to Lake Michigan in 1827, township lines were soon run over much of this area.[45] Following the 1836 Ottawa cession that opened lands north of Grand River to settlement, northern surveys proceeded rapidly and included no fewer than three correction lines to compensate for the converging meridians. Surveyors completed the meridian to the Straits of Mackinac in 1840, and within the next decade they had laid out and subdivided all but a few townships at the northern end of the peninsula.[46]

Although the survey of Lower Michigan followed the sequence of treaty cessions, the transfer of land to private ownership did not always mirror the sequence of survey. Actual land sales were influenced by a number of additional factors associated with the administrative context in which its alienation took place, and the temporal pattern of surveys provided only a framework for such sales.

Under the auspices of the General Land Office, or GLO, the federal government offered tracts of land for sale in contiguous blocks in order of the completion of their survey. It organized the available territory into districts, each administered by the staff of a land office conveniently located to serve the prospective inhabitants. These land offices oversaw the marketing of federal land, collecting payment for purchases and recording the locations of the sold parcels. In response to the availability of unsold land, the government created, altered, or closed land districts and offices. The alienation of federal territory was also affected by the creation of special categories of lands, such as those set aside as Indian reservations, as well as various types of state lands set aside to generate funds for special purposes. The evolution of land districts provides a framework for examining the administrative organization of public land sales in Michigan.

Congress recognized Detroit as the paramount administrative center for land distribution in Michigan when it established a land office there in 1804 with jurisdiction over all ceded lands in what became the Michigan Territory. The importance of the Detroit Land Office increased markedly after the War of 1812, as the implementation of the 1807 treaty and the execution of the 1819 cession extended the district's boundaries well into the interior of Lower Michigan. The difficulty of administering such an extensive territory from a single office, however, soon became apparent. Immigrants traveling by way of the lakes and wishing to settle in the southern portion of Michigan had to make an additional journey up the Straits of Detroit to enter their land. The management of the western lands acquired in the Treaty of 1821 added to the inconvenience of those wishing to purchase property in Michigan.[47]

In response to these needs, Congress created a new land district in 1823 with an office at Monroe. Its boundaries extended across the peninsula and included all the territory south of a line between Townships 3 and 4 South (fig. 5.2). The Detroit Land District included all ceded lands north of this. Three years later, the northern boundary of the Monroe Land District west of the meridian was moved northward to the base line (fig. 5.3). In 1831 the GLO again redrew the land district boundaries in response to the needs of immigrants to western Michigan. A new office far to the west at White Pigeon in St. Joseph County replaced the one at Monroe. The land district boundaries were also altered dramatically, with all ceded lands west of the Meridian assigned to the Western District and those to the east returned to the Detroit District (fig. 5.4).[48]

The abandonment of the Monroe Land Office apparently afforded little improvement. Although land seekers in western Michigan now had access to a land office, inhabitants of the southeastern part of the territory felt that this would cause their region to be bypassed by immigrants for lands further west. As a result of their concerns, the old Monroe Land District was reinstated in 1833, with its western boundary at the line between Ranges 5 and 6 West. This created three land districts in southern Lower Michigan (fig. 5.5). The expansion of settlement in southwestern Michigan prompted the removal of the land office for the Western District from White Pigeon to Kalamazoo, then called Bronson, in 1834. This resulted in a slight adjustment in the western limit of the Monroe Land District (fig. 5.6).[49]

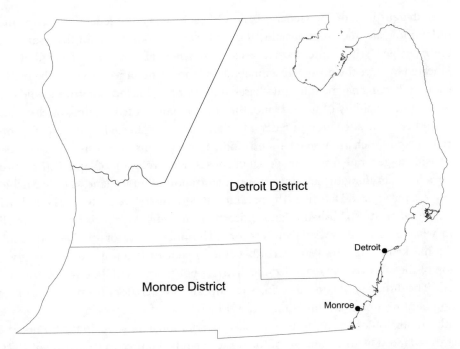

FIGURE 5.2. *LAND DISTRICTS AND LAND OFFICES IN SOUTHERN MICHIGAN IN 1823*. (Sources: see text).

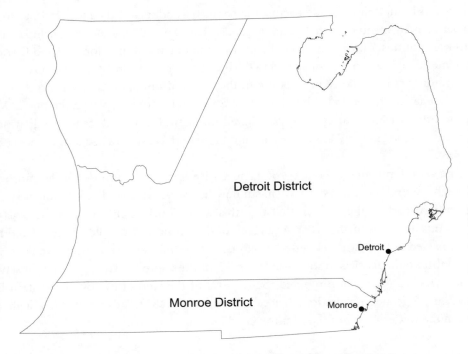

FIGURE 5.3. *LAND DISTRICTS AND LAND OFFICES IN SOUTHERN MICHIGAN IN 1826*. (Sources: see text).

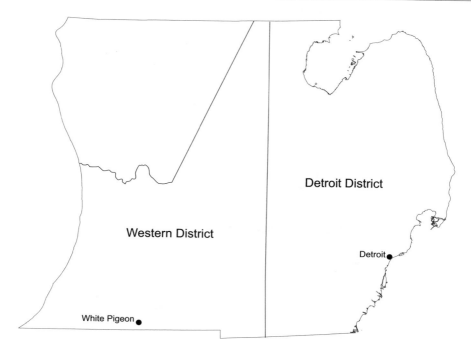

FIGURE 5.4. *LAND DISTRICTS AND LAND OFFICES IN SOUTHERN MICHIGAN IN 1831.* (Sources: see text).

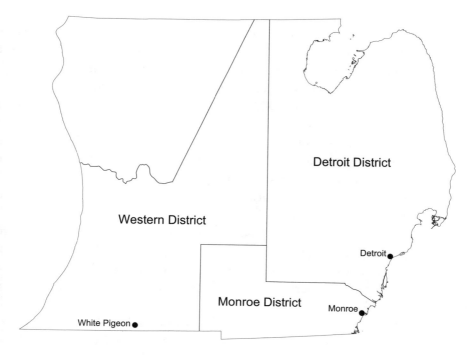

FIGURE 5.5. *LAND DISTRICTS AND LAND OFFICES IN SOUTHERN MICHIGAN IN 1833.* (Sources: see text).

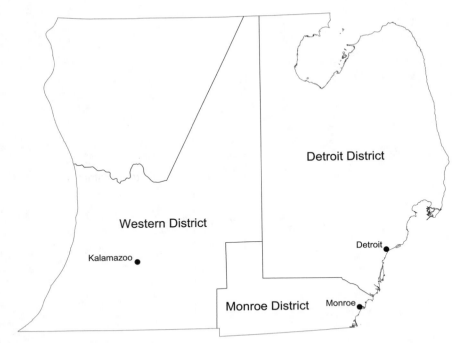

FIGURE 5.6. *LAND DISTRICTS AND LAND OFFICES IN SOUTHERN MICHIGAN IN 1834.* (Sources: see text).

The opening of lands north of Grand River by the Ottawa cession and an increase in immigration into the Saginaw Bay region provided the impetus for two northern land districts in 1836 (fig. 5.7). These were formed by detaching much of the region south of Saginaw Bay from the Detroit Land District to constitute the new Saginaw Land District and combining the northern part of the Western District with the recently acquired Ottawa lands to form the Grand River Land District. Flint, on the Flint River, and Ionia, on the Grand River, became the respective sites of the new land offices. The perception that northern Michigan offered no inducements for agricultural settlement temporarily halted the creation of additional land districts. Only in 1854, after Americans discovered that conditions favorable to crop production extended northward along the Lake Michigan shoreline, was a separate northern district established with its office in Traverse City.[50]

The GLO attempted to place federal lands in market as soon as possible, and the order in which it made Michigan lands available for sale generally followed that in which they were surveyed. This practice resulted in the sequential pattern revealed in figure 5.8. The availability of lands did not guarantee their purchase, however, because a number of other factors also affected the success of land sales.[51]

During the time in which the Detroit Land District administered all land sales in Michigan, several large tracts in the eastern peninsula were surveyed and offered for sale. These included the interior north of Detroit, a wide area west of Monroe, and an extensive

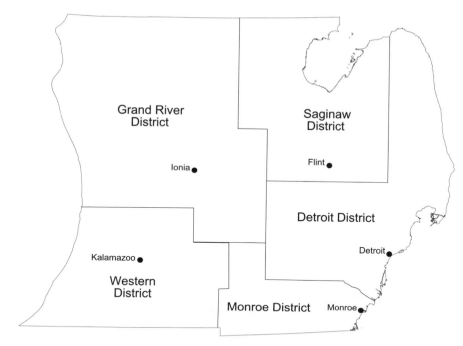

FIGURE 5.7. *LAND DISTRICTS AND LAND OFFICES IN SOUTHERN MICHIGAN IN 1836.* (Sources: see text).

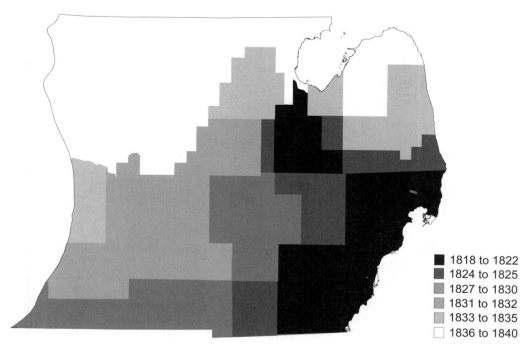

FIGURE 5.8. *SEQUENCE OF LANDS OPENED TO SETTLEMENT FROM 1823 TO 1836.* (Sources: see text).

territory south of Saginaw Bay. Despite the ambitious scope of its plans, sales by the Detroit Land Office were initially slow. Large tracts remained unsold, especially those located far from the entrepôt. The opening of the second land office, at Monroe in 1823, promoted settlement in southern Michigan. During the 1820s, the two offices administered land sales over increasingly larger areas, and by the close of the decade, the Monroe District offered tracts across the entire peninsula.[52]

Early land sales in eastern Michigan included areas along its southern extreme that would later become part of the state of Ohio. Lands extending as far as two townships below the present southern boundary east of the meridian were included in the land sales of 1820. The boundary between Michigan and Ohio had been imprecisely defined at the time of the latter's admission as a state in 1803, and subsequent attempts to establish a line based on the language of the Northwest Ordinance had resulted in conflicting claims by the two parties. By the time this controversy erupted into open political conflict in the 1830s, much of the region had been settled. The subsequent "Toledo War," as the dispute became known, did not affect the region's colonization, and settlers on each side of the boundary became residents of their respective states upon its conclusion.[53]

The establishment of a Western Land District in 1831 corresponded with the opening of vast areas south of the Grand River. Between 1831 and 1834 nearly all of the ceded lands in the western portion of the peninsula were placed in market, and land sales in this region far exceeded those in either the Detroit or Monroe Districts. The northward movement of the land office in 1834 accompanied the expansion of land sales in the Western District. Sales at Kalamazoo rose to such a volume in the spring of 1836 that the register and receiver closed the land office for eighteen days to bring their books up to date. Although sales declined as the amount of available land diminished, this office still accounted for half the sales in Michigan as late as 1838. In addition to the western lands, additional tracts were offered southwest of Saginaw Bay and in the Thumb.[54]

The cession of the Ottawa lands north of the Grand River in 1836 opened the remainder of the western peninsula to settlement. The creation of two new land districts, with offices at Ionia and Flint, facilitated the marketing of northern lands, but their sales were slower than in areas previously colonized. This was due in part to their marginal geographical position, as well as to the depressed economic conditions at the time in which the lands were placed in market.[55]

The transfer of substantial tracts of federal land to state control further affected settlement in Michigan. The GLO placed these parcels, together with control over the conditions of their sale, in the hands of the State of Michigan, in order to raise public revenues. Michigan received federal lands primarily to generate funds for education and internal improvements. The Ordinance of 1787 established the precedent of reserving Section 16 of every township for the support of public schools, and funds realized from the sale of these tracts were granted directly to state governments for such purposes in 1836. Michigan also received an allocation of seventy-two sections for the support of universities in 1837, and its legislature petitioned Congress for additional lands to support a normal school and an agricultural college. Support for the latter finally materialized in 1855 with the donation of twenty-two sections of federal land. Michigan also acquired lands to support the construction of public buildings, as well as for internal improvements such as roads, railways, canals, river navigation, and the draining of swamps. In addition, the state was allotted the revenue from the sale of up to twelve salt springs. Each of these valuable mineral resources included six contiguous sections.[56]

The State of Michigan assessed values and assigned prices to state lands, which usually exceeded the $1.25 per acre minimum price set for federal land in 1820. The legislature, for example, established minimum prices of school and salt spring lands at $5.00 an acre, and university lands sold for a minimum of $15.00 an acre. State building lands, most of which lay in urban areas, were offered at prices from $12.00 to $45.00 an acre.[57]

The sale of state lands at higher prices did not have a dramatic impact on overall settlement in southern Lower Michigan. Most tracts were widely scattered, and their presence had little effect on the occupation of the surrounding region. University lands consisted of small parcels distributed over the southern portion of Michigan in Berrien, St. Joseph, Branch, Kalamazoo, Calhoun, and Jackson Counties. Salt spring lands followed the distribution of these mineral deposits at isolated locations in Wayne, Macomb, St. Clair, Gratiot, and Kent Counties. School lands occupied a complete section near the center of each township. Situated in Kent County near the site of Grand Rapids, in Berrien County near the settlements of Niles and Bertrand, and in Ingham County in the platted site of Lansing, state building lands also comprised small, scattered tracts.[58]

Although initially high, the purchase price of state lands came to more closely approximate those paid for nearby lands as settlers occupied the area, boosting land values. As a result, state lands became as attractive to buyers as any other tract. Some state tracts, such as university lands, were selected for their high agricultural quality, a factor that justified their cost to prospective buyers, who often purchased them earlier than other land. Because the price of state lands did not significantly deter colonization, their presence was not a barrier to settlement in Lower Michigan.[59]

The alienation of internal improvement lands, on the other hand, markedly affected the distribution of Michigan's settlement. The bulk of these lands formed a large area north of the Grand River, with several smaller parcels composed of contiguous tracts in the Saginaw drainage, southern Kalamazoo County, and Oceana County. Because the state wished to sell these tracts rapidly to generate funds for important construction projects, it purportedly chose them on the basis of their high agricultural quality. When placed in market at minimum price in 1843, they sold slowly and their price remained low. The high cost of these vast tracts undoubtedly deterred prospective buyers in the depressed economy of the early 1840s, and their proximity to the perceived northern boundary of agriculture made them less attractive to some. The Michigan Legislature exacerbated this situation with its decision to remove internal improvement lands from general sales to use as payment for state construction projects. Placing government lands on the tax rolls helped a cash-poor state government finance much needed works, but the conveyance of large tracts into the hands of corporations rather than individuals did not encourage immediate settlement. The noticeably slower colonization of internal improvement tracts produced pockets of late settlement of lands north of the Grand River.[60]

The long European presence in eastern Michigan complicated and impeded the settlement of the Eastern Shore. Upon acquiring the territory, the United States government found itself charged with adjudicating claims for grants made by the previous French and British governments, whose authority predated American rule. Concentrated in a relatively small area stretching along the shore of Lake St. Clair and the Detroit River and another farther south at the mouth of the River Raisin, these early tracts were foci of initial American settlement in Michigan. Federal authorities recognized the need to adjudicate and verify previous land grants in the Land Act of 1796, which established procedures for processing such claims through a land commission. Hearings regarding land ownership were delayed in Michigan and hindered by incomplete or absent documentation and illegal encroachments on Indian lands, all of which complicated the confirmation of French and British claims. The War of 1812 further prolonged the work of the land commission, which was not revived again until 1820 and required several more years to complete its task. By the time these claims were resolved, the availability of extensive and more desirable interior lands helped turn the direction of immigration away from the Eastern shore.[61]

6

The Settlers' Acquisition of Land

Antebellum American land policy remained consistent with Jeffersonian ideals that favored establishing individual yeoman farmers as producers of commercial agricultural commodities on lands transferred directly to them. Successful settlement, however, required sufficient funds to buy and establish a farm on undeveloped land, and the cost of frontier farm-making in antebellum Michigan affected the transfer of land to prospective settlers. Immigrants were not guaranteed easy or immediate access to new lands and the economic bounty they promised. Although the purchase price of unimproved western tracts was perhaps half that of established farmland in the East, access to frontier lands was still limited by the immigrant's resources. Land and farm-making costs and the strategies pioneers developed to surmount them helped shape the form of settlement in southern Lower Michigan.[1]

THE COSTS OF LAND AND FARM-MAKING

Immigrants had to procure land before they could start farms, and most settlers purchased it directly from the U.S government. The perceived quality, availability, state of improvement, or accessibility of land determined its cost, and the value of land generally increased as a region was colonized. "Every farmer who comes into the country with his family," wrote James Lanman of Michigan, "every artisan who is to build a house, a boat, or a mill; and every settler who erects a log house on the land or clears an acre for cultivation, tends to advance the value of property."[2] Land values and prices rose as the length of time a region was occupied increased, but other variables also affected the actual value of particular tracts.

The agricultural potential of land affected its value to prospective buyers; however, this was not reflected in the arbitrary minimum price of $1.25 for which it initially sold. Because the vast amount of land surveyed and placed in market in Michigan exceeded the needs of perspective buyers, they tended to purchase the most attractive lands, leaving those of lesser quality unsold. This not only deterred settlement in some areas, but also held down land prices generally and retarded federal revenues from land sales. Eastern capitalists and western agricultural interests, seeking to increase western populations and expand markets, proposed to remedy this situation by graduating the price of land downward relative to the length of time it remained unsold. Although supported by the Michigan legislature, fears arose in Congress that price reductions would invite speculation in frontier property by large outside investors who would manipulate prices and discourage settlement.

Congressional doubts and the opposition of conservative interests prevented ratification of federal graduation legislation until 1854, by which time the frontier had drawn to a close in southern Lower Michigan.[3]

Because of the failure of federal land policy to recognize variation in land quality, prices of newly opened federal lands in Michigan remained relatively constant, usually selling at the minimum price of $1.25 an acre throughout the Lower Peninsula. Jane Comstock, a newly arrived resident of Eaton County, expressed these sentiments to her parents. "Tis great chances here for buying land," she wrote. "If you know anybody complaining of not having a farm, send them here. They can get a good farm very cheap." If the ratio of buyers to good lands was high, the cost of particular tracts occasionally rose above the minimum level in competitive bidding at government land auctions; however, even then the cost of federal lands remained low. For example, in a discussion of prices of lands sold in the Western Land District during the peak year of 1837, the *Kalamazoo Gazette* reported that the average cost per acre was only "three cents over government price."[4]

The consistently low cost of government land resulted in the early sale of the best lands. In 1843, an early resident of LeRoy Township in Calhoun County commented that the only lands available at government price were marshes. All other property was in private hands and valued at $5.00 an acre. Unimproved land offered by individuals appears to have sold at prices of from $2.50 to $6.00 an acre across much of Michigan in the 1830s and 1840s. These included prairie lands in the St. Joseph drainage, oak openings in Eaton County, pinelands in western Michigan, forested bottoms along the lower Grand River, mixed wooded and open lands along the upper Grand and Shiawassee River drainages, and older timbered lands in southeastern Michigan. Even at prices higher than the government minimum, however, the cost of land in Michigan was considerably lower than that in the eastern states, and the price of land in itself is unlikely to have been a detriment to immigration. Secondhand lands offered another advantage, in that their owners were often willing to sell on credit. Although entailing a higher cost overall, credit purchase permitted the immigrant short on capital to pay for the land on time out of the profits of production.[5]

In spite of the fact that frontier land in Michigan was initially cheap, even when resold, its value inflated when it and surrounding tracts were improved. Martin L. Daniels, a resident of Lenawee County, advised a friend in 1837 that such lands "around Clinton and Tecumseh and in the country about there is worth from ten to forty dollars per acre and land [further west] in the country about Jonesville is rising very fast." Improved lands in areas undergoing settlement along the Flint River drainage apparently sold at between $15.00 and $40.00 per acre, a range comparable to that in Lenawee and Hillsdale Counties. The rapid rise in the value of such lands affected dramatically the real estate costs of subsequent immigrants, a condition that is likely to have encouraged the expansion of settlement onto cheaper, unimproved lands.[6]

All lands, however, did not appreciate in value. Those perceived as less desirable for agriculture often retained a lower value despite the development of the surrounding countryside. For example, Sylvanus Bachelder, who established a farm in low-lying Bath Township in Clinton County in 1846, noted that nine years after his arrival the land just across the road from his improved acreage was still selling for only $4.00 an acre. Its price reflected the area's image as an undesirable environment.[7]

When federal law graduating the price for unsold government land was finally enacted in 1854, it stimulated the sale of lesser-quality lands. An article in the *Grand River Times* called attention to unsold government lands in Montcalm, Kent, and Ottawa Counties that could be purchased for 75 cents an acre and admonished prospective immigrants to become actual settlers before development of the region inflated land prices. The lowering of land prices encouraged the rapid sale of lands.[8]

The value of state lands varied with the circumstances under which they were alienated. Internal Improvement lands awarded to road contractors in payment for their services failed to increase in value and actually decreased in price because many recipients did not intend to settle them. Most, in fact, wished to sell them at the earliest opportunity, to avoid property taxes. John Ball of Kent County recalled that warrants for these tracts were commonly purchased for 40 cents an acre, a condition that attracted a continual flow of immigration. Other state lands also became bargains when the prices of surrounding lands rose. For example, William Redding found the $6.00 per acre price of state university lands in southern Berrien County a modest investment relative to the cost of comparable farmland elsewhere in 1852.[9]

Tax lands retained a low price, regardless of their actual value. These consisted of properties for which purchasers had failed to pay state, county, or local taxes for a period of three years, and were sold by the state at auction. Frontier farmers often could not pay their taxes while beginning production in a region where markets were not yet fully developed and transportation links were still being built. Severe economic downturns exacerbated this situation, increasing the amount of land available at tax sales to prospective settlers. Bela Hubbard remarked that lands auctioned for taxes in Ionia and Kent Counties in 1842 sold for 25 to 75 cents an acre, far below their actual value. Later the state also employed tax sales to dispose of unsold and unredeemed state lands and offered lands not sold at auction to applicants at a minimum price.[10]

The cost of land, however, was only a fraction of the investment necessary to create a profitable farm in the wilderness. Immigrants had to clear land and acquire livestock, tools, and equipment necessary for subsistence and production. In addition, they needed to erect houses, barns, fences, and other structures necessary to accommodate their households, livestock, and production activities. Provisions needed for survival until the first harvest were also part of the start-up costs. The amount spent on these items varied with the size of the tract developed, the requirements for improvements, and the accessibility of the farm.[11]

Federal land legislation affected farm size on the Michigan frontier. Most settlers purchased their farms under the terms of the Land Act of 1820. This legislation set the minimum price of land at $1.25 an acre and permitted sales in tracts as small as 80 acres. A second land act, passed in 1832, allowed the sale of some lands in 40-acre parcels. A survey of Midwestern farms in 1860 found that 80-acre farms were the most common, followed by farms of 160 and 40 acres. In Lower Michigan a similar pattern prevailed. "The primitive American farm averaged less than 160 acres," wrote Edward W. Barber of Eaton County in the 1840s. "[It] rarely covered a half section of 320 acres, and often was as small as 40 acres." His estimate of 175 farms to the rural township implies a mean size of just over 131 acres.[12]

In assessing the quality of wilderness land, prospective settlers considered the expense of preparing it for the plow. Consequently, they preferred prairies, and, to a lesser extent, openings, rather than bear the high costs of clearing heavily forested tracts. For example, T. E. Gidley of Jackson County remarked that, "It is better for a first settler to pay $10 an acre for plains, where he can accommodate his farm, . . . than $1 where the land is covered with a heavy growth of timber." Estimated costs to establish a farm ranged from $800 to $1,200 for a 40-acre farm, $1,333 to $2,000 for an 80-acre farm, and $2,000 to $3,000 for a 160-acre farm. Generally, the lower figures represent the costs of established farmers who brought livestock, supplies, and equipment from a previous operation. Labor expended in clearing land ranged from as little as $1,600 to prepare a 160-acre prairie farm to $2,400 for one of comparable size in a wooded area.[13] Contemporary estimates of farm-making expenses confirm the costs. In 1833 a Washtenaw County farmer declared that the value of improvements on a farm with 20 acres cleared and fenced together with livestock, exclusive of land costs, was under $300, just under half the amount projected for a 40-acre tract. O. Wilder's and Sidney Smith's figures for clearing, planting, and harvesting tracts in southwestern Michigan that same year were $1,500 for an 80-acre farm and $2,600 to $3,100 for a farm of 160 acres.[14]

These figures can be misleading, because they carry with them the assumption that all land purchased was immediately cleared, but pioneer farmers realized that the limited resources available and the limited market for surpluses made this impractical. Instead, they followed a strategy of gradual farm development aimed at providing sufficient arable land for immediate subsistence. In almost all cases, the size of the tract believed adequate for subsistence was only a fraction of the total acreage. Mrs. M. L. Sanford felt that breaking 25 of her 40 acres of land in southern Newaygo County would be sufficient to produce a crop of wheat. Nathan Fay considered an 80-acre tract in Shelby Township in Macomb County with 16 acres cleared to be adequate for his immediate needs. One immigrant to Washtenaw County purchased an "improved" quarter section of which only 40 or 50 acres were in cultivation. Estimated rates of farm-making varied for different types of land; however, most farmers brought their land into production long before it was fully cleared.[15]

STRATEGIES FOR LAND ACQUISITION

The majority of colonists settling land in Lower Michigan purchased frontier lands property, often with capital obtained by selling their farms in the East. John Blois observed that,

> The immigrants are mostly either young or middle aged, many of them wealthy, or in independent circumstances, who have sold their lands in the east and have come hither to better their fortunes. Very few do not own, or possess the means of owning a farm."[16]

The scenario of established eastern farmers induced to leave their property and resettle in the West is repeated many times in pioneer accounts. Harriet Munro Longyear, for example, recalled how her father's sale of their New York property for $10,000 in 1836 allowed her family to obtain a large farm in recently settled Clinton County. Successful small businessmen, such as Moses Chamberlain of Concord, New Hampshire, could also afford to enter frontier farming comfortably. Selling his merchandise store and small acreage in the East, he purchased 960 acres in Berrien County in 1836 where his family later settled.[17]

Not all immigrants were as prosperous as these, and many purchasers of smaller acreage invested most of their savings in farm-making. The G. W. Dryer family invested all of its funds in a 160-acre tract of oak openings in Calhoun County. Chandler W. Church recalled that after completing initial improvements on his 160-acre farm just north of Albion in 1834, he and his wife "had just two shillings [25 cents] left, and spent that for postage on a letter to the 'old folks at home,' telling them of the new home in the West."[18]

Others had little money left after purchasing land and were scarcely able to afford the improvements. People such as Rowland S. Van Scoy of DeWitt Township in Clinton County triumphed through careful planning despite their meager beginnings. Nearly exhausting his funds in the purchase of 80 acres in 1839, Van Scoy cleared 10 acres a year, gradually expanding his base of production. He systematically invested a portion of his profit each year in additional land and eventually accumulated holdings totaling 400 acres, all of which he placed in cultivation. Not all were as diligent and fortunate as Van Scoy, however, and many failed.[19]

Establishing a frontier farm also involved the expense of locating and evaluating land suitable for settlement. Visits by "land lookers" were not uncommon in Lower Michigan. A typical example, appearing in the *Detroit Gazette,* noted the arrival of "a number of gentlemen . . . whose object it is to explore a portion of the country with a view of purchasing tracts for families who are anxious to remove, should their reports be favorable." Land looking could be a lengthy process, and often required several visits to procure the desired tracts. For example, William Nowlin recalled that his father spent six to eight weeks exploring Wayne County in 1832 before purchasing eighty acres only twelve miles from Detroit. Land looking, however, was beyond the means of most prospective pioneers in Michigan.[20]

Many prospective immigrants, faced with the prospect of buying land with a limited knowledge of its actual quality, sought to mitigate the risks of acquiring poor land by pooling their resources to employ an agent. These individuals were charged with evaluating potential settlement areas and purchasing large, contiguous parcels to be subdivided among the group's members. Various immigrant associations, ranging from loose bands of citizens to business partnerships to formal "colonies" bound together by religious or ethnic ties, used this strategy to successfully overcome many of the difficulties found in locating land individually.[21]

Because organized communities consisted of absentee buyers, they depended heavily upon the services of the agent who served as their representative. Land-buying agents had to be reliable individuals with a knowledge of farming and the environmental requirements of successful agri cultural production. William Chamberlain, of Pembroke, New Hampshire, was such an agent. In 1830 a group of seven residents of nearby Loudon who desired to emigrate to southwestern Michigan hired him, to "examine the country, the best mode of conveyance [there], and to make any other inquiries that the emigrant may suggest."[22]

Reliance upon an agent, while beneficial in defraying the expenses and risks involved in land buying, occasionally presented unanticipated problems for land seekers if the agent were dishonest. For example, a corrupt representative for a group of Pennsylvania immigrants near South Bend, Indiana, just across the Michigan border, acquired title to a large tract, which the group proceeded to clear cooperatively. When the land was ready for occupation, the agent violated their communal agreement by reserving the best lands for himself and distributing the poorer "broken, marshy land" to the group's members. Although not common, this incident reveals the potential hazard in group purchase that may have influenced prospective immigrants to avoid such schemes.[23]

For those who could not immediately afford to acquire their own land in frontier Michigan, tenancy offered an alternative strategy for realizing this goal. Many prospective immigrants, like Asa P. H. Kelsey of Middleburgh, New York, lacked the necessary capital to establish themselves in the new country. "I feel that it will cost considerable to go to Michigan and a grait [sic] deal to start upon," he wrote, "but I will try to do the best I can." Kelsey's situation mirrored that of poor pioneers in the West generally, yet like many others he eventually succeeded as a frontier farmer. Kelsey and his contemporaries employed a scheme that, if managed carefully, could lead to land ownership. He began as a tenant farmer, renting land from another to acquire the capital to purchase and equip a farm of his own.[24]

Although it was never a prevailing form of land tenure, tenancy was always present on the American frontier. In the West many large tracts were owned by individuals who could not immediately resell them or place them in production. The necessity of paying taxes and other costs on such lands required that they be placed in production to generate income, a condition that encouraged tenancy as both a temporary and a permanent arrangement. The need for tenant labor offered immigrants the opportunity to enter farming with substantially less capital than was required for purchase. "The . . . poor man," wrote William Kirkland, "can hire both ground and oxen if he has not the money to buy them, paying the hire in a portion of the fruits raised." Danhof estimated that a farmer with about $500 capital in livestock, equipment, and cash could enter into an agreement and obtain a two-thirds division of the product of a forty-acre tract in Michigan, or with just over half this amount might secure a half-and-half division. Tenant capital required for larger tracts was also substantially less than for ownership.[25]

Tenancy entailed risks for the renter but provided a means for accumulating capital at a much faster rate than at wage labor. The benefits of tenancy outweighed the threats of crop failures, low prices, and practices of unscrupulous landlords. For some farmers tenancy was a better investment of capital and labor than the purchase of an inexpensive farm on less productive land. Because they would not derive the long-term benefits expended for capital improvements on property they did not own, renters instead attempted to maximize short-term gains by expanding production of the highest-yield crops and placing a higher proportion of their land in production.[26]

The rate of tenancy in frontier Michigan is difficult to ascertain because of the absence of enumerated data, the transient state of tenancy, the different arrangements under which this form of land tenure existed, and its existence as both a permanent and a temporary arrangement. Although dismissed as a rarity by contemporary promotional literature, many farmers probably employed tenancy as a strategy to acquire land. Joseph Shipman, for example, recalled how he arrived in Sheridan Township in Calhoun County in 1843 with "but two dollars and a half in his pocket." Living with his brother, he worked the farm of an uncle for three years in order to amass the cash necessary to purchase a tract of nearby land, where he later settled. Shipman was representative of a large number of people who used tenancy as a transition to ownership.[27]

Many immigrants with insufficient capital worked and saved their wages to purchase a farm in Michigan. This strategy involved little or no entry cost and provided poor people with a means of economic mobility. The key to its success lay in the relatively high return that labor demanded on the thinly populated frontier. "This is the country for a poor man to come to," wrote William Richards of Washtenaw County in 1833, "a laboring man will get one dollar a day and his board in harvest, and six shillings [75 cents] in spring and Fall, and half a dollar in the winter . . . A young man that hires out by the year will get from 120 to 150 dollars per year to work on a farm and if industrious he will soon save enough to buy him 80 acres of land." His statement was echoed by the *Kalamazoo Gazette* several years later, in an article that cited numerous examples of successful farmers who arrived without even the means to bring their families to Michigan, and yet had "by their enterprise secured a competency in life, and are now considered rich."[28]

The adult children of immigrants, already resident in Michigan, frequently worked for wages to establish themselves as independent farmers. John Fedewa of Dallas Township in Clinton County, for example, worked for a number of years in the "saleratus works" in nearby Lyons to acquire the cash necessary to reimburse his pioneer father for forty acres of the family's quarter section.[29]

The encouraging language of successful settlers and journalists, however, often failed to emphasize the delay involved in accumulating funds sufficient for land purchase and entry into farming. A potential pioneer farmer might need the savings of ten years' work to provide the funds necessary to acquire a frontier farm and place it in production. Afterward, farm income usually increased rapidly, allowing the family to enjoy a much higher standard of living. Matthew Brown worked for eleven years as a farm laborer in Oakland County in order to purchase 120 acres in Keene Township in Ionia County. Brown then continued to hire out for several more years, presumably to acquire the cash necessary to establish himself on his new property. Martha Munsell Grainger's family followed a similar pattern in obtaining their Comstock Township farm in Kalamazoo County. Her father came to Michigan in 1842 to build stone culverts on the Central Railroad and was joined by her mother the following year. The family lived in Kalamazoo for eleven years, until their savings were adequate to purchase an 80-acre farm. As long as wages on the frontier remained high and the cost of land relatively low, the strategy for land acquisition through wage labor remained viable in southern Michigan.[30]

SPECULATION AND FRONTIER DEVELOPMENT

By the time Michigan's settlement began in the 1820s, the federal government conducted all land sales for cash. Many people believed that earlier credit sales had precipitated the inflationary conditions in the financing of western lands after the War of 1812 and led to the collapse of the western land bubble in 1818, an event that contributed to the national depression the following year. Congress felt that by eliminating credit and lowering the price of land, speculation would be curtailed, thereby preventing a repetition of this disaster. The Land Act of 1820, however, ignored the important role played by credit in financing the sale of federal lands, and encouraged the entry of speculators who purchased frontier tracts for the purpose of reselling them, on credit, at a profit. These individuals filled a need for cash-poor pioneers and played a significant role in the transfer of western frontier lands before 1860.[31]

Speculators stood as commercial middlemen who conducted their business for personal gain. As such, their actions may be seen to have interfered with the settlement process when it conflicted with private interests. The success of speculation, however, was closely linked to that of colonization, and the symbiotic relationship between them tempered personal greed with the necessity of creating a workable system for transferring land on credit at reasonable rates. Central to this was the provision of credit through the mortgaging of land.[32]

The economic significance of the mortgage to immigrants without the available cash to buy land for farm-making cannot be overestimated. The mortgage introduced a mechanism by which such people could capitalize on their labor. Indeed, the mortgage offered by the speculator was often the only source of capital available for productive enterprises in an agricultural frontier region. The speculator might be despised as one profiting from others' misfortune, but nonetheless he was accepted as an economic necessity in the absence of financial institutions common in longer-settled areas.[33]

If speculation was to be economically worthwhile, the speculator could usually afford to hold land unsold only a short time while anticipated profits earned by resale remained greater than taxes. If the public remained unconvinced of the land's value, the speculator ran the risk of making no profit or even losing money. It was the failure of speculative ventures rather than their success that retarded frontier settlement.[34]

Because of the amount of capital and risk involved, only large investors with access to information regarding land markets engaged in extensive speculation. Their success depended upon their ability to promote the rapid turnover of land, but their schemes were not always as profitable as many imagined them. The risks were even greater for smaller-scale speculators without specialized knowledge, who needed to sell lands even more quickly to realize a profit.[35]

Inflation in the price of frontier lands was the key to success for speculative ventures, and the expansion of the national economy in the first half of the nineteenth century provided the impetus for widespread investment in western real estate. Following the War of 1812, a post-war boom fueled by commercial and industrial expansion and international trade, and abetted by an unregulated banking system, resulted in the uncontrolled expansion of business credit. Although land speculation occurred in the upper Mississippi and Ohio Valleys, Michigan was largely bypassed. The subsequent Panic of 1819 brought a devastating drop in prices and a collapse of the agricultural economy, which curtailed land sales and prompted the revision of federal land legislation the following year.[36]

Sustained economic growth in the late 1820s and 1830s spurred the agricultural colonization of Michigan. Rapid growth and diversification in industry, coupled with expansion of the internal transportation infrastructure and an increase in foreign trade, created an economic environment that favored the sale of Michigan lands. The happy combination of enhanced productivity and falling prices gave rise to increasingly more speculative and unwise investments in the mid-1830s. Westward expansion made land a potentially lucrative commodity for such activity in spite of the requirement that it be could no longer be purchased on credit.[37]

Land values in lower Michigan bear witness to the national economic trend of the period. Residents in the early 1830s commented on the slow but steady rise in land prices that reflected demand by immigrants. This steady increase was perceived by Elizabeth Chandler of Lenawee County, who commented in 1832 that "Even uncultivated lots are frequently valued twice the original price." Three years later, inflation caused her brother to remark that, "Property has sold higher this season by far than heretofore." Inflation was not confined to agricultural property. The value of urban lots also increased. In the village of Plainwell in Allegan County a resident remarked that "ground bought four years ago for 1–1_ $ now will sell for 100." In Detroit, urban real estate had appreciated enormously, leaving American observers struck with disbelief at the reluctance of French-Canadian owners to relinquish their ancestral holdings for the higher prices they commanded.[38]

The inflation of land prices in Michigan led to an increase in sales for investment. Some, like Jonathan Wood, made quick fortunes. "Real estate is rising rapidly," he wrote in 1836, "I probably cleared over $1,000 last season." So lucrative was the Michigan land market in the 1830s that Warren Chase recalled, "Michigan was . . . full of speculators and land hunters, and [was] the best school to study the speculating side of humanity that the nation had to offer." Speculators profited from the sale of property itself as well as from the sale of interest in it. George C. Bates of Detroit, for example, explained that in a two-year period from 1834 to 1836 he accumulated $17,000 profit by buying and selling lots, "when in no single case had the deeds been made to him." He accomplished this by acquiring the right to purchase a lot and then selling it at an advance, "and pocketed the difference."[39]

The rapid growth of settlement that accompanied the boom in speculation of the mid-1830s was reflected by mushrooming land sales in Michigan. Receipts of sales by the territory's land offices show a marked rise during the first half of the 1830s (table 6.1), and in the peak year of 1836 they were twenty-eight times greater than those of six years earlier. The jump in land sales was encouraged by the sudden availability of credit provided by the growth of banking in the West.

TABLE 6.1. *RECEIPTS FROM PUBLIC LAND SALES IN MICHIGAN UNDER THE LAND ACT OF 1820*

Year	Amount	Year	Amount
1820	$11,000	1841	$28,000
1821	$9,000	1842	$36,000
1822	$26,000	1843	$17,000
1823	$38,000	1844	$29,000
1824	$94,000	1845	$34,000
1825	$136,000	1846	$36,000
1826	$75,000	1847	$67,000
1827	$55,000	1848	$94,000
1828	$33,000	1849	$63,000
1829	$90,000	1850	$93,000
1830	$185,000	1851	$193,000
1831	$403,000	1852	$49,000
1832	$323,000	1853	$331,000
1833	$563,000	1854	$668,000
1834	$623,000	1855	$410,000
1835	$2,272,000	1856	$160,000
1836	$5,242,000	1857	$45,000
1837	$969,000	1858	$24,000
1838	$122,000	1859	$37,000
1839	$175,000	1860	$46,000
1840	$33,000		

Source: Cole, "Sale of Public Lands," 234-35.

Federal deregulation of banking in 1836 led to the rise of numerous state banks and an explosion of money lending that fueled land speculation and inflation in the West. This phenomenon came about following the failure of the federal government to recharter the Second Bank of the United States in 1832, a decision that resulted in the redistribution of federal deposits to state-controlled banks and prompted the central bank itself to expand its lending policy. A rise in the volume of lending followed; however, it did not result from an increase in real wealth. Rather, it represented an attempt on the part of financial entrepreneurs to generate quick profits without risking or even possessing capital.[40]

Many of these banks were established solely to provide easy access to funds for speculative economic ventures, and their success depended upon continued inflation. On the other hand, lending by such banks offered the only means by which profits could be generated rapidly in an economically peripheral region. Many western states, including Michigan, enacted particularly lax banking laws that encouraged their creation.[41]

As might be expected, many state-chartered banks were fraudulent schemes intended to serve only the interests of land speculators. Many "wildcat" banks issued paper notes backed by little or no security, because they were not fully capitalized. These banks lent money solely to speculators, who, in turn, used the notes to pay for their lands. The land offices immediately returned the money to the banks as federal deposits, and the cycle began again. Wildcat money served principally as a device by which speculators granted themselves continuous credit to finance their business. F. A. Dewey, an early settler in Lenawee County, later recalled that, "In the year 1836 . . . lots . . . sold for fabulous prices, and wildcat money circulated in uncut reams." The expansion of credit backed by largely worthless paper currency launched land sales into an upward spiral in the 1830s and ultimately increased its cost to actual settlers.[42]

Only direct federal intervention curtailed the excesses of the fraudulent banking system. The excesses of nonresident speculation in the West and a desire to maintain lower prices for actual settlers prompted President Andrew Jackson's "Specie Circular" in 1836, requiring that government lands be purchased only with federal metallic currency. This also reflected his party's belief that the restoration of specie, or "hard money," as currency would prevent the cyclical inflationary business expansion and economic contraction that accompanied the overissuance of bank notes and the subsequent depreciation of paper currency. The Specie Circular curtailed the operations of most fraudulent western banks, including those in Michigan, by rendering their unsupported notes worthless. It also forced other state banks to borrow heavily from eastern banks. The specie drain resulting from these demands came at a time when these banks' resources were also threatened from other directions.[43]

In the second quarter of the nineteenth century the United States remained a semi-peripheral area in the European world economy. Its reliance upon agricultural exports in international trade made the country particularly vulnerable to fluctuations in European markets, particularly those involving American credit. By 1836 the wave of prosperity in the United States had increased the purchase of European manufactured goods, resulting in a markedly unfavorable balance of trade. This condition occurred at the same time that British banks attempted to avoid a financial crisis in their banking system by stemming the acceptance of foreign bills or securities, particularly those from America. The tightening credit situation prompted a dramatic fall in the price of American export cotton and led to the failure of American brokerage houses in the spring of 1837. The specie demands on American banks brought on by the credit crisis were exacerbated further by a new federal requirement that the government surpluses held in the principal banks be redistributed to state banks. By May 1837, their resources depleted, the eastern banks suspended specie payments. This action brought on a national economic depression, bankrupting firms, creating widespread unemployment, and temporarily bringing business to a standstill.[44]

Although the Panic of 1837 had its greatest impact in the East, its repercussions were felt in the West as well. Land speculators in Michigan experienced its immediate effect, as the volume of immigration lessened sharply and the cash supply dwindled. Land became a drug on the market in the late 1830s, and receipts of sales plummeted at the Michigan land offices (table 6.1). Sales that had totaled over five million dollars in 1836 reached a low of $17,000 in 1843.

"I have more lands than I wish to hold," complained J. Seymour, a speculating investor from Rochester, New York, admonishing his Michigan agent that he was "more desirous to sell than buy."[45]

As the depression deepened, land values declined further. "Fifteen thousand acres of good Michigan land, lying in Lapeer and adjacent counties was sold at auction in Boston on the 31st ult.—one half section at $92^1/_2$, and the balance at $37^1/_2$ to 62 cents per acre," bemoaned the editor of the *Monroe Advocate,* adding that

> The land was purchased of Government at $1.25 for purposes of speculation! Had all the money which was sunk during the visionary years of wealth been expended in making improved farms, putting machinery into operation, &c., how different, now, would be the prospects of Michigan.[46]

The national depression marked the end of the economic expansion during which much of Michigan's early agricultural settlement occurred. Between 1837 and 1843 agricultural prices fell. Western farmers suffered the loss of savings deposited in frontier banks and a decline in the profitability of their work. Most managed to survive, however, because a growing frontier population maintained the demand for foodstuffs, and the volume of regional trade actually grew during the course of the depression.[47]

Unlike the inflated wilderness lands owned by speculators, improved farmland on the frontier often appreciated in value. In 1844 Henry S. Sanford noted that the worth of settled lands in Berrien County had increased over the preceding five years.[48] The following year, Henry Waldron of Hillsdale pointed with equal optimism to conditions in his locale. He commented on

> the extraordinary increase in value which property has undergone here in the short space of six years. . . . It has not taken place during times of feverish expansion and unhealthy speculation, but when those days had passed away and been succeeded by times of deep commercial depression. Our village has prospered in spite . . . of adverse times and contending elements.[49]

By the mid-1840s the depression had run its course and the national economy began to improve, bringing a period of growth that lasted for more than a decade. Although demand for new lands increased during this time, prices remained relatively low, because speculators were trying to divest themselves of large amounts of land. In 1844 a Saginaw newspaper noted that they "were constrained . . . not only to enter into competition with the Government, but to sell at a price less than a minimum of the Government [and] the best lands produce nothing more than the minimum price of $1.25 per acre." The relatively low value of unimproved land also affected the value of state lands, especially those coming into market. The Kalamazoo *Michigan Telegraph* estimated that they were worth 60 to 70 cents an acre, but warrants for them could be purchased for as little as 30 to 56 cents on the dollar. Dampened perhaps by the abundance of private sales of lands acquired before the Panic of 1837, much federal land remained unsold, and the rate of transfer of public lands in southern Michigan rebounded slowly from its nadir in 1843 (table 6.1). Only in the 1850s, when sales had shifted to lands along the Western Shore and areas outside the agricultural region, did this rate approach the average for public land sales in other developing western states.[50]

THE INFLUENCE OF SPECULATION IN SOUTHERN MICHIGAN

Several types of land speculators operated in Michigan, as they did throughout the American West. They included nonresident eastern capitalists who bought up large tracts in anticipation of resale and carried out their operations through agents. In Michigan, organizations such as the American Land Company invested huge sums of capital in potential farmlands as well as urban properties. Resident speculators operated on a smaller scale and remained a part of the community in which their clients resided. They included immigrants who purchased more land than they could farm as well as nonfarmers who became dealers in real estate, mortgagors of land purchased at tax sales, and proprietors of tenant estates. Both hoped to add to their fortunes through selling land.[51]

The scale on which they operated drew attention to absentee speculators and led many to exaggerate their preoccupation with profit and lack of interest in promoting settlement during the land boom of the 1830s. A Kalamazoo newspaper reported that, "the great moneyed associations of the east have been sending their agents amongst us like a legion of evil spirits and their coming has everywhere brought a curse." Critics claimed that speculators perpetrated criminal frauds, including bribing land officers to accept only their bids at auctions and selling lands they didn't own, as well as employing illegal means to prevent legitimate settlers from purchasing desirable tracts.[52]

When a legitimate settler outwitted the large speculator or his agents, it was considered a laudable feat. In his later years, Alvah Brainard, an early pioneer in Grand Blanc Township in Genesee County, recalled with satisfaction how, when asked "to show people land for homes," he would determine if they were settlers. "If they wanted it to speculate, [he] did not know of any such lands in the country." Jacob A. Crawford of Ray Township in Macomb County recounted how he outsmarted a speculator with designs on land he wished to settle by traveling day and night to beat the man to the Detroit Land Office to claim the tract for himself.[53]

The nonresident speculator also became a stock character in thinly disguised fictional literature of the Michigan frontier. Caroline Kirkland described how canny frontiersmen justifiably sold shares in a tract of land, "purchased for four hundred dollars just a week before," to greedy but gullible "eastern buyers" for $3,000. Jerome J. Wood's fictional residents of Hudson also outmaneuvered speculators who attempted to lure them into a fraudulent development scheme. In spite of their reputation, however, outside speculators often succeeded and became wealthy through careful investment in Michigan lands.[54]

Most speculators realized, as did John M. Gordon, that success required the selection of lands likely to appreciate and sell rapidly. "Mere speculators, generally speaking, cannot hold on for any length of time. If they have bought or borrowed capital, then their investments are not permanent." Gordon felt that the way to minimize risk was to choose land judiciously. The successful speculator anticipated the direction of settlement and purchased land accordingly. Investors relied upon maps prepared from survey notes and information supplied by paid agents to inform them of the agricultural quality of available lands. This resulted in speculators acquiring huge chunks of good land. In southwestern Michigan, where forested lands were considered desirable, Henry Chamberlain of Three Oaks recalled that, "the timberland of this section was all taken up by speculators, so that by June 1836, there were no government lands of any value subject to entry."[55]

By far the greatest amount of speculation involved agricultural lands. Determining those lands "in the column of immigration" required knowledge of likely routes of access to the frontier. In 1825 the *Detroit Gazette* reported that attempts to purchase lands along the projected route of the first major interior road resulted in their being withheld for auction to the highest bidder. Tracts along the path of the second inland road attracted similar attention from speculators four years later. Albert Baxter of Grand Rapids recalled that "valuable lands along the Grand river, and some not very valuable, were 'gobbled' by non-resident speculators; and the same may be said of the country along the territorial or State roads."[56]

Often absentee buyers preferred to acquire large tracts of unimproved farmland over other lucrative real estate, because of its lower development costs. When faced with a choice between buying an Eaton County mill site of four hundred contiguous acres or five thousand to six thousand acres of land in other locations, speculator J. Seymour advised his Michigan agent against the mill site. Although he felt that "it would be a profitable investment," the development and management of a production site required a resident agent, the cost of which made the potential gain less than that which might accrue from the sales of large acreage of farmland, which would need no supervision.[57]

Many land companies found it worthwhile to employ resident agents to oversee extensive holdings in Michigan. Usually members of a frontier community, these agents knew the land and had a stake in the region's economic development. Many who served in this capacity went on to distinguished careers in Michigan business and politics, including banker Charles C. Trowbridge, politician Elon Farnsworth, attorney Theodore Romeyn, and congressman and senator Lucius Lyon. Because their success was linked closely to the development of frontier Michigan, all contributed heavily to the regional economy. In this sense, outside land speculation became a form of local investment. Profits placed capital in the hands of resident entrepreneurs, in whose interest it was to establish the infrastructure necessary for commercial production.[58]

Some speculators, however, caught up in the land frenzy of 1836, bought extensive tracts sight unseen. Joseph Beers and Samuel Sherwood of New York City, for example, purchased a total of 2,386 acres in Kalamazoo County in only eleven days in November 1835. Such large-scale and indiscriminate acquisition of lands for resale created a pattern of speculator ownership that bore little relationship to that of immigrant settlement. Large investors often held onto lands not in immediate demand for years in hopes of profiting from rising prices. This practice retarded their sale until surrounding lands selling at the government price were taken up. Unless taxes forced their sale, such tracts became "speculator deserts," a phenomenon that certainly inhibited settlement and affected settlement patterning in many parts of southern Lower Michigan following the Panic of 1837. For example, in Kalamazoo County settlement was retarded by speculator retention of large parcels of land. Immigrant C. Parker lamented that much of the land around St. Joseph was "owned by speculators . . . living in New York & New England and was held at enormous prices, which prevented the place from improving. . . . I was astonished to find so much wild land about the place." In Eaton County, outside investors held "a monopoly of large tracts [that] delayed settlement and improvement [in Benton and Chester Townships] . . . for twenty-five years."[59]

Successful urban speculation also shaped settlement patterning on the frontier. The resale of lands for prospective town sites proved to be the most lucrative form of investment in frontier property. Frontier towns functioned as centers of economic, social, and political activities for a wide region, and smaller nucleated settlements contained crucial processing and storage facilities, such as grain and flour mills and warehouses, as well as retail services and repair shops necessary to support agricultural production. These settlements were crucial to the development of the frontier economy, and property values in these settlements increased rapidly as their functions expanded. To a speculator perceptive enough to choose the right site, the return on investment might be dramatic. Since Michigan's sparsely settled frontier could accommodate only a limited number of central settlements, competition to locate them was fierce and investing in them risky. In spite of these drawbacks, there was no shortage of town-site speculators on the Michigan frontier.[60] Nonresident investors recognized the necessity and value of urban settlements. New Yorker John M. Gordon noted in his diary that Michigan, "has now none or few towns, and that its population is pouring in at a rate of 50 thousand a year." Because, he argued, "they are accustomed to and must have their villages, . . . it will be perceived that these town speculations have a real basis of intrinsic value," unlike similar investments in older established areas. Although Gordon himself preferred to invest in less risky ventures, others did not follow his example. Investors considered several factors with regard to the location of town sites. The first was access to waterpower needed to operate heavy machinery. Sites along streams providing the proper volume and slope necessary for mills were among the earliest choices for towns in the interior. Pontiac was recognized as an "eligible point" for such a town because of the presence of "excellent mill seats and other water privileges." The distribution of the agricultural population was a second factor. An area where production was likely to expand needed the services provided in a nucleated settlement. Finally, access to transportation routes was advantageous to settlements serving as regional collection and redistribution points. Promoters attempted to place town sites on existing or future routes of transportation and communication.[61]

Anticipation of transportation routes was a key factor in town-site speculation. In 1853, for example, John Swegles formed a joint-stock company that purchased land in Clinton County. Swegles, in his former position as state auditor general, had learned that the Detroit & Milwaukee Railroad, then building westward across the peninsula, intended to pass through the lands his groups purchased. No sooner had the railroad marked the locations of the line and depot then Swegles's surveyors began laying out town lots, which sold rapidly as economic activity gravitated toward this new transportation hub, named St. Johns.[62]

A new town's success also depended on the hard work of enterprising promoters. In Kalamazoo County, Titus Bronson's efforts insured the future of his town site at the expense of its two rivals. The selection of Bronson's site as the county seat came about because he alone argued his case before the government commission charged with determining the seat's location. The rise of Bronson (later Kalamazoo) as an administrative center in 1831 provided the impetus for the community to rapidly outdistance competing settlements and acquire the complex functions of a frontier town.[63]

Town-site speculation in Lower Michigan reached its peak before the Panic of 1837. Although many of these enterprises resulted in successful settlements, many failed because they were founded on fraudulent schemes designed to take advantage of unwise investors. George C. Bates recalled that during the mid–1830s such schemes proliferated in Detroit, where frontier entrepreneurs gathered. "The walls of Michigan Exchange, the National hotel, the American hotel, Uncle Ben's, and all the other hotels of Detroit were papered over with plats, maps and diagrams of new cities," that were up for sale. Many, like Caroline Kirkland's fictional New-New York, were simply ill-sited and remained "paper towns," often situated in uninhabitable locations. The city of White Rock, for example, was platted beneath the waters of Lake Huron.[64]

The success of a town depended on its maintaining its position in rapidly shifting frontier transportation networks. Changes in this network led to the decline or abandonment of many early town sites, such as Keene, in western Lenawee County. When faced with the prospect of being bypassed by the railroad in 1841, the town was moved literally by its citizens to a new site and became Hudson. DeWitt, the original seat of Clinton County, also showed a marked decline after St. Johns became the county seat in 1857 and assumed the central economic and political functions of the earlier settlement.[65]

Political actions intended to alter the organizational structure of the colonial region also changed the patterning of urban settlement. The decision of the state legislature in 1847 to place Michigan's new capital in a relatively unpopulated location near the geographical center of the state, for example, created a new focus for services and economic activities and altered the structure of transportation in the central timberlands. The arbitrary creation of an urban center in a "howling wilderness" had clear implications for the distribution of settlement in this region at mid-century.[66]

Michigan pioneers often availed themselves of the opportunity to sell real estate that had appreciated in value, and many immigrated west with the intent of becoming resident speculators. The inherent rise in land values following initial purchase made every frontier landowner a potential speculator. Abundant and cheap land, the high cost of labor, and limited markets encouraged a strategy of purchasing and partially improving a tract, selling it at a profit, and acquiring a larger property with the proceeds. In this sense, a large proportion of the immigrants to Michigan and other frontier areas could be considered speculators.[67]

Resident speculation took several forms, all of which affected the patterning of pioneer settlement. Perhaps the most obvious involved immigrants who acquired a large amount of land within a small area for the purpose of reselling it. The subsequent rise in land prices made this a worthwhile investment for many. Anticipated expansion of settlement also enhanced interest in land investment by those occupying adjacent territory. Ruth Evans, who lived north of Adrian in 1835, was certainly aware of the potential profits to be obtained through the resale of government lands lying along Bean Creek in western Lenawee County and expressed her intentions to take advantage of this situation. "We wish to invest our money in unimproved land there," she wrote, "as it more than doubles in value every year."[68]

The opportunity for land investment appealed to immigrants with capital to invest in rural or urban real estate on the Michigan frontier. Individuals such as Louis Campau of Grand Rapids, Rix Robinson of Ada, and the Williams Brothers of Owosso had all amassed wealth in the Indian trade in Michigan. Others, such as Moses Chamberlain of New Buffalo, Titus Bronson of Kalamazoo, and William Swarthout of Victor Township in Clinton County, brought capital with them from earlier business enterprises. Their success as speculators rested on their ability to resell the lands they purchased within a short time, an endeavor that was enhanced by their intimate knowledge of the region and active participation in the promotion of settlement.[69]

David Scott, who immigrated to southern Clinton County in 1833, successfully promoted DeWitt Township after buying 1,426 acres there. DeWitt lay on the Looking Glass River, a principal tributary of the Grand, and the Grand River Trail, a principal overland route. To encourage settlement of his land, Scott established farms for his family and his son and erected a store and hotel where the trail crossed the Looking Glass. The first county courts held their sessions in Scott's buildings, and the settlement, first known as "Scotts," became the county seat of DeWitt. DeWitt's location on a major road at a waterpower source encouraged its further economic growth. As an early frontier center, DeWitt drew immigration to the surrounding region and permitted Scott to successfully promote the sale of his extensive holdings.[70]

Resident speculators encouraged the sale of their lands by providing pioneers with flexible terms of purchase. Investors found it more profitable to offer buyers lenient terms, especially in hard economic times, than to refuse purchase or foreclose on a mortgage. William Swarthout, for example, offered John and Sarah Parker a farm of 160 acres for nothing down in the depression year of 1837 and loaned them a horse team to break the land. Profits from the Parker farm soon permitted them to pay off the mortgage and later expand their holding in Clinton County's Victor Township. Such agreements often bound the purchaser not only to regular payments, but also to a schedule of improvements that insured the land's increase in value.[71]

Because of their central role in developing frontier communities, pioneers perceived resident speculators much differently than they did their absentee counterparts. By providing assistance to newcomers and needed services to local residents, resident speculators invariably became central figures in the communities they helped to settle. Many early resident speculators, such as B. O. Williams, acquired civil and political offices and ended their days in comfortable retirement. Others, like Louis Campau, fell into financial poverty, yet retained a high social status in later life. The general respect, if not affection, for such individuals was reflected in their contemporaries' use of the honorific terms "Uncle," "Captain," and "Judge" to connote their influential yet familiar position in the pioneer community.[72]

Some pioneers capitalized on the transfer of smaller tracts by repeatedly buying, improving, and selling frontier properties. Elizabeth Chandler observed this form of speculation in Lenawee County during the 1830s and explained its appeal to both buyer and seller.

> Breaking up and fencing land is allowed to raise its value [from $1.25] to ten dollars an acre though selling a farm bears a higher rate than that. But farms are not sold here as yet by the acre generally, but in the lump. This makes the selling of a partially improved farm quite a profitable affair very often; and improved land is often a considerable object to persons coming in who have large families to provide for, because they can so much more derive their support from the land, a second move into the woods is not near so formidable, while the additional capital they acquire can be invested to excellent profit. This occasions frequent changes and removals in a new settlement, especially among those [who] are not so well off, or have anything *speculative* in their dispositions.[73]

Unlike the nonresident speculator, who had to absorb the cost of maintaining unimproved land that returned no income, the settler-speculator employed the land to support a household and pay taxes while its intrinsic value increased. Immigrants with limited capital could rapidly increase their wealth through the rising equity of their real estate alone and could establish a financial base capable of underwriting larger agricultural endeavors in the future. Immigrant correspondence is full of references to the rapid and profitable turnover of the property. "Peter has sold his land and gone to the [land] office for more," wrote Betsey Landon of her brother's 1836 dealings in Spring Arbor Township in Jackson County. Similarly, Melancthon Bagg anticipated that the impending sale of his partially improved lots in Marengo, Calhoun County, would more than pay his debts and allow him to "begin anew." The success achieved by the repetitive sale of frontier farms is reflected in the experience of Charles P. Klingensmith, of Jefferson Township in Hillsdale County, who began with a 45-acre tract in the 1840s. After "buying and selling several times, making something on each sale, . . . he was enabled to secure possession of [a] . . . farm of 190 acres."[74]

For many pioneer farmers the sequential sale and acquisition of property was quite rapid. Sylvanus Bachelder, for example, obtained the Bath Township property that he occupied for the rest of his life after a whirlwind of real estate activity in which he "sold and traded farms five times in two years." For others the process occupied many years. Lewis Townsend of Marengo Township settled on 25 acres of unimproved land in Washtenaw County in 1838. Thirteen years later he purchased 440 acres in Calhoun County on the proceeds of the sale. Harvey Bump waited eleven years to realize a substantial profit from the sale of his Hillsdale County farm in 1854, capital that he used subsequently to develop a larger acreage in Montcalm County.[75]

Resident farmers, like others who speculated in land values, had to be careful not to overextend their resources in a capricious land market. E. Lakin Brown, of Kalamazoo County, recalled how his family's overpurchase of lands in southwestern Michigan just before the Panic of 1837 left them with larger holdings than they could farm and which for the time being could not be sold. His eventual disposal of much of the property for less than its original cost led him to conclude later that, "The affair was a loss to all parties."[76]

Large resident investors differed from nonresident speculators because they were enmeshed in the region's development. Outsiders had no stake in the frontier beyond the funds invested; but residents committed the bulk of their profits to developing the regions they promoted. By gambling all of their resources on the successful growth of settlement, they ventured their futures in these speculative enterprises. Large-scale resident speculators found it in their interest to sell land to actual settlers as rapidly as possible, and their efforts were directed toward encouraging this process.

Resident speculators sought to create a regional infrastructure, which accelerated the rate of agricultural expansion and the concomitant rise in land values. They were also instrumental in attracting regional economic and political institutions to towns they promoted. The establishment of DeWitt as the initial seat of Clinton County on Captain David Scott's land, the choice of Titus Bronson's tract for the location of the land office and seat of Kalamazoo County, and the development of the Williams brothers' property at Owosso as Shiawassee County's economic focus were not fortuitous events. Neither was the selection of pioneer Judge Samuel Dexter's early settlement and mills as the seat of Ionia County and the location of the Grand River District Land Office. These central institutions attracted population to the newly created towns and promoted their growth.[77]

SQUATTING AND PREEMPTION

Many immigrants without sufficient capital to acquire land or a desire to assume tenancy chose instead to settle illegally on government lands not yet brought into market, unsold federal and state lands, or unimproved lands held by absentee owners. These "squatters" employed a strategy that allowed them to obtain subsistence and enter production at minimal cost. Not unique to the American West, squatting was a widespread practice in many parts of the world. It was a strategy that arose among marginal social and economic groups seeking permanent or temporary access to land for residence or production. Where land use was denied for economic or political reasons, squatting arose as an extralegal means to accommodate this purpose. Subordinate ethnic groups in Europe had long employed rural agricultural squatting as a response to the uncertainties of production in poor environments, and they carried it to North America along with other immigrant cultural traditions. In colonial America squatting became a common response to conditions of marginalization on the frontier, and by the nineteenth century it was a recognized, though still largely illegal, means of land acquisition.[78]

The tradition of squatting on frontier lands developed in response to conditions created by increasing population pressure on the limited land resources of the British colonies. Expansion westward was frustrated by the conflicting land claims of the Eastern Seaboard provinces and the desire of the Crown to preserve the trans-Appalachian region as a reserve for its Indian allies. In the absence of a legal framework for expansion, western settlement could take place only by illegal squatting, which increased following the American Revolution and the loss of British authority. Only the presence and strength of aboriginal peoples limited squatting on western lands as the United States formulated land policy at the end of the eighteenth century.[79]

Colonial land distribution policies encouraged squatting by leaving settlement site choice to individual immigrants. This practice, particularly prevalent in the middle and southern colonies, fostered "indiscriminate location," characterized by expansive and uncontrolled settlement. Several colonial and early state governments also gave tacit support to squatting by recognizing the rights of settlers to subsequently claim the lands that they had illegally occupied, a precedent that later affected federal land policy in the West.[80]

By the 1780s squatting had become commonplace in the Northwest Territory, despite the efforts of the U.S. government to discourage incursions on Indian lands or unsold federal reserves. Although the Indian Wars delayed large-scale migration of settlers in the 1790s, illegal settlement in the West increased afterward in defiance of national policy. Federal officials possessed the authority to remove squatters, yet were reluctant to disrupt western settlements that were opening the interior to colonization and promoting economic expansion by the new nation. Western squatting thus became a quasi-legal activity.[81]

Squatting gained legal recognition as the result of a cumulative political process that allowed the preemption of government lands by people who occupied tracts but did not own them. At the beginning of the nineteenth century, the first onslaught of American colonization in the Old Northwest created large concentrations of squatters on lands where legal jurisdiction was uncertain or ownership was unclear. In western Ohio, settlers on a large unsurveyed private tract between the Great and Little Miami Rivers had been conveyed lands outside the limits of the original grant by its owner, John Cleves Symmes. Congress granted them preemption rights in 1799 in the first such federal relief act. In 1813, American settlers in Illinois received preemption rights to lands some had occupied as squatters for nearly three decades. In addition to such specific cases, Congress allowed limited general preemption under the Land Act of 1820, which provided for settlers who had been forced to relinquish land for nonpayment under the earlier credit system of purchase.[82]

In the 1820s federal attitudes toward squatting changed markedly in response to its perceived role in western settlement. A report issued by the Congressional Committee on Public Lands in 1828 concluded that squatters actually encouraged the opening up of new lands to settlement and their improvements increased the value of wilderness tracts. Consequently, it was argued that their contribution to colonization entitled squatters to first right of purchase. In 1830 Congress passed a general preemption act with the strong endorsement of President Andrew Jackson. This law entitled a settler who had occupied and cultivated any part of a tract up to 160 acres in 1829 to purchase that land at the minimum government price. Because it limited the time for filing claims to a year, pressure arose to expand its provisions, especially the dates of eligibility. During the following decade, Congress passed other acts that facilitated preemption and more clearly defined its conditions.[83]

The Preemption Act of 1841 finally made the provisions of the earlier legislation permanent and established squatting as a legitimate means of land acquisition. It also restricted preemption to small farmers by stipulating that land be used for agricultural purposes only, and discouraged profiteering by forbidding individuals in trade or who owned 320 or more acres in any state or territory to preempt public land. The passage of this act helped place immigrants of moderate means on a level comparable to those with greater capital. In this it ameliorated to some degree the impact of speculation on frontier settlement expansion.[84]

In Michigan, squatter settlement ranged well ahead of official land openings, spreading rapidly across the interior. As early as 1826, a correspondent to a Monroe newspaper reported that settlers already occupied much of the St. Joseph Valley, "anxiously waiting for the lands in that quarter to be brought into market." Three years later, immigrant Thaddeus Smith bitterly reported that much of the prairie land he sought to purchase in southwestern Michigan had been occupied by "trespassers or squatters, composed to Tom, Dick, Harry, the Devil & his Imps." Another observer also noted the considerable extent of squatting across much of western Michigan. Clearly the anticipation of a general preemption law encouraged the expansion of settlement.[85]

Most Michigan residents welcomed preemption legislation as a means of increasing the rate of frontier settlement. They believed it would improve the accessibility of new lands, increase the rate at which they were placed in production, and enhance the value of frontier real estate. Preemption had an immediate impact on the amount of land sold. Only five months after the passage of the Act of Preemption of 1830, the Monroe *Michigan Sentinel* observed that "considerable quantities of land are claimed under it." Figures kept by the General Land Office revealed a substantial number of initial land claims filed in 1830, followed by a decline and then a dramatic increase in the middle of the decade (table 6.2). The onslaught of preemption claims placed an immediate burden on the land offices, which were now obliged to process squatters' petitions in addition to normal land sales. So numerous did preemption claims become in western Michigan that the Kalamazoo Land Office had to set aside separate days to hear and determine them, apart from regular land sales.[86]

TABLE **6.2.** *QUANTITIES OF LAND IN MICHIGAN SOLD UNDER PRE-EMPTION LAWS THROUGH 1835.*

Year	Number of Acres Sold
1830	6,192.95
1831	2,237.58
1832	1,374.99
1833	693.93
1834	4,362.67
1835	37,044.81

Source: ASP/PL/8/1525/1836.

Immigrants employed preemption to acquire agricultural land, and the accounts of many squatters turned successful farmers appear in the pioneer literature of the late nineteenth century. Many of these people related experiences in the western portion of the peninsula, which had been the destination of many illegal immigrants following the 1821 treaty cession. Subsequently, preemption accounted for a large number of the land claims filed in the Western Shore region. The *Grand River Times* reported that of 3,500 claims in northwestern Oceana County, 1,000 were filed by squatters. Many of these immigrants, like Edward Ingalls of Otisco Township in Ionia County, were nearly destitute. Having failed at farming poor land in New York, he worked his way westward until he located on unclaimed land, which he cleared and placed in production. From the proceeds of his work he was subsequently able to purchase the tract through preemption.[87]

Although preemption was intended to assist agricultural settlers, town-site speculators also benefited from its provisions. By selecting land-possessing characteristics amenable to the development of urban functions, entrepreneurs secured valuable tracts at minimal cost. One such man was Rix Robinson, whose intentions seemed obvious to John M. Gordon, who learned of his plans in 1836.

Robinson has squatted on an 80 acre lot opposite the Grand Rapids under the expectation of securing it at government price by means of future preemption Law. The waterpower which it commands will, with its adaptation to the site of a town, make it very valuable. I am informed that if put up at public sale the 80 acres would bring $1,000 or $15.00 per acre. He has placed a brother (of whom he has six) at all of the best points from the mouth to the sources of the Grand River, with view to getting the title by occupancy. One is at the mouth of Grand River, one of the best Harbours on Lake Michg., another is at the mouth of the Thorn apple, a good point for transshipment, and a third at the junction of the flat and Grand, . . . all of which [places] . . . will become towns or places of transshipment.[88]

Robinson's strategy allowed his family to establish valuable landholdings at Ada, Lowell, Grand Rapids, and Grand Haven, properties that soon became nucleated settlements on the lower Grand River drainage. The rapid development of the last two as processing and shipping centers, and the accompanying inflation of their value as real estate, permitted Robinson to live comfortably and devote his time to a variety of pursuits, including politics.[89]

Michigan extended the scope of preemption legislation to include state lands reserved to generate funds to support education and other public projects. Many of these tracts were occupied illegally because their boundaries were unclear to prospective immigrants or had been established after squatter settlement had begun. To avoid conflict over these lands, the state legislature resolved to allow preemption on state tracts already settled in exchange for other unoccupied federal lands.[90]

Squatters sometimes acquired tracts purchased by absentee owners who had forfeited land due to unpaid taxes. This situation was especially prevalent in the wake of the depression of the late 1830s. The state disposed of tax-delinquent properties at sales. For the nominal sum of the taxes owed, a squatter could acquire a tax title deed, which did not convey the land he occupied outright, but gave the occupant rights to all improvements he had made on it. The absentee owner could, of course, reclaim the land by repaying the back taxes and interest, but this amount plus the value of the settler's improvements soon exceeded the worth of the property. At this point practical ownership of the land passed to the squatter.[91]

Although tax lands provided an opportunity for immigrants unable to afford the cost of land, these settlers risked losing their property through the machinations of a legal system many did not fully understand and often feared. Because the possession of absentee-owned land on the basis of tax deeds did not produce immediate or clear title, those who held such deeds occasionally found their status challenged by swindlers who took advantage of ambiguities in the law. In Michigan, people purporting to represent the interests of landowners attempted to defraud preemptors of "nominal fees" for their client's interest in the claim. The passage of state legislation curtailed corrupt practices by awarding ownership of tax lands to immigrants who remained on them for a period of twenty-one years.[92]

Squatters assumed a greater risk by settling without benefit of a tax deed. Those who occupied a tract in anticipation of its sale could find themselves obliged to move, if the land were reclaimed. While traveling in Kalamazoo County in 1844, Henry Sanford encountered a number of deserted squatter cabins on tax lands, all of which had been abandoned when their occupants learned that the tracts would not be offered for sale.[93]

Squatters attempted to protect their rights by organizing regional "claim associations." Such groups arose in the West in the 1820s to promote the cause of preemption and provide mutual support and protection for immigrants on federal lands. Claim associations helped regulate the distribution of land among their members in a fair manner and facilitate the transfer of property when it officially came on the market. They also created a stable political situation in the absence of official administrative institutions, so that immigrants might "improve the public land as though they already had titles from government."[94]

John M. Gordon encountered a claim association composed of three hundred settlers in Kent County in 1836 and described its operations.

> They are said to keep a land office of their own in which each squatter's name and section or lot are entered as evidence of title when Congress passes another pre-emption Law, and all persons coming among them are required to join the association. They have caused surveyors of their own to extend the lines . . . of the old survey, so that each makes a description of his location as exact as those kept at Govrt. Land offices. They doubtless, by their early preparation and close combination have ulterior views of enforcing Lynch law in case it becomes necessary thus to support their claims.[95]

This organization included the provision for mutual aid found in the constitutions of most squatter's associations. This involved the support of fellow members at land sales, where a bidder selected to represent all members at the sale insured that the price of land remained low. John Ball of Grand Rapids served in this capacity for squatters in Kent and Ottawa Counties in 1843 and successfully secured their claims to state lands at a minimal price.[96]

Gordon's reference to "Lynch Law," however, reveals that mutual aid could also involve the intimidation of those who challenged claims of association members. Preemptors usually directed this at those described as speculators, and their actions ranged from the "score of snapping eyes" aimed at an outside bidder at an Indiana auction to threats with pistols that Illinois squatters employed to discourage "New York speculators" in Chicago. Irate squatters from Kent County were so fearful that speculators would bid off their lands in 1839 that they went to the Ionia Land Office "with clubs to fight them off." Although this incident remained peaceful when the anticipated speculators failed to appear, another confrontation at the same land office witnessed the spectacle of an unsuccessful outside bidder, "going from Ionia like a streak of blue lightning; a yelling, infuriated score of squatters raising a cloud of dust in his wake." Incidents of actual violence appear to have been rare in Michigan, since squatters' associations protected their members from competing claimants to their lands.[97]

By the mid-1820s pioneers generally anticipated preemption, and following its legal recognition in 1830, squatting became increasingly popular in areas they expected to be opened for settlement. The use of preemption as a strategy was most prevalent in western Michigan, an area perceived to possess great agricultural value. The General Land Office, anticipating that preemption would precipitate rapid growth, urged the completion of surveys of recently obtained federal lands as quickly as possible. The preemption acts, which provided a filing period of a year after the surveys were completed, encouraged early settlement, and the rush of immigrants to secure choice lands in western Michigan increased the rate of settlement expansion.[98]

Preemption did not create areas of dense settlement, but rather encouraged its dispersal. Legislation limited the size of the tracts each preemptor could claim and promoted the ownership of smaller units of land. It also left settlers free to choose the location of their lands. By permitting settlement before sale, the government temporarily lost systematic control of land allocation, resulting in a rapid but indiscriminate occupation of a large portion of the Lower Peninsula. The extremely scattered distribution of settlement produced by preemption affected the growth of settlement in frontier Michigan.[99]

The timing of preemption legislation also influenced the rate of settlement. Preemption in Michigan increased with the impending passage of federal legislation in the late 1820s and accelerated with the land boom of the mid-1830s. Areas that had been obtained by the United States through cession but had not yet come into market were the most likely to be settled by squatters. These include the south central and southwestern parts of the Lower Peninsula acquired in the Treaty of 1821 and the Grand River country obtained in the Treaty of 1836. The increase of squatting pushed settlement beyond the boundaries dictated by official land openings shown in figure 5.8. Although the pattern of preemptive holdings is largely undocumented, it is likely to have been similar to that of general settlement. Squatters shared the same perceptions about Michigan's environment and Native inhabitants as other immigrants, and followed the same routes into the interior. Consequently, their contribution to the frontier landscape was one of accelerating expansion rather than altering its form.

7

Strategies for Settlement

MOTIVATIONS FOR COLONIZATION

Those who immigrated to Michigan came voluntarily to the new country; but their choice to do so entailed more than simply making a decision to relocate. Although most perceived that the benefits of resettlement would justify the cost of movement, immigration was an expensive and disruptive experience, and one not lightly undertaken without expectations of an improved life. In addition to the monetary costs of travel and farm-making, immigration also involved the social cost of leaving kin groups, churches, established communities, and familiar environs. People migrated in response to worsening circumstances in the homeland or a markedly better situation on the frontier, or both. Laborers, tenant farmers, fugitive slaves, European farmers, established eastern agriculturists, and capitalist entrepreneurs had quite different incentives to migrate, but all found inducements strong enough to attract them to Michigan.[1]

Most of Michigan's pioneers had participated in the American economy and had no desire to leave it behind. Instead, they sought to expand its geographical arena and lay claim to a greater share of its wealth. The abundance of land in Michigan attracted easterners wishing to increase their fortunes in farming, as well as others seeking opportunities for success. In the eyes of the editor of the *Grand River Times,* "eastern emigrants, the farmer—the mechanic—the professional man and the capitalist seem alike attracted to this 'land of promise.'"[2] A growing obsession to possess frontier lands prompted Michigan resident D. L. Porter to report that

> [an] emigration mania or fever is prevailing very extensively in the western part of New York, in all the middle states & most of the eastern states. There have been pioneers from every section of the middle and eastern states to examine the country. I am not aware of an instance in which they have returned to their friends without purchasing a lot first.[3]

Although Porter exaggerated the extent of land purchases, he captured the enthusiasm that gripped many easterners.

Driven by economic motives, many immigrants contracted Michigan fever, including James Lanman, who captured the attitudes of recent settlers:

he state of Michigan is rapidly filling up with an active class of people from the east, who have left the Atlantic frontier to improve their fortunes, or perhaps from that reckless and migratory character which belongs to this country. . . . Wealth and honor . . . are the grand motives of emigration.[4]

Hiram Arnold, of Kalamazoo County, recalled explicitly immigrating to "improve his financial condition in a new country." Polly Ely, of Poplar Ridge, New York, observed that fifteen people who had recently left her community for Michigan did so principally "to increase in wealth."[5]

The degree to which Michigan pioneers valued economic success and placed business above all other endeavors in life impressed visitors from the East, although not always favorably. The Reverend James Selkirk, for example, found the residents of St. Joseph "so engaged in making money that they seemed to have left religion in their former place of abode."[6] British diarist James Platt Clapham, who journeyed to the Old Northwest in 1836 to seek his fortune, conveyed the economic imperative for western settlement with quintessential simplicity. "If I did not see my chance of making money, he noted, I would not stay one *minute* on this side of the Atlantic."[7]

Changing economic conditions on the Eastern Seaboard induced emigration. Rapid population growth, from natural increase and European immigration, placed increasing pressure on limited land resources. Traditional farming became increasingly unprofitable because of higher operating costs, increased land values, competition from western agriculture, and often declining output from worn-out lands. Although many eastern farmers found employment in manufacturing, others looked toward resettlement in the West as a solution to these conditions.[8] Their perceptions found their way into popular verse in the "Michigan Emigrant's Song."

> And there's your Massachusetts,
> Once good enough, be sure;
> But now she's always laying on
> Taxation and manure;
> She costs you pecks of trouble,
> But de'il a peck can pay;
> While all is scripture measure
> In Michigania.[9]

The low cost of Michigan land encouraged easterners to move westward. To Alvah Brainard, a young immigrant to Grand Blanc from Monroe County, New York, cheap land offered the only way to enter farming. He concluded, "I would have to go west, where it could be had cheap. . . . [T]here was no alternative but to go." The opportunity to acquire tracts of agricultural land at relatively low cost permitted many immigrants of moderate means to enter farming in Michigan.[10]

The frontier held for some the opportunity to rebuild fortunes lost in the East. More than one immigrant would share the experience of Bethuel Farrand, of Ann Arbor, who recalled that "Pecuniary losses, and the prospect of the successful prosecution of an extensive business enterprise were the motives which induced me to emigrate." W. R. McCormick, whose family was forced to sell its farm near Albany, New York, to cover a debt on a countersigned note, turned to "the wilderness of the great West . . . to . . . retrieve the fortunes that had been so suddenly wasted." The availability of land provided eastern farmers a second chance, and landless farmers often perceived western land as offering them a chance to achieve agricultural prosperity.[11]

The promise of cheap and abundant land also reached beyond the United States to attract Europeans from regions where agriculture was undergoing stressful changes. In Great Britain, uneven harvests and the effects of the Napoleonic Wars played havoc with the production and marketing of foodstuffs. Furthermore, the Industrial Revolution led to the rapid commercialization of agriculture, which displaced farmers and prevented others from taking up this occupation. In Germany, many small farmers lost access to arable land as a result of "reform movements" that redistributed peasants' lands to large landholders. In southern and western Germany, land shortages forced farmers to turn to more intensive forms of agriculture, particularly viticulture and raising potatoes. The intermittent failure of these crops, together with the loss of foreign grain markets, created massive agricultural unemployment that induced many farmers to emigrate. The economy of the Netherlands also recovered slowly in the aftermath of the Napoleonic Wars. The situation worsened with the loss of the potato crops in the mid–1840s. Although famine was avoided, conditions of economic poverty prompted the Dutch government to promote organized emigration as a means of alleviating the troubles at home. Many saw the American West as a viable alternative to their unhappy economic situation and elected to seek their fortunes there.[12]

America appeared to offer this growing surplus agricultural population the resources necessary to become independent farmers. British observer Henry Fearon portrayed the American West as a refuge where poor immigrants might find the means to support their families and prosper. "I can safely say of this country," he wrote, "that every industrious man may make a living here." In a similar vein, W. Faux appealed to "those of *decreasing* means, and *increasing* families, uprooted, withering, and seeking a transplantation somewhere; to find . . . independence . . . [in] America." Clearly, economic motivations directed the movement of British and European agriculturists to the American West.[13]

Success in frontier agriculture, however, required capitalization to establish a farm. A German traveler, reporting on the success of his countrymen as western farmers, echoed the need for adequate resources. "Labor by itself, although richly rewarded, gets one ahead but slowly," wrote Karl Neidhard. "However, capital and labor combined lead to quick prosperity. He who has neither one nor the other had best stay at home." Although poor, most European farmers were not destitute. One contemporary characterized them as "small capitalists," who perceived their livelihood as threatened. For example, grain farmers, faced with market losses, declining profits, and an inability to adjust production, comprised the majority who came to the United States during the peak of British immigration. Seldom did they lack the means, skills, or experience necessary to become successful commercial farmers. To immigrants with the skills and means necessary for farm-making, Michigan offered a potential for economic success otherwise unobtainable.[14]

The family formed the central unit of commercial farm production and the context in which it was replicated. As a basic social institution, kin groups have always played an important role in rural economies. Kinship was a central element of British colonial society on the Eastern Seaboard, and the maintenance of kin ties was a powerful motivation shaping the settlement of the West. English immigrants created a precedent for kinship systems in British North America. Lacking complex lineage and extended family structures, they established a pattern of single-family households interlinked through marriage and the exchange of children as servants and apprentices. The households controlled access to all land, making each a focus of economic and social power within the agricultural community. As a consequence, members of the next generation of farmers were entirely dependent upon their elders for obtaining the means of their livelihood, a situation that served to link several generations in a form of extended family occupying a more-or-less contiguous territory.[15]

An agricultural economy based on single-family households was well adapted to conditions of abundant land and low population. Its success, measured in a rapidly expanding population, also threatened its existence, however, if the amount of land remained finite. Overpopulated agricultural regions could not accommodate continued growth, and each generation produced surplus farmers. Economic conditions discouraged the maintenance of multigenerational households when already subdivided family estates could no longer accommodate sons and nearby farmland was taken up by others. Migrating westward to newly opened lands offered the only opportunity for many to remain in agriculture.

Separation from the parent kin group, however, was a traumatic experience that severed social contacts and deprived individuals of the significant assistance provided by relatives. Shared labor was integral to the organization of farm activities, and the interaction within kin groups formed the basis for simple commodity production. Kin groups also provided protection and security for members, assisting those who suffered economic or personal calamity and caring for those unable to do so for themselves. Clearly, breaking this bond entailed hardships for those who moved away, as well as for those left behind.[16]

Women played a central role in maintaining rural households, and took part in extensive social interaction with their relatives. Separated from kin, they became socially isolated, with few opportunities for forming new relationships. The economic flexibility of men, in contrast, frequently took them away from home and placed them in regular contact with others engaged in business. Caroline Kirkland recognized this disparity and urged frontier women to extend, "a feeling of hostess-ship" toward the newcomer. "I speak only of women," she added, observing that their involvement in "the race of enterprise, i.e. making money," provided men ample opportunity for social interaction. Many women feared the loss of established bonds and the prospect of living alone in a wilderness of strangers more than they did the more obvious uncertainties of pioneering.[17]

As the cement that held rural society together, kinship offered the mutual support necessary to establish farms and businesses in unfamiliar surroundings. Many agriculturists realized the advantages of maintaining a larger kin group and relocated together. In this sense, kinship itself became a motivation for colonization. The desire to provide for the larger kin group was almost certainly in the mind of Michigan promoter John T. Blois when he pointed out that, "a father may sell his small farm in the East for a sum that will purchase a dozen large ones in the West. . . . He may thus . . . settle a handsome property upon each of his family, who, in a few years, may become wealthy and independent." Faced with the prospect of remaining on "worn-out" farmlands in Vermont, Edward W. Barber's father and others "saw better opportunities for themselves and their children" in the West.[18]

Many heads of families believed that maintaining a network of close relatives helped secure the welfare of the families' younger members and justified the cost of uprooting and moving to Michigan. Grand Blanc pioneer Enos Goodrich recalled that his father's family was typical of others. "The old hive got full and there must be a swarming," he wrote. The "ominous" prospect of losing six sons and a daughter, however, "caused the parents many an anxious thought," and they resolved to sell their farm in western New York and emigrate west together. Another Grand Blanc resident told a poignant story. Raised on a farm in Monroe County, New York, Alvah Brainard resolved to leave for the West with his new bride, his sister, and her husband.

> I introduced the subject to my father. . . . Oh, the affections of parents for the welfare of their children. Father thought the subject over a short time, then answers us in this wise: "Children, you see me and your mother here, and we are now quite advanced in years. It is affecting to us to have you leave us and go to the woods, from us. I propose to sell out and go with you, if you will promise to settle down by us and stay by us whilst we live." What child would not be touched to have sacrifice made like this for them from their parents?[19]

Often immigrants attempted to entice relatives still living in the East to join them. Sylvanus Bachelder, for example, harangued his brother James for years to become his neighbor in Bath Township. When James later settled in Kalamazoo, Sylvanus entertained the notion of relocating himself to be near him. N. M. Thomas expressed a similarly strong interest in reuniting his family in the West. Apprising them of the prairie lands in Kalamazoo County, he was careful not only to point out the economic advantages of settling in Michigan but also to emphasize that "the rest of the family, if they ever think of emigrating, could be all accommodated with land at one place."[20]

Many immigrants to the West left their homes to flee intolerable circumstances. Antebellum Michigan became a destination for those who sought to practice dissenting religions, avoid political persecution, and escape slavery and racial discrimination. These motivations helped shape their strategies for colonization.

Religious motivations encouraged emigration from the Northeast as well as from Europe. In New England, Calvinist theology encouraged dissent, and church communities often resolved differences through fragmentation, with the dissenters seceding and establishing separate communities. This process of religious bifurcation and physical resettlement of dissenters facilitated westward movement from the northeastern states. During the first half of the nineteenth century, a religious upheaval known as the Second Great Awakening resulted in the formation of new groups with distinctive doctrines. These people escaped constraints on their religious practices by establishing settlements in the West among others who shared their beliefs.[21]

Europeans migrated to the frontier in the American West to escape religious prosecution. Political changes in several European nations increased pressure on groups that had broken with established state churches or held views perceived to be injurious to state unity. Pietists, in particular, opposed what they saw as an increasingly formal and superficial orthodoxy in the established state churches, and they formed their own churches. The strength of their religious convictions did not actually result in dissenting groups being banished from their homelands, but discrimination often made remaining there difficult, if not impossible. Pietists from the Netherlands and Germany organized colonies that immigrated to Michigan in the second quarter of the nineteenth century.[22]

European political refugees also sought a safe haven in the United States. Americans took pride in the new republic's image as a refuge for skilled and useful immigrants, a perception captured in an 1848 congressional report on internal commerce.

> The evils and oppressions, moral and political, which now urge the emigrant to leave the land of his nativity, to seek a home in a new and distant country, will have to be abated, or Europe will be deprived of its most profitable and most enterprising population. . . . Evils emanating from restricted civil rights are not so easily cured. These will, without doubt, turn the attention of the emigrant to this country for years to come.[23]

Popular uprisings occurred in France, Germany, Belgium, Hungary, and Poland in the 1830s and 1840s, and repression motivated many to emigrate to the United States. Unlike dissenting religious groups, who often migrated as communities, political refugees usually arrived as part of the general movement of immigration.[24]

Political conditions in the British province of Upper Canada during the 1830s encouraged a substantial number of refugees to immigrate to Michigan. Although Michigan bordered Upper Canada, migration between the two regions had not been extensive before the Rebellion of 1837, a movement by radical elements opposed to a Canadian government they felt ignored their interests and discouraged economic development.[25] As the resulting armed conflict passed into its second year, the number of refugees to the United States increased. A Detroit newspaper reported that

> Emigration . . . , now instead of being composed of men of strong political feelings, embraces the most cautious and industrious classes. . . . Military clangor keeps one portion of the people from brooding over the general depression, while a morbid melancholy seems to have seized others, who are apathetic as to the consequences of passing events, and look upon emigration as a panacea for all their ills.[26]

A substantial number of Canadians passed into Michigan seeking land. A St. Joseph resident, traveling across the state in 1838, reported that "the roads are alive with travellers from Canada, and . . . [I] counted in one cavalcade eighty-six teams loaded with these unfortunate people and their effects." Many settled in southwestern Michigan.[27]

Americans of African descent escaping slavery and racial discrimination also sought residence in Michigan. They comprised a distinctive type of political refugee because their racial status separated them from other groups of immigrants, and the legal status of some made their presence controversial. Black people came to Michigan as free people, fleeing economic and social conditions in the American South, or as fugitive slaves, seeking escape from bondage.

Free blacks occupied a tenuous position in racially divided antebellum southern society. Obliged to support themselves, yet denied full participation in society, they remained marginal people of low status. They were frequently resented by slaves, who looked upon then as having betrayed those still in bondage. Distrusted by whites as well as by slaves, free lacks often emigrated from the South. Independence gave them higher expectations and encouraged their movement to places that offered opportunities. Many believed that they could best achieve economic independence by resettling as farmers on the frontier, and the chance to create their own agricultural communities was a powerful motivation for coming to Michigan. Settlements of black immigrants added a distinctive feature to Michigan's antebellum landscape.[28]

Slaves, on the other hand, were property and, unless freed by their owners, could change the terms of their status only through extralegal means. Escape offered freedom, and the desire to achieve it became a strong motivation to migrate to free states. In response, many southern states enacted increasingly repressive legislation to discourage fugitives seeking asylum in the North. This movement culminated in the federal Fugitive Slave Act of 1850, which prevented free states from offering refuge to runaway slaves. At the same time, however, court decisions established important precedents that supported the rights of manumitted slaves and the children of fugitives born in free states. These conditions encouraged the formation of the "Underground Railroad" to move fugitive slaves through free states and territories to Canada.[29]

The Underground Railroad established an infrastructure capable of transporting fugitives over long distances. Its network of routes passed through the Old Northwest, and Michigan's proximity to Canada gave it strategic importance. Although the Underground Railroad was supported by black communities, white organizations, particularly the Quakers, were the primary organizers and operators of the system. Quaker settlements in southern Michigan became integral components of the Underground Railroad as well as places for resettling former slaves.[30]

COMMUNITIES OF ACCRETION: AN AMALGAM OF DIVERSITY

The success of individual pioneers depended on their participation in larger networks that offered mutual support. Despite the social and economic attenuation of the frontier, immigrant households participated in "open-country communities" similar to those found in other rural regions. These communities integrated dispersed settlers by means of complex and well-established social, religious, and political linkages that supported cooperative activities and institutions around which pioneer society was organized.[31]

Most Michigan pioneers settled in communities of accretion that grew with the arrival of new residents, who often possessed no earlier connections and lacked mutual ties. In the absence of social institutions, ties between residents revolved largely around trade. As one early observer remarked, "the inhabitants appear to form no connections, or habits, beside those which naturally grow out of bargain and sale." Although they lacked the mutual support provided by organized colonies, communities of accretion possessed a flexibility that allowed them to absorb immigrants with more diverse interests and backgrounds.[32]

The extensive influx of northeasterners led many to see Michigan as an extension of New England. Blois's *Gazetteer* estimated that New Englanders and their descendants comprised over two-thirds of the state's population in 1838. By mid-century, people coming directly or indirectly from the Northeast accounted for slightly over half of Michigan's residents and more than 80 percent of those born outside the state. A common place of origin helped shape the character of institutions in Michigan communities. Michigan settlements perpetuated the names of northeastern towns, local government and school systems followed New England models, and religious denominations on the frontier had roots in the Northeast. These patterns, however, greatly belie the importance of the diverse motivations that attracted immigrants, minimize the impact of the strategies they followed, and mask the presence and influence of other groups who migrated to the region.[33]

Most immigrants to Michigan joined developing frontier communities that were as yet only loosely formed. Here social and economic institutions developed around perceptions of social group identity, religion, and kinship. Contemporary accounts suggest that many newcomers from the Northeast made an effort to locate in the vicinity of former neighbors or others who had migrated from their area of origin.[34] "Our society too, is unusually good, for a place so newly settled," wrote Sarah Allen, who had recently settled in Schoolcraft. "Most of the inhabitants of this ville are Vermonters, & the greater part from Cavendish. So you see we feel quite at home on that account." Sylvanus Bachelder, attempting to entice his brother to join him in Bath Township, emphasized that in coming he would "not be among strangers. There is Alverson and Mr. Jeffes, your neighbors from York State within two miles. Nathan Alverson from Perry has moved in this fall, and in fact nearly all the inhabitants are from York State." Margaret Lafever recalled that the presence of former neighbors in Eaton County was a key factor in enticing her parents to leave their Orleans County, New York, home and journey to Michigan in 1836.[35]

Often the desire to remain among former neighbors prompted people from one locale to all settle in the same vicinity on the frontier. These people did not constitute formally organized groups, but individuals or families who moved over a period of time to a common destination to which their neighbors had migrated earlier. A resident of Marcellus, New York, for example, reported that as many as two dozen residents of that area were immigrating to Michigan. Most were headed to St. Joseph County, where Marcellus residents had already settled. The St. Joseph country was also the destination of as many as 150 families from Chatauqua County, New York, who began arriving in the spring of 1830. The Reverend Ira Allen recalled that his portion of Clinton County was settled by emigrants from Ohio in the 1850s. Within six years, he witnessed the arrival of "fifty families that he knew in Ohio, and they all settled within a few miles of Elsie."[36]

The common origin of community members is reflected in the repetitious use of northeastern settlement names or places, many of which settlers first brought with them to western New York and Ohio and later took to other areas farther west. Names such as Albion, Athens, Batavia, Kinderhook, Lancaster, Lewiston, Manchester, New Buffalo, Northville, Ovid, Pittsford, Plymouth, Rochester, Utica, Watertown, Vermontville, and Wayland attest to the origins of their immigrant founders.[37]

Yet not all immigrants shared a common New England heritage. The second quarter of the nineteenth century witnessed the arrival in America of increasing numbers of European agriculturists. Although some came in organized groups, others joined the general flow of immigration and were accommodated within existing open-country communities. Their settlement, too, was often influenced by the presence of those with whom they perceived an affiliation. Lutheran Germans entered Michigan and Ohio in search of agricultural lands. Upon their arrival, many became aware of the previous German settlement of Westphalia in western Clinton County, a tightly organized community of Catholic Germans whose social and religious institutions remained closed to outsiders. Common ethnicity and language, however, induced many Lutherans to settle in its vicinity and participate in the regional economy. Once a Lutheran presence was established, it attracted additional German immigrants and formed the basis for a distinct rural community that maintained its own social and religious institutions.[38]

In addition to the Clinton County community, concentrations of German immigrants appeared elsewhere in antebellum Michigan. Often their settlements gravitated toward areas occupied by Americans of German ancestry who came to Michigan from New York and Pennsylvania. Common language and ethnicity eased their integration into the regional economy of the frontier. Among these were rural communities near Owosso in Shiawassee County, in western Washtenaw County, and in portions of Macomb and St. Joseph counties. Many Germans also settled in English-speaking areas across southern Lower Michigan.[39]

Free blacks and some fugitive slaves formed a community of accretion centered on Calvin Township in Cass County in southwestern Michigan. It grew in response to the desire by freed slaves to relocate in the North and a need to provide settlements of people of African descent to support the Underground Railroad in Michigan. Creating a black rural community on the frontier was not an easy task, given the costs of farm-making and the widespread racial prejudice. The Quakers stepped in to supply the wherewithal and guidance to insure their success. As a group whose religion rejected a social system based on inequality, many Quakers actively supported movements that advocated black emigration and resettlement, as well as the abolition of slavery. They believed that the successful establishment of frontier settlements consisting of former slaves would demonstrate the validity of their beliefs.

Quakers began immigrating to Michigan in the 1820s, settling mainly in Lenawee County, where they organized their first meeting in 1831. Although they did not come as part of an organized migration, common beliefs and a desire for social interaction with those who shared their religion promoted the geographical grouping of their settlements. Areas where they congregated became centers for antislavery activities. Prolific abolitionist writer Elizabeth Chandler and ardent organizer Darius Comstock organized abolitionist sentiment at Adrian and stimulated similar activities in the Quaker settlements at Battle Creek in Calhoun County and Young's Prairie in Cass County, the latter of which supported the development of the rural black community in Calvin Township.[40]

Situated at the junction of Underground Railroad routes passing through Indiana and Illinois, Cass County proved an ideal location to assist fugitive slaves on their way to Canada. Its distance from the slave states created a perception of safety that encouraged settlement not only by freedmen but also by fugitive slaves who saw the area as a refuge provided by a supportive community. The presence of a black rural community in southwestern Michigan attracted former slaves residing in nearby states as well as those recently emancipated in the South. Material support for immigrants came not only from Quaker sources but from funds willed to emancipated slaves by former owners. In one case, funds provided to resettle slaves freed at the death of their Virginia owner were used to purchase land for forty-seven people in Cass County.[41]

In the late antebellum period the black population of Cass County expanded, rising from 8 in 1840, to 389 in 1850, and to nearly 1,400 by the eve of the Civil War. People of African descent comprised a quarter of the population of Calvin Township at mid-century and over half in 1860. Over two-thirds of these people owned land, totaling more than 2,100 acres in Calvin and adjacent Porter Townships in 1850. Their numbers continued to grow over the next twenty years, creating a nearly contiguous open-country community of black farmers in southwestern Michigan. Resettlement proved to be a successful strategy for both refugee freedmen and fugitive slaves, who together formed a significant component of the area's population.[42]

As a settlement strategy, kin group migration invariably offered advantages that were unavailable to the individual pioneer. Ties of blood provided mutual support through a structure of obligatory social and economic relationships that served to pool the resources of capital and labor necessary for production. Kin groups thus formed a basis for frontier community organization, although their size affected their ability to carry out community functions.

Easy access to western lands motivated many large families to migrate to the frontier, where they could acquire estates large enough to insure an equitable distribution of land among their members. The family of Enos Goodrich moved to Michigan in 1835 for just this reason. Unable to maintain a family of seven children on a 114-acre New York farm, they sold their property and with the proceeds purchased 1,000 acres on Kearsley Creek in Genesee County. Two years earlier, Alvah Brainard's family, consisting of the parents, five children, and two spouses, bought a tract of 480 acres in Grand Blanc Township where all might live contiguously. Purchasing the land collectively in the name of the older married son, they later allocated parcels to individual group members.[43]

On family-owned tracts, younger family members often worked to establish the family homestead before starting their own farms. This reduced the time needed to create a production base on undeveloped land, a process that required the labor of as many hands as could be employed. By delaying the establishment of their own farms they also deferred the expenses of farm-making until they could accumulate the capital and resources to pay for them. Terrence and Patrick McCleer, for example, postponed work on their tracts until the clearing of their parents' Livingston County farm was completed. Similarly, Moses Wright, of Tecumseh, was willing to "work for the benefit of the family" before receiving his share of the land. All eventually acquired their own farms.[44]

Maintaining a kin group on communal property also allowed younger family members time to amass capital for the acquisition of additional land. Wages received for work while living at home helped pioneers such as the McCleer brothers to purchase tracts to supplement their share of the parental estate. A similar strategy was followed by the McCleers' neighbors, James and Edward Birney. In both cases, sons attempted to purchase land as close to the family tract as possible, which enlarged the territory occupied by the kin group and the resource base it controlled.[45]

Kin groups usually immigrated as small family units. The ever-observant Elizabeth Chandler carefully recorded the arrival of an extended family in her neighborhood in 1833.

> As we were going to meeting yesterday a couple of wagons passed us completely loaded with people. We afterwards learned they had just come into the country from one of the eastern states, and were part of the *family* of a friend Aldrich, who purchased land here last season, and expected to bring altogether forty persons—twenty-five of them arrived yesterday—his children, grandchildren, &c.[46]

As a contiguous family group, the Aldriches formed part of the growing Quaker community in Lenawee County.

Although it was not always possible to establish contiguous family properties, large groups of relatives often assembled close to one another. If a kin group migrated over a much more extended period, an initial settlement usually served as a focal point for later immigration. Traveling between Pokagon and Niles in 1844, Henry Sanford observed the arrival of a Mr. Silver, who intended to settle in the vicinity. "He was the last one of the family left behind," Sanford confided in his journal, "all the others having moved to Michigan." In all, forty-one members of Silver's extended family had migrated from New Hampshire during the previous decade and taken up residence in Berrien County.[47]

Kinship, like ethnicity, provided a powerful integrating mechanism on the frontier. Its bonds brought cohesion to open-country agricultural communities and allowed members to persist and overcome adversities. Indeed, links of fictive kinship often arose to unite the members in communities of accretion. The social and economic support of kin groups promoted successful colonization among people of disparate background, but remained inherently limited by a reliance on blood ties.[48]

As colonization swept across the Lower Peninsula, religious institutions introduced by evangelical Protestant denominations played an important role in integrating the heteroge- neous immigrant communities of accretion on the frontier. Following the War of 1812, the Presbyterians, Congregationalists, Baptists, and Methodists organized and systematized their missionary activities on a national scale to proselytize the disparate populations in the West. They dispatched missionaries and itinerant ministers over circuits throughout southern Michigan, where they endeavored to make converts and establish new congregations.[49]

Missionary societies directed their efforts primarily at communities of accretion. In many frontier settlements, church services, prayer meetings, and revivals became major social events, and churches assumed a crucial role in organizing what were often collections of strangers. Presbyterian missionary Samuel Newbury remarked that "constant emigration" maintained a high level of diversity in the frontier communities he served in western Michigan. At the rapidly growing St. Joseph River port of Niles, Methodist missionary J. N. Parsons noted that residents "complained that they were strangers to each other," but responded favorably to his call for "a church meeting, to get acquainted." His regular services and weekly prayer meetings became a focus of religious activity in Niles and drew adherents from the surrounding rural population. The Reverend Elijah Pilcher recalled the explosive impact of an impromptu revival at Battle Creek. Requested to preach while passing through the settlement in 1839, his sermon so inspired residents that they requested him to continue his services. Over the three months he remained there, he drew increasingly larger audiences and established a permanent Methodist church in the settlement.[50]

Evangelical church organizations established in new settlements were well suited to the socially diverse character of the communities they encountered. These frontier religious insti- tutions did not require membership and reinforced the idea of volunteerism to manage and maintain their congregations. Integral to the formation of new social structures, voluntary choice and individual responsibility helped forge networks of social and economic linkages necessary to integrate open-country communities on the frontier. Missionary churches intro- duced the group discipline that provided a model for establishing bonds of mutual support among people for whom no previous ties existed.[51]

As a force of social cohesion in nascent rural communities, evangelical religion often affected settlers' choice of location on the Michigan frontier. The formation of missionary churches often became a divisive force that encouraged members of different denominations to move so that they might live among others who shared their beliefs. Quaker immigrants, for example, sought to settle together, and formed distinctive rural communities in southern Michigan. In 1833, Barney Harris left his Lenawee County farm of twenty improved acres to resettle. "He belongs to the Methodist Society," reported a Quaker neighbor, "and is anxious to be amongst them and there is a settlement of them . . . where he intends going." When denom- inational loyalty led pioneers to shift location, the strong links forged by religious unity served to discourage rather than promote persistence on the Michigan frontier.[52]

In communities of accretion, persistence rested on the success of immigrants in bringing farms into production, and many failed. Ethnic, religious, and kin group solidarity helped pioneers, but did not insure success if pioneers' attempts fell short of their expectations. A belief that farming was untenable frustrated many settlers in southern Michigan. As early as 1822, J. V. K. Ten Eyck, a correspondent to the *Detroit Gazette,* warned that

> The history of the settlement of every part of the western country, offers instances in which the disappointment of too sanguine expectations . . . has turned back with disgust a portion of the emigrants from situations possessing every advantage which could be reasonably looked for. . . . It ought not be a matter of surprise should we find occasional disappointment among emigrants. . . . The national tendency to indulge the imagination . . . is apt to raise his expectations beyond what a rational calculation would justify.[53]

Nearly a dozen years later, the editor of the *Democratic Free Press* echoed these sentiments.

> This is not fairy land or paradise. The warm imagination and discontented spirits of New England, if their wayward fancies are not in some degree restrained, will be exceedingly liable to disappointment in the reality of its dark forests and pestiferous marshes. . . . Though not enchanted, Michigan is on the whole an inviting country; . . . but as for those who are determined to be *fevered up* by high wrought anticipation before they emigrate, they must expect to be agued down after wards.[54]

Accommodation to life on the frontier involved adjusting one's expectations to privation, and those most adept at doing so had the greatest success in dealing with this transition. Although studies have shown that colonists with the most impoverished backgrounds were best suited to enduring the deprivation associated with resettlement, they were the least likely to possess substantial capital for farm-making. A successful immigrant had to possess enough wealth to establish a farm, yet be realistic enough not to anticipate immediate rewards.[55]

Caroline Kirkland recognized the role this balance played in the relative success of settlers in southern Livingston County in the 1830s. She observed that older farmers who sold eastern farms in the hope of acquiring more property and wealth in the West suffered the most from the loss of conveniences in adjusting to frontier life. They learned "too late . . . that it kills old vines to tear them from their clinging places. . . .People with broken fortunes, or who [had] been unsuccessful in past undertakings" likewise found it hard to cope with frontier adjustments. Unable or unwilling to succeed as farmers, they constituted a bitter lot who became disappointed in their attempts at establishing themselves as frontier producers.

In contrast, Kirkland found that the most successful colonists were

> young married people just beginning in the world; simple in their habits, moderate in their aspirations, . . . These find no fault with their bare loggeries. With shelter and a handful of furniture they have enough. . . . These people are contented, of course.

The capable pioneer with low expectations for immediate material rewards was most likely to prevail on the Michigan frontier. Kirkland's conclusion recognized that immigrants with the most realistic hopes possessed the greatest likelihood of achieving their goals.[56]

Persistence in frontier communities of accretion depended on more than an ability to endure temporary deprivation, and varied directly with a region's rate of development. In general, the early years of colonization, when the rate of settlement was the most rapid, experienced the greatest turnover of population. Persistence rates rose and stabilized only after a region had been occupied for a decade or more.[57]

Settlers in Michigan communities of accretion possessed slight initial ties to the land, and the prospect of greater opportunity frequently beckoned. Pioneer author H. H. Riley captured the feeling in the following passage from *Puddleford Papers*:

> How is it in a new country? Not one resident in ten is permanently located. Every man expects to move somewhere else, at some time. Here is no association, no tie, to bind him to the soil. The pioneer is but a passenger, who has stopped overnight, as it were, and he holds himself ready to push forward, at the blow of the trumpet. Villages, and even whole townships, change inhabitants in short periods.[58]

The continual opening of new frontiers offered the western immigrant the constant promise of greener pastures and greater return on investment. The availability of land elsewhere explains, in part, the high rate of pioneer transience. The lure of better or more abundant soil, together with the opportunity for realizing a profit from selling current holdings, was a constant incentive to move on, and often difficult to ignore. "The . . . settlers here cannot, of course, be expected to remain satisfied with what they have found," wrote Cyrus P. Bradley of Michigan immigrants of the 1830s. "They are going to Illinois—the next jump . . . will be to some unnamed territory in the region of the Rocky Mountains." As a consequence, many western farmers felt themselves compelled to remove frequently, and their behavior insured a high turnover rate for most newly occupied regions.[59]

Removal also offered a new start to those who failed. Many attributed failure to the character of those involved. Caroline Kirkland, for example, spoke of unsuccessful colonists as a distinct group of people. She recognized them as

> a class of settlers whose condition has always been inexplicable to me. They seem to work hard, dress wretchedly, and live in the most uncomfortable style in all respects, apparently denying themselves and their families everything beyond the absolute necessities of life. . . . Yet in spite of increasing their means by these penurious habits, they grow poorer every day.[60]

Another contemporary described those who failed as "a transient class, [who] soon fall in a new country, . . . [and] when broke down retreat to the western wilderness to gain and again to lose."[61]

Although few pioneers left accounts dealing with failure exclusively, many who eventually succeeded in Michigan described earlier failures in frontier farming. The family of Theodore

Potter moved no fewer than eight times during their first fourteen years in the state. Following their settlement in Saline in 1830, the family occupied seven farms in four counties and had planned a move to Wisconsin when the father died suddenly. Stranded on their Eaton County property in 1846, the Potters eventually succeeded as farmers, and some members became life-long residents of the area. P. S. Richards' family endured a similar experience. They moved four times in thirteen years and attempted farm-making in four different counties before settling permanently in Jackson County's Leoni Township in 1838. Other newcomers, such as Joseph Waldron, attempted to make a living by a number of different means on the Michigan frontier. He tried farming, storekeeping, and operating a mill before finding eventual success as a Jackson County farmer in 1842. The experiences of other people suggest that the Waldron, Richards, and Potter families were typical. Many who eventually succeeded failed more than once.[62]

Pioneer persistence increased the likelihood of economic success and establishing social ties on the frontier, both of which increased the likelihood of staying in one place. The longer a farmer remained in operation, the greater was his opportunity to enlarge the size and extent of production. Growth introduced economies of scale that further enhanced the level of productivity and provided additional incentive to continue operating. Longer-term residents acquired more extensive social and economic relationships, which they strengthened through intermarriage. Newly created kin networks served as a basis for economic cooperation and social integration on the frontier.[63] Although economic optimization certainly affected pioneer farmers' decisions to remain on their farms, persistence did not correlate with economic opportunity alone. In western Kalamazoo County, for example, ownership of larger, high-valued tracts gave settlers access to favorable environmental zones, facilitated larger farm operations by kin groups, and provided excess land that could be rented to tenants or sold to newcomers. Despite these advantages, many high-valued tracts turned over rapidly, while lower-valued lands often remained in continuous ownership. In frontier communities of accretion, the strength of social links often made the difference in the decision of farmers to remain on their land or leave and try again elsewhere.[64]

Although successful immigrants prepared the way for others, their preemption of access to both agricultural resources and societal institutions introduced an inherent inequality that favored long-term settlers over newcomers. Such conditions encouraged a high turnover rate among later settlers and helped structure the regional social and economic hierarchy that developed at the close of the frontier. Frontier communities of accretion thus created a structure for successful colonization by a heterogeneous population, although they were not equally beneficial for all their members.[65]

COVENANTED COMMUNITIES: CITIES UPON A HILL

Covenanted communities offered immigrants continuity and security amidst the uncertainty of relocation and became distinctive and successful settlements on the Michigan frontier. Organized around a "covenant," these communities possessed a common set of rules or expectations that provided a sense of unity and coherence and formed a basis for institutions that linked the elements of frontier society. The community provided people sharing common motivations with a strategy designed to share the risks of colonization and thereby increase the likelihood of their success. Organized settlement provided the economic advantages of scale and the social benefits of maintaining established relationships and institutions on the frontier. The exclusive membership of covenanted communities also offered ideological, ethnic, and religious solidarity that might not be possible elsewhere. Three general types of covenanted communities appeared in antebellum Michigan: communities based on common economic interests and ideals, and often a common faith; those settled by foreign colonists bound by religion, ethnicity, language, and a formal organization; and experimental communities organized around communitarian principles. Each of these produced distinctive colonization strategies that affected the nature of rural settlement in frontier Michigan and added distinctive patterning to the regional landscape.[66]

Groups seeking to replicate in Michigan an earlier community formed the least complicated covenanted communities. Blois's *Gazetteer* described the manner in which immigrants to Michigan might organize such a project, as well as the advantages it offered its members.

> Ten, thirty, or fifty families of a neighborhood, might agree upon the project, appoint a competent and trusty agent to select and locate a body of lands, suitable and sufficient for the company. . . . By uniting in this scheme, . . . they might all remove and locate at the same time, and take their portions in severalty. In the clearing and improving their lands, they might render each other mutual assistance. Such a community would have all possible advantages of making the best order of social society, and being united, might monopolize all its benefits. By proper vigilance, the vulgar and immoral could easily be excluded. . . . In short, such a colony . . . would possess all the advantages of society they before enjoyed, together with the means of raising it to the highest state of perfection.[67]

Settlements at Vermontville and Olivet in Eaton County and the Rochester colony in Clinton County were typical communities of common interest. Their histories provide a detailed picture of this type of covenanted community and the role it played in colonization. The "Union Colony," a sectarian organization composed of emigrants from several towns in Vermont, founded Vermontville in sparsely settled Eaton County in 1836 (fig. 7.1). Under the leadership of the Reverend Sylvester Cochrane, a Congregational minister from East Poultney, Vermont, its members signed a contract binding them to migrate and settle in a contiguous area and establish institutions for mutual support. Although the contract obliged the signers to adhere to certain moral principles, such as observing the Sabbath and refraining from the consumption of alcohol, it did not establish a particular religion or otherwise attempt to regulate their behavior.[68]

The colony's "Code of Laws" dealt almost entirely with the settlement's physical infrastructure. It authorized the purchase of at least 5,760 acres and provided for its division into village lots and farms to be distributed among the group's members. These lands were to be

FIGURE 7.1. *LOCATIONS OF COVENANTED COMMUNITIES IN MICHIGAN.* (Sources: see text).

selected and purchased by three agents, who were assigned the task of examining Michigan for suitable sites. They accomplished their work in the winter of 1836, and the first immigrants took up residence in the spring.[69]

The Vermontville Colony grew within a limited area because the contiguous layout of tracts distributed its population within a small area that focused its activities on Vermontville Village. Settlers built a meeting house, church, and academy, institutions that integrated the rural community. All remain standing today. The organization of Vermontville provided mutual support for its colonists and insured their high rate of persistence. The colony became a focus for trade and other activity and its success promoted settlement of the surrounding area. This covenanted community became a magnet for regional growth, and its village developed as a regional center during the pre-railroad era.[70]

In the winter of 1836, twenty-six families from Rochester, New York, formed the nonsectarian Rochester Colony for the purpose of settling in the West and hired agents to procure a large, contiguous tract of land. The colony acquired more than four thousand acres in an unsettled portion of northeastern Clinton County and subdivided the land into farm and village tracts for its members (fig. 7.1). Colonization began in the fall of 1836. Although the Rochester Colony's members occupied the tract and soon developed strong community social and economic links, the colony lacked a rigid organizational structure. As a result, when residents organized a church and a school, they dispersed the locations of these key integrating institutions. The proposed central settlement at Mapleton remained only a mill site on the Maple River.[71]

The Rochester Colony created a stable setting conducive to the persistence of its settlers. Indeed, the mutual support it provided allowed its residents to overcome what others perceived as a less than hospitable environment. "Almost shut in by swamps, [they] believe themselves occupying one of the best sections of the state," confided surveyor Bela Hubbard in his journal. Impressed by their persistence, he added, "I am convinced that if farmers can do better on such land as this, it must be because industry is stimulated by the difficulties it is forced to overcome." Although it failed to develop a nucleated settlement, the Rochester Colony endured as a rural community in northeastern Clinton County.[72]

The Congregational community at Oberlin, Ohio, founded a Christian community and college at Olivet under their missionary leader, the Reverend John Jay Shipherd (fig. 7.1). Originally intended as a planned settlement funded by outside subscribers, the financial downturn of the late 1830s delayed Olivet's founding until 1843. At that time a group of colonists from Oberlin organized to purchase a large tract of land in southern Eaton County. Although the colony lacked a formal covenant, its members shared a common origin and purpose, and were selected to insure that the colony possessed the skills necessary for its success. Its early settlers included farmers, millwrights, educators, and other crafts specialists. Several wealthy members of the colony organized a milling company, and within two years they operated a gristmill and a sawmill. Their presence insured the economic survival of the settlement and helped generate capital to support the settlement's members and to underwrite other community ventures.[73]

From the beginning, Olivet's organizers planned a college as a central community institution. They organized Olivet Institute under the auspices of the Congregational Church within a year of the settlement's founding, and it began operation by the close of 1844. Although not officially chartered until 1859, the college operated as an institution of higher learning from the early days of settlement and served, together with the church, as a central focus for the Olivet community.[74]

The presence of Olivet, Vermontville, and the Rochester Colony affected the distribution of settlement in antebellum Michigan. Because covenanted communities needed large, contiguous blocks of unsold land, they located away from areas favored by previous settlement. Olivet, Vermontville, and the Rochester Colony were all situated in vacant areas. Their appearance established a pioneer presence in the central timberlands and encouraged growth in this area. The allocation of farm sites introduced a relatively dense, evenly spaced pattern of settlement that often included lands that might otherwise have been avoided as undesirable. Communal control of land acquisition also limited individual tract size and prevented land investment by pioneers, thereby discouraging both speculation and the rapid turnover of property.

Southern Michigan witnessed the arrival of three separate covenanted communities from Europe during the antebellum period, and each made a substantial contribution to regional settlement. Churches served as the central institution around which these communities were organized, and common religious affiliation became the focus for foreign immigrant communities. Church organizations managed the immigration and settlement of their members and formed bastions of cultural cohesiveness on the frontier. Although the foreign covenanted communities in Michigan were not dedicated solely to a church mission, the economic and social institutions that formed the core of these territorially based groups had their roots in a common religious faith.[75]

Catholic Germans emigrating from the Prussian provinces of Westfalia and the Rhineland established the earliest foreign covenanted community in Michigan. Their settlement reflected the active role played by the Roman Catholic Church as an agent of colonization. It established a separate diocese for Michigan and the Northwest at Detroit in 1832, and a German bishop served existing German Catholic populations in Michigan. Settlement at Westphalia began in the fall of 1836, when several families occupied land in western Clinton County purchased by the Reverend Anton Kopp, a Catholic priest (fig. 7.1). This became the nucleus of a substantial community that developed over the next thirty years on a large tract of land.[76]

The success of the Westphalia community derived from the central role of the Catholic Church. Its traditional position of leadership in German villages made it the key institution for social integration and gave the village priest paramount status as a community leader. Membership in the church admitted one to a covenant that was administered by its representative. The Reverend Kopp, appointed as priest to Westphalia by the bishop of Detroit in 1837, became a central figure in the frontier community. He organized the parish church and school to serve as the foci of this open-country community. Upon Westphalia's organization as a township in 1839, its priest became the first supervisor, extending the existing community organization to its civil government. Although the church later ceased to dominate public offices in Westphalia, it remained a central element in the community.[77]

Rapid population increase required spatial expansion, and the Westphalia colony managed this growth in a manner that allowed it to retain its distinctiveness. Traditional land inheritance practices and the strong intergenerational ties of German farming families influenced the spatial form of expansion. Westphalia's pioneers came from a region of Germany characterized by partible inheritance, a practice that divided estates between all eligible children and resulted in individual holdings made up of small, scattered plots that were redistributed as each generation inherited the family estate. This practice provided farmlands for all heirs and maintained a contiguous community over time. As population expanded, however, the continual subdivision of land made farming less and less efficient and induced many to emigrate to America, where abundant western land could provide farms for all heirs. Available lands in Michigan permitted family members to preserve traditional patterns of contiguous settlement and sustain the strong bond between farmers and the land they occupied. [78]

On the Michigan frontier, purchase of large tracts allowed German pioneers to perpetuate family links while insuring an inheritance for all those of the younger generation. After working cooperatively to establish the parental household as a base of production, the remainder of each estate, as well as adjacent tracts acquired later, was subdivided to provide farms to children as they came of age. Continuous population growth and a widespread preference for contiguous kin-based settlement helped Westphalia develop as a culturally distinct region, a covenanted community based on common religion and ethnicity.[79]

Within a decade of the founding of the Westphalia community, a second mass immigration by Germans created an ethnic enclave in the Saginaw Valley (fig. 7.1). Organized by the Lutheran Church, the colony consisted of emigrants fleeing poor economic conditions in the Middle Franconia province of Bavaria. Its origins grew out of a German Lutheran missionary movement directed by the Reverend Wilhelm Loehe of Neudettelsau in Bavaria. Upon learning of efforts by Lutheran pastors to minister to settlers in Michigan and carry out missionary work among the Chippewas of Saginaw Bay, Loehe proposed that both interests could be combined through the establishment of a Lutheran colony in the Saginaw region.[80]

Loehe's plan for colonization called for several settlements in portions of the Cass and lower Saginaw drainages. The relative absence of previous American settlement here left a large, contiguous area on which the colony might locate and expand with minimal outside interference. Immigrants collectively purchased land at several locations. The first of these Loehe called Frankenmuth, or "Courage of the Franconians," to commemorate its role in initiating settlement. Laid out in 1845, Frankenmuth began as a dispersed collection of farms that expanded with the influx of settlers the following year. In order to maintain cohesion as settlement expanded, a second settlement was begun two years later. Frankentrost, or "Consolidation of the Franconians," became the first of several settlements intended to insure the integrity of the Lutheran community in the Saginaw region. In the next three years, Frankenlust, or "Joy of the Franconians," and Frankenhilf, or "Aid of the Franconians," appeared, their names proclaiming the colony's success and its role as an outlet for economically deprived Germans. Although not united officially, all of the settlements shared a common faith expressed through parallel social covenants laid out in their constitutions.[81]

The Lutheran Church imposed order in the colony through church constitutions that constituted a moral and civil code as well as a de facto legal system that maintained the settlers' cultural integrity. These covenants contained regulations that insured religious conformity among community members, specified the mutual obligations of members, oversaw individual conduct and the resolution of disputes, and provided for the support of public improvements. These powerful instruments of social control regularized behavior within the German settlements and insured the continuance of traditional lifeways in Michigan. The institutional structure provided by the covenants insured that farmers received the cooperative support necessary for success in the new country. Although the covenants made no attempt to isolate the colonists from other immigrants, the closeness of the Franconian community and its internal orientation set it apart and created a perceptual barrier that discouraged non-Germans from settling among them.[82]

Agricultural settlement in the Franconian colony rapidly dispersed despite initial plans to concentrate settlement around the church, stores, mills, and other unifying activities at central village sites. Geography and the nature of inheritance systems influenced the form of settlement expansion within this rapidly growing population. The low, wet, conditions in the Saginaw Valley led immigrant farmers to avoid many areas in order to select the best lands. Difficulty in making poorly drained soils of the Saginaw Valley arable discouraged agricultural expansion at Frankenlust and Frankentrost. Lands with greater agricultural potential at Frankenmuth, Frankenhilf, and elsewhere attracted the attention of colonists in search of farms.[83]

Although the Franconian region retained its cultural homogeneity, settlement did not follow the contiguous pattern found in Westphalia. Highly variable land quality characterized the Saginaw Valley and prevented immigrants from amassing tracts extensive enough to permit division into contiguous farms. Instead of subdividing the parental farm, partible inheritance took the form of partible division, in which one child received the parental tract, while the family estate assisted other children in acquiring new lands. When good land nearby was taken up, second-generation farmers moved away from the original parental holding. Those in Frankenmuth, for example, found that the closest available lands were in Frankenhilf. This practice encouraged the rapid geographical dispersal of German settlement in the Saginaw Valley.[84]

Active promotion by both official and private sources apart from the Reverend Loehe's organization brought additional Protestant Germans to the Saginaw Valley. As part of a campaign to attract foreign immigrants, the Michigan Legislature authorized the appointment of an agent to advertise the state in Europe. Saginaw County also supported the dissemination of promotional literature, and a privately published German-language account of the Saginaw Valley attracted immigration directly to the region. The presence of the Franconian community encouraged the persistence of settlers in a region heretofore avoided by pioneers, and its success served as a magnet for immigration and a catalyst for regional development in the lower Saginaw Valley.[85]

During the 1840s, Hollanders migrated to an area of western Michigan lying between the Grand and St. Joseph Rivers, where they formed a community united by a covenant grounded in a common religion (fig. 7.1). As in Michigan's other covenanted communities, the church organization dominated both spiritual and secular affairs of the colonists, and its pervasive presence integrated activities within each of the Dutch settlements and united the immigrant population as a single regional community.

Although worsening economic conditions compelled the Netherlanders to leave Europe, they migrated for religious reasons as well. During the first quarter of the nineteenth century, reforms in the organization of the state church in the Netherlands led to opposition by members who remained devoted to the discipline of older Calvinist teachings. The failure of these parties to resolve their differences led to the formation of a Seceder movement that formally separated from the Netherlands Reformed Church in 1834. The Seceders suffered official discrimination and repression, which led many in the movement to envision migration as a means to start anew.[86]

As a closely knit religious community, the Seceders realized the advantages of group colonization and turned to their leaders to develop strategies for resettling their members abroad. In 1846 the Seceder movement organized a society for the emigration of its members to the United States, regardless of their ability to pay. Its constitution provided a set of rules to insure that the society's colonies maintained an ethnically homogeneous population in a contiguous area and established the Reformed Church as the central institution responsible for administering the colony and insuring community integrity.[87]

The Reverend Albertus C. Van Raalte, one of the leaders of the Seceder movement, came to the United States in the fall of 1846 and examined large tracts of unsettled forested land in western Michigan. Van Raalte selected lands along Black River that were well suited for farming and accessible to outside markets by way of the lake. By 1847 he had acquired title to a substantial acreage, and made preparations for the movement of immigrants to the site of de Kolonie, or the Holland Colony, a name that became associated with all Dutch settlements in southwestern Michigan.[88]

As director of Dutch immigrant Reformed churches in the colony, the Reverend Van Raalte managed the church's administrative role in the colony's affairs. He oversaw the distribution of land, conducted relations with the outside world, and worked to create an infrastructure to support the community's growth. His secular leadership reinforced the position of the Reformed Church as the central integrating institution in the community and the covenant's role as the colony's organizing charter. Almost from the beginning colonists established local meetings to manage community activities and public works. Drawing on a common cultural tradition of self-rule, the meetings implemented rules to allow residents to conduct their affairs more efficiently.[89]

The church remained the key institution among the Dutch communities of western Michigan. Although the Reformed Church was rent by a schism in the 1850s, Dutch churches continued to play a central integrating role in the Dutch settlements. Despite divisions in the larger community, its members continued to perceive of themselves as possessing a distinctive common ethnic entity. This unity played an important role as the Holland Colony expanded its territory.[90]

Colonists established five new settlements organized around congregations in 1847 and 1848. They included Graafschap, situated south of Holland, Zeeland, to the northeast, and Overisel, Drenthe, and Vriesland lying further to the east in an arc along the Black River drainage. Like Holland, each possessed a covenant that organized the community under the direction of church leaders. Later agricultural settlements appeared at Noord Holland, Noordeloos, and Zuid Holland and Groningen, a lumber-milling and stave-making settlement developed east of Holland in 1849 (fig. 7.1). Although massive immigration in the 1850s increased the number of Dutch settlers in Michigan, their settlements remained clustered in southern Ottawa and northern Allegan counties. Their close geographical proximity helped maintain the ethnic and cultural homogeneity desired by the colony's founders. By 1860, Dutch immigrants and their descendants comprised an overwhelming majority of the population, and the Dutch community continued to dominate these counties long after the close of colonization.[91]

The Dutch extended their economic hinterland beyond the contiguous boundaries of the Holland Colony. They employed a strategy in which younger members from the Holland settlements temporarily migrated to find wage work elsewhere in western Michigan. Working as domestic servants, farmhands, lumbermen, and laborers, they acquired capital to begin and improve farms in the home colony. Dutch farms also centered round the multigenerational family, and additional income from outside work was entirely compatible with traditional practice. Supplemental income helped Dutch immigrants overcome the financial uncertainties of frontier farm-making and insured the colony's success.[92]

Colony members working elsewhere in Michigan maintained a sense of unity that emphasized their distinctness from non-Dutch settlers. The Reformed Church fostered ethnic awareness among temporary workers, and Reformed congregations soon appeared in the growing manufacturing center of Grand Rapids, an emerging woodworking and furniture-making center. Grandville, Grand Haven, and Kalamazoo also lured skilled craftworkers and urban immigrants who hoped to practice their trades, and Reformed Church services were held in lumber camps at Saugatuck and Singapore on the Kalamazoo River. Although living in American settlements geographically removed from the Holland Colony, Dutch inhabitants remained tied to the Black River community through a common faith, and this helped them to maintain their distinctiveness in western Michigan.[93]

The development of transportation links in western Michigan insured the economic success of the Holland Colony. By mid-century, state and federal roads gave farmers access to markets on the Grand and Kalamazoo River drainages, and the developing port of Grand Haven provided a regional gateway for shipping on Lake Michigan. With the completion of harbor improvements at Holland in 1858, the lower Black River became an outlet for lumber, wood, and other regional products. This trade underwrote the colony's development as an integral component of western Michigan's emerging commercial economy.[94]

During the first half of the nineteenth century the Second Great Awakening gave rise to a number of utopian religious movements in the United States. They shared the millennial belief that an imminent Apocalypse would bring the return of Christ, the triumph of good over evil, and salvation to the faithful. They maintained further that the advent had already occurred and that prophets had received divine revelations to guide the formation of communities that might work actively toward the building of a perfect society on earth. When they accomplished this task and society achieved perfection, history would end. These groups sought to reach their goal through small, partly isolated cooperative communities characterized by the collective ownership of property. Members of these communitarian socialist communities believed that voluntary, experimental organizations would demonstrate, on a small scale, how immediate reform might be achieved through non-revolutionary means while preserving harmony and order. They anticipated that their success would inspire emulation by the larger society and lead to its regeneration.[95]

The western frontier offered the isolation many groups needed to carry out their activities unmolested, and over a dozen successful communitarian communities existed in the Old Northwest by the late 1830s. Two appeared in Lower Michigan.[96] The Alphadelphia Association grew out of the millennial aims of the Universalist Church and the philosophy of the French socialist Charles Fourier. Universalists believed they could bring about universal salvation by reshaping the structure of society according to a natural social order that eliminated its conflicts and inequities. Achieving a divine social order depended upon establishing communal agricultural communities, called Phalanxes, the success of which would foster universal harmony and hasten the coming of God's kingdom.[97]

In July 1844, Michigan Universalists founded the Alphadelphia Phalanx in Comstock Township, near Galesburg in Kalamazoo County, on 2,814 acres, about a third of which were already under cultivation (fig. 7.1). Those joining the venture relinquished land, tools, and other property in exchange for stock in the association and would receive a return on their investment from its profits. All received housing, supplies, and a uniform wage for their work. Despite the initial success of agricultural and craft activities, the community proved unable to support all of its members, who became increasingly distrustful of its leaders' ability to manage the community's business. Accusations of unfairness and profiteering hastened the departure of most members within four years of its founding, and the Alphadelphia Phalanx soon collapsed.[98]

German separatists founded Michigan's second communitarian colony in the vicinity of Wildfowl Bay in northwestern Huron County (fig. 7.1). The community was sponsored by the German Methodist Church, an evangelical denomination centered in Cincinnati and popular among immigrants in the Old Northwest. One of its missionaries, Emil Baur, had been impressed with communitarian socialist communities in the East and determined to found a Methodist community in Michigan. In 1862 he organized the German Christian Agricultural and Benevolent Society of Ora et Labora, Latin for "pray and work." The colony's organization and code of behavior reflected Methodist beliefs and intended to preserve German customs and language. Members of this joint-stock venture received stock in return for their property, worked on communal projects, and were remunerated for their labor from a common store. Ora et Labora provided members housing, livestock, and a half-acre plot for their own use.[99]

The State of Michigan provided seven thousand acres of marshland for the colony on condition that the settlers successfully drain the tract. Clearing and draining began under the

direction of a state reclamation supervisor in the fall of 1862, and colonists arrived the following spring. Economic conditions limited Ora et Labora's development and prompted its early
demise. The investment required to prepare the marshlands created a severe capital shortage,
and its isolated location, far from markets and sources of supply, limited income from trade.
Disheartened by the poor economic prospects, settlers lost faith in the communitarian way of
life. Only fourteen families remained when the colony disbanded in 1867. Although Ora et
Labora failed as community, its experience changed perceptions of the northern Thumb and
opened a previously unsettled territory to settlement.[100]

COLONIZING STRATEGIES AND SETTLEMENT PATTERNING

With the exception of the communitarian experiments, settlers in Michigan's covenanted
communities enjoyed a high rate of persistence. Their success derived from the presence of
central institutions that maintained a high level of group integration through mutual support
often absent in communities of accretion. Covenanted communities did not attempt to manage the regional economy or direct its expansion. Leaders confined their activities largely to
distributing land, assisting newcomers, maintaining social relations, and promoting public
works, leaving the control of production and the development of trade to individual colonists.
Without interference, the frontier economy grew in response to regional market forces. Local
producers enjoyed the flexibility needed to adjust their output and direct their exchange as
they believed advantageous. The absence of a rigid economic structure, combined with the
security of community institutions, increased their members' chances for success in a developing economy.[101]

Because of their distinctive organization and the need to maintain cultural homogeneity,
covenanted communities took on spatial characteristics absent elsewhere on the frontier. To
sustain such a colony, it was necessary to acquire a territory substantial enough to accommodate its entire population as well as its immediate anticipated growth, and yet permit the communication necessitated by their corporate structure. The need for large, contiguous tracts
limited settlement to those left unoccupied by previous immigrants to Michigan. Such tracts
were frequently those avoided because of the perception that they were of poorer quality. Their
colonization shifted the impetus of general settlement away from older agricultural areas,
resulting in dramatic changes in settlement patterning during the period in which covenanted
communities entered Lower Michigan.

The migration of successful covenanted communities to frontier Michigan produced a
pattern of settlement, the form of which reflected factors other than environment and economy. Their presence altered the flow of immigration to the poorly drained lands of the lower
Saginaw Valley, the northern Thumb, portions of the sandy pinelands of the Western Shore,
and previously overlooked tracts of heavy woodlands on the upper Grand River drainage.
Organized settlement brought about a stable occupation with a complex institutional infrastructure. These, in turn, encouraged the rapid growth of rural communities and the early
appearance of a mature agricultural landscape.

Communities of accretion also influenced regional settlement patterning. Although their members had diverse origins and initially lacked strong integrative institutions, economic factors dictated the spatial requirements of this colonization strategy. These communities came into being as soon as land was made available for settlement, and their distribution followed the expansion of land sales, although some communities squatted on unsold lands in hope of preempting their purchase later. Because such communities came into being quickly, settlement could extend across all available territory with minimal delay. Perceptions of environmental potential and accessibility for exchange also affected pioneers' choice of lands. Communities of accretion sought out the best arable lands, whose locations offered the greatest potential for trade. These two factors influenced the distribution of most settlement on the Michigan frontier.

8

Michigan's Frontier Economy in 1845

Antebellum American economic expansion stimulated the growth of Michigan's frontier economy. As the Northeast emerged as a national center of commercial and industrial activity in the new nation, its commercial centers sought access to wider resources, and incorporated more geographically dispersed areas into a national system of production and marketing. This process required that peripheral regions such as Michigan become commodity producers, an endeavor that offered pioneers the promise of wealth, yet demanded that a base for commercial production be constructed in the wilderness.

Establishing a commercial economy on the Michigan frontier, a difficult and lengthy undertaking, required building a complex infrastructure to support production and marketing on a national scale. The development of this infrastructure reflected the struggle of settlers to establish and expand agriculture and trade with limited financial resources. Furthermore, it entailed adaptations that influenced the form and nature of its frontier landscape. Michigan's settlement had much in common with that of other colonial regions; however, historical and geographical conditions also made its development and patterning distinctive.

Immigrant farmers came to Michigan anticipating that they would become food producers for growing urban markets in the East. Although they were initially isolated by distance and a lack of adequate transportation, the low cost of western lands and the potential of gaining wealth through expanded production provided incentives enough for them to endure the process of relocation and the delay in entering commercial agriculture. The correspondence of high grain prices to the peak periods of western land sales in 1816–18, 1832–36, 1846–47, and 1850–56 illustrates the strong link between pioneer aspirations and the growth of the national economy. Immigration to Lower Michigan responded to larger market fluctuations, and the period of national economic growth of the 1830s clearly contributed to its greatest burst of settlement.

The nature of Michigan's frontier economy reflected both the goals of pioneer agriculturists and the limitations of geography and transportation. Successful colonization required that immigrants establish a production base sufficient to permit the survival and growth of settlement. Such production had to accommodate the needs of an expanding society with minimal resources and restricted external trade, yet at the same time anticipate incorporation within national markets. To meet these seemingly contradictory demands, pioneers developed diverse strategies that allowed them to maintain maximum flexibility while retaining the option to specialize when conditions changed. These strategies created a regional economy, the organization of which was crucial to the structure of frontier settlement patterning in Michigan.

INITIAL ECONOMIC ADAPTATIONS ON THE MICHIGAN FRONTIER

Early pioneer strategies arose from the settlers' own experience as well as that of others living in the region. Americans' experiences in trading with Indians and their adoption of French agricultural practices helped shape the regional economy on the Michigan frontier. Interaction with these groups offered solutions of significant value to agriculturists faced with the necessity of sustaining themselves in a region largely isolated from their homeland. Although the ultimate intent of American colonization was to develop commercial agricultural production in Lower Michigan, it was necessary first to settle an immigrant population, establish farms, and develop an infrastructure capable of sustaining the regional production upon which the colony's survival depended.

The lengthy relationship between Europeans and Indians in the Great Lakes centered round exchange, a process that introduced European industrial technology to Native societies and focused Native production round specialized exchange items. Europeans created a demand by Native groups for manufactured goods and opened channels for their distribution. Trade bound Indians and Europeans economically and encouraged interaction between them. Always active participants in the trade, Indians adapted consciously to it in a manner that permitted them to retain as much cultural autonomy as possible. Their ability to do so was tested severely during the American period, when agricultural expansion threatened to deprive them of the traditional lands that were the basis of their political and economic independence.

An increased market for foodstuffs and other items created by American settlement intensified trade and expanded its scale and scope. Not only did the number of its participants increase, so did the variety of the products exchanged. By broadening trade to accommodate this market, Native peoples employed their traditional subsistence base to maintain their economic viability and retain control over the lands they occupied. Although they ultimately lost most of their territories in Lower Michigan, the participation of Indians in the broad-based trade in subsistence products contributed substantially to the initial frontier economy.

Pioneer accounts of early settlement frequently mentioned trading with Indians for food that was crucial for survival. Many echoed the sentiments of Michael Shoemaker of Jackson County, who recalled poignantly that

> The first winter, that of 1830–31, was the most trying of any our little settlement of Jacksonburgh had to endure. Food was scarce and prices high. . . . It was here that a great benefit was derived from our red brethren. . . . The supplies of venison, game, maple sugar, berries and fish furnished . . . were of the last importance to our pioneers during the long winter and the first of spring.[1]

Among the most common items supplied were meat, particularly venison, wild turkey, and other game. One early settler from Ionia County later remembered the "many cheap saddles of venison" provided by the Ottawas, who "were of considerable service to the early settlers." William Forbes, of Plainwell Township in Allegan County, acquired fish regularly, on one occasion purchasing forty, "averaging three to five pounds each of different kinds [including] pickerel, bass, mullet, suckers, trout, and sturgeon, from Indians who had speared them."[2]

Indians also traded gathered seasonal foods, especially berries, to settlers. In the vicinity of Paw Paw, Potawatomis "flocked to the swamps, and for a few weeks . . . trade was lively," recalled Edwin D. Smith. Similarly, Julia Belle Towner, of Vernon in Shiawassee County, remembered, "when it was no uncommon sight for 'Old Chief Fisher' to come into the village with his little tribe, all riding astride their Indian ponies, each with a sack of huckleberries or cranberries thrown over their ponies' necks to exchange."[3]

Maple sugar, produced by Indians, proved to be an essential staple for recent immigrants. Both Indians and Europeans used it as a preservative, a dietary supplement in late winter, and a seasoning. Maple sugar was thus an important component of the fur trade. Native people manufactured it on a large scale and packed it in bark vessels, called mococks, for exchange with settlers. Pioneers frequently mentioned it as a principal item of subsistence supplied to them. The volume of the sugar trade increased markedly after the War of 1812, propelled by the consumption needs of immigrants moving into the region, as well as by demand in the Northeast.[4]

The key role of Indians in the provisions trade gave them a dominant position in frontier exchange. Americans acknowledged that Native people controlled certain natural resources as long as they occupied the land. For example, pioneer George W. Lawton recalled that most early settlers in western Michigan recognized that the Ottawas and Potawatomis had "an 'unalienable right' to possess the fisheries, the huckleberry and cranberry swamps, and held a monopoly of the basket business" in the region.[5] As suppliers of crucial foodstuffs, Native people also exercised control over aspects of the trade itself. Indians fixed prices for their products by requiring "equal measure" of pioneer items, such as flour, meal, bread, corn, potatoes, and pork. Writing of his dealings with the Saginaw-Chippewas in Genesee County, Alvah Brainard recalled that, "Whatever they had to exchange, they wanted the same measure back as they gave. They would bring us a bushel of cranberries and swap for a bushel of potatoes." A similar practice was noted among the Potawatomis in Branch County, who demanded equal volume measure regardless of a product's value as a commodity. While the exchange of berries for potatoes might be in a settler's favor, trading equivalent amounts of items such as salt might prove to be a costly bargain for a needy immigrant. Immigrants with previous experience in trade and more complete knowledge of the value of Native products in pioneer society, on the other hand, could also turn the practice of equal measure to their advantage. Recalling trade with the Potawatomis in Jackson County, Michael Shoemaker observed that "of all classes of men the Indian has the least and poorest ideas of values, and our sharp, shrewd first settlers from New York and New England were not very scrupulous in their dealings with those upon whose good will they were so dependent."[6]

The provisions trade was not limited to the exchange of items. Cash also played a role, and Indians' recognition of its value and their use of it as a medium of exchange made them participants in the "money economy" of the frontier. Michigan Indians received money in their annuities from the U.S. government under the cession treaties. The British government also made cash payments to them as a reward for their loyalty in time of war. The use of cash by its recipients was necessarily restricted, however, because, unlike blankets or farming tools, it could not be employed in its original form. Instead, it was converted, often immediately, into objects of need or desire that were supplied by traders anxious to take advantage of the periodic influx of specie. Early Kalamazoo resident Henry Parker Smith recalled that the Potawatomis

> went once a year to Detroit or some point in that region to receive their pay for their land relinquished to the state. When they came back they had money for their powder and lead . . . , when it was exhausted they had to obtain their goods by exchanging venison and furs for them.[7]

Similar behavior was witnessed by other contemporary observers, who noted the sharp increase in business conducted by traders around annuity payment time.[8]

Although cash in their hands often fell into the clutches of unscrupulous traders, Indians also recognized its value for other purposes. Here again, money was not invested for purposes of profit, but employed as part of a larger strategy of resistance to colonial encroachment. Occasionally, insightful leaders were able to amass and employ substantial amounts of cash for projects of long-term benefit. Leopold Pokagon, for example, used funds acquired from annuity payments and sales of other lands to purchase the substantial tract that would become a center for Potawatomi persistence in southwestern Michigan.[9]

Native people also accepted cash in transactions with Americans. Numerous accounts record exchanges in which Indians were compensated for supplies with money. Immigrants often mentioned purchasing game. Mary M. Hoyt, the daughter of an innkeeper at Yankee Springs in Berry County during the 1830s, recalled that her parents regularly bought venison haunches for twenty-five cents each, "no more, no less." Fish and wild turkey were also purchased frequently, for unspecified amounts. Similar prices for venison were reported by Livingston County resident Caroline Kirkland and Edward A. Foote of Eaton County, the latter of whom emphasized the Indians' insistence on the use of coinage for such transactions: "They would as soon take chip as paper money." Jacob Gerrish, a storekeeper in New Buffalo, recorded numerous transactions with resident Potawatomis involving payment in cash and other products. Over a period of five years he paid cash for such items as furs, deerskins, and maple sugar, most of which were acquired for resale.[10]

Pioneer accounts reveal that cash also passed into Indian hands for services rendered. For example, they received monetary bounties for wolves killed in Davidson Township in Genesee County in the 1840s. Judge Albert Miller of Saginaw found himself obliged to pay several "silver coins" for the assistance of an Indian guide in a search for a missing business associate along the Flint River in 1832. In an attempt to collect damages for injuries inflicted on one of their members by an employee of Kalamazoo resident Jesse Turner, a group of Potawatomis demanded $20 cash. Although Turner's antagonists were ameliorated by other means, it is clear that cash in exchange for goods and services flowed both ways in the Indian trade during the time of Michigan's colonization.[11]

Several generalizations can be made regarding the nature of trade between Indians and American settlers and its role in shaping the initial economy of colonial Michigan. First, the Indian trade introduced a substantial number of nonagricultural subsistence products. Foods obtained by hunting, gathering, and collecting played an important role in the pioneer diet, particularly in the time before farms were established and crops raised. Although such products were known to immigrant settlers in their previous homes, their use had been much less pervasive. A reliance on wild products on the Michigan frontier established a precedent for their regular use. Because they comprised a major component of the economy, the nature of their acquisition had implications for the nature of immigrant production during the settlement period.

The Indian trade also influenced the early colonial economy through its emphasis on exchange on an individual basis, occasioned largely by need. Game was hunted, berries collected, and sap processed into sugar with particular receivers in mind. The aim of the trade was not to produce surpluses, but to meet the general subsistence needs of newcomers to Michigan. Specialized production by Native people of subsistence items for exchange was well established in the region, and the experience of trade facilitated the distribution of these products.

Americans moving into Lower Michigan encountered an earlier French colonial population whose agricultural settlements were scattered along the rivers of the Eastern Shore. The French had established these communities to provide a regional source of provisions for trading and military settlements in the Great Lakes. French settlement was not part of an expanding agricultural frontier but rather an adjunct activity to a specialized form of colonization. The fur trade, like other endeavors associated with cosmopolitan frontiers, reflected narrow economic interests, the development of which was the primary cause of colonial change. The abrupt collapse of French hegemony in the Great Lakes at the conclusion of the Seven Years' War in 1763 had far-reaching implications for the nature of French agriculture in Michigan.

Created to support more highly valued activities, French production was controlled by law and influenced by the small size of the colonial population, which discouraged agricultural growth. After the Seven Years' War, the French settlements were effectively isolated, and they languished under three decades of British administration that curtailed immigration and remained largely indifferent to the region's agricultural development.[12]

French agriculture in Michigan differed markedly from that in British America. The regional French economy puzzled and frustrated American observers accustomed to the agriculture of the Northeast and its increasingly capitalist orientation. Newcomers encountered a population in Michigan that possessed very different notions of production. The nature of the crops raised by the French settlers, called *habitants,* as well as the extent and manner of their cultivation, was a result of their unique experience.

The agricultural economy of French Michigan revolved around the production of wheat, although *habitants* also grew corn and other "grains," as well as hemp and grass for forage. Gardens supplemented farms, and their cultivation comprised a major aspect of agricultural production. Fruit orchards, located throughout French-occupied lands, supplied a vital part of the colonists' diet. The first American survey of the French settlements, conducted by Indian agent Charles Jovett in 1804, revealed that agriculture was practiced at several locations along the Eastern Shore. Principal concentrations of farmers occurred at the mouths of Otter Creek, the River Raisin, Sandy Creek, and the Huron and Rouge Rivers, at Detroit, and at points along the western shore of Lake St. Clair.[13]

Despite the length of time that French settlers had lived in Michigan, the scale of their farming remained small and its practice conservative. Jovett found that most farm tracts were only partially improved, providing room for only meager crops. The scale of production was much less than Americans were accustomed to, and the lack of extensive improvements made the French settlements appear primitive and poverty-stricken. Seeking an explanation, most observers, like Agent Jovett, attributed this condition to an "indolence and want of skill in agriculture which so conspicuously marks the Canadian character in this country." Contemporary sources interpreted the use of the simple plow, hoe cultivation, and the planting of corn in irregular rows as evidence of a lack of proper agricultural knowledge by a backward people resistant to change.[14]

Particularly galling to the Americans was the absence of any effort to improve or maintain soils. "The farms in this territory are very old, and as the proprietor of them seldom or never strengthened the soil by manure, they are in a great measure exhausted," reported the *Detroit Gazette*.[15] Americans were fond of relating instances of what they perceived to be illogical behavior. One early resident informed visitor Henry Sanford that when he arrived,

> The French would, in the winter, . . . cast their manure onto the ice in order that it would be carried off in the spring, or the more slack farmers . . . would, as the manure accumulated around their shanties & barns, move them off to another place and then again in due time move them again.[16]

The failure of the French farmers to renew continuously cropped lands appalled American immigrants, whose misunderstanding of its causes led to persistent ridicule.

In addition to their claims of French mistreatment of the land, American observers accused the French of wasting agricultural produce and failing to efficiently utilize the resources to which they had access. Evidence of neglect was seen in the apparent decayed state of many French dwellings and other structures, and the French were perceived by Americans to lack any inclination to establish a higher standard of living. Indeed, the general use of the term "muskrat Frenchman," alluding to the hutlike dwellings of the poorer colonists, reflected the derogatory attitude of many Americans toward the agricultural practices of these small-scale farmers.[17]

Americans saw a reluctance to increase the size of the agricultural base, even when additional land became available, as the best evidence for French disinterest in improvement. Salmon Keeney expressed such sentiments in 1827 when he noted with disbelief the failure of farmers on the River Raisin to take advantage of nearby lands for the expansion of their farms. The "French people . . . are wilfully & Stupidly ignorant," he wrote. "They are the poorest farmers I ever saw, considering the chance they have. . . . The French raise little except in their gardens." In their use of resources, as well as in their agricultural methods, the French colonists exercised restraint.[18]

French fruit production, however, impressed early American colonists. Along the Eastern Shore they discovered orchards of apple, pear, peach, and cherry trees that yielded fruit of exceptional quality. "Perhaps there is no part of the United States or its territories," proclaimed the *Detroit Gazette*, "where the climate and soil are more favorable to the cultivation of fruit trees, than in this section of Michigan Territory; and . . . there are but few orchards in the U. S. so beautiful as those on the banks of the Detroit river." Many of the trees were reputed to have been brought from France in the first half of the eighteenth century and planted in the settlements on either side of the Detroit River from the River Raisin to Lake St. Clair. Usually well cared for, the orchards produced in abundance, providing both fresh fruit and the ingredients for cider and brandy in quantities beyond the consumption needs of their owners.[19]

Fruit alone appears to have been traded widely between settlements. In 1804, Agent Jovett remarked that "their . . . orchards produce fruit and cider in sufficient abundance for the consumption of the country, and even for the supply of many of the Canadian settlements, to which they are exported." A dozen years later the *Detroit Gazette* remarked that many of the "settlements up and down the [Detroit] river . . . are dependent on this place for that article." In fact, the same source noted that the produce of the orchards "furnishes, generally, the greatest share of the owner's gains."[20]

The intentional production of an abundance of orchard fruit from which an income was derived appears incongruous in an economy characterized by indifferent farming and restrained yields. American perceptions of the French colonial economy were, however, misleading, in that they imply that no agricultural surplus existed and that all food was grown for its cultivator's subsistence. Even contemporary sources pointed out that the habitants produced quantities large enough to satisfy "the small local demand among themselves." Indeed, the *Detroit Gazette* noted that many French residents "buy bread of the baker and vegetables of their more enterprising neighbors." This regional exchange of foodstuffs is suggestive of a household mode of production, an arrangement that would also encompass many of the features associated with the limited scope and scale of French agriculture.[21]

Although regional exchange limited the production of most crops, orchards bore continuously, once established, and growers found it difficult to regulate the size of their crops. If there were no takers, they simply discarded excess fruit, a phenomenon observed frequently in early Michigan. The availability of surplus orchard fruit at a time when American immigrants' need for foodstuffs increased demand markedly made fruit sales an immediate, if unplanned, source of household income for the *habitants*. The conversion of fruit to liquid form to enhance its preservation and transportability only added to its value as an exchange item in a suddenly expanded regional economy.[22]

The fur trade dominated the economy of French Michigan and influenced regional settlement. *Habitants* lived in close proximity with Indian peoples, and interaction between the two groups was extensive and generally friendly. Many Europeans, in fact, adopted elements of aboriginal culture as part of their general subsistence strategy, and hunting and trapping became particularly important activities. American observers recalled that some French colonists depended almost wholly on hunting for their living, while others relied on the fur trade. A reliance upon hunting, gathering, trapping, and foraging was an attractive alternative to agriculture for people whose part-time participation in the fur trade occupied them for extended periods. It provided subsistence as well as a means to acquire foodstuffs and other products in regional exchange. As a small, geographically isolated population faced with surviving in a region of diverse resources, the French found an economy incorporating mixed strategies to be an efficient adaptation.[23]

The American settlement of Lower Michigan gradually brought an end to the conditions that had shaped the economy of the French colony. The passage of political power to a new regime, however, did not immediately affect the influence of the *habitants*, who played a significant role in regional economic and social affairs immediately following the War of 1812. Although immigration by farmers with very different notions of production would bring about change, the survival and establishment of the newcomers entailed their incorporating, to more than a small measure, strategies developed by earlier European residents.[24]

French agriculture was an intelligent adaptation to conditions on the Great Lakes frontier. Created in response to the limited needs of the fur-trade settlements, the deliberate restriction of production was well suited to a region with a relatively fixed population and no outside markets. Although the practice proved problematic in areas undergoing rapid settlement, maintaining a limited and diversified agricultural output until links with the larger economy were established had advantages during the initial period of American settlement.

French emphasis on subsistence products instead of those with high value in export markets was another important precedent for an immigrant population attempting to establish a production base in a new country. Subsistence crops insured success by providing the foodstuffs necessary for survival and creating a production base that could be adapted for intraregional exchange. Early production of a diversity of subsistence items would be a key to the rapid establishment of an agricultural colony, as well as to maintaining its economic unity during the crucial period of initial settlement.

EARLY PIONEER STRATEGIES OF SUBSISTENCE

The process of farm-making required time, and the most pressing problem facing pioneer settlers in Michigan was to survive until they had harvested their first crops. J. B. LaRowe, an early settler of Howell Township in Livingston County, recalled that upon his arrival in 1837, "Our main object was to get something to eat. We all lived in anticipation of better days." His concern was echoed by others, such as M. Shoemaker of Jackson, who stressed the critical nature of the first year of settlement. Faced with a need for foodstuffs beyond the limited supplies brought with them or obtained by trade, immigrants developed nonagricultural strategies to supplement their diet.[25]

Relatively abundant wildlife provided an immediate source of food for Michigan's settlers. Although hunting continued as a leisure activity long after the establishment of agricultural production, it played an extensive, and even critical, role in initial subsistence. To the settler from the East, the abundance of game animals was astonishing. "You can go out any time and get a saddle of venison, lots of deer and bears, turkeys . . ." wrote Sylvanus Bachelder of the situation in Bath Township in Clinton County. "We have all kinds of game from the smallest to the largest." In addition to the larger species, particularly deer, a number of smaller animals and fowl are mentioned in contemporary accounts. These include rabbits and squirrels as well as turkeys, partridges, quail, ducks, and passenger pigeons.[26]

Hunting was not always restricted to indigenous wild species, but included introduced animals that had escaped and become feral. Col. M. Shoemaker of Jackson provided an example of this phenomenon. In 1830, he recalled,

> Some hogs brought into the neighborhood got into the woods and ran wild. They were not pleasant objects to meet without firearms, and were really more dangerous than the wolves, bears, or any other of the wild beasts of our forests. They, however, at this juncture, served a good turn, . . . [as] they were systematically hunted. . . . There was plenty of shack in the woods, and the hogs were not plenty, so that they were generally in very good condition for the pot, to which they were as welcome as flowers in May.[27]

Whether it involved native or introduced game, hunting was an important aspect of early subsistence among Michigan immigrants.[28]

Pioneer reliance on hunting also reflected the relatively important role of meat in the antebellum American diet. During this period Americans consumed foods rich in calories with an emphasis on fats and salt. Foods such as salt pork, lard, and butter comprised a large part of this diet, often to the exclusion of fluid milk, fresh fruit, and green vegetables. Meat was considered a necessary foodstuff, and its significant role in the pioneer diet encouraged the unrestrained exploitation of available wildlife in newly settled areas.[29]

The demand for meat by newly arrived immigrants and the growing number of people living in Detroit and other urban settlements encouraged the growth of market hunting in Michigan. Many pioneers killed game far beyond their own subsistence needs, and the meat obtained provided a much-needed item of exchange. Individuals such as Ebeneezer Hough of Lapeer County supplemented a tenuous income by periodically "killing a load of game and taking it to Detroit, where he found a ready market." Pioneers perceived game as limitless, but regular subsistence hunting destroyed animal populations and their habitats. Only the abundance of wildlife permitted widespread hunting to continue unabated.[30]

Fish from Michigan's numerous streams, rivers, and interior lakes were an important source of protein. "Our lakes are well stocked with excellent fish," wrote L. D. Watkins, who settled in southeastern Jackson County in 1834. "Bass, pike, pickerel, perch, sunfish, and bluegills were the most common and easily taken." Settlers with access to water fished extensively, and fish constituted a regular part of many an immigrant's diet. The *Emigrant's Guide* proclaimed that "fish . . . will give variety to the tables of the rich, while they afford at the same time a needful supply to the poor." Fish abounded in the Great Lakes bordering the Michigan peninsulas. Whitefish, sturgeon, trout, and herring taken from the lakes were important foodstuffs. Although fishing in the Great Lakes remained in the hands of specialized fishing companies, and outside markets took much of its product, Michigan residents consumed at least a quarter of the fish caught, which contributed a "needful supply" to the diet of its growing population.[31]

Whortleberries, blackberries, huckleberries, whiteberries, raspberries, gooseberries, black currants, and crab apples also enriched the diets of immigrant settlers in southern Lower Michigan. "The pioneer found that kind nature had anticipated his wants in an abundant supply of wild fruits and nuts," recalled L. D. Watkins. "In succession came the delicious wild strawberry, blue berry, grapes, plums, and cranberries. Nuts were abundant, hickory, black walnut, butternut and hazelnut, . . . were gathered and stored away for the . . . long winter."[32] Harvesting berries was frequently a social occasion for household members. Describing her family's regular seasonal foraging activities, Elizabeth Chamberlain of New Buffalo wrote that

> Fruit of all kinds is abundant and we have fine times gathering it. I jump into the ox wagon with Willie for driver, along with Henry and generally some of the neighbors, and away we go over the roots and stumps, through the mud until we come to the marsh where we stay most of the day.[33]

Preserved wild foods, collected during the first summer in the new country, constituted an important food source for the immigrant family struggling to establish agricultural crops. Stockpiled for later use, these foods were integral to the pioneer diet and provided insurance if other sources of subsistence failed. Immigrants stored nuts and dried fruit or made them into preserves. They brought the knowledge and technology necessary for "putting up" with them and were familiar with storing both wild and domestic plant foods. Wild foods remained part of the pioneer diet long after farms were established. Entrepreneurs such as surveyor Bela Hubbard developed plans to harvest cranberries commercially on lands they owned, particularly in eastern Michigan. Farmers also sold berries they found growing on their unused lands. Ainsworth Reed of Clinton County, for example, regularly exchanged the cranberries gathered on the wetlands of his Victor Township farm with itinerant buyers as late as the 1850s.[34]

Pioneers found honey plentiful and gathered it in substantial quantities. They obtained it from the nests of bees encountered in land clearing or sought out by experienced "bee hunters." Long-time Clinton County resident Bub Able declared, "The woods are full of bees and every little while I fell a bee tree where I am clearing, that has all the way from ten gallons to a barrel and a half of nice strained honey in it." Bee hunters, versed in the lore of locating nests and removing their contents, became standard characters of frontier folklore. H. H. Riley introduced such a character, Venison Styles, in his collection of tales of early Constantine in St. Joseph County, where honey was an integral part of the settlers' subsistence. Perhaps because of the mysterious skills required for obtaining it, the fortuitous nature of its acquisition, and its association with male subsistence activities, honey was often mentioned together with products of the hunt.[35]

Maple sugar was another product that contributed greatly to the regional frontier economy. Manufactured by Native peoples in Michigan long before the arrival of American settlers, its use as a preservative, a dietary supplement, and a seasoning made it important to both Indians and Europeans. Its compact and highly portable nature, combined with its varied uses, made maple sugar a staple of the Indian trade in the closing years of the eighteenth century. By the mid–1820s "Indian sugar" had become one of Michigan's principal exports, and it appeared regularly in shipping manifests of the period. Maple sugar production in Michigan increased over time, and by 1860 the state's output ranked third in the nation.[36]

The demand for maple sugar encouraged immigrants from New York and New England to carry out its manufacture during the early spring lull in farm work. Many pioneers, like Thomas Chandler of Lenawee County, purchased their property with an eye toward the presence of a concentration of maple trees, referred to as a "sugar bush." Sugar making required minimal equipment, and sugar makers maximized production to take advantage of their product's value in trade "for goods or family supplies." Maple sugar was thus widely exchanged. A contemporary observer estimated that a pioneer family could easily acquire the family's yearly needs with each spring's sugar production and still have a substantial amount left over. It became a staple item of regional exchange and generated cash necessary to purchase manufactured items from the outside.[37]

Immigrants from the Northeast brought knowledge of potash making with them to Michigan, where they turned it into an important frontier industry. Michigan farmers found a ready market for the ashes of hardwood trees cut down to clear fields. Ashes formed the basic ingredient for potash, and its purified derivative pearlash. These products were used in soap and glass-making, formed a component of medicines, and constituted the major element of saleratus, a leavening agent. Indeed, the final form of potash would often return to Michigan as a finished good.[38]

Settlers found the sale of ashes a reliable way of obtaining cash or exchange in the early years of settlement. "Had it not been for the black salts and maple sugar," wrote Edward Barber, "it is difficult to tell how taxes could have been paid." Indeed, in an effort to increase their earnings some early settlers were reported to have "cleared up their farms more rapidly because the ashes [could readily] . . . be transmuted to articles indispensable to family comfort." Henry Sanford went so far as to observe that because of their relatively high demand, "the ashes that [a farmer] can get from the trees he cuts will be sufficient to support his family for the first year." The good market for potash also encouraged its processing in the region. Detroit merchants advertised for finished potash in the early years of settlement expansion. Enterprising frontier entrepreneurs such as Jacob Gerrish of New Buffalo found it in their interest "to go into the pot & pearling business." In many frontier settlements, such as Grand Rapids, multiple potash-making facilities arose by the 1840s.[39]

Pioneers conducted shingle making as an adjunct to farm-making, and it provided an important item for use in regional exchange. Needed in the construction of houses, barns, and other buildings, shingles were manufactured from coniferous logs felled in clearing land, or from pine timber cut for that purpose. Demand for shingles resulted in extensive harvesting of the pinelands in the lower Grand River Valley and the Western Shore, as well as around Saginaw Bay. "If the settler wanted something more costly, as flour or pork," wrote Grand River pioneer Henry Griffin, "his only alternative was to get up a shingle shanty, and make shingles." David

Realy and James Dalton found shingle making more lucrative than farming the poor soil of their Ottawa County farms and made shingles full time, using timber cut on unsold federal lands.[40]

With the transition to agriculture as a primary means of subsistence, many of the early strategies declined in importance. Agricultural production became the principal task of the rural population in southern Michigan and its demands precluded maintaining the diversified forms of subsistence that had accompanied initial settlement. Some, like hunting, wild food collecting, and sugar making, continued to supplement agriculture as long as the resources remained available. Others, such as potash and shingle making, became increasingly specialized activities.

Farm-making on the frontier was hardly a haphazard venture. Most prudent immigrants followed the same advice that John P. Powell gave his son, who planned to farmland in Ionia County. Before commencing, the younger Powell was instructed to "take a general survey of your farm so as to locate your buildings judiciously for convenience of the land, water and the roads, find the best site for a garden, and orchard, and shape all doings in conformity to the grand design of beauty and use." A "grand design" of farm-making helped not only in planning the layout and composition of the agricultural settlement, but also in setting out the order of its completion.[41]

Farm-making was the most difficult and formidable task for immigrant farmers. It required an extensive investment of labor and capital, and a pioneer's success depended upon an understanding of the requirements of production and planning. A. C. Glidden recalled the laborious process of "cutting brush, piling and burning logs, and then the breaking, for which all previous work was but preliminary." Forested lands, oak openings, and prairies could be converted to agricultural production only after the immigrant farmer had cleared and prepared fields for planting and constructed houses, barns, outbuildings, fences, and other structures necessary for the cultivation, processing, and storage of crops.[42]

Settlers timed their arrival on frontier land to keep the time to first harvest as short as possible. Inauspicious timing could make or break a prospective farmer. George W. Thayer recalled how pioneers in the oak openings planned their settlement to permit efficient preliminary clearing and planting:

> A pioneer would go onto his land in the late summer or early fall, build his log house of the smaller oaks, girdle a few trees to prevent the leaves from growing in the spring and forming a shade, plough, drag in a crop of wheat right among the standing oaks, and in spring plant corn and potatoes, and secure a fine crop of each.[43]

Betsey Landon, who settled near Spring Arbor in Jackson County, advised her father in the East to "move out next fall or this summer," as her family had done the previous year. She emphasized that this time of arrival would not only allow the planting of both winter and spring crops, but also permit the cutting of marsh hay necessary to sustain livestock over the first winter.[44]

Settlers in heavily wooded areas had to remove the timber before they could plant a crop. Eugene Davenport recalled that immigrants who arrived in the winter or spring carried out initial cutting the following summer and sometimes planted a small crop of wheat that fall among the stumps. More often the cut trees were left to dry until the following summer, when they were burned. Contemporary accounts of woodland settlers indicate that preparation of their lands required a long time. "Father's place looks quite farmlike," wrote Henry Chamberlain of Berrien County. "Two years ago the land was covered by heavy timber, all was a wilderness. Now 25 acres is [sic] cleared . . . and everything [has] a thriving appearance." Even at this point, however, Chamberlain recognized that land preparation was still incomplete: "The stumps still raise their heads and are a great impediment to the successful cultivation of the soil." It took at least five years for the stumps to begin to rot so that they could be burned out, leaving the ground ready for normal plow tillage.[45]

Winter provided a break in the production cycle when farmers turned to tasks associated with consolidating their improvements and expanding the agricultural production base. During this season, farmers cleared additional land, piled and burned logs, and removed brush in preparation for planting the following spring. Winter also provided time for threshing and transporting grain, breaking steers and colts for farmwork, splitting rail fencing, and procuring timber and shingles for building.[46]

Immigrants made building a permanent house a high priority, but its expense and labor conflicted with the development of a production base. Settlers usually resolved this dilemma by building in stages, constructing at first only minimal protection from the elements. In the warm June weather of 1829, pioneer Thaddeus Smith wrote to his wife Elizabeth that he had "seen 10 large families ploughing and planting without any other house than an open tent made of their bedding," but anticipated that they "will put up log huts this summer." Log huts, or cabins, were small temporary dwellings, often with a single-slope roof and dirt floor, and a chimney made of sticks set in mud or clay mortar. After a pioneer family brought their farm into production, they turned their attention to erecting a larger hewn-log house, usually a story and a half in height, with a puncheon floor, gable roof, and a stone or brick chimney. Frequently clapboarded on the exterior, many also had plastered interior walls. As farm families' wealth increased, they replaced their log houses with larger frame houses, to accommodate their growing households and to advertise success through the possession of dwellings exhibiting contemporary architectural styles.[47]

In time, farmers constructed barns for storing hay and equipment as well as housing livestock and processing farm products. Often years passed before immigrants completed these large structures, because of the time and labor required to build them. Elizabeth Chandler remarked that in the vicinity of Tecumseh, the occurrence of barn raisings reflected not only the length of time the settler had been in residence but also the density of local settlement from which labor could be drawn.[48]

In order to succeed at farming, immigrant farmers first had to achieve a level of production adequate to meet their families' immediate needs. Contemporary accounts, such as that by Jackson County resident Michael Shoemaker, emphasized that soon after their arrival, "crops were raised so that in the winter of 1830–31 the pioneers had not to depend entirely upon having the means of livelihood brought from abroad." In order to accomplish this, farmers chose crops that were capable of thriving in the newly cleared soil and likely to yield a substantial harvest.[49]

Cultivating corn proved advantageous to those arriving in Michigan between the previous harvest and the time for spring planting. Pioneers who settled on new farm sites in a forested environment immediately set about girdling trees and clearing and burning brush to produce a small clearing in which they planted corn with a hoe or stick. This provided a subsistence crop sufficient to carry the family through the following winter, during which time they extended the cleared land. On open land, larger summer corn crops could be planted after breaking the soil with a plow. For example, Henry Parker Smith recalled that his party planted corn immediately upon their arrival at nearby Prairie Ronde, in order "to feed everyone another season." In the oak openings of Eaton County, Theodore Potter's family was able "to clear seven acres and get in the spring . . . corn" to tide them over until the following year.[50]

Corn could be processed easily with a minimum of tools and equipment. Michigan pioneers frequently mentioned the use of samp mills, or hominy blocks, for crushing the kernels. Mrs. Alvin Cross of Ypsilanti Township later recounted how the resulting material was "carefully separated, the fine used for bread, and the coarse for samp [porridge]." Other accounts indicate that corn bread, or "johnny cake," was much more common in pioneer households than wheat bread and that cornmeal mush formed a substantial part of the immigrant farmer's daily diet.[51]

Corn generally grew well in southern Michigan and often produced surprising initial yields, but it also had drawbacks. Continuous cultivation rapidly depleted some soils of the nutrients needed for other crops. Those on J. M. McMath's farm at Willow Run in Washtenaw County deteriorated particularly rapidly. He discovered that after two seasons, "all the elements that go to produce the usual cereals seem to have been exhausted." Other disasters plagued the corn farmer as well. In 1832, Albert Miller of Saginaw reported that "clouds of blackbirds from the marshes" destroyed his corn crop. The disadvantages of corn prompted farmers to supplement its cultivation with other grains.[52]

Although farmers cultivated wheat extensively in Michigan, the delay in obtaining a first crop curtailed its use on new farms on timbered lands. Wheat's growing cycle required that it be planted in the fall to be harvested the following summer, making it necessary to clear land a year before the earliest yield of grain. The time and labor required to prepare woodlands for wheat discouraged farmers from sowing it as an early crop, and they often postponed planting wheat for several years. The perception that forest soils were less suitable for growing wheat further limited the extent of its cultivation.[53]

Settlers viewed openings and prairies as wheat country because the lack of heavy vegetation in these areas made plowing easier. Mitchell Hinsdill and his neighbors prepared their prairie farms for wheat by simply breaking the soil prior to planting. Even a settler like the Reverend Thomas Sprague, whose ministry frequently called him away from his Calhoun County farm, managed to cultivate a small acreage of wheat on the openings during his first year of residence.[54]

The complex procedure involved in processing wheat discouraged even open land farmers from planting it extensively. Making flour from wheat was more complicated than producing cornmeal. Wheat had to be threshed to separate the grain, ground at a mill to make flour, and bolted to sift it for fineness. Although a few immigrants improvised by grinding and bolting wheat at home, most relied on mills. The difficulty and expense of erecting these facilities in newly settled lands limited their appearance in Michigan, and their scarcity forced many farmers to transport wheat long distances. As the number of mills increased, so did the popularity of wheat. Resulting surpluses permitted the grain to emerge as a staple in Michigan's frontier economy.[55]

The early pioneer diet reflected both the relative scarcity and desirability of wheat. R. C. Crawford of Oakland County recalled that "Wheat was a luxury when it came, [and] was for Sabbath eating."[56] Early Kent County settlers also hoarded wheat flour,

> for such state occasions as quiltings, weddings, Thanksgiving and other holidays, when the good wife was want to exercise her culinary skill in compounding short-cake to grace the bountifully-spread table. It was also considered the proper thing to have a loaf or two of wheat bread in the house should the clergyman or other respected visitor come to take tea.[57]

In addition to corn and wheat, garden vegetables sustained early settlers. Many planted high-yielding root crops in newly cleared land with a minimum of effort and subsisted off them while awaiting their first harvest of grain. In 1835 Jonas Clark of Eagle Township in Clinton County "planted . . . potatoes and turnips that the family might have something to live upon the following winter." Pioneer accounts describe large returns on these root crops. The Chandler farm, for example, produced 100 bushels of potatoes from a half-acre tract, and an acre field yielded 150 bushels of turnips. Squash, gourds, pumpkins, watermelons, cantaloupes, and other melons supplemented potatoes and turnips in the diets of early farm families.[58]

The crops employed for early subsistence were crucial to the success of immigrant settlement in Michigan. Although access to outside markets did not yet exist on the frontier, trade was central to the development of internal markets. Such markets became the basis for a regional economic infrastructure that supported the growth of farms and villages in the new country.

THE ORGANIZATION OF THE FRONTIER ECONOMY

Michigan's economy centered around agricultural production on family farms, but the nature of frontier production differed from that in older settled areas because of the conditions of relative isolation under which it was carried out. These circumstances required pioneer farmers to modify household patterns of work and social organization characteristic of a capitalist economy in which farmers grew crops for cash, participated in larger markets, and consumed finished goods made elsewhere. In capitalist agriculture, farming centered around "simple commodity production," within which kinship affected the role of labor and its relationship to the ownership and means of production. Unlike the factory, the family farm did not share the firm class divisions separating owners and laborers. Whereas factory owners controlled the means of production and labor had no role in decision making and remained subject to the owners' interests, on family farms household members performed labor and additional temporary help came from other farm households. Wages did not represent a social division within farm households. Instead they were a means of redistributing capital within and between farm households and served to finance the establishment of new farms and to overcome labor discrepancies among existing farm households. Simple commodity production provided stability that protected farmers from the vicissitudes of a capitalist economy. It also established a structure that permitted production to be adapted to economic conditions encountered on the periphery of settlement.[59]

In Michigan, farm households adapted production to conditions that restricted external trade and minimized the influence of national markets. Without a cash market for their crops, adequate long-distance transportation, and wide access to imported finished goods, they produced surpluses of food and goods for exchange with others on the frontier. This regional trade was necessary because established colonists were not self-sufficient, and immigration created a persistent demand for supplies. These circumstances did not alter the structure of simple commodity production but rather redirected its cooperative organization to different ends. Colonists adopted a "household mode of production," an arrangement directed toward producing and distributing goods on the basis of need rather than price. Under this scheme, a product's use value to consumers was greater than its value as a commodity. Exchange served to meet the economic needs of the pioneer community, and its role in maintaining social relationships among its members took precedence over maximizing profit.[60]

Although the exchange of goods did not subordinate their value to a pricing system, its use of cash distinguished it from institutionalized barter. To colonists accustomed to assigning cash values to goods and services, the use value of a product expressed as a cash equivalent provided a means of comparison, and did not actually turn goods or labor into money. Rather, each party sought to insure that he or she might receive something equal to that given. People did not enter into exchange with one another to transform their products into a universal equivalent and maximize monetary surpluses. Instead, they sought to obtain goods or services with comparable use values directly and without the mediation of money. This form of exchange inhibited capital formation and mitigated the appearance of a capitalist economy.[61]

The role of cash in transactions also differed from that in a market economy. Parties used cash values to assign equivalencies between the items exchanged, not to create surplus wealth. Selling a product or service for cash offered no advantage, and cash was used for maintaining balances between producers. It was another product with a specific use value that it retained while in circulation. Although pioneers needed cash to purchase land and pay taxes, as long as people exchanged frontier products on the basis of need, cash remained an alternative form of payment. When this condition changed, so did the role of cash in the frontier economy.[62]

The household mode of production was an efficient adaptation to the situation encountered by Michigan's agricultural pioneers. It provided a mechanism to establish and expand production and created networks of regional exchange in the absence of substantial ties with the larger economy. The expanding production base created by a growing population did not alter the nature of exchange on the frontier; however, its presence marked the intent of the larger economy to incorporate the new land and its resources and impose market relations on products and services formerly exchanged on the basis of need.

Frontier agriculturists followed several concurrent strategies to provide for their subsistence and establish an efficient production base. Some increased the number of subsistence products raised on their farms, especially corn and tuberous vegetables that could be harvested soon after arrival and processed on the farm. They had no intent of making individual households self-sufficient, but instead expanded production to meet the needs of wider regional markets. Pioneers followed the wider practice of colonial and antebellum northern farmers, who produced 20 to 40 percent or more of their crops for trade. From the beginning, pioneer farms participated in a larger economy.[63]

Many farm households diversified production in order to cope with an uncertain produce market. This strategy offered a greater range of crops, which helped insure against the potential failure of newly introduced cultigens. Diversification also involved producing specialized household items, such as brooms and tools, and providing repair services for other pioneer households. Specialized production appeared early and accompanied regional exchange. It made a greater variety of goods available to Michigan settlers, including the products and services of craftsmen and other specialists whose contributions were crucial to establishing and maintaining settlements and creating the economic infrastructure of a farming region.[64]

Michigan's frontier economy depended upon the creation of a system of internal transportation and communications capable of handling the exchange of foodstuffs and other locally made products within the region. This overland network took its dendritic form from a series of long-distance routes opened to provide pioneers access from Detroit to the undeveloped hinterland. The road network reflected the central government's ambivalent constitutional role in funding internal improvements, which resulted in the absence of a "great road" tradition in the United States before the 1830s. Limited federal construction passed the responsibility for building other roads to the states and territories. Michigan, largely inhabited by a dispersed population, had few resources to draw upon for additional internal improvements. The dendritic form of the federal immigration routes, however, severely inhibited exchange within the region and necessitated the construction of internal overland networks. These additional roads provided access to areas far from principal immigration routes and linked pioneer settlements and production sites to mills, river landings, or towns. The inward focus of these regional networks supported pioneer settlement, but their layout mitigated the development of an export-oriented economy.[65]

The absence of lateral routes was apparent to early residents such as the Reverend Elijah H. Pilcher, an itinerant Methodist minister whose circuit during 1831 included a large area in southern Michigan. Pilcher preached in Branch, Hillsdale, and Lenawee Counties, all situated along the road that ran through the southern part of the territory, as well as in Calhoun, Jackson, and western Washtenaw Counties, lying on a more northerly road. He lamented the lack of connecting routes between points along these roads, recalling that to travel from Marshall to Coldwater, lying directly to the south, he had to first retrace his path east as far as Ypsilanti, where the roads came together. Frustrated by the four weeks consumed by this circuitous passage, he determined to find someone to guide him through the "trackless" intervening country. Pilcher overcame the disadvantages of the early road network only by creating his own "cross-roads."[66]

The slow development of Michigan's overland system and the inadequate condition of its roads also inhibited internal trade. As late as 1819, only unimproved trails penetrated Michigan's interior. Systematic road construction did not begin until the late 1820s, when immigrants began to move across the peninsula in substantial numbers. Describing the passage through the southernmost counties of the territory in 1828, Abraham Edwards recalled that "The country . . . was almost a trackless wilderness, very few wagons having passed over it. The Indian trail therefore had to be our guide, as it was very difficult to keep the road track." His words were echoed by contemporary traveler A. D. P. Van Buren, who found that the route was marked only by the passage of vehicles over it. They and other pioneer settlers found their way into Michigan's interior by following the trails attributed to the Indians.[67]

Even when improved to accommodate wheeled vehicles, frontier roads were often barely adequate to handle the traffic. Roads were particularly bad on poorly drained lands. George C. Bates described a region through which nearly all immigrants to Michigan were obliged to pass:

> for forty miles in every direction around Detroit lies one heavy timbered, level, muddy plain, where the soil is alluvial on the surface and a cold, squeasy, heavy clay beneath, through and over which . . . transit is almost impossible . . . Through a forest . . . a black, sticky road was cut, and when the rush of emigration commenced in 1830, all those highways were cut up with slough holes, dug-ways, and morasses, through which it seemed impossible to drag a stage coach or a heavy laden wagon . . . Except through the Black Swamp, . . . there were no more fearful and horrid roads to be found than all those leading out from Detroit in 1833 to 1837.[68]

Early immigrant Enoch Chase likened the poorly drained roads on the Eastern Shore to "an almost continuous mudhole." Early roads paralleling Lakes Erie and St. Clair often failed to bridge streams or marshes, "rendering their passage both dangerous and difficult."[69]

Principal roads elsewhere were little better. Harriet Martineau, traveling westward across the peninsula in 1836, found the main road in St. Joseph County "absolutely impassable," requiring her coach to detour "above a mile through the *wood,* where there was no track, but where the trees are blazed, to serve as guideposts, summer and winter." The same year residents claimed that conditions on this road were so poor "that a waggon cannot be drawn through with the least burthen upon it," concluding that "The road in its present condition is perfectly useless." The principal road leading westward from southwestern Michigan along Lake Michigan to Chicago actually lay "in some places under water for several miles," making "travelling . . . hazardous during the prevalence of certain winds." Martineau remarked that "whenever it was *dangerous* for the carriage, . . . we were obliged to get out" and continue the journey on foot. The following year, George Taylor took a coach from Detroit to Ypsilanti, a distance of only thirty miles, "nearly one third of which some of us walked, and helped the stage along."[70]

Bad roads posed a great risk for cargoes being shipped overland and restricted long-distance trade. A complaint voiced by the *Detroit Gazette* in 1825 addressed the danger to anyone attempting to move goods over the road network in Michigan. "It is truly discouraging to the emigrant," wrote the editor, "after having transported his goods safely for three or four hundred miles, to have them dashed to pieces on our broken causeways, within ten miles of this place." The condition of frontier roads slowed the rate and raised the cost of moving cargo. Poor roads provided little encouragement to immigrants whose livelihood depended on the safe shipment of goods. The time required to travel over bad roads could be staggering. For example, in 1828 the 30-mile journey from Detroit to Ypsilanti took three days and the 170-mile trip from Detroit to Edwardsburg in western Cass County lasted eighteen days. Two years later a round trip with a load from Detroit to Ann Arbor via Plymouth involved a week's travel. "Difficulty of access," remained the greatest obstacle in the territory."[71]

The survival and success of immigrants depended upon their ability to move goods and services among rural buyers and sellers. In 1824 a Michigan editorial writer emphasized that

> Perhaps there is no labor which will so quickly enhance the value of farms, and increase the comforts of the farmer, as that bestowed on the highway, leading from the principal market places to the agricultural districts. . . . A farm is more or less valuable, according to the ease with which it can be approached—a Paradise, in the centre of an *ocean of mud,* would not be considered as worth sixpence, yet an ordinary piece of land, if situated on a good road leading immediately to a market, would be looked upon as valuable.[72]

Bad roads made profitable trade difficult, and the cost of shipment could easily outweigh that of production. "The price of purchase is the great question with the practical farmer, declared the editor of the *Detroit Gazette,* who then asked rhetorically, "Of what use is a superabundant crop, if for want of demand it must perish upon the spot where it grew?" Contemporary observers clearly recognized that high shipping costs were the principal barrier to outside trade.[73]

The obstacles experienced by early Michigan farmers in traveling to grain milling sites illustrate the effect of inadequate roads on the internal economy. An initial absence of lateral roads encouraged millers to place these facilities along the principal immigration routes into the interior, locations that were inconvenient to many parts of the interior and forced many settlers to make long, arduous trips to convert their grain into an exchangeable product. Early settlers in Barry County required two days or more to get their wheat ground at a Gull Prairie mill in neighboring Kalamazoo County. In 1830, residents of Jackson County likewise found it necessary to make "tedious and unprofitable trips to the grist mill in Dexter." The mills at Coldwater in Branch County were not unusual in being "patronized by nearly all the inhabitants for from twenty to forty miles." James Lanning of Lenawee County recalled that the mills at the county seat of Tecumseh also regularly attracted customers from a forty-mile radius. N. H. Hart of

Lapeer County spent nearly a week in 1831 traveling to and between mills in Oakland County before returning with ground flour.[74]

Farmers returned home with processed grain after milling to feed their households and exchange the surplus. The nature of customer demand and degree of accessibility by road determined the direction and patterning of internal exchange. The form and extent of Michigan's frontier economy reflected the context in which producers met consumer requirements in a newly settled region, a phenomenon called the provisions market.

Newly arrived settlers needed time to establish farms. Supplying their needs constituted an important component of Michigan's regional economy. Describing the agricultural situation in Oakland County in 1829, David L. Porter remarked, "Little is exported, [all] being consumed by emigrants." The situation he observed reflected the struggle of initially low production to meet expanding demand. The intensity of immigration between 1815 and 1835 caused contemporary sources to remark on its effect. "The rapid increase of population in Michigan is beyond example," reported the *Democratic Free Press,* "so much so that we learn that farmers in the interior find it difficult to reserve sufficient produce for their own families." James Lanman observed in the 1830s that the frontier farmer had "a market for his produce at his own door." Although perhaps exaggerated, these statements clearly demonstrate that a self-contained market for foodstuffs dominated Michigan's early regional economy.[75]

Subsistence depended on a variety of agricultural staples, especially wheat, corn, and oats. In Elizabeth Chandler's Lenawee County household, the wheat raised was in such great demand that her brother was obliged to "part with all he could spare." Farmers raised corn and oats for food and fodder, and both were in high demand by newly arrived immigrants. Pioneer farmers planted both in expectation of selling the surplus. Wheat production grew rapidly in frontier Michigan and surpassed that of both corn and rye, as well as other food crops, during the 1830s. Other provision crops included potatoes; animal products such as beef, pork, and lard; and dairy products.[76]

Because vicissitudes of the environment affected crop production, and uneven levels of immigration created an unpredictable market for foodstuffs in Lower Michigan, farmers found it difficult to plan for future demand. As long as the influx of settlers continued, the sellers' market remained good and prices high. In Detroit, consistent scarcity kept demand and prices high. "Nothing surprises a stranger in Detroit so much as the high price of everything that is brought to its market by the farmer," complained the editor of the *Detroit Gazette* in 1829, who stressed the growing provisions market as an incentive for prospective western farmers. On the other hand, overproduction dramatically lowered the value of foodstuffs. A rapid decline in immigration to Shiawassee County in 1837 diminished the demand for grain sharply and its value dropped to less than a quarter of what it had been the previous year. Similarly, Prairie Ronde preemptors raised large crops in 1828 only to find few new buyers in this lightly settled area.[77]

The availability of provisions, as well as their relative value, varied seasonally. The experience of Martin L. Daniels of Tecumseh illustrates the effect of a seasonal demand on a fixed resource during the winter. "Provision is plenty here now," he wrote in the spring, "but when we staid [sic] through the winter it was more scarce." Extreme weather only exacerbated these conditions. "Times are extremely hard. The winter has been long & severe," reported Anson W. Halbert of Portland. "Provisions of all kinds are *scarce* & *double in price* what they were four months ago." Demand, however, might also vary from one item to another and, despite general scarcity, individual prices fluctuated dramatically. Describing such conditions in New Buffalo in 1837, merchant Jacob Gerrish wrote, "Provisions this winter have been very high . . . but some . . . articles have fallen while others have risen."[78]

In times of extreme shortage, foodstuffs imported from adjacent regions supplemented those produced in Michigan. During the early years of settlement the large number of newcomers created a market for Ohio foodstuffs. Estwick Evans, who traveled to Michigan in 1819, observed that

> Along the south shore of Lake Erie the markets will, for some time to come, be very good. Depots of provisions are established here by the farmers of New York, Pennsylvania, and Ohio; and vessels on the lake transport them, during spring and fall, to Detroit.[79]

Increasing immigration in the 1830s created an expanding market for grain that made the region dependent on Ohio foodstuffs for a number of years. In 1831 Oakland County resident David L. Porter observed that

> The greatest scarcity prevails at this time & the demand is incessant from the emigrants. The surplus wheat of this country was at least 8 to 10,000 bushels last harvest and now we have to depend on Detroit for breadstuffs. [The price of] produce must fall when navigation opens as we can then obtain supplies from Ohio. Another month will remedy the evil.[80]

As late as 1837 settlements in southeastern Michigan remained largely dependent on Ohio flour and shipments of Ohio grain through Detroit even reached as far as Grand Rapids. So significant was the immigrant market for grain in Michigan in the 1830s that the editor of the *Democratic Free Press* predicted it might result in shortages in eastern markets and increase the importation of foreign grain.[81]

Immigrants to Michigan also imported livestock. Pork was an important component of the pioneer diet. In her autobiographical account of life in Livingston County, Caroline Kirkland described the residents' preference for pork as exceeding even that for sugar and whiskey. The ease with which hogs could be raised, together with the popularity of their meat, created a lucrative market for hog raisers. Hog production was an important component of the economy of the antebellum South, and the states bordering the Ohio River formed an early focus of hog production in the West before the Civil War. Like their neighbors in the upland South, hog raisers on the Ohio served urban markets east and west of the Appalachians and were important suppliers to adjacent frontier regions where pioneers had yet to establish their own herds.[82]

Unlike provisions that had to be shipped, livestock could be driven overland to market, even in the absence of roads. New settlements in Michigan often obtained pork in this manner. "Of pork we shall be deficient," wrote O. Wilder of Marshall in 1833, "not yet having had time to raise a supply. Our stock . . . are driven in from the Wabash and Illinois counties." Henry Little of Kalamazoo County recalled that two years earlier their provisions had included "a drove of one hundred hogs from Indiana." The importance of hog imports to Michigan is reflected in a local appeal that was reprinted in a Detroit newspaper on behalf of immigrants to the St. Joseph country. Directed to "our well-fed neighbors in Indiana and Ohio," it implored them to "Send a few thousand hogs . . . into these parts, and take away some of our hard dollars."[83]

The provisions market in Lower Michigan created a structure of centralized exchange that defined the form of the regional economy. Nucleated settlements served as points of exchange for their surrounding areas and drew distant travelers to procure provisions. The most important regional market was Detroit. "The market for country produce in Detroit is always high," wrote Estwick Evans in 1819, "and large sums of money are annually paid there for provisions." As Michigan's entrepôt, it was a principal source of foodstuffs for newly arrived settlers. William Clark, who moved to Livingston County in 1837, recalled that, "Almost everything . . . pork, beef, flour, etc., had to be brought from Detroit, at a cost of one to two dollars a hundred to Brighton, forty miles." Even with "an energetic teamster and an enterprising team," the round trip to Detroit "usually took three to four days if not longer." Settlements, such as Tecumseh, Ann Arbor, and Pontiac, arose in central locations in the interior transportation network to become points of exchange for regional produce and sources for imported finished goods.[84]

The substantial distances involved in reaching central settlements and the difficulties of travel led settlers to find alternative modes of trade. Exchanges between producers and consumers were the simplest arrangement. In his travels through Michigan in the early 1840s, William Thompson observed that throughout much of the interior, "There are no great fairs or . . . markets. . . . It is a general rule, both in agriculture and mercantile business, that those who wish to buy, look out for and call on those who wish to sell." E. Clark, an early settler in western Washtenaw County, recalled that "before we had facilities for transporting produce to market, . . . it was the object to induce emigrants to come among us to settle. They made a home market for the surplus provisions and stock we had to spare."[85]

Farmers also transported their foodstuffs to convenient locations in areas undergoing settlement. In 1838, for example, George Thurston and several other residents of Sturgis Prairie in St. Joseph County drove wagons loaded with produce to the rapids of the Grand River with the intent of selling produce to immigrants just entering this newly opened territory. Although Thurston's party met with mixed success, farmers in Allegan and Ottawa Counties found a lucrative market for their produce following the mass movement of Dutch settlers to the mouth of the Black River in the 1840s.[86]

Frontier conditions in Michigan created a regional economy characterized by diversified household production and regional consumption, still largely isolated from national markets. Nowhere was the impact of this economy as evident as in the nature of farming. "It must be concluded," wrote the editor of the *Michigan Farmer* in 1845,

> that farming . . . has been, by no means a money-making pursuit. Indeed, the assertion is often
> made that a farm, well broken, fenced, and stocked, and with suitable buildings erected, a man

cannot hire his labor, and obtain anything like simple interest on the amount of capital invested.[87]

The nature of frontier agriculture reflected adjustments by settlers to current restraints on the nature and scale of production, but not Michigan's potential for commercial agriculture.

Farmers did not immigrate to Michigan to avoid the larger national economy or remain cut off from their parent society. Pioneers intended to enter commercial production as soon as it became feasible, but in the meantime developed an efficient strategy of diversified production and regional trade that established a production base and supported growth until they gained access to external markets. The requirements of the frontier economy, however, restricted the size and scope of production and limited the expansion of agriculture. The demands of regional markets determined the amount of production and also affected the nature of frontier exchange.[88]

Regional exchange served to achieve a "communal self-sufficiency" among frontier households rather than to maximize return on investment. This economic arrangement offered security because it ensured farmers a reliable supply of food at fixed production costs.[89] It provided "a safe, comfortable, independent living, even in the worst of times." Lenawee County pioneer Alanson Bang's characterization of Monroe as a place to sell farm produce as well as to "purchase the food necessary for the sustenance of life" reveals the symbiotic nature of the foodstuffs trade in the regional economy.[90]

Regional trade in Michigan depended upon establishing standard values for products exchanged. In an economy characterized by production based on need, a product's use determined its worth. By comparing recognized use values for specific products, pioneers developed a system of equivalencies that facilitated trade. They always expressed the values of crops or other farm products in dollar amounts. These monetary values standardized equivalencies for products and services and, even in the absence of actual cash, provided a framework in which exchange could be conducted in a systematic manner.[91]

References to the cash values of particular items appear frequently in contemporary accounts. For example, the fixed value of shingles in Kalamazoo permitted one resident there to use them to make regular payments on a tract of land. Similarly, a Marshall newspaper noted that the assignment of standard prices to wheat permitted a considerable amount of trade for merchandise with very little specie changing hands. The pervasiveness of barter by equivalency is evidenced in a letter written by an Eaton County immigrant to an eastern relative. "I had a good crop of wheat this summer, but it will not sell for cash at all," he lamented. "It is worth only three shillings [37¢] in barter. . . . It is a hard case to git [sic] cash to pay our taxes in this state and intirely [sic] out of the case to collect a det [sic] unless in taking property in exchange." Although cash itself did not frequently change hands in frontier Michigan, it provided a constant standard by which to balance the myriad exchanges that took place in its regional economy.[92]

Berrien County pioneer Henry Chamberlain left a detailed account of exchange in southwestern Michigan in the 1840s. He characterized the economy as one in which "Transportation was difficult and expensive and . . . it was of importance that all the necessities of life should, as far as possible, be purchased or manufactured in the vicinity." In addition to goods and services intended for household use, Chamberlain recalled that additional quantities were produced for exchange. He described how women spun flax into thread, and wove it into fabric for their families "or exchanged [it] for goods." Likewise, "socks, stockings, and drawers were knit and frockings and flannels were woven for domestic purposes or exchanged for other articles. . . . These male and female weavers went from house to house to weave the woollen and linen clothes." Millers and other specialists offered their services for a share of the product. "The tanner and currier took from the farmer the hides and skins of his cattle and returned half of the leather," Chamberlain wrote, and "the work at saw mills was done in consideration of a share of the lumber produced from the logs furnished by the customer."[93]

Others with special skills, however, exchanged their products and services for foodstuffs or labor, especially people who did this on a full-time basis. Alvah Brainerd recalled how he and most other Grand Blanc Township pioneers paid for the services of a local carding mill in produce, "which was better again to us than having to pay money. Labor debts were commonly used to compensate craftsmen who were also farmers. Henry Chamberlain mentioned masons and carpenters who performed work during the off-season for which they would be repaid in kind during planting and harvest. Edward Parsons of Oakland County, for example, worked off his debt to a blacksmith by cutting marsh hay and cradling oats in exchange for repairs made on his wagon.[94]

Occasionally a group of people contributed labor toward the completion of facilities that benefited all of them. Such was the case in southern Berrien County in the fall of 1844 when Asa A. Jacobs, a miller from Ohio, built a sawmill in Three Oaks Township. Although Jacobs owned only the mill site itself, his neighbors desired his services badly enough to erect the mill structure and advance him supplies in return for sawing their lumber when it was completed. Similarly, Thomas Chandler participated in a sawmill raising near Adrian as part of a communal effort to build a mill in central Lenawee County.[95]

Labor exchange also extended to production. Frontier barn raisings were almost legendary. Carried out to reduce the costs of farm-making, this communal activity diffused the burden of making capital improvements by spreading it among the residents of an area. Elizabeth Chandler commented that "These raisings are quite a tax upon the time in a new settlement," but admitted, "these are things that cannot very well be done without." Despite the sacrifice involved, raisings helped to establish a production base that was beneficial to pioneer farmers.[96]

Another common form of labor exchange involved trading regular farm work. This helped farmers avoid high expenditures during labor-intensive times in the agricultural cycle. Such arrangements benefited the immigrant farmer with few resources, because his labor was equal in value to that of any other member of the group. "As far as getting his grain out is concerned," wrote William T. Kirkland, "he is no worse off than the richest man in the neighborhood." Communal labor also helped alleviate the chronic labor shortage encountered in newly settled areas. Writing of her brother's agreement to share labor, Elizabeth Chandler emphasized not only the cost savings it provided, but also the assurance that labor would be available when needed.[97]

Pioneers also exchanged the use of tools and other implements associated with manufacture, repair, or specialized activities. One settler recalled that "Borrowing sometimes, was the very means that helped [him] out of difficulty and set his enterprise along again. Everyone borrowed and everyone lent; and by it business was kept prosperous and suffering often avoided." For the most part, borrowing was necessitated by availability. Describing the custom in the East, immigrant Thomas Wright wrote, "When I wanted a tool I went and bought, for I laid down as a first principle that I would neither borrow or lend tools for carrying on my business." Upon his arrival in Oakland County, however, he soon discovered that "[tools] were not to be bought and I was, contrary to my rule, compelled to borrow." The compulsion to borrow and the propensity for individuals to lend was supported by an ethos of equality in which items of general use became communal property regardless of their ownership. Such values seemed onerous to Caroline Kirkland, whose relative wealth set her household apart from those of other pioneer families in Livingston County. Her experience at Pinckney soon taught her that "A store of anything, however simple or necessary, is . . . a subject of reproach, if you decline supplying whomsoever may be deficient." Despite her disapproval, the sharing of artifacts, like that of labor, proved an adaptive response to a situation characterized by scarce resources, and insured the completion of activities crucial to establishing a production base.[98]

The shortage of cash also discouraged the accumulation and investment of capital wealth in Michigan's frontier economy because production based on need and exchange linked to use values mitigated the accrual of substantial debts and profits. Although transactions did not always compensate all parties fairly, and people benefited unequally from them, the excesses derived from such exchanges could not be immediately converted to cash, and the incentive for accumulation remained much lower than in places with outlets for surplus production.

Michigan's initial settlers complained universally about the scarcity of cash. "In the good old days of Michigan," Alvah Brainard recalled, "there was not any money to speak of floating around from hand to hand." "Money indeed hardly exists in this western country," wrote Sylvester Cochrane in 1840. In his two and one-half years of work as a Presbyterian minister in Michigan he had received "but one five dollar bill for ministerial services." The Reverend Cochrane's plight was shared by most pioneer residents. Adrian furniture-maker C. B. Stebbins recalled that his firm "made and sold $3,000 worth of furniture in 1844, on account of which but $130 in money passed through our hands," and merchant Moses Chamberlain observed that farmers had difficulty "selling anything for money in this country."[99]

The shortage of cash stemmed largely from the low volume of outside sales by frontier producers. The amount of cash received was always far less than that which flowed out of the region for land purchases and purchases of imported items. "There was but little money to spend among our settlers after they had paid for their lands, bought their teams and stock, built their log houses, and made such improvements as the scant time left after this was accomplished would allow," wrote M. Shoemaker of Jackson. So acute was the shortage of cash that periodic influxes of specie were seen as windfalls by local residents. The distribution of Indian annuities or the arrival of a large number of immigrants, such as the Dutch on the Western Shore in the late 1840s, provided irregular but necessary additions of this medium to the frontier economy.[100]

Although cash was the only medium flexible enough to balance accounts of transactions, its scarcity restricted its actual use in frontier Michigan. When it was necessary, pioneers minimized the amount needed to close a deal. Early Grand Rapids resident John Ball recalled that a contemporary, Judge Morrison, prided himself in the fact "that in building a pretty good house he paid out but one dollar," adding that, like many other transactions, the work was largely arranged "by exchange or 'dicker.'"[101]

The use of cash to continually balance transactions further precluded the accumulation of funds and relegated the function of cash to that of a unit of exchange rather than one of investment. As such, cash was not distinguished from other items exchanged, a condition reflected in an exchange proposal made by a Springwells Township resident to her cousin in Royal Oak. Seeking to acquire a quantity of pork, she offered to trade him and his neighbors cloth, adding that if any differences in the value of these items could not be resolved, they could be made up "in money."[102]

The regional economy of antebellum Michigan was an impermanent condition that represented an adaptive response by pioneer producers to geographical isolation, the incomplete development of agriculture, and restricted transportation within the area of colonization. The nature of production and exchange, and particularly the role of money, affected the form of the frontier economy and imposed limitations on Michigan's pioneer residents. Economic organization was also manifested in the patterning of pioneer activities during the time of Michigan's occupation and the distribution of its population, the form and growth of regional transportation, and the hierarchical structure of settlements all developed in response to conditions arising from the frontier economy. These combined to create a landscape of colonization.

Frontier production and exchange laid the foundation for Michigan's integration within the larger national economy. They established the region as a potential producer of valuable agricultural commodities as well as a vast market for finished industrial goods. Michigan's transition to a commercial economy could not occur until its agricultural base was sufficiently developed to attract the outside investment necessary to create adequate transportation and communications systems linking the region to national markets and build a new infrastructure to support large-scale production.[103]

9

Population Expansion, Transportation, and Settlement Patterning on the Michigan Frontier, 1845–1860

By the mid–1840s, the distribution, interconnectedness, and function of Michigan's settlements constituted a cultural landscape that marked the culmination of the region's frontier development and formed the basis for its growth as a commercial region. This settlement patterning exhibited broad characteristics common to agricultural frontier regions, yet factors particular to the time and place of its colonization also affected its form, direction, and sequence of expansion. Pioneer perceptions of the environment, the nature of land acquisition and distribution, the nature of production and exchange in the context of an evolving frontier, and the strategies of colonization employed by its settlers all worked to create a distinctive landscape.

Settlement patterning in Michigan between 1815 and 1845 may be observed in several ways. First, a series of maps based on a spatial analysis of the particular factors discussed in the previous chapters can provide an accurate estimate of settlement spread across the region. Employing a Geographic Information System (GIS) permits the simultaneous analyses of multiple categories of data necessary to construct these images. Next, the actual distribution of individual settlements over time may be discerned from their sequential appearance, evidenced here by the establishment of post offices on the frontier. Patterns of settlement interconnections, evidenced by the form of the evolving transportation network, can reveal the organization of production and marketing in early Michigan. Finally, an analysis of settlement content will permit us to identify the function of inhabited places in the region. Michigan's economy was organized around frontier towns that also served as the principal social and political centers. Smaller, less complex nucleated and seminucleated settlements performed fewer of these tasks and served as secondary centers of activity. The distinctive roles of these two types of settlements should provide the key to the hierarchical structure of Michigan's frontier economy.

ESTIMATING THE EXPANSION OF POPULATION

A flood tide of immigration overran Lower Michigan, occupying much of the region by 1845. The movement and changing distribution of its pioneer population are the keys to observing the overall form of settlement. Tracing the historical distribution of Michigan's population is complicated by an absence of contemporary sources portraying actual land occupancy. Settlement spread may be estimated, however, by analyzing Lower Michigan as a colonial agricultural region whose occupation

FIGURE 9.1. *ESTIMATED SPREAD OF SETTLEMENT THROUGH 1818.* (Sources: see text).

was influenced by the distinctive conditions examined in the previous chapters. This task must consider the relative significance of these variables and the changing role that some played over time. For example, environmental perception was far more important to pioneer land evaluation for farm location than was the distribution of Native peoples. Nonetheless, images of Indians' willingness to help or hinder immigrants both deterred and encouraged settlement in different parts of Michigan.

The complex task of comparing all of the variables involved in settlement patterning to create a graphic portrayal of settlement over time is facilitated by employing a Geographic Information System (GIS). This computer-based methodology utilizes programs designed to conduct simultaneous spatial analyses of multiple classes of data, such as vegetation, watercourse, and roads, and permits their spatial relationships to be portrayed in graphic form. A GIS analyzed particular variables to generate accurate maps of settlement growth in Michigan at intervals throughout the frontier period.[1]

Figure 9.1 shows the confined distribution of Michigan's nonaboriginal population at the close of the War of 1812. Occupying enclaves along the Detroit River and an initial interior pocket in Oakland County, early immigrant settlements remained concentrated around Detroit and the smaller ports of Monroe and Mt. Clemens; however, favorable reports prompted inland expansion into newly opened lands northwest of Detroit.

Between 1819 and 1823, a rapid expansion of settlement occupied available lands in the southern part of Michigan west of Detroit and Monroe. The attractiveness of the interior

FIGURE **9.2.** *ESTIMATED SPREAD OF SETTLEMENT FROM 1819 THROUGH 1823.* (Sources: see text).

environment, the ease of access from the two ports, the opening of a second land office at Monroe, and the absence of hostile Native peoples all encouraged this growth. In contrast, perceptions of poorer environments, a large, resentful Native population, and difficult access discouraged expansion in the north into lands south of Saginaw Bay (fig. 9.2).

By the mid–1820s, tracts of wet forestlands were in market north of Detroit and south of Saginaw Bay. Their perceived unsuitability for agriculture and the proximity of the latter to the Chippewa reserves on Cass River prevented them from being settled immediately. Open lands and dry forests in Lapeer County lay adjacent to settlement in Oakland County and would have drawn settlement in spite of an absence of roads.

A large block of open lands lying in Oakland, Livingston, and Shiawassee Counties was made available in 1824. Situated adjacent to lands already undergoing settlement, the opening of this region encouraged movement into the central portion of the peninsula. The presence of extensive forests on the Grand River drainage encouraged immigrants to seek out the more easily cultivated lands available on the upper Shiawassee drainage. The region was linked to Detroit by trails, and the upper Shiawassee and Looking Glass Rivers also provided desirable waterpower sites. Further south, the availability of extensive open lands in Oakland, Livingston, Washtenaw, Lenawee, and Hillsdale Counties extended settlement west of the Principal Meridian. The area's easily cleared openings and abundant hydraulic power enhanced the image of the southern peninsula and turned the flow of settlement away from the adjacent timberlands (fig. 9.3).[2]

Key
Unsuitable Lands

Suitable Lands

Not Open to Settlement

FIGURE 9.3. *ESTIMATED SPREAD OF SETTLEMENT FROM 1824 THROUGH 1826.* (Sources: see text).

By the late 1820s, the amount of available land had grown substantially, to include portions of territory acquired in the 1819 and 1821 treaties. This included open and forested lands in the upper Grand drainage, but perceptions of these land types encouraged immigrants to settle north and south of the forested zone. Movement was facilitated by roads extending from Detroit to Pontiac and Ann Arbor, though a lack of access into the forested zone further deterred its early occupation.

Open land and prairie land in the southern counties were magnets for the western settlement. The newly opened Chicago Road and the St. Joseph River, emptying into Lake Michigan, facilitated regional development. The presence of the Potawatomis, and their role in the regional frontier economy, further encouraged settlement. Although the substantial distance between western lands and the administering land office in Monroe deterred some land purchasers, their absence was tempered by an increase in squatting. Encouraged by national preemption legislation in 1830, squatters occupied lands in Michigan prior to their sale and hastened the movement of immigrants onto desirable lands in the southwest. As the legal status of preemption became more secure, its practice encouraged the spread of settlement on such highly regarded lands. As a result, pioneer population momentarily skipped over less well-perceived environments (fig. 9.4).[3]

During the early 1830s, the remaining lands acquired in the 1819 and 1821 treaties were opened to settlement. Perceptions of the land and its accessibility to immigrants guided expansion. Settlement gravitated toward the openings and prairies and remained heaviest in the

Key
Unsuitable Lands
Suitable Lands
Not Open to Settlement

FIGURE 9.4. *ESTIMATED SPREAD OF SETTLEMENT FROM 1827 THROUGH 1830.* (Sources: see text).

southern and central portions of the region, through which roads in the southern row of counties and the Kalamazoo drainage passed. A third immigration route extended into the Grand River drainage and afforded access to the open lands of the Thornapple Valley.

The creation of the Western land district in 1831 facilitated settlement in western Michigan; however, as desirable open lands filled, purchasers and squatters turned to the interior forests. The impending expansion of the public domain encouraged further expansion into this region, portions of which were still unceded. Access to the central timberlands by the Grand River Road now channeled immigration directly into the interior following the tongue of open land that penetrated the forested zone. The rise of absentee speculation that accompanied the Michigan land boom of the 1830s affected settlement distribution on these lands. Although the practice promoted settlement, the Panic of 1837 left many unsold and unoccupied tracts out of market, resulting in an uneven distribution of settlement in open and timbered lands. Despite the opening of overland routes to Saginaw and several of the Indian reserves, poorly developed roads made the southern Thumb and adjacent lands inaccessible to immigrants. Negative perceptions of the environment and the persistence of a substantial resident aboriginal population also continued to discourage settlement, and lands here sold slowly (fig. 9.5).[4]

With the Ottawa cession of 1836, the public domain of Michigan expanded to include all of the Lower Peninsula. Within a year, the federal government acquired title to nearly all Indian reserves created by previous treaties. This affected settlement by opening a tremendous tract of

FIGURE 9.5. *ESTIMATED SPREAD OF SETTLEMENT FROM 1831 THROUGH 1835.* (Sources: see text).

dry forested land north of the Grand River and removing the Native occupants of the Saginaw Valley. Additional factors also modified the impact of these changes.

Lands placed in market by 1840 extended as far as the perceived northern limit of agriculture, and by mid-century the remainder of the Lower Peninsula had been surveyed and brought into market. In the lower Saginaw drainage, perceptual barriers still deterred settlement, and the complicated alienation of state lands left many areas north of the Grand River unoccupied. Although the creation of two new land districts facilitated northern immigration, the lack of access to older settled parts of Michigan from these regions resulted in only marginal expansion in the north by the 1840s. Even the Lake Michigan shoreline, now seen as valuable for agriculture, was not immediately settled. Elsewhere, however, roads extended across the peninsula, through the central timberlands, and penetrated the Kalamazoo drainage and Grand River drainages. By 1840, American settlement covered nearly all of Lower Michigan, and frontier expansion was almost complete in this region (figure 9.6).[5]

The contours shown on these maps constitute an accurate estimate of the spread of Michigan's immigrant population. These patterns are large-scale, however, and do not reveal either relative population density or settlement distribution across southern Michigan, or changes in either over time. Such information may be obtained by comparing other types of data pertaining to the distribution of population between 1815 and 1845.

FIGURE 9.6. *ESTIMATED SPREAD OF SETTLEMENT IN 1836 AND AFTERWARD.* (Sources: see text).

EVIDENCE FOR SETTLEMENT DISTRIBUTION IN FRONTIER MICHIGAN

At first glance, the expansion of frontier settlement in Michigan appears to have been a straightforward phenomenon, in which areas were occupied in the order just described. Although documentary sources reveal the sequence in which land came into market and was sold, they provide little direct evidence regarding when it was actually occupied or the density of its settlement. Available records are incapable of showing the spatial arrangement of settlement on a small scale, and shed little light on the formation of frontier communities. The absence of direct evidence, however, does not preclude the investigation of these questions. Rather, it requires that we examine other variables capable of yielding information about the origin and distribution of frontier settlement.[6]

The appearance of post offices accompanied the extension of the agricultural frontier in Michigan, and the sequence of their appearance reveals the distribution of settlement. Hundreds of post offices were established in Michigan before 1845, and their placement provides the key to the movement and distribution of agricultural settlement. Mail service was integral to the social and economic integration of newly occupied regions. The flow of mail and the information and materials it contained linked settlements in Michigan with one another and with the East. The federal government established post offices at convenient central locations where patrons delivered and picked up their parcels and letters. In rural areas without nucleated settlements, the post office occupied the local postmaster's house, which was centrally located within the area it served. Because people traveled by foot or horse-drawn vehicles, the radius of travel to each office was limited and their locations marked the foci of dispersed pioneer populations. As new areas were settled, pioneer residents, eager to maintain social as well as economic ties with correspondents in the East, demanded access to postal service. Since post offices had to be moved and additional ones created as population expanded, their locations and dates of appearance are good indicators of population spread and distribution in Lower Michigan. Outside of the agricultural frontier, post offices appeared only in widely separated central settlements, such as the lumber port of Muskegon in western Michigan. These few dispersed post offices served the often-transient extractive activities of the northern interior, and their distribution mirrored the structure of those industries.[7]

Tracing the changing distribution of Michigan's antebellum population by post office establishment dates offers advantages over using other types of data. County census figures provide the only evidence of population growth by comparable geographical units. Although they reveal expansion and gross changes in population density, the relatively large scale on which they measure change obscures details of settlement disposition within them. This is complicated further by the fact that many counties initially administered areas much larger than their final boundaries. Relying on counties also ignores settlement beyond the bounds of these organized political units. Documenting the edge of pioneer settlement is crucial to observing the spatial patterning of frontier population spread, and the inability of county census data to do so seriously limits its usefulness here. Overall, these figures provide only a general idea of settlement distribution and density over time.[8]

Another potential measure of settlement distribution is the appearance of civil townships. As the smallest units of political and administrative organization, each township offered services for the inhabitants of a six-mile square surveyed area. Because townships came into existence when the need for services arose, their appearance followed colonization. On the frontier, civil townships often preceded county organization, and the sequence of their creation indicates the direction of initial population spread. They often encompassed large areas of widely dispersed settlement, however, the actual form and extent of size of which is obscured, making it difficult to calculate changes in population density over time. These shortcomings restrict the usefulness of employing civil township formation data to observe settlement distribution in frontier Michigan.[9]

Post office locations present perhaps the most complete picture of frontier settlement distribution in Michigan. Changes in the patterning and density of their locations should reveal the form and direction of expansion and provide clues to the nature of regional economic organization. Six maps show the distribution of post offices in southern Lower Michigan between 1815 and 1845.[10]

Immediately following the War of 1812, post offices along the Eastern Shore marked the limited geographical concentration of the early American occupation around areas of established

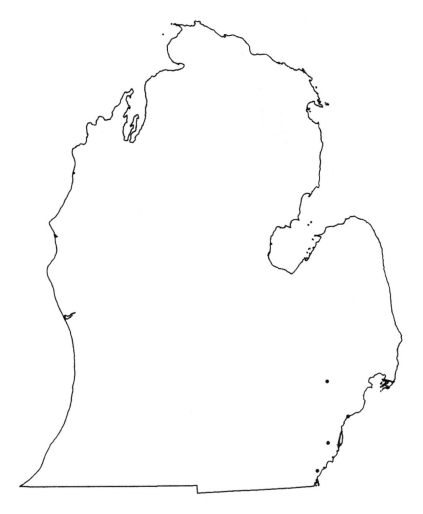

FIGURE 9.7. *DISTRIBUTION OF LOWER MICHIGAN POST OFFICES IN OPERATION IN 1820.* (Source: Ellis, *Michigan Postal History*).

French settlement. Two additional offices marked the beginnings of expansion along the Eastern Shore and the occupation of newly opened interior lands in Oakland County (fig. 9.7).[11]

The expansion of interior settlement between 1820 and 1825 reveals movement into the dry woodlands beyond the wet forest zone. It clustered in eastern Oakland and western Macomb Counties around Pontiac, west of Detroit in the vicinity of Ann Arbor, and in western Monroe and eastern Lenawee Counties as far west as Tecumseh. New post offices attest to continued growth of population along the eastern lakeshore. The larger concentration of post offices around Pontiac reveals rapid growth in the oldest focus of interior settlement (fig. 9.8).[12]

FIGURE 9.8. *DISTRIBUTION OF LOWER MICHIGAN POST OFFICES IN OPERATION FROM 1821 THROUGH 1825.* (Source: Ellis, *Michigan Postal History*).

In the second half of the 1820s, settlement expanded southwestward onto the newly opened old Potawatomi lands as far as Lake Michigan. Post offices appeared in the southern counties following the belt of open lands and farther north in Washtenaw and Jackson Counties as far as the Principal Meridian. Their widely dispersed and uneven placement reveals that settlement was concentrated in the southwestern part of the territory. In eastern Michigan the inland settlement expanded just inland of the wet forests, forming a nearly continuous occupation from Macomb to Lenawee and Monroe Counties. Settlement had yet to penetrate the extensive wooded lands of the Saginaw drainage, and the post office at Grand Blanc marked its northward extent in the territory. On the eve of its period of peak

FIGURE 9.9. *DISTRIBUTION OF LOWER MICHIGAN POST OFFICES IN OPERATION FROM 1826 THROUGH 1830*. (Source: Ellis, *Michigan Postal History*).

immigration, Michigan's population had just begun to venture into the region's interior. Settlement on the Eastern Shore remained concentrated along the shoreline near the mouths of major rivers, with scattered extractive activities to the north along the St. Clair River (fig. 9.9).[13]

Between 1830 and 1835, settlement expanded westward throughout the open lands of the lower two rows of counties, concentrated along the two principal overland routes and the territory between them. In the east, settlement increased in intensity and expanded into the dry forests and open lands as far west as Genesee and Livingston Counties. Isolated settlements at the mouths of the Kalamazoo and Grand Rivers and at Saginaw mark the appearance of

FIGURE 9.10. *DISTRIBUTION OF LOWER MICHIGAN POST OFFICES IN OPERATION FROM 1831 THROUGH 1835.* (Source: Ellis, *Michigan Postal History*).

riverine centers of lumbering in western Michigan and the Saginaw Valley. Industrial activities frequently dominated settlement in poorly perceived environments (fig. 9.10).

The final half of the 1830s brought noticeable changes in the distribution of settlement, which exhibited an intensive and much more evenly spaced distribution in the eastern and southern counties as well as an expansion north of the Kalamazoo drainage, along the Grand and Thornapple Rivers, and into the upper Saginaw Valley. This patterning reveals a general movement away from heavily occupied open lands into the adjacent forested environments. Movement from a number of directions into the central timberlands resulted in an uneven occupation. By 1840, settlement was concentrated along the lower Grand River in Ionia and

FIGURE 9.11. *DISTRIBUTION OF LOWER MICHIGAN POST OFFICES IN OPERATION FROM 1836 THROUGH 1840*. (Source: Ellis, *Michigan Postal History*).

Kent Counties, but had yet to expand into available lands further north. No extensive tracts of vacant lands remained in the central timberlands. Agricultural settlement still avoided the Western Shore and the Saginaw drainage generally, but began to intrude on their peripheries. Despite the availability of lands, colonization had yet to extend north of Grand River. It also avoided the Thumb region and was sporadic in western Michigan and the lower Saginaw Valley (fig. 9.11).[14]

Figure 9.12 reveals that the area of American settlement in Michigan remained roughly the same between 1840 and 1845. Its distribution became more evenly spaced across the region as vacant areas were filled, particularly in the central timberlands as well as in the older settled

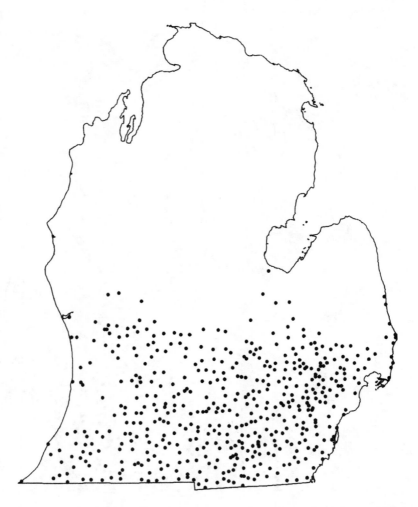

FIGURE 9.12. *DISTRIBUTION OF LOWER MICHIGAN POST OFFICES IN OPERATION FROM 1841 THROUGH 1845.* (Source: Ellis, *Michigan Postal History*).

areas of the southern and eastern counties. Greater density of settlement in longer-settled areas reveals an intensification of agricultural production and infrastructure development marking the beginning of a shift in the frontier economy from regional to export production. Expanding settlement in the wet forests of the Eastern Shore implies that a need to increase production justified the use of these heretofore avoided lands. Agricultural settlement was still largely absent along much of the Western Shore, and did not extend far north of the Grand River.

The locations of post offices in frontier Michigan reveal a pattern of settlement distribution similar to that indicated earlier for population spread. The direction and density of colonization independently corroborate the importance of the factors employed to estimate regional expansion and indicate that both regional conditions and the insular frontier process influenced settlement patterning. Settlement distribution was important in shaping Michigan's colonial landscape because it formed the framework upon which the infrastructure of production and transportation was developed. The survival and success of frontier settlements depended on a transportation network that provided the linkages necessary for regional economic interaction. Trade and communications bound together settlements and provided access to markets. The form of the network also determined a settlement's role in the regional economic hierarchy. Frontier Michigan was bound together by a network of regional exchange, the form and composition of which shaped the second element of settlement patterning on this transitional landscape.

THE DEVELOPMENT OF ROADS IN A FRONTIER ECONOMY

The mid–1840s marked the zenith of Michigan's regional economy, the organization of which created a landscape shaped by the adaptation of agriculture to the peripheral position of the frontier economy. A network of roads evolved that followed the distribution of interior settlement, and its configuration mirrored the spatial organization of the economy and its supporting infrastructure. Because the positions of settlements in this transportation network were linked directly to their functions, the layout of roads often determined the roles of individual settlements in the regional economic hierarchy. Network changes that accompanied the growth of the frontier economy also witnessed changes in the roles of frontier settlements. Settlement interconnectedness was an important aspect of initial settlement patterning in frontier Michigan and is the key to understanding the organization of its landscape.

Successful colonization in Michigan depended on the creation of a transportation infrastructure that allowed pioneers access to frontier lands and facilitated the establishment of regional exchange necessary to sustain them. Roads offered the advantages of flexibility, ease of construction, and low cost, all of which suited them to the needs of a rapidly growing region. Although unimproved roads could not accommodate heavy, bulky cargoes shipped over the long distances necessary for external trade, they were ideal for short-distance transportation in a region with limited resources. Roads were well adapted to serving Michigan's regional economy.

The transportation system of frontier Michigan included two types of roads; each met different needs. The network of central roads facilitated immigration and administration, tasks that required the most efficient communications between Detroit and outlying regions. The necessity of working with scarce resources favored a network with the fewest number of links, one that took on the classic dendritic form associated with agricultural colonization. The configuration of the central road network took advantage of the extensive network of long-distance Indian trails employed in the fur trade period. These provided access to lands along all major river drainages in Lower Michigan and were found suitable for improvement into roads capable of handling wheeled traffic. The network also facilitated administration of the frontier. A central network alone, however, could not bring about regional economic development (fig. 9.13).[15]

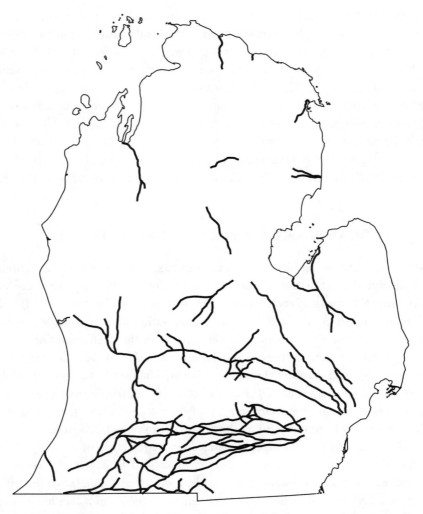

FIGURE 9.13. *THE NETWORK OF INDIAN TRAILS IN LOWER MICHIGAN.* (Source: Comer et al., *Michigan's Native Landscape*).

The need for exchange organized around internal markets necessitated the construction of a regional transportation network linking settlements dispersed over an expanding region. This required an optimal number of direct ties between producers and consumers located at many points. Building regional roads required a massive investment in construction at a time when financial resources were limited. As a result, a network of unimproved and poorly maintained roads developed, often consisting of circuitous point-to-point routes and frequently incorporating existing Indian trails.[16]

Regional road networks extended outward to reach lands farther from the central road corridors but did not develop in a systematic manner and often constituted an irregular system

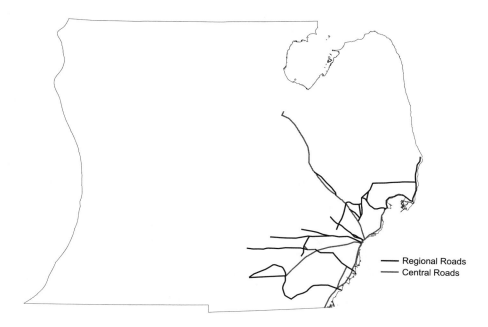

FIGURE 9.14. *THE TRANSPORTATION NETWORK IN SOUTHERN MICHIGAN IN 1826.* (Sources: see text).

whose form traces the growth of Michigan's frontier economy. These road networks may be reconstructed by examining a variety of early sources. Contemporary immigrant guide maps, continually updated during the settlement period, provide detailed, large-scale depictions of the region. Other sources include large-scale county maps published by the state geological survey, surveyors' plats of road surveys, postal routes, and pioneer accounts of travel and trade. Michigan maps were drawn to high professional standards, making them valuable sources for road and settlement data. A series of maps traces the growth of Michigan's transportation network from 1815 to 1845 and reveals this network's evolving role in the settlement landscape.[17]

Michigan's routes of overland transportation followed early frontier growth closely. Prior to the War of 1812, roads linked Detroit and Frenchtown (Monroe) with Cincinnati, Cleveland, and points in the East. Following the war, roads expanded along the Eastern Shore and penetrated inland to Oakland County and the Saginaw country. John Farmer's first comprehensive immigrant map, issued in 1826, revealed internal networks in southern Oakland and western Macomb Counties, as well as in eastern Washtenaw and Lenawee Counties. These linked settlements and provided access to areas between the central routes leading from Detroit. The intensity of inland route development formed a basis for the integration of settlement on the interior open lands (fig. 9.14).[18]

By the close of the 1820s, Michigan's road network had expanded to accommodate the opening of lands in the southwest and the growth of pioneer settlement in previously opened

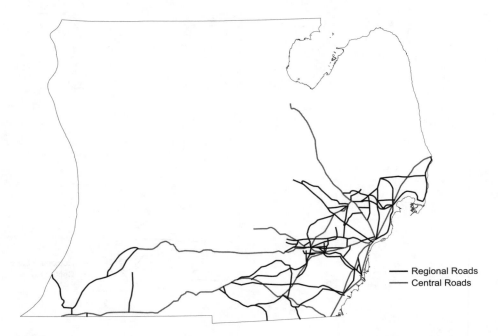

FIGURE 9.15. *THE TRANSPORTATION NETWORK IN SOUTHERN MICHIGAN IN 1830.* (Sources: see text).

areas. The central road network extended across the southern two tiers of counties, and regional roads linked Pontiac and Ann Arbor and provided access between the Lake Erie shoreline and points along the major rivers of the Eastern Shore. The appearance of secondary roads in the dry forests and open lands undergoing intensive settlement marked a significant expansion of the regional network to provide the transportation access necessary for the emergence of regional trade. The number of roads linking Michigan with surrounding states also increased, providing Michigan farmers with access to Ft. Wayne and the country south and west of Lake Michigan, as well as to the Maumee River settlements in Ohio (fig. 9.15).[19]

Michigan's road system of 1836 reveals uneven development. The first half of the decade witnessed the expansion of the central road network with the opening of a northern route as far as Grand Rapids, the extension of the Territorial road westward to Lake Michigan, the completion of roads to the mouth of the Saginaw River and the lower Thumb region, and the beginning of a second route to the upper Grand drainage. The western roads provided direct access from Detroit to the lower drainages of the Kalamazoo and Grand Rivers and encouraged immigration toward the central woodlands. Roads in eastern Michigan attempted to encourage movement into areas that had previously attracted few settlers. New road networks expanded throughout the region in response to new settlement. Complex systems at the rapids of Grand River expanded south into the Thornapple Valley, and in southwestern Michigan road networks grew extensively in many counties (fig. 9.16).[20]

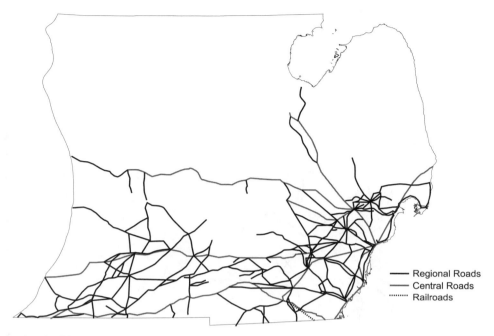

FIGURE 9.16. *THE TRANSPORTATION NETWORK IN SOUTHERN MICHIGAN IN 1836.* (Sources: see text).

An increase in the number of roads to Indiana indicated emerging ties between regional economies in western Michigan and its neighboring state as well as the development of the St. Joseph River as an inland transportation route. This waterway offered an outlet on Lake Michigan as well as a connection between Michigan and Indiana settlements along its route. In 1836 a railroad linking southeastern Michigan with the Ohio port of Toledo also served as a regional trade conduit.[21]

Between 1835 and 1840 the central road network expanded and existing regional networks grew. The extension of the government road into the central timberlands allowed access to the Grand River drainage as far as Grand Rapids, but the newly opened area had yet to develop a regional network. Networks expanded elsewhere in the central timberlands, particularly along its southern periphery, and in the Saginaw valley, connecting its settlements with the Grand River country and the southern Thumb region. In western Michigan, regional networks now extended along the Western Shore, but avoided areas of nonagricultural production, such as the lower Grand Valley (fig. 9.17).[22]

The expansion of regional road networks accompanied population growth and density, and the increasing complexity of the regional networks testifies to an intensification of transportation activity between interior settlements. Roads to Indiana and Ohio attest to the increasing integration of frontier Michigan with the economies of neighboring states. Although railroads were constructed by 1840, these small and geographically isolated lines did not alter the structure of regional transportation. Early railroads, for the most part, augmented

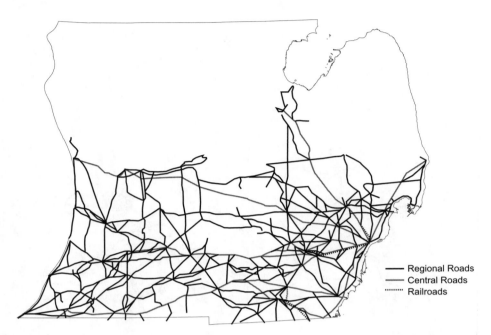

FIGURE 9.17. *THE TRANSPORTATION NETWORK IN SOUTHERN MICHIGAN IN 1840.* (Sources: see text).

the central road network, conveying immigrants inland and carrying goods and information along established routes. Only after mid-century, when forged into larger interstate systems, did they play a key role in expanding commercial export trade.[23]

The early 1840s saw the consolidation of overland transportation in Lower Michigan. The central road network's completion permitted immigrants access to all areas of settlement, and regional networks filled in places previously bypassed. The completion of the southern Grand River Road encouraged the growth of regional road networks in the upper Grand drainage, and the northern Grand River Road continued to serve as a basis for route development on the northern edge of settlement. Further east, road networks in the Grand and Saginaw drainages and the lower Thumb region began to merge. In western Michigan, however, regional roads followed the Grand and Kalamazoo river corridors as settlers continued to avoid the lakeshore. To the north, lengthy routes to distant points and an absence of ancillary road networks marked the growth of specialized lumber milling activity in Newaygo and Montcalm Counties as well as in the Thumb counties of Tuscola and Sanilac (fig. 9.18).[24]

Michigan's railroads expanded into the peninsula's interior, but their routes remained incomplete in 1845. Although they moved goods and people with increasing efficiency, their transportation potential could not be realized as long as they constituted an unconsolidated system. Their growth, however, created an important component of the infrastructure for commercial trade, and their routes became a central factor in shaping future patterns of commercial trade.[25]

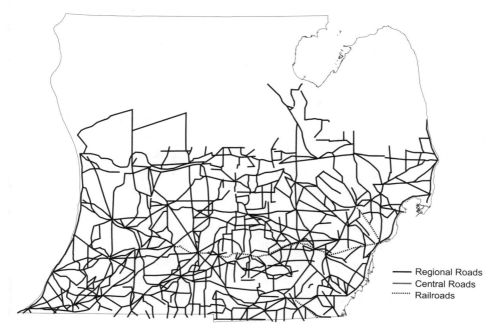

FIGURE 9.18. *THE TRANSPORTATION NETWORK IN SOUTHERN MICHIGAN IN 1845.* (Sources: see text).

The consolidation of Michigan's road networks in the mid–1840s accompanied the maturation of the regional economy. Roads now provided access to almost all parts of the area and increased the number of routes by which goods, people, and information could travel between points. The foci of such networks became central places in the developing system of regional settlement. Settlements took on specialized roles in trade, the hierarchical structure of which facilitated the increasing volume of internal exchange. The economic functions of individual settlements defined their place in the colonization gradient and were reflected in their composition and the nature of their connections.

THE ORGANIZATION OF SETTLEMENT IN THE COLONIAL ECONOMY

The function of Michigan's frontier settlements corresponded to the role each played in the hierarchically arranged regional economy. Because a settlement's role was also linked to its position in the colonial transportation network, function can be recognized by analyzing the network's form. The low population density on the frontier limited the number of larger settlements containing most of the central activities to which residents of the region required access, and the number of routes leading to these few settlements increased with their economic importance. We may thus identify the functional importance of Michigan's frontier settlements by comparing the number of roads emanating from them.[26]

Michigan's frontier towns were the highest-ranking interior settlements. Their importance required that they be situated at key points along the central road network that provided direct connections to the entrepôt of Detroit. Frontier towns became jumping-off points for immigrants entering the interior, and the principal termini of the regional transportation network. These central places were focal points for regular economic, social, administrative, and religious activity, and stores, warehouses, repair facilities, mills, markets, banks, land offices, churches, schools, and municipal services could be found there. As regional centers of activity, frontier towns grew larger and acquired more substantial populations than surrounding settlements, and possessed a greater number of connections to other points. The role of frontier towns in the colonial economy gave them advantages for development, but did not guarantee their continued success if their inhabitants failed to adapt to conditions imposed by an increasingly commercial market.

Michigan's frontier economy also depended upon secondary settlements that served as smaller centers of trade. Nucleated settlements contained stores, mills, and other processing and storage facilities and served as markets for more restricted areas. Many possessed administrative functions as county seats or sites of land offices, but most social and religious activities occurred there more sporadically and on a smaller scale. The size of nucleated settlements varied with the population density of the surrounding region, and could grow rapidly as settlement expanded. Some of those in newly occupied areas became frontier towns over time, while others served as subsidiary economic foci linking central places.

Seminucleated settlements often consisted of isolated specialized activities, such as stores or mills, or a small cluster of activities that operated irregularly on demand. Their restricted functions generated less traffic and allowed them to be placed away from the central road network, although they still possessed a number of connections to other places. As immigration increased and the frontier economy expanded, seminucleated settlements could take on new roles, although the inability of regional trade to support substantial growth often prevented them from becoming very large. Nonetheless, they occasionally became subsidiary centers with connections to central places.[27]

The position of Michigan settlements in the expanding transportation network before 1845 provides a picture of their evolving roles during the period of colonization. It reveals a pattern of areal growth that saw the sequential appearance of a settlement hierarchy following the occupation of new lands. Within this hierarchy, fourteen central places eventually emerged to form the core of the frontier economy in 1845, and numerous nucleated settlements arose as secondary foci of trade. In the following section, we will examine the growth of these centers and their role in forming the economic landscape.[28]

Michigan's settlement structure had begun to assume a basic form by the mid–1820s (figs. 9.14 and 9.19). Detroit formed the terminus of the central road network, and several interior settlements had arisen as nodes along its major routes. All of the interior centers lay adjacent to rivers and developed into regional milling sites. Pontiac, on the Saginaw Road, possessed links to many surrounding interior settlements and became an early milling and industrial center and a county seat. To the south, Ypsilanti lay at the junction of two principal interior routes,

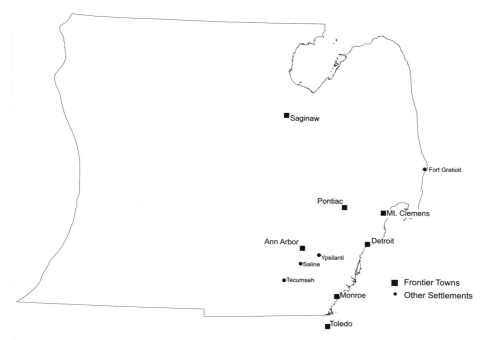

FIGURE 9.19. *FRONTIER TOWNS AND OTHER SETTLEMENTS IN SOUTHERN MICHIGAN IN 1826.* (Sources: see text).

the Territorial Road leading to the county seat of Ann Arbor, and the Chicago Road leading to Saline and Tecumseh. Although a developing nucleated settlement, Tecumseh still lacked the centralizing features of a frontier town.[29]

The mid–1820s also witnessed the emergence of secondary eastern ports, linked to Detroit by the central road network. Mt. Clemens and Monroe provided additional routes of access to the interior, but neither became a major port or a competitor to the entrepôt. Far from expanding settlement on the Eastern Shore, Saginaw remained isolated, as did the outliers along the St. Clair River.[30]

By the close of the 1820s, additional settlements appeared on the map of Michigan, joined by a number of new roads, including many between older established places. New settlements arose in the western part of the territory, and the occupation of the eastern interior expanded substantially, as indicated by the dramatic growth in the number of links and settlements (figs. 9.15 and 9.20).

Detroit remained the focus of the central road network, and earlier interior nodes also continued to dominate eastern Michigan. Pontiac was firmly established as a frontier town. To the south, Ann Arbor had grown substantially, encouraged by its location on the Territorial Road. Other nucleated settlements emerged or remained as secondary points. On the Chicago Road, Tecumseh and Adrian emerged as twin nodes in southern Michigan. Their comparable economic growth evidenced a competition that remained unresolved until the mid–1830s.[31]

FIGURE 9.20. *FRONTIER TOWNS AND OTHER SETTLEMENTS IN SOUTHERN MICHIGAN IN 1830.* (Sources: see text).

Along the eastern shore, Monroe gained additional connections to the interior, and Mt. Clemens expanded its network northward. The growth of regional route networks north and west of Detroit led to the emergence of Romeo, Rochester, and Auburn as nucleated settlements. Their appearance accompanied the growth of Pontiac and Mt. Clemens as frontier towns and illustrates the increasing complexity of the linkages in this part of Michigan.[32]

Western settlements emerged along both the Chicago and Territorial Roads before 1830. Jackson lay at the edge of northern expansion. Jonesville marked the terminus of several routes that intersected the Chicago Road. The appearance of several settlements in southwestern Michigan revealed rapid colonization in this portion of the territory. The largest of these was Niles, situated at the point where the Chicago Road crossed the lower St. Joseph River and intersected a trail leading to Jackson. Neither St. Joseph, at the mouth of the St. Joseph, nor Edwardsburg as yet possessed functions associated with nucleated settlements.[33]

By the mid–1830s, three principal overland routes spanned Michigan's Lower Peninsula from Detroit, accompanied by the creation of new frontier towns and other regional centers whose distribution showed the effect of earlier settlement patterning (figs. 9.16 and 9.21). Detroit and the established eastern frontier towns remained transportation nodes, with an increasing number of connections. Pontiac had grown into the largest interior town in the territory and lay at the junction of central roads leading to Saginaw and the Grand River Valley. A major road now connected it directly to Ann Arbor, providing an important trade and communications link between them.[34]

FIGURE 9.21. *Frontier Towns and Other Settlements in Southern Michigan in 1836.* (Sources: see text).

In eastern Michigan, settlements grew up at Farmington and Plymouth on secondary roads connecting Pontiac and Ann Arbor. North of Detroit, the network of routes centered on Rochester expanded to link Mt. Clemens with the St. Clair River settlements and those in the southern Thumb. The lack of route development around other earlier settlements implies that none had become centers of regional trade. Ann Arbor dominated the central interior, with links to Dexter, Dixboro, and other surrounding settlements, as well as to older nucleated settlements along the central road network and major settlements on the Eastern Shore.[35]

In southern Michigan, Adrian emerged as a frontier town. Its strategic economic position relative to western settlements along the Chicago Road was enhanced by a railroad connection to Toledo, and it replaced Tecumseh as the county seat. The latter remained an important nucleated settlement with connections to the interior and points along the Eastern Shore. The Lake Erie ports of Mt. Clemens and Monroe both increased the number of links to interior settlements and assumed more diversified economic roles. Mt. Clemens's hinterland, however, was restricted by the unfavorable Eastern Shore environment. Monroe grew rapidly as a port, acquiring direct links with inland frontier towns and other interior points. Its proximity to the principal western immigration routes and its land office insured Monroe's continued influence as the Michigan frontier expanded. Although engaged in increasingly intense competition with Toledo for a share of the interior trade, Monroe emerged as Michigan's second-most-important commercial port.[36]

Southwestern Michigan experienced extensive route development in the early 1830s, and several important places emerged as centers of regional networks along the Chicago Road.

Niles solidified its position as the center of trade on the lower St. Joseph River. Farther east, White Pigeon became the focus of a road network extending throughout southwestern Michigan and northern Indiana. Its strategic location influenced its choice as the location for the western land office in 1831. Jonesville also maintained a number of overland ties to eastern Michigan.[37]

Along the Territorial Road, several frontier towns had appeared by the early 1830s. A county seat and economic center with diverse functions, Marshall possessed numerous connections with southwestern Michigan and the Thornapple Valley. Kalamazoo's road network extended over a large part of western and southwestern Michigan, and the removal of the White Pigeon land office to Kalamazoo in 1834 made it the dominant settlement in western Michigan at mid-decade. Although a regional network was centered at Battle Creek, it had not yet become a nucleated settlement. Jackson lay about midway between Marshall and Ann Arbor on the Territorial Road and was the focus of a regional road network linking the upper Grand drainage with older areas of settlement along the Chicago Road. West of Kalamazoo, Paw Paw marked the center of settlement. Its roads connected it with growing settlements to the south, and it remained a small nucleated settlement.[38]

A number of settlements situated away from the central road network also provided important road connections. Cassopolis, Schoolcraft, Centreville, Union City, Homer, and Napoleon arose as small commercial centers with extensive regional links between the Chicago and Territorial roads. North of the Territorial Road, the networks of Otsego and Geloster (present-day Richland) extended into the lower Kalamazoo drainage and along the Thornapple Valley into the lower Grand River region. Middleville linked these settlements and others with those on Grand River. Along the northern route to the Grand River country, Byron connected settlements in Oakland and Washtenaw counties with those further west. Few roads linked other northern settlements to the more heavily settled part of Michigan, and those in the southern Thumb, the Saginaw drainage, and on the Grand River remained relatively isolated. None were yet foci of frontier transportation.[39]

The second half of the 1830s witnessed the extension of Michigan's regional economy and the coordination of trade through a greater number of centers (figs. 9.17 and 9.22). South of the Grand River a consolidation of settlement and road networks increased the number of nodes and the complexity of the links between them. Farther north, regional networks expanded to fill in newly occupied lands. Road network development left its mark on the structure of frontier trade by altering the function of some settlements and promoting continuity in others.

Pontiac continued to dominate trade north of Detroit, and promoters of a planned railroad from Detroit sought it as a terminus. In contrast, Mt. Clemens failed to expand its direct overland routes, and many of the nucleated settlements in the region developed connections to the southern Thumb and small ports on the St. Clair River. Further south, Farmington, Plymouth, and Dearborn developed substantial regional networks with links to Detroit, Pontiac, and Ann Arbor. The choice of Dearborn as the site of the United States arsenal reflected its rising importance.[40]

FIGURE 9.22. *FRONTIER TOWNS AND OTHER SETTLEMENTS IN SOUTHERN MICHIGAN IN 1840.* (Sources: see text).

Ann Arbor remained the frontier town for the central interior, with a network extending in all directions. The Central Railroad connected it directly to Detroit in 1839 and Ann Arbor became the site of the state university. Ypsilanti, Saline, and Dixboro all provided connections to other parts of the interior, and Dexter emerged as a focus for trade and communications to semi-nucleated settlements in the upper Grand Valley. Adrian remained the regional frontier town of the southern interior, and railroads now connected it with two lake ports. Several smaller regional nodes also emerged as overland route networks expanded in southeastern Michigan. As the eastern terminus of the Southern Railroad, Monroe retained its role as a frontier town.[41]

A substantial amount of road network development accompanied the settlement of lands between the Territorial and Chicago Roads. In the south, Jonesville and Coldwater became nucleated settlements. Jackson became a frontier town, although White Pigeon, having lost its land office, declined in status. The frontier towns of Marshall and Kalamazoo found themselves at the center of increasingly complex regional networks extending north and south of the Kalamazoo Valley. Lying between them, Battle Creek and Comstock possessed a substantial number of regional links. Paw Paw remained the only nucleated settlement west of Kalamazoo.[42]

Niles remained the frontier town for western Michigan. By 1840 its network linked the settlements of New Buffalo and St. Joseph, and the newly established county seat of Berrien Springs. Cassopolis, Constantine, and Centreville emerged as nucleated settlements whose road networks provided economic services to support the dramatic growth of settlement along the Chicago and Territorial Roads, including the semi-nucleated settlements of Schoolcraft, Three Rivers, Union City, Homer, and Concord.[43] Settlement expanded rapidly south of the Grand River in the late 1830s, accompanied by the development of routes linking settlements on the Territorial Road with those on the northern and southern Grand River Roads. The nucleated settlements of Allegan, on the lower Kalamazoo, and Bellevue, on the upper Thornapple, became centers of new regional road networks, and the semi-nucleated settlements of Middleville, Yankee Springs, Vermontville, Hastings, and Geloster emerged as important intermediate trading points between the Grand and Kalamazoo drainages.[44]

Grand Rapids lay at the center of a vast overland network, and the Grand River provided steamboat connections with Lake Michigan and settlements upriver. Its central position made it the frontier town for the lower Grand Valley. Nucleated settlements grew up at Grand Haven, at the river's mouth, and farther east at Grandville. The settlements of Ada and Lowell appeared at the confluence of major tributary streams along the Grand. A regional center of trade and the site of the land office for the Grand River District, Ionia became the second frontier town on the Grand, while Lyons and Portland arose as small settlements farther upriver. DeWitt became a focus of settlement on the road linking the region with the upper Shiawassee drainage.[45]

Regional road networks also developed between the upper Grand and Saginaw drainages, and Howell developed as a center of transportation on the Grand River Road. Howell grew rapidly as a frontier town with a large and diverse commercial component. The semi-nucleated settlement of Hamburg connected Howell with settlements farther east, and four small settlements along the Shiawassee River, including the county seat of Corunna, accompanied expanding route networks to accommodate growth in the upper Saginaw valley. The focus of a regional network, Flint possessed connections that bound the settlements of the Saginaw valley together and tied them to adjacent regions. This county seat and trading center became the frontier town for the upper Saginaw region. Lapeer emerged as a nucleated settlement whose connections linked the lower Thumb with the upper Saginaw drainage and the Eastern Shore. Farther north, Saginaw's linear road network linked new settlements nearer Saginaw Bay with those to the south.[46]

During the first half of the 1840s, road network growth followed the continued consolidation of settlement south of the Grand River and its expansion into the Saginaw valley and the lower Thumb region. (figs. 9.18 and 9.23). Michigan's road system now afforded access to nearly all settled parts of the southern Lower Peninsula, and the ties between individual settlements and their neighbors in all directions attest to a relatively high degree of regional economic integration in the late frontier period. In most cases, the additional connecting routes supported the existing settlement hierarchy, because improved access enhanced the importance of established central settlements.

Road networks expanded in this period between Monroe and Detroit in response to Monroe's growing role in trade and the settlement of a region bypassed by earlier immigrants. Farther west, road networks expanded in Michigan and Indiana. Hillsdale lay at the center of

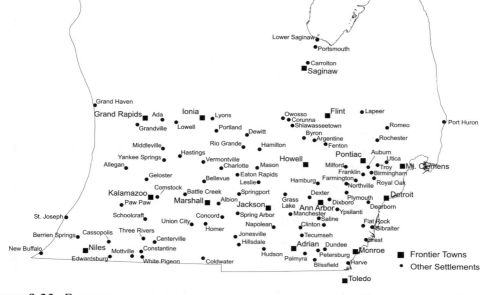

FIGURE 9.23. *FRONTIER TOWNS AND OTHER SETTLEMENTS IN SOUTHERN MICHIGAN IN 1845.* (Sources: see text).

this growth, and the arrival of the railroad and the settlement's designation as a county seat enhanced its economic role. Lagging settlement, however, prevented its becoming a frontier town. The largest regional networks in southwestern Michigan centered round the nucleated settlements of Cassopolis, Centreville, White Pigeon, and the small river port of Union City. Niles remained the frontier town for southwestern Michigan. St. Joseph developed an extensive interior network and emerged as the principal port for overland travelers headed for Chicago.[47]

The rapid extension of the Michigan Central Railroad enhanced the growth of the principal settlements through which it passed. Ann Arbor remained the dominant frontier town in the east and Jackson grew in importance as its network expanded in the rapidly settling center of the state. The arrival of the Michigan Central in 1844 dramatically reduced the time of transit to Marshall from Detroit and made the frontier town a major transportation hub. Its extensive road network reached out in all directions to connect this rapidly expanding frontier town with those of neighboring regions. Marshall's economic growth and expanding role in transportation, coupled with its central position with regard to the state's expanding population, made it a strong candidate for the site of the new capital during the late 1840s.[48]

Kalamazoo grew in size during this period and broadened the range of its commercial and manufacturing activities. The arrival of the railroad there at the beginning of 1846 made it a terminus of western immigration and encouraged further economic expansion. Its road network now extended over much of western Michigan, linking it to regional centers such as Allegan and Paw Paw and connecting it to the lower Grand Valley as well as to the St. Joseph

River settlements to the south. The nearby nucleated settlement of Battle Creek possessed an extensive route network, and it remained an important link between Marshall and Kalamazoo.[49]

Grand Rapids lay at the center of a growing network of routes that now extended to settlements along the Western Shore and to recently established lumber mills in Muskegon and Montcalm Counties. Much of its hinterland remained sparsely settled in the poor economic climate of the mid–1840s, and Grand Rapids remained a small frontier town whose growth still lay ahead. Other settlements along the river remained small and often specialized. Ionia's growth insured its position as the frontier town for the middle Grand Valley, and road network expansion increased its trading hinterland. With the completion of the southern Grand River Road, route networks developed throughout the upper Grand drainage. One, centered at Mason, intersected other networks expanding from the south, east, and west and precipitated the formation of several semi-nucleated settlements. Firmly established as the frontier town for the upper Grand Valley, Howell grew into a substantial settlement. Its extensive network of roads allowed it to capture the trade of the newer settlements to the west.[50]

In the upper Saginaw Valley, trade networks expanded outward from the frontier town of Flint through a number of smaller settlements to the east and south. Although Saginaw became the focus of an expanding regional network, it failed to provide direct access to many parts of the interior, and large portions of the region remained unsettled. Nevertheless, Saginaw's role as a center of regional trade made it the frontier town for the lower Saginaw Valley.[51]

The Late Frontier Landscape in Michigan

In 1845, the landscape of Lower Michigan consisted of a hierarchy of settlements connected by a road network that had grown in response to regional development over the previous three decades. The structure of this late frontier economy was based on the differential distribution of activities between settlements and the nature of trade and marketing in the region. An examination of Michigan's early transportation network has identified the frontier towns that rested at the apex of the regional hierarchy. The positions of other settlements, however, remain unclear from their locations alone, and it is uncertain which of them served as secondary centers on the Michigan frontier. To examine this aspect of Michigan's frontier economy, we now turn to evidence pertaining directly to the wider role of settlements in the development of the region.

A settlement's hierarchical position in Michigan's regional economy reflected its function, which, in turn, manifested the nature of the activities carried out there. Those settlements with a greater diversity of activities possessed more central functions. In general, frontier towns dominated the colonial economy, followed by nucleated settlements, which played a secondary role. Each may be distinguished by comparing the activity diversity of Michigan's frontier settlements. Blois's *Gazetteer* of 1838 offers the only comprehensive source of detailed settlement information by which to observe activity variation during the late frontier period. Where possible, other contemporary sources have supplemented these data to provide as complete a picture as possible of settlement function in the 1840s. Although expansion was not yet complete in 1838, the road network extended over much of Lower Michigan, and the regional economy encompassed much of the region. The hierarchical structure of the frontier should thus be evident in the function of settlements.[52]

Our analysis compares variation in four broad activity categories, the occurrence of which increased with a settlement's relative importance in the frontier economy. These include: (1) governmental and administrative, (2) commercial and retail, (3) manufacturing, processing, and storage, and (4) religious, public, and educational activities. Because government and administrative facilities were important to acquiring a central role on the frontier, the occurrence of county, state, and federal offices can identify places with central administrative functions. The variety and diversity of commercial and retailing activities indicates a settlement's role in trade and its position within the regional economic network. Manufacturing, processing, and storage activities usually varied with economic function. Finally, the presence of churches, academies, and other public buildings should reveal those settlements with central social, religious, and political functions.[53]

Michigan settlements of the late 1830s exhibited a great disparity in the occurrence of activities. Although some settlements had multiple activities in all of the categories, most exhibited diversity in only a few. If we assume that those settlements with a greater number of activities in the most categories possessed greater social and economic complexity, and such complexity reflected a settlement's relative placement in the regional hierarchy, then Michigan's frontier settlements may be ranked according to their importance by examining their activity diversity. A comparison of these settlements (table 9.1) reveals that at least fifteen of them contained three or more activities in at least three activity categories. These include Detroit and fourteen frontier towns that have previously been identified as central places on the basis of their positions in the route network and other descriptive information: Monroe, Adrian, Niles, Kalamazoo, Marshall, Jackson, Ann Arbor, Mt. Clemens, Pontiac, Howell, Flint, Grand Rapids, Ionia and Saginaw (table 9.1).

A number of secondary market centers may be identified on the basis of their having multiple activities in at least one category, although they exhibited less activity diversity in all categories (table 9.1). Of lesser complexity than frontier towns, these nucleated settlements nonetheless played an important role in Michigan's frontier economy. They include: Algonac, Allegan, Auburn, Battle Creek, Bellevue, Birmingham, Cassopolis, Centreville, Clinton, Coldwater, Comstock, Constantine, Corunna, Dearborn, Dexter, Dundee, Grand Haven, Grandville, Harve, Jonesville, Lyons, Milford, Northville, Palmer, Palmyra, Paw Paw, Plymouth, Port Huron, St. Joseph, Tecumseh, Utica, and Ypsilanti. Michigan's secondary market centers all lay on major roads connecting frontier towns and were often the foci of smaller route networks. In the late 1840s, however, the degree of settlement development across the region was still uneven. Consequently, the total number of activities in settlements varied, with towns in older areas having more than those more recently settled. In some areas occupied early, such as Oakland County, several settlements exhibited substantial diversity in several activity categories. Here the secondary centers were assumed to be those with activities in the greatest number of

TABLE 9.1 *ACTIVITY DIVERSITY IN MICHIGAN'S FRONTIER SETTLEMENTS IN 1838*

Entries indicate the number of examples of each activity category found in each settlement.

Name of Settlement	Government & Administrative	Retail & Commercial	Mfr., Processing, & Storage	Religious, Public, & Education
Entrepôt				
Detroit	10	11	7	12
Frontier Towns				
Adrian	2	10	7	2
Ann Arbor	3	8	7	2
Pontiac	2	10	6	2
Mt. Clemens	4	7	7	0
Monroe	3	4	7	4
Marshall	2	8	4	2
Jackson	2	6	4	2
Kalamazoo	3	5	4	2
Grand Rapids	2	6	3	2
Niles	1	6	4	2
Saginaw	3	7	3	0
Howell	2	5	2	2
Flint	2	5	3	0
Ionia	3	3	3	0
Secondary Market Centers				
Tecumseh	1	8	4	1
Ypsilanti	1	6	6	1
Centreville	2	6	2	1
St. Joseph	2	6	2	1
Dearborn	2	2	5	1
Northville	1	3	5	1
Dundee	1	5	3	1
Palmer	2	5	2	1
Bellevue	1	4	4	1
Port Huron	2	4	3	0
Constantine	0	6	2	1
Dexter	1	5	3	0
Utica	1	3	3	2
Grand Haven	2	4	3	0
Grandville	1	4	4	0
Clinton	0	5	3	1

(continued on next page)

TABLE **9.1** *(continued)*

Name of Settlement	Government & Administrative	Retail & Commercial	Mfr., Processing, & Storage	Religious, Public, & Education
Secondary Market Centers				
Battle Creek	0	5	4	0
Plymouth	1	6	0	1
Auburn	0	3	3	2
Allegan	2	5	1	0
Coldwater	2	4	1	1
Jonesville	2	4	1	1
Birmingham	0	4	3	0
Milford	1	2	4	0
Palmyra	1	4	2	0
Corunna	2	1	3	0
Paw Paw	1	2	2	1
Algonac	2	2	1	1
Comstock	1	3	2	0
Cassopolis	2	3	1	0
Harve	1	2	1	0
Lyons	0	4	0	0

Source: Blois, Gazetteer.

categories. Secondary centers in newly settled or bypassed areas possessed relatively fewer activities overall, but clearly possessed more than their neighbors. Taking these subjective differences into consideration, we can identify thirty-two nucleated settlements that served as secondary market centers.

Information concerning activity diversity supports earlier conclusions regarding the identity of the central settlements in frontier Michigan and provides insights into the structure of its regional economy. Scattered across Lower Michigan, the placement of frontier towns maximized accessibility to central services in a region still dominated by internal trade. The distribution of nucleated settlements at locations intermediate to frontier towns also indicates a functional relationship between the two levels of settlement in the frontier economy. This tie between settlement form and economic structure is one that bears further investigation (fig. 9.24).

The distribution of frontier towns and nucleated settlements serving as secondary centers in Michigan was directly tied to the regional organization of the frontier economy around internal markets. The presence of regional economic organization may be observed by employing a central place model that recognizes that the organization of trade determines the spatial relationship between central settlements and those of the next-lower order of importance. This relationship

FIGURE 9.24 *FRONTIER TOWNS AND SECONDARY SETTLEMENTS IN SOUTHERN MICHIGAN IN 1838.* (Sources: see text).

can be seen in the arrangement of the two settlement types. Expressed schematically, each central settlement lies in the center of a hexagonal trade area abutting areas of adjacent centers. Smaller market settlements lie on the boundaries of these trade areas at points between the centers. The structure of the links between the centers and the secondary settlements reflects the organization of trade. Regions organized around internal markets seek to maximize accessibility between central settlements and smaller market centers. Consequently, each lower-ranking center is located at the midpoint between three higher-level centers (fig. 9.25). If we superimpose market area boundaries around Michigan's frontier towns and straighten their boundaries out to diagrammatic form, the schematic arrangement of frontier towns and nucleated settlements clearly exhibits the anticipated pattern for regional economies dominated by internal trade (fig. 9.26).[54]

Although Michigan's late frontier economy possessed a structure associated with internal market systems, several gaps indicate the absence of secondary settlements. Such breaks are particularly noticeable where market area boundaries met north of the Grand River, in the lower Saginaw Valley, among the Central Timberlands on the upper Grand, and in the Thumb, regions still undergoing colonization, where an uneven population distribution, inadequate transportation networks, and poorly developed trade delayed the formation of substantial nucleated settlements.

The rapidly evolving frontier economy of western Michigan also produced two pairs of competing nucleated settlements that had grown up close to one another. Comstock's proximity to

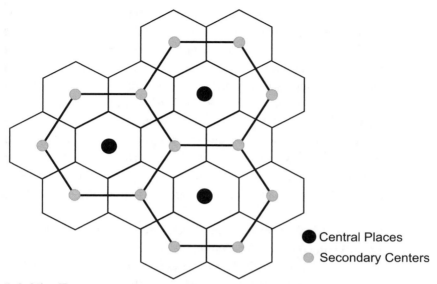

FIGURE 9.25. *The arrangement of market areas and settlements in a region character- ized by internal trade and organized according to the marketing principle. The K-3 net- work formed by this arrangement places each lower-ranking secondary center at the midpoint between three higher-ranking central places.* (Sources: see text).

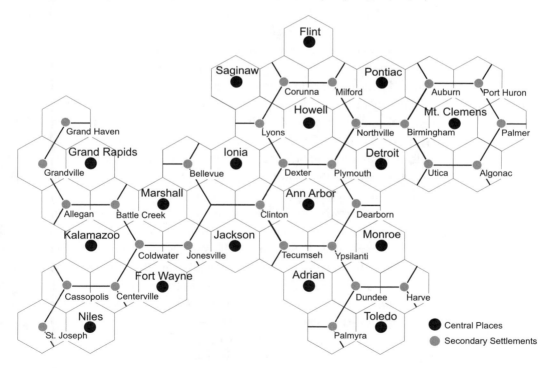

FIGURE 9.26. *The arrangement of market areas and settlements in southern Michigan during the 1840s.* (Sources: see text).

Kalamazoo restricted its economic hinterland; however, and prevented it from developing as a separate market center. Lying only ten miles apart, rivals Centreville and Constantine each possessed advantages that enhanced their economic importance. The latter emerged early as a trading point on the St. Joseph River, but Centreville's role as a county seat with numerous links to the north and east permitted it to supersede its neighbor as a secondary settlement.[55]

The arrangement of secondary settlements along the state's southern border testifies to the integral role frontier towns in adjacent states played in Michigan's frontier economy. Fort Wayne dominated the interior trade of northern Indiana, and the Lake Erie port of Toledo was the economic center of northwestern Ohio. Both played an important role in the development of southern Michigan and maintained links to its frontier towns through a number of key nucleated settlements. The schematic diagram portrays the position of these central places as integral elements of Michigan's late-frontier cultural landscape.[56]

In the 1840s, settlements stretched across Lower Michigan, linked together by routes still followed today by those traversing the state. Yet, despite the familiarity of early place names and their historical continuity with towns and cities of the present, much of Michigan's late-frontier landscape would appear alien to us today. Large portions of the region's physical landscape remained uncleared or unmodified, and the regional economy was incapable of supporting a complex infrastructure of production and trade. A central component of this landscape was its simplified settlement structure, which concentrated many key economic, political, social, and religious institutions in frontier towns, while others were distributed in smaller nucleated and semi-nucleated settlements elsewhere in the region.

Michigan's frontier towns were the most extensive and diversified settlements in the interior. In spite of their volume of activity, however, they remained relatively small, with populations generally around one thousand persons, far below those of comparable municipalities in older settled areas. The limited capacity of frontier industries and other urban activities to employ large numbers of resident workers and the absence of a substantial resident farming population in the surrounding countryside limited their growth in the context of the regional trade, and these towns grew substantially only after the region's entry into the national economy.[57]

Nucleated settlements served to collect, process, and redistribute produce and services and as focal points of social activity. Their relatively limited range of facilities and the seasonality of some activities, such as milling, restricted their development, but many of them became secondary centers in the regional economy. Generally they were much smaller in size than frontier towns. Battle Creek, for example, had fewer than half as many people as nearby Marshall, and Niles had a population ten times larger than that of neighboring Berrien Springs in 1838. Nucleated settlements possessing extraordinary resources, however, occasionally acquired larger populations. St. Joseph's position as a lake port, for example, permitted its rapid growth during the 1830s. Still, most nucleated settlements lacked the means to support large populations and remained small villages throughout the frontier period.[58]

Semi-nucleated settlements ranged from isolated activities, such as Mr. Jones's stage house and farm, which constituted Jonesville in 1831, to the collection of hotel buildings at Yankee Springs, to the half dozen houses and the grist and saw mill that comprised early Hastings.

Most were loosely integrated farming settlements with the addition of at least one specialized activity that operated at least periodically to process, manufacture, repair, or redistribute goods or services. Michigan's semi-nucleated settlements remained small activity centers throughout the frontier period.[59]

The integration of Michigan's regional economy, the infrastructure of which was nearly complete by the mid–1840s, produced the structural patterning of frontier towns and secondary centers. his landscape persisted as population growth, technological change, expanding production, and intensified and improved transportation introduced greater complexity, while outside market forces worked to restructure the economic organization in Lower Michigan after 1845.

Michigan's landscape and the distinctive types of settlements that grew up on it changed rapidly with the transition of the region's economy in the 1850s. Although many settlements retained significant roles after this time, others did not. Their fate and the character of the new landscape of which they became a part were determined by the manner in which Michigan was integrated into the national economy. Made possible by the revolution in long-distance transportation brought about by the railroad, technological developments in agriculture, and the reorganization of marketing, Michigan's transitional economy was shaped by forces far different from those that produced the cultural landscape of the frontier.

10

Long-Distance Transportation and External Trade

By the fourth decade of the nineteenth century, agricultural settlement had spread over much of southern Michigan, and farmers raised a range of staple crops for a largely internal market. Although most immigrants hoped to increase production and participate in wider trade, their efforts were thwarted by the lack of access to outside markets. The region's isolation from the urban markets of the East limited the scale and diversity of agriculture until conditions favored long-distance exchange. The transformation of Michigan's frontier economy came in response to growing external demands which set in motion a series of changes in transportation, technology, and the organization of marketing that altered the geography of agriculture on the western frontier. Rapid growth in the scale and organization of production, processing, and marketing infrastructures occurred in the second quarter of the nineteenth century to permit the expansion of the American economy on an unprecedented scale, a phenomenon that historian George Rogers Taylor called the "transportation revolution."[1]

Integrating the frontier economy of Lower Michigan with that of the eastern United States required a network of efficient and economical long-distance transportation capable of moving heavy, bulky materials between widely separated points as rapidly as possible, while avoiding transfer from one means of carriage to another en route. The creation of this network occurred during a period of substantial innovation in the technology of transportation which changed the form and scope of trade and the means by which it was carried out. The transportation revolution altered Michigan's internal economy and moved it toward commodity production. This impact is best seen in the larger context of evolving antebellum transportation technology and long-distance trade.

OVERLAND TRANSPORT IN EXPANSION AND DEVELOPMENT

In the first quarter of the nineteenth century, roads offered the widest access to the American interior, but the technology of overland transportation limited their use largely to immigration. The development of western settlement and trade required flexibility in routing. Roads could be built quickly and adapted to a wide range of environments. In contrast, water routes reached only portions of the interior, and much of the West lay beyond navigable streams, even though water transport remained a more efficient means of moving large cargoes over long distances. Overland routes dominated expansion into the West and contributed significantly to the development of frontier regions, including southern Michigan.[2]

The nature of conveyances and the composition of roads limited long-distance trade. Wagons, carts, and other wheeled vehicles carried relatively small cargoes and moved slowly, especially in bad weather. The cost and labor required to ship heavy loads restricted freight to valuable and durable items. The form of road networks designed for short-range exchange further limited their use in national trade. In the absence of consistent support by the national government, the construction of internal improvements lay in the hands of states or private corporations, who built improved roads, called "turnpikes," to serve the interests of internal rather than national trade.[3]

Nevertheless, the expansion of roads and turnpikes created an overland network that facilitated immigration to newly opened areas. As early as 1819, Americans followed established overland routes to the Old Northwest, and in the 1820s the National Road opened the Ohio Valley and the region south of the Great Lakes to immigration. The construction of turnpikes and the development of stage routes connecting the Lake Erie port of Buffalo with population centers of the Northeast increased the accessibility of Michigan to immigrants from New York and New England, and at least one stage company offered transportation from Buffalo to Detroit via the southern shore of the lake.[4]

Most of Michigan's settlers came from the Northeast. Their principal route passed along the southern Lake Erie shore by way of Erie, Pennsylvania, and Cleveland, Ohio; past Sandusky and Miami Bay; and north through the Black Swamp to Detroit. A second land route went westward through Canada along the northern shore of Lake Erie. These routes were heavily traveled in the 1830s, especially during the winter months, when ice closed Lake Erie and the frozen ground permitted rapid travel over streams, swamps, and other obstacles that might have slowed travel during warmer weather. Farmers found the overland passage to Michigan particularly attractive because it permitted them to move their stock inexpensively. In warm weather, immigrants followed this route as far as Cleveland, where they procured lake passage to Detroit. Although never able to compete with water routes for long-distance trade and immigration, overland travel around Lake Erie offered an alternative path to Michigan (fig. 10.1). Many people came from the southeastern United States to Michigan over newly constructed roads across the Appalachians. Southern immigration into the Old Northwest was extensive during the 1820s, and during one month in 1829 at least nine thousand immigrants from Virginia and South Carolina were reported to have passed through Charleston, "bound for Indiana, Illinois, and Michigan."[5]

Roads also laid the groundwork for the economic integration of southern Michigan. Its residents clearly understood the importance of an internal overland network to the development of commercial agriculture, and perceived that its construction was necessary for their successful participation in the national economy. "It is a fact often forgotten," wrote the editor of the *Michigan Farmer* in 1847,

> that the value of lands depends not only—and often not chiefly—on the state of improvement they are in—nor on their productiveness, but essentially, on the facilities for communication between them and market. *Roads make farms,* and the want of them unmakes them, or leaves them unmade.[6]

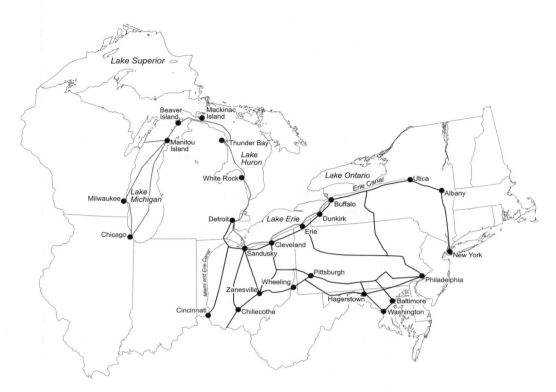

FIGURE 10.1. *OVERLAND, CANAL, AND LAKE ROUTES TO MICHIGAN BY 1830.* (Sources: Meinig, *Atlantic America,* 5, 226; Parkins, *Historical Geography of Detroit,* 257; Darby, *Tour,* xlv–xlvi; Hewitt, *American Traveller,* 54.

Seeking the construction of roads to link the principal settlements of the Kalamazoo Valley, a contemporary newspaper declared that "the increasing importance of such communication . . . is acknowledged by all, . . . we assert that there is not a farmer, a merchant, or any citizen engaged in business in western Michigan, who will not derive some benefit from such an improvement." Early entrepreneurs, such as B. O. Williams of Owosso, recalled that creating "an outlet for the products of the country" was crucial to "the success of settling our portion of the country."[7]

By the 1830s, Michigan had begun constructing an internal road network connecting interior points to central locations along major immigration routes. Territorial funds built some roads, such as those linking the seats of Branch, St. Joseph, and Cass Counties to the port of St. Joseph in 1832. Residents also sought federal support for roads perceived to have strategic value "in times of war," or those intended to encourage settlement and improve access to interior settlements. By 1845, internal roads became the basis for the infrastructure of internal trade and communications across Michigan. This network, however, still did not provide an efficient means to cheaply transport heavy, bulky, farm produce long distances to eastern markets. Roads built for immigration were inadequate for commercial trade, and export-oriented production had to await the introduction of adequate means of transportation.[8]

THE ERIE CANAL AND THE LAKE PASSAGE TO MICHIGAN

The development of water routes linked lower Michigan to northeastern markets and population centers and opened the region to long-distance trade and immigration. Navigable water offered the only practical method of extending commercial trade to the Old Northwest in the early nineteenth century. Constructing western water routes, however, required the efforts of both private and government interests to circumvent the natural barriers that separated Michigan from markets in the East. Efforts to improve water transport took the form of river improvements, as well as the construction of canals to open entirely new routes. During the eighteenth century, canal construction transformed the landscape of industrialized nations in northern Europe, and in the 1790s, states along the Atlantic Seaboard began extensive programs of canal construction to link coastal markets with inland producers and canalize many of the coastal rivers and waterways. Canals stimulated competition among seaboard cities for control of the most extensive hinterlands. New York's ascendancy as the center of antebellum American trade was due as much to its capture of an extensive western hinterland as to its control of the cotton trade and the export trade to Europe. It accomplished this feat by constructing a canal tying the Hudson River and the port of New York with the extensive drainage of the Great Lakes.[9]

Finished in 1825, the Erie Canal played a critical role in developing a water transportation system to the West because it opened a route capable of carrying heavy cargoes cheaply and efficiently and permitted the expansion of commercial production into the continent's interior. Its completion opened an extensive economic hinterland for New York City by opening western lands to its central market for breadstuffs.[10]

The canal's construction also established a precedent of government support for public transportation projects intended to encourage settlement and commercial production. The State of New York underwrote the costs of this ambitious project in 1817, and its success in promoting agricultural settlement in western New York and trade in the western lakes led to its intensive use. Its tolls quickly repaid the cost of its construction and established canals as an affordable means of developing the West. In the three decades following the completion of the Erie Canal, Ohio, Indiana, and Michigan all sponsored canal construction. Although the success of the western canals never approached that of the Erie, they expanded the transportation infrastructure of commercial agriculture.[11]

Michigan residents recognized the significance of the Erie Canal as crucial for expanding the regional economy. Months before the canal's 1825 opening, editorialists from Michigan's Lake Erie ports anticipated its impact on agricultural marketing and production. "The great canal of New York will, when completed, afford us a cheap transportation of our surplus produce to the great commercial emporium of America," proclaimed the *Detroit Gazette,* and the *Michigan Sentinel* attributed the territory's "present rapid increase in population, and general advancement in wealth," to the anticipated opening of long-distance water transportation.[12] The Erie Canal completed a network of water transport connecting Michigan and the Northeast, and its opening altered the scope of exchange between western producers and eastern markets.

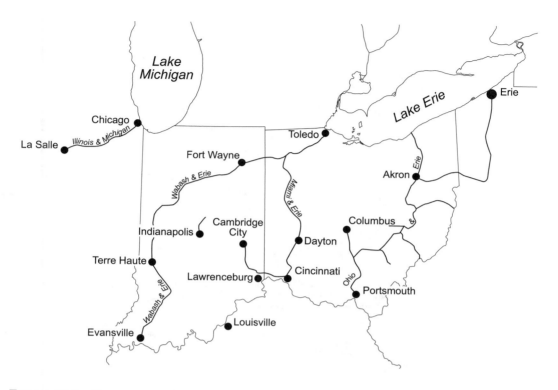

FIGURE 10.2. *THE NETWORK OF CANAL ROUTES IN THE OLD NORTHWEST.* (Sources: Shaw, *Canals for a Nation*, 128, 136).

The success of Erie Canal and the construction of canals south of the Great Lakes encouraged Michigan's residents to consider their use for internal transportation. By the 1830s, canals in the Old Northwest formed a network that linked much of its interior with the Great Lakes and with the extensive drainage of the Ohio and Mississippi Rivers (fig. 10.2). In 1837 the State of Michigan undertook the ambitious task of making a series of internal improvements designed to create a system of canal and railroad transportation providing access to Michigan's interior. Canal advocates planned two large projects to exploit the region's extensive river network (fig. 10.3). The Clinton & Kalamazoo Canal was intended to pass from the mouth of the Clinton River on Lake St. Clair, through the third tier of counties, to the mouth of the Kalamazoo River on Lake Michigan. Its supporters saw it as a conduit for commerce to Lake Michigan, bypassing the longer route through the Straits of Mackinac and making Mt. Clemens a major shipping port. The Saginaw Canal hoped to link the Saginaw drainage with that of the Grand River. Beginning at Saginaw, its route proceeded westward to the Maple River, along which improvements permitted traffic to flow into the Grand. Similar improvements on the Flint River would provide access to central Genesee County.[13]

A shortage of funds resulting from the national depression in 1837, mismanagement, and competition between the political supporters of different projects doomed Michigan's program

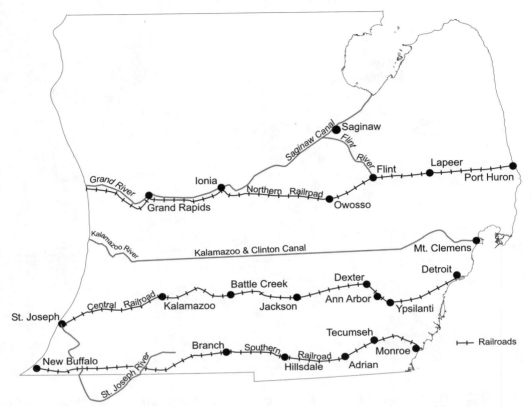

FIGURE 10.3. *PROJECTED ROUTES OF STATE-SPONSORED CANALS AND RAILROADS IN MICHIGAN.* (Sources: Keith, "Internal Improvements"; Parks, *Democracy's Railroads,* 35).

of canal construction to failure. Although about eight miles of the Clinton & Kalamazoo Canal were opened along the Clinton River in 1845, lack of funding and insufficient receipts from tolls prevented proper maintenance, and the canal was closed within two years. Work on the Saginaw Canal never proceeded beyond initial excavations.[14]

Although Michigan's canal projects failed, the state improved several of its major rivers. These projects were not intended to create major interregional trade arteries. Rather, efforts to clear major portions of the St. Joseph, Kalamazoo, Grand, Flint, and Maple Rivers opened existing navigable routes to larger vessels and heavier traffic, changes that promoted trade by increasing access to interior points not yet served by completed internal improvements.[15]

The Erie Canal's economic potential could be realized only by increasing the scale and volume of shipping and developing port facilities on the lakes capable of handling greater trade and communications. Prior to the opening of the canal, only forty small sailing craft moved furs, lumber, sugar, and other western products to Buffalo, carrying supplies, provisions, and immigrants on their return journeys. The completion of the Erie Canal in 1825 had an immediate effect on the volume of traffic on Lake Erie. "America may, perhaps with modesty, assert supremacy on her own fresh water seas," wrote a traveler in 1833, who noted that Lake Erie was "a sea of busy commerce." The growth in total ship tonnage of states operating on this body of water testifies to the increase in lake traffic. The growth in tonnage, from 980 tons in 1818, to 24,045 in 1836, 29,995 in 1837, and 57,793 in 1845, represents a greater number of vessels as well as increasing vessel capacities. During the second quarter of the nineteenth century, shipbuilding at Buffalo, Cleveland, Detroit, and Chatham, Ontario, supported the growing volume of import and export trade on this inland waterway.[16]

The needs of immigration shaped the technology of lake travel. Steam power, adapted to drive vessels on American rivers, now powered boats on the Great Lakes. The first passenger steamboat, the *Walk-in-the-Water,* entered service in 1818, and three others joined it by 1825. Steamboats passing between Buffalo and Detroit stopped at the Ohio ports of Grand River, Cleveland, Sandusky, and Put-in-Bay during the three-day trip.[17]

Immigration from the Northeast to Michigan accounted for a substantial part of the traffic on Lake Erie. Observers described the influx of newcomers in the 1830s as "a torrent." An estimated two thousand persons per week arrived in Detroit in the spring of 1831, double the number of two years earlier. Contemporaries perceived the rate of immigration to Michigan as indicative of the level of regional economic growth, and the phenomenal increase in traffic in 1836 was seen to reflect favorably on "the business of Detroit and of the West in general."[18]

The position of Lake Erie made it a strategic route for commerce that was generated south and west of the Great Lakes. Exports of western grain accounted for much of the new trade. Although Michigan shippers first exported wheat and flour in 1826, the flow of wheat was insubstantial and did not begin to grow significantly until the 1830s. The amount of grain passing through Buffalo rose from 304,990 bushels in 1836 to more than a million bushels three years later. So great was the increase in grain traffic that it exceeded the capacity of the Erie Canal, necessitating its enlargement in 1836. By 1844 the amount of grain shipped through Buffalo had doubled to more than two million bushels, and this quantity tripled within the next three years. Of the more than twenty-four million dollars worth of exports that passed through Lake Erie ports in 1848, however, only 15 percent originated in Michigan ports.[19]

The expansion of trade and settlement to the shores of Lake Michigan extended waterborne trade to the western lakes. The volume of regular water traffic on Lake Michigan developed later than that on Lake Erie. After the War of 1812, erratically scheduled vessels supplied soldiers and traders on the upper lakes and carried out furs and other exports. Throughout the 1820s, American settlement on the lakeshores above Detroit was limited largely to military garrisons and trading posts at the head of the St. Clair River, the Straits of Mackinac, Green Bay, and Chicago.[20]

By the 1830s, the settlement of northern Illinois and Wisconsin resulted in a dramatic increase in traffic on the western lakes. Passenger steamboats operated on Lake Michigan as early as 1831, and by 1834 150 vessels plied the lake's waters. Regularly scheduled shipping on Lake Michigan was established by the middle of the decade, and steamboats served Chicago by 1836. Traveling by schooner that year, a visitor to Michigan reported that the trip from Detroit to Chicago took ten days.[21]

The lake route through the Straits of Mackinac and Lake Michigan presented other impediments to travel that were not immediately apparent. Rapidly developing and extremely strong
storms were the greatest danger to shipping. Although a hazard on all the Great Lakes, sailors
especially feared storms on Lake Michigan, because its lack of natural harbors and tricky cur-
rents made it a dangerous place to ride out a storm. When winds blew strongly from the north
or south, its elongated shape made it particularly perilous for sailing, and it has claimed more
ships than all the other lakes combined.[22]

The expansion of water traffic opened the entire shoreline of the Lower Peninsula of
Michigan to settlement. Contemporary marine technology restricted waterborne traffic to
points possessing deep water in close proximity to land, conditions that often occurred at the
mouths of rivers. These locations offered increased protection from storms and provided safe
anchorages for lake shipping. Michigan's first ports developed along the western shore of Lake
Erie (fig. 10.4). Detroit's site on the deep channel of the Detroit River insured access by ships
of all sizes during the ice-free season, which lasted from late March or early April to the beginning of December. Following the fire of 1805, the city was redesigned to accommodate anticipated economic and population growth, and by the late 1810s its waterfront burgeoned with
new wharves, storehouses, ferry accommodations, hotels, livery stables, stores, taverns, banks,
markets, and other facilities to serve the increased flow of passenger and freight traffic into
southern Lower Michigan.[23]

Monroe, located at the mouth of the River Raisin, possessed a natural harbor located conveniently for immigrants seeking access to the southern tier of counties. Initially small and isolated, Monroe grew dramatically during the 1820s, when lands were offered for sale in its
vicinity and it became a destination for immigrants who traveled there by water from Detroit.
Although it possessed a natural harbor, a bar at the mouth of the River Raisin created an
impediment that required ships to land passengers and cargoes by lighter craft until the late
1820s, when federal funding for a ship channel and piers facilitated access to the port. The
placement of Michigan's customs office at Detroit, however, denied Monroe the mercantile
business upon which its development as a port depended. Although shipping later served
Monroe directly, its volume never equaled that of Detroit.[24]

Above Detroit, water traffic on the lakes stopped at Mt. Clemens, at the mouth of the
Clinton River on Lake St. Clair. A secondary port, it served a limited region north of Detroit
and became the terminus of Michigan's only internal canal. Shipbuilding further enhanced Mt.
Clemens's role in marine trade on the lakes. The minor ports of Fort Gratiot and Port Huron
lay at the confluence of the Black and St. Clair Rivers. Situated outside the region of agricultural settlement, the military garrison and a small shipbuilding industry generated the bulk of
their early traffic. These settlements were served by steamboats from Detroit and were regular
stops for ships bound for the western lakes.[25]

Water traffic also reached the settlements of Lower Michigan via Saginaw Bay on Lake
Huron, and the port of Saginaw grew in importance as the region developed. Although poorly
connected by roads, rivers offered access to much of the vast lower Saginaw River drainage.
Because Saginaw lay twenty miles from the head of the bay, ships stopping there had to depart

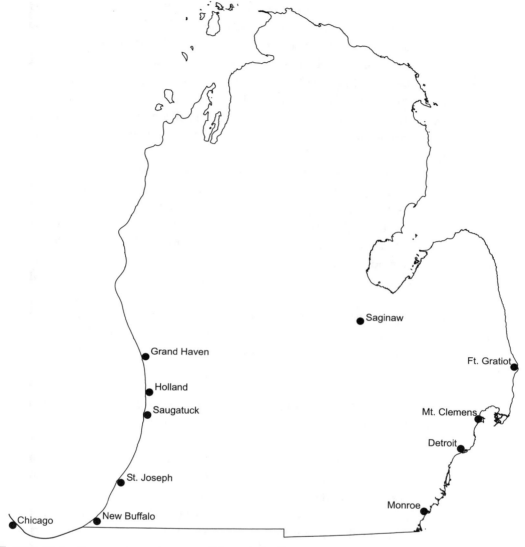

FIGURE 10.4. *PRINCIPAL LAKE PORTS IN MICHIGAN DURING THE SETTLEMENT PERIOD.* (Sources: Hewitt, *American Traveller*, 55–56; Mitchell, *Traveller's Guide*, 68; Tanner, *American Traveller*, 34).

from their lake routes, and initially only ships dedicated to trade with regional settlements visited Saginaw. Only two steamers plied regularly between Detroit and Saginaw in the mid–1830s, and by the early 1850s five were in regular service on the Saginaw River. At mid-century, annual arrivals at Saginaw averaged around twenty-five, and as many as ten or fifteen ships connected Saginaw with Buffalo and other lake ports.[26]

Ports on Lake Michigan were less important to settlement than those of the Eastern Shore, for several reasons. First, the land offices were located at Detroit, Monroe, or inland locations along a dendritic road network that funneled western settlement through Lake Erie ports. The placement of these administrative facilities all but precluded the development of western immigration ports. Second, the volume of commercial shipping on Lake Michigan expanded only after the settlement of much of western Michigan was already well under way. Third, the perception of Michigan's western shore as a hostile coastline for shipping also delayed development of western lake ports. Blois's 1838 *Gazetteer* noted that south of Grand Traverse Bay only two potential harbors existed, at the mouths of the Grand and St. Joseph Rivers, and both required improvements to make them navigable. Ten years later, a national mercantile journal reported that, of the natural harbors at the mouths of major rivers, all but that on the St. Joseph were "shut up by bars and obstructions."[27]

The development of western Michigan ports came only with the emergence of Chicago as an entrepôt for lands being colonized west of Lake Michigan. Its location and access to waterborne communications presented an opportunity for eastern investors to create at Chicago a western market with a potentially vast hinterland. By the mid–1830s, observers recognized Chicago's prominence as an economic center. Patrick Shirreff found the growing village to be "a place of considerable trade, supplying . . . a large tract of that country to the south and west; and [it] cannot fail of rising to importance."[28] Traveler Charles Fenno Hoffman predicted that

> As a place of business, its situation at the head of the Mississippi Valley will make it the New Orleans of the North; and its easy and close intercourse with the most flourishing eastern cities will give it the advantage, as its capital increases, of all their improvements in the mode of living.[29]

Chicago's emergence as a significant port in the late 1830s attracted shipping to the southern end of Lake Michigan and generated a volume of water traffic extensive enough to support secondary ports along the western Michigan shoreline.[30]

St. Joseph became western Michigan's principal port because of its early settlement and its proximity to Chicago. The settlement grew during the 1830s in response to the need of farmers in southwestern Michigan for an outlet for trade. An extensive trade flourished on the St. Joseph River despite delays in clearing that limited the use of steamboats until the 1840s, but by this time railroads had begun to siphon off trade and destroy commerce on the river.[31] Early travelers from western Michigan passed through St. Joseph on their way to Chicago by lake, and many preferred the lake voyage to the onerous overland route subsequently constructed over the wet lowlands around Lake Michigan. By the late 1830s steamboats offered daily service between Chicago and St. Joseph, and steamboats sailing between Chicago and Buffalo regularly stopped there. The port's role in the lake trade led the federal government to develop its harbor by constructing a breakwater and removing the bar to provide a harbor to shelter vessels in bad weather. Harbor improvements insured the settlement's prominence in the expanding Lake Michigan trade.[32]

Several other lake ports arose near natural harbors on the Lake Michigan shore. New Buffalo developed at the mouth of the Galien River during the 1830s. Its residents engaged in some trade with other lake ports, primarily Chicago and Milwaukee, Wisconsin, but it was not an export center. Dutch immigrants founded Holland in the late 1840s near the head of the

Black River and used its unimproved harbor largely for local trade and landing immigrants. Saugatuck developed in the late 1830s in response to the growth of lumbering on the lower Kalamazoo River. Situated near its mouth, Saugatuck imported freight and supplies and exported forest products. River trade above Allegan expanded, and by 1838 a steamboat made regular trips to Allegan and flatboats traveled as far as Kalamazoo.[33]

Grand Haven, at the mouth of the Grand River, grew slowly as the hub of a regional lumber and wood products trade, primarily with Chicago. Steamboats and other vessels traveled regularly from there as far inland as Grand Rapids. Some immigrants entered western Michigan via this port, and improvements to its harbor eventually permitted heavy shipping. Further north, settlements appeared at Grand Traverse Bay and the mouth of the Muskegon River during the late 1840s. Supplies for lumbering and provisioning settlements in these areas constituted the only lake traffic to these points and, although they possessed good natural harbors, neither was developed as a port until after 1860.[34]

The Erie Canal and the introduction of steam-powered ships reduced the time and cost involved in the movement of goods to eastern markets, and water transport offered Michigan a means by which to conduct external exchange throughout most of the year. Successful export trade, however, required a transportation system capable of moving agricultural commodities efficiently from the interior to lakeshore ports in all seasons. Such a task was beyond the capacity of the internal road network created to foster settlement and could only be accomplished through the use of innovative steam technologies just coming into use in the second quarter of the nineteenth century.

RAILROAD EXPANSION AND WESTERN COMMERCE

Possessing advantages over other means of transportation, railroads introduced a revolutionary form of technology capable of moving large volumes of cargo throughout the year across all sorts of terrain. Railroads combined the hauling capacity of canals with the flexibility of roads to bring about the rapid expansion of an export-oriented transportation system. First, they were not limited by the course of natural waterways or topography. If sharp grades were avoided, track could be laid over ground of varied elevation to reach almost any location. Trains could carry heavy, bulky cargoes to and from disparate settlements. Seasonal floods, droughts, ice, and snow had less effect on railroads, making their networks accessible throughout the year. Direct routes between points, fewer delays, and an ability to maintain constant rates of movement made shipment by rail far faster and more reliable than by road or canal.[35]

Transportation by rail also permitted reliable scheduling, and the need for efficiency in operations encouraged the use of standardized time to coordinate activities. The timely movement of goods eliminated unpredictable delays and a need for merchants to maintain large stocks. Because retailers could now acquire items expeditiously, wholesalers maintained greater control of their inventories and the prices they charged, and manufacturers could plan production according to demand. These developments increased the efficiency of production and marketing, which promoted economic integration on a larger scale. The efficiency of railroads directly affected agricultural production. Railroads moved produce quickly and with greater ease to regional entrepôts, thereby dramatically cutting the time farmers spent traveling to market. Savings could be reinvested in enlarging production and expanding the agricultural base, the fruits of which would now find an expanding and more reliable external market.[36]

The growth of railroads coincided with western expansion, and the flexibility of their technology provided the impetus for their recognition as the most suitable mode of transport in the West. The success of isolated rail routes encouraged economic growth in underdeveloped regions seeking external outlets, a pattern that encouraged the development and interconnection of smaller systems into larger networks. At the same time, the scale and nature of railroad transportation changed as a result of improvements in steam motive power, rolling stock, and track and roadbed construction, as well as in the standardization of track gauge.[37]

The terrain of lower Michigan proved ideal for the creation of a railroad network. The gently rolling to near level topography impressed early observers with its suitability for the construction of railroads. In 1835, Lt. John M. Berrien, a U.S. Army engineer, surveyed prospective routes across the peninsula and described its advantages in a report to the state railway convention meeting in Detroit.

> Throughout this route, but especially the western portions of it, extensive plains are met with, admitting of the construction of a [rail]road varying but little from the natural surface of the ground and nearly level. But few deep cuts are anywhere to be encountered, and heavy embankments may in most instances be avoided, and, the expense of grading will therefore be materially less than upon most other important [rail]roads, none of which I imagine traverses a country more admirably adapted to improvements of the kind, so far as regards facilities of construction.[38]

Chicago's emergence as the prime center of trade for the trans-Mississippi West stimulated railroad construction in Michigan. Since Chicago's role as a regional economic center depended on securing an extensive hinterland, the creation of a far-reaching railroad network permitted the city to capture overland trade, to become a western entrepôt as well as a major outlet for the produce of adjacent areas. Chicago's proximity to the Lower Peninsula stimulated Michigan's frontier economy by offering a second outside market, and its railroad links with older eastern markets drew Michigan into a developing national transportation system. The rise of Chicago as a railroad center hastened Michigan's transition from a frontier to a commercial agricultural region.[39]

By the 1830s, people interested in developing Michigan's economy believed that railroads would provide the most efficient means of opening the interior to trade. As a result, the territorial government granted charters for twenty-five railroad companies between 1830 and 1837. Of these, three managed to amass enough capital to actually begin construction. They were the Erie & Kalamazoo, to extend from the port of Toledo (then still within Michigan's boundaries) inland to Adrian in Lenawee County; the Detroit & St. Joseph, to be built westward from Detroit; and the Detroit & Pontiac, to link these two settlements (fig. 10.5).[40]

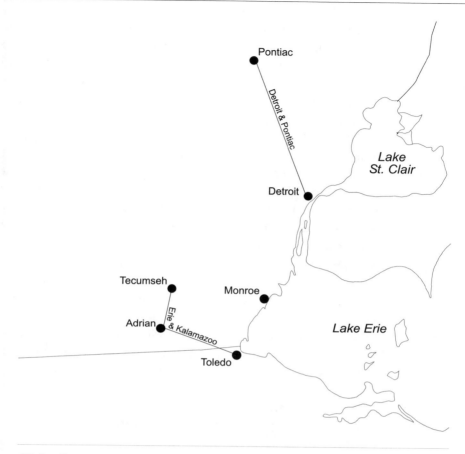

FIGURE 10.5. *ROUTES OF PRIVATELY FUNDED RAILROADS COMPLETED IN SOUTHERN MICHIGAN BY 1838.* (Sources: Parks, *Democracy's Railroads,* 51; Meints, "Michigan Railroad Construction," 2–3).

The Erie & Kalamazoo and Detroit & Pontiac were the first operating railroads north of the Ohio River. In 1837 the former carried freight by steam power along its entire length, and the next year the latter began running between Detroit and Royal Oak. Despite the limited extent of their operations, these pioneer railroads demonstrated their potential to increase the volume of trade to and from interior areas. Their presence had an immediate impact on the roles of frontier settlements. The placement of the terminus of the Erie & Kalamazoo at Adrian, for example, greatly enhanced the role of this small settlement as a shipping center. Its central location allowed it to immediately begin attracting grain and produce from a wide area, which promoted the expansion of trade and attracted other centralizing activities.[41]

The increase of trade at both Adrian and Pontiac, however, failed to attract large sums of private capital. Early Pontiac resident and railroad promoter Sherman Stevens noted that the cost of transporting a barrel of flour to Detroit fell from $1.25 to 18 3/4¢, an occurrence he claimed "was sufficient to double the value of wheat land in the country." Similarly, Mrs. Frank P. Dodge of Adrian recalled how the price of a barrel of Syracuse salt dropped from $15 to $9 after the completion of the Erie & Kalamazoo.[42] Despite their success in encouraging local economic growth, however, the limited financial return on developmental railroads made capitalists reluctant to invest in their construction. The frustration caused by the inability of private resources to underwrite internal improvement growth led the state to choose the dramatic, and disastrous, alternative of public sponsorship.

When the State of Michigan assumed responsibility for constructing internal improvements in 1837, it planned three railroads across the peninsula (fig. 10.3). Two stretched westward to the Lake Michigan shore, linking Detroit to St. Joseph and Monroe with New Buffalo, to connect proposed Canadian rail lines and Lake Erie shipping with Lake Michigan and the Mississippi Valley. These railroads also provided access to the agricultural settlements in Michigan's interior and diverted their produce from the rival port of Toledo. The route of the Northern Railroad passed westward from Palmer (present-day St. Clair), on the St. Clair River, through the northernmost area of settlement to the mouth of the Grand River.[43]

Following the Panic of 1837, Michigan attempted to salvage its internal improvement program by concentrating its resources on the two southern railroads. During the 1840s the Central was completed westward from Detroit through Ypsilanti, Ann Arbor, Jackson, and Battle Creek, to Kalamazoo. The Southern Railroad linked the port of Monroe with Adrian and Hillsdale (fig. 10.6). Greater support from the state made possible the more extensive development of the Central. Its short length and limited hinterland, coupled with the poorly developed harbor at Monroe, handicapped the Southern. Competition from the Erie & Kalamazoo, an established railroad with excellent port facilities at Toledo, also retarded the development of this line. The deficiencies of the Southern contributed to its reputation as a badly maintained railroad. Lack of funding prevented any construction on the Northern Railroad. Declining state revenues and inadequate operating receipts prevented the completion of either the Central or Southern, and motivated the state to sell all of its railroads to private interests in 1846.[44]

After 1846, private investors developed an efficient internal transportation system that focused on the Central, the Southern, and the Detroit & Pontiac Railroads. The owners extended routes into the interior to increase the size of their shipping territories. In order to maintain close ties with the national economy, they anchored their lines in Detroit, which had firm links to the industrial centers of the Northeast. They also understood the growing significance of transportation connections between the Northeast and the Mississippi Valley, and they planned the routes of Michigan railroads to become portions of national trunk lines passing from Chicago around Lake Erie.

The Michigan Central extended its line southwestward from Kalamazoo to New Buffalo in 1849. Two years later, construction on the Michigan Southern Railroad reached as far west as White Pigeon. Together the two railroads established trunk lines across southern Michigan, linking the Kalamazoo and St. Joseph River Valleys with the eastern part of the state. In what was perhaps a more extraordinary development, a third railroad was built westward from Pontiac to Grand Haven. This line, called the Detroit & Milwaukee, incorporated the older Detroit & Pontiac Railroad in 1855 and within three years was extended across the peninsula

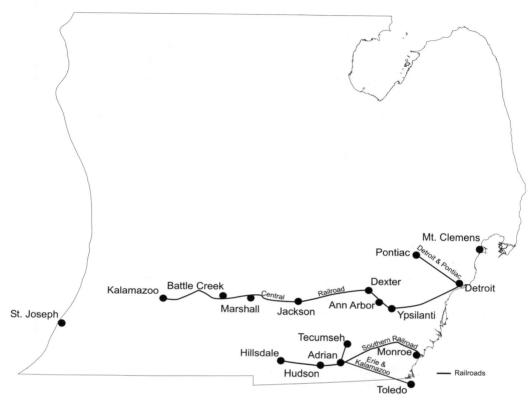

FIGURE 10.6. *ROUTES OF STATE-SPONSORED RAILROADS COMPLETED IN SOUTHERN MICHIGAN BY 1846.* (Sources: Parks, *Democracy's Railroads,* 132; Meints, "Michigan Railroad Construction," 3–7).

through the Grand River Valley to the shore of Lake Michigan. Although envisioned primarily as a bridge line linking the Wisconsin port of Milwaukee with eastern markets, its completion also provided a means of transportation capable of supporting commercial agriculture in the northernmost settled portion of southern Lower Michigan.[45]

Rail lines now reached all settled parts of Lower Michigan, and the access to trade they offered encouraged the development of improved feeder roads to accommodate the increased traffic to and from farms. Plank roads helped create these badly needed routes. Constructed cheaply in frontier regions where timber was abundant, plank roads provided a hard surface over which freight, produce, and passengers could travel more or less unimpeded for short distances during all seasons. In Michigan, plank roads became popular as feeder lines to the railroads in the 1840s and were constructed as toll roads by private companies under state charter. Their numbers proliferated as traffic increased, which led to the replacement of plank roads by more efficient means of transportation.[46]

The 1850s witnessed the growth of railroad feeder lines in Michigan in response to the increased volume of trade. A 1855 state law expedited the incorporation of railroads to meet these needs, and federal legislation the following year granting lands to aid railroad construction provided a financial stimulus for the extension of rail lines into all parts of the interior. By 1857, a dozen railroads were formed in the state, and sixteen others followed in the next two years. Although an integrated rail network did not appear in Michigan until after the Civil War, its roots had taken hold by 1860. In little more than a decade after the sale of the state's railroads, the system was well on its way to fulfilling the intent of its original planners, who saw this mode of transportation as the key to opening the frontier to commercial trade.[47]

In order to facilitate Michigan's export trade, the regional railroads centered the transportation network in Detroit. The city's port furnished facilities capable of handling large quantities of freight and its location provided a direct water route to Buffalo and other eastern Lake Erie ports. The Michigan Central had always maintained a terminal at Detroit, and the choice of the Detroit & Pontiac as the basis for the northern route anchored this railroad in the entrepôt as well. Finding itself without a Michigan terminus, the Michigan Southern constructed and leased a line linking it with Detroit.

The choice of Detroit as a terminus by Michigan's principal railroads strengthened the city's position as a regional entrepôt. Railroads established the city as the center of a transportation system that made export-oriented agricultural production feasible in southern Michigan. With the provision of a central wholesale market for Michigan, the cost of selling frontier crops fell markedly and farm income increased. As agricultural producers and trades people realized greater wealth, Detroit emerged as the focus of trade and manufacturing in Michigan and its major urban center. Detroit's central role in export trade insured its continued economic dominance.[48]

To the eastern interests that backed the construction of Michigan's railroads, however, the opening of a peninsular hinterland was not the final goal in the establishment of the new transportation lines. The proximity of southern Michigan to the commercial artery of the eastern Great Lakes and Chicago provided an opportunity for railroads crossing the peninsula to establish crucial overland transportation links between Chicago and the Northeast and gain a monopoly over western trade. The owners of Michigan's southernmost railroads attempted to take advantage of this situation.[49]

Although the charters of both the Michigan Central and the Michigan Southern restricted the length of their routes and obliged them to build lines, respectively, to the Lake Michigan shore and the St. Joseph River, each planned its route so as to continue further westward to Chicago. The Michigan Southern, having reached White Pigeon in 1851, linked its western terminus with the Northern Indiana Railroad through the lease of a private line constructed northward from South Bend expressly for that purpose. The owners of the Michigan Southern, having purchased an interest in the Northern Indiana and the Chicago, Rock Island & Pacific, used these railroads' rights-of-way to open traffic from western Michigan to Chicago in the winter of 1852. Three years later the Michigan Southern and Northern Indiana merged to form a single corporation.[50]

Having extended its line from Kalamazoo to New Buffalo in 1849, the Michigan Central followed the lead of its sister railroad in extending its line westward beyond the state's boundaries. It, too, obtained use of a western right-of-way by assisting an Indiana line, the New

Albany & Salem, and arranged joint use of track with the Illinois Central to gain entry into Chicago. The Michigan Central began operating trains between Detroit and Chicago in the spring of 1852.[51]

The completion of the Michigan Central and Michigan Southern lines opened the first rail links between Lake Erie and Chicago. Both railroads, however, still depended upon lake shipping for their connection with eastern markets. In order to overcome the seasonal disadvantages of water transportation on Lake Erie, which froze over in winter, and establish reliable, year-round freight routes to the Northeast, the railroads extended their connections eastward around the lake to Buffalo. The Great Western Railroad of Canada accomplished this in the 1850s when, with financial assistance from the Michigan Central, it built a line from Windsor to Buffalo. The consolidation of a number of short lines south of Lake Erie linked Buffalo to the Michigan Southern terminus at Toledo via the "Lake Shore Route." Together these two systems formed overland trunk lines from Buffalo to Chicago, and their operators held a monopoly over this lucrative interregional trade until the end of the 1850s. Although other routes would subsequently be established to Chicago and the West, the early entry of the Michigan railroads into long-distance trade assured the state a permanent role in western commerce. This development further accelerated Michigan's incorporation within the national economy.[52]

The railroads' success as long-distance carriers enriched their owners and changed the nature of trade in the regions through which they passed. As principal shippers of western grain, Michigan railroads hauled not only the produce of their own state, but also that of other places. Indeed, the access they provided for western grain-growing areas helped reorient much of their trade away from the Mississippi River corridor toward the Northeast.[53]

11

The Restructuring of Michigan Agriculture

A Focus on Marketable Crops

S uccessful commercial agriculture in the West depended upon the production of farm commodities for which there was demand sufficient to justify the costs of specialization. The transformation of the national economy, particularly the rise of urban markets in the East, brought about a geographical reorganization of production on American farms. Crops likely to yield the highest income per unit of land tended to gravitate toward urban markets, while those requiring greater acreage and fetching lower prices remained peripheral to them. This process not only altered the nature of eastern agriculture, but extended the production of less valuable commercial crops westward. Occurring at a time when the national population itself was growing rapidly, these changes opened a market for farmers on newly settled Michigan lands.

Corn for Food, Feed, and Drink

Corn was the all-purpose subsistence crop in nineteenth-century America, and it was produced in greater quantities than any other crop in antebellum Michigan (table 11.1). Its popularity had less to do with its commercial potential than its unique role in the regional economy of the frontier. As the basis for such staple foods as johnny cake, corn mush, hominy, and corn fritters, it became a mainstay of the farm diet. Corn was a major component of feed for work animals and was used extensively for fattening meat animals. Its wide range of uses made it ideal for Michigan farmers, who required a crop adaptable to the varied needs of diversified production during the settlement period.[1]

Although Lower Michigan lay at the northern edge of the corn-growing zone of North America, settlers perceived its land as suited for the production of corn, even though yields fell short of those realized in Ohio, Indiana, and Illinois. Corn was sensitive to Michigan's climate, and a distinctive geographic pattern in its production emerged early and persisted throughout the antebellum period (figs. 11.1 and 11.2). Although extremely hot weather could injure or reduce its yields, corn was not affected by the diseases and insect pests that threatened other grains.[2]

Corn was an ideal frontier crop. Since it produced relatively large yields per weight in seed, settlers could bring enough seed with them to plant their first crop, using few tools, in land that was only minimally cleared. Corn seldom failed, could be harvested gradually at low cost, and was easily stored. These advantages made corn crucial to the survival of pioneers such as Henry Rowland

TABLE 11.1 *PRODUCTION OF AGRICULTURAL CROPS IN MICHIGAN FROM 1810 THROUGH 1864.*

Product	1810	1836	1840	1850	1854	1860	1864
Wheat (bu)	12,000	1,014,896	2,157,108	4,893,141	7,027,932	8,171,688	9,687,627
Rye (bu)	-	21,994	34,236	102,260	-	525,716	-
Corn (bu)	10,000	791,427	2,227,039	5,704,172	7,630,658	13,372,877	11,007,284
Oats (bu)	8,000	1,116,910	2,114,051	1,843,134	-	4,063,528	-
Barley (bu)	100	-	127,802	70,801	-	302,951	-
Potatoes (bu)	12,540	-	2,109,205	2,333,020	2,917,434	5,258,628	4,059,271
Wool (lbs)	-	-	153,375	2,007,598	2,680,747	6,929,113	7,249,934
Hay (tons)	-	-	130,805	424,070	496,041	-	843,346
Flour (bbls)	-	-	202,880	784,684	998,503	761,156	1,319,923
Buckwheat (bu)	1,308	64,022	-	476,811	-	523,687	-
Orchard Production	-	-	$16,075	$130,552	-	$1,116,219	-

Sources: Blois, *Gazetteer*, 392; U. S. Census, 1810, 1840, 1850, 1860; Michigan Census, 1854, 1864; Evans, *Pedestrious Tour.*

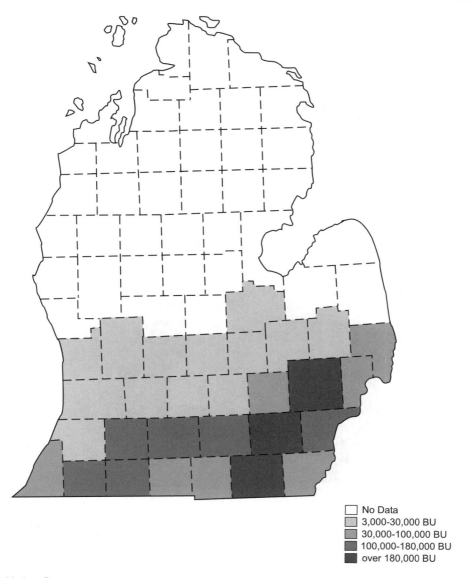

FIGURE 11.1. *CORN PRODUCTION IN SOUTHERN MICHIGAN IN 1840.* (Source: U. S. Census, Agriculture, 1840).

and his neighbors in Clinton County. In their first year of residence, he and four Eagle Township neighbors subsisted on the corn they harvested and ground on a shared hand mill. In the next year they raised a crop of wheat, which had to be transported to Portland, in neighboring Ionia County, to be milled. Contemporary accounts reported that corn yielded forty to fifty bushels per acre on a variety of soil types.[3]

Throughout most of the antebellum period there was no substantial external market for Michigan corn harvested as grain, but a portion of the crop found a wider market. Many farm

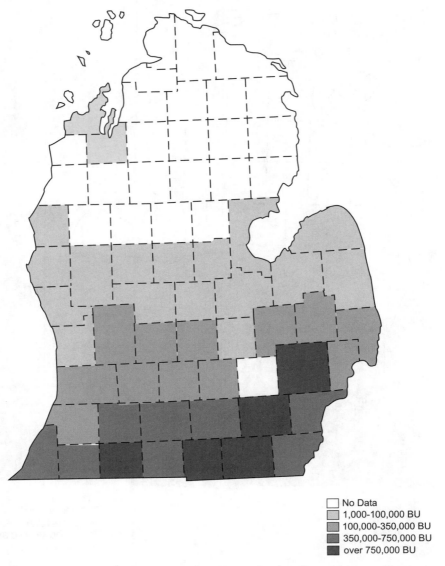

FIGURE 11.2. *CORN PRODUCTION IN SOUTHERN MICHIGAN IN 1860*. (Source: U. S. Census, Agriculture, 1860).

families made brooms from broomcorn grown expressly for this purpose. Michigan pioneers, such as Thomas Wright of Tecumseh, engaged in broom-making as a winter activity. Jeremiah D. Williams of Washtenaw County recalled that several Webster Township residents engaged in broom-making in 1835. By mid-century, farmers grew broomcorn widely in Michigan, although by this time broom-making had moved from farms to factories in the larger settlements.[4]

Since corn could be converted into meat for both subsistence and trade, the raising of livestock became an increasing source of income for Michigan residents (table 11.2). Driving animals to market required no roads or vehicles, but livestock farmers needed corn to fatten cattle prior to and during the drives. Michigan residents, such as White Cleveland of Raisin Township in Lenawee County, engaged in "mixed husbandry," farming as well as feeding cattle for sale each spring. Romain Putnam, of Burton Township, bought stock in Genesee County for sale in Detroit. Similarly, William Baker, a merchant from Hudson, drove stock acquired in Lenawee County to Toledo for sale. Residents of southwestern Michigan fattened cattle that were sold in Indiana, from whence they were driven to New York markets. Leonard Miller, of Scipio Township in Hillsdale County, and other cattle dealers drove their herds directly to markets in the Northeast.[5]

Michigan corn could be converted to cash by raising hogs, and farmers found hogs an ideal product for wider markets. Quick to reach maturity and requiring little skill and labor to handle, hogs were well adapted to conditions on the frontier and were relied upon almost universally by pioneer farmers for domestic consumption and income. Frontier hogs ran loose during the year, surviving on acorns, nuts, roots, and other natural fodder, and then were fattened with corn before slaughter in the fall. Butchers at regional markets converted hogs into pork and shipped the barreled product eastward via the canal and lake system. This practice subjected the shipment of pork to the limitations of water transportation, which allowed only a short period between fall slaughter and the winter close of navigation.[6]

Michigan settlers also converted corn into another saleable product which had a distinctive role in the pioneer diet. During the first thirty years of the nineteenth century, Michigan followed a national trend of increasing alcohol consumption, generating a growing demand for distilled beverages on the frontier.[7] John F. Hinman commented dryly that in the 1820s, "Hard drinking was indulged in until old age scarcely enabled a man to see snakes." Liquor played an extensive social role in pioneer communities. In the absence of formal institutions, gatherings brought a dispersed and diverse population together to engage in the communal activities, rituals, and ceremonies necessary for farm-making and maintaining social integration.[8] When Macomb County was settled in the 1820s, early resident John E. Day remembered

> the use of intoxicants on all noted occasions, and indeed upon the most common events of pioneer life. . . . At births, weddings, and deaths, its inspiring aid was sought. Prominent in the history of each new township were the bees, for the progress of work which one alone could not very well accomplish, such as loggings and raisings.[9]

Pioneers consumed notorious amounts of distilled spirits at communal building projects and, for occasions such as barn raisings, saw liquor as a necessary libation, "to exhilarate and fire the spirit and to put enthusiasm and life into the gathering." A participant in the raising of the frame for the new state capital in Lansing attributed the success of the endeavor to the convivial atmosphere created by the free liquor and food provided for the volunteer workers. Many farmers believed the invigorating effect of whiskey maintained their health when carrying out heavy labor.[10]

Because a bushel of corn converted to whiskey yielded five times its worth as grain and could be transported easily, it became a commonly traded item in Michigan's frontier economy.

TABLE 11.2 *PRODUCTION OF LIVESTOCK AND LIVESTOCK PRODUCTS IN MICHIGAN FROM 1836 THROUGH 1864.*

Product	1837	1840	1850	1854	1860	1864
Wool (lbs)	-	153,375	2,007,598	2,640,747	6,929,113	7,249,934
Pork (lbs)	-	-	-	11,258,841	-	33,137,002
Butter (lbs)	-	-	7,056,896	7,924,896	15,498,047	13,836,452
Cheese (lbs)	-	-	1,112,646	779,530	1,610,097	1,580,945
Sheep	22,684	99,618	756,382	964,333	1,266,680	2,053,363
Hogs	109,096	295,890	202,588	239,832	366,572	385,889
Cattle	89,610*	185,190	117,043	141,253	240,428	210,382
Milch Cows	-	-	97,557	139,260	189,441	232,188
Working Oxen	-	-	56,203	67,033	62,055	60,643

* Includes all cattle, milch cows, and working oxen

Sources: Blois, *Gazetteer*, 392; U. S. Census, Agriculture, 1840, 1850, 1860; Michigan Census, 1854, 1864.

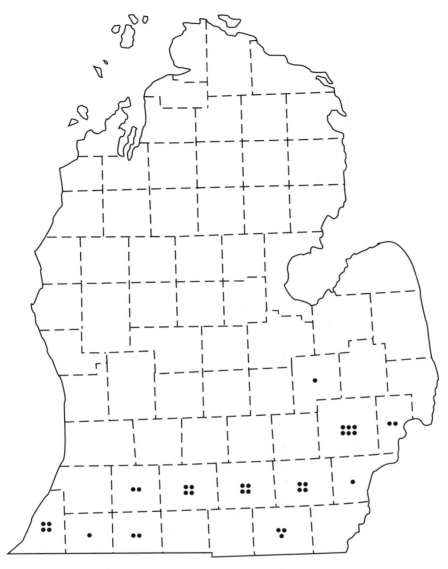

FIGURE 11.3. *DISTRIBUTION OF DISTILLERIES BY COUNTY IN SOUTHERN MICHIGAN IN 1840.* (Source: U. S. Census, Agriculture, 1840).

Residents produced distilled spirits sufficient for internal distribution and limited export sales, and state administrators found it nearly impossible to effectively control an inexpensive product that was distributed by grocers, merchants, and small retailers scattered over an extensive region. Some Michigan distillers also exported a portion of their production. In southwestern Michigan the navigable St. Joseph River provided an early outlet for whiskey via Lake Michigan as early as the 1820s. Whiskey also found its way into illegal trade with Native peoples, and some distilleries operated intentionally for the Indian market. One St. Joseph County operation,

TABLE 11.3. *PRODUCTION OF DISTILLED LIQUOR IN MICHIGAN FROM 1810 THROUGH 1864.*

	1810	1820	1822	1837	1840	1850	1854	1860	1864
Liquor (gal)	20,400	2,160	-	-	337,761	873,920	260,340	-	284,332
Distilleries	8	4	4	16	34	29	13	7	17

Sources: U. S. Census, 1810, 1820; U. S. Census, Agriculture, 1840, 1850, 1860; ASP/F 4/1823/662; Michigan Census, 1854, 1864; Blois, *Gazetteer*, 390.

TABLE 11.4. *PRODUCTION OF BEER IN MICHIGAN FROM 1840 THROUGH 1864.*

	1840	1850	1854	1860	1864
Number of Brewers	10	-	28	42	95
Quantities Produced (bbl)	(7,529)	-	36,392	57,671	54,926
Quantities Produced (gal)	308,696	-	(1,492,072)	(2,364,511)	(2,251,884)

Numbers in parentheses are estimates based on 1 bbl = 41 gals.

Sources: U. S. Census, Agriculture, 1840, 1850; U. S. Census, Manufactures, 1860; Michigan Census, 1854, 1864.

recalled Three Rivers resident Ruth Hoppin, carried out an extensive trade with the nearby Potawatomi reservation.[11]

The distribution of distilleries in Lower Michigan followed the growth of settlement. The earliest recorded distillery was erected in Macomb County in 1797, and by the 1820s distillers also operated in neighboring St. Clair County. Agricultural expansion in the subsequent decade encouraged the spread of distilling across the peninsula, where its manufacture gravitated toward those counties producing the greatest volume of corn (fig. 11.3). In 1840, Kalamazoo, Calhoun, St. Joseph, Oakland, Washtenaw, Berrien, and Lenawee were the largest liquor-producing counties.[12]

Distilled alcohol production in Michigan reflected a rising national trend in the output and consumption of distilled spirits, especially in areas where grain surpluses existed. Despite a dearth of quantitative data for antebellum Michigan, census returns provide a record of whiskey making for some years (table 11.3). These figures reveal an apparent decline in production immediately after the War of 1812, followed by a marked and continuing increase in both the quantity of spirits manufactured and the number of distilleries operated. Michigan distillers increased their per capita output so that the greatest amount of liquor was actually manufactured after the number of distilleries had begun to decline. The volume of whiskey making in Michigan reached its height around mid-century.[13]

Two broader trends in antebellum America intervened to alter the role of corn as a commercial crop. First, a decline in national per capita alcohol consumption after 1835 lowered demand for distilled products and precipitated a falling off of the whiskey market. Encouraged by a growing religious and social movement advocating temperance or abstinence as necessary steps toward achieving spiritual salvation and material improvement, Americans began to favor malt beverages with a lower alcohol content.[14] In Michigan, a statewide temperance society campaigned vigorously to restrict or prohibit liquor use, and its efforts resulted in the passage of a state law in 1855 forbidding all traffic in distilled spirits. Unaffected by the prohibition law of 1855, beer consumption increased rapidly to fill the void left by spirituous liquor, and beer and malt liquor production rose as distilling declined (table 11.4).[15]

An increased national demand for grain had even greater significance for the production and use of corn. Reduced costs of transporting western produce to eastern markets created a national feed grain market that enhanced the value of corn dramatically. As the price of corn overtook that of whiskey, the latter became more expensive to produce. By mid-century, Michigan farmers found alternative markets for corn. Markedly rising receipts for corn shipped through Toledo and Buffalo in the 1850s imply the diversion of a significant portion of Michigan's corn from alcohol to feed grain. The growth of a national feed market sustained increased corn production in Michigan, insuring its place as a leading export crop.[16]

Wheat, the Market Grain of Choice

In the eyes of Michigan's settlers, wheat's high value as a cash crop made it the most desirable grain to produce. Always in demand, it kept well and could be cultivated with relatively little capital investment. On a cleared farm, wheat required only seasonal labor, which was well within the capabilities of a dispersed agricultural population. By the time pioneers introduced wheat in southern Michigan, it was already a successful staple crop in the Old Northwest. "This is emphatically a wheat country," wrote a correspondent to the *Genesee Farmer* in 1833. Contemporary sources reported substantial yields of wheat in frontier Michigan. Observers claimed that between twenty and forty bushels per acre could be raised in various parts of Michigan; however, recent research suggests yields rarely reached the upper end of this range.[17]

The increasing size of wheat harvests in antebellum Michigan reveals a marked expansion in its cultivation for market purposes following the opening of transportation links to the Northeast (table 11.1). The exponential growth of wheat production after 1836 also attests to an increasing emphasis on this marketable crop by Michigan settlers as they expanded their farms. At mid-century, wheat occupied a greater acreage than any other crop in Michigan, taking up one-fourth of all improved land and one-half of the land currently in use.[18] Farmers grew so much wheat that at harvest time they clogged the roads, hauling wheat to market. Traveling between Hillsdale and Monroe in 1849, the editor of the *Michigan Farmer* bore witness to this spectacle:

> What particularly attracted our attention along the road was the immense quantities of wheat and flour coming into market. Long trains of cars were loaded down with these commodities, going into Monroe; the warehouses were, to a considerable extent, filled with them, and the streets were blockaded with trains. A gentleman informed us, that he stood and counted fifty teams in the streets of Hillsdale at one time on Saturday, and doubtless a much larger number might have been counted at Adrian.[19]

Wheat production gravitated toward those counties possessing large areas of openings and prairie lands that could be rapidly placed in cultivation. This pattern was already evident in 1840, when the greatest production was concentrated in Oakland, Washtenaw, and Lenawee Counties and the counties of the upper Kalamazoo and St. Joseph river drainages (fig. 11.4). Two decades later wheat production had increased markedly in all counties, but its distribution still indicated a preference for open lands (fig. 11.5). One visitor to the St. Joseph River described the country as, "one uninterrupted field of wheat."[20]

Farmers grew several varieties of winter wheat, to improve the reliability of yields. Among those mentioned in contemporary accounts were white chaff and flint, which were reliable but produced low yields; red chaff, an uncertain variety capable of large yields; and blue stem, a reliable, widely cultivated type that produced good yields.[21]

Wheat farmers experienced risks because of the grain's extreme susceptibility to diseases that could destroy an entire crop, threatening the livelihood of the growers. Farmers feared black stem rust, which shriveled the grain. Long prevalent in the eastern United States, rust had spread to Michigan by the 1830s, and attacked crops grown under wet conditions. William Nowlin, an early settler farmer in Dearborn, recalled rust as a common plague on wheat grown in the poorly drained lands of eastern Michigan. Yet rust also occurred in areas where wheat

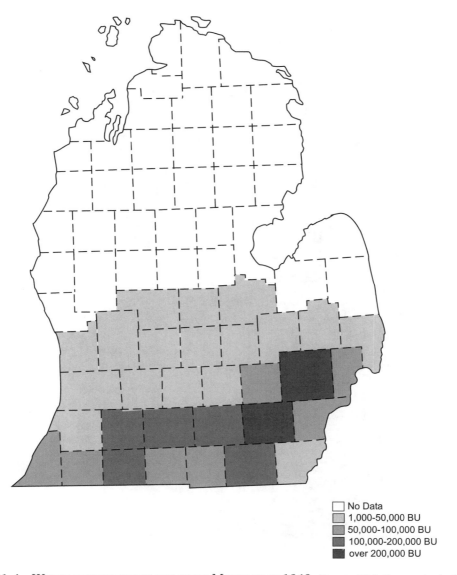

No Data
1,000-50,000 BU
50,000-100,000 BU
100,000-200,000 BU
over 200,000 BU

FIGURE 11.4. *WHEAT PRODUCTION IN SOUTHERN MICHIGAN IN 1840.* (Source: U. S. Census, Agriculture, 1840).

normally grew well. In the St. Joseph country, for example, an exceedingly wet spring devastated the wheat crop in 1834.[22]

Other enemies of wheat included the Hessian fly and the midge. The larvae of the Hessian fly fed on the plant stalks, and the midge, or weevil, attacked wheat kernels. Introduced on the Eastern Seaboard during the American Revolution, the Hessian fly spread rapidly westward in the 1820s. By the 1830s this "mysterious and destructive insect" had reached Michigan, affecting crops in Oakland County, and by the end of the decade it had spread across the peninsula.

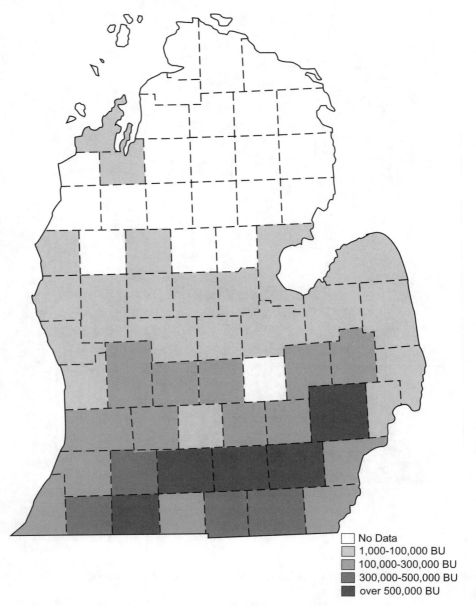

FIGURE 11.5. *WHEAT PRODUCTION IN SOUTHERN MICHIGAN IN 1860.* (Source: U. S. Census, Agriculture, 1860).

Pioneer explorer and geologist Bela Hubbard observed crops reduced by this pest to half their normal size and reported that the destruction of wheat in Kalamazoo County and southwestern Michigan was so extensive in 1840 that many farmers plowed up their fields in the late spring to plant other crops. The midge migrated southward from Lower Canada before 1830 and spread quickly over the northern United States, reaching Michigan by the 1840s.[23]

Although destructive, damage by insects and disease could be reduced by varying agricultural practices. Farmers found that by planting after fall frosts had destroyed the Hessian fly larvae, they could interrupt the cycle of infestation and protect new crops from this insect. They controlled rust by reducing moisture in the soil through draining and deep-plowing. Farmers also employed deep-plowing to destroy the midge larvae, and rotated crops and eliminated weeds to protect new wheat crops planted in previously infested fields.[24]

Wheat continued to be grown successfully in Michigan despite these destructive agents, yet the lessons learned from the experience caused many farmers to question their reliance on a single commercial crop. The *Michigan Farmer,* a rising advocate of agricultural reform, argued in 1849 that the economic precariousness of relying on a single crop placed the state's farmers at the mercy of weather and crop pests and warned that the exhausting effects of wheat cultivation on soil would cause its steady deterioration and reduce its ability to produce crops. However, the diversification of market agriculture promoted by such journals was not immediately forthcoming. Wheat continued to dominate commercial production in the 1840s and 1850s as improved transportation and high prices encouraged the expansion of production in the newly settled western lands.[25]

Field Crops, Fruit, and Specialty Crops

Michigan farmers raised barley, hay, potatoes, and other cultigens for market sales as well as home consumption (table 11.1). Immigrant farmers grew barley as food for themselves and their animals. Barley was a hardy crop, often sown in place of wheat when the latter was threatened or had been destroyed by midge or other diseases. Like corn, barley possessed the advantage of being easily converted into a product whose popularity increased demand. As a principal ingredient in beer, barley found a growing market among Michigan brewers. As the popularity of beer increased in the late antebellum period, so did the commercial role of barley, and by 1860 its production was largely devoted to beer making.[26]

Michigan farmers harvested large quantities of hay, to feed their livestock over the winter and to sell to nonfarmers who depended heavily on animal power all year round. The grasslands of Michigan afforded settlers a natural hay that could be harvested for home use or the maintenance of cattle being driven to eastern markets. Lansing Swan, traveling through southern Michigan in 1841, remarked on the "great number of natural meadows of hundreds of acres, never cultivated in the least. All the farmer has to do is, when the grass is ready, send on his men and mow it down." After visiting the wild hay marshes in Allegan County, Bela Hubbard noted that "Very little cultivated hay is raised in any county we have entered west of Calhoun, and the farmers go great distances to cut hay in these marshes." Western hay found use as fodder for the farmers' own stock, but was also shipped to cities or other settlements where animals powered transport. Farmers who raised specialized livestock, such as dairy cows and sheep, also purchased hay to feed their stock. In response to rising demand, commercial hay production expanded rapidly in Michigan in the 1850s (table 11.1).[27]

Immigrant farmers also grew the Irish potato, a New World cultigen that was well adapted to northern soils. Potatoes yielded prodigious harvests in the small clearings of pioneer farms and were among the earliest crops planted. Michigan farmers produced potatoes for regional consumption until long-distance transportation opened a wider market in the Northeast.[28]

Demand for western potatoes rose rapidly in the 1840s with the appearance of the "potato disease," or "rot," which devastated northeastern crops before spreading to Europe. In spite of the disease, the continued opening of new lands in the West actually permitted output to increase in the United States, and Michigan's potato crop grew moderately in the unhappy decade (table 11.1). Cheaper long-distance transport, together with the development of disease-resistant strains and improved planting practices, encouraged the expansion of potato production in the 1850s, and Michigan's output more than doubled by 1860 (table 11.1). Quick to take advantage of the higher prices in a growing market, many farmers curtailed wheat production in favor of potatoes, and in some areas, including St. Joseph County, they became a major crop.[29]

Michigan settlers planted three other grains (table 11.1). They produced buckwheat and rye for home or local consumption only. Oats delivered large yields on a variety of soils, and farmers fed the crop to their livestock and sold oats as fodder, but their low ratio of food value to bulk made long-distance shipping unprofitable. Farmers discovered that when they used oats as a rotation crop, they enhanced the production of wheat. The moderate increase in oat production in Michigan between 1840 and 1860 stemmed from farm growth and the modification of agricultural practices, rather than the expansion of markets.[30]

Michigan possessed an environment amenable to several orchard crops. Perhaps the most important of these was the apple. Apples grown in the French enclave settlements yielded both fruit and cider, and orchards were established by the time of American settlement. Apples had also been a staple on farms in the Northeast, and their demonstrated success in Michigan, as well as their introduction into Ohio and Indiana by agricultural promoters such as John Chapman (Johnny Appleseed), encouraged their adoption by immigrants familiar with this fruit.[31]

Settlers perceived the lands of the Michigan interior to be congenial to apple growing, and they planted orchards as soon as possible. An immigrant to Schoolcraft in Kalamazoo County proclaimed proudly that her family had immediately set out fifty apple trees, and predicted that "in five years [we] shall have fruit in abundance." A similar sentiment of optimism was expressed by a farmer near Eaton Rapids, whose 180 apple trees had begun to bear in their third year. "I had two bushels this year," he wrote. "Last year I had forty apples. I think next year I will have twenty to thirty bushels."[32]

Most pioneers set out seedling apple trees obtained from nurseries. John Daniels, of Jackson, for example, planted the first orchard in the county with trees sent him by his father from Detroit. Settlers in Kent County also set out seedlings. So great was the demand for seedling trees that they became an item of exchange in the frontier economy. Several immigrants to Ionia County established a nursery upon their arrival in order to supply apple trees to new settlers in the late 1830s. A large nursery in Oakland County supplied farmers throughout the state and even exported trees to Wisconsin. By the 1840s, the sale of seedling trees was big business in Lower Michigan.[33]

Frontier orchards soon produced enough apples for the regional economy, and later for export to eastern markets. In 1851, surveys of Michigan apple growers revealed that at least twenty-one varieties were grown in the state, many of which were produced specifically for long-distance marketing. The success of market-oriented production of apples resulted in an eightfold increase in the size of the crop between 1840 and 1850 and a comparable increase during the next ten years (table 11.1).[34]

Settlers grew peaches in many locations across the Lower Peninsula, and immigrants established small orchards with imported trees and seedling stock. By 1830, extensive orchards existed in the southeastern part of the state. The ameliorating effect of Lake Michigan also produced a climate conducive to fruit growing along the western shore, and specialized production of peaches began in the lower St. Joseph Valley in the 1830s. The fruit's susceptibility to late frosts limited peach growing elsewhere.[35]

Access to external markets by way of Lake Michigan permitted peach growing to emerge as a commercial enterprise in western Michigan. The first peaches were shipped via the lake to Chicago in 1839, and within a year the regular export of Michigan fruit commenced. The growth of the Chicago market created an impetus for expansion, and several large orchards were producing fruit by the late 1840s. In 1850 growers shipped an estimated ten thousand baskets of peaches through St. Joseph. Although the fruit-growing area of western Michigan remained confined to the southwestern portion of the state before the Civil War, the success of production there would encourage the subsequent northward expansion of agriculture along the western shore during the second half of the nineteenth century. Pioneers also planted plum, pear, nectarine, and apricot trees for home or local consumption, but none produced substantial yields in 1860. Cherries began to draw the attention of growers, but their commercial success as a market crop also came much later.[36]

Michigan entrepreneurs produced peppermint oil exclusively for the commercial export market. In response to rising demand for peppermint as a flavoring agent, growers began cultivating plants on White Pigeon Prairie in St. Joseph County in 1835 and extracted oil two years later. By 1846, about 25 percent of the total American output of peppermint oil originated in Michigan, although its restricted market limited production to a small portion of St. Joseph County. Michigan peppermint oil producers owed their success largely to their exporter, the New York firm of E. C. Patterson and Company, whose agents paid rival New York growers to discontinue the crop in order to create a shortage of the oil. The rising market price of oil enhanced the firm's profits and provided a monopoly for Michigan producers as well as a steady market for their crop.[37]

During the 1830s, many Michigan farmers responded to the promotion of silk production and attempted to produce it from the cocoons of silkworms. They found the prospect especially attractive because it offered a valuable cash crop that would bear the cost of long-distance transportation, and proponents predicted that it would become one of the state's principal crops. A number of farmers planted the "Chinese" mulberry tree (*Morus multicaulis*), upon which the silkworms fed, but only a few, such as Abel Page of Kent County, successfully raised silkworms and sold the cocoons. Michigan's silk cocoon output for 1840 was only 266, and it had declined to 180 a decade later, by which time the silk craze had run its course in the United States.[38]

Promoters also attempted to introduce sugar beets as a livestock feed and a source of sugar for human consumption. Farmers successfully raised sugar beets in Massachusetts, Ohio, and northern Illinois, and their experience led promoters to view Michigan as an ideal place for the production of this potentially lucrative cash crop. Supported by legislative bounty on sugar manufactured from beets, entrepreneurs organized the White Pigeon Sugar Beet Manufactory in St. Joseph County in 1838. Although sugar beets grew successfully in Michigan, lack of expertise and resources doomed the venture to failure. Only much later in the century did the manufacture of beet sugar develop as a successful industry in the peninsular state.[39]

Dairying and Wool Production

The development of dairying in Michigan arose in response to its growth in the Northeast. The reorganization of agriculture that accompanied industrialization created new demands for dairy products in growing urban markets. Dairying underwent changes that increased the quantity and quality of its products and lowered the costs of production as it evolved from an ancillary farm activity to one of major commercial importance. These included improving the care of farm stock, crossing native and imported purebred milk cattle, and increasing the scale and organization of production. These improvements, together with more efficient transportation to distant markets, led to the expansion of dairy farming into the Old Northwest.[40]

Although dairying developed slowly in Lower Michigan, early settlers produced and traded butter and cheese. Butter became a common item of exchange in the regional economy of Michigan because people who did not possess livestock desired it as a regular part of their diet. Contemporary observers noted an uneven availability of dairy products. In southeastern Michigan, an Adrian farmer with ten cows informed traveler George David in 1833 that he realized more than $400 a year from the butter and cheese he supplied to surrounding residents. In contrast, for Henry Sanford, traveling in southwestern Michigan eleven years later, "good butter [was] extremely hard to find." As late as 1850, a Wayne County farmer commented that in spite of the lower cost of land and cattle, and the high price of cheese in Michigan, he was the only one in Redford Township engaged in dairying."[41]

Contemporary sources attributed the slow emergence of dairy farming to the uncertain market and the difficulty of establishing a dairy. Farmers with limited means found it advantageous to maintain cattle that could serve multiple purposes. Many early cattle were kept as working oxen, as well as a source of meat or milk. Cows subsisted well in the summer, grazing in the woods or openings, but ate poorly in the winter. As a result, the milking season was short. One observer remarked that "By far the best of it is over within two months." By the 1850s, conditions allowed better maintenance of livestock and experience had shown that animals well fed and cared for in winter produced more milk. Farmers came to rely on pasture only in the summer, and fed their cows on corn stalks in the fall and hay and grain in the winter. The introduction of breeds of European dairy cattle, including Devons, Herefords, and Ayrshires, also increased milk production.[42]

Improved livestock care, combined with the opening of wider markets, increased dairy production dramatically in the West during the 1850s, and in 1860 Michigan ranked fourth in the region in output of both butter and cheese (table 11.2). Even though dairying grew rapidly in Michigan, the state's production of dairy products still ranked far below that in the Northeast. Dairying remained a small-scale farming activity and produced a relatively limited marketable surplus of butter and cheese. Dairying prospered only in the seven eastern counties, where farmers could easily sell their products in urban markets.[43]

By the 1820s, sheep raising had become a specialized form of agriculture, producing wool for industrial markets. During the 1830s, specialized wool production began to supplant other types of farming in parts of the Northeast, and sheep farming expanded into the West. Wool's relatively low investment cost, its high intrinsic value, and its relatively low bulk made it an ideal frontier crop. The potential profitability of wool during tough economic times in the 1840s encouraged the movement of sheep raising beyond Ohio, into Michigan and more distant parts of the Old Northwest.[44]

Promoters proclaimed the potential value of wool production for Michigan. Ever mindful of encouraging interior settlement, the *Detroit Journal and Michigan Advertiser* proclaimed in 1831 that the openings of Oakland County were "well adapted to the raising of the finer breeds of sheep," and admonished immigrants to "provide themselves early with a select flock, as much of the prosperity of an inland country must depend on the encouragement of manufactures, as well as a proper attention to agriculture." Outside investors, such as New York banker Arthur Bronson, also recognized Michigan's potential for sheep raising and were quick to sense the opportunity for western wool production. By the mid–1830s the perception of Michigan as a location favorable for wool production appears to have been widespread, setting the stage for the introduction of sheep raising in frontier Michigan.[45]

In the 1830s, contemporary observers began noting increased investment in wool production in southwestern Michigan. In 1838, Calhoun County farmers brought several flocks of Saxon and Spanish Merino sheep from New York to improve the wool output of "native" sheep. Three years later, Bela Hubbard "saw frequent flocks of sheep, lately introduced," in adjacent Kalamazoo County. A Marshall newspaper estimated that twenty thousand sheep were kept in that county in the previous year. Farmers built structures to maintain their flocks over the winter. In eastern Allegan County, Bela Hubbard found buildings designed to house three thousand animals. The same day he passed one thousand sheep being driven from Ohio to Kent County. He estimated that half of these were Merinos.[46]

Michigan farmers kept sheep for the value of their wool, and the wool breeds, such as the Merino, Saxony, and Leicestershire, dominated sheep raising. A Grand Blanc farmer informed the editor of the *Michigan Farmer* that the importance of wool in the frontier economy was great enough to outweigh all other uses of sheep in Michigan. The value of wool even overcame the long-held preferences of immigrant English sheep farmers, who traditionally judged the animals "by their mutton-making properties." Although these farmers introduced English mutton breeds, namely the Cotswold and South Down, to Michigan, they were raised for mutton only along the Eastern Shore, where farmers had ready access to the Detroit market.[47]

Wool was light and could be transported with only minimal processing, and agents purchased it directly from producers for shipment to the East. As early as 1838, Marshall resident Charles Dickey, "engaged in wool buying for eastern parties, and bought . . . the first of that staple ever sold for money in the counties of Calhoun, Branch, Kalamazoo, Jackson, Eaton, and Barry." At shearing time, wool buyers regularly converged on nucleated settlements to purchase the clip of area sheep farmers, who had to transport their wool only the short distance from their homes. In Washtenaw County, for example, periodic wool markets at Ann Arbor, Dexter, Saline, and Ypsilanti placed no resident farther than twenty miles from a buyer.[48]

By the mid–1840s, immigrant farmers had great expectations for the profitability of growing wool in Michigan. Reuben Landon, who came to Michigan from Poplar Ridge, New York, was typical of future sheep farmers. Landon's uncle summarized Reuben's intentions:

> He calculates to go through Ohio and buy a drove of sheep (a small one), say about two hundred he thinks, . . . David White tells him he can make more money growing wool in that country than any other business that he can go into. Dave knows, for he has been into it for so long that he has made himself rich at it, which makes Reuben wide awake for it, and it is tended with a little labor and a good profit.[49]

An article in a major contemporary economic journal reported that by 1847 Michigan's wool trade was "already respectable," and "destined for a great increase," and two years later the *Michigan Farmer* noted that wool was becoming a profitable export, "which always commands money." The steady increase in antebellum wool production in Michigan (table 11.5) reflected the crop's expanding market and high price. Michigan's remarkable rise in the 1850s to become the second-largest wool producing state in the West reveals the significant role of wool in the state's economy, as well as the increasing importance of western wool in the national market, made possible by improved long-distance transportation.[50]

Wool production provided Michigan's changing economy with an alternative staple to grain. Wool helped to avert financial disaster if the grain crop failed, and its sale in the spring proved especially beneficial when farmers needed income at the end of the winter. The combination of sheep raising and wheat farming was also an economically wise combination, because the manure of sheep pastured on fallow fields restored fertility.[51]

Sheep raising, perhaps more clearly than other frontier agricultural strategies, revealed settlers' intentions to raise a valuable crop that would permit them to enter the national economy. Although cattle, pork, and liquor also possessed a high intrinsic worth and portability, none had the economic impact of wool before 1860. In addition, wool played a dual role as subsistence good and commercial commodity.

AGRICULTURAL INNOVATIONS AND IMPROVEMENT

The growth of national produce markets and interregional competition led to extensive experimentation and innovation, which transformed antebellum American agriculture. The changes

TABLE 11.5. *PRODUCTION OF WOOL IN MICHIGAN FROM 1845 THROUGH 1864.*

	1845	1846	1847	1848	1849	1850	1854	1860	1864
Weight (lbs)	550,000	716,000	968,000	1,200,000	1,500,000	2,007,598	2,640747	6,929,113	7,249,934

Sources: *Michigan Farmer*, 1850, 292; U. S. Census, Agriculture, 1850, 1860; Michigan Census, 1854, 1864.

were so profound that they compelled farmers to acquire and implement new methods and technologies in all regions attempting to enter the national market. Frontier Michigan possessed the natural resources necessary to enter national agricultural markets, but its residents recognized that the production of commercially viable commodities required expanded output as well as consistent quantity and quality over time. The need to adapt frontier farming to meet these demands, together with competition from other parts of the country, gave Michigan farmers an incentive to continuously improve the efficiency of their production in order to maintain or enhance crop yields.[52]

Agricultural improvement was the result of innovations from many sources, particularly Great Britain. In the second half of the eighteenth century, new farming techniques developed in Britain found their way into American practice. British farmers restructured field and rotation systems to eliminate fallow periods and improve output. Introducing clover and legumes into the rotation of crops helped eliminate weeds and restored the soil. It also provided substantial fodder for winter livestock forage, thereby improving the quality of their products and the amount of manure available for fertilizer.[53]

British reformers also sought to increase agricultural output by improving soil quality and introducing new varieties of plants and animals. British farmers enriched soils by using animal manures to increase organic content and revived the ancient custom of adding marl, natural deposits containing a substantial amount of calcium carbonate, to restore exhausted soils. The discovery of the beneficial effects of calcium and nitrogen resulted in the extensive use of bone products and imported guano and led to development of artificial fertilizers, such as calcium superphosphate, which came into widespread use before 1850. Improved varieties of crops and animals increased the volume and quality of agricultural outputs. Among those that influenced antebellum northern agriculture were specialized breeds of dairy cattle as well as sheep for wool production. The sugar beet, whose inauspicious trial in antebellum Michigan belied its future success, had its beginnings in the European movement to improve agriculture.[54]

Agricultural innovation in the United States grew out of the research and experimentation of private citizens and public agencies. Practical experimentation demonstrated that artificial drainage improved soils, and academic research established the relationship between plant nutrition and the chemical composition of soil. These efforts profoundly affected the cultivation of grains and crops that exhausted soils. By the 1840s, the use of Peruvian guano, the rotation of grains with leguminous plants or turnips, and the addition of artificial fertilizers such as nitrates and superphosphate of lime had become accepted in the United States as methods of restoring soils and maintaining or increasing output.[55]

In the first half of the nineteenth century, state governments increasingly subsidized agricultural research. State agricultural societies and boards of agriculture encouraged innovation through reports and fairs that displayed new products, techniques, and improvements, while geological surveys carried out basic research in geology and soil chemistry. States assisted farmers by combating the spread of diseases, controlling farm product quality, and establishing staple standards and inspection laws. Particularly relevant to Michigan farmers were New York laws pertaining to flour and Ohio regulations for the packaging of meat. Consistent standards allowed products to be compared, evaluated, graded, sorted, and priced, all of which facilitated marketing on a national scale and promoted consumer confidence.[56]

The federal government played a passive but important role in antebellum agricultural change by introducing and testing foreign crops. Systematic plant collection began in 1819, and by 1836 the Office of the Patent Commissioner had taken over the role of plant introduction and evaluation, a task it pursued vigorously for the next quarter of a century. This agency imported and examined large numbers of foreign plants, and its efforts led to the adoption of sorghum, alfalfa, fescue, lima beans, sesame, and other crops that would otherwise have remained unknown to American farmers.[57]

Private organizations and government agencies played the principal role in dispersing knowledge of new crops and techniques. The generally literate agrarian audience read a growing body of almanacs, weekly newspapers, farm journals, and books. This widely distributed literature contained articles on improving crop yields and farmlands through proper tillage practices, drainage, application of fertilizers, rotation, and other means. Farmers learned about new crops and horticultural matters, especially the specialized treatment of fruits and vegetables. Articles were regularly devoted to livestock, including their selection, care, and feeding, and to treatment of diseases and conditions. Articles also touched on the human element of farming when they discussed such diverse topics as the efficient scheduling of farm work and household activities. Editors of periodical literature emphasized market production and commercial crops, regularly quoting current prices and encouraging innovation to maximize profit.[58]

State agricultural societies and boards of agriculture, supported by increasingly generous legislative appropriations, advanced the dissemination of information through annual publications, which included statistics of crops and livestock as well as research reports. The New York State Agricultural Society diligently presented reports of current work conducted by leading academic authorities. These accounts significantly influenced publications by agricultural societies in Michigan, Ohio, and Wisconsin. In the 1840s, agricultural societies, with the backing of state governments, supported the creation of schools dedicated to applying scientific principles to general agricultural practice. Over the next two decades, Pennsylvania, Wisconsin, and Michigan initiated academic programs in agriculture. Agricultural education played an auspicious role in promoting the innovations necessary to bring this about.[59]

The U.S. government published agricultural information through several organs, including the U.S. Census, which tabulated statistics on agriculture in all states beginning in 1840. Census reports provided detailed information, including articles on crops, innovative farming practices, new technologies, and marketing farm products. Beginning in 1837, the annual reports of the U.S. Patent Office carried a wide array of information and statistics obtained from the office's agricultural studies and experiments and journals. The reports also contained information about newly patented farming machinery and articles dealing with crops, livestock, fruit, use of manures, and combating diseases. The office laid the groundwork for a permanent federal role in agriculture, which fostered a national agricultural policy and led to the creation of a separate executive Department of Agriculture in 1862.[60]

In Michigan a movement arose to distribute information regarding innovations in agriculture to farmers preparing to enter commercial production. The editor of the *Detroit Journal and Michigan Advertiser* advocated the establishment of agricultural societies in Michigan. He argued that "the information which such societies are capable of collecting and disseminating, tending to point out the most profitable and economic mode of conducting a farm, must be as useful in a new as in an old country." Supporters also advocated the formation of an "Agricultural State Society, with its branches in every county," with funding and logistical assistance from the state.[61]

The Michigan legislature first encouraged the growth of agricultural organizations at the county level through official acts. These authorized county boards of supervisors to levy taxes to match amounts raised by agricultural societies to award as prizes for the "diffusion of agricultural knowledge." In 1849 the Michigan State Agricultural Society was incorporated by law and charged with disseminating agricultural knowledge and supporting innovations in crop and livestock raising across Michigan. Like the county societies, it received state matching funds for premium awards.[62]

The creation of the Michigan State Agricultural Society further encouraged the increase of county societies, and by 1858 at least twelve counties in Lower Michigan had permanent agricultural organizations. All held annual fairs and awarded premiums for crop and livestock competitions, carried out agricultural experiments, and distributed seeds and cuttings. Many published formal transactions.[63] A description of a fair in Kalamazoo County bore testimony to the importance of these events:

> For four years past, [Kalamazoo County] has had her agricultural organization, and her annual Fairs, . . . The spirit of agricultural improvement was breathed into its organization, and became to it a living soul. From year to year, it has held on its way, every succeeding exhibition being more interesting than the one that preceded it. Its own spirit has been diffused into every section of the state and several county organizations have been effected during the past year, and are already on the high road to usefulness.[64]

Publications devoted to agriculture accompanied the agricultural society movement in Michigan. Immigrant farmers relied on eastern journals, such as the *Genesee Farmer,* published in western New York, and the state's growing rural population formed an eager audience for a Michigan "agricultural paper." In the 1840s several farm journals appeared, including the *Farmers' Advocate,* which began in Kalamazoo in 1841, the *Michigan Farmer and Western Horticulturist,* issued at Jackson from 1843 to 1847, and the *Western Farmer,* which began publication at Detroit in 1841 and subsequently became the *Michigan Farmer.* By the end of the decade, a correspondent to this journal congratulated the state's agricultural press for having "done more in a few years . . . to promote the cause of agriculture by intellectual efforts, by causing the triumph of mind over matter, animating and encouraging the spirit of invention, and by a general diffusion of knowledge."[65]

Michigan took a leading role in agricultural education by founding Michigan Agricultural College, the first institution of higher learning devoted to this specialty. The state's newly formed State Agricultural Society enthusiastically supported the establishment of the college under state auspices, and the state constitution of 1850 authorized the institution. Although originally proposed as a branch of the University of Michigan, proponents recognized the need to include an experimental farm as an integral part of the school and successfully pressed for its creation as a separate entity. In 1855 the legislature authorized the founding of the Agricultural College near Lansing and appropriated land for its financial support. Funding for the agricultural college was enhanced by the federal Morrill Act of 1862, which set aside government lands for the endowment, support, and maintenance of state colleges devoted to "agriculture and the mechanic arts." A separate governing board for the school insured its independence and clarified its paramount role in scientific agricultural research and training in Michigan and as the state's center for collecting and disseminating agricultural information. The opening of Michigan Agricultural College in 1857 emphasized the role played by scientific innovation in the state's emerging agricultural economy.[66]

Michigan farmers applied new ideas and innovations to improve the results of frontier agriculture. This knowledge helped them devise effective ways to expand farmland through drainage. Farmers perceived that standing water or substantial subsurface moisture made soil infertile and wetlands dangerous for livestock. New technology restored wet soils and made them suitable for cultivation. Wetlands could be drained through ditches that carried the surface runoff elsewhere or by wells that allowed moisture to pass through impermeable layers of clay near the surface into gravelly subsoils. The subsoil plow broke up heavy soils and was considered necessary for preparing newly drained lands. Correspondents to the *Michigan Farmer,* one of whom had converted "comparatively barren wastes" into valuable hayfields, attested to the productivity of these technologically modified soils. So useful did draining become that state law regulated drain construction as early as 1839, and in areas where extensive drainage was necessary, provided for their construction and management by drain commissions.[67]

Crop rotation helped farmers stem the loss of soil fertility. Although many frontier farmers believed that some virgin soils possessed infinite fertility, experience soon demonstrated otherwise and led them to seek means of restoring agricultural lands. Chemists established the link between soil depletion and a deficiency of nitrogen, and showed that planting clover as a second crop alleviated this problem. Michigan's agricultural press promoted the widespread use of scientific crop rotation, and knowledge of its benefits led to its increasing popularity among farmers.[68] As early as 1832, "J. B.," a correspondent to the *Michigan Emigrant,* wrote that,

> Experience must have shewn every farmer that he cannot raise a good crop of wheat, corn, and flax, &c. upon the same field, for several years in succession. And why? Because every species of plant takes from the soil a specific food which others do not take . . . and soon impoverishes the soil.[69]

Farmers followed his recommendation, even wheat farmers, who had seen diminishing soil fertility, insect pests, and disease curtail grain yields on continuously cropped land. By 1860 they employed crop rotation in varying forms throughout Lower Michigan.[70]

CHANGES IN AGRICULTURAL TECHNOLOGY

Technological innovations altered the nature of agriculture in frontier Michigan. The impetus for adopting new agricultural technology in the nineteenth century derived from a need to meet growing market demands in the absence of an expanding labor force. Agricultural producers resolved this dilemma by increasing the efficiency of labor through the use of technology, which produced high-quality yields of greater value than its cost. Investment in machines encouraged specialization in commercial staples.[71]

The first half of the nineteenth century witnessed a revolution in agricultural technology. Antebellum innovations involved the redesign of traditional implements and their incorporation into larger machines that combined and automated tasks, yet still were operated largely by animal power. This permitted the new technology to be introduced without altering the organization of farming or entailing a substantial investment in supporting infrastructure. As soon as farmers acquired access to markets, the new technology could be used to expand production.[72]

The mechanization of frontier agriculture enmeshed farmers in the larger economy while preserving the structure of family farming. Farmers adopting improved technology became more reliant on outside manufacturers, who possessed the capital, skills, and organization to produce it. New tools and machines were expensive to make and ship from central locations to farming areas. Financing of farming operations required credit, and farmers began to rely on lending institutions to meet day-to-day business expenses. Although the mechanization of agriculture placed new constraints on farmers, it multiplied the results obtained from labor and helped preserve the farm family household as the unit of commercial agricultural production.[73]

Technological innovations enabled farmers to plant, cultivate, harvest, and process their crops more efficiently. Pioneer farmers benefited greatly from improvements in the plow. Early immigrants to Michigan brought with them the European-style plow. This large wooden implement, with an iron-covered share and moldboard, remained in common use through the 1820s, but poor control, slow and difficult tilling, and unreliable performance made it inefficient for western farming. These disadvantages prompted a series of revolutionary innovations in plow technology. Factory-made plows of improved design with interchangeable cast iron parts possessed practical advantages quickly discerned by pioneer farmers. Although improved plows were expensive and replacement parts difficult to obtain, they became popular in the West.[74]

The use of steel in place of iron reduced the friction of plows in the clayey soils found in western prairies. Introduced by John Deere, an Illinois blacksmith, the steel plow was so successful that it increased the demand for this efficient implement and led to a proliferation of new plows, including two designed specifically for rough western soils. The Eagle plow and the Michigan Double plow, introduced in the 1840s and 1850s, respectively, became popular in Michigan and were heavily promoted by the Michigan State Agricultural Society.[75]

Specialty plows also appeared to meet the needs of settlers on the prairie lands of southwestern Michigan. The large breaking plow, a wooden devices plated with iron strips and pulled by as many as ten yoke of oxen, permitted farmers to penetrate the tough root structure of the prairie grasses and turn the rich heavy soils. Introduced in the 1820s, this heavy, bulky implement was gradually improved after 1840, sharply reducing the number of animals and workers required to operate it. The narrow-bladed subsoil plow permitted farmers to deepen furrows, allowing greater penetration by moisture and roots in poorly drained, wet, and tightly compacted soils. Farmers used the paring plow, or "marsh plow," with its wide, triangular blade, to remove "the peaty surfaces of marshes preparatory to seeding them to tame grass."[76]

The harrow, used to pulverize soil and cover seed, also changed dramatically. Stronger, lighter harrows replaced untrimmed tree branches and homemade frames with wooden teeth. By the 1840s, the Geddes folding harrow, a flexible, triangular implement with two sections of steel teeth, came into wide use. It became especially popular in Michigan, where its efficiency in working recently cleared soils and uneven surfaces impressed contemporary observers, who noted its superiority to earlier harrows.[77]

The seed drill replaced hand broadcasting as a means of sowing grain, and its efficiency permitted cultivation on a larger scale. Coming into use in the 1840s, this horse-drawn machine opened furrows, deposited seed, and covered it in a single operation. Subsequent improvements allowed the precise distribution of seed. Before 1850, Michigan farmers used grain drills on prairie lands in the southwestern counties, where the topography offered ideal conditions for their use and railroads could deliver the machines. The grain drill facilitated commercial farming, and by 1860 one source estimated that at least 20 percent of the wheat in Michigan was planted by drilling.[78]

Antebellum inventors also improved the efficiency of corn planting, with the introduction of the shovel plow and corn drill. In contrast to broadcast grains, agriculturists traditionally planted corn in hills spaced several feet apart using a dibble stick or hoe. The horse-drawn shovel plow, designed to turn the soil to either side of a narrow, shallow furrow, permitted farmers to plant corn by plowing, dropping in the seed, and covering it with a succeeding furrow. On the prairie lands of southwestern Michigan, plow planting produced high yields with little subsequent cultivation. The corn drill, introduced in the 1850s and used extensively in Michigan by the end of the decade, offered considerable labor savings.[79]

In the first half of the nineteenth century, grain harvesting underwent the greatest change of all agricultural activities. At the close of the eighteenth century, all grain was cut by hand, using either the sickle or the scythe. Pioneer farmers brought both of them to the Michigan frontier, where the cradle scythe rapidly proved itself the more efficient tool. The scythe remained popular throughout the antebellum period, despite the introduction of mechanized harvesters.[80]

The introduction of reaping machines heralded extensive and rapid change in the harvesting of grain. In 1826 a wheat harvester built by British inventor Patrick Bell employed a revolving reel that pulled the grain toward a set of reciprocating blades, trimmed it off near ground level, and laid it on a platform. These features became integral parts of two later American machines that found much wider acceptance. Obed Hussey and Cyrus McCormick introduced harvesting machines in 1833 and 1834, respectively, and developed reliable reaping

machines by mid-century. The expiration of their original patents in the mid–1840s made harvester technology widely available, increasing competition and promoting an innovative
atmosphere in the antebellum farm machinery industry.[81]

Mechanical reapers cut more grain, faster, and more cleanly, outperforming manual labor
and reducing waste. Their use permitted Michigan farmers to cultivate greater acreages of wheat
and to time its harvest more accurately. Because they increased the potential volume of production, reapers rapidly gained acceptance in the West, where excess farmland outstripped capability of available labor. Cyrus McCormick successfully introduced the mechanical reaper in
southern Michigan in 1844, and a White Pigeon farmer purchased one. A Hussey reaper was in
use on Prairie Ronde in Kalamazoo County three years later. The relocation of McCormick's
manufacturing plant to Chicago in 1847 to take advantage of the western market provided a
boost to regional sales. McCormick aggressively marketed his machines through advertising,
and commission merchants, who sold on credit, shipped reapers and parts by rail and repaired
broken machines. By 1860 farmers in southwestern Michigan relied almost exclusively on
McCormick's machines.[82]

Since reapers reduced the need for manual labor, farmers could harvest crops even when
workers were unavailable. The resulting efficiency permitted agriculture to keep pace with
rapidly expanding markets. Those who could not afford harvesters of their own pooled their
resources with other farmers to purchase one jointly. With the cost borne by more than one
owner, farmers realized a profit based on the cost savings obtained from machine use.
Although statistics on joint ownership of machines are unavailable, many Michigan farmers
engaged in this widespread practice.[83]

The mower, a horse-drawn machine, designed to replace the scythe in cutting hay, found
only limited acceptance in antebellum Michigan. Obed Hussey introduced the first successful
model in 1833. Although mowers achieved some popularity in the 1840s and the 1850s,
Michigan farmers adopted this machine only in the 1860s, when intense wartime labor shortages and increased production demands made mechanization of this task necessary.[84]

Farmers employed large comblike devices called horse rakes to collect hay or straw into
windrows or heaps. In widespread use by northern farmers by 1820, contemporaries claimed
this harvesting tool could accomplish the work of ten men. Improvement in the design of horse
rakes encouraged their use among antebellum grain farmers in Michigan. Mr. Starkweather, a
progressive Ypsilanti farmer, reported that the use of the rake in gleaning not only hastened the
completion of his task, but actually increased his yield per acre. Horse rakes may have been
manufactured in Michigan as early as the 1850s.[85]

With the harvest completed, crops had to be processed further before shipment or consumption. Grain required the most extensive processing. Farmers first threshed it, to separate
the seed from the chaff, and then winnowed it, to remove waste. The fanning mill modified the
winnowing process by utilizing a rotating fan to separate the grain. Introduced from Britain in
the late eighteenth century, the fanning mill was a standard implement in American wheat-
growing regions by the 1830s. Although the fanning mill required three people to operate, it

greatly increased the amount of grain that could be cleaned. An enterprising manufacturer in Detroit advertised fanning mills as early as 1818, but they did not come into common use until about 1830.[86]

Horse-powered threshing machines revolutionized the processing of wheat in the United States. During the 1820s and 1830s, small horse-powered threshing machines appeared. Initially attached to treadmills, they later employed horse-operated sweeps to increase their capacity. The first combination thresher and winnower was introduced in 1837, followed by more efficient designs during the next two decades. The new machines permitted farmers to thresh the larger crops obtained with improved harvesting technology. Many wheat farmers adopted them in southwestern Michigan in the 1830s. By the mid–1840s, combined threshers and separators were also used.[87]

Some Michigan farmers had sufficient capital to purchase threshing machines for their exclusive use, but most could not afford to buy one. Many farmers hired the use of a thresher, and by the late 1850s the increased capacity and efficiency of machines encouraged the rise of itinerant threshing crews, whose speedy work permitted the farmer to bring his crop to market faster. Thomas Wright of Tecumseh recalled that the cost of a hired threshing machine was offset by the higher price he received for an early crop.[88]

Farmers often entered into cooperative arrangements with their neighbors to purchase a threshing machine. Pioneer Eugene Davenport recalled that for many Michigan residents, threshing "was a general time for changing works." William Kirkland, a Livingston County resident, observed that,

> You pass a stack of wheat, near which a threshing machine is planted, around which you will see some twelve and twenty men and boys busily employed. The owner ... is to pay each of his co-labourers a day's work when called upon; and so far as getting out his grain is concerned, he is no worse off than the richest man in the neighborhood.[89]

Communal threshing allowed individual households to maintain control of production and encouraged the development of simple commodity production in a region emerging from frontier isolation into a market economy. Moreover, the trading of labor at threshing time served as a means of social interaction as the threshing machine moved from farm to farm, bringing members of neighboring families together.[90] Charles E. Weller remembered threshing in the frontier Michigan of his childhood, when the arrival of the machine, with its horses and crew, signaled the beginning of a period of intensive activity:

> With what wondering eyes we would watch, listening to the ceaseless tramp of the horses, combined with the terrific grinding noise of the machinery, as bundle after bundle of the golden sheaves was pitched from the barn loft into the constantly moving carrier, passing from thence through the thresher, ... while at a wooden spout at the bottom of the far end of the machine was flowing the precious grain, pouring into the empty sacks.[91]

Children, especially young boys, found threshing an almost mystical experience that allowed them to transcend the isolation of everyday existence through participation in this annual event. The economic and social aspects of shared capital and labor that arose from communal threshing helped integrate frontier society and shaped the structure of production as Michigan entered the commercial economy.[92]

Less conspicuous, smaller tools and devices also improved the efficiency of agriculture. The hay fork was an implement that permitted the application of horsepower to the movement of hay from wagon to loft. Hand-operated mechanical fodder choppers and feed mills, designed to process cattle forage with less waste, entered Michigan in the 1840s and 1850s. About the same time, mechanical corn mills, designed to replace the hominy block, and corn stalk cutters, used to prepare fodder, came into widespread use. The corn sheller, which appeared prior to 1820, removed kernels from the cob. By the 1840s, farmers rapidly adopted efficient hand-cranked designs, and higher capacity horse-powered machines became available.[93]

The expansion of mechanized agriculture gave Michigan an important role in the development of new harvesting technology. Hiram Moore, of Climax Prairie, with the financial support of his neighbor John Hascall, built the first combine, designed to accomplish the tasks of both the reaper and the thresher. Between 1835 and 1854 he tested five models of this enormous machine in southwestern Michigan, where its efficiencies suited the large scale of prairie farming. Although the Moore-Hascall combine saw only limited use in antebellum Michigan, the technology it introduced set the stage for the massive machines later employed on the large farms farther west.[94]

THE INFRASTRUCTURE OF PROCESSING AND SETTLEMENT PATTERNING

The development of a commercial economy in Lower Michigan required a service infrastructure capable of collecting and processing agricultural commodities. Wheat and corn had to be reduced to flour or meal that could be easily transported and stored. This task was carried out at mills, which became the central industry of Michigan's economy and an important factor in determining the roles of settlements in this evolving region. Mills attracted business, brought urban functions to frontier settlements, and influenced the development of transportation networks. Consequently, the distribution of mills shaped the patterning of settlement in late antebellum Michigan.

Antebellum mills depended on flowing water for power, and sites where it was abundant became foci of frontier settlement in Michigan. Although French settlers built windmills at Detroit as early as 1703, American settlers did not make use of them. Moving water provided the energy for hydraulic mill machinery and required locations adjacent to a river or stream with adequate fall. Vertical waterwheels powered most mills because the large overshot wheel provided the most efficient operation. Overshot wheels, however, required great height of fall and could be constructed along only those rivers with descent adequate to provide this fall. Introduced in the 1840s, the turbine significantly improved the efficiency of hydraulic machinery because it generated more energy, reduced its mechanical complexity, and simplified its maintenance. Since turbine technology did not reach full development until after mid-century, builders of antebellum industrial mills in Michigan still favored sites along swiftly flowing streams with sufficient descent.[95]

Early explorers looked for sites suitable for mills. One of the first organized parties to examine the lands northwest of Detroit reported the difference between the fast-moving interior rivers and the "slow water" nearer the lakeshore and proclaimed that "as to seats for mills, there will be no want, one may be found in every neighborhood." All interior rivers did not present equally opportune hydraulic conditions, however, and mill construction in Michigan's interior gravitated toward those that were most favorable. In the region around Saginaw Bay, for example, the sluggish nature of the Saginaw River caused millers to initially avoid it and erect their water-powered establishments on its faster-running tributaries, the Cass, Tittabawassee, Chippewa, Flint, and Thread Rivers.[96]

Grist-milling sites offered waterpower for additional industries, the presence of which enlarged the surrounding settlements. The waterpower at Pontiac, for example, ran an iron foundry and fulling and carding mills as well as its grist and saw mills. Carding and fulling mills were crucial to the success of wool production, and their erection came soon after the introduction of sheep in the 1820s and 1830s. Other hydraulic-powered industries included snuff-grinding, cider-making, the manufacture of hemp, and the processing of flax for linseed oil. All of these industries helped increase the economic diversity of Michigan's frontier economy.[97]

Despite the dominance of hydraulic power for grist milling, the industrial use of steam increased rapidly in late antebellum America. Steam was not tied to the availability of flowing water, but it was more expensive to use. By 1830 more efficient steam engines powered machinery used for on-site processing of products, such as lumber and lead. Because of their higher operating costs, steam engines could not compete with hydraulic power, and their use was limited to sites lacking adequate waterpower.[98]

Comparative statistics for the use of steam power are unavailable before 1850, but later data show a marked disparity in the relative roles of steam and water power in grist and saw milling (table 11.6). A comparison of the relative popularity of each power source reveals that grist millers clearly favored hydraulic power, and water-driven machinery dominated the industry. The popularity of steam-powered sawmills, on the other hand, was perceptibly higher and increased steadily. By the 1860s, steam engines powered half the sawmills in southern Michigan and encouraged lumber-making to expand rapidly into remote areas without adequate waterpower.[99]

Steam power also permitted grist mills in areas lacking flowing water. By late antebellum times, the availability of steam-powered grist mills facilitated agricultural settlement in previously neglected portions of Lower Michigan. These included the Western Shore and the area stretching from the lower Saginaw valley across the Thumb to the St. Clair River. The creation of a more convenient processing infrastructure made these regions attractive to immigrants and helped facilitate accelerated movement into these areas during the 1850s.

Transportation costs of the materials processed at mills dictated their geographical placement. Grist mills were usually built near markets because little or no weight loss occurred after

TABLE 11.6. *Number and Percentage Frequencies of Water-Powered and Steam-Powered Grist and Lumber Mills in Michigan, 1850–64.*

Grist Mills	1850		1854		1860		1864	
Water-Powered Grist Mills	180	91%	220	90%	243	79%	323	81%
Steam-Powered Grist Mills	18	9%	24	10%	63	21%	74	19%
Total Number of Grist Mills	198		244		306		397	

Lumber Mills	1850		1854		1860		1864	
Water-Powered Lumber Mills	351	72%	618	70%	462	52%	523	50%
Steam-Powered Lumber Mills	134	28%	217	30%	431	48%	531	50%
Total Number of Lumber Mills	85		835		893		1,054	

Sources: U. S. Census, 1850, 1860; Michigan Census, 1854, 1864.

the kernels were ground into flour or meal. Millers dispersed these industries to permit more convenient access to scattered rural settlements. In contrast, timber processed by sawmills encountered a large weight loss during processing, and these mills were situated in often remote locations, close to their raw materials. The distinctive requirements of these two commodities affected mill locations in Michigan and had strong implications for the patterning of its commercial infrastructure.[100]

Grist mills followed the spread of early settlement across Lower Michigan. The state's first comprehensive statistical account of industries in 1837 revealed a distribution of mills similar to that of the pioneer population. Only five of the twenty-nine southern counties lacked grist mills. More than one-third of the grist mills were situated in Oakland, Washtenaw, and Lenawee Counties, each of which was settled early and had substantial populations as well as hydraulic resources. By 1854 all of the southern counties possessed grist mills. Their use had spread into more recently settled areas in the Thumb and north of the Grand River, but it did not extend beyond the state's agricultural region. In response to the growth of agricultural production in Michigan, concentrations of mills had grown up in the populous western counties of Jackson, Calhoun, Kalamazoo, and St. Joseph, and in Livingston and Genesee Counties on the upper Grand and Saginaw River drainages (table 11.7).

By mid-century, grist-milling centers had become the foci of regional networks in Lower Michigan. As destinations for trade, mill settlements acquired additional economic activities and became magnets for exchange, warehousing, repair, and manufacturing, all of which increased their size and importance. Many settlements that acquired key economic functions early continued to play central roles in regional development and formed the basis for the service infrastructure of Lower Michigan.[101]

In contrast, saw milling had a very different relationship to settlement patterning in Michigan. Although the need for lumber made sawmills integral to antebellum industry in Michigan settlements, their distribution extended well beyond the state's agricultural areas and urban centers. Responding to the demand for building materials, lumbermen built sawmills near stands of abundant timber, or at locations where logged timber could easily be transported by water and later rail. Lumbering was even illegally carried out on government lands not yet sold.[102]

Sawmills nearly always preceded agricultural settlement, and often lay in remote areas or at the periphery of settlement. Substantial numbers of mills in counties having few grist mills, such as Ottawa, Allegan, and Berrien Counties on the Western Shore; Barry, Ingham, Kent, and Moncalm Counties in the central timberlands; and St. Clair, Lapeer, and Sanilac Counties in the Thumb, reveal this trend. The growth of Michigan lumber exports further concentrated lumber milling in areas of pine timber, and by the 1850s milling extended into the northern Lower Peninsula and the Upper Peninsula, as lumbering spread well beyond the bounds of agricultural settlement (table 11.7). Distant lumbering settlements often remained transitory and specialized, and usually failed to attract substantial permanent populations or centralizing activities. Only occasionally did lumber ports, such as Allegan, become markets for surrounding agricultural areas, foci of transportation networks, or seats of regional economic and social

TABLE 11.7. *MICHIGAN GRIST AND SAWMILLS IN 1837 AND 1854 BY COUNTY.*

County	Grist Mills		Saw Mills	
	1837	1854	1837	1854
Allegan	1	5	17	29
Barry	0	2	2	22
Berrien	5	8	26	45
Branch	4	6	10	32
Calhoun	4	13	20	34
Cass	5	6	19	25
Chippewa	0	0	0	1
Clinton	0	1	2	8
Eaton	1	5	5	18
Emmet	0	0	0	2
Genesee	1	11	13	26
Grand Traverse	0	0	0	12
Hillsdale	1	9	15	47
Houghton	0	0	0	9
Ingham	0	4	0	15
Ionia	2	8	3	18
Jackson	5	14	21	22
Kalamazoo	3	12	21	30
Kent	2	7	15	36
Lapeer	3	6	11	32
Lenawee	14	17	13	54
Livingston	3	15	11	26
Mackinac	0	0	1	2
Macomb	6	9	25	32
Monroe	7	7	25	31
Montcalm	0	1	0	13
Newaygo	0	2	0	7
Oakland	17	25	40	46
Ontonagon	0	0	0	4
Ottawa	0	2	3	40
Saginaw	1	1	5	2
Sanilac	0	1	0	16
Shiawassee	1	3	4	5
St. Clair	1	4	40	39
St. Joseph	8	12	13	21
Tuscola	0	1	0	6
Van Buren	0	3	0	21
Washtenaw	11	22	36	39
Wayne	5	13	27	55

Source: Blois, *Gazetteer,* 390; Michigan Census, 1854.

institutions. Unlike grist milling, saw milling played a minimal role in shaping settlement patterning in Lower Michigan.[103]

The development of a technological infrastructure for grain processing supported the growth of Michigan's regional economy and, with improvements in transportation and changes in farming, made possible the transition to commercial agricultural production. Milling was a central component of the regional economic system and influenced the distribution of central settlements in the region. The operation of a commercial economy, however, also depended on institutions to oversee production and exchange and provide the services necessary to carry out trade with external markets.

12

The Organization of Production and Marketing

Michigan's transition to a commercial economy hinged upon the introduction of external capital and financial expertise. These were provided by eastern capitalists who saw investment in the West as a way to promote national growth and expand business opportunities, from which they expected to profit. The westward flow of capital to finance frontier enterprises was not a uniform and efficient process, however. A multiplicity of interests conducted business in a loosely organized and sometimes unstable national economy constrained by the changing nature of money, banking, and credit. The nature of investment in Michigan and the institutions of production, processing, and trade it created reflected the milieu in which its participants operated.

BANKING, CREDIT, AND THE EXPANSION OF PRODUCTION

The creation of a commercial economy depended on the availability of cash for transactions and the existence of financial institutions capable of meeting the needs of people seeking to invest capital in Michigan. The form of cash and the institutions through which it flowed reflected the nature of contemporary money and banking in the United States, and constituted the major components of a loosely organized national financial system that was adapting to conditions imposed by geographical expansion and economic growth. During the antebellum period, this system evolved to provide the credit and the medium of exchange needed by the changing American economy.

Banking in the United States was still in its formative stages when the young nation found itself thrust into an economic arena characterized by expansion and instability. Early banks organized by federal charter and succeeding commercial banks helped ameliorate the effects of these conditions by providing a stable currency. They did this by using specie contributed by their subscribers to back the bank's notes, which were, in turn, redeemable in coin. In the absence of large amounts of circulating specie, bank notes were not usually redeemed immediately, and instead passed from hand to hand as currency. The credit made available to banks by the issuance of notes offered the promise of financing the expansion of production, trade, and settlement in the United States. The success of a currency based on private banknotes, however, rested on the notes' soundness.[1]

The federal government attempted to manage American banking through its support of the Second Bank of the United States (BUS), organized as a national repository as well as a commercial venture. With government backing, the BUS rapidly expanded the scope of its operations, opening branches in many parts of the country. As the nation's central bank, it served essentially as a bankers' bank and could restrain credit to state banks in order to curtail overexpansion and expand loans during times of crisis in order to ease the impact on the business and financial community. Although the BUS helped make credit and currency available outside of the Eastern Seaboard states, its conservative policies in managing other banks' activities limited the raising of capital for development in the South and West.[2]

Conservatively managed banks followed the doctrine that to remain liquid—that is, able to pay off liabilities on short notice—a bank should lend money only for the short-term and on the safest security. This tenet restricted banks to furnishing credit for trade rather than production, because the former usually involved relatively rapid transactions, with the goods in transit providing the necessary security. Most banks also refused to make land a basis of credit, and controlled loans tightly, policies that found little favor in sections of the country that were heavily dependent on agriculture and chronically in debt. The inability of conservative policy to accommodate the credit requirements of an expanding economy exposed a weakness in the banking system that forced entrepreneurs in the West to turn to alternative but inherently dangerous banking institutions to overcome the absence of growth capital on the frontier.[3]

State banks came to play an increasingly larger role as creditors. Unlike the BUS, state banks were organized by their investors for financial gain, and these investors governed their operations with weak and often ineffective regulations. Such institutions had no inherent interest in safe currency or business stability. Because their profits derived from extending loans, they sought to maximize their note issue and avoid paying out specie. In times of expanding credit, demand for specie remained low and state banks remained solvent. On the other hand, if an unusual demand for specie occurred, such institutions might be unable to meet the demand for specie and thus fail. The regulatory powers of the BUS held the excesses of state banking in check until 1836. Political controversy had arisen over the BUS's role as a central bank, however, and President Andrew Jackson vetoed the renewal of its federal charter in 1832. The subsequent removal of government deposits from the BUS and their distribution among state banks diminished its control over the operations of these institutions, leaving them free to expand their lending.[4]

The second quarter of the nineteenth century witnessed the growth of state banking as well as an expansion of its role in facilitating economic development. Many financiers embraced a more liberal doctrine that encouraged banks to supply funds to underwrite new enterprises in agriculture and industry. Credit for the development of production, known as "accommodation" loans, was necessary to support economic expansion, and these loans were justified to those who saw such development as likely to yield a good return in both the short and long term. Backing ventures that might be unsuccessful made accommodation loans risky for investors. An unproductive farm or a failed mill would leave a lending institution with little chance of recouping its investment. Although crucial to establishing frontier production and creating a supporting infrastructure, extensive long-term credit could threaten the stability of banks and encourage dangerous fluctuations in the larger economy.[5]

In the 1830s, rapid economic growth, fueled by the rapid, and often reckless, expansion of credit to meet the needs of a mushrooming economy, created a precarious situation. This decade witnessed the introduction of "free banking," a policy that loosened the standards for organizing banks. Based on the assumption that the creation of more banks increased competition, eliminated monopolistic practices, and provided expanded credit, free banking gained popularity and banks proliferated. Residents of western states in dire need of credit grasped the advantages of having more currency available. Michigan passed a free banking law in 1837, and within a year it possessed three times as many banking associations as state-chartered banks. Although this legislation produced a number of legitimate banks, which strengthened Michigan's economic infrastructure, it also gave rise to many poorly or corruptly managed ventures created solely to generate quick profits. The "wildcat banks" of the 1830s typified uncontrolled private banking run amok. Organized with little or no capital and inaccessible to note holders, such institutions detracted from rather than contributed to the frontier economy.[6]

Trust companies played a particularly important role in frontier production because of their ability to make large, long-term loans. Their development demonstrates the role of eastern capital in creating financial institutions on the frontier. Trust companies, functioning as financial intermediaries, invested the funds of depositors on a long-term basis. Entrepreneurs who were accumulating surplus capital from their expanding eastern businesses but lacked financial expertise relied on trust companies to invest their funds. Because they sought long-term returns, trusts often turned to accommodation loans in agriculture, trade, and manufacturing, investments that were likely to yield steady interest over the years.[7]

The Ohio Life Insurance and Trust Company (OLTC), among others, made capital available to western farmers seeking mortgages to underwrite improvements, and to merchants and artisans attempting to expand their businesses. In Michigan, large trusts provided eastern capital to fund the infrastructure of production. The OLTC's capital investment in real estate mortgages and conservative approach to lending insured the company against the overissuance of notes and permitted it to function as a secure financial institution in a developing region. Although financial difficulties eventually befell the OLTC as a result of mismanagement, its role in providing a conduit for eastern investment capital helped insure the economic success of settlers in Michigan and surrounding regions.[8]

Eastern capitalists also controlled the operations of Michigan's leading banks. The Dwight family of New York and Massachusetts and other eastern financiers were majority stockholders in the Bank of Michigan, the state's oldest and most influential financial institution. Other New York investors maintained stock control over the largest of the early chartered state banks as well.[9] Eastern-owned banks made money available for mortgages on farms and for larger development projects. Credit obtained from such banks frequently provided the substantial funds needed to acquire, survey, and promote town sites. When, for example, entrepreneur John Allen established the town site of Ann Arbor in the 1820s, he borrowed funds from the Bank of Michigan. Eastern capital from Michigan banks permitted him to repeat this process with varying degrees of success elsewhere in southern Michigan.[10]

Banking and credit institutions on the frontier depended on the transfer of funds, and the nature of money determined the nature of exchange. In the loosely organized structure of unregulated American banking, money differed from its modern counterpart. The only national currency in circulation consisted of metallic coinage, or specie. Although valued everywhere, the expense and difficulty of transporting gold and silver coins made their use awkward. In addition, the supply of specie remained inadequate and uncertain during the first half of the nineteenth century. The mint produced coins slowly, and the fluctuating value of precious metals as bullion often reduced circulating coinage, the contents of which became more valuable if melted down or shipped abroad. Out of necessity, Americans used a heterogeneous mixture of foreign and domestic coins for exchange, an awkward combination that complicated business transactions. American coinage did not begin to meet the needs of circulation until after 1853.[11]

Although the operation of Michigan's regional economy did not require a large number of specie transactions, settlers needed currency for purchasing land, paying taxes, and acquiring imported goods. They also wanted a secure medium with which to assign values to items exchanged. Specie remained highly valued, especially during times of depression, and its absence could drastically curtail production and trade.[12] Referring to the shortage of hard currency, the editor of a Pontiac newspaper proclaimed:

> It is the farmers' turn next. . . . His wheat and oats and corn must be estimated in value proportionately to the security of a circulating medium. The miller and the flour dealer cannot afford to give more than four or five shillings [50–62 cents] for wheat, because *they can get but little money* for their flour. . . . Everything must descend to the standard of what little circulating medium the administration has been pleased to let us have.[13]

A merchant in Hillsdale, Thomas W. Stockton, attributed the "dullest times I have ever known in any country" to the absence of cash. A Marshall resident claimed that because cash was so scarce, merchants lacked the capital to purchase goods and settle debts with suppliers or even to pay the shipping on the goods they were able to obtain.[14]

Immigrants brought specie into Michigan as savings or the proceeds from the sale of earlier properties. Settlers from Europe introduced foreign currency that also circulated as cash. Annuity payments, paid to Michigan Indians as compensation for lands or past services, also contributed specie to the Michigan economy. Although some annuity money was saved for land or other large purchases, much of it quickly passed into the hands of traders, merchants, and others, to become part of the circulating medium.[15]

In Michigan and other frontier regions, banknotes comprised much of the circulating currency. Unlike specie, notes did not constitute a national currency, possessed no intrinsic value, and played a more limited role in exchange. Issued by the BUS, state, and private banks, and by other financial institutions, promissory notes were payable to the bearer in specie on demand. Most banknotes, however, remained unredeemed, and circulated as paper money. Because their value in exchange rested on the reputation of the issuing institution, all notes were not of equal worth, and their use entailed some risk. A banknote's value as cash was discounted when exchanged for other currency or merchandise, and the rate of discount varied with the issuing bank and the distance from its place of issue. Overissuance and other abuses by many banks caused the exchange value of their notes to depreciate considerably and placed note holders at a financial disadvantage. In an attempt to discourage the use of unsound banknotes, large banks regularly published discount rates and lists of notes they would receive for deposit.[16] The financial depression of the 1830s exacerbated this situation. By 1841, confidence in western banks had fallen to such a point that the editor of the *Jonesville Expositor* proclaimed,

> The local currency of one State is worthless in another; and it can only be used at a ruinous rate of discount. The notes of Michigan Banks cannot be used as currency in Ohio or Indiana; and the notes of the Banks of these States are in reality as worthless as those of Michigan.[17]

Nevertheless, banknotes substituted for specie and sufficed for regional trade in Michigan. As long as such currency remained unredeemed and in restricted use, its intrinsic value was less relevant than the fact that it permitted exchange equivalencies to be maintained within the regional economy. In order to facilitate trade in the absence of adequate amounts of circulating currency, some municipalities and private businesses issued their own due bills as notes. "Shinplasters" constituted a large portion of the currency in Detroit after the War of 1812 and in other portions of Michigan undergoing rapid growth. The village of Grand Rapids, for example, issued $300 worth of unsecured notes in 1838 for the payment of local taxes, dues, and debts. These, together with promissory notes issued by private individuals, circulated locally as fractional currency for several years.[18]

The weakness of Michigan banknotes affected financial transactions and trade between state residents and people living elsewhere. The difficulty in exchanging western money for specie or the notes of sound eastern banks lowered its relative exchange value. Eastern notes, on the other hand, were acceptable in the West and even convertible to specie to purchase federal land or pay taxes. In a story related in the *Monroe Advocate*, a New York resident who journeyed to Michigan to pay taxes on his lands exchanged eastern bills for those of a Michigan bank. He received such a favorable rate that the $1,000 he brought to pay his taxes at par was also sufficient to cover the cost of his trip, as well as his stay in Detroit while conducting business. Eastern bills, however, remained difficult to obtain, and the high cost of redeeming them at their source banks effectively prohibited their use as currency in the West.[19]

To overcome the shortcomings of banknotes, Michigan residents used bank drafts as a means of conducting external business. Drafts drawn on accounts in eastern banks, unlike notes, represented actual funds on deposit and were redeemable at face value. Easterners carried drafts to the West and sold them to those in need of currency to purchase goods or carry on commerce with eastern businesses. Because western merchants were dependent on wholesalers in New York, Boston, and other eastern market centers for their goods, it was imperative that they acquire a medium of exchange acceptable to their eastern suppliers. When Moses Chamberlain, a merchant of Scipio, Ohio, could not procure eastern merchandise for western currency, he made an arrangement with Jeremiah Wilkins, an associate from his home state of New Hampshire. Wilkins made drafts on Boston banks and brought them west to exchange for western bills that he used for purchases in Ohio. Chamberlain, in turn, traveled eastward with the bank drafts to restock his inventory. A decade later, Chamberlain, then settled in New Buffalo, Michigan, purchased drafts from New York banks from brokers who dealt in western products. He then settled accounts with eastern suppliers with funds drawn on these banks.[20]

The shortage of money in the West, together with the confusing proliferation of paper currency, encouraged widespread counterfeiting. Michigan newspapers frequently carried warnings against bogus banknotes circulating in the western states. Forgers often imitated notes of the Bank of the United States and large state banks, but some even copied village currency. In Kalamazoo the appearance of counterfeit shinplasters in 1838 caused great confusion among local citizens and resulted in the issuance of new bills. Entrepreneurs also attempted to produce false specie. F. A. Downing, when exploring Cambridge Township in western Lenawee County in 1832, discovered a secluded furnace and forge that purportedly turned out $500 in bogus half dollars during each day of operation.[21]

The nature of currency in frontier Michigan exposed the deficiencies of antebellum banking and monetary policy in the United States. The problems it caused remained unsolved until the creation of a national banking system in the 1860s permitted the free movement of currency between East and West. Although unable to fully meet the demands of economic expansion and the growth of external trade, the available currency met the needs of Michigan's regional economy. The limitations of the monetary system impeded but did not exclude the external exchange upon which Michigan's economic transformation depended. Export trade, made possible by technological advances in transportation and communications, together with a rising demand for western products, expanded within the context of an exchange system that continued to influence both its structure and its organization.[22]

EXTERNAL EXCHANGE IN A FRONTIER ECONOMY

Michigan's emergence as a commercial agricultural region depended on the development of an infrastructure capable of supporting exchange and marketing on a scale adequate to accommodate a high volume of regular, long-distance trade. Two factors shaped the evolution of this infrastructure and the nature of trade carried out over long distances. The first was the method of financing of export shipments. The slowness of water transport to the East placed a burden on both buyers and sellers, because one of them had to retain ownership of goods during shipment. To address this need, credit was extended through bills of exchange to people exporting frontier products. These bills, which the seller drew on the buyer at the time of the sale, ordered the buyer to pay for the goods when they arrived at their destination. A third party, usually a bank, purchased these bills and transferred the funds to the seller immediately, in effect granting credit during the time that the goods were in transit. The discounted price the bank paid for the bills reimbursed it for its services. Bills of exchange facilitated trade by reducing the turnaround time on producers' investments, and they became the principal financial instrument by which western grain was transferred to eastern markets.[23] Transportation technology dictated how produce was shipped and formed the second crucial element in the infrastructure of export marketing. Until mid-century, watercraft carried out Michigan's export trade, and their design restricted cargoes to small containers, such as sacks and barrels. The labor required to handle them increased both the time and cost of transit. In addition to being slow, water transport was subjected to climatic delays each winter.

To meet the needs of long-distance trade, country merchants and commission merchants worked to link western producers with eastern buyers. The country merchant coordinated the movement of commodities from producer to market. As the central figure in frontier exchange, these individuals constituted the pioneer farmers' principal contact with outside markets and played a pivotal role in organizing and directing trade. Country merchants served as buyers of frontier products destined for export shipment. Because most farmers lacked the time, knowledge, and financial ability to market their own produce, country merchants became regional buyers who arranged for the subsequent shipment of most commodities. In Michigan, merchants specializing in the export of grain rapidly established themselves at interior settlements following the extension of adequate transportation between those points and lakeshore ports at Detroit, Monroe, Toledo, and St. Joseph.[24]

Merchants generally acquired agricultural produce by paying cash. Smith & Co., country merchants of Hillsdale County, sought to attract sellers through advertisements offering cash for their wheat. Paying cash for agricultural commodities required that merchants obtain credit on which to make these purchases. Often they issued bank drafts drawn on the accounts of eastern creditors that would be repaid upon the sale of the wheat, when it reached the market. When, for example, Sidney S. Allcott sought cash to buy and process wheat in Calhoun County, his brother William advised him to obtain "a part of this . . . in Eastern funds at Detroit or Marshall, . . . which could be obtained on drafts at three or four months or even six months." Borrowers had to time these transactions carefully. In order to avoid tying up investment capital any longer than necessary, they attempted to minimize the period over which such drafts were drawn. At the same time, they had to allow adequate time for transporting and selling the western commodities.[25]

The country merchant supplied the capital for indigenous frontier investment, upon which commercial production was dependent. Farmers had to be reimbursed upon sale of their produce. If they were not, it became difficult for them to purchase imported goods and to meet other cash expenses, jeopardizing their well-being and that of the merchants who depended on expanding export grain sales. Curtailed production, resulting from delayed payment, placed a merchant's future business at risk. During the business depression of the late 1830s, knowledgeable observers attributed hundreds of business failures to the acquisition of grain on credit. Although it was in the merchant's interest to maintain a flow of cash to pioneer producers, this had to be done in a manner calculated to assure adequate profits.[26]

Their isolation from eastern markets placed country merchants at a disadvantage because it denied them information crucial to making marketing decisions regarding frontier commodities. In a national economy characterized by fluctuating supply and demand, Michigan merchants agonized over the price of wheat in markets constantly responding to the independent actions of producers and eastern buyers. Farmers, recalled the editor of the *Michigan Farmer*, responded to rising prices by holding back sales in the expectation that prices might

go even higher, "and never have we known the time when farmers have thus held on, that they
were not compelled to sell in the end, at a greatly reduced price." Prices of grain in eastern markets fluctuated with urban demand in America and Europe and were difficult to predict. Some
merchants, like Sidney Alcott, attempted to protect their interests and those of their farmer
clients by offering current prices in advance of harvest. These merchants believed that a guaranteed price benefited the farmer by assuring him the sale of his grain and protected the merchant from abrupt rises in cost.[27]

Country merchants also oversaw the distribution of imported goods in newly settled areas
and had to maintain a wide variety of merchandise. A prospective country merchant was wise
to heed the advice of New Buffalo storekeeper Jacob Gerrish:

> In regard to goods, you had better purchase, principally staple articles, a large amount of
> domestics, home made clothes, but little tea and a large amount of coffee, 200 bbls of salt, which
> you would buy at Buffalo, in other respects, a small stock, but as of general assortment as you
> would buy for a country store in New Hampshire.[28]

The sale of finished goods provided the means to acquire the cash and credit necessary to
maintain retail businesses and buy produce. Indeed, merchants' access to capital in an economically peripheral region often permitted their expansion into additional activities, such as
operating grist and sawmills, inns, livery stables, and banks.[29]

The intermittent nature of long-distance trade constrained the extent of the country merchant's business by delaying shipments of produce and tying up capital. The difficulties in and
length of time required for travel prior to the coming of the railroads allowed country merchants only two trips per year to eastern centers to replenish their merchandise. Between these
times, produce was accumulated and stored and goods were gradually sold off. The widely
spaced purchasing of goods, together with the seasonality of the agricultural cycle, required
careful management of the merchant's capital. If deteriorating winter weather prevented the
shipment of fall produce until spring, it tied up capital during the time when the merchant's
resources had been expended to purchase the fall harvest but not yet reimbursed by its sale.
Because farmers quickly expended harvest income on supplies, mortgage payments, capital
improvements, and farm expenses, goods had to be sold on credit throughout much of the
winter.[30]

The necessity of maintaining a substantial capital to accommodate the boom and bust
nature of income favored the establishment of partnerships that allowed individual merchants
to pool their resources. Jacob Gerrish was later joined by Moses Chamberlain, who contributed
capital from his former retail businesses in Vermont and Ohio. Later, Chamberlain's son-in-
law, Hale B. Crosby, brought an additional stock of merchandise into the New Buffalo business.
Other frontier merchants, such as Jonas Allen of St. Joseph, acquired nonresident partners who
became, in effect, absentee investors in frontier retailing.[31]

Country merchants sought to minimize their risk by distributing their goods as widely as
possible. Those operating out of major ports, such as Monroe, actively advertised for interior

customers. Jacob Gerrish extended his mercantile activities across southwestern Michigan and northern Indiana, often trading along the Lake Michigan shore as far as Chicago and Milwaukee. Maintaining a wide network of customers assured a steady trade and a regular income.[32]

Country merchants often accepted goods other than grain in exchange for their wares. Joseph M. Griswold of Brooklyn recalled that,

> The necessities of the times, the want of a reliable currency, compelled . . . barter trade, and to handle all its varied ramifications successfully required knowledge, sagacity, boldness, [and] untiring vigilance. . . . At that time few firms in Michigan had credit in the eastern markets . . . so this firm [Harmon & Cook of Brooklyn] became the purchasers of the grain, the cattle, the pork, the wool, the beans, the butter, the wood, the ashes and everything else grown or raised, of a great circle of country around them.[33]

Indeed, the skill of the country merchant in assessing "the value of all the queer commodities that would be brought into him for exchange for his goods" became a legendary aspect of the frontier economy. Despite the desire on the part of merchants to place sales on a cash basis, the exchange of farm produce remained an integral part of the country merchant's trade as long as economic conditions inhibited the flow of funds and delayed the movement of cargo.[34]

Commission, or forwarding, merchants provided the link between Michigan and eastern urban markets. They handled the storage, transportation, and sale of produce acquired by the country merchant, who paid them a commission for their services. In addition, commission merchants frequently provided country merchants with cash advances necessary to purchase the harvest and offer credit to frontier producers. The growing market for western agricultural produce attracted commission merchants to Michigan as early as the 1820s. Rival firms competed for the trade in grain, advertising advantages in cost, speed of shipment, and business connections with eastern wholesalers and importers. Many erected warehouses at Detroit, Monroe, and other major ports, as well as at convenient collection points along the lakeshore. In western Michigan, for example, commission merchants established a warehouse at St. Joseph to store grain harvested throughout the St. Joseph River drainage. Others later appeared at the small settlements of New Buffalo and Grand Haven.[35]

Under the system of commission sales, ownership of produce remained with the shipper, usually the country merchant, until it reached its final point of sale. Produce traveled in sacks, which allowed individual owners' grain to remain separated throughout its journey. Numerous people coordinated the long-distance movement of produce and goods to and from the West, through a cumbersome process. Edwin D. Worcester, a successful railroad administrator in the 1870s, looked back on the complex problems faced by the commission merchant of earlier days:

> In the then ordinary way of doing business, a man shipped his property to a certain point, say the terminal of some route, and when it got there it was subject to his order. If he was not there

himself, he got an agent or consignee to take it. The business of that agent or consignee would be to pay the charges if not prepaid when the property was shipped, deliver it to the next party in the line of transportation after making his bargain with such party, and so on, for every point of reshipment.[36]

Consignment shipping required careful organization to minimize problems inherent in long-distance transportation.[37]

The risks involved in long-distance shipping required insurance against loss. Grain and flour could spoil or suffer water damage during its voyage eastward, a trip that might also become dangerous during the late fall season. The responsibility for insuring cargoes fell on the country merchants, who bought insurance from commission merchants to ameliorate their risk. Although shippers continued to own their grain on its way to market, middlemen began to play an increasingly larger role by protecting their clients' interests, a change that set the stage for a dramatic restructuring of trade. This transformation needed only the nudge provided by technological innovation in the closing years of the antebellum period.[38]

THE RAILROAD, THE ELEVATOR, AND THE RESTRUCTURING OF TRADE

The railroad, the grain elevator, and telegraphic communication changed the manner in which trade was carried out in the American West. The expansion of export trade depended on the creation of an efficient long-distance transportation infrastructure, and railroads offered reliable, year-round access to eastern markets. Although residents of southern Michigan lacked the means to develop rail routes to the East, the technological advantages railroads brought to shipping made them a worthwhile investment for eastern capitalists seeking to develop commercial production in the West.

Corporate investors, with funds amassed in trade and manufacturing, possessed the capital and expertise to organize, construct, and maintain Michigan's railroads after their divestiture by the state. Eastern investors insured the success of Michigan's first railroad, the Erie & Kalamazoo. When western entrepreneurs failed to raise sufficient capital for its construction, Charles Butler and several New York capitalists gained control of the company's stock, and their agent assumed supervision of the railroad's construction. They also acquired the affiliated Erie & Kalamazoo Railroad Bank, an institution created to supply credit to finance the line's construction. Their management of the bank provided the confidence to attract the additional eastern investment necessary to complete the railroad to Adrian in 1836 and begin operations the following spring.[39]

Eastern investors played a key role in completing Michigan's two state-owned railroads. Investors Tennis van Brant and George Bliss, builder of the Boston & Albany, purchased the Michigan Southern from the state and rebuilt it with funds provided by the New York relatives of Detroit attorney Elisha Litchfield. Van Brant became president of the Michigan Southern. The Litchfields, Bliss, and other investors facilitated the expansion of the railroad's network by acquiring the Erie & Kalamazoo and extending its line westward through Indiana to Chicago.

John Murray Forbes of Boston, Erastus Corning of Albany, and a number of smaller New England financiers provided capital to purchase and improve the Michigan Central. They negotiated the extension of the railroad to Chicago and played a key role in financing the construction of the Great Western Railroad of Canada between Buffalo and Windsor. This line formed the crucial overland link between the Michigan Central's Detroit terminus and the markets of the Northeast.[40]

British capitalists financed the construction of a northern rail line across the Lower Peninsula. Their funding revived the faltering Detroit & Pontiac Railroad and extended its route to the port of Grand Haven on Lake Michigan, from which they hoped to establish a cross-lake connection to Milwaukee. British investors saw the Detroit & Milwaukee Railroad as the natural western extension of the recently finished Great Western Railroad through Canada north of Lake Erie, and the Detroit & Milwaukee soon fell under the control of the Great Western.[41]

The railroad dramatically lowered the country merchant's capital costs. By linking Detroit and Toledo directly with eastern markets, railroads enhanced these cities' roles as distribution centers and altered the manner in which business was conducted in the interior. Urban wholesalers could now stock goods on short notice, and country merchants no longer had to invest so much of their capital in merchandise. The ability to make frequent buying trips to a regional center, such as Detroit, obviated the need for a large inventory and the cost of maintaining it.[42]

Railroads increased the scale of retail activity in Michigan by making it possible for merchants with very little capital to buy grain. Since they could ship it to market without the expense of warehousing, merchants could expend more of their capital buying rather than storing produce. Rail transport permitted merchants in Michigan to penetrate the region's interior along the lines of the expanding rail network. Here, as elsewhere in the West, merchants gravitated to strategic points where they could buy wheat from surrounding farms, load it, and ship it eastward. The rise of this new type of merchant is illustrated by the rapid success of John Hicks of Clinton County. An immigrant to Michigan in the 1850s, Hicks began his business career as a clerk for James Sturgis, a country merchant and miller in DeWitt. The extension of the Detroit & Milwaukee Railroad through the county in 1857 caused him to reassess his business strategy. Selling out his interest in the DeWitt store, in which he had become a partner, Hicks moved to the nascent settlement of St. Johns. There he invested much of his capital in the acquisition of grain, which he shipped by rail directly to eastern markets. The rapid turnaround on his investment subsequently permitted Hicks to expand and diversify his business activities in St. Johns on minimal credit. By the late 1860s, he was a leading commercial figure in the community.[43]

The year-round access provided by railroads greatly benefited producers with late crops. In 1850, the editor of the *Michigan Farmer* observed that heretofore they were obliged to sell grain at low prices to "speculators," who comprised the only late-year market. The value of late crops was diminished because they could not be shipped until spring. The opening of winter trade eliminated the need for storage by expanding the market for late grain crops and providing a more reliable income for western farmers.[44]

The steam-powered grain elevator provided the second element of the complex infra-structure needed to support export production. The elevator offered substantial savings in the cost of handling grain and transformed it from a product bought and sold in its own right to an abstract commodity traded for profit. A grain elevator was essentially a vertically arranged warehouse that employed steam-driven machinery to weigh, sort, and move grain in and out of storage bins. Its automatic features increased the ease with which large amounts of grain could be processed, expediting its shipment. Elevators effectively converted the flow of grain from a slow, piecemeal procession of sacks to a "river of grain," flowing from its western col-lection point to its eastern destination. Grain elevators first appeared at the Great Lakes receiv-ing port of Buffalo in 1843 and were soon constructed at grain shipping ports. Toledo acquired an elevator in 1847 and another was built at Detroit in 1851. Not unexpectedly, both accom-panied the convergence of railroads at these Michigan ports.[45]

Because the elevator required that individual owners' grain be mixed prior to shipping, it introduced an economy of scale that brought about two important changes in the organization of the grain trade. First, it moved the point of sale to the shipping port. Ownership of grain in sacks had traditionally remained with the seller until delivery at an eastern market. Mixing the grain at the elevator broke the visible link between western producers and eastern merchants and enhanced the role of middlemen in this process.[46]

Grain elevators also facilitated the regulation of grain quality. Boards of trade established standard grades as a means of sorting large lots of wheat based on plumpness, purity, cleanli-ness, and weight. These private groups arose in the export centers on the Great Lakes. Organized to represent collectively the business interests of these cities, boards of trade suc-cessfully managed the increasing amount of grain shipped from this region. Detroit's Merchants' Exchange and Board of Trade, incorporated in 1848, regulated and coordinated the growing commercial trade through Michigan's entrepôt.[47]

The storage of grain, graded on the basis of standardized criteria of quality, also created the means to expand credit in the West. Elevator operators provided sellers with a receipt based on the grade of the grain sold. Acceptable within the business community, receipts could be traded widely and quickly throughout eastern market centers. In addition, the quality and value of grain stored in western elevators permitted it to function like a gold reserve. Receipts drawn on stored grain acted as collateral for advances from local banks, eastern capitalists, or grain merchants. Farmers, merchants, and businessmen relied on this expanding source of credit to acquire more manufactured goods, finance grain purchases, build railroads, and fund diverse investments that served to enmesh Michigan ever more tightly within the national economy.[48]

The development of the telegraph in the 1840s facilitated the almost instantaneous com-pletion of contracts between distant partners. It changed the economic landscape of the United States by widely disseminating price data and other information pertaining to commodity availability and demand. This information promoted price stabilization, decreased the risks involved in long-distance commerce, and significantly lowered the cost of doing business. Transshipment centers of the western grain trade, particularly Buffalo, received information on a daily basis regarding conditions in the New York and European markets, as well as those at Great Lakes ports.[49]

Equal access to information and the benefits it bestowed did not accompany the availability of telegraphic communication. The greatest number of telegraph messages passed directly between dealers and clients at larger western ports, such as Chicago, Detroit, and Toledo. This practice concentrated market power, at the expense of trading centers that received less information. The monopolization of information helped consolidate Detroit's role as Michigan's major economic center.[50]

Michigan's growing role in the grain trade encouraged the development of a telegraph network, and by mid-century lines linked most of the major settlements in southern Michigan with the national network. Builders of a line westward from Buffalo selected Detroit as the center for its Michigan lines in 1847. The state legislature authorized telegraph lines along "any public roads or highways, and across any waters or bridges within the limits of this state," and by the fall of 1847 operators transmitted the first telegraph messages between Detroit and Ypsilanti along wires paralleling the Michigan Central tracks. During the following spring, telegraphic communication linked Detroit with Chicago and New York, giving Michigan businessmen direct access to eastern markets as well as the growing center of western commerce on Lake Michigan. The legislature supported the expansion of intrastate telegraphic service in Michigan, and by 1852 three separate companies operated in the state. The telegraph completed Michigan's commercial infrastructure by incorporating the state within a national information network.[51]

ECONOMIC CHANGE AND SETTLEMENT PATTERNING

During the 1840s and 1850s, more efficient long-distance transportation, improvements in agriculture, and the development of a service infrastructure altered the regional economy of southern Michigan. Increasingly organized around simple commodity production, the scale of agriculture expanded, while it became focused around a narrower range of staple crops. These changes provided greater return for farmers to invest in production and changed the appearance of the agricultural landscape. They also influenced land use and modified the pattern of settlement. Michigan's transformation from a regional to an export-based economy altered the infrastructure of production and brought changes in the distribution and function of settlements.[52]

As the focus of the regional rail network and connecting point to long-distance transportation, Detroit remained Michigan's central settlement. Its role as the state's wheat market and subsequent growth as an industrial center had a profound effect on the nature of its growth. The "immense influx" of immigrants responding to the demand for urban labor was evident to contemporary writer Sidney Smith, who referred to Detroit in his 1849 guidebook as the "Constantinople of the West." The rapid inrush of industrial workers brought an enlargement of the city's physical size, restructured the distribution of activities to accommodate factories and associated workers' neighborhoods, and increased the ethnic and class diversity of its population. All of these variables drastically modified the urban settlement pattern of Detroit and permitted it to maintain its central role as Michigan entered the national economy.[53]

The railroad shaped settlement patterning throughout southern Michigan. Railroads ignored earlier patterns of movement to establish direct routes between points of production and markets. The form of their networks encouraged the creation and growth of settlements along the new transportation routes, thereby altering spatial relationships among settlements on the frontier landscape. Rail transportation created a need for interior centers or internal central places to accommodate marketing activities. Changing settlement roles reflected an altered distribution of economic services and other urban functions in Michigan's hinterland and an increased disparity in settlement size. A new regional hierarchy emerged to replace that of the frontier period.[54]

The infrastructure of long-distance marketing provided the impetus for change in rural settlement patterning in Michigan. Expanding markets encouraged farmers to adopt simple commodity production, the surpluses of which underwrote the adoption of new crops and innovative practices. Labor-saving equipment allowed farmers to place larger tracts in production and increase the scale of their operations. Changes in agriculture occurred as many of the children of early settlers came of age. As members of simple commodity households, this second generation had access to the means of purchasing and bringing into cultivation new farms of their own. This insured the continued dominance of family farming in Michigan and encouraged an expansion of farming into areas previously overlooked or sparsely settled and markedly changed the distribution of rural settlement in Michigan.

13

The Consolidation of Settlement and Transportation in a Transitional Economy

During the 1850s the insulation of Michigan's frontier economy dissolved as improvements in transportation technology and changes in marketing allowed pioneer producers to participate in larger national markets. This mid-century transformation was evidenced by dramatically changing patterns of transportation and settlement.

The expansion of the state's railroad system made much of Lower Michigan accessible to external trade and provided a catalyst for the transformation of its internal regional economy. As railroads altered the structure of transportation, they affected the economic roles of the settlements they linked together. Builders of new rail lines, and of the improved roads built to support the traffic they generated, arranged their routes to promote export production and organize its activities efficiently in space. The resulting transportation network differed markedly from that developed to serve internal frontier markets. Its new form created the framework for a settlement hierarchy that superseded that of the frontier period and established the foundation for Michigan's subsequent economic development.

By this time Michigan's farming population occupied most of the southern Lower Peninsula. The distribution of post offices in operation in 1860 illustrates expansion and consolidation as pioneers took up the remaining vacant lands. They moved northward as far as Newaygo and Isabella Counties, perceived to lie on the margin of agriculture, and began to fill in the upper Grand River drainage and the eastern Thumb. The successful transplantation of substantial covenanted communities facilitated settlement on large portions of the Western Shore and in the lower Saginaw Valley. Permanent shoreline settlements as far north as Little Traverse Bay served as a precursor to later agricultural growth along the Lake Michigan Shore. Population density also increased on the long-neglected Eastern Shore, partially in response to Detroit's growing urban market (fig. 13.1).

RAILROADS AND MARKET EXPANSION

Following a slow start in the 1840s, railroad construction in Michigan expanded rapidly, and the form of their networks added a new dimension to the patterning of settlement. External trade now dictated rail routes, and new lines constructed in the 1850s were built to facilitate the shipment of goods to eastern markets rather than to link settlements within the region or promote immigration. Where a route incorporated an older frontier town and made it a center of trade, the latter retained its importance; however, railroad placement did not always reinforce the earlier hierarchy, and promoted the fortunes of many settlements based on the needs of export trade.

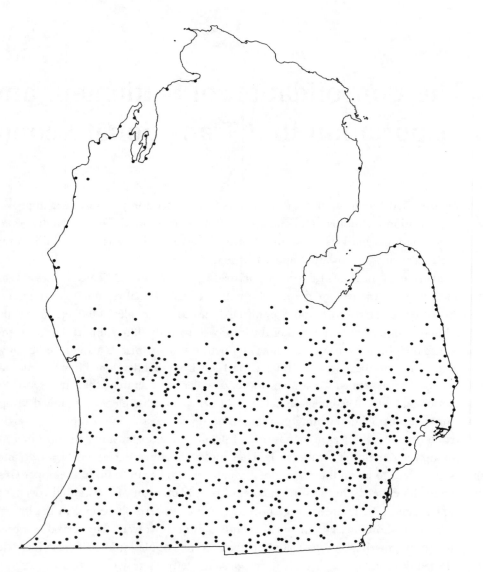

FIGURE 13.1. *DISTRIBUTION OF MICHIGAN POST OFFICES IN OPERATION FROM 1851 THROUGH 1860.*
(Source: Ellis, *Michigan Postal History*).

By 1850 the two state railroads, which had recently come into private ownership, had extended their routes across the Lower Peninsula (fig. 13.2). Construction on the Michigan Central reached Michigan City, Indiana, and the Michigan Southern, following delays resulting from its reorganization, extended as far as Coldwater. The older portions of both routes followed the courses of roads that linked together older frontier towns, but the western extension of the Michigan Central bypassed nearly all of Michigan's Western Shore to follow the lakeshore to reach Chicago (fig. 13.2).

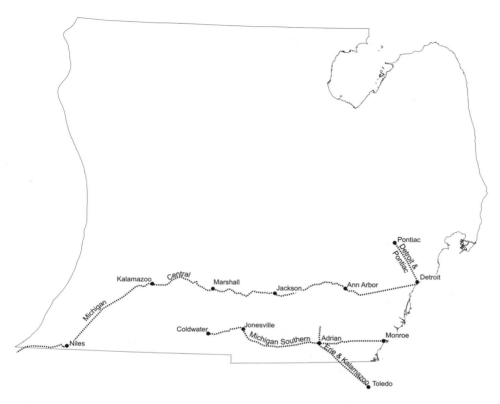

FIGURE 13.2. *THE RAILROAD NETWORK OF SOUTHERN MICHIGAN IN 1850.* (Sources: see text).

In the early 1850s the Michigan Southern completed its line across the Lower Peninsula. Extending its trades southward into Indiana to avoid the route of the competing Michigan Central, the Michigan Southern completed its route to Chicago in 1852. Together these two railroads became interregional trunk lines linking the new metropolis of the west with the Lake Erie ports.[1]

Throughout southern Michigan the rail network expanded to obtain more direct access to frontier production, and lines branched out from established regional centers. The Michigan Southern extended its track northward into a portion of the St. Joseph Valley and opened its Tecumseh branch as far inland as Manchester in 1855, linking the settlements along the River Raisin to its hub at Adrian (fig. 13.3).[2]

The completion of the Detroit & Milwaukee to the Lake Michigan shore at Grand Haven in 1858 opened a third cross-peninsular route in the north. Its owners hoped to develop a western trunk line employing ferry boats across Lake Michigan, and the location of its route influenced the creation of central places in more recently settled territory. Although its use as an interregional route did not produce the anticipated revenues, the Detroit & Milwaukee prospered by providing an outlet for the agricultural products of the Grand River Valley and the northern settled counties of Lower Michigan.[3]

FIGURE 13.3. *THE RAILROAD NETWORK OF SOUTHERN MICHIGAN IN 1855.* (Sources: see text).

Additional branch line expansion occurred in the late 1850s. The Michigan Southern completed its Adrian line from Manchester to Jackson, connecting it directly with a settlement on the line of the rival Michigan Central. Another railroad, presumptuously named the Amboy, Lansing, & Traverse Bay, began construction southward from the Detroit & Milwaukee line at Owosso with the intent of providing a rail link to the new capital at Lansing (fig. 13.4).[4]

Detroit consolidated its position as the state's center of rail transportation with the construction of two railroads that linked the major ports along the eastern shoreline. The Detroit, Monroe & Toledo formed a bridge line connecting Detroit with Toledo, where the Lake Shore line offered a direct route for Michigan products destined for eastern markets. Farther north, the Chicago, Detroit & Canada Grand Trunk Junction Railroad linked Detroit with producers in Macomb and St. Clair counties and provided an outlet to the East via the Grand Trunk through Canada (fig. 13.4).

Although still incomplete in 1860, Michigan's rail network already formed the heart of a vast new infrastructure shaped by the functional requirements of export trade. As the state emerged from its frontier status, it possessed a transportation system capable of supporting the growth of an export economy and restructuring the settlement hierarchy in the region. Despite being the central element in the new transportation system, however, railroads depended on

FIGURE 13.4. *THE RAILROAD NETWORK OF SOUTHERN MICHIGAN IN 1860.* (Sources: see text).

the development of additional routes to efficiently handle the increasingly higher volume of long-distance traffic.[5]

THE SYSTEM OF FEEDER ROADS

Plank roads offered the means for providing a secondary network of routes over which heavy, bulky freight could be carried from the interior. Although the rising volume of travel over short distances from farm to rail lines could not justify the cost of additional railroad construction, it was sufficient to support the building and maintenance of plank roads over which farmers could move heavy loads of goods expeditiously in wagons during all seasons. Proponents argued that plank roads complimented railroads, dramatically lowering the cost of transportation and increasing the accessibility of markets to farmers. Their use resulted in more reliable trade and reduced fluctuation in produce prices. The low cost and availability of sawn lumber made their construction and maintenance cheaper than that of paved roads, and state governments usually passed these costs on to profit-oriented private corporations authorized to operate plank roads and collect tolls.[6] Plank roads proliferated in the Old Northwest between 1844 and the mid-1850s. The State of Michigan clearly saw the economic value of plank roads and

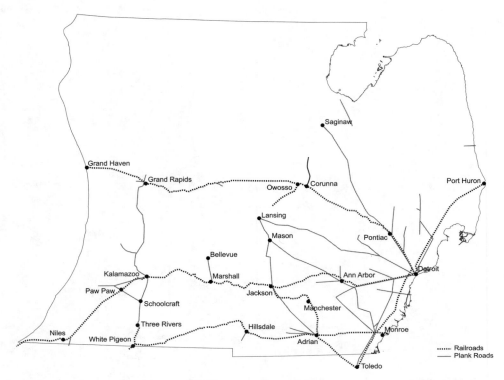

FIGURE 13.5. *The network of plank roads and railroads of southern Michigan in 1860.*
(Sources: see text).

issued 170 charters to companies between 1837 and 1860. A substantial number of these were completed.[7]

Michigan's plank roads formed an integral part of a larger network oriented toward export trade. Superimposing the routes of plank roads on the railroad network of 1860 reveals the spatial relationship of these two forms of transportation (fig. 13.5). Plank roads of varied lengths linked portions of the interior with central locations, usually along the routes of rail lines, and became a secondary network capable of providing feeder traffic to the railroads connecting Michigan with the outside world. The longer plank roads in southern Michigan provided access to distant locations in areas beyond the reach of existing railroads. Several of these roads led to Lansing and the rapidly developing region on the upper Grand Valley, and one directly linked the new state capital and Detroit. Others joined settlements in the lower Grand and Kalamazoo Valleys with western railroad centers and tied the developing Saginaw Valley region to a rail line at Pontiac.[8]

Plank road construction lasted only a relatively short time. National depressions in 1854 and 1857 hit the West especially hard, and when proponents realized that the costs of building and maintenance exceeded estimates, they curtailed the building of new roads in the late 1850s. As a result, the plank road network remained incomplete and failed to meet all the needs of a secondary road system in late antebellum Michigan.[9]

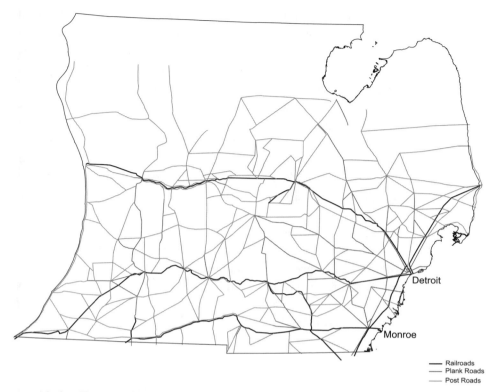

Detroit

Monroe

— Railroads
— Plank Roads
— Post Roads

FIGURE 13.6. *THE NETWORK OF PLANK ROADS, POST ROADS, AND RAILROADS OF SOUTHERN MICHIGAN IN 1860.* (Sources: see text).

The development of federal postal routes in Lower Michigan integrated the region within the nation communications system, and a desire to increase delivery rates encouraged the improvement of the roads along which mail traveled. The post office department organized its routes to permit information and goods to pass throughout the state. By 1860 these routes formed an extensive system that made up the remainder of the secondary road network. The increase of business and commercial mail that accompanied the expansion of retail trade integrated mail routes more closely with the transportation system created by the railroads, whose lines were already designated as post routes.[10]

Figure 13.6 illustrates the network of postal routes, plank roads, and rail lines in 1860. Together they formed a system that reached nearly all areas of agricultural settlement, providing farmers access to markets and opening Michigan's interior to commercial trade. These routes extended beyond the state's borders to enmesh the Michigan's villages and towns in a network linking them by land or water with central places in neighboring states and creating an infrastructure capable of integrating frontier Michigan with the national economy. Extended transportation routes also tied Lower Michigan to the growing number of isolated extractive industries in the north and the Thumb.[11]

Michigan's emerging transportation system exhibited several characteristics that facilitated the development of a commercial economy in southern Michigan. First, the completion of the three major rail lines obviated the need to traverse lengthy unimproved roads to reach markets. In areas far distant from rail lines, secondary routes converged around intermediate centers, such as Schoolcraft in southern Kalamazoo County, that possessed direct access to railroad settlements. Secondary routes spaced more or less evenly across most of the region formed complex systems that often provided producers direct links to more than one railroad settlement. For example, farmers living in southern Calhoun County had access to Battle Creek and Marshall on the Michigan Central Railroad or Coldwater on the Michigan Southern. Finally, secondary roads provided the principal connections with the new state capital of Lansing, hastening its emergence as a political center in direct communication with Detroit and other central settlements.[12]

By 1860, southern Michigan possessed a transportation network capable of supporting the entry of its producers into the national economy. The completion of these internal connections is usually associated with the emergence of dominant interior centers that generate higher traffic flows between them. The patterning of interconnections in Michigan's transportation network marked a phase of development that altered the function of key settlements, and its form may be used to identify those that played important roles in Michigan's transitional economy.[13]

TRANSPORTATION AND SETTLEMENT STRUCTURE IN 1860

The relative importance of Michigan settlements in the emerging commercial economy of the 1850s is reflected in the nature and number of their transportation links. Placement on a railroad line was most advantageous for a settlement, because it enhanced its potential as a trading center. The number of secondary roads emanating from a particular railroad settlement directly affected the volume of its commerce and its economic importance. Because Michigan's rail network remained incomplete in 1860, the foci of secondary route networks of plank roads and post roads also marked central settlements.

The layout of the transportation system in 1860 placed a number of settlements at key locations. Central places included towns on rail lines with the greatest number of secondary routes emanating from them. Table 13.1 shows that of seventy-four railroad settlements, thirty-five possessed three or more secondary routes and six marked railroad junctions. Many of settlements not situated on railroads also became the focal points of a number of secondary routes. Four or more routes met at eighteen settlements on plank roads (table 13.2). Since the plank roads terminated at rail lines, they represented heavy traffic links in the primary transportation network, and regional centers arose along them or at their junctions. The fact that railroads extended their lines to Lansing, Flint, and Saginaw within the next decade attests to the importance of central places in recently settled areas. Six additional settlements marked the foci of networks of five or more postal routes (table 13.3). Although these secondary roads could not carry a volume of goods comparable to plank roads, their networks also supported a substantial level of trade.[14]

TABLE 13.1 *RANKING OF RAIL SETTLEMENTS BY TOTAL NUMBER OF SECONDARY ROUTES*

8 or More Routes	7 Routes	6 Routes	5 Routes
Detroit*	Ionia	Grand Rapids	Dearborn
	Pontiac	Ann Arbor	Battle Creek
	Mt. Clemens	Kalamazoo	Monroe*
	Ypsilanti	Owosso*	Adrian*
	Marshall	Jackson*	

4 Routes	3 Routes	2 Routes	1 Route
Lowell	Grand Haven	Fenton	Ovid
Bloomfield	Port Huron	Holly	Chelsea
Columbus	Ada	Birmingham	Comstock
Dexter	Saranac	Wayne	Wyandotte
Niles	Lyons	Leoni	Brownstown
White Pigeon*	St Johns	Decatur	Petersburg
	Corunna	Dowagiac	Owosso
	Royal Oak	Constantine	Bronson
	Albion	Three Rivers	
	New Buffalo	Napoleon	
	Tecumseh	Manchester	
	Blissfield	Clinton	
	Hillsdale	Jonesville	
	Coldwater	Quincy	
		Sturgis	

* Railroad Junction Settlement
(Source: see text.)

TABLE 13.2. *RANKING OF NON-RAILROAD SETTLEMENTS ON PLANK ROADS BY TOTAL NUMBER OF SECONDARY ROUTES*

7 Routes	6 Routes	5 Routes	4 Routes
Lansing*	Romeo*	Washington*	Mason*
Paw Paw*	Schoolcraft*	Farmington*	
	Grand Blanc*	Almond	
	Saline	Plymouth	
		Flat Rock	
		Mooreville	
		Whitmore Lake	
		Howell	
		Allegan	
		Flint	
		Saginaw	

* Plank Road Junction Settlements
(Source: see text.)

TABLE **13.3.** *RANKING OF NON-RAILROAD SETTLEMENTS ON POSTAL ROADS BY TOTAL NUMBER OF SECONDARY ROUTES*

8 Routes	6 Routes	5 Routes
Lapeer	Charlotte	Otisco
		St. Joseph
		Cassopolis
		Centreville

(Source: See text.)

Figure 13.7 illustrates the locations of settlements identified as foci in the primary and secondary route networks of late antebellum Michigan. The different types of routes linking them and the number of connections associated with each indicate that the level of trade at each varied and that their economic roles differed. This information, by itself, is insufficient to clearly recognize functional distinctions among places of economic significance or to identify a hierarchy of relative importance. The patterning of transportation routes in 1860, however, reveals several important characteristics of the region's new economic landscape.

Perhaps the most noticeable feature of this landscape was the continued dominance of Detroit. Situated at the junction of rail lines, plank roads, and other secondary routes, the entrepôt's role as a conduit for immigration became less important than its function as a center for western trade. Detroit's success as a regional transportation hub encouraged the expansion of manufacturing there and laid the basis for its emergence as the heart of industrial development in southeastern Michigan.[15]

The number of important transportation centers also increased markedly by 1860. All of the frontier towns retained positions of importance as the hubs of secondary route networks. With the exception of Saginaw and Flint, all of them were connected by rail lines by 1860. Although these older towns continued to play a central role in regional transportation, there were now many other centers with large, and often more extensive, secondary networks. Their appearance implies greater competition between central settlements and a reduction in the geographical size of their economic hinterlands.

The number and distribution of central settlements in 1860 also testify to a consolidation of agricultural production during the 1850s. Only a few areas in the central and western part of southern Michigan remained outside the reach of markets on the new overland network. The denser occurrence of transportation hubs made the central services associated with commercial trade (such as retail and wholesale trade, warehousing, banking, and manufacturing) available across the region and encouraged Michigan's incorporation in the larger national economy.

EXPLORING SETTLEMENT FUNCTION

Summarizing the abruptness of change in the community of Hillsdale, contemporary resident Henry Waldron remarked, "Although it is true that Rome was not built in a day, yet it is no less

FIGURE 13.7. *A HIERARCHICAL ARRANGEMENT OF SOUTHERN MICHIGAN'S SETTLEMENTS IN 1860 BASED ON THEIR POSITION IN THE REGIONAL TRANSPORTATION NETWORK.* (Sources: see text).

true that Hillsdale was built in a few. In the short space of three years its buildings, its inhabitants, and its business have increased tenfold. . . ."[16] Waldron's observations described more than the growth of the regional economy in the 1850s. They acknowledged the metamorphosis undergone by Michigan's settlements as they responded to regional economic reorganization. The rise of a market-oriented economy dramatically altered the roles of rural centers in southern Michigan and created a far more complex hierarchy than that of the frontier. A settlement's role in the larger economy determined its function, which is expressed in the nature of the centralizing activities that took place there. These included retailing and wholesaling, processing and storage, manufacturing and repair, banking, courts, churches, public accommodation, and professional services. Such activities served as a magnet for immigration, and settlement growth accompanied increasing functional complexity. The largest and most complex settlements ranked highest in the settlement hierarchy and constituted Michigan's central places.

Because number of inhabitants correlates with size, an examination of comprehensive population records can provide a comparative overview of Michigan's settlements during the 1850s. Federal and state censuses of 1854, 1860, and 1864 contain population figures acquired through direct and extensive survey, but include data for relatively few individual settlements,

TABLE 13.4. *COMPARISON OF THE ORDER OF SETTLEMENTS IN THE 1864 MICHIGAN CENSUS AND THE 1859, 1863, AND 1864 GAZETTEERS*

Gazetteers		Census	
Detroit	70,000	Detroit	53,170
Grand Rapids	10,500	Saginaw/East Saginaw	8,928
Saginaw/East Saginaw	9,500	Grand Rapids	8,770
Adrian	9,000	Adrian	7,041
Jackson	7,500	Kalamazoo	6,797
Ann Arbor	7,102	Ann Arbor	5,731
Kalamazoo	6,500	Jackson	5,544
Port Huron	6,200	Monroe	4,214
Ypsilanti	5,500	Marshall	4,192
Niles	5,500	Ypsilanti	4,189
Lansing	5,000	Port Huron	4,025
Coldwater	5,000	Coldwater	3,977
Monroe	4,500	Battle Creek	3,856
Flint	4,500	Lansing	3,573
Marshall	4,200	Flint	3,297
Battle Creek	4,000	Niles	3,095
Pontiac	3,200	Pontiac	2,531
St. Clair	2,200	St. Clair	1,676
Owosso	1,500	Owosso	1,346

(Source: see text.)

and many are not reported consistently. Consequently, only a few may be compared over time (see appendix 1).[17] On the other hand, Michigan gazetteers contain extensive statistical listings of individual settlements for this period. Intended as reference works as well as promotional documents, gazetteers published in 1859, 1863, and 1864 include consistent and comprehensive population data on many more municipalities than are found in the censuses (see appendix 2). A comparison of gazetteer and census data identified Michigan's nineteen largest cities and towns and ranked them in nearly the same order (table 13.4). Although the gazetteers generally inflated population size, they did so consistently and offer a reliable means of estimating the relative size of Michigan's settlements.[18]

A graphic comparison of the populations of Michigan's settlements produces a frequency distribution that reveals substantial disparities in size. This patterning implies considerable variation in their functional complexity (fig. 13.8), but also indicates clustering around several peaks that allow us to group them into five categories (table 13.5).

One hundred and sixty-one villages in the fifth category contained the lowest populations. Nonetheless, most were larger than the majority of settlements of the frontier period, and some surpassed many earlier frontier towns. Size did not preclude the presence of integrating institutions, and this group included at least three county seats, while most were at least township centers. The fourth-largest group included a number of county seats and three former frontier

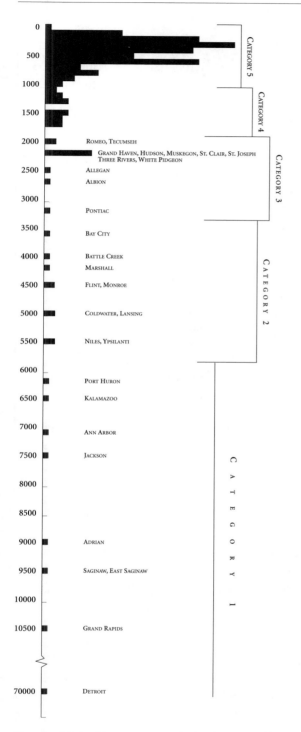

FIGURE 13.8. *FREQUENCY DISTRIBUTION OF SETTLEMENTS IN SOUTHERN MICHIGAN BASED ON POPU-LATIONS PROVIDED BY GAZETTEERS OF THE EARLY 1860S.* (Sources: see text.)

TABLE 13.5. *RANKED CATEGORIES OF SETTLEMENTS BASED ON GAZETTEER POPULATIONS.*

1 Over 6,000	2 3,500-5,500	3 2,000-3,000	4 1,100-1,800	5 Under 1,000
Detroit *	Ypsilanti	Pontiac +*	Corunna *	161 Villages
Grand Rapids +*	Niles +	Albion	Jonesville	
Saginaw/	Lansing	Allegan *	Sturgis	
East Saginaw +*				
Adrian +*	Coldwater *	Grand Haven *	New Baltimore	
Jackson +*	Monroe +*	Hudson	Mt. Clemens +*	
Ann Arbor +*	Flint +*	Muskegon *	Ionia +*	
Kalamazoo +*	Marshall +*	St. Clair	Dowagiac	
Port Huron *	Battle Creek	St. Joseph *	Owosso	
	Bay City	Saline	Fenton	
		Three Rivers	Grass Lake	
		White Pigeon	Constantine	
		Romeo	St. Johns *	
		Tecumseh	Paw Paw *	
			Addison	
			Galesburgh	
			Berrien Springs	
			Howell +*	
			Dexter	
			Buchanan	

+ Former Frontier Town
* County Seat
(Source: see text.)

towns. Howell, Ionia, and Mt. Clemens were all situated at important rail and secondary over-land route junctions. The third-largest cluster consisted of thirteen smaller regional centers situated at rail and/or secondary route junctions and transportation centers associated with lake and river traffic. Nine larger regional centers form the second-largest group. Over half of these lay on rail lines and formed junctions of secondary overland routes. All were lake ports or foci of inland trade. This group included the new state capital of Lansing.[19]

Michigan's primary transportation centers possessed the largest populations and comprised the first category of settlements. They include, in increasing order of size, Port Huron, Kalamazoo, Ann Arbor, Jackson, Adrian, Saginaw/East Saginaw, Grand Rapids, and Detroit. Railroads provided access to all of them by the early 1860s, and several lay at junctions of rail networks. With an estimated population of 70,000, Detroit stood apart from the others. Its size and growing rail connections enabled the city to dominate the state's economy as the latter became increasingly oriented toward national trade (fig. 13.9).[20]

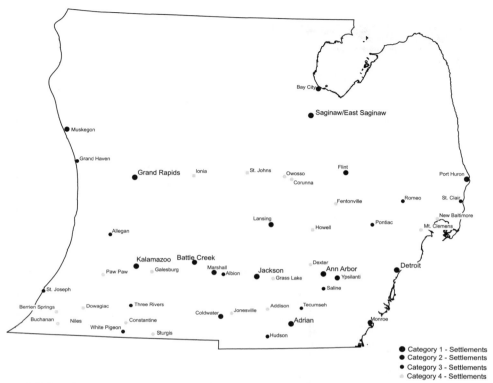

FIGURE 13.9. *A HIERARCHICAL ARRANGEMENT OF SOUTHERN MICHIGAN'S SETTLEMENTS IN THE EARLY 1860S BASED ON POPULATION SIZE.* (Sources: see text).

The differences in population among Michigan's settlements reveal markedly differential growth by the early 1860s, a pattern produced by their changing roles in a transitional economy increasingly dependent on commercial trade. Nearly all of the fifty settlements with populations of more than one thousand lay on major overland routes, especially railroads, and two-thirds of them were major transportation hubs; however, the fact that half of the settlements situated at route junctions still had populations of fewer than one thousand indicates that the economy's development remained incomplete. Important functional differences already existed in Michigan's settlements by this time, and these are evident in the nature of activities carried out there.[21]

Because economic complexity rather than size alone determined a settlement's relative importance, we must compare the kinds of economic activities in each settlement to reveal its centrality in the emerging hierarchical structure of late antebellum Michigan. In a commercial economy, a settlement's complexity increased directly with the variety of economic activities (retailing, wholesaling, manufacturing, and services) performed there as well as with their total number. Functional variation is measured by deriving and comparing index numbers for each settlement based on the frequency and variety of these activities. These variables can be compared statistically on a region-wide basis and the results expressed through functional index

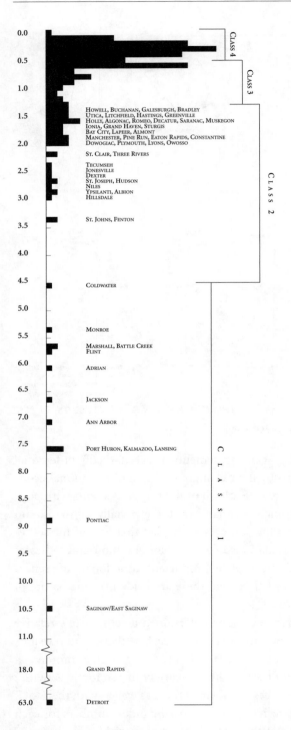

FIGURE 13.10. *FREQUENCY DISTRIBUTION AND RANKING OF SOUTHERN MICHIGAN'S SETTLEMENTS THE EARLY 1860S BASED ON FUNCTIONAL INDEX NUMBERS.* (Sources see text).

FIGURE 13.11. *DISTRIBUTION OF SOUTHERN MICHIGAN'S CENTRAL PLACES AND SECONDARY SETTLEMENTS IN THE EARLY 1860S.* (Sources: see text).

numbers for each settlement. Because settlements with larger index values possessed greater economic complexity than those with lower numbers, a settlement's numerical ranking indicates its relative position in the regional hierarchy. The nature and distribution of activities in Michigan were derived from lists of businesses in contemporary gazetteers. These revealed that nearly one hundred separate activities were carried out in 276 different Michigan communities during the early 1860s (see appendix 3).[22]

A comparison of functional index numbers revealed a great disparity in the economic activity carried out in the settlements examined and permitted us to place them into four ranked classes. Most settlements clustered in two groups at the lower end of the functional complexity scale. These classes included the villages and smaller towns then emerging as local service centers. Two other classes of settlements exhibited a markedly greater complexity, however, and are clearly distinguishable from the others. These settlements would have occupied key positions in the functional hierarchy of southern Michigan in 1860 and represented its central places and secondary settlements (fig. 13.10).[23]

Michigan's central places comprised a group of fifteen settlements whose range of economic activities set them apart from the rest. All possessed substantial populations and together constituted the state's larger cities and towns. In order of importance, the central places were the port of Detroit, Grand Rapids, Saginaw/East Saginaw, Pontiac, Port Huron, Kalamazoo, Lansing,

Ann Arbor, Jackson, Adrian, Flint, Marshall, Battle Creek, Monroe, and Coldwater. Functional index numbers also identified a class of forty-one secondary settlements.

In descending order of functional index values, these are: St. Johns, Fenton, Hillsdale, Ypsilanti, Albion, Niles, St. Joseph, Hudson, Dexter, Jonesville, Tecumseh, St. Clair, Three Rivers, Dowagiac, Plymouth, Lyons, Owosso, Manchester, Pine Run, Eaton Rapids, Constantine, Bay City, Lapeer, Almont, Ionia, Grand Haven, Sturgis, Holly, Algonac, Romeo, Decatur, Saranac, Muskegon, Utica, Litchfield, Hastings, Greenville, Howell, Buchanan, Galesburg, and Bradley. Among these were older settlements that had once played central roles in the frontier economy, but many in this group had arisen more recently as newly occupied areas came into production (fig. 13.11).

Although these cities and towns differed in size and volume of trade, each exhibited a degree of economic diversity that identify it as having played an important role in Michigan's developing commercial economy. It is significant that all central places and secondary settlements lay on railroads or primary overland routes. Each derived its economic importance from its participation in long-distance trade, and this enhanced reliance on transportation made a settlement's centrality within the network structure correspond to its position in the economic hierarchy. Because the structure of the transportation network reflected the nature of trade, an analysis of the links between central places and secondary settlements should reveal patterning indicative of Michigan's emerging commercial economy and the formation of its post-frontier landscape.

14

The Landscape of Settlement in Southern Michigan in 1860

The structure of Michigan's settlement in 1860 was shaped by the development of long-distance trade linking its producers with external markets. Because the success of this commerce depended on keeping transportation costs down, distance became an increasingly important factor in the placement of settlements important in trade. Just as Michigan's frontier economy emphasized access between central settlements and secondary market centers, the new export-oriented economy underscored the importance of minimizing the distance over which goods moved to major transportation arteries. This encouraged the placement of as many secondary settlements as possible along routes linking the central places that provided the connections with external markets. In emerging commercial economy, the central place model anticipates that a transport principle would influence the organization of the settlement hierarchy to facilitate such a pattern. In a regular lattice of hexagonal trade areas, a larger number of secondary centers would have been arranged on transportation routes midway between each pair of central places to create the network illustrated in figure 14.1.[1]

The pattern of transportation routes linking pairs of central places identified on the basis of their functional complexity provides vital clues to the structure of Michigan's 1860 settlement network. Using the locations of intervening secondary settlements to mark the market boundaries of trade between central places allows us to estimate market area boundaries for each of the higher-order settlements. The juxtaposition of central places and secondary settlements and the network of railroad, plank road, and post road connections between them reveals the pattern anticipated by the transport principle. The form of Michigan's commercial settlement network is apparent when the market area boundaries are straightened out and expressed as hexagons to reveal the hierarchical organization of settlement (fig. 14.2).

On the eve of the Civil War, the structure of Michigan's settlement network had begun to take on a form that facilitated the growth of commercial production. The locations of economic centers minimized the distance separating farmers from the major transportation routes by which their produce moved to external commercial markets and over which they received increasingly greater quantities of finished goods in return. The transition to a commercial economy was not entirely completed by 1860. In several places secondary centers had not yet arisen, while elsewhere multiple settlements combined to take on this role. Some secondary settlements served more than one central place, and in one instance two cities competed for dominance. Nonetheless, a remarkable change had overtaken southern Michigan and left its mark on the new regional landscape.

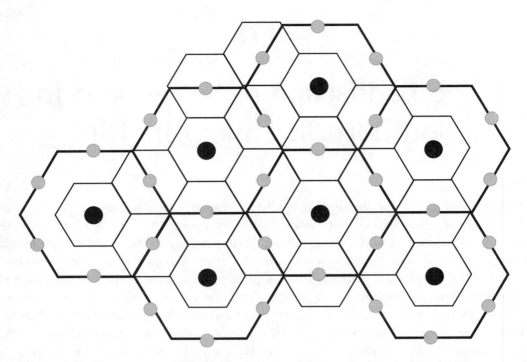

FIGURE 14.1. *THE ARRANGEMENT OF MARKET AREAS AND SETTLEMENTS IN A REGION CHARACTER-IZED BY EXTERNAL TRADE AND ORGANIZED ACCORDING TO THE TRANSPORT PRINCIPLE. THE NETWORK FORMED BY THIS ARRANGEMENT PLACES EACH LOWER-RANKING SECONDARY CENTER AT THE MIDPOINT BETWEEN FOUR HIGHER-RANKING CENTRAL PLACES.* (Sources: see text).

Not surprisingly, Detroit dominated the state's economy. As Michigan's center of trade, it extended commercial connections to major American and foreign cities. Detroit's importance as an industrial center expanded rapidly after 1840 as improved transportation permitted manufacturers to gather raw materials, such as wood, copper, and iron, and ship finished goods more efficiently. The city became home to firms turning out a variety of finished and semi-finished products and grew to dominate regional manufacturing in Michigan and parts of adjoining states.[2]

Detroit maintained direct railway links with the nearest interior central places, the old frontier towns of Adrian, Ann Arbor, and Pontiac. All had used available water power to become important manufacturing centers whose foundries, factories, and machine shops turned out steam engines, agricultural implements, stoves, and other finished products. Flour milling remained an integral business in these cities, and each developed substantial retail trade with its surrounding areas. In addition, all retained their political function as county seats.

Although similar in function, each city had already begun to develop a distinctive charac-ter. Observers noted that Pontiac's influence extended into adjacent Lapeer, Livingston, and Genesee Counties and emphasized its image as "a place of bustle and business, and quite as well deserving the cognomen of city." In contrast, visitors to Ann Arbor were struck by "its pleasant

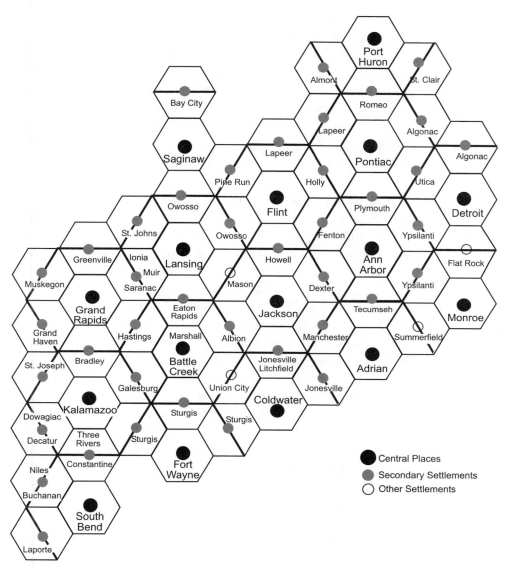

FIGURE 14.2. *THE ARRANGEMENT OF MARKET AREAS AND SETTLEMENTS IN SOUTHERN MICHIGAN DURING THE EARLY 1860S.* (Sources: see text).

location, the beauty of its scenery, its healthful position," and the attractiveness of its buildings, parks, and gardens. The University of Michigan and the state medical college enhanced Ann Arbor's image as a diversified community that included education and the arts as well as industry and trade. As an early railroad junction with a direct connection to Lake Erie, Adrian became the transportation hub of southeastern Michigan. Its rapid growth distinguished Adrian from surrounding communities in southeastern Michigan, and its "well laid-out streets, large blocks of stores, and elegant private residences" typified the city as a center of wealth and enterprise.[3]

A number of secondary settlements linked pairs of urban centers in eastern Michigan, and in one instance connected three of these central places. Although always overshadowed by the neighboring county seat of Ann Arbor, Ypsilanti arose as a center of flour milling in the lower Huron Valley. Its industries produced lumber and plaster and manufactured steam engines and agricultural machinery. Ypsilanti lay at the center of a road network that linked Ann Arbor with Detroit and Monroe and possessed direct access to several urban centers, and the town provided services and commercial outlets for a densely settled agricultural region.[4] Tecumseh, whose mills on the River Raisin had established its importance, expanded its role as a retail center and shipping point for agricultural products to the larger markets at Ann Arbor and Adrian.[5]

Farther north, Utica lay between Detroit and Pontiac. Although slow growth in northern Macomb County initially limited its commercial development, by the 1850s it had become the produce market for a "well-settled and well-cultivated" area with direct transportation links to Detroit. One observer noted that its favorable location allowed Utica to thrive as a place of enterprise.[6] Algonac served as a secondary settlement for two central places in Michigan. Situated on the St. Clair River, it offered both Detroit and Pontiac direct access to Canada. The "thriving village" of Plymouth, in western Wayne County, maintained commercial ties with Ann Arbor, Pontiac, and Detroit, and its mills and merchants were all "doing good business."[7]

Although railroads had reduced Monroe's role as a grain port, they enhanced its position as a central place. Linked by rail with Toledo and Detroit, as well as with the interior, Monroe thrived as a service center, transportation hub, and market in southeastern Michigan. Because of the relatively slow growth of agriculture on the Eastern Shore, secondary settlements failed to develop near Monroe; however, Summerfield and Flat Rock, situated approximately midway on the rail lines linking the port with Adrian and Detroit, were foci of economic activity and may have served as intermediate markets for traffic between these central places.[8] On the River Raisin, the community of Manchester grew up rapidly as a milling and manufacturing center in the 1850s. Even a disastrous 1853 fire that destroyed its flour mill and fourteen businesses failed to halt its development. By 1860, Manchester's railroad connections linked farmers to markets at Jackson and Adrian and made it the market for a substantial area.[9] Railroads also linked Dexter with the central places of Ann Arbor, Jackson, and Detroit. As a regional focus of flour and wool production, Dexter's steam- and water-powered mills processed large quantities of farm produce for shipment to larger markets.[10]

To the west, Coldwater and Jackson remained central markets and transportation hubs, and began to emerge as manufacturing centers. In addition to their mills, both produced a variety of goods, including tools and agricultural equipment, and conducted business over the central part of southern Michigan. Coldwater, the seat of Branch County, lay in the center of a developed agricultural district. The settlement grew rapidly following the arrival of the railroad in 1850. Despite two disastrous fires, "new . . . buildings rose phoenix-like from the ruins of the old, and in a short time all evidence of the late calamity was effaced." In addition to its flour and saw mills, tanneries, foundries, banks, and retail businesses gravitated there and Coldwater became the regional market for farm produce.[11]

By 1860 Jackson was well on its way to becoming a diversified industrial center. Its twenty-eight manufacturing establishments engaged in eighteen different types of production. Jackson's choice as the site of the Southern Michigan Prison promoted industrial growth in this county seat. The city's entrepreneurs took advantage of the state's penal system, which permitted prisoners to be contracted out as a means of rehabilitation. This practice provided manufacturers of wagons, agricultural implements, and other products with a pool of cheap captive labor that greatly enhanced the rate of business expansion in Jackson. The prison and its industries also became a market for local supplies and produce. The availability of coal, sandstone, and other raw materials further benefited the development of manufacturing there in the late 1850s.[12]

Jonesville and the nearby county seat of Hillsdale constituted the only substantial municipalities south of Jackson, between Coldwater and Adrian. Both lay along the railroad, which provided direct transportation links east and west, and together they served three central places. Although "burned to the ground" in 1849, Jonesville rebuilt its mills and grew rapidly in the 1850s to become the principal market for the recently settled agricultural lands in central southern Michigan. By the mid-1850s, Michigan Central College (later Hillsdale College) was relocated in Hillsdale and the town had taken on an imposing appearance with several substantial public buildings. Together, Jonesville and Hillsdale developed considerable retail trade prior to 1860.[13]

Expanding agriculture on the openings west of Jackson provided Albion's mills with large quantities of wheat. Both Jackson and Marshall drew produce from this important secondary settlement. Its hydraulic resources drew a variety of manufacturing activities to Albion and provided a basis for industrial growth. One local industry, the Gale Manufacturing Company, exemplified this trend. Established as a shop in 1844, it underwent a phenomenal growth during the next fifteen years to include a foundry and a threshing machine factory, as well as other manufacturing businesses. Although known for its industry, the addition of the Wesleyan Seminary, which became Albion College, distinguished the village from other emerging milling and manufacturing centers.[14]

In general, secondary settlements separated Michigan's central places, but Battle Creek and Marshall lay too close together to permit an intervening market center. This situation resulted from Battle Creek's rapid rise as an industrial, commercial, and transportation center, and an agricultural market, which allowed it to draw away business from the older frontier town and county seat. Marshall's failure to develop its regional trade led to its gradual economic decline, but this process was far from complete in 1860. Consequently, the two cities became the bifurcated center for a rich agricultural district in the upper Kalamazoo Valley, from which transportation routes extended to neighboring communities on all sides.[15]

Kalamazoo emerged as the agricultural market and manufacturing hub for southwestern Michigan. Its industries included foundries, tanneries, flour and saw mills, sash and blind factories, and a blast furnace producing stoves and other castings. An observer commented that "Its businessmen appear to have the bump of go-a-head-a-tiveness strongly developed . . . we cannot conceive [of] sending east for an article that can be procured at home." The image of

Kalamazoo also became that of a rising commercial center with extensive trade in agricultural produce. Transportation arteries provided this county seat access to other central places in the state as well as to those in neighboring Indiana, and led beyond to the western entrepôt of Chicago. Its role as an economic center attracted other institutions. Kalamazoo College, a seminary and theological school, was established there, and the Michigan legislature recognized its status as an urban center by placing one of the state's major public institutions in Kalamazoo. The state mental hospital, or asylum, opened there in 1859.[16]

Galesburg developed as a secondary settlement on the highly productive prairie lands between Kalamazoo and Battle Creek. Lacking advantages for extensive industrial development, it became primarily a trade and transportation center.[17] Farther south, the secondary settlement of Sturgis shipped agricultural produce to both Battle Creek and Kalamazoo, and connected each with Fort Wayne, an established central place that dominated railroad and canal transportation in northern Indiana.[18] Although a secondary settlement was absent between Battle Creek and Coldwater, Union City could well have filled this role. A regional road junction since the frontier period, it developed as a milling and retail center in the upper St. Joseph Valley.[19]

Farther west, Three Rivers and Constantine occupied strategic water-power sites and had become the principal milling centers in the St. Joseph Valley. Linked by rail, they formed a dual market center for this developed agricultural region, with access to Kalamazoo as well as South Bend, Indiana. Constantine had emerged from the "miscellaneous" collection of buildings that characterized its Puddleford roots to become an important milling settlement and focus of retail trade. Three Rivers also rose in prominence in the 1850s as a result of its rapid industrial growth. By the close of the decade, its factories produced agricultural machinery as well as a variety of finished goods, and its mills exported large amounts of flour.[20]

The economy of southwestern Michigan had always extended beyond the state's political borders, and in 1860, the railroad center of South Bend, Indiana, served as a focus for trade in the lower St. Joseph Valley. South Bend tapped the hydraulic resources of the St. Joseph River in the 1850s and became an important milling, manufacturing, and commercial center in northern Indiana. The growth and diversification of its industries and other institutions extended its economic influence into southwestern Michigan. To the west, the smaller secondary settlement of LaPorte gave this central place access to produce from the area south of Lake Michigan.[21]

South Bend also maintained important connections with the Michigan settlements of Niles and Buchanan in Berrien County. Situated on the navigable lower St. Joseph, Niles was an important river port and former frontier town with extensive economic ties. The absence of a dam on the St. Joseph restricted its hydraulic resources and limited its growth as a milling and manufacturing center in 1860. Although much smaller than Niles, the nearby river port of Buchanan also possessed a variety of commercial activities, and supplemented its neighbor as a focus of trade.[22]

Several secondary settlements provided markets for Kalamazoo in western Michigan. Decatur and Dowagiac grew up in the late 1840s along the railroad in Van Buren and Cass

Counties. This mode of transportation offered an outlet for regional produce, and both communities expanded rapidly, adding manufacturing and retail businesses to their flour milling facilities. So rapid was its growth that Dowagiac occupied parts of four townships three years after it was surveyed.[23]

The port of St. Joseph provided Kalamazoo with an outlet to Lake Michigan and Chicago. Although towns on the new rail routes south of the lake offered farmers a more convenient market for their produce, water traffic remained an important means of shipping their produce. St. Joseph's harbor facilities allowed local producers to participate directly in commercial trade, and made it an important transportation hub through which commodities such as lumber, grain, and fruit might reach larger markets with access to the lake.[24]

The region separating the lower drainages of the Grand and Kalamazoo Rivers remained sparsely populated even in the 1850s, and Bradley grew up as a secondary settlement midway between Kalamazoo and Grand Rapids on the plank road connecting the two central places. Although it still lacked substantial industries by 1860, its location permitted Bradley to develop as a center of retail trade, and it possessed a number of retail and processing activities.[25]

Grand Rapids dominated trade in western Michigan. A milling and marketing center, it expanded rapidly as a regional transportation hub in the 1850s following the completion of the plank road to Kalamazoo and the railroad to Detroit. By the close of the decade this county seat was Michigan's second-largest city and conducted substantial retail trade. Damming the Grand River at its rapids provided power for a variety of manufacturing industries, including tanneries; flour, lumber, and veneer mills; machine shops; woolen factories; foundries; and tools and agricultural equipment manufacturers. By 1860 Grand Rapids had already begun to emerge as a center of furniture making as well as the home of numerous service industries.[26]

The railroad linked Grand Rapids to the port of Grand Haven, whose large harbor made the village an outlet on Lake Michigan, providing western Michigan's urban center with connections to Milwaukee, Racine, Southport [Kenosha], and Chicago. Although its business still rested largely on lumber milling, Grand Haven began to attract other commercial activities, and expanded its retail trade.[27] The lumber port of Muskegon offered access to the northern portion of western Michigan via water and by overland routes paralleling the shoreline.[28]

To the east, Hastings lay at the center of a network of post roads in the sparsely settled region south of the Grand River. This secondary settlement occupied a strategic position in the Thornapple Valley because it lay on the road linking Battle Creek with Grand Rapids. Still largely a milling settlement in 1860, it was home to several merchants and a bank. These, together with its role as a transportation hub and political importance as the seat of Barry County, made up for a lack of substantial industry, and allowed Hastings to develop an extensive retail trade in this newly occupied area.[29]

Ionia retained its role as a market center on the railroad between Grand Rapids and Lansing. This former frontier town remained a county seat and kept the federal land office, but the slowness of agricultural development north of the Grand River restrained its growth and prevented its dominating trade in this region. Lyons and Saranac, possessing rail connections and water power, also arose as foci of manufacturing and processing and, together with Ionia, comprised a dispersed secondary settlement that served as a market for farmers in this portion of the Grand River Valley.[30]

In the center of the state, the capital of Lansing grew rapidly as a central place. A plank road hub with approaching railroad connections, Lansing acquired the communications links needed to serve both the state government and the agricultural college. Its role as Michigan's political center spurred the development of trade, and retailing expanded to augment the growth of industry. Residents erected several flour and saw mills, and the appearance of machine shops and foundries signaled the establishment of a manufacturing base. Lansing's emergence as an urban center in a poorly settled part of the state served as a magnet to immigration and encouraged the rise of several nearby settlements.[31]

Southwest of Lansing, the milling center of Eaton Rapids became the focus of retail trade and industry between Lansing and Battle Creek and Marshall. Described as "quite a brisk little place," its size and business began to grow as farming expanded in the upper Grand Valley.[32] Mason lay on the plank road from Lansing to Jackson. Although still a village that had not yet reached the complexity of other secondary settlements, it served as the seat of Ingham County and had become a center for retail trade and service industries in this recently settled part of the state.

Owosso occupied an excellent waterpower site on the Shiawassee River, and this small retail center grew up around its mills. By 1860 railroad construction made it a focus of transportation in the upper Saginaw drainage and permitted the expansion of manufacturing and trade in an area still undergoing settlement. Incorporated as a city in 1859, its industries included a foundry; a furniture, sash, door, and blind factory; a brewery; and flour and cloth mills, and one bank had already opened its doors. As the largest area market with railway and road connections linking Lansing with both Saginaw and Flint, Owosso became a secondary settlement serving two pairs of central places.[33]

During the 1850s Flint grew rapidly as this former frontier town became the agricultural market and focus of retail trade and manufacturing in the eastern Saginaw drainage. The growth of lumbering in the Saginaw Valley served as an impetus for expanding industry in this county seat during the 1850s. In addition to larger sawmills, entrepreneurs built new plants for the manufacture of salt, iron tools, carriages, machinery, and other goods, and laid the basis for Flint's rise as a central place.[34]

The old frontier town of Howell retained an important economic role as the market center for the region lying between Flint and Jackson. Its location on the Grand River plank road promoted the steady growth of retail businesses as well as milling and industries in the 1850s. The absence of railroad connections to neighboring central places kept the cost of transportation high and restrained commercial development in Howell. The seat of Livingston County remained a secondary settlement in 1860.[35]

Fenton became the market for farmers in the area south of Flint, and its hydraulic advantages attracted milling and manufacturing to this community. Railway and plank road connections provided excellent transportation access and made the village an important link between the upper Saginaw Valley and Ann Arbor.[36] The development of overland transportation in the 1850s also promoted the rapid growth around the mills at Holly, and the settlement grew as a market between Flint and Pontiac.[37] The village of Pine Run, in northern Genesee County, became another important focus of commercial activity. Located on the plank road between Flint and Saginaw, it served as the major center of retail trade between these central places.[38]

The county seat of Saginaw and neighboring East Saginaw expanded rapidly with the growth of saw milling in the Saginaw Valley. An increasing demand for wood products accompanied that for lumber and provided an impetus for the manufacture of lath, shingles, and staves. Lumber milling also facilitated the development of other industries, such as salt making. The greater accessibility offered by plank roads and the navigable Saginaw River permitted this double community to become the regional center of trade. Agricultural colonists in the lower Saginaw drainage found a market here, and by 1860 the volume and diversity of its activities made it Michigan's northernmost central place.[39]

Port Huron's strategic position at the head of the St. Clair River led to its emergence as a central place in the lower Thumb. Road and railway connections, together with the river trade, made it the transportation hub for the eastern Thumb region. As a port of entry, Port Huron extended its influence across the Canadian border. Although lumbering remained the area's largest industry, Port Huron became the central market for the produce of interior settlement. Its central role in trade supported steam mills and attracted other manufacturing activities to this growing central place.[40]

Two secondary settlements connected Port Huron to developed areas nearby. The established nucleated settlement of Romeo expanded its role as a retail center and market in the 1850s as plank road connections to Pontiac allowed it to capture the produce trade in northern Macomb County.[41] The port of St. Clair linked Port Huron to settlements along the St. Clair River and as far inland as Macomb and Lapeer Counties. In addition to its role as a regional market, St. Clair developed as an industrial center producing heavy machinery and equipment.[42]

Along the periphery of agricultural production in southern Michigan, a number of secondary settlements served areas undergoing recent colonization. These northern gateways provided markets for developing regions by tying them directly with established central places. In the west, Greenville arose as a center of commercial activity north of the Grand River. Linked by a complex of post roads to Grand Rapids and the surrounding area, it became "the chief emporium of the county of Montcalm, and until 1860 its seat of justice."[43]

North of Lansing, St. Johns grew rapidly following the construction of the railroad in 1856. It soon became the principal market for farmers in the growing agricultural region on the upper Grand, and its major shipping point. Lacking waterpower, entrepreneurs employed steam to run the machinery for milling and manufacturing. St. Johns's factories made machine parts, agricultural equipment, furniture, and other products. Expanding mercantile activity made the village a center of retail trade, and it became the seat of Clinton County in 1857.[44]

Bay City emerged as a secondary settlement following the influx of colonists into the lower Saginaw drainage in the 1850s. Located at the mouth of the Saginaw River and connected by road to Saginaw, it became the transportation hub for this region and an important lumber shipping point. Although saw milling remained its dominant industry, Bay City also served as the produce market and retail center for this region.[45]

The ongoing expansion of agriculture in the lower Thumb saw the emergence of Lapeer as a secondary settlement that served a wide area. Linked directly to both Flint and Pontiac, Lapeer provided immigrant farmers access to both central places and permitted this small county seat village to develop as a retail center and agricultural market for a wide area. Flour milling and small manufacturing industries grew up in Lapeer during the 1850s, and a heavy dependence on lumber milling further enhanced its role as a regional business center.[46]

Almont served as an interior market for Port Huron. With an economy based on lumbering and agriculture, its plank road connections encouraged trade and the development of manufacturing before 1860. Described as "a village of bustle and business," Almont attracted a number of business enterprises that helped diversify its trade.[47]

By 1860 Michigan's settlement patterning exhibited a structure that manifested its emerging role in the national economy. The state possessed many substantial central places and secondary centers, which were larger, more numerous, and exhibited greater economic complexity than their counterparts of two decades earlier. Their hierarchical structure increasingly facilitated export trade and their arrangement more closely resembled that found in older settled regions with well-integrated economies.

Although economic integration produced the settlement structure of late antebellum Michigan, the patterning of its distinctive economic landscape owed much to the process of frontier change that preceded it. All of the new central places emerged from frontier towns, and many secondary settlements arose from earlier nucleated settlements. For many settlements, however, importance in the frontier hierarchy failed to guarantee later success. If a settlement's situation no longer suited the changing structure of trade, its role diminished as its market area shrank, and many substantial early settlements failed to grow, or even disappeared. Frontier perceptions of Michigan's environment also continued to affect settlement, inhibiting northward agricultural expansion and discouraging the development of secondary centers in some areas.

In addition to delineating the form of the state's economy in 1860, Michigan's settlement network defined directions for its future growth. Secondary centers lying adjacent to areas undergoing settlement established markets, to which subsequent production gravitated and from which transportation routes spread. Already some of these secondary centers linked southern Michigan with nascent settlements to the north and had begun to facilitate the exploitation of its natural resources. With the increased availability of capital and demand for resources in the 1860s, these centers formed an infrastructure for commercial expansion as the state entered an era of economic growth following the Civil War.

15

Epilogue

The settlement patterning of Michigan's 1860 landscape represented the state's adaptation to the needs of an emerging commercial economy. The emerging structure of production and transportation, largely in place by the beginning of the Civil War, accommodated the new demands brought by more extensive involvement in national trade. Although the introduction of new industries and greater scales of production continued to modify Michigan's economy, they entailed no further alteration of an infrastructure flexible enough to provide a basis for subsequent development.

The era of the Civil War marked a further intensification of economic activity in Michigan and the Old Northwest. Agriculture remained the dominant economic strategy; however, growth altered the scale and organization of production and substantially increased the rate of return. Commercial demand for northern agricultural products increased markedly after 1860 in response to military needs and European crop failures, and rising prices for farm produce offered farmers unparalleled financial opportunities. Wartime deficits in labor were met by a greater reliance on mechanization. Michigan farmers turned increasingly to machines to increase the efficiency of cultivation and to free household labor for field tasks. Their adoption of new crops and practices and systematic land use resulted in a substantial increase in the percentage of improved acres per farm and the consolidation of croplands. Michigan agriculture accelerated its trend toward greater and more specialized production.[1]

The restructuring of bank finance supported the growth of farm production by overcoming the limitations of antebellum exchange. The Bank Act of 1863 provided a secure medium of exchange and encouraged capital flows necessary to expand the scale of business. The growing volume and complexity of commercial and industrial investment promoted the growth of regional centers as clearing houses and concentrated bank finance in central urban locations. Detroit arose as a national banking center, and other cities, such as Grand Rapids, Kalamazoo, and Saginaw, became foci of regional banking. These banking centers forged networks of tributary hinterlands where they, rather than outside sources, provided entrepreneurs with loans and opportunities for investment. Financial institutions enhanced existing connections between Michigan cities, and these links played a crucial role in developing business and industry and helped define the position of urban centers in the regional settlement structure.[2]

Postbellum expansion in Michigan's urban centers brought further commercial diversification and growth. Cities that enlarged the scale of their wholesale trade attracted larger populations that, in turn, intensified demand for retailing and services and promoted the growth of local market industries. Such an environment encouraged technological and organizational innovation, which stimulated further expansion and diversification in many aspects of the urban economy.[3]

Because settlements with better access to raw materials and markets stood a greater chance to increase their wholesale trade, their success depended increasingly on the state's principal transportation system. The expansion of the rail network in the 1860s permitted favored cities to expand their economic bases and emerge as an industrial urban hierarchy. Kalamazoo, Grand Rapids, Lansing, Jackson, Saginaw, and other transportation centers became foci of trade and manufacturing. As the hub of Michigan's rail network, as well as its financial center, Detroit's expanding trade underwrote phenomenal growth and economic diversification. Manufacturing took on an increasingly larger role in Michigan, concentrated around heavy industries, such as iron and steelmaking, as well as the production of paper, construction materials, agricultural machinery, industrial goods, pharmaceuticals, furniture, chemicals, steamboats, stoves, and railway cars.[4]

The restructuring of bank finance, the commercialization of agriculture, and the expansion of trade and transportation all worked to complete an infrastructure capable of extending economic services over Michigan's interior. These developments did not, however, measurably alter the settlement structure of 1860. The inextricable continuity between the late-antebellum landscape and subsequent settlement patterning emphasizes the importance of the frontier experience in shaping what came afterward and the degree to which the process of settlement permeated all facets of the new landscape.

Although the closing of the frontier did not create the modern State of Michigan, it played a central role in developing the "agricultural commonwealth" upon which the region's economic growth rested, as George Fuller recognized more than eighty years ago. As the crucial process underlying the success of commercial farming, frontier colonization shaped a landscape that provided the basis for a complex economy closely integrated with national markets. The milieu of the new economy diversified production and expanded services, launching Michigan's modern commercial growth. In this sense, today's Michigan is, indeed, a legacy of the frontier.[5]

Appendix 1

Population of Michigan Settlements Based on Census Returns in 1854, 1860, and 1864

Settlements	Michigan Census 1854	U. S. Census 1860	Michigan Census 1864
Adamsville	-	105	-
Adrian	4,857	6,194	7,044
Albion	-	1,720	-
Allegan	-	940	-
Ann Arbor	3,339	4,447	5,731
Battle Creek	-	3,508	3,856
Bay City	-	1,585	-
Breedsville	-	252	-
Brooklyn	-	331	-
Buchanan	-	910	-
Burlington	-	150	-
Burr Oak	-	666	-
Canandaigua	-	139	-
Centreville	-	473	-
Clarkston	-	376	-
Clinton	-	680	-
Coldwater	-	2,905	3,977
Corunna	-	864	-
Decatur	-	564	-
Detroit	40,373	45,387	53,170
Dowagiac	-	1,180	-
East Saginaw	-	3,005	5,725
Eaton Rapids	-	582	-
Edwardsburgh	-	241	-
Fentonville	-	783	-
Flint	-	3,052	3,297
Flushing	-	406	-
Grand Rapids	4,278	8,090	8,770
Grass Lake	-	479	-
Greenville	-	399	-

(continued on next page)

Settlements	Michigan Census 1854	U. S. Census 1860	Michigan Census 1864
Hastings	-	888	-
Hillsdale	-	2,173	-
Holly	-	542	-
Howell	-	757	-
Jackson	3,326	4,799	5,544
Jonesville	-	1,008	-
Kalamazoo	-	6,075	6,797
Lansing	-	3,085	3,573
Lawrence	-	339	-
Lawton	-	420	-
Lexington	-	690	-
Lockport	-	312	-
Marshall	-	3,580	4,192
Mason	-	363	-
Medina	-	211	-
Mendon	-	1,141	-
Monroe	3,889	3,895	4,214
Morenci	-	459	-
Mt. Clemens	-	1,428	-
Muskegon	-	1,448	-
Niles	-	2,789	3,095
Northville	-	621	-
Okemos	-	75	-
Orion	-	292	-
Paw Paw	-	1,098	-
Plymouth	-	821	-
Pokagon	-	122	-
Pontiac	-	2,576	2,531
Port Huron	-	4,376	4,025
Quincy	-	573	-
Saginaw	-	1,699	3,203
Owosso	-	1,169	1,346
St. Clair	-	1,670	1,676
South Haven	-	308	-
Summerville	-	130	-
Teconsha	-	135	-
Tecumseh	-	1,640	-
Three Rivers	-	960	-
Wayne	-	304	-
Ypsilanti	-	3,956	4,189

Appendix 2

Population of Michigan Settlements Based on Gazetteer Data in 1859, 1863, and 1864

Settlements	Hawes 1859	Clark 1863	Hawes 1864
Ada	-	300	350
Adamsville	500	200	250
Addison	400	-	475
Adrian	8,000	7,881	9,000
Albion	2,500	-	2,700
Algonac	800	500	650
Allegan	2,000	-	2,500
Almont	3,000	-	2,600
Ann Arbor	8,000	7,102	-
Armada	400	-	450
Augusta	-	200	-
Auchville	-	-	300
Austerlitz	1,200	-	-
Austin	-	500	-
Base Lake	48	-	75
Battle Creek	4,000	4,000	-
Bay City (Lower Saginaw)	3,000	3,000	3,500
Bedford	300	250	-
Belle River (Newport)	1,500	500	600
Belleville	250	300	350
Bellevue	1,000	500	700
Berlin	200	200	250
Berrien Springs	1,000	1,000	1,200
Bertrand	-	300	300
Big Rapids	300	300	350
Birmingham	-	500	550
Blissfield	-	500	600
Bloomingdale	-	700	-
Bradley	250	200	300
Brady	150	200	-
Breedsville	500	300	400

(continued on next page)

Settlements	Hawes 1859	Clark 1863	Hawes 1864
Brest	150	150	150
Bridgeport Center	100	200	250
Brighton	-	500	550
Brockway	-	100	150
Bronson's Prairie	-	300	350
Brooklyn	600	200	300
Buchanan	1,000	1,000	1,100
Buck Creek	-	100	150
Buell	-	-	275
Burr Oak	-	700	800
Byron	300	-	-
Canandaigua	200	150	300
Cannonsburgh	150	250	350
Carlton	-	-	400
Carrolton	-	300	-
Cassopolis	-	500	600
Cedar Springs	-	350	400
Centre	-	200	300
Centreville	1,500	600	800
Ceresco	150	150	200
Charlotte	-	800	1,000
Chelsea	800	700	1,000
Clark City	200	-	-
Clarkston	-	400	-
Clinton	-	700	900
Coldwater	4,000	4,500	5,000
Coloma	300	200	300
Columbiaville	500	-	300
Constantine	-	1,200	1,300
Corunna	-	1,500	1,700
Danby	400	200	-
Davisburgh	300	200	350
Day	75	-	400
Dayton	-	300	400
Decatur	-	-	800
Dearborn	-	300	400
Deerfield	540	300	400
Delhi	-	150	-
Denmark	-	-	400
Detroit	70,000 (est.)	70,000	70,000
DeWitt	-	300	400

(continued on next page)

Settlements	Hawes 1859	Clark 1863	Hawes 1864
Dexter	1,500	1,000	1,100
Disco	-	200	-
Dowagiac	1,500	1,500	-
Dundee	500	500	600
East LeRoy	-	100	150
East Saginaw	4,000	5,000	-
Eastmanville	-	500	600
Eaton Rapids	700	800	-
Edwardsburgh	300	300	400
Egleston	-	200	-
Elsie	200	200	300
Erie	-	200	300
Fair Haven	-	-	300
Fallasburgh	300	-	400
Farmers Creek	-	200	300
Farmington	300	500	600
Fentonville	1,500	1,500	-
Fillmore	-	-	800
Fitchburg	-	100	200
Flat Rock	-	500	600
Flint	4,500	4,000	4,500
Florence	-	-	200
Flushing	-	500	600
Forestville	500	300	600
Fowlerville	-	300	400
Franciscoville	100	-	-
Frankenmuth	-	200	300
Franklin	250	300	400
Fremont	-	100	150
Gaines Station	200	200	300
Galesburgh	-	1,200	-
Ganges	125	-	-
Grand Blanc	-	200	300
Grand Haven	1,500	2,000	2,200
Grand Ledge	225	-	300
Grand Rapids	12,000	10,000	10,500
Grandville	-	200	300
Grass Lake	-	1,500	-
Gravel Run	-	200	300
Greenville	500	500	600
Hadley	-	200	250

(continued on next page)

Settlements	Hawes 1859	Clark 1863	Hawes 1864
Hastings	1,500	-	-
Hickory Corners	-	150	200
Hillsdale	3,500	-	4,000
Holly	700	700	900
Homer	400	500	600
Howell	1,000	-	1,200
Hudson	2,500	1,800	2,200
Ionia	-	1,500	1,600
Jackson	7,000	7,000	7,500
Jonesville	2,000	1,500	1,700
Kalamazoo	7,000	-	6,500
Kelloggville	-	100	150
Lansing	5,000	4,000	5,000
Lapeer	1,000	1,000	-
LaSalle	-	-	300
Lawton	-	500	500
Leoni	-	300	-
Lexinton	1,000	700	-
Linden	400	-	450
Lowell	-	800	900
Lyons	1,000	-	-
Maple Rapids	-	-	600
Marathon	200	-	-
Marshall	4,000	4,000	4,200
Marysville	175	300	-
Mason	-	500	-
Matherton	200	-	300
Mattawan	500	500	550
Meads Mills (Waterford)	220	-	-
Medina	-	300	400
Memphis	-	400	500
Mendon	-	500	600
Merrillsville (Yale)	300	-	400
Millburgh	500	-	600
Mill Point	-	500	600
Monroe	-	5,000	4,500
Morenci	-	500	-
Mosherville	75	125	200
Mottville	-	-	900
Mt. Clemens	2,000	1,500	1,600
Muskegon	-	2,000	2,200

(continued on next page)

Settlements	Hawes 1859	Clark 1863	Hawes 1864
Nankin	-	300	350
New Baltimore	1,000	1,000	1,600
New Buffalo	600	500	550
New Casco	-	-	450
Niles	5,000	5,000	5,500
North Brownville	-	300	-
Northville	-	600	700
Norvell	150	100	150
Nunica	-	-	700
Oakwood	200	-	300
Okemos	-	200	200
Olivet	300	350	400
Orangewood Mills (Orangeville)	700	300	400
Orion	-	500	600
Ortonville	60	-	-
Ovid	450	-	-
Owosso	-	1,300	1,500
Oxford	500	-	-
Parkville	-	140	200
Paw Paw	-	1,300	-
Pere Marquette (Ludington)	1,500	300	400
Pinckney	-	500	550
Pine Run	300	-	500
Plainfield	-	50	150
Plymouth	-	1,000	-
Pokagon	-	300	400
Pontiac	4,000	3,000	3,200
Port Austin	-	500	-
Port Huron	4,500	6,000	6,200
Portsmouth	500	500	600
Ridgeway	-	300	-
Rochester	-	500	600
Romeo	-	2,000	-
Saginaw	3,500	-	4,500
St. Charles	500	500	600
St. Clair	3,000	2,000	2,200
St. Johns	1,000	1,000	1,300
St. Joseph	-	2,000	2,200
St. Louis	-	200	250
Salina	-	500	-
Saline	-	2,000	2,200

(continued on next page)

Settlements	Hawes 1859	Clark 1863	Hawes 1864
Saranac	600	-	700
Saugatuck	400	-	600
Sturgis	1,500	1,600	1,700
Summerville	-	200	-
Sylvanus	-	150	-
Taras Hall	75	200	250
Tecumseh	2,000	2,000	-
Three Oaks	700	700	800
Three Rivers	2,000	2,000	2,200
Traverse City	-	500	600
Trenton	-	1,000	-
Union City	600	-	800
Utica	1,000	-	-
Vassar	600	-	700
Vernon	100	-	-
Wacousta	-	100	150
Walled Lake	200	-	250
Waterloo	-	500	550
Watervliet	150	-	-
Watrousville	-	200	250
West Windsor	400	-	500
White Pigeon	1,200	1,800	2,200
Whitmore Lake	100	-	150
Wolf Creek	500	-	-
Ypsilanti	5,000	4,500	5,500

Appendix 3

Hierarchical Order of Central Settlements in Michigan in 1860 Based on Functional Index Values

Settlements	Retailing Activities	Wholesaling Activities	Production Activities	Service Activities	Functional Index Numbers
Detroit	444	125	306	489	62.97
Grand Rapids	110	38	83	133	17.88
Saginaw/East Saginaw	28	9	26	45	10.51
Pontiac	39	22	39	52	8.93
Port Huron	63	14	42	56	7.63
Kalamazoo	68	12	46	70	7.60
Lansing	53	15	47	50	7.58
Ann Arbor	62	9	73	72	7.19
Jackson	75	8	46	69	6.71
Adrian	67	7	49	60	6.08
Flint	45	7	65	62	5.78
Marshall	71	6	46	52	5.71
Battle Creek	42	10	46	39	5.66
Monroe	58	8	31	46	5.44
Coldwater	46	7	28	38	4.59
St. Johns	31	6	20	24	3.43
Fentonville	35	3	45	32	3.40
Hillsdale	33	3	27	33	3.00
Ypsilanti	46	6	33	43	2.90
Albion	28	3	28	32	2.85
Niles	40	0	34	45	2.78
St. Joseph	27	4	22	21	2.75
Hudson	35	3	18	23	2.68
Dexter	31	2	34	19	2.56
Jonesville	26	3	23	23	2.51
Tecumseh	16	3	29	28	2.43
St. Clair	33	0	29	32	2.21
Three Rivers	26	2	23	20	2.18
Dowagiac	26	2	15	19	2.00

(continued on next page)

Settlements	Retailing Activities	Wholesaling Activities	Production Activities	Service Activities	Functional Index Numbers
Plymouth	21	0	42	25	1.97
Lyons	22	1	26	25	1.95
Owosso	24	2	15	19	1.94
Manchester	10	0	16	15	1.92
Pine Run	10	0	22	9	1.92
Eaton Rapids	19	0	38	29	1.91
Constantine	24	1	29	15	1.87
Bay City	22	1	12	33	1.83
Lapeer	22	0	22	34	1.78
Almont	12	0	44	26	1.76
Ionia	28	0	28	18	1.70
Grand Haven	16	2	9	24	1.68
Sturgis	15	2	17	15	1.67
Holly	8	3	20	19	1.63
Algonac	13	2	21	13	1.61
Romeo	23	0	26	19	1.59
Decatur	11	3	8	14	1.58
Saranac	14	0	39	18	1.56
Muskegon	14	0	26	31	1.56
Utica	12	0	33	26	1.54
Litchfield	16	0	31	22	1.54
Hastings	11	2	13	19	1.51
Greenville	15	0	26	27	1.51
Howell	14	0	27	24	1.44
Buchanan	13	0	31	21	1.43
Galesburgh	14	0	28	22	1.42
Bradley	7	2	20	13	1.41
Armada	13	0	33	15	1.35
Linden	11	1	23	14	1.34
Centreville	10	0	33	18	1.32
Brooklyn	9	1	24	25	1.32
Corunna	16	1	15	13	1.31
Rochester	18	0	29	9	1.30
Dryden	12	0	27	18	1.26
Mt. Clemens	16	0	14	28	1.26
Farmington	10	0	22	25	1.24
Lexington	11	0	27	18	1.23
Berrien Springs	11	0	18	27	1.23
Millburgh	5	2	20	6	1.21

(continued on next page)

Settlements	Retailing Activities	Wholesaling Activities	Production Activities	Service Activities	Functional Index Numbers
Summerfield	10	0	26	19	1.20
Allegan	8	0	27	21	1.20
Dundee	6	0	37	13	1.18
Chelsea	17	0	18	15	1.17
Cassopolis	12	1	13	13	1.15
Mason	12	0	17	21	1.12
Reading	9	0	25	17	1.11
Belle River	19	0	16	11	1.11
New Baltimore	7	0	16	28	1.09
Maple Rapids	9	0	25	14	1.05
Birmingham	10	1	16	7	1.03
Paw Paw	6	0	21	21	1.02
Union City	10	0	27	19	1.02
Northville	7	0	20	10	1.02
Homer	9	0	22	15	1.01
Lowell	13	0	15	16	1.01
Vassar	8	0	19	19	1.00
Ovid	13	0	18	12	0.99
Saline	15	0	17	10	0.99
Belleville	6	0	24	15	0.96
Deerfield	6	0	25	14	0.96
Clinton	10	0	21	12	0.96
DeWitt	2	0	30	15	0.96
Davidburgh	4	1	15	13	0.95
Morenci	8	0	19	15	0.92
Burlington	12	0	12	14	0.88
White Pigeon	12	0	11	15	0.88
Newport	4	2	4	7	0.88
Byron	8	0	20	11	0.86
Grass Lake	10	0	15	13	0.86
Mattawan	12	0	13	12	0.86
Olivet	4	0	21	16	0.86
Burr Oak	9	0	16	13	0.85
Grand Ledge	7	0	19	12	0.83
Memphis	8	0	18	11	0.82
Ruby	7	0	22	8	0.81
Saugatuck	11	0	14	10	0.81
Lawrence	6	0	23	8	0.80
New Buffalo	12	0	11	10	0.78

(continued on next page)

Settlements	Retailing Activities	Wholesaling Activities	Production Activities	Service Activities	Functional Index Numbers
Three Oaks	3	0	24	10	0.77
Breedsville	9	0	12	12	0.75
Fairfield	2	0	25	9	0.74
Trenton	4	0	16	15	0.74
Mendon	10	0	16	12	0.74
Portland	8	0	15	9	0.72
Elsie	6	0	22	5	0.72
Bangor	4	0	22	8	0.72
Fallasburgh	5	0	14	13	0.69
Cannonsburgh	5	0	21	6	0.69
Schoolcraft	11	0	9	9	0.69
Blissfield	8	0	17	5	0.68
Ransom	4	0	19	9	0.68
Fowlerville	8	0	13	9	0.68
Adamsville	3	0	20	9	0.67
LaSalle	1	0	21	11	0.67
Franklin	7	0	13	10	0.67
Lawton	12	0	12	3	0.66
Lamont	6	0	15	9	0.66
Ganges	7	0	14	8	0.65
Bellevue	3	0	18	27	0.65
Brady	1	0	24	7	0.65
Macon	5	0	18	7	0.65
Bronson's Prairie	7	0	12	9	0.63
Flushing	4	0	20	5	0.62
Oxford	6	0	13	9	0.62
Orion	5	0	11	12	0.61
Matherton	3	1	6	6	0.60
Delhi Center	8	0	12	6	0.60
Addison	4	0	13	11	0.60
Flat Rock	8	0	8	10	0.60
Ludington	7	0	12	7	0.59
Forestville	4	0	14	9	0.58
Waterloo	4	0	15	8	0.58
Brockway	8	0	9	8	0.58
Clarkston	5	0	11	10	0.57
Gravel Run	4	0	6	16	0.56
Columbiaville	4	0	14	8	0.56
Cambridge	2	0	14	11	0.56

(continued on next page)

Settlements	Retailing Activities	Wholesaling Activities	Production Activities	Service Activities	Functional Index Numbers
Augusta	3	0	14	9	0.55
Ceresco	4	0	17	4	0.54
Brighton	6	0	10	8	0.54
Troy	6	0	12	6	0.54
Danby	3	0	15	7	0.53
Vermontville	3	0	18	4	0.53
Austerlitz	6	0	11	6	0.52
Erie	4	0	11	9	0.52
Barryville	4	0	10	10	0.52
Dallas	3	0	11	10	0.51
North Brownsville	7	0	10	5	0.51
Frankenmuth	5	0	13	5	0.51
Ridgeway	2	0	14	8	0.50
St. Charles	6	0	5	11	0.50
Marcellus	0	0	15	10	0.50
Vernon	4	0	9	10	0.50
Manlius	5	0	12	5	0.49
St. Louis	5	0	9	8	0.49
Bloomingdale	1	0	11	12	0.49
Hickory Corners	3	0	11	9	0.49
Tompkins	0	0	16	8	0.48
Edwardsburgh	3	0	11	8	0.47
Ada	5	0	14	9	0.47
Grand Blanc	2	0	13	7	0.46
Medina	2	0	12	8	0.46
Pokagon	4	0	8	9	0.46
Hartwellville	3	0	12	6	0.45
Berlin	3	0	11	7	0.45
Grandville	6	0	8	5	0.44
Port Austin	6	0	5	8	0.44
Fair Grove	0	0	15	7	0.44
Coloma	4	0	10	6	0.44
Oakwood	3	0	13	4	0.43
Watervliet	3	0	8	9	0.43
Sylvanus	2	0	10	8	0.42
Walled Lake	2	0	10	8	0.42
Mill Point	1	0	12	7	0.41
Canois	1	0	11	8	0.41
Ray Center	0	0	12	8	0.40

(continued on next page)

Settlements	Retailing Activities	Wholesaling Activities	Production Activities	Service Activities	Functional Index Numbers
Novi	4	0	9	5	0.40
DuPlain	4	0	7	7	0.40
Marathon	6	0	4	7	0.40
Crimea	4	0	8	6	0.40
Parkville	3	0	8	7	0.39
Kalamo	3	0	8	7	0.39
Portsmouth	2	0	6	10	0.38
Zeeland	6	0	8	2	0.38
Paint Creek	0	0	12	7	0.38
Fremont	3	0	8	6	0.37
Wheatland	1	0	12	5	0.37
Okemos	4	0	8	9	0.36
Farmers Creek	4	0	7	5	0.36
Orangewood Mills	2	0	10	5	0.36
Ravenna	2	0	11	4	0.36
East LeRoy	2	0	8	7	0.36
Leoni	3	0	8	5	0.35
Cheshire	3	0	5	5	0.35
LaGrange	1	0	14	2	0.35
Bristolville	2	0	7	7	0.34
Whitmore Lake	0	0	10	7	0.34
Traverse City	3	0	2	10	0.33
Marysville	4	0	3	7	0.32
Big Rapids	2	0	6	7	0.32
Carlton	0	0	10	6	0.32
Dayton	3	0	6	5	0.31
Eastmanville	3	0	6	5	0.31
Norvell	5	0	6	2	0.31
Ortonville	2	0	10	2	0.30
Bethel	0	0	10	5	0.30
Daltons Mills	4	0	4	5	0.30
Goodland	0	0	9	6	0.30
Fitchburg	1	0	9	4	0.29
Gaines Station	5	0	1	6	0.29
Clark City	1	0	6	7	0.29
North Plains	5	0	2	5	0.29
Camden	2	0	4	7	0.28
Berrien Centre	0	0	11	7	0.28
Egleston	2	0	6	5	0.28

(continued on next page)

Settlements	Retailing Activities	Wholesaling Activities	Production Activities	Service Activities	Functional Index Numbers
Batavia	0	0	10	4	0.28
Cass	0	0	7	7	0.28
Nankin	1	0	8	4	0.27
Washington	1	0	11	1	0.27
West Windsor	0	0	8	4	0.26
California	0	0	10	3	0.26
Centre	2	0	5	5	0.26
Westphalia	2	0	3	7	0.26
Brest	1	0	5	6	0.25
Disco	1	0	5	6	0.25
Bertrand	1	0	7	4	0.25
Tuscola	2	0	6	3	0.24
Bennington	0	0	10	2	0.24
Mosherville	2	0	5	4	0.24
Farmers Creek	1	0	6	4	0.23
Hamilton	3	0	5	2	0.23
New Casco	1	0	6	4	0.23
Elk Rapids	3	0	4	3	0.23
Cascade	1	0	2	8	0.23
Nebraska	1	0	4	6	0.23
Clarendon Center	2	0	6	2	0.22
Campbellton	2	0	5	3	0.22
Hadley	0	0	4	7	0.22
Bush Creek	0	0	7	4	0.22
Caledonia	0	0	4	6	0.20
Taras Hall	0	0	5	5	0.20
Burns	0	0	8	1	0.18
Bowne	0	0	8	1	0.18
Porter	0	0	9	0	0.18
Spring Brook	0	0	6	3	0.18
Bridgeport Center	1	0	4	3	0.17
Franciscoville	0	0	5	3	0.16
Jay	0	0	4	4	0.16
Holland	4	0	0	2	0.16
Canandaigua	1	0	4	4	0.15
Kelloggville	1	0	3	3	0.15
Wolf Creek	0	0	6	1	0.14
Monterey	2	0	2	2	0.14
Conway	0	0	3	4	0.14

(continued on next page)

Settlements	Retailing Activities	Wholesaling Activities	Production Activities	Service Activities	Functional Index Numbers
Austin	1	0	3	2	0.13
Marr	3	0	2	0	0.13
Ida	2	0	1	2	0.12
South Assyria	0	0	3	3	0.12
Summerville	0	0	5	1	0.12
Edinburgh	1	0	1	4	0.10
Meads Mills	0	0	5	0	0.10
Merrillsville	0	0	4	1	0.10
Clay Banks	1	0	1	2	0.09
Bass Lake	0	0	3	1	0.08
Glen Arbor	0	0	2	2	0.08
Plumb Brook	0	0	0	4	0.08
Union	0	0	1	0	0.02
Total Functional Units	3,169	377	4,657	4,134	
Locational Coefficients	.03	.27	.02	.02	

Endnotes

CHAPTER 1

1. The term "southern Lower Michigan" precisely delineates that portion of Michigan's Lower Peninsula lying below an imaginary line drawn from Muskegon to Saginaw Bay. This region has a number of physiographic characteristics that set it apart from the remainder of the state. These, together with cultural factors, encouraged Michigan's early agricultural settlement to be confined largely within its boundaries. The terms "southern" and "Lower" alone can also refer to this area, and for stylistic reasons their use in this text will follow this practice.

2. Fuller's ideas were first set forth in "An Introduction to the Settlement of Southern Michigan from 1815 to 1835," *Michigan Pioneer and Historical Collections* [hereafter *MPHC*] 38 (1912): 538–79. These were expanded in his Ph.D. dissertation, which subsequently appeared as *Economic and Social Beginnings of Michigan: A Study of the Settlement of the Lower Peninsula during the Territorial Period, 1805–1837* (Lansing, Mich.: Wynkoop Hallenbeck Crawford, 1916).

3. Classic definitions of concept of landscape stressed the role of human societies in creating landscapes and influencing their form over time. See Carl Ortwin Sauer, "The Morphology of Landscape," in *Land and Life: A Selection from the Writings of Carl Ortwin Sauer*, ed. John Leighly (Berkeley: University of California Press, 1963), 343; idem, "Forward to Historical Geography," in *Land and Life*, 360–61; and John Leighly, "Some Comments on Contemporary Geographic Method," *Annals of the Association of American Geographers* 27 (1937): 134. More recently, geographers have seen landscapes as an outcome of human activities and a reflection of the societies that created them. See Peirce F. Lewis, "Axioms for Reading the Landscape: Some Guides to the American Scene," in *The Interpretation of Ordinary Landscapes*, ed. Donald W. Meinig (New York: Oxford University Press, 1979), 11–32; John R. Stilgoe, *Common Landscapes of America, 1580 to 1845* (New Haven, Conn.: Yale University Press, 1982); and James Duncan and Nancy Duncan, "(Re)Reading the Landscape," *Environment and Planning D: Society and Space* 6 (1988). Landscapes may also be perceived in differing contexts based on the particular experiences of the individuals or groups involved. See David Lowenthal, "Geography, Experience, and Imagination: Towards a Geographical Epistemology," *Annals of the Association of American Geographers* 51 (1961): 260; and D. W. Meinig, "The Beholding Eye, Ten Versions of the Same Scene," in *The Interpretation of Ordinary Landscapes*, ed. D. W. Meinig (New York: Oxford University Press, 1979), 43–45.

4. R. Knowles and J. Wareing, *Economic and Social Geography* (London: W. H. Allen, 1976), 28–31.

5. Archaeologists have emphasized the importance of settlement patterning as a crucial aspect of past landscapes, relating to the adjustments of peoples and cultures to environment and their level of social and economic complexity. Studies of settlement patterning have observed variation at the household, community, and regional levels, allowing the influence of variables to be examined at widely different scales. See Gordon Willey,

Prehistoric Settlement Patterns in the New World, Smithsonian Institution, Bureau of American Ethnology, Bulletin no. 155 (Washington, D.C.: Government Printing Office, 1956), 1; and Bruce Trigger, "The Determination of Settlement Patterns," in *Settlement Archaeology,* ed. K. C. Chang (Palo Alto, Calif.: National Press, 1968), 53–78.

6. This definition of frontier is derived from a number of works, by scholars in several fields. They include: Frederick Jackson Turner, "The Significance of the Frontier in American History," in *Annual Report of the American Historical Association for the Year 1893* (Washington, D.C.: Government Printing Office, 1893), 199–227; Isaiah Bowman, *The Pioneer Fringe,* American Geographical Society, Special Publication no. 13. (New York: American Geographical Society, 1931); C. A. Dawson, *The Settlement of the Peace River Country: A Study of a Pioneer Area,* Vol. 6 of *Canadian Frontiers of Settlement,* ed. W. A. Mackintosh and W. L. G. Joerg (Toronto: Macmillan, 1934); James G. Leyburn, *Frontier Folkways* (New Haven, Conn.: Yale University Press, 1935); Walter Prescott Webb, *The Great Frontier* (Boston: Houghton Mifflin, 1952); A. Irving Hallowell, "The Impact of the American Indian on American Culture," *American Anthropologist* 59 (1957): 201–16; Walker D. Wyman and Clifton Kroeber, eds., *The Frontier in Perspective* (Madison: University of Wisconsin Press, 1957); H. C. Allen, *Bush and Backwoods: A Comparison of the Frontier in Australia and the United States* (East Lansing: Michigan State University Press, 1959); Ladis K. D. Kristof, "The Nature of Frontiers and Boundaries," *Annals of the Association of American Geographers* 49 (1959): 269–82; Owen Lattimore, *Studies in Frontier History* (London: Oxford University Press, 1962); Joseph B. Casagrande, Stephen I. Thompson, and Philip D. Young, "Colonization as a Research Frontier: The Ecuadorian Case," in *Process and Pattern in Culture: Essays in Honor of Julian H. Steward,* ed. Robert A. Manners (Chicago: Aldine, 1964), 281–325; J. R. V. Prescott, *The Geography of Frontiers and Boundaries* (Chicago: Aldine, 1965); Marvin W. Mikesell, "Comparative Studies in Frontier History," in *Turner and the Sociology of the Frontier,* ed. Richard Hofstadter and Seymour Martin Lipset (New York: Basic Books, 1968), 152–71; Stephen I. Thompson, "Pioneer Colonization: A Cross-Cultural View," *Addison-Wesley Modules in Anthropology* 33 (Reading, Mass.: Addison Wesley, 1973); Robert D. Mitchell, *Commercialism and Frontier: Perspectives on the Early Shenandoah Valley* (Charlottesville: University Press of Virginia, 1977); and William W. Savage Jr. and Stephen I. Thompson, "The Comparative Study of the Frontier: An Introduction," in *The Frontier: Comparative Studies,* vol. 2, ed. William W. Savage Jr. and Stephen I. Thompson (Norman: University of Oklahoma Press, 1979), 3–24. See also Kenneth E. Lewis, "Sampling the Archaeological Frontier: Regional Models and Component Analysis," in *Research Strategies in Historical Archaeology,* ed. Stanley South (New York: Academic Press, 1977), 151–201.

7. Comparative analyses of frontier colonization have revealed parallel changes under similar circumstances as an adaptation of industrialized state societies to conditions on the periphery of settlement. Two studies from which many of the generalizations employed here have been drawn are, Casagrande, Thompson, and Young, "Colonization," 314; and Stephen I. Thompson, "San Juan Yapacani: A Japanese Pioneer Colony in Eastern Bolivia," Ph.D. diss., University of Illinois (Ann Arbor, Mich.: University Microfilms, 1970), 198–99.

8. Immanuel Wallerstein, *The Modern World System, Capitalist Agriculture and the Origins of the European World Economy in the Sixteenth Century* (New York: Academic Press, 1974), 15–17, 348, introduced the term "world economy" to distinguish systems associated with the expansion of competing states, such as those of post-medieval Europe. He contrasted these economies with "empires" that were characterized by the central political control of a single state. Fernand Braudel, *The Perspective of the World,* vol. 3 of *Civilization and Capitalism, 15th-18th Century,* trans. Sian Reynolds (New York: Harper & Row, 1984), 69–70, on the other hand, adopted a wider definition of world economy, stressing that the economic structure of precapitalist empires, rather than political dominance, defined their limits and organization. Indeed, the fact that the capitalist world economy grew out of an earlier network of economic

relationships in the Mediterranean region has been employed to argue that, although structurally distinct, the two economies represent a continuity in development. See Timothy C. Champion, introduction to *Centre and Periphery: Comparative Studies in Archaeology* (London: Unwin Hyman, 1989), 7–8. Because of the pervasive role played by capitalism in the development of the American economy and in the organization of production in its frontier regions, Wallerstein's narrower definition of world economy will be followed here.

9. Immanuel Wallerstein, *The Modern World System II, Mercantilism and the Consolidation of the European World Economy* (New York: Academic Press, 1980), 179, 238–39; J. D. Gould, *Economic Growth in History, Survey and Analysis* (London: Methuen & Co., 1972), 335–36. Braudel, *Perspective of the World,* 56, 263–66; Wallerstein, *Modern World System,* 350.

10. Eric R. Wolf, *Europe and the People without History* (Berkeley: University of California Press, 1982), 79, 265; Aidan Foster-Carter, "The Modes of Production Controversy," *New Left Review* 107 (1978): 74.

11. Paul M. Sweezy and Harry Magdoff, "Capitalism and the Distribution of Income and Wealth," *Monthly Review* 39, no. 5 (1987): 3.

12. Wolf, *Europe,* 302; Kristof, "Frontiers and Boundaries," 274; Hans W. Weigert, Henry Brodie, Edward W. Doherty, John R. Fernstrom, Eric Fischer, and Dudley Kirk, *Principles of Political Geography* (New York: Appleton-Century-Crofts, 1957), 115; H. Peter Gray, *A Generalized Theory of International Trade* (New York: Holmes & Meier Publishers, 1976), 126–27.

13. The term "cosmopolitan frontier" was introduced by Jerome O. Steffen in "Insular vs. Cosmopolitan Frontiers: A Proposal for Comparative Frontiers Studies," in *The American West: New Perspectives, New Dimensions,* ed. Jerome O. Steffen (Norman: University of Oklahoma Press, 1979), 94–123; and developed more extensively in *Comparative Frontiers: A Proposal for Studying the American West* (Norman: University of Oklahoma Press, 1980), esp. xii–xvii. The development of one particular type of cosmopolitan frontier is discussed in Donald L. Hardesty, "Evolution on the Industrial Frontier," in *The Archaeology of Frontiers and Boundaries,* ed. Stanton W. Green and Stephen M. Perlman (Orlando, Fla.: Academic Press, 1985), 216–18.

14. This model was originally developed in D. W. Meinig, "Spatial Models of a Sequence of Transatlantic Interactions," *XXIII International Geographical Congress, International Geography '76,* Sec. 9: *Historical Geography* (Moscow: n.p., 1976), 31–34 and later presented in idem, *Atlantic America, 1492–1800,* vol. 1 of *The Shaping of America: A Geographical Perspective on 500 Years of History* (New Haven, Conn.: Yale University Press, 1986), 65–76.

15. Steffen, *Comparative Frontiers,* xii, xvii–xviii.

16. The economic relationship between insular frontiers and the core state also reflected mercantilist policies that attempt to protect home industries by limiting strictly the importation of competitive goods. This encouraged a diversification of production and promoted the development of alternative markets for colonial-produced commodities. Success depended more on a broad-based adaptation to local conditions than on the maintenance of close ties with the homeland. The colonial economy of an insular frontier was also less responsive to the policies of core state capitalist interests, who found it difficult to manipulate the colony's development. Greater political and economic insularity fostered endemic growth and was coincident with more pervasive colonial change. Gray, *Theory of International Trade,* 130; Robert E. Baldwin, "Patterns of Development in Newly Settled Regions," *Manchester School of Social and Economic Studies* 24 (1956): 167–68.

17. The classic definition of economic distance was made by Johann Heinrich von Thünen, who illustrated its principles by modeling a central market on a homogeneous plain surrounded by concentric rings of increasingly lower rent-yielding production. See *Isolated State: An English Translation of Der Isolierte Staat,* trans. Carla M Wertenberg, ed. and intro. Peter Hall (Oxford: Pergamon Press, 1966).

18. Richard Peet, "Von Thünen and the Dynamics of Agricultural Expansion," *Explorations in Economic History* 8 (1970–71): 188–90; Eric Pawson, *Transport and Economy: The Turnpike Roads of Eighteenth-Century Britain* (London: Academic Press, 1977), 11.

19. Mitchell, *Commercialism and Frontier,* 5, 7, 190; Baldwin, "Patterns of Development," 176. Thompson, "Pioneer Colonization," 14; Percy Wells Bidwell and John I. Falconer, *History of Agriculture in the Northern United States, 1620–1860* (Washington, D.C.: Carnegie Institute, 1925; reprint, New York: Peter Smith, 1941), 164–65. Peet, "Dynamics of Agricultural Expansion," 191; Bowman, *Pioneer Fringe,* 67.

20. Casagrande, Thompson, and Young, "Colonization," 312. Although these were new routes in the sense that they were created to support colonization, they often incorporated earlier existing networks that served this purpose. Indeed, the existence of an extensive precolonial transportation network can promote frontier expansion. Routes that do not promote the penetration of the interior are ignored, resulting in their abandonment. Peter W. Rees, "Origins of Colonial Transportation in Mexico," *Geographical Review* 65 (1975): 334; Martin T. Katzman, "The Brazilian Frontier in Comparative Perspective," *Comparative Studies in Society and History* 17 (1975): 269; B. J. Garner, "Models of Urban Geography and Settlement Location," in *Models in Geography,* ed. Richard J. Chorley and Peter Haggett (London: Methuen & Co., 1967), 309; John Davis, "Transportation and American Settlement Patterns," in *The American Environment: Perceptions and Policies,* ed. J. Wreford Watson and Timothy O'Riordan (London: John Wiley & Sons, 1976), 169; E. J. Taaffe, R. L. Morrill, and P. R. Gould, "Transport Expansion in Underdeveloped Countries: A Comparative Analysis," *Geographical Review* 53 (1963): 528.

21. D. W. Meinig, "American Wests: Preface to a Geographical Interpretation," *Annals of the Association of American Geographers* 62 (1972): 173; Taaffe, Morrill, and Gould, "Transport Expansion," 503–5, 514.

22. Garner, "Models of Urban Geography," 306. The term "colonization gradient" was introduced in Casagrande, Thompson, and Young, "Colonization," 311, who employed it to describe variation in settlement function through time as well as over space.

23. For a summary of the role of function in settlement hierarchies, see Brian J. L. Berry, *Geography of Market Centers and Retail Distribution* (Englewood Cliffs, N.J.: Prentice-Hall, 1967), 33–34. The definition of the entrepôt is from Casagrande, Thompson, and Young, "Colonization," 312.

24. Casagrande, Thompson, and Young, "Colonization," 312–13.

25. Ibid., 287; 313. Isolated administrative centers are discussed in Kenneth E. Lewis, *The American Frontier: An Archaeological Study of Settlement Pattern and Process* (Orlando, Fla.: Academic Press, 1984), 82.

26. Casagrande, Thompson, and Young, "Colonization," 314; H. Roy Merrens, "Settlement of the Colonial Atlantic Seaboard," in *Pattern and Process: Research in Historical Geography,* ed. Ralph Ehrenberg (Washington, D.C.: Howard University Press, 1975), 239–40. Bidwell and Falconer, *Agriculture in the Northern United States,* 254–55; Mitchell, *Commercialism and Frontier,* 4.

27. The processing requirements of bulky, weighty, and perishable products contrast markedly with those of more compact, nonperishable products such as tobacco and coffee. As a result, the number and distribution of frontier settlement types varies between insular frontiers according to the crops produced. See Carville Earle and Ronald Hoffman, "Staple Crops and Urban Development in the Eighteenth-Century South," *Perspectives in American History* 10 (1976): 11; Thompson, "Pioneer Colonization," 14; Katzman, "Brazilian Frontier," 279; Paul W. Gates, *The Farmer's Age: Agriculture, 1815–1860,* vol. 3: *The Economic History of the United States* (New York: Holt, Rinehart and Winston, 1960), 158; and Lewis, *American Frontier,* 73.

28. The model of settlement distribution was introduced in John C. Hudson, "A Locational Theory for Rural Settlement," *Annals of the Association of American Geographers* 59 (1969): 365–81. Its three phases are, "colonization," "spread," and "competition." Casagrande, Thompson, and Young, "Colonization," 314, also discuss the role of competition on the fate of frontier settlements.

29. Casagrande, Thompson, and Young, "Colonization," 314–15; Lewis, *American Frontier*, 86. Factors affecting the post-frontier development of a region include the ecological effects of production on the regional environment; the changing nature of relations with core economic interests; the impact of additional colonization, especially in adjacent areas; and finally the effect of rising regional elites in the former colony and their efforts to control, manipulate, and centralize internal surpluses and alter the nature of production there. See Robert W. Paynter, "Surplus Flows between Frontiers and Homelands," in *The Archaeology of Frontiers and Boundaries,* ed. Stanton F. Green and Stephen M. Perlman (Orlando, Fla.: Academic Press, 1985), 199–200.

30. Regional studies of frontier areas have demonstrated a strong relationship between specific factors and the distribution of initial settlement. A consideration of such variables has been particularly useful in developing comprehensive explanations for the forces that resulted in such patterning. See Roger D. Mason, *Euro-American Pioneer Settlement Systems in the Central Salt River Valley of Northeast Missouri,* Publications in Archaeology 2, (Columbia: American Archaeology Division, University of Missouri-Columbia, 1984), 88–90.

CHAPTER 2

1. For discussions of the North Atlantic fishery and its significance to the nations of northern Europe, see, Samuel Eliot Morrison, *The European Discovery of America, the Northern Voyages, A.D. 500–1600* (New York: Oxford University Press, 1971), 270–73; George Masselman, *The Cradle of Colonialism* (New Haven, Conn.: Yale University Press, 1963), 13–15; Braudel, *Perspective of the World,* 189–90; and Meinig, *Atlantic America,* 58.

2. See Charles Verlinden, *The Beginnings of Modern Colonialism, Eleven Essays with an Introduction,* trans. Yvonne Freccero (Ithaca, N.Y.: Cornell University Press, 1970); Wallerstein, *Modern World System,* 261; Carl Bridenbaugh, *Vexed and Troubled Englishmen, 1590–1642* (New York: Oxford University Press, 1968), 394–400; and David Beers Quinn, *England and the Discovery of America, 1481–1620* (New York: Alfred A. Knopf, 1974), 484–85. Population growth in England responded to conditions that occurred under Tudor rule, chiefly domestic peace, a rapid expansion of industrial production, specialization in agriculture, and economic diversification linked to England's increasingly advantageous position in a world economy now centered in northern Europe. See M. W. Flinn, *An Economic and Social History of Britain, 1066–1939* (New York: Macmillan, 1965), 76; K. W. Taylor, "Some Aspects of Population History," *Canadian Journal of Economics and Political Sciences* 16 (1950): 308.

3. France suffered from several handicaps that retarded its development as a core state. This failure had broad implications for the nature of French colonization in the New World. Its long-range trade was curtailed by Dutch and English competition for its home markets and by a virtual Dutch monopoly of French overseas exchange. French production reflected strong regional diversity and self-sufficiency focused on established commodities and luxury goods, for which there were substantial markets. Such markets, however, were regional in nature and did not encourage the establishment of nationwide trading networks. Regional capitalist interests also remained at odds with the aim of the monarchy to establish a unified state. Braudel, *Perspective of the World,* 256–57 and idem, *History and Environment,* vol. 1 of *The Identity of France,* trans. Sian Reynolds (New York: Harper and Row, 1988), 66–67. Central to the establishment of the French monarchy's administrative authority was a recognition of the distinction between public and private business. This concept permitted the acceptance of that authority by a traditionally powerful nobility, yet dramatically retarded the economic integration of the nation and the penetration of capitalism into all sectors of the national economy. Edward W. Fox, *History in Geographic Perspective: The Other France* (New York: W. W. Norton & Co., 1971), 74, 97–98.

In contrast to its English counterpart, the French state never integrated the political interests of the ruling aristocracy with the economic concerns of rising capitalists, and instead tried to subordinate the latter rather than incorporate them on a national scale. The sixteenth century also saw civil war and religious division plague France. These further retarded the creation of a national economy, while providing conditions that encouraged the monarchy in establishing direct administrative control of the state to maintain order. Wallerstein, *Modern World System,* 290–97; Fox, *The Other France,* 96; Fernand Braudel, *The Structures of Everyday Life,* vol. 1 of *Civilization and Capitalism, 15th-18th Century,* trans. Sian Reynolds (New York: Harper and Row, 1981), 54.

4. Paul Chrisler Phillips, *The Fur Trade* (Norman: University of Oklahoma Press, 1961), 1:13; W. J. Eccles, *The Canadian Frontier, 1534–1760* (New York: Holt, Rinehart, and Winston, 1969), 19; Harold A. Innis, *The Fur Trade in Canada: An Introduction to Canadian Economic History* (New Haven, Conn.: Yale University Press, 1962), 12.

5. Morrison, *European Discovery of America,* 273; Eccles, *Canadian Frontier,* 19; Hubert Charbonneau, *The First French Canadians: Pioneers in the St. Lawrence Valley,* trans. Paola Colozzo (Newark: University of Delaware Press, 1993); Leslie Choquette, *Frenchmen into Peasants: Modernity and Tradition in the Peopling of French Canada,* Harvard Historical Studies vol. 123 (Cambridge, Mass.: Harvard University Press, 1997).

6. Edward C. Kirkland, *A History of American Economic Life* (New York: F. S. Crofts and Co., 1939), 8; Eccles, *Canadian Frontier,* 34, 83–85; Wallerstein, *Modern World System II,* 147. Sigmund Diamond, "An Experiment in 'Feudalism:' French Canada in the Seventeenth Century," in *Essays on American Colonial History,* ed. Paul Goodman (New York: Holt, Rinehart and Winston, 1967), 55–60; Meinig, *Atlantic America,* 113; Carl Wittke, *A History of Canada* (New York: F. S. Crofts and Co., 1941), 28.

7. Innis, *Fur Trade in Canada,* 82–83; Richard White, *The Middle Ground: Indians, Empires, and Republics in the Great Lakes Region, 1650–1815* (Cambridge: Cambridge University Press, 1991), x–xi.

8. Meinig, *Atlantic America,* 113.

9. The English resettled people overseas for the purpose of producing a variety of commercial commodities. Employing joint-stock companies as extensions of the state, England had successfully established control of the Scottish Highlands, the Hebrides, and portions of Ireland by the sixteenth century. This experience formed the basis for initial settlement in North America and introduced precedents for production, political organization, and relationships with aboriginal populations that would have implications for the region's subsequent development. See William Christie MacLeod, *The American Indian Frontier* (New York: Alfred A. Knopf, 1928), 157; E. L. J. Coornaert, "European Economic Institutions and the New World: The Chartered Companies," in *The Cambridge Economic History of Europe,* vol. 4: *The Economy of Expanding Europe in the Sixteenth and Seventeenth Centuries,* ed. E. E. Rich and C. H. Wilson (Cambridge: Cambridge University Press, 1967), 226; J. H. Parry, *The Age of Reconnaissance* (New York: Mentor Books, 1963), 222–24; Quinn, *England and the Discovery of America,* 337–38; Bridenbaugh, *Vexed and Troubled Englishmen,* 396–397; and C. E. Carrington, *The British Overseas,* Part 1: *Making of the Empire* (Cambridge: Cambridge University Press, 1968), 28. Colonies founded at Plymouth and Massachusetts Bay in the 1620s and 1630s expanded rapidly. Settlers moved southwestward into the Connecticut Valley and northward into present-day New Hampshire. To the south, settlement also grew in Virginia, where the first successful colony was founded in 1607. See James A. Henretta, *The Evolution of American Society, 1700–1815: An Interdisciplinary Analysis* (Lexington, Mass.: D. C. Heath, 1973), 8; and Meinig, *Atlantic America,* 95–96.

10. When the English realized that the Hudson River lay in a strategic position for controlling the interior, they captured New Amsterdam in 1664 to transform the peripheral Dutch colony into the focus of its North American empire. Meinig, *Atlantic America,* 120–21; Phillips, *Fur Trade,* 1:247; Wolf, *Europe and the People without History,* 161; Thomas Elliot Norton, *The Fur Trade in Colonial New York, 1686–1776*

(Madison: University of Wisconsin Press, 1974); David A. Armour, *The Merchants of Albany, New York, 1686–1760* (New York: Garland, 1986).

11. Merrens, "Settlement of the Colonial Atlantic Seaboard," 239–40; Russell G. Handsman, "Early Capitalism and the Center Village of Caanan, Connecticut: A Study of Transformations and Separations," *Artifacts* 9 (1981): 3; Henretta, *Evolution of American Society,* 9–11; Meinig, *Atlantic America,* 356–59.

12. Helen Hornbeck Tanner, ed., *Atlas of Great Lakes Indian History* (Norman: University of Oklahoma Press, 1987), 30–31; Innis, *Fur Trade in Canada,* 55, 89; Almon Ernest Parkins, *The Historical Geography of Detroit* (Lansing: Michigan Historical Commission, 1918), 50–51; Eccles, *Canadian Frontier,* 136–37.

13. Iroquois expansion displaced a number of indigenous groups from Michigan. They were seasonally migratory, egalitarian societies, most of which based their subsistence on a mixed hunting-farming economy. Among these were the Sauks, the Foxes, and the Kickapoos, who purportedly inhabited the Saginaw Valley and other parts of the eastern peninsula; the Mascoutens, whose territory extended westward from the Saginaw drainage to Lake Michigan; the Potawotomis, who inhabited the southwestern portion of Michigan from the St. Joseph Valley as far north as Ludington; and the Miamis, whose range extended westward from the St. Joseph Valley around the southern shore of Lake Michigan. By the third quarter of the seventeenth century, all had retreated west of Lake Michigan, leaving the Lower Peninsula largely depopulated. Its former inhabitants, together with other displaced peoples, remained refugees until the Iroquois threat subsided. See George T. Hunt, *The Wars of the Iroquois: A Study of Intertribal Trade Relations* (Madison: University of Wisconsin Press, 1967), 110–11, 116; Ives Goddard, "Mascouten," in *Handbook of North American Indians,* vol. 15, *Northeast,* ed. Bruce G. Trigger (Washington, D.C.: Smithsonian Institution, 1978), 668–69; James A. Clifton, *The Pokagons, 1683–1983: Catholic Potawatomi Indians of the St. Joseph Valley* (Latham, Md.: University Press of America, 1984), 1; and Charles Callender, "Miami," in *Handbook of North American Indians,* vol. 15, *Northeast,* ed. Bruce G. Trigger (Washington, D.C.: Smithsonian Institution, 1978), 681.

14. James M. McClurken, "We Wish To Be Civilized: Ottawa-American Political Contests on the Michigan Frontier," (Ann Arbor: University Microfilms, 1988), 33–34, 48. Johanna Feest and Christian F. Feest, "Ottawa," in *Handbook of North American Indians,* vol. 15, *Northeast,* ed. Bruce G. Trigger (Washington, D.C.: Smithsonian Institution, 1978), 772; Tanner, *Atlas,* 62.

15. McClurken, "We Wish to Be Civilized," 48; Margaret Mary Montfort, "Ethnic and Tribal Identity among the Saginaw-Chippewa of Nineteenth-Century Michigan" (Master's thesis, Michigan State University, 1990), 34; E. S. Rogers, "Southeastern Ojibwa," in *Handbook of North American Indians,* vol. 15, *Northeast,* ed. Bruce G. Trigger (Washington, D.C.: Smithsonian Institution, 1978), 760–61; Tanner, *Atlas,* 58–59, 61.

16. Clifton, *Pokagons,* 20–21; Tanner, *Atlas,* 58–59, 63; R. Cole Harris, *Atlas of Canada,* vol. 1, *From the Beginning to 1800* (Toronto: University of Toronto Press, 1987), 87; Helen Hornbeck Tanner, "The Location of Indian Tribes in Southeastern Michigan and Northern Ohio, 1700–1817," in *Indians in Northern Ohio and Southeastern Michigan,* comp. and ed. David Agee Horr (New York: Garland Publishing, 1974), 326–27; Rogers, "Southeastern Ojibwa," 773–74; R. David Edmunds and Joseph L. Peyser, *The Fox Wars: The Mesquakie Challenge to New France* (Norman: University of Oklahoma Press, 1993); Joseph L. Peyser, ed. and trans., *Letters from New France: The Upper Country, 1686–1783* (Urbana: University of Illinois Press, 1992).

17. The international rivalry in North America was a regional manifestation of a series of European wars fought on a worldwide scale. The first three conflicts (King William's War, 1689–97; Queen Anne's War, 1701–13; and King George's War, 1739–48) involved French and British interests in North America, but affected the West only indirectly. The French and Indian War (1754–60), however, involved the Great Lakes region, and its results had profound implications for the future of the region and its inhabitants. See Tanner, *Atlas,* 49.

18. Innis, *Fur Trade in Canada,* 45; Phillips, *Fur Trade,* 1:361; Eccles, *Canadian Frontier,* 130; Ida Amanda Johnson, *The Michigan Fur Trade* (Lansing: Michigan Historical Commission, 1919; reprint, Grand Rapids, Mich.: Black Letter Press, 1971), 54–55, 61–62; Carolyn Gilman, *Where Two Worlds Meet, the Great Lakes Fur Trade,* Minnesota Historical Society, Museum Exhibit Series, no. 2 (St. Paul: Minnesota Historical Society, 1982), 2–3.

19. For a discussion of the origins and growth of Métis society and its role in the development of the fur trade, see, Jacqueline Peterson, "Many Roads to Red River: Métis Genesis in the Great Lakes Region, 1680–1815," in *The New Peoples: Being and Becoming Métis in North America,* ed. Jacqueline Peterson and Jennifer S. H. Brown (Winnipeg: University of Manitoba Press, 1985), 37–71.

20. Wolf, *Europe and the People without History,* 174. The term "middle ground" was introduced by Richard White in his perceptive analysis of the development of European-Indian relations in the Great Lakes region before the American occupation. It is a geographical concept, in that the middle ground represents a region between cultures and peoples, a zone that separates the boundary of empire from the world characterized by less-complex levels of political organization. Its occurrence between "the foreground of European invasion and occupation and the background of Indian defeat and retreat" clearly differentiates processes associated with such a region from those found in areas of settlement colonization; however, as agents of change and inducements for increasing interdependence, middle ground processes help create conditions conducive to the establishment of the strong links between homeland and periphery upon which cosmopolitan frontier colonization depends. White's emphasis on the political role of the fur trade also permits such processes to be seen as more than an outcome dictated solely by restricted economic interests, but rather as a reflection of larger national interests as well. See Richard White, *The Middle Ground,* x–xi, 51–53, 483–86.

21. Pontiac's War, inspired by an Ottawa leader from southeastern Michigan, involved a number of groups from Michigan and the Ohio country and intended both to restore perceived past lifeways and to expel the British. See Anthony F. C. Wallace, *The Death and Rebirth of the Seneca* (New York: Alfred A. Knopf, 1970), 115–21; Tanner, *Atlas,* 49–50; Harris, *Atlas of Canada,* 89; and Wolf, *Europe and the People without History,* 174–75. In its aftermath, the British established an "imperial system" that imposed a political solution to the conflicting interests of trade and settlement. Initially this attempted (albeit unsuccessfully) to reserve all lands west of the Appalachian Mountains for Indian use. Although this policy restored the allegiance of the western Indians, it alienated eastern colonists, who considered western Indian lands a zone for agricultural expansion. The necessity of regulating the increasingly competitive trade prompted an additional move to insure stability in the West. The Quebec Act, passed in 1774, extended the jurisdiction of this province southward into the Ohio country and effectively placed the western trade in the hands of established British commercial concerns in Canada in whose interest it was to continue the political and economic relationships established with native peoples during the previous French period. See Innis, *Fur Trade in Canada,* 176, 179; and Phillips, *Fur Trade,* 1:625–26. Many of the colonies held charter claims to parts of this territory and regarded current boundaries as only temporary impediments to the growth of western settlement. See Meinig, *Atlantic America,* 378–79.

22. Tanner, *Atlas,* 91; SLUS/1795/7:49–54.

23. Initially the Northwest Territory was subdivided into administrative areas containing an existing center of population. Wayne County, centered around Detroit, included Michigan's Lower Peninsula and portions of present-day Ohio, Indiana, Illinois, and Wisconsin. This area was subsequently reduced in size as westward-expanding American populations occupied the lands south of the Great Lakes, and portions of the original Northwest Territory were set off as smaller political units. It was anticipated that this process would serve as the basis for creating new states. See Proclamation, Aug. 15, 1796, TPUS/NWT 2:567–68; and George N. Fuller, *Michigan: A Centennial History of the State and Its People* (Chicago: Lewis Publishing Co., 1939), 1:113–14.

24. SLUS/1807/7:105–7; SLUS/1808/7:112–13; Tanner, *Atlas,* 158.

25. Eccles, *Canadian Frontier,* 187; Phillips, *Fur Trade,* 2:9; F. Clever Bald, *Detroit's First American Decade, 1796–1805* (Ann Arbor: University of Michigan Press, 1948), 79.

26. Wayne E. Stevens, "The Michigan Fur Trade," *Michigan History* 29 (1945): 501; Phillips, *Fur Trade,* 2:160; Johnson, *Michigan Fur Trade,* 144–45, 152–53.

27. This conflict extended up the St. Lawrence Valley to merge with a regional Indian uprising near the western end of Lake Erie. Smoldering Indian resentment of American expansion had coalesced around a Shawnee leader, Tecumseh, and his brother, the Prophet, who attempted to establish a pan-Indian confederacy of groups living east of the Mississippi. An American attack on Tecumseh's forces in 1811 commenced hostilities and provided British authorities in Canada with organized Indian allies that were employed in the formal war that began the following year. Since 1808 Great Britain had actively sought to identify itself with Indian interests and establish military alliances with aboriginal groups against a potential common enemy who had settlement designs on their territory. See Tanner, *Atlas,* 108; and Fred C. Hamil, "Michigan in the War of 1812," *Michigan History* 44 (1960): 258.

    In the West, British and Indian forces worked together in a series of successful military campaigns that defeated American forces on the western Great Lakes and captured strong points at Detroit and the Straits of Mackinac. A decisive American naval victory on Lake Erie in the fall of 1813, however, made the British position in southeastern Michigan untenable. The subsequent land campaign in Upper Canada defeated Indian forces at the Battle of the Thames, where Tecumseh was killed. Despite their reoccupation of Detroit and the surrounding region, American forces failed to recapture Fort Mackinac to the north or expand their campaign against the Indians into Michigan's interior. See Robert S. Allen, "His Majesty's Indian Allies: Native Peoples, the British Crown and the War of 1812," *Michigan Historical Review* 14 (1988): 11–12; Tanner, *Atlas,* 117–18; and Hamil, "Michigan in the War of 1812," 285.

28. Smallpox struck the Potawatomis in the Detroit area in 1752 and along the St. Joseph River in 1757 and 1762. In 1778 an unknown disease prevailed among the Ottawas at the mouth of the Grand River and in 1787–88 a localized epidemic of smallpox affected the Wyandots near Detroit. Finally, in 1813–14 an epidemic of whooping cough or typhoid swept across eastern Michigan, striking the Ojibwas north of Lake St. Clair as well as the Potawatomis living west of Detroit. See Tanner, *Atlas,* 169–73.

29. Allen, "His Majesty's Indian Allies," 23; SLUS/1815/7:131–32; Act. Gov. Woodbridge to Act. Sec. of War, 8 May 1815/TPUS/MT/10:536–37; Gov. Cass to Sec. of War, 3 August 1819/TPUS/MT/10:853; HR/1826/42; H. N. Bissell, "The Early Settlement of Mt. Clemens and Vicinity," *MPHC* 5 (1884): 463.

30. Francis Paul Prucha, *The Great Father: The United States Government and the American Indians* (Lincoln: University of Nebraska Press, 1984), 1:21–22. For the texts of the Saginaw and Chicago treaties, see SLUS/1819/7:203–6; SLUS/1821/7:218–21.

31. Divesting the Indians of lands also had the philosophical connotation of consigning "vacant" land to civilized use, an act that Americans believed would encourage the Indians' adoption of a European way of life. See Bernard W. Sheehan, *Seeds of Extinction: Jeffersonian Philanthropy and the American Indian* (New York: W.W. Norton, 1974), 167; Clifton, *Pokagons,* 36–38; Alec R. Gilpin, *The Territory of Michigan, 1805–1837* (East Lansing: Michigan State University Press, 1970), 116–28; and Elizabeth Neumeyer, "Michigan Indians Battle Against Removal," *Michigan History* 55 (1971): 287–88.

32. Johnson, *Michigan Fur Trade,* 127–28; McClurken, "We Wish To Be Civilized," 83–86; Montfort, "Ethnic and Tribal Identity," 69–72. For a discussion of the impact of capitalist trade on traditional societies and the nature of native adaptations to participation in this activity, see Wolf, *Europe and the People without History,* 194.

33. French Jesuit missionaries explored the Michigan shoreline as early as the 1630s, and by the 1680s maps appeared that accurately portrayed both the configuration of the Great Lakes and Michigan's position among

them. French and later British cartographers added more details, and made reasonably accurate renditions of militarily important areas, such as the Straits of Mackinac and St. Mary's River in the north, as well as the Detroit River region between lakes Erie and St. Clair. For a review of early mapping in Michigan, see LeRoy Barnett, "Milestones in Michigan Mapping: Early Settlement," *Michigan History* 63 (September/October 1979): 34–43. The classic annotated work on Michigan maps is Louis C. Karpinski, *Bibliography of the Printed Maps of Michigan, 1804–1880* (Lansing: Michigan Historical Commission, 1931). See also idem, "Early Maps of Michigan and the Great Lakes Region," *Michigan History* 27 (1943): 143–55; idem, "Michigan and the Great Lakes upon the Map, 1636–1802," *Michigan History* 29 (1945): 302; and idem, "Early Michigan Maps: Three Outstanding Peculiarities," *Michigan History* 29 (1945): 507–8. More recent listings of Michigan maps before 1800 may be found in Renville Wheat, *Maps of Michigan and the Great Lakes, 1545–1845* (Detroit: Detroit Public Library, 1967); LeRoy Barnett, comp., *Checklist of Printed Maps of the Middle West to 1900*, vol. 5, *Michigan*, gen. ed. Robert W. Karrow (Boston: G. K. Hall, 1981); and Keith R. Widder, "Mapping the Great Lakes: 1761 Balfour Expedition Maps," *Michigan History* (May/June 1991): 24–31.

34. An 1813 account of Michigan's topography noted, "In the centre the land is high, from whence there is a descent in all directions." John Melish, *A Statistical Account of the United States, with Topographical Tables of the Counties, Population, etc.* (Philadelphia: G. Palmer, 1813), 34. For a discussion of the myth of the central ridge, see Karpinski, "Early Michigan Maps," 506.

35. Edward Tiffin to Josiah Meigs, 30 November 1815/ASP/PL/ 3/1816/238.

36. Jedidiah Morse, *The American Gazetteer, Exhibiting, in Alphabetical Order, a Much More Full and Accurate Account, than has been Given, of the State, Provinces, Counties, Cities, Towns, . . . of the American Continent* (Boston: S. Hall, 1797); C. Jouett to Henry Dearborn, 25 July 1803/ASP/PL/1/1804/97; ASP/PL//1/1806/126; Report of Judge Augustus C. Woodward, "Land Titles in Michigan Territory," ASP/PL/1/1806/126; Melish, *Statistical Account*, 33; idem., *A Geographical Description of the United States, with the Contiguous British and Spanish Possessions* (Philadelphia: By the author, 1816), 34.

37. Lewis Cass to Josiah Meigs, 11 May 1816/TPUS/MT/10:636.

38. James Abbot to Josiah Meigs, 30 June 1816/TPUS/MT/10:655–57. The reputed role of the Tiffin report on perceptions of the Michigan landscape dates from the settlement period itself. John Blois's *1838 Gazetteer of the State of Michigan* (Detroit: Sydney L. Rood & Co., 1838; Reprint, Knightstown, Ind.: Bookmark, 1979), 22, attributed the slow growth of early settlement in the territory to contemporary knowledge of this document, and other antebellum authors repeated this conclusion. See, for example, James H. Lanman, *History of Michigan, Civil and Topographical, in a Compendius Form; With a View of the Surrounding Lakes* (New York: E. French, 1839), 319; and J. R. Williams, "Internal Commerce of the West: Its Condition and Wants, as Illustrated by the Commerce of Michigan," *Merchants' Magazine and Commercial Review* 19 (1848): 20. The myth of the Tiffin report's influence was circulated widely in later nineteenth-century literature (see, for example, Madison Kuhn, "Tiffin, Morse, and the Reluctant Pioneer," *Michigan History* 50 [1966]: 120–21), and was even mentioned in Fuller's discussion of the impact of physical factors on Michigan's settlement (Fuller, *Economic and Social Beginnings*, 50–51).

39. In his comprehensive study of urban development in the American West, historian Richard Wade observed that towns were often planted far in advance of the line of settlement and provided focal points in the West for the approaching settlers. He noted that all of the five early major urban centers south of the Great Lakes arose as isolated outposts, each occupying a location strategic to regional trade, defense, or administration. See Richard C. Wade, *The Urban Frontier: Pioneer Life in Early Pittsburgh, Cincinnati, Lexington, Louisville, and St. Louis* (Chicago: University of Chicago Press, 1959), 1, 20, 26. See also Bert Hudgins, "Evolution of Metropolitan Detroit," *Economic Geography* 21 (1945): 212; Bela Hubbard, *Memorials of a Half-Century in Michigan and the Lake Region* (New York: G. P. Putnam's Sons, 1888), 114; and Parkins, *Historical Geography of Detroit*, 46–50, 62–63.

40. Woodward to Proctor, 20 August 1812/TPUS/MT/10:406. For a general discussion of the adaptive advantages of line villages, see, Lowry Nelson, *Rural Sociology* (New York: American Book Co., 1952), 67; and T. Lynn Smith, "Brazilian Land Surveys, Land Division, and Land Titles," *Rural Sociology* 9 (1944): 270. See also discussions in Terry G. Jordan, "Antecedents of the Long-Lot in Texas," *Annals of the Association of American Geographers* 64 (1974): 80–81; and Smith, "Brazilian Land Surveys," 256.

41. Meinig, *Atlantic America,* 242. The persistence of these landholdings long after the close of the frontier was noted by contemporary American observers. See Hubbard, *Memorials,* 352–53; and I. P. Christiancy, "Recollections of the Early History of the City and County of Monroe," *MPHC* 6 (1883): 373. For discussions of the advantages of French farming strategies in colonial North America, see R. Cole Harris, "The Extension of France into Rural Canada," in *European Settlement and Development in North America: Essays on Geographical Change in Honor and Memory of Andrew Hill Clark,* ed. James R. Gibson (Toronto: University of Toronto Press, 1978), 45; and Howard S. Russell, *A Long, Deep Furrow: Three Centuries of Farming in New England* (Hannover, N.H.: University Press of New England, 1976), 258. A contemporary evaluation appeared in Lanman, *History of Michigan, Civil and Topographical,* 318.

42. Charles Jouett to Henry Dearborn, 25 July 1803/ASP/PL/1/1804/97. David Ferrell, "Settlement along the Detroit Frontier, 1760–1796," *Michigan History* 52 (1968): 96–102, 107; William Hull to D. B. Woodward, ASP/PL/1/1805/112; Gov. Hull to Sec. of War, 20 July 1810/TPUS/MT/10:320.

43. Parkins, *Historical Geography of Detroit,* 55, 96, 100, 131–32; D. B. Warden, *Statistical, Political, and Historical Account of the United States of America; from the Period of their First Colonization to the Present Day* (Edinburgh: Archibald Constable and Co., 1819), 3:75; Lina Gouger, "Montreal et le peuplement de Détroit, 1701–1765," *Proceedings of the Eighteenth Meeting of the French Colonial Historical Society, Montreal, May 1992,* ed. James Pritchard (Cleveland: French Colonial Historical Society, 1994), 46–58.

44. Bald, *Detroit's First American Decade,* 23–24; Parkins, *Historical Geography of Detroit,* 79, 97.

45. MLCLC/1825/MTL/1:283–85; Sec. of War to Gov. Hull, 23 July 1805/TPUS/MTL/10:23–24. Gilpin, *Territory of Michigan,* 35. For a discussion of the Woodward Plan of Detroit and its antecedents, see John W. Reps, *Town Planning in Frontier America* (Columbia: University of Missouri Press, 1980), 255–58. Detroit's role as an entrepôt was reflected in the perceptions of early writers who always specified it as the preferred entryway to Michigan. See, for example, Estwick Evans, *A Pedestrious Tour of Four Thousand Miles, Through the Western States and Territories, During the Winter and Spring of 1818* (Concord, N.H.: Joseph C. Spear, 1819), 121; Sec. Woodbridge to John C. Calhoun, 4 March 1819/TPUS/MT/10:819; *Emigrant's Guide, or Pocket geography, of the United States: and from the Eastern to the Western States* (Philadelphia: Phillips & Spear, 1818), 169; Blois, *Gazetteer,* 107–8.

46. This involved the settlement of the Connecticut Western Reserve and the Sufferers' Land, or Firelands, immediately to the west a decade later. The relative economic isolation of this region, however, caused its development to lag far behind that of the Ohio Valley to the south. Only after the opening of canal routes to the East and South in the 1820s provided markets for Great Lakes agricultural commodities could frontier production expand and the lake trade flourish. Harlan Hatcher, *Lake Erie* (Indianapolis: Bobbs-Merrill, 1945), 61–62. A graphic study of the distribution of these lands appears in Thomas Aquinas Burke, *Ohio Lands: A Short History* (Columbus: Ohio Auditor of State, 1987), 7–8; John Biddle, "Discourse Delivered Before the Historical Society of Michigan," in *Historical and Scientific Sketches of Michigan* (Detroit: Stephen Wells and George L. Whitney, 1834), 163; Frederick L. Paxon, "The Gateways of the Old Northwest," *MPHC* 38 (1912): 143–44; Harlan Hatcher, *The Western Reserve: The Story of New Connecticut in Ohio* (Indianapolis: Bobbs-Merrill, 1949), 76, 109–14; and ASP/M/1/1808/250.

Lake Erie is unique among the Great Lakes, in that its bottom lies well above sea level. The lake's relative shallow depth, averaging only sixty feet, makes it especially prone to freezing over during the winter months. See John A. Dorr Jr. and Donald F. Eschman, *Geology of Michigan* (Ann Arbor: University of

Michigan Press, 1988), 165; Val L. Eichenlaub, *Weather and Climate in the Great Lakes Region* (Notre Dame, Ind.: University of Notre Dame Press, 1979), 286; and Hatcher, *Lake Erie,* 68–70.

    Routes across the lake varied, but most included Cleveland and Sandusky as regular stops, as well as the Bass Islands at the head of Lake Erie and the British settlements of Amherstburg, Malden, and Sandwich on the Canadian side of the Straits of Detroit. See William Darby, *A Tour from the City of New York, to Detroit, in the Michigan Territory, made Between the 2d of May and the 22d of September, 1898* (New York: By the author, 1819; reprint, Chicago: Quadrangle Books, 1962), xlv–xlvi; *Detroit Gazette* 28 August 1818, 11 June 1919; and George Clark, "Recollections," *MPHC* 1 (1877): 503. Travel times by sailing craft were reported in "A Visit with a Lady Who Knew Detroit as a Frontier Post," *MPHC* 14 (1889): 537; Ephraim S. Williams, "Personal Reminiscences," *MPHC* 8 (1886): 234; and *History of Washtenaw County, Michigan* (Chicago: Charles C. Chapman, 1881), 431. Those by steamboat are taken from *Detroit Gazette,* 28 August 1818, 29 May 1820; Mrs. E. M. S. Stewart, "Childhood's Recollections of Detroit," *MPHC* 18 (1891): 458–59; and Melvin D. Osband, "My Recollections of Pioneers and Pioneer Life in Nankin," *MPHC* 14 (1889): 433.

    Water transport beyond Detroit was limited largely to the supply of the military posts at Fort Gratiot, Mackinac, Chicago, and Green Bay. No overland routes as yet reached these places, and their support depended solely on lake shipping. See Blois, *Gazetteer,* 107, 108; C. Colton, *Tour of the American Lakes, and Among the Indians of the North-West Territory, in 1830: Disclosing the Character and Prospects of the Indian Race* (London: Frederick Westley and A. H. Davis, 1833), 1:29; Charles C. Trowbridge, "Detroit, Past and Present," *MPHC* 1 (1877): 383; Milo O. Quaife, *Lake Michigan* (Indianapolis: Bobbs-Merrill, 1944), 133–34; and Hatcher, *Lake Erie,* 90.

47. Anthony Wayne to Sec. of the Treasury, 4 September 1796/TPUS/NWT/2:570; SLUS/1795/7:49–54.
48. Darby, *Tour,* 201; William T. Mitchell, "History of St. Clair County," *MPHC* 6 (1883): 406; George H. Cannon, "History of the Township of Shelby, Macomb County, Michigan," *MPHC* 17 (1890): 425.
49. SLUS/1808/7:112–13; SLUS/1811/2:668–69; Reasin Beall to Josiah Meigs, 16 January 1815/TPUS/MT/10:558–59; ASP/M/2/1812/298. Martin R. Kaatz, "The Black Swamp: A Study in Historical Geography," *Annals of the Association of American Geographers* 45 (1955): 1–2, 12. ASP/M/2/1820/491; *Detroit Gazette,* 30 January 1818; SLUS/1827/:231–32; Talcott E. Wing, "Continuation of the History of Monroe," *MPHC* 6 (1883): 374; Salmon Keeney, "Salmon Keeney's Visit to Michigan in 1827," ed. Helen Everett, *Michigan History* 40 (1956): 442; SLUS/1804/2:275–77. Both travelers and immigrants managed to negotiate the swamp, and one enterprising Detroit resident attempted to initiate an overland passenger route during the winter months between Buffalo and Detroit. See *Detroit Gazette,* 8 January 1819; Evans, *Pedestrious Tour,* 101; and Clark, "Recollections," 504.
50. Henry A. Ford, "The Old Moravian Mission at Mt. Clemens," *MPHC* 10 (1886): 113; Aura P. Stewart, "Recollections of Aura P. Stewart, of St. Clair County, of Things Relating to the Early History of Michigan," *MPHC* 4 (1883): 327. Presentment of Grand Jury, 22 September 1810/TPUS/MT/10:327–28; MLCLC/1815/MTL/1:290–94; Alexander Macomb to Sec. of War, 23 November 1816/TPUS/MT/10:670; MLCLC/1816/MTL/1:295–98; MLCLC/1817/MTL/1:306–10; Alexander Macomb to Sec. of War, 2 November 1818/TPUS/MT/10:785.
51. Thomas J. Drake, "History of Oakland County," *MPHC* 4 (1883): 565; Edmund A. Calkins, "Old Trails of Central Michigan," *Michigan History* 12:329; Tanner, *Atlas,* 121.
52. HR/1826/42; HR/1826/68; Fuller, *Economic and Social Beginnings,* 76–78; J. M. McMath, "The Willow Run Settlement," *MPHC* 14 (1889): 485; Henry B. Pierce, *History of Calhoun County, Michigan* (Philadelphia: L. H. Everts, 1877), 14.
53. References to the St. Joseph Trail appear in Fuller, *Economic and Social Beginnings,* 78; Douglas H. Gordon and George S. May, ed., "The Michigan Land Rush in 1836, Michigan Journal, 1836, John M. Gordon,"

Michigan History 43 (1959): 445; J. Q. A. Sessions, "Ann Arbor—A History of Its Early Settlement," *MPHC* 1 (1877): 335; Calkins, "Old Trails of Central Michigan," 339; Mrs. E. M. S. Stewart, "Early Settlement of Ann Arbor—Account Given to Mrs. E. M. S. Stewart in 1852 by Mr. Bethuel Farrand, Who Died in Ann Arbor, July 23, 1852," *MPHC* 6 (1883): 445; C. B. Seymour, "Early Days in Old Washtenaw County," *MPHC* 28 (1897–98): 392; Henry Little, "Fifty Years Ago, Jacksonburg and Jackson County—1829–1879," *MPHC* 4 (1883): 510; and MTL/183/3:888.

The Thornapple Trail is described in, Martin Davis et al. to Delegate Wing, 7 December 1831/TPUS/MT/11:395; L. D. Watkins, "Settlement of the Township of Bridgewater and Vicinity, Washtenaw County," *MPHC* 28 (1897–98): 568; Enos Northrup, "First Trip to Michigan," *MPHC* 5 (1884): 69. Calkins, "Old Trails of Central Michigan," 336–37; "Pioneer History of the Settlement of Eaton County," *MPHC* 22 (1893): 519; Margaret Lafever, "Story of Early Day Life in Michigan," *MPHC* 38 (1912): 672–73.

For the Saginaw Trail, see, Fuller, *Economic and Social Beginnings,* 76; Drake, "History of Oakland County," 565, 568; B. O. Williams, "Sketch of the Life of Oliver Williams and Family," *MPHC* 2 (1880): 38–39. *Detroit Gazette,* 26 February 1819; and MLCLB/1822/MTL/1:265–66.

The Grand River Trail is referred to by William Bronson, "Pioneer History of Clinton County," *MPHC* 5 (1884): 326; Elijah H. Pilcher, "Forty Years Ago," *MPHC* 5 (1884): 83. Munnis Kenny, Diary, 1828/KFP/MHC; Agnes Pike, "Clinton Co. History, Interesting Reminiscences Read Before DeWitt Grange," *Clinton County Republican,* 6 November 1902; Calkins, "Old Trails of Central Michigan," 331–33; H. H. Carson, "Village Trails and Mounds in Michigan," *American Antiquarian* 9 (July 1887): 237–38.

54. Triangular patterns of exchange characterized the Atlantic trade. One involved the shipment to the Northeast of West Indian sugar and molasses, which were subsequently turned into rum to be exchanged in West Africa for the slaves that were in constant demand in the West Indies. A second triangle saw the movement of sugar and molasses directly to Britain, from which manufactured goods were sent to the Northeast, which in turn supplied provisions to the plantation islands. The relevance of the triangular trade to the economic development of Britain's northern American colonies is discussed in Wallerstein, *Modern World System II,* 237; Henretta, *Evolution of American Society,* 44–47; and Ernest Mandel, *Marxist Economic Theory* (New York: Monthly Review Press, 1968), 1:106–10.

55. Henry Adams, *The United States in 1800* (Ithaca, N.Y.: Cornell University Press, 1955), 6. Douglass C. North, *The Economic Growth of the United States, 1790–1860* (New York: W. W. Norton, 1966), 52; Baldwin, "Patterns of Development," 172–74; Earle and Hoffman, "Staple Crops and Urban Development," 67.

56. North, *Economic Growth of the United States,* 36, 41–43; Paul A. Groves, "The Northeast and Regional Interaction, 1800–1860," in *North America, the Historical Geography of a Changing Continent,* ed. Robert D. Mitchell and Paul Groves (Totowa, N.J.: Rowman & Littlefield, 1987), 199; Baldwin, "Patterns of Development," 176–77; and Carville Earle, "Regional Economic Development West of the Appalachians, 1815–1860," in *North America, the Historical Geography of a Changing Continent,* ed. Robert D. Mitchell and Paul Groves (Totowa, N.J.: Rowman & Littlefield, 1987), 174.

57. Winifred B. Rothenburg, "The Market and Massachusetts Farmers, 1750–1855," *Journal of Economic History* 41 (1981): 311–12; idem, "The Emergence of a Capitalist Market in Rural Massachusetts, 1730–1838," *Journal of Economic History* 45 (1985): 806; Diane Lindstrom, "Southern Dependence upon Interregional Grain Supplies: A Review of the Trade Flows, 1840–1860," *Agricultural History* 44 (1970): 101–13 ; Russell, *Long, Deep Furrow,* 266; and George Rogers Taylor, *The Transportation Revolution, 1815–1860,* vol. 4: *The Economic History of the United States* (New York: Rinehart and Co., 1951), 17.

58. Curtis P. Nettels, *The Emergence of a National Economy,* vol. 2, *The Economic History of the United States* (New York: Holt, Rinehart & Winston, 1962), 121–22.

59. Ibid., 203–4, 275–76; North, *Economic Growth of the United States*, 57; S. P. Lee and P. Passell, *A New Economic View of American History* (New York: Norton, 1979), 146–52.

60. North, *Economic Growth of the United States*, 178–80. Victor Clark, *History of Manufactures in the United States*, vol. 1, *1607–1860* (Washington, D.C.: Carnegie Institute, 1929; reprint, New York: Peter Smith, 1949), 322; Paul A. Groves, "The Northeast and Regional Integration," 202.

61. Robert Greenhalgh Albion, *The Rise of New York Port (1815–1860)* (New York: Charles Scribner's Sons, 1939), 95–97.

62. Albert Fishlow, "Antebellum Interregional Trade Reconsidered," *American Economic Review* 54 (1961): 362–363; Groves, "Northeast and Regional Integration," 203; Henretta, *Evolution of American Society*, 204–5.

63. North, *Economic Growth of the United States*, 159–160.; Clark, *History of Manufactures*, 436. David R. Meyer, "Emergence of the American Manufacturing Belt: An Interpretation," *Journal of Historical Geography* 9 (1983): 149. Robert W. Paynter, *Models of Spatial Inequality, Settlement Patterns in Historical Archaeology* (New York: Academic Press, 1982), 81–82.

64. The development of these specialized forms of agriculture are discussed in detail in Russell, *Long, Deep Furrow*, 327, 351–77. See also Clarence H. Danhof, *Change in Agriculture: The Northern United States, 1820–1870* (Cambridge, Mass.: Harvard University Press, 1969), 20; and Taylor, *Transportation Revolution*, 153–56.

65. Groves, "Northeast and Regional Integration," 205; Albion, *Rise of New York Port*, 89–90.

CHAPTER 3

1. These perspectives are discussed in geographer John Jakle's recent study of nineteenth-century traveler's perceptions of the Ohio Valley, *Images of the Ohio Valley: A Historical Geography of Travel, 1740–1860* (New York: Oxford University Press, 1977), 89.

2. The origins and development of this view of nature are traced in Lynn White Jr., "The Historical Roots of Our Ecological Crisis," *Science* 155, no. 3767 (1967): 1205–6.

3. Wilderness represented alien space, which invoked fear; however, it was not immutable. Wilderness could be modified for the benefit of humankind, and to do so demonstrated not only a mastery over nature, but also the conversion of chaos to order. Such an assumption invited the appropriation of natural resources for human use as a necessary step in improving lands that had heretofore constituted only waste. See John R. Stilgoe, *Common Landscape of America*, 7–11. The image of America as wilderness was as much poetic metaphor as reality. It reflected values that stressed the importance of unceasing manipulation and mastery of the forces of nature, including human nature. By exaggerating dangers posed by the frontier environment and native peoples to the establishment of a new civilization in a land of plenty, the need for an aggressive, controlled, and well-disciplined society was justified. Groups such as the New England Puritans favored a wilderness image to characterize land they chose to settle. See Leo Marx, *The Machine in the Garden: Technology and the Pastoral Ideal in America* (London: Oxford University Press, 1964), 42–44.

4. Alexis de Tocqueville, *Democracy in America*, vol. 2, ed. Phillips Bradley (New York: Vintage Books, 1954), 46.

5. Jakle, *Images of the Ohio Valley*, 9.

6. Willis F. Dunbar, *Michigan: A History of the Wolverine State*, rev. by George S. May (Grand Rapids, Mich.: William B. Eerdmans, 1980), 294.

7. Although the Romantic movement served as an organizing principle for antebellum images of the environment, the notion that the natural world was an important influence on the development of behavior

had much earlier roots and played an important role in Elizabethan perceptions of America. The natural abundance noted by early English observers led them to characterize its environment as a "garden," an idyllic world in which to create a new civilization. As a metaphor for a utopian existence, providing bounty, freedom, leisure, and harmony without the deprivations associated with complex state structures, the garden offered the potential of improving society through its beneficence, rather than its constituting an obstacle to be overcome. See Marx, *Machine in the Garden,* 39–40, 42–43. For a discussion of the influence of the garden myth in shaping American images of the wilderness, see Henry Nash Smith, *Virgin Land: The American West as Symbol and Myth* (Cambridge, Mass: Harvard University Press, 1950), 44–45. The role of changing historical perceptions of wilderness in Western thought is treated in detail in Roderick Nash, *Wilderness and the American Mind* (New Haven, Conn.: Yale University Press, 1967), chap. 3.

8. The influence of pristine nature on the development of the American character became a cornerstone of transcendentalism, an American manifestation of the Romantic movement, and later became a central theme in Frederick Jackson Turner's influential interpretation of the frontier's role in shaping American history. See Ray Allen Billington, *Land of Savagery, Land of Promise: The European Image of the American Frontier in the Nineteenth Century* (New York: W. W. Norton, 1981), 80. The impact of the western frontier on American Transcendentalism is discussed in Rod W. Horton, *Backgrounds of Literary Thought* (New York: Appleton-Century-Crofts, 1952), 112–13, 134–35; and Lucy Lockwood Hazard, *The Frontier in American Literature* (New York: Frederick Unger, 1927), 149–50.

9. Ray Allen Billington, *Westward Expansion: A History of the American Frontier* (New York: Macmillan, 1967), 80. Sacrificing the environment to provide raw materials did not necessarily involve the loss of the garden's influence. The industrial development of America, which required the acquisition of resources from nature, was seen by contemporary observers as an equally important force for personal renewal. A persistent belief that the revolution in technology and industrial organization would bring about a new golden age of civilization in America helped create a parallel myth that the "workshop," as well as the garden, would serve as a rejuvenating moral force on the population of the United States. See Marvin Fisher, *Workshops in the Wilderness: The European Response to American Industrialization, 1830–1860* (New York: Oxford University Press, 1967), 37–42.

10. Hazard, *Frontier in American Literature,* xviii.

11. For a discussion of these themes, see Vernon Louis Parrington, *The Romantic Revolution in America, 1800–1860* (New York: Harcourt, Brace and Co., 1927), 161–62. Parrington's treatment of literature as an expression of larger political, economic, and social ideas is particularly relevant in that it emphasized the importance of the images presented in fiction and their general acceptance by contemporary audiences. See also Richard Hofstadter, *The Progressive Historians, Turner, Beard, Parrington* (New York: Alfred A. Knopf, 1968), 354–55. Indeed, it has also been suggested that early fictional literature set in the West introduced characters whose personalities and actions formed the basis for the development of a frontier mythology that permeated American perceptions of expansion throughout the nineteenth century. See Richard Slotkin, *The Fatal Environment: The Myth of the Frontier in the Age of Industrialization, 1800–1890* (New York: HarperCollins, 1985), chaps. 5 and 6. Discussions of the Romantic approach in western literature include Everett Carter, *The American Idea: The Literary Response to American Optimism* (Chapel Hill: University of North Carolina Press, 1977), 196; and William S. Osborne, *Caroline M. Kirkland* (New York: Twayne Publishers, 1972), 40.

12. Charles Fenno Hoffman, *A Winter in the West* (New York: Harper & Bros., 1835), 1:139, 183–84, 216.

13. James Fenimore Cooper, *The Oak-Openings; or the Bee Hunter* (New York: Hurd and Houghton, 1848); Caroline Matilda Kirkland [Mary Clavers], *A New Home—Who'll Follow? Or Glimpses of Western Life* (New York: C. S. Francis, 1839); H. H. Riley, *Puddleford Papers, or, Humors of the West* (New York: Derby and Jackson, 1857); Benjamin F. Taylor, *Theophilus Trent, Old Times in the Oak Openings* (Chicago: S. C.

Griggs, 1887); Orlando B. Willcox, *Shoepac Recollections: A Way-side Glimpse of American Life* (New York: Bunce and Brother, Publishers, 1856); Jerome James Wood, *The Wilderness and the Rose: A Story of Michigan* (Hudson, Mich.: Wood Book Co., 1890). Useful background on these authors, together with selections from their works, appear in a recent anthology. See Larry Massie, *From Frontier Folk to Factory Smoke: Michigan's First Century of Historical Fiction* (Au Train, Mich.: Avery Color Studios, 1987).

14. Examples of travel accounts included Evans, *Pedestrious Tour,* and Darby, *Tour,* while among the travelers' guides could be found Samuel Brown, *The Western Gazetteer; or Emigrant's Directory, Containing a Geographical Description of the Western States and Territories* (Auburn, N.Y.: H. C. Southwick, 1817); John Melish, *Information and Advice to Emigrants to the United States and from the Eastern to the Western States* (Philadelphia: By the author, 1819); Andrew Miller, *New States and Territories, or the Ohio, Indiana, Illinois, Michigan, North-Western, Missouri, Louisiana, Mississippi and Alabama, in Their Real Characters, in 1818* (Keene, N.H.: By the author, 1819); Warden, *Statistical, Political, and Historical Account;* and *Emigrant's Guide.*

15. Among the most widely read journal accounts were those by H. S. Tanner, *Memoir on the Recent Surveys, Observations, and Internal Improvements in the United States, with Brief Mention of the New Counties, Towns, Villages, Canals, and Railroads Never Before Delineated* (Philadelphia: By the author, 1829) and Patrick Shirreff, *A Tour through North America; Together with a Comprehensive View of the Canadas and the United States, as Adapted for Agricultural Emigration* (Edinburgh: Oliver and Boyd, 1835). Directories, guides, and gazetteers included those by John Melish, *The Traveller's Directory through the United States; Containing a Description of all the Principal Roads through the United States, with Copious Remarks on the Rivers and Other Objects* (New York: By the author, 1825); D. Hewitt, *The American Traveller; or National Directory, Containing an Account of All the Great Post Roads, and Important Cross Roads, in the United States* (Washington, D.C.: Davis and Force, 1825); William Chapin, *A Complete Reference Gazetteer of the United States of North America* (New York: W. Chapin and J. B. Taylor, 1839); James Hall, *Statistics of the West, at the Close of the Year 1836* (Cincinnati: J. A. James and Co., 1836); idem, *Notes on the Western States; Containing Descriptive Sketches of Their Soil, Climate, Resources, and Scenery* (Philadelphia: Harrison Hall, 1838); Samuel Augustus Mitchell, *Mitchell's Traveller's Guide through the United States, Containing the Principal Cities, Towns, &c.* (Philadelphia: Thomas Cowperthwait and Co., 1836); John Mason Peck, *A New Guide for Emigrants to the West, Containing Sketches of Ohio, Indiana, Illinois, Missouri, Michigan, with the Territories of Wisconsin and Arkansas, and the Adjacent Parts* (Boston: Gould, Kendall, and Lincoln, 1837); Blois, *Gazetteer;* James H. Lanman, *History of Michigan, Civil and Topographical;* Grenville Mellen, *A Book of the United States, Exhibiting Its Geography, Divisions, Constitution, and Government . . .* (Hartford, Conn.: Frederick Sumner, 1842); O. L. Holley, *The Picturesque Tourist; Being a Guide Through the Northern and Eastern States and Canada* (New York: J. Disturnell, 1844); and H. Phelps, *Phelps' Traveller's Guide through the United States; Containing Upwards of Several Hundred Railroad, Canal, and Stage and Steam-Boat Routes, Accompanied by a New Map of the United States* (New York: Ensigns and Thayer, 1848).

16. Barnett, "Milestones in Michigan Mapping: Early Settlement," 38.

17. Terry Jordan and Matti Kaups argue that the rapid expansion of agriculture across the eastern woodlands was made possible by adaptations in architecture and agricultural strategies that originated in Europe's Scandinavian periphery and were rapidly disseminated among colonists from other areas. See *The American Backwoods Frontier: An Ethnic and Ecological Interpretation* (Baltimore: Johns Hopkins University Press, 1989), 94–95. For the changing perception of open lands in the West, see, Bernard C. Peters, "Changing Ideas about the Use of Vegetation as an Indicator of Soil Quality: Example of New York and Michigan," *Journal of Geography* 72 (1973): 19–21; and Brian Birch, "British Evaluations of the Forest Openings and Prairie Edges of the North-Central States, 1800–1850," in *The Frontier, Comparative*

Studies, vol. 2, ed. William W. Savage and Stephen I. Thompson (Norman: University of Oklahoma Press, 1979), 174–75. A useful comparative study of the role of perceptions of open lands in western agricultural settlement is Terry G. Jordan, "Pioneer Evaluation of Vegetation in Frontier Texas," *Southwestern Historical Quarterly* 76 (1973): 254.

18. Billington, *Land of Savagery, Land of Promise,* 89–90.

19. Frank Leverett, *Surface Geology and Agricultural Conditions in Michigan,* Michigan Geological and Biological Survey, Publication no. 25 (Lansing, Mich.: Wynkoop Hallenbeck Crawford Co., 1917), 105; Lawrence M. Sommers, *Michigan, a Geography* (Boulder, Colo.: Westview Press, 1984), 53–54. For a discussion of the impact of the Pleistocene glaciations and changing lake levels on the landforms of Michigan, see Dorr and Eschman, *Geology of Michigan,* 159–68; and Curtis E. Larsen, "A Century of Great Lakes Levels Research: Finished or Just Beginning," in *Retrieving Michigan's Buried Past: The Archaeology of the Great Lakes State,* ed. John R. Halsey, Cranbrook Institute of Science, Bulletin no. 64 (Bloomfield Hills, Mich.: Cranbrook Institute of Science, 1999), 1–30.

20. Leverett, *Surface Geology,* 108.

21. The landforms described are based on those identified by Sommers, *Michigan, a Geography,* 58–61. See also Richard A. Santer, *Michigan: Heart of the Great Lakes* (Dubuque, Iowa: Kendall/Hunt, 1977), 94–96; and J. O. Veatch, *Soils and Land of Michigan* (East Lansing: Michigan State College Press, 1953), 14–16.

22. Sommers, *Michigan: A Geography,* 61, 69; Veatch, *Soils and Land,* 6–7.

23. Bert Hudgins, *Michigan: Geographic Backgrounds in the Development of the Commonwealth* (Detroit: By the author, 1961).

24. Charles M. Davis, "The Hydrographic Regions of Michigan," *Papers of the Michigan Academy of Science, Arts, and Letters* 16 (1932): 212–13; Santer, *Michigan,* 100.

25. Elton B. Hill and Russell G. Mawby, *Types of Farming in Michigan,* Agricultural Experiment Station, Special Bulletin no. 206 (East Lansing: Michigan State College, 1954), 68, 70–80. E. P. Whiteside, I. F. Schneider, and R. L. Cook, *Soils of Michigan,* Agricultural Experiment Station, Special Bulletin 402, (East Lansing: Michigan State University, 1959), 8; Sommers, *Michigan: A Geography,* 68–69.

26. Whiteside, Schneider, and Cook, *Soils of Michigan,* 41–42, 44, 51; Sommers, *Michigan: A Geography,* 69–70; Hill and Mawby, *Types of Farming,* 73–76, 80.

27. Dewey A. Seeley, "The Climate of Michigan and Its Relation to Agriculture" (Master's thesis, Michigan State College, 1917), 5; Jay R. Harman, "Environmental Significance of a Great Lakes Location," in *Michigan: A Geography,* by Lawrence M. Sommers (Boulder, Colo.: Westview Press, 1984), 71–72.

28. Eichenlaub, *Weather and Climate,* 36, 41–44.

29. Harman, "Environmental Significance," 75–76; Eichenlaub, *Weather and Climate,* 81–82, 131–37, 146–51.

30. Thomas E. Niedringhaus, "A Climatology of Michigan," Ph.D. diss., Michigan State University (Ann Arbor, Mich.: University Microfilms, 1966), 187–89.

31. Ibid., 193–96.

32. These climatic fluctuations are best documented in Europe. Wind circulation patterns are believed to be associated with climatic change, however, and similarities in these patterns over eastern North America and Europe suggest that the two continents have historically shared similar climates. This assumption has been corroborated by limited historical evidence. See Eichenlaub, *Weather and Climate,* 231–27; and R. C. Kedzie, "Soil, Productions, and Climate," in *Michigan and Its Resources,* comp. Frederick Morley (Lansing, Mich.: W. S. George and Co., 1881), 62.

33. Lee R. Dice, *The Biotic Provinces of North America* (Ann Arbor: University of Michigan Press, 1943), 3–6, 14–17; idem, "A Preliminary Classification of the Major Terrestrial Ecologic Communities of Michigan, Exclusive of Isle Royale," *Papers of the Michigan Academy of Science, Arts, and Letters* 16 (1932): 221–23, 225–27; J. O. Veatch, "The Dry Prairies of Michigan," *Papers of the Michigan Academy of Science, Arts, and*

Letters 8 (1927): 277–78; Harman, "Environmental Significance," 86–89; Tanner, *Atlas*, 14–15. Kimberley E. Medley and Jay R. Harman, "Relationships between the Vegetation Tension Zone and Soils Distribution across Central Lower Michigan," *Michigan Botanist* 26 (1987): 86; Veatch, *Soils and Land*.

34. Tanner, *Atlas*, 13.

35. The role of fire in the maintenance of open lands was demonstrated by Edgar Nelson Transeau, "The Prairie Peninsula," *Ecology* 16 (1935): 434, and investigated more recently by Michael Fleckenstein and Richard W. Pippen, "A Prairie Grove in Southwest Michigan," *Michigan Botanist* 16 (1977): 149. Pioneer observers noted the impact of Native peoples in maintaining open environments (see W. R. McCormick, "Sketch of Early Life in the Saginaw Valley," *MPHC* 4 [1883]: 365; Franklin Everett, *Memorials of the Grand River Valley* [Chicago: Chicago Legal News Co., 1878; reprint, Grand Rapids, Mich.: Grand Rapids Historical Society, 1984], 40; and Edward A. Foote, "Historical Sketch of the Early Days of Eaton County," *MPHC* 4 [1883]: 379), and remarked on the spatial extent of such tracts (see *Detroit Journal and Michigan Advertiser*, 9 November 1831; and Mary E. Shout, "Reminiscences of the First Settlement at Owosso," *MPHC* 30 [1905]: 346).

36. Hudgins, *Michigan*, 34; Seeley, "Climate of Michigan," 29–30.

37. Hill and Mawby, *Types of Farming*, 43–44, 72–73, 78–79.

38. Veatch, *Soils and Land*, 55–58.

39. Ibid., 57–58.

40. Hill and Mawby, *Types of Farming*, 25; Sommers, *Michigan: A Geography*, 131–33.

41. The rapid expansion of early landscape knowledge may be discerned from contemporary accounts. See, for example, Evans, *Pedestrious Tour*, 119; A. D. P. Van Buren, "Pioneer Annals: Containing the History of the Early Settlement of Battle Creek City and Township, with Vivid Sketches of Pioneer Life and Pen Portraits of the Early Settlers," *MPHC* 5 (1884): 238; and *Owosso Weekly Press*, 7 October 1885. As early as 1824 the trustees of the University of Michigan reported with pride that "The prospects of the Territory are greatly changed. The fertility of its soil, and the salubrity of its climate are no longer unknown." See Memorial to Congress, 30 July 1824/TPUS/MT/11:613.

42. *Detroit Gazette*, 13 November 1818; *Detroit Gazette*, 15 September 1820, 10 October 1821, 15 February 1822, 2 August 1822, 17 October 1823, 7 September 1821; *Emigrant*, 25 March 1831; S. C. Coffinberry, "Incidents Connected with the First Settlement of Nottawa-Sippi Prairie in St. Joseph County," *MPHC* 2 (1880): 490.

43. *Michigan Statesman and St. Joseph Chronicle*, 28 January 1834.

44. Willcox, *Shoepac Recollections*, 331; Wood, *Wilderness and the Rose*, 12–13, 17.

45. Memorial to Congress by Inhabitants of Macomb County, 7 November 1818/TPUS/MT/10:786. Thaddeus Smith to Elizabeth Smith, 14 June 1829/SBSFC/WMUARHC.

46. *History of Jackson County, Michigan* (Chicago: Inter-State Pub. Co., 1881), 194. For a similar statement, see Monroe *Michigan Sentinel*, 22 May 1830.

47. *Western Statesman*, 12 March 1840; Edward Parsons Diary, 26 May 1835/PaFP/MSUAHC.

48. Warren Chase, *The Life-Line of the Lone One; Or Autobiography of the World's Child* (Boston: Bela Marsh, 1857), 50; "Interesting Paper Concerning the Township of Unadilla, By James Craig, Read Before the Pioneer Society at the Courthouse, Howell, June 13, 1879," *Livingston Republican*, 13 June 1879; *Western Emigrant*, 12 November 1829; Edward Cook to Henry Waldron, 7 September 1837/HWP/MSUAHC.

49. MAL/R/1845/30:167–68. Lucy B. Jones to Laura Hall, 2 August 1846/HFL/MSUAHC; D. Landon to Hermon Landon, 15 February 1836, in *Stray Leaves from Pioneer Days*, comp. Mrs. Herman Landon Brown (Parma, Mich.: Parma News Printers, 1920): 17. The editor of the *Jackson Michigan State Gazette*, 8 April 1841, remarked that this noticeable change in image had taken place since the late 1820s.

50. *Detroit Gazette*, 29 January 1819, 18 July 1823; *Emigrant's Guide*, 167–68; Miller, *New States and Territories*, 24; Evans, *Pedestrious Tour*, 119; *Detroit Gazette*, 30 July 1819; Melish, *Information and Advice*

to Emigrants, 3–4; *Michigan Sentinel,* 14 October 1826; *Western Emigrant,* 12 November 1829; Thaddeus Smith to Elizabeth Smith, 14 June 1829/SBSFC/WMUARHC; Henry R. Schoolcraft, "Natural History . . . Extracts . . . Taken from a Lecture Delivered before the Detroit Lyceum," in *Historical and Scientific Sketches of Michigan* (Detroit: Stephen Well and George L. Whitney, 1834), 179–80.

51. James H. Lanman, *History of Michigan, from Its Earliest Colonization to the Present Time* (New York: Harper and Brothers, 1841), 18. The distribution of this and other perceived land types is based on information derived from J. O. Veatch, *Presettlement Forest in Michigan,* map on 2 sheets, 79 x 55 cm. and 56 x 79 cm., scale 1:500,000 (East Lansing: Department of Resource Development, Michigan State University, 1959); and P. J. Comer et al., *Michigan's Presettlement Vegetation, as Interpreted from the General Land Office Surveys, 1816–1856* (Lansing: Michigan Department of Natural Resources/Nature Conservancy, Michigan Natural Features Inventory, 1995). See also Peck, *New Guide for Emigrants,* 186; *Emigrant,* 25 May 1831; *The Western Traveller's Pocket Directory and Stranger's Guide; Exhibiting the Principal Distances on the Canal and Stage Routes in the States of New York and Ohio, in the Territory of Michigan, and the Province of Lower Canada, &c.* (Schenectady: S. S. Riggs, 1834), 52; and Blois, *Gazetteer,* 23–24.

52. Charles Lanman, *A Summer in the Wilderness; Embracing a Canoe Voyage Up the Mississippi and Around Lake Superior* (New York: D. Appleton and Co., 1847), 170; Lanman, *History of Michigan, from Its Earliest Colonization,* 18; Lanman, *History of Michigan, Civil and Topographical,* 251; *Emigrant,* 25 May 1831; *Niles Gazette and Advertiser,* 5 March 1836; *Western Emigrant,* 12 November 1829; Blois, *Gazetteer,* 24.

53. Hall, *Statistics of the West,* 102.

54. Lanman, *History of Michigan, Civil and Topographical,* 251, 254. See also W. J. Beal, "Pioneer Life in Southern Michigan in the Thirties," *MPHC* 32 (1902): 241–42; and Nicholas P. Hardeman, *Shucks, Shocks, and Hominy Blocks: Corn as a Way of Life in Pioneer America* (Baton Rouge: Louisiana State University Press, 1981), 53–56.

55. Lois Kimball Mathews, *The Expansion of New England: The Spread of New England Settlement and Institutions to the Mississippi River, 1620–1865* (Boston: Houghton-Mifflin Co., 1909), 288; Eugene Davenport, *Timberland Times* (Urbana: University of Illinois Press, 1950), 19–22.

56. The philosophical role of Transcendentalism in justifying expansion and the active conquest of the frontier environment, particularly that represented by the western forest, is discussed in Philip Durham and Everett L. Jones, eds., *The Frontier in American Literature* (New York: Odyssey Press, 1969), 30–31; and Hazard, *Frontier in American Literature,* 150–52.

57. Henry S. Sanford, Journal, 15 August 1844/HSSP/Box 3/GSML.

58. *Detroit Journal and Michigan Advertiser,* 13 April 1831.

59. Petition to Congress by Inhabitants of the Territory, 7 October 1825/TPUS/MT/11:706; Hoffman, *Winter in the West,* 1:156; *Detroit Gazette,* 2 August 1822; Lanman, *Summer in the Wilderness,* 170; Blois, *Gazetteer,* 24; Bernard C. Peters, "Pioneer Evaluation of the Kalamazoo County Landscape," *Michigan Academician* 3 (1970): 23.

60. *Calhoun County Patriot,* 13 November 1840; *Democratic Free Press and Michigan Intelligencer,* 22 September 1831; Peck, *New Guide for Emigrants,* 185; Lanman, *History of Michigan, Civil and Topographical,* 324; Blois, *Gazetteer,* 25; *Western Traveller's Pocket Directory,* 52; Douglas H. Gordon and George S. May, eds., "The Michigan Land Rush in 1836, Michigan Journal, 1836, John M. Gordon," *Michigan History* 43 (1959): 263; Cooper, *Oak-Openings,* 11.

61. Lanman, *History of Michigan, Civil and Topographical,* 254, 324; *Niles Gazette and Advertiser,* 5 March 1836; D. L. Porter to W. P. Porter, 1 November 1829/DLPP/CHL; *Western Traveller's Pocket Directory,* 53; Peck, *New Guide for Emigrants,* 19; Blois, *Gazetteer,* 418.

62. D. L. Porter to W. P. Porter, 1 November 1829/DLPP/CHL; *Jackson Michigan State Gazette,* 8 April 1841.

63. *Democratic Free Press and Michigan Intelligencer,* 22 September 1831; Timothy Dwight, *Travels; in New*

England and New York (New Haven, Conn.: T. Dwight, 1822), 4:63; Peters, "Changing Ideas," 20–21. Lands characterized by grasslands and scattered oak woodlands were also known as "barrens." See J. B. Killebrew, *Introduction to the Resources of Tennessee* (Nashville, Tenn.: Tavel, Eastman and Howell, 1874; reprint, Spartanburg, S.C.: Reprint Co., 1974), 112, 792; and Peck, *New Guide for Emigrants,* 185. A resident of New Buffalo in Berrien County, who had formerly lived on the frontier in Ohio, referred to such lands in Michigan as barrens in a letter to his son in New York. See Moses Chamberlain to Mellen Chamberlain, 3 March 1848/CFP/MSUAHC; Fuller, *Economic and Social Beginnings,* 257–58; and Harriet Martineau, "Harriet Martineau's Travels in and around Michigan, 1836," *Michigan History* 7 (1923): 60.

64. *Democratic Free Press and Michigan Intelligencer,* 6 October 1831; Martineau, "Travels in and around Michigan," 78; Fuller, *Economic and Social Beginnings,* 249–50, 311.

65. *Detroit Gazette,* 21 January 1820; Blois, *Gazetteer,* 25; Albert F. Butler, "Rediscovering Michigan's Prairies," *Michigan History* 31 (1947–48): 267–86; 32 (1948): 15–36; 33 (1948): 117–30, 220–31; Hall, *Statistics of the West,* 98–99; *Western Traveller's Pocket Directory,* 57. Henry S. Sanford, Journal, 14 August 1844/HSSP/Box 3/GSML; Lansing B. Swan, *Journal of a Trip to Michigan in 1841* (Rochester, N.Y.: George P. Humphrey, 1904), 30; Lanman, *Summer in the Wilderness,* 170; Martineau, "Travels in and around Michigan," 57–58.

66. *Calhoun County Patriot,* 18 November 1840; Blois, *Gazetteer,* 25–26; *Tecumseh News,* 17 July 1884.

67. The lakebed explanation appeared in the *Detroit Gazette,* January 21, 1820; *Michigan Farmer* 1849:124. Gordon and May, "Michigan Land Rush," 277 and Blois, *Gazetteer,* 25–26, both mention the role of fire in the creation of prairies. See also Bernard C. Peters, "Early American Impressions and Evaluations of the Landscape of Inner Michigan, with Emphasis on Kalamazoo County," Ph.D. diss., Michigan State University, 1962 (Ann Arbor, Mich.: University Microfilms, 1969), 124–26.

68. Peck, *New Guide for Emigrants,* 185; *Niles Gazette and Advertiser,* 5 March 1836; *Detroit Journal and Michigan Advertiser,* 24 November 1830; *Democratic Free Press and Michigan Intelligencer,* 6 October 1831. Corn and wheat yields are given by Lanman, *History of Michigan, Civil and Topographical,* 252; idem, *History of Michigan, from Its Earliest Colonization,* 21; Blois, *Gazetteer,* 25; *Michigan Sentinel,* 6 March 1830; and *Michigan Farmer* 1849:124. The adequacy of prairie soils for wheat is mentioned in Lanman, *Summer in the Wilderness,* 170; *Calhoun County Patriot,* 13 November 1840; *Democratic Free Press and Michigan Intelligencer,* 22 September 1831; and Lanman, *History of Michigan, Civil and Topographical,* 325. Peck, *New Guide for Emigrants,* 186; Blois, *Gazetteer,* 26; and Lanman, *History of Michigan, Civil and Topographical,* 252, commented on the use of wet prairies for pasture.

69. *Emigrant,* 25 May 1831; Hall, *Statistics of the West,* 102; Sarah Allen to J. A. Barney, 31 March 1839/SBSFC/WMUARHC; *Detroit Journal and Michigan Advertiser,* 24 November 1830; *Calhoun County Patriot,* 13 November 1840; Hall, *Statistics of the West,* 99. The relatively expeditious manner in which prairie lands could be prepared for cultivation led James Hall to advise, "A farmer had better settle in the midst of a prairie and haul his fuel and rail five miles, then to undertake to clear a farm in the forest" (103). Costs of clearing prairie land are found in *Democratic Free Press and Michigan Intelligencer,* 9 September 1831; *Emigrant,* 25 May 1831; Blois, *Gazetteer,* 25; and Lanman, *History of Michigan, Civil and Topographical,* 325.

70. Blois, *Gazetteer,* 26; Lanman, *History of Michigan, Civil and Topographical,* 325; idem, *History of Michigan, from Its Earliest Colonization,* 22.

71. Lanman, *History of Michigan, from Its Earliest Colonization,* 21.

72. *History of Jackson County,* 221–22.

73. Bela Hubbard, Notebook, 9 August 1842/BHP/Box 1/MHC; Blois, *Gazetteer,* 26. A Lenawee County contributor to the *Tecumseh News,* 17 July 1884, recalled how the "Big Prairie" in Ridgeway Township was

used extensively by early settlers as a source of hay for livestock. The same source also related how the same land, after draining, had produced cultivated grass, oats, wheat, and other crops.

74. Hoffman, *Winter in the West*, 1:126–27; Munnis Kenny, Diary, 29 July 1828/KFP/MHC.

75. Clarence Frost, "The Early Railroads of Southern Michigan," *MPHC* 38 (1912): 498.

76. Harman, "Environmental Significance," 85; Lawrence M. Sommers, "Economy," in *Atlas of Michigan*, ed. Lawrence M. Sommers (East Lansing: Michigan State University Press, 1977), 145; Joshua C. Goodrich Diary/20 May 1835/EHC/WMUARHC; Sec. Woodbridge to Sec. of War, 4 March 1819/TPUS/MT/10:818–21. Kaatz, "Black Swamp," 22–25.

77. Blois, *Gazetteer*, 23.

78. Truman B. Fox, *History of Saginaw County, from the Year 1819 Down to the Present Time* (East Saginaw, Mich.: Enterprise Print, 1858; reprint, Mt. Pleasant, Mich.: Central Michigan University Press, n.d.), 25; D. Bethune Duffield, "The Underdeveloped Regions and Resources of the State of Michigan, with Some Practical Suggestions in Reference to Their Early Occupancy and Development," in *Three Lectures Delivered before the Michigan State Agricultural Society at Its Annual Meeting at Lansing, January 17, 1865* (Lansing, Mich.: John A. Kerr, 1865), 10–11.

79. Ormond S. Danford, "The Social and Economic Effects of Lumbering on Michigan, 1835–1890," *Michigan History* 26 (1942): 348–49; Duffield, "Underdeveloped Regions and Resources," 10; J. R. White to Lucius Lyon, 20 May 1836/LACC/SAM.

80. Sidney Smith, *The Settler's New Home; or the Emigrant's Location, Being a Guide to Emigrants in the Selection of a Settlement, and the Preliminary Details of the Voyage* (London: John Kendrick, 1849), 27.

81. Jean M. Grove, *The Little Ice Age* (London: Methuen, 1988), 355. Michigan's remoteness, together with the unsystematic manner in which weather records for the United States as a whole were collected before 1871, has left extensive gaps in our knowledge of its antebellum climate. In Lower Michigan the earliest records date back only as far as 1830, and regular records were not kept before 1849. A discussion of early weather reporting in the United States appears in David M. Ludlam, *Early American Winters, 1604–1820* (Boston: American Meteorological Society, 1966), ix. A contemporary summary of antebellum meteorological records may be found in the pioneering work by Lorin Bloget, *Climatology of the United States, and the Temperate Latitudes of the North American Continent* (Philadelphia: J. P. Lippincott and Co., 1857), 48–49.

82. General temperature trends in the northern hemisphere between the 1770s and 1850 are revealed in two long series of observations taken at London and at Zwanenberg, in the Netherlands. A comparison of the average annual mean temperature of each decade to the average mean of the series (fig. 3.10) shows that temperatures declined sharply from the 1770s to the 1780s, followed by an amelioration in the 1790s and 1800s. The decade of the 1810s was cold again, followed by a warm-up in the 1820s, a slight cooling in the 1830s, and an even warmer period in the 1840s. This pattern of change is also seen in winter mean temperatures from other reporting stations in Europe, whose figures show periods of warm winters in the 1790s, 1800s, 1820s, and 1840s, with colder winters in the 1810s and 1830s. See Bloget, *Climatology of the United States*, 489–90; and Emmanuel Le Roy Ladurie, *Times of Feast, Times of Famine: A History of Climate Since the Year 1000*, trans. Barbara Bray (Garden City: N.Y.: Doubleday and Co., 1971), 83, 94. In North America, twenty years of cold weather closed the eighteenth century, followed by an amelioration after 1800. Cold summers characterized the next decade, particularly in 1812 and 1816. Observations in Maine indicate a generally cool period before 1820, with summer frosts occurring in 1800, 1807, 1816, and 1817. See Bloget, *Climatology of the United States*, 35, 146–47, 149; D. C. Smith et al., "Climatic Stress and Maine Agriculture, 1785–1885," in *Climate and History, Studies in Past Climates and Their Impact on Man*, ed. T. M. L. Wigley, M. J. Ingram, and G. Farmer (Cambridge: Cambridge University Press, 1981), 455–56; Joseph B. Hoyt, "The Cold Summer of 1816," *Annals of the Association of American Geographers*

48 (1958): 118–31; David M. Ludlam, *Early American Winters;* and idem, *Early American Winters II, 1821–1870* (Boston: American Meteorological Society, 1968).

83. M. W. Harrington, "Notes on the Climate of Detroit," *American Meteorological Journal* 2 (1885): 318.

84. Russell, *Long, Deep Furrow,* 274–75; Smith et al., "Climatic Stress," 456–57.

85. Thomas Jefferson proposed the notion of a warmer western climate in 1785, and Comte de Volney expanded it in 1804. They assumed that as one approached the summit of the Appalachians, the climate became progressively colder; however, upon descending toward the Mississippi, the opposite effect occurred, until western temperatures exceeded those on the Eastern Seaboard. This idea was formalized by Jefferson in *Notes on the State of Virginia,* ed. W. Peden (Chapel Hill: University of North Carolina Press, 1955), 75. See also Bloget, *Climatology of the United States,* 126; and Ludlam, *Early American Winters,* 232–233. This argument was particularly attractive to promoters of western immigration. So appealing was its promise for agriculture that allusions to warmer western climates appeared in immigration literature of the Mississippi Valley states well into the second half of the nineteenth century. Killebrew, *Resources of Tennessee,* 7, for example, attributed warmer temperatures in western Tennessee to this phenomenon.

86. *Emigrant's Guide,* 170; Evans, *Pedestrious Tour,* 119–20; *Detroit Gazette,* 29 January 1819, 30 July 1819; Warden, *Statistical, Political, and Historical Account,* 3:69; *Genesee Farmer* 3 (1833): 10; Mellen, *Book of the United States,* 143–46; Shirreff, *Tour Through North America,* 393; Lanman, *History of Michigan, Civil and Topographical,* 254; *Detroit Gazette,* 6 November 1830; Nathan Hoskins, *Notes Upon the Western Country, Contained Within the States of Ohio, Indiana, Illinois, and the Territory of Michigan; Taken on a Tour Through that Country in the Summer of 1832* (Greenfield, Mass.: J. P. Fogg, 1833), 22; Blois, *Gazetteer,* 116, 124; Samuel Augustus Mitchell, *A General View of the United States; Comprising, also, a Description of Each Individual State and Territory in the Union* (Philadelphia: By the author, 1846), 85; Smith, *Settler's New Home,* 91. The *Michigan Sentinel,* 29 December 1827, declared, "this country is far removed from the region of tempests; for here we have no storms, nor violent commotions of the elements."

87. *Atkinson's Casket,* "Views of the West, Michigan," 5 (1833): 223–24.

88. *Michigan Farmer,* 1850:244; Frederick B. Goddard, *Where to Emigrate, and Why* (New York: Frederick B. Goddard, 1869), 315.

89. *Atkinson's Casket,* "Michigan," 223; *Livingston Courier,* 6 September 1843; Goddard, *Where to Emigrate,* 315, 321; *Detroit Gazette,* 7 January 1820; *Michigan Sentinel,* 29 December 1827; Peck, *New Guide for Emigrants,* 63–64.

90. *Florida Star,* 15 January 1885.

91. *History of Saginaw County, Michigan* (Chicago: Chas. C. Chapman, 1881), 245; *Detroit Gazette,* 17 May 1825.

92. *Detroit Gazette,* 25 February 1825.

93. The Monroe newspaper observed that the winter "took many farmers and mechanics upon surprise; the former with a scanty supply of feed for their cattle—and the latter with . . . a moderate supply of wood for their fireplaces" (*Michigan Sentinel,* 5 May 1826). For reactions to the colder winters, see *Detroit Gazette,* 26 February 1826; and Lucius Lyon to William Lytle, 27 January 1831/TPUS/MT/12:248. The year was also accompanied by a severe frost in August, spoiling fall crops. See *History of Saginaw County,* 245; *Detroit Courier,* 8 December 1831. See also Ludlam, *Early American Winters II,* 146; Thomas Wright, Diary, 16 January 1832/TWD/MSUAHC; and *History of Jackson County,* 183.

94. *Democratic Free Press,* 12 December 1832; *Genesee Farmer* 1833:317; *Michigan Statesman,* 24 January 1835; *Democratic Free Press,* 23 July 1834, 18 April 1836, 26 April 1836/PaFP/MSUAHC; *History of Jackson County,* 208. Shortages of hay caused hardships for many pioneer farmers unprepared for the harsh winter. James Birney of Livingston County reported that cattle in Unadilla Township survived only because

farmers cut down trees to provide them with browse. See Robert Edward Stack, "The McCleers and the Birneys—Irish Immigrant Families—Into Michigan and the California Gold Fields, 1820–1893," Ph.D. diss., St. Louis University (Ann Arbor, Mich.: University Microfilms, 1972), 140–41.

95. A contributor to the *Kalamazoo Gazette*, 16 September 1837, advanced a theory that postulated the existence of warm and cold periods linked to "the relative position of the earth relative to the heavenly bodies." The rapid return to warmer winters, he felt, implied that Michigan was in a warm period. See Edward W. Barber, "Recollections and Lessons of Pioneer Boyhood," *MPHC* 31 (1902): 211.

96. Severe November storms wrecked at least eighteen ships on Lake Erie alone, and in Lower Michigan the ground was frozen from November to April and snow remained until the following month. See Ludlam, *Early American Winters II*, 153; *Livingston Courier*, 8 March 1843; *Adrian Daily Times and Expositor*, 20 November 1888; and Jacob Gerrish to Moses Chamberlain, 16 February 1843/CFP/MSUAHC. Like their counterparts six years earlier, farmers, such as Edward Barber of Vermontville and a man named Wells of Oakland County, resorted to cutting trees for cattle feed. See *Livingston Courier*, 8 March 1843; Barber, "Recollections and Lessons," 214; "Life of William Fulton," p. 16/SHPF/MSUAHC; and *Adrian Daily Times and Expositor*, 20 November 1888.

97. Ludlam, *Early American Winters*, 233; Idem, *Early American Winters II*, 155.

98. Henry S. Sanford, Journal, 15 August 1844/HSSP/Box 3/GSML.

99. Carried to North America by infected European and African populations in the seventeenth century, malaria became established early on the Eastern Seaboard. From there it spread westward, presumably along the Gulf Coast and into the Mississippi Valley, as well as overland across the Appalachian divide. See E. C. Faust, "Clinical and Public Health Aspects of Malaria in the United States from an Historical Perspective," *American Journal of Tropical Medicine* 25 (1945): 186; and David Charles Nutter, "Malaria in Michigan," (Master's thesis, Michigan State University, 1988), 14–17. General Anthony Wayne established the American occupation at Detroit in the midst of a malaria outbreak in the summer of 1796 and, together with many of his troops, suffered from the disease. See Warden, *Statistical, Political, and Historical Account*, 3:76; and *Detroit Gazette*, 10 September 1819, 7 September 1824.

100. Victims of malaria attacks characteristically exhibit chills, a rapid rise in temperature, headaches and myalgia, and diffuse sweating. See Nutter, "Malaria in Michigan," 9; and Davenport, *Timberland Times*, 149. The contemporary attitude toward the disease was reflected by a resident who informed Charles Fenno Hoffman that as a factor "in the general health of the country, [malaria] was hardly to be considered." See Hoffman, *Winter in the West*, 1:153. See also *Democratic Free Press*, 22 May 1833. When, for example, the central character of *Theophilus Trent* acquired the symptoms of the disease and felt that he was "near death," he was given assistance by strangers who countered his grave concerns with the reply, "Why, you've got the ague,—fever and ague—, that's all!" (Taylor, *Theophilus Trent*, 240). The effects of malaria were recounted in M. A. Leeson, *History of Macomb County, Michigan* (Chicago: M. A. Leeson, 1882), 279–80.

101. Henry Chamberlain to Amos Chamberlain, 18 March 1845/CFP/MSUAHC; Davenport, *Timberland Times*, 149. The infrequent mention in pioneer accounts of the employment of drugs to effect a cure implies that they were not used extensively in the antebellum West. Malaria was one of the few maladies known to be treatable with drugs, and the effectiveness of quinine, made from cinchona bark, was widely understood by the contemporary medical community. Nevertheless, its use as a treatment for malaria was not universal, nor were its limits in treating other diseases well understood. These factors, together with misperceptions regarding the seriousness of the illness, are likely to have affected the extent of the drug's use in treating malaria, especially on the western frontier, where supplies of quinine were less than adequate. James H. Cassedy, *Medicine and American Growth, 1800–1860* (Madison: University of Wisconsin Press, 1986), 23n. 33; Jack Larkin, *The Reshaping of Everyday Life, 1790–1840* (New York: Harper and Row, 1988), 90.

102. Shirreff, *Tour through North America,* 345–46; Smith, *Settler's New Home,* 91; Hoffman, *Winter in the West,* 1:193, 194; *Western Statesman,* 21 November 1839; *Detroit Journal and Michigan Advertiser,* 25 May 1831. Among those who commented on this phenomenon were Nancy Bagg of Marengo Township in Calhoun County, to John L. Powell, 25 March 1835/PFP/MSUAHC; Henry F. Lyster, "The State with Reference to Malarial Diseases," in *Michigan and Its Resources,* ed. Frederick Morley (Lansing, Mich.: W. S. George, 1881), 70–71; and Nutter, "Malaria in Michigan," 4. The association of diseases with the occurrence of certain climatological conditions was a widespread belief in antebellum scientific circles; however, the causes of malaria were generally attributed to germs that circulated in the air and water and whose multiplication was governed by topographical, hydrographical, and meteorological conditions. Cassedy, *Medicine and American Growth,* 49–51.

103. Blois, *Gazetteer,* 125; *The Democratic Free Press,* 11 October 1832, observed that the healthiness of the St. Joseph country was attributed to the fact that the river did not overflow its banks. D. L. Porter to W. P. Porter, 1 November 1829/DLPP/CHL; *Democratic Expounder and Calhoun County Democrat,* 9 September 1841. Antebellum scientific opinion associated the occurrence of malaria with topographic features that produced standing water. As a result, land drainage was promoted generally as a practical step toward improving health. Cassedy, *Medicine and American Growth,* 36–37; *Western Statesman,* 21 November 1839; *Michigan Statesman,* 24 January 1835; L. H. Powers to George Smith, 7 December 1835/GNSP/MSUAHC; Erwin H. Ackerknecht, "Diseases in the Middle West," in *Essays in the History of Medicine in Honor of David J. Davis, M.D., Ph.D.* (Chicago: University of Illinois Press for the Davis Lecture Committee, 1965), 169–71.

104. Warden, *Statistical, Political, and Historical Account of the United States,* 3:76; Blois, *Gazetteer,* 126–27; Earl E. Kleinschmidt, "Prevailing Diseases and Hygienic Conditions in Early Michigan," *Michigan History* 25 (1941): 58–59.

105. *Detroit Gazette,* 17 May 1825; 30 May 1826; 6 August 1829; *Oakland Chronicle,* 12 November 1830; *Grand River Times,* 28 April 1852; Kleinschmidt, "Diseases and Hygienic Conditions," 69; Dunbar, *Michigan,* 210; *Detroit Journal and Michigan Advertiser,* 1 August 1832; Fuller, *Economic and Social Beginnings,* 137. Cholera was not the only epidemic to strike frontier Michigan. Ackerknecht, "Diseases in the Middle West," 172–75, notes that epidemics of erysipelas in the 1830s and typhoid in the 1840s were particularly devastating. See also Thomas Wright, Diary, 16 January 1832/TWD/MSUAHC; Moses Chamberlain to Hale E. Crosby, 4 February 1844/CFP/MSUAHC); Andrew Huggins, "History of the Epidemic of 1848 in Shiawassee County," *MPHC* 28 (1897–98), 506–11; and James L. Scott, *Journal of a Missionary Tour through Pennsylvania, Ohio, Indiana, Illinois, Iowa, Wiskonsin, and Michigan* (Providence, R.I.: By the author, 1843), 192. One immigrant family, recently arrived from England, barely survived an unidentified epidemic that carried off three of the children and left the mother critically ill. See Charles E. Weller, *Yesterday, a Chronicle of Early Life in the West* (Indianapolis: Cornelius Printing Co., 1921), 13–14.

106. At the close of the second epidemic, a White Pigeon newspaper reported that in spite of the prevalence of "much sickness . . . during the present season; . . . we are able to state that our citizens have mostly resumed their usual good health." *Michigan Statesman and St. Joseph Chronicle,* 25 October 1834; Fuller, *Economic and Social Beginnings,* 271, 357.

107. *Detroit Gazette,* 8 November 1825; D. L. Porter to W. P. Porter, 2 May 1830/DLPP/CHL. MTL/1827/2:30.

108. Warden, *Statistical, Political, and Historical Account,* 3:76–77; *Detroit Gazette,* 16 November 1821, 23 November 1821, 22 February 1822; J. L. Cole, "J. L. Cole's Journal of a Pedestrian Tour from Detroit to Sagana River in 1822," *MPHC* 2 (1880): 473; *Western Traveller's Pocket Directory,* 78–84. These maps are discussed in detail in a later chapter.

109. Recognizing the importance of aboriginal trails to the success of agricultural settlements, one influential guidebook carefully mentioned such routes leading to potential settlement sites on the lower Grand River. See *Western Traveller's Pocket Directory*, 82–84; *History of Jackson County*, 168.

110. Hardeman, *Shucks, Shocks, and Hominy Blocks*, 58; and H. Roy Merrens, "The Physical Environment of Early America: Image and Image Makers in Colonial South Carolina," *Geographical Review* 59 (1969): 553–54 discuss the importance of old fields to pioneer agriculture generally. See also Shout, "First Settlement at Owosso," 346. Visiting the site of Grand Rapids in 1837, John M. Gordon observed that the entire bluff directly across the Grand River appeared "once to have been in cultivation." Gordan and May, "Michigan Land Rush," 456. Bela Hubbard, traveling along the Shiawassee River a year later, noted that, "Many of the Indian clearings stretched for several continuous miles, and many acres bordering the river were covered with luxuriant maize, . . ." Hubbard, *Memorials*, 70. See also Foote, "Early Days of Eaton County," 397. Pioneer recognition of aboriginal corn hills is noted in David Scott, "Early History of Clinton County, Michigan," *MPHC* 17 (1890): 413; Edward W. Barber, "Beginnings in Eaton County: Its Earliest Settlements and Settlers," *MPHC* 28 (1899–1900): 347; and Samuel W. Durant, *History of Kalamazoo County, Michigan* (Philadelphia: Evarts and Abbot, 1880), 409.

111. McCormick, "Early Life in the Saginaw Valley," 365; Daniel B. Harrington, "Daniel B. Harrington," *MPHC* 5 (1884): 140; Sherman Stevens, "Sketch of Early Pioneer Life," *MPHC* 7 (1886): 94; William M. Carr, "Settlement of Williamstown—Pioneer Life," *MPHC* 18 (1891): 448; Barber, "Beginnings in Eaton County," 366. The placement of pioneer settlements near old fields is mentioned in Barber, "Beginnings in Eaton County," 347; *History of Jackson County*, 177; Foote, "Early Days of Eaton County," 391–92; John Ball, "Physical Geography of Kent County," *MPHC* 1 (1877): 216; "The City of Ionia: Its First Settlement and Early History," *MPHC* 3 (1881): 470; and Everett, *Memorials*, 40.

112. Durant, *History of Kalamazoo County*, 67–70; Foote, "Early Days of Eaton County," 379; Bissell, "Early Settlement of Mt. Clemens," 464; Scott, "Early History of Clinton County," 413; *Detroit Gazette*, 15 February 1822; Barber, "Beginnings in Eaton County," 347. Attributing prehistoric structural remains to "lost races" was not unique to Michigan's early residents. This interpretation arose from a wider debate among scholars, speculators, and others interested in investigating America's ancient past. During the antebellum period, the quest to explain these relics centered round the "Moundbuilder question," a controversy that surrounded the origin of prehistoric North American earthworks. Most observers saw no link between these structures and contemporary Indian societies, and instead attributed them to known early civilizations in the Old World or the Americas, or to "lost" civilizations, such as Atlantis. For discussions of the Moundbuilder question and its role in the development of American prehistory, see Robert Silverberg, *Mound Builders of Ancient America: The Archaeology of a Myth* (Greenwich, Conn.: New York Graphic Society, 1968); Gordon R. Willey and Jeremy A. Sabloff, *A History of American Archaeology* (San Francisco: W. H. Freeman, 1974), 30–36; and Stephen Williams, *Fantastic Archaeology: The Wild Side of American Prehistory* (Philadelphia: University of Pennsylvania Press, 1991), 39–57.

113. John S. Schenck, *History of Ionia and Montcalm Counties, Michigan* (Philadelphia: D. W. Ensign, 1881), 30; Memorial to Congress by Citizens of the Territory, 3 October 1832/TPUS/MT/12:529; *Detroit Journal and Michigan Advertiser*, 9 November 1831; SLUS/1843/5:624–25.

CHAPTER 4

1. Darby, *Tour*, 198–200. Williams, "Life of Oliver Williams," 38–39; *Detroit Gazette*, 13 November 1818.
2. *Detroit Gazette*, 26 February 1819, 23 May 1826, 30 May 1826.

3. O'Shea Wilder, Diary, 18 November 1831/MHC; *Detroit Journal and Michigan Advertiser,* 11 May 1831; William Nowlin, *The Bark Covered House, or Back in the Woods Again; Being a Graphic and Thrilling Description of Real Pioneer Life in the Wilderness of Michigan* (Detroit: By the author, 1876; reprint, Chicago: R. R. Donnelley & Sons, 1937), 37.

4. *Detroit Gazette,* 15 February 1822, 1 March 1822; *Macomb Statesman,* 22 September 1837; *Detroit Gazette,* 1 March 1822; Lanman, *History of Michigan, Civil and Topographical,* 284; *Detroit Journal and Michigan Advertiser,* 4 May 1831.

5. Sec. of the Treasury to Christopher Rankin, 3 April 1822/TPUS/MT/11:232–33; *Michigan Sentinel,* 16 August 1834; Wing, "History of Monroe," 381; "Copy of a Letter from a Gentleman in the Michigan Territory to His Friend in Connecticut, Dated Oct. 1, 1823," *MPHC* 7 (1886): 75.

6. *Detroit Gazette,* 12 October 1821; *Michigan Sentinel,* 20 May 1826; Memorial to Congress by Inhabitants of Part of the Southern Land District, 11 January 1831/TPUS/MT/12:236; *Detroit Gazette,* 4 August 1820, 28 June 1822, 2 August 1822, 17 October 1823; *Michigan Sentinel,* 20 March 1830. Later observations may be found in Lanman, *History of Michigan, Civil and Topographical,* 283.

7. *Detroit Gazette,* 27 May 1825; E. M. Chandler to Jane Howell, 13 December 1830/EMCP/Box 1/MHC; E. M. Chandler to Jane Howell, 2 September 1833/EMCP/Box 1/MHC; Elizabeth Chandler to Jane Howell, 15 April 1831/EMCP/Box 1/MHC; Bela Hubbard, Notebook, 29 June 1839/BHP/Box 1/MHC; *Michigan Farmer,* 1849:259.

8. *Western Emigrant,* 12 November 1829.

9. Thomas Andrews to Mary Andrews, 27 July 1833/TAL/CHL.

10. *Western Emigrant,* 27 January 1830; Joshua C. Goodrich Diary, 19 May 1835/EHC/WMUARHC.

11. *Detroit Gazette,* 16 November 1821, 22 February 1822, 1 March 1822.

12. Josiah Orvis to Jacob Hooper, 11 May 1838/MHC; Petition to Congress by Inhabitants of the Territory, 7 October 1825/TPUS/MT/11:706–7; *Detroit Journal and Michigan Advertiser,* 9 November 1831; *Michigan Farmer* 1850:285.

13. *Detroit Gazette,* 22 February 1822, 1 March 1822; Cole, "J. L. Cole's Journal," 470–73. B. Frank Emery, "Fort Saginaw," *Michigan History* 30 (1946): 487–88; Fox, *History of Saginaw County,* 6–7; J. L. Whiting, "Pioneer Sketch Relative to the Military Occupation of the Saginaw Valley, and Other Reminiscences," *MPHC* 2 (1880): 460–61.

14. William Brookfield to Rev. Gabriel Richard, 3 March 1824/TPUS/MT/11:529; Robert Clark to Micajah T. Williams, 21 June 1831/TPUS/MT/12:300–301; Hervey Parke to Micajah T. Williams, 14 July 1831/TPUS/MT/12:309; Hervey Parke to Robert T. Lytle, 11 November 1835/TPUS/MT/12:1011. Fox, *History of Saginaw County,* 7; Robert Clark Jr. to Micajah T. Williams, 28 July 1831/TPUS/MT/12:313–15.

15. Letter from 'Emigrant,' *Oakland Chronicle,* 30 September 1830; Fox, *History of Saginaw County,* 11; Lew Allen Chase, *Rural Michigan* (New York: Macmillan, 1922), 45; *Detroit Journal and Michigan Advertiser,* 25 May 1831; Lanman, *History of Michigan, Civil and Topographical,* 292; Blois, *Gazetteer,* 238.

16. Leslie A. Kenoyer, "Forest Distribution in Southwestern Michigan as Interpreted from the Original Land Survey (1826–32)," *Papers of the Michigan Academy of Science, Arts, and Letters* 11 (1934): 107; Lawrence G. Brewer, Thomas W. Hodler, and Henry A Raup, "Presettlement Vegetation of Southwestern Michigan," *Michigan Botanist* 23 (1984): 153; Comer et al., *Michigan's Presettlement Vegetation;* Knox Jamison, "The Survey of the Public Lands in Michigan," *Michigan History* 42 (1958): 204.

17. Joshua C. Goodrich, Diary, 22 May 1835/EHC/WMUARHC; Charles J. Lanman and Robert Clark to George Graham, 7 December 1827/TPUS/MT/11:1136; *Michigan Sentinel,* 4 September 1830; *Genesee Farmer,* 1833:316.

18. Robert Clark and Charles J. Lanman to George Graham, 15 January 1828/TPUS/MT/11:1155; Joshua C. Goodrich, Diary, 24 May 1835/EHC/WMUARHC.

19. *Democratic Free Press and Michigan Intelligencer,* 11 October 1832; Jacob Gerrish to Moses Chamberlain, 6 July 1840/CFP/MSUAHC; Peters, *Early American Impressions,* 82–84.

20. *Democratic Free Press and Michigan Intelligencer,* 11 October 1832; *Detroit Gazette,* 20 October 1828; Peters, "Early American Impressions," 88–90.

21. Gordon and May, "Michigan Land Rush," 277; Joshua C. Goodrich, Diary, 24 May 1835/EHC/WMUARHC; *Emigrant,* 25 May 1831. The perception of fertility derived from the soil's appearance and consistency. Comparing prairie soils with the "gravelly loams" of the oak openings, a Calhoun County farmer told traveler Charles Fenno Hoffman that the former were, "four feet deep, and so fat it will grease your fingers." *Winter in the West,* 1:184, 187–88, 216; Lanman, *History of Michigan, Civil and Topographical,* 286; *Detroit Journal and Michigan Advertiser,* 15 January 1831.

22. Jamison, "Survey of the Public Lands in Michigan," 204.

23. Kenoyer, "Forest Distribution," 109; Brewer, Hodler, and Raup, "Presettlement Vegetation," 155.

24. *Jackson Sentinel,* 19 January 1839; Joshua C. Goodrich, Diary, 29 May 1835/EHC/WMUARHC; Betsey Landon to Thomas Cranson, 2 May 1836, in Brown, *Stray Leaves,* 24; *Democratic Free Press and Michigan Intelligencer,* 11 October 1832; Lanman, *History of Michigan, Civil and Topographical,* 287; Blois, *Gazetteer,* 225.

25. W. H. Perrine, "Notes on the Settlement of Townships in Calhoun County," *MPHC* 2 (1880): 244; *Jackson Sentinel,* 19 June 1839; Lucius Lyon to William Lytle, 27 January 1831/TPUS/MT/12:249. Although Deputy Surveyor Calvin Britain noted succinctly that, "The district [in western Allegan County] is know[n] to be one of the worst description from the multiplicity of its swamps as well as the thickness of the timber and undergrowth which everywhere abound," the editor of the *Michigan Farmer* emphasized that "the timber has not the dense growth of that around Detroit, possessing more nearly the character of the 'beech and maple land' of the Eastern states, with a rolling surface and gravelly soils, abounding in springs and streams." Calvin Britain to William Lytle, 18 May 1831/TPUS/MT/12:289; *Michigan Farmer* 1849:354.

26. Kenoyer, "Forest Distribution," 109; Lucius Lyon to William Lytle, 27 January 1831/TPUS/MT/12:249; G. A. Morgan, "Township of Pine Plains—A Historical Sketch," *MPHC* 3 (1881): 293–94.

27. Memorial to Congress by the Legislative Council, 10 February 1831/TPUS/MT/12:254; John Biddle to Edward Tiffin, 30 June 1826/TPUS/MT/11:983.

28. *Detroit Journal and Michigan Advertiser,* 9 November 1831; *Democratic Free Press,* 16 May 1838; *Grand River Times,* 14 May 1856; Harriet Munro Longyear, "The Settlement of Clinton County," *MPHC* 39 (1915): 360. The forest soils varied from sandy to clayey in composition, although both were seen as equally adaptable to the production of commercial crops, especially wheat. The principal distinction between them, according to two contemporary Ionia County observers, lay in the immediate fertility of the former versus the durability of the latter. W. Janes to Frederick Hall, 1 June 1848/HFL/MSUAHC; Myron Tupper to Edward Merrill, 10 April 1846/HHCP/Box 1/MHC; John L. Powell to Joseph R. Powell, 19 October 1846/PFP/MSUAHC; *Democratic Free Press,* 18 October 1837;

29. Foote, "Early Days of Eaton County," 386; *Grand River Times,* 14 May 1856. The *Democratic Free Press,* 5 May 1838, quoting a local source, described these timbered lands as

> one of the finest tracts of farming land that we have anywhere seen, [and that], as a whole, ... no section of the state presents stronger inducements to the agriculturalist. ... Although it has not the inviting prairies of the southern section of the state, its rich and durable soil, its freedom from marshes and ponds, and the thousand clear and rapid brooklets that everywhere meet the observer's eye, give at least equal advantage.

30. Petition to Congress by Inhabitants of Washtenaw County, 20 December 1825/TPUS/MT/11:835; Petition to Congress by Inhabitants of the Territory, 30 January 1826/TPUS/MT/11:938; Munnis Kenny, Diary, 5 August 1828/KFP/MHC; J. Seymour to Sidney S. Allcott, 5 April 1837/AFC/MSUAHC.

31. French and British posts were situated near the mouths of the St. Joseph, Kalamazoo, and Grand Rivers. See Quaife, *Lake Michigan,* 52–59; Johnson, *Michigan Fur Trade,* 61–63; and Clifton, *Pokagons,* 21. By the close of the War of 1812 the Western Shore had "been very generally explored and . . . delimited with considerable correctness." Prior to 1820, a United States military survey of the area mapped the locations of all rivers flowing into Lake Michigan and evaluated their suitability as harbors. See *Detroit Gazette,* 4 December 1819; 7 January 1820.

32. *Detroit Journal and Michigan Advertiser,* 24 November 1830; *Atkinson's Casket,* "Michigan," 223; H. S. Tanner, *The American Traveller: Or Guide through the United States* (Philadelphia: By the author, 1836), 64.

33. This variety of forest vegetation ranged from beech-maple forest in the entisol soils of the south to a mixed beech-maple-white pine forest stretching northward from Van Buren County on spodosol soils. Interspersed among these were areas of white pine growth, usually associated with patches of wetter histosol soils. See J. O. Veatch, "Reconstruction of Forest Cover Based on Soil Maps," *Michigan Quarterly Bulletin* 10 (1928): 119; Brewer, Hodler, and Raup, "Presettlement Vegetation," 155; Comer et al., *Michigan's Presettlement Vegetation;* Calvin Britain to William Lytle, 3 January 1831/TPUS/MT/12:229; Everett, *Memorials,* 495, 498; *Three Oaks Press,* 28 April 1899; *Atkinson's Casket,* "Michigan," 223; and G. Van Schelven, "Early History of Holland," *MPHC* 26 (1894–95): 570–71.

34. Everett, *Memorials,* 458; Jamison, "Survey of the Public Lands in Michigan," 205. *Grand River Times,* 12 March 1856, 21 May 1856; *Michigan Farmer* 1853:172; Duffield, "Underdeveloped Regions and Resources," 14.

CHAPTER 5

1. Dwight L. Smith, "The Land Cession: A Valid Instrument of Transfer of Indian Title," in *This Land Is Ours: The Acquisition and Disposition of the Public Domain* (Indianapolis: Indiana Historical Society, 1978), 88–89; TPUS/NWT/2:39–49; Willard W. Cochrane, *The Development of American Agriculture: An Historical Analysis* (Minneapolis: University of Minnesota Press, 1979), 39; Roy M. Robbins, *Our Landed Heritage: The Public Domain, 1776–1970* (Lincoln: University of Nebraska Press, 1976), 5. American territorial claims to the region were reiterated in early American legislation, particularly the Northwest Ordinance of 1787. See Bernard W. Sheehan, "The Northwest Ordinance: An Annotated Text, Article the Third," in *The Northwest Ordinance, 1787: A Bicentennial Handbook,* ed. Robert M. Taylor Jr. (Indianapolis: Indiana Historical Society, 1987), 62–63.

2. For discussion of the change in antebellum Indian policy, see Prucha, *The Great Father,* 64–77; and Sheehan, *Seeds of Extinction,* chap. 9.

3. Henry R. Schoolcraft, *History of the Indian Tribes of the United States: Their Present Condition and Prospects, and a Sketch of Their Ancient Status* (Philadelphia: J. B. Lippincott and Co., 1857), 406–7.

4. Robbins, *Our Landed Heritage,* 21–22, 50–54.

5. Evans, *Pedestrious Tour,* 128; Lanman, *History of Michigan, Civil and Topographical,* 311; Everett, *Memorials,* 273, 279; Greenman, "Indians of Michigan," *Michigan History* 45 (1961): 1–33; Tanner, *Atlas,* 100–3, map 98–99; see also maps in Clifton, *Pokagons,* 70, for Potawatomi villages, McClurken, "We Wish To Be Civilized," xi, for Ottawa villages, and Montfort, "Ethnic and Tribal Identity," 50, 59, for Saginaw-Chippewa villages.

6. McClurken, "We Wish To Be Civilized," 23–25; Montfort, "Ethnic and Tribal Identity," 22. Clans represented perhaps the most complex corporate units found among Michigan's Native peoples. As unilineal descent groups tracing ancestry to a fictitious totemic ancestor, clans formed a basis for social integration and political solidarity as well as a mechanism for expansion. Although clans were well developed among the Potawatomis when they expanded out of Wisconsin in the 1670s, their existence among the Ottawas and Saginaw-Chippewas and their role in structuring community relations and promoting tribal solidarity in these groups is uncertain. See Clifton, *Pokagons*, 4–5, 8–13; Montfort, "Ethnic and Tribal Identity," 21–22; McClurken, "We Wish To Be Civilized," 25–27; and Charles E. Cleland, *Rites of Conquest: The History and Culture of Michigan's Native Americans* (Ann Arbor: University of Michigan Press, 1992), 102–3.

7. Stephen Cornell, "The Transformation of Tribe: Organization and Self-Concept in Native American Ethnicities," *Ethnic and Racial Studies* 11 (1988): 32.

8. SLUS/1795/7:49–54.

9. James A. Clifton, *The Prairie People: Continuity and Change in Potawatomi Indian Culture, 1665–1965* (Lawrence: Regents Press of Kansas, 1977), 151; Smith, "Land Cession," 96–97.

10. These ceded lands included that portion of the Lower Peninsula lying east of a line drawn from the junction of the Auglaize and Miami Rivers northward to the latitude of the outlet of Lake Huron and then northeastward to intersect the shoreline of that lake. See SLUS/1807/7:105–7; Gilpin, *Territory of Michigan*, 40; and Montfort, "Ethnic and Tribal Identity," 54.

    The American policy of forced acculturation rested on the belief that the Indian was a "noble savage," whose way of life was formed by a submersion in nature. It presupposed that environment was the primary force in shaping culture and that aboriginal practices could be altered in a desired direction if the Native peoples were exposed to different circumstances. Americans felt that confining Indians to reservations would provide a new environment that would civilize them, so that they might be incorporated into the society of European America. The inherently disruptive effects of this process on Native societies led to its ultimate failure, however, and the federal government subsequently turned to removal as a means of dealing with aboriginal peoples, a policy that only delayed the ultimate consequences of expansion through enforced separation of Indians and colonists. For a more complete discussion of antebellum Indian policy and its philosophical roots, see Sheehan, *Seeds of Extinction*, chaps. 4–6; Prucha, *The Great Father*, 229; and Gilpin, *Territory of Michigan*, 127–28. The treaties eliminating the southern reservations were signed at Chicago (SLUS/1833/7:442–48) and Washington (SLUS/1836/7: 491–97). See also McClurken, "We Wish to Be Civilized," 283–85; Clifton, *Pokagons*, 38–41; and Tanner, *Atlas*, 163–66.

11. Gov. Hull to Sec. of War, 25 April 1811/TPUS/MT/10:355.

12. The eastern shore of Michigan had recently been a theater of a war that had witnessed well-known American defeats at the River Raisin and Detroit. In the popular imagination it was a scene of recent tragedies and home to an Indian foe who, abetted by British allies, had participated enthusiastically in military actions against American forces as well as in harassing civilians living in occupied areas. See Act. Gov. Woodbridge to Sec. of War, 8 May 1815/TPUS/MT/10:536–37; Gov. Cass to Act. Sec. of War, 7 July 1815/TPUS/MT/10:563. Gov. Cass to Sec. of War, 30 July 1816/TPUS/MT/10:661; and Gov. Cass to Sec. of War, 3 August 1819/TPUS/MT/10:853. See also John E. Day, "Sketches and Incidents Concerning the Settlement of Macomb County," *MPHC* 4 (1881): 313; and Bissell, "Early Settlement of Mt. Clemens," 463.

13. Gov. Cass to Sec. of War, 6 January 1819/TPUS/MT/10:808. Gov. Cass to Sec. of War, 27 May 1819/TPUS/ MT/10:827–28; Gov. Cass to Sec. of War, 6 January 1819/TPUS/MT/10:808; SLUS/1819/7:203–6; Tanner, *Atlas*, 133.

14. Gov. Cass to Sec. of War, 25 April 1822/TPUS/MT/11: 236–237; Emery, "Fort Saginaw," 502; Johnson, *Michigan Fur Trade,* 137–38; William H. Sweet, "Brief History of Saginaw County," *MPHC* 28 (1897–98): 486–87.

15. Johnson, *Michigan Fur Trade,* 150.

16. The locations of the 1819 Treaty reservations are illustrated in Montfort, "Ethnic and Tribal Identity," 50, and the failure of the agricultural programs is discussed in ibid., 75–76.

17. Ibid., 74. SLUS/1837/7:528–32; SLUS/1836/7:503–4; Tanner, *Atlas,* 164–65, map 31, 174; Dunbar, *Michigan,* 181–82.

18. SLUS/1818/7:180; SLUS/1827/7:305; SLUS/1842/11:581–85; Greenman, "Indians of Michigan," 28; Tanner, *Atlas,* 164–65, map 31.

19. HR/1826/42. So intimidating was their presence initially that one newspaper editor declared, "there is no portion of the frontier of the United States, which so loudly demands from the government the immediate establishment of a permanent defense as this" (*Detroit Gazette,* 27 June 1823). See also *History of Washtenaw County,* 452; Beal, "Pioneer Life in Southern Michigan," 237. Perrine, "Townships in Calhoun County," 209–10; Coffinberry, "Settlement of Nottawa-Sippi Prairie," 499–500; and Thomas Andrews to Mary Andrews, 27 July 1833/TAL/CHL.

20. Sessions, "Ann Arbor," 335; Barber, "Vermontville Colony," 227; Melville McGee, "The Early Days of Concord, Jackson County, Michigan," *MPHC* 21 (1892): 425; *Portrait and Biographical Album of Kalamazoo, Allegan, and Van Buren Counties, Michigan* (Chicago: Chapman Bros., 1892), 1079.

21. SLUS/1817/7:160–70; SLUS/1821/7:218–21; SLUS/1827/7:305–6; SLUS/1828/7:399.

22. SLUS/1832/7:399–400; SLUS/1833/7:442–48. SLUS/1830/4:411–12.

23. The Potawatomis' acceptance of the educational programs of the Baptist mission, organized west of Niles in 1820, reinforced the perception that these Native peoples were not opposed to emulating American culture. In addition, they agreed to and participated in educational programs provided by the various cession treaties, schemes intended largely to convert Indians into Christian farmers. Knowledge gained by the Potawatomis as a result of these experiences later proved useful to bands seeking to retain possession of their lands in the face of mounting pressure for removal. See Clifton, *Pokagons,* 17–19, 49; and Damon A. Winslow, "Early History of Berrien County," *MPHC* 1 (1877): 121.

24. Clifton, *Pokagons,* 69–71; Susan Sleeper-Smith, *Native Women and French Men: Rethinking Cultural Encounter in the Western Great Lakes* (Amherst: University of Massachusetts Press, forthcoming), 362–63.

25. Everett, *Memorials,* 35; *City of Grand Rapids and Kent County, Michigan, Up to Date, Containing Biographical Sketches of Prominent and Representative Citizens* (Logansport, Ind.: Bowen, 1900), 575; Longyear, "Settlement of Clinton County," 364.

26. SLUS/1836/7:491–97; Gilpin, *Territory of Michigan,* 170. James M. McClurken, "Ottawa Adaptive Strategies to Indian Removal," *Michigan Historical Review* 12 (1986): 36, 46–47; idem, "We Wish To Be Civilized," 193, 343–46.

27. Gordon and May, "Michigan Land Rush," 465–66; McClurken, "Ottawa Adaptive Strategies," 46–47; Susan E. Gray, "Limits and Possibilities: White-Indian Relations in Western Michigan in the Era of Removal," *Michigan Historical Review* 20, no. 2 (1994): 78.

28. McClurken, "Ottawa Adaptive Strategies," 51–54.

29. SLUS/1855/11:621–29.

30. Malcolm J. Rohrbough, *The Land Office Business: The Settlement and Administration of American Public Lands, 1789–1837* (New York: Oxford University Press, 1968), 5–6.

31. The distinctive characteristics and implications of this system of land survey and alienation are discussed in John Fraser Hart, *The Look of the Land* (Englewood Cliffs, N.J.: Prentice-Hall, 1975), 54–55, and Richard A. Bartlett, *The New Country: A Social History of the American Frontier, 1776–1890* (New York: Oxford University Press, 1974), 68.

32. Hart, *Look of the Land*, 51–52; Bartlett, *New Country*, 69.

33. Nettels, *Emergence of a National Economy*, 140, 142; Robbins, *Our Landed Heritage*, 5.

34. TPUS/NWT/2:12–15; SLUS/1796/1:464–69. Bartlett, *New Country*, 71; Burke, *Ohio Lands*, 11–12.

35. Hart, *Look of the Land*, 57.

36. Henry S. Sanford, Journal, 14 August 1844, 15 August 1844/HSSP/Box 3/GSML.

37. Rohrbough, *Land Office Business*, 8–9.

38. SLUS/1800/2:73–78; SLUS/1812/2:716–18.

39. Robbins, *Our Landed Heritage*, 13–14; Benjamin Horace Hibbard, *A History of the Public Land Policies* (Madison: University of Wisconsin Press, 1965), 2–4.

40. SLUS/1800/2:73; SLUS/1804/2:277. Robbins, *Our Landed Heritage*, 30–32; Cochrane, *Development of American Agriculture*, 46.

41. SLUS/1820/3:566. Rohrbough, *Land Office Business*, 151; Wayne D. Rasmussen, "Introduction to U.S. Land Policies, 1783–1840," in *Agriculture in the United States, a Documentary History*, ed. Wayne D. Rasmussen (New York: Random House, 1975), 278.

42. *Detroit Gazette*, 9 August 1822.

43. *Western Emigrant*, 12 November 1829.

44. Benjamin Hough to Edward Tiffin, 20 May 1815/TPUS/MT/10:539. When completed in 1816, the base line survey was so inaccurate that it had to be rerun eight years later to reconcile discrepancies in individual townships. Although the eastern and western base lines were to intersect at the meridian, inaccuracies occurred when the eastern line was extended through lakes and rough country in 1816. Its 1824 resurvey discovered that it intersected the meridian 938.8 feet north of the western base line. Earlier surveying errors also made the last sections east of the meridian a half mile short. As a result, Michigan's base line has a jog midway across the peninsula and two initial points from which land measurements east and west of the meridian are taken. See Billy D. Buckler, "Why Does Michigan's Meridian-Baseline Have Two Initial Points?" in *Special Instructions to Deputy Surveyors in Michigan, 1808–1854* (Lansing: Michigan Museum of Surveying, 1990), 376–77; Gov. Lewis Cass to Josiah Meigs, 11 May 1816/TPUS/MT/10:636; Sec. of the Treasury to Josiah Meigs, 19 March 1817/TPUS/MT/10:693; Josiah Meigs to Gov. Cass, 16 July 1816/TPUS/MT/10:659; and Jamison, "Survey of the Public Lands in Michigan," 204. Persistent problems caused by errors in the eastern base line resulted in settler complaints that, "the surveys have been so imperfectly done as to be utterly worthless." In order to resolve the problem finally, the commissioner of the GLO was directed by Congress to assess damages claimed by Michigan residents resulting from "erroneous or fraudulent surveys" so that compensation might be awarded. See SR/1844/49; SLUS/1846/9.

45. As late as 1835, the commissioner of the General Land Office reported that much of the land around Saginaw Bay remained unsurveyed. See MAL/R/1842/8:156–57; ASP/PL/VIII/1835/1339. The subdivision of the region east of the meridian was also hindered by errors. Initial survey errors, compounded by a failure to compensate for the inevitable northward convergence of meridian lines caused by the earth's spherical shape, produced the irregular shapes of many townships situated just east of the meridian. See Jamison, "Survey of the Public Lands in Michigan," 202.

46. HD/1841/38; HD/1842/24; SED/1849/1, pt. 2; Jamison, "Survey of the Public Lands in Michigan," 205.

47. SLUS/1804/2:277–83; SLUS/1820/3:577; Sec. of the Treasury to Christopher Rankin, 3 April 1822/TPUS/MT/11:232–33.

48. SLUS/1823/3:778–79; SLUS/1826/4:167–68. Memorial to Congress by Inhabitants of the Southern Land District, 11 January 1831/TPUS/MT/12:236; Petition to Congress by Inhabitants of the St. Joseph Country, Oct. 1829/TPUS/MT/12:85; George Graham to Samuel F. Vinton, 10 January 1829/TPUS/MT/12:4; SLUS/1831/4:442–44.

49. Petition to Congress by Inhabitants of the Southeastern Part of the Territory, Nov. 1831/TPUS/MT/12:386; Blois, *Gazetteer*, 74; SLUS/1833/4:610–11; SLUS/1834/4:682.

50. SLUS/1836/5:48–49; Ethan A. Brown to the President, 9 July 1836/TPUS/MT/12:1203; HR/1842/512; SLUS/1854/33:275; Goddard, *Where to Emigrate*, 578.

51. Figure 5.8 was constructed from information contained in Michigan, State Land Office, *Tract Books*, MHC, 1818–40, as well as the following sources: Proclamation of Land Sales in Detroit, 31 March 1818/TPUS/MT/10:739–40; Proclamation of Land Sales in Detroit, 15 March 1820/TPUS/MT/11:18–19; Proclamation of Land Sales in Detroit, 19 September 1820/TPUS/MT/11:59; Proclamation of Land Sales in Detroit, 16 May 1822/TPUS/MT/11:239–40; Proclamation of Land Sales in Detroit, 2 February 1824/TPUS/MT/11:505–7; Proclamation of Land Sales in Monroe, 22 July 1824/TPUS/MT/11:571–72; Proclamation of Land Sales in Detroit and Monroe, April 1825/TPUS/MT/11:675–76; Proclamation of Land Sales in Detroit, 12 March 1827/TPUS/MT/11:1060–61; Proclamation of Land Sales in Monroe, 28 June 1828/TPUS/MT/11:1188–89; Proclamation of Land Sales in Monroe, 2 February 1829/TPUS/MT/12:16–17; Proclamation of Land Sales in Detroit, 24 February 1829/TPUS/MT/12:27; Proclamation of Land Sales in Detroit and Monroe, 5 June 1830/TPUS/MT/12:175–76; Proclamation of Land Sales in Monroe, 25 March 1831/TPUS/MT/12:274–75; Proclamation of Land Sales in Monroe, 2 July 1832/TPUS/MT/12:498–500; Proclamation of Land Sales at White Pigeon, 3 September 1833/TPUS/MT/12:609–10; Proclamation of Land Sales at Detroit and Bronson, 7 July 1834/TPUS/MT/12:784; Proclamation of Land Sales at Detroit, 6 May 1835/TPUS/MT/12:904–5; and Gov. Cass to Josiah Meigs, 3 April 1818/TPUS/MT/10:741. Geographer LeRoy Barnett has recently constructed a map of Michigan lands offered for sale by year. It may be found in "Mapping Michigan's First Land Sales," *Michigan Out-of-Doors* 53, no. 2 (1999): 46.

52. These included lands north and south of the base line east of Range 8 East, opened in 1818; a large tract west of this and south of the base line, offered in 1820; and a third area lying north of the base line and south of Saginaw Bay, opened in 1822. In 1824 and 1825 lands offered for sale at the Detroit Land Office included a number of tracts left unsold or forfeited by earlier purchasers. Land sales were extended westward and northward into portions of Livingston, Genesee, and Shiawassee Counties and northward into Lapeer County and an area adjoining the original Saginaw tract offered in 1822. In the Monroe District, lands advertised also included unsold tracts as well as an area lying directly west of the region offered in 1820. In 1827, lands included in the 1821 cession were first placed in market, and over the next three years a continuous strip extending to the Lake Michigan shoreline was made available for settlement. Farther to the north, in the Detroit District, land sales were extended west of the meridian to include territory in Ingham and portions of Eaton and Clinton Counties. See *Detroit Gazette*, 7 February 1826. See also Barnett, "Michigan's First Land Sales," 46.

53. Burke, *Ohio Lands*, 27–28; George J. Miller, "The Establishment of Michigan's Boundaries: A Study in Historical Geography," *American Geographical Society Bulletin* 43 (1911): 342.

54. These northern tracts further east in Isabella, Midland, and Gratiot Counties were placed in market, as were portions of the thumb region in Tuscola and Sanilac Counties. See Barnett, "Michigan's First Land Sales," 46; *Democratic Free Press*, 8 August 1834; ASP/PL/VIII/1836/1546; Ethan A. Brown to Ratliff Boon, 28 April 1836/TPUS/MT/12:1183; *Kalamazoo Gazette*, 4 February 1837; and *Democratic Free Press*, 6 June 1838.

55. Barnett, "Michigan's First Land Sales," 46. ASP/PL/VIII/1836/1546.

56. SLUS/1787/2:175; SLUS/1836/5:59; *Kalamazoo Gazette*, 27 January 1838; MAL/R/1850/3:452; MAL/R/1850/20:462–63; Hibbard, *History of the Public Land Policies*, 325; Blois, *Gazetteer*, 77; SLUS/1841/5:318–19; 453–58; SLUS/1847/9:181–82.

57. MAL/L/1842/27:44–47; MAL/L/1841/67:157–58; MAL/L/1845/90:119–21; LeRoy Barnett, "State Building Lands: Giving Michigan Grounds for Complaint," *Michigan Surveyor* 22, no. 6 (1987): 10.

58. Barnett, "State Building Lands," 10.

59. Henry Sanford remarked at his good fortune in acquiring such a tract in Brady Township in Kalamazoo County. Prior to its being placed in market the land around it had been settled by immigrant farmers, whose improvements had caused property in the vicinity to rise in value. Consequently, he felt the price he paid for the land was much less than its current worth. See Journal, 15 August 1844/HSSP/Box 3/GSML.

60. Sen. William Woodbridge to Gov. John S. Barry, 18 April 1842/MREOCAONMS/Box 5/SAM. MDNRI-ILC/1843–59/27; LeRoy Barnett, "Internal Improvement Lands: A Down-to-Earth Solution for Developing Michigan Transportation," *Michigan Surveyor* 25, no. 5 (1990): 10, 12

61. SLUS/1796/1:464–69; Sec. of State to Gov. St. Clair, 18 September 1797/TPUS/NWT/2:629; SLUS/1807/2:437–39; ASP/PL/ I/1805/112; SLUS/1808/2:502–4; SLUS/1812/2:710–11; Petition to Congress by Citizens of the Territory, 31 December 1816/TPUS/MT/10:683–84; SLUS/1820/3:572–73; Gilpin, *Territory of Michigan*, 36, 130–31.

CHAPTER 6

1. *Western Emigrant,* 12 November 1829; Danhof, *Change in Agriculture,* 102. For traditional discussions of the safety valve notion, see Frederick Jackson Turner, *The Frontier in American History* (New York: Henry Holt, 1920), 259, 297; and Jeremy Atack and Fred Bateman, *To Their Own Soil: Agriculture in the Antebellum North* (Ames: Iowa State University Press, 1987), 143–44.

2. Lanman, *History of Michigan, Civil and Topographical,* 297.

3. Daniel Feller, *The Public Lands in Jacksonian Politics* (Madison: University of Wisconsin Press, 1984), 79–81, 147–48; Sres/1838/160; ASP/PL/V/1828/675; *Detroit Gazette,* 20 March 1828; Robbins, *Our Landed Heritage,* 169.

4. Hoffman, *Winter in the West,* 1:128–29; Jane Comstock to Samuel and Nancy Hickson, 29 August 1845/JCL/MSUAHC; *Kalamazoo Gazette,* 27 January 1838.

5. Asa Post Hull Kelsey to Hannah P. H. Hinckley, 26 February 1843/HHL/CHL. See Shirreff, *Tour through North America,* 219; *Niles Gazette and Advertiser,* 5 March 1836; Jacob Gerrish, Diary, 13 April 1837/JGP/MSUAHC; and Sue I. Silliman, "Overland to Michigan in 1846," *Michigan History* 5 (1921): 429, for prices of prairies lands; Anson W. Halbert to Harrison Halbert, 29 December 1839/HFP/SAM; and Wealthy A. Searles to Zelotes B. Searles, 27 September 1840/JSP/CHL, for oak openings; *Grand River Times,* 28 April 1852, for pinelands; Mrs. S. L. Withey [Marion Louise Hinsdill], "Personal Recollections and Incidents of the Early Days of Richland and Grand Rapids," *MPHC* 5 (1884): 437, for forested bottoms; Josiah Orvis to Jacob Hooper, 11 May 1838/MHC, for mixed woods and open lands; and Ruth Evans to Jane Howell, 5 March 1835 /EMCP/Box 1/MHC; and *Portrait and Biographical Album of Hillsdale County, Michigan* (Chicago: Chapman Bros., 1888), 629, for older timbered lands.

6. Martin L. Daniels to Isaac Arnold, 19 March 1837/MHC; Josiah Orvis to Jacob Hooper, 11 May 1838/MHC.

7. Sylvanus Bachelder to James Bachelder, 5 September 1855, in Glen L. Bachelder, comp., *Bachelder Family Letters, 1835–1935* (East Lansing, Mich.: By the compiler, 1989).

8. *Grand River Times,* 14 May 1856; Everett, *Memorials,* 491.

9. Ball, "Physical Geography of Kent County," 214; Michigan Land Patent 3940, Book G, p. 307/CFP/MSUAHC.

10. Blois, *Gazetteer,* 69–70; Jacob Gerrish to Moses Chamberlain, 29 January 1838/CFP/MSUAHC. Bela Hubbard, Notebook, 6 August 1842/BHP/MHC; MAL/L/1846/14:13–14; MAL/L/1849/254:334–36.

11. Danhof, *Change in Agriculture,* 107.

12. SLUS/1832/4:503. Atack and Bateman, *To Their Own Soil,* 140; Barber, "Beginnings in Eaton County," 394.

13. *Jackson Sentinel,* 19 June 1839. The average costs necessary to bring a given amount of land into cultivation provide a better picture of the expenses faced by a pioneer farmer in the southern Lower Peninsula. Excluding the land itself, this amount included clearing; fencing; erection of a dwelling house, barns, and other farm structures; livestock; tools; vehicles and equipment; seed; and provisions. Projections of these expenses for Midwestern farms are based on earlier comparative analyses of contemporary data by Clarence Danhof as well as more recent studies by Atack and Bateman, which generally affirmed Danhof's figures. See Clarence H. Danhof, "Farm-Making Costs and the 'Safety Valve': 1850–60," *Journal of Political Economy* 49 (1941): 327; and Atack and Bateman, *To Their Own Soil,* 142–43.

14. William Richards to Herman Richards, 2 March 1833/MHC; *Genesee Farmer,* 1833:316; Smith, *Settler's New Home,* 91.

15. Mrs. M. L. Sanford to Amanda Sanford, 25 December 1859/MLSL/CHL; Nathan Fay to Joshua Fay, 11 February 1827/JFFC/CHL; William Richards to Herman Richards, 2 March 1833/MHC.

16. Blois, *Gazetteer,* 158.

17. Longyear, "Settlement of Clinton County," 360–61; Henry Chamberlain, "A Michigan Octogenarian," *MPHC* 35 (1907): 665; *Three Oaks Press,* 21 April 1899.

18. Pierce, *History of Calhoun County,* 145; Perrine, "Townships in Calhoun County," 251.

19. Beal, "Pioneer Life in Southern Michigan," 237; Danhof, *Change in Agriculture,* 115; *Portrait and Biographical Album of Shiawassee and Clinton Counties, Michigan* (Chicago: Chapman Bros., 1891), 196.

20. *Detroit Gazette,* 24 May 1825; Nowlin, *Bark-Covered House,* 19–20.

21. A discussion of the role of such agents is found in John Denis Haeger, *The Investment Frontier: New York Businessmen and the Development of the Old Northwest* (Albany: State University of New York Press, 1981), 72.

22. Agreement, 9 August 1830/CFP/MSUAHC; Barber, "Vermontville Colony," 203; Bronson, "Pioneer History of Calhoun County," 329–30.

23. T. G. Turner, *Gazetteer of the St. Joseph Valley, Michigan and Indiana* (Chicago: Hazlitt & Reed, 1867; reprint, Grand Rapids, Mich.: Black Letter Press, 1978), 48–49.

24. Asa P. H. Kelsey to P. H. Hinkley, 7 May 1838/HHL/CHL.

25. Gates, *Farmer's Age,* 66; Bidwell and Falconer, *Agriculture in the Northern United States,* 449; William Kirkland, "The West, the Paradise of the Poor," *United States Magazine and Democratic Review,* n.s., 15 (1844): 182; Danhof, *Change in Agriculture,* 92–93. Data accumulated for the Midwest in general support this figure. See Atack and Bateman, *To Their Own Soil,* 131, 134.

26. Gates, *Farmer's Age,* 97; Danhof, *Change in Agriculture,* 94; Atack and Bateman, *To Their Own Soil,* 135.

27. For an examination of tenancy in antebellum Kalamazoo County, see John T. Houdek and Charles F. Heller, "Searching for Nineteenth Century Farm Tenants: An Evaluation of Methods," *Historical Methods* 19 (1986): 59–60. Blois dismissed the role of tenancy among Michigan immigrant farmers *Gazetteer,* 158. On the other hand, immigrant accounts, like that of Adam D. Storms of Orangeville Township in Barry County, described tenancy as an accepted practice. Storms contracted with a Mr. Tilton to work a farm on shares, paying the latter five bushels per acre in rent. Within five years, Storms had "paid for his land with wheat," despite the depressed price of agricultural produce in the late 1830s. See Pierce, *History of Calhoun County,* 144; and *Portrait and Biographical Album of Barry and Eaton Counties, Michigan* (Chicago: Chapman Bros., 1891), 578.

28. William Richards to Herman Richards, 2 March 1833/MHC; *Kalamazoo Gazette,* 5 August 1837.

29. *Portrait and Biographical Album of Shiawassee and Clinton Counties,* 631.

30. Estimates on immigrants' use of wage earnings and other outside income to enter frontier farmering is presented in Frank D. Lewis and M. C. Urquhart, "Growth and the Standard of Living in a Pioneer

Economy: Upper Canada, 1826–1851," *Willam and Mary Quarterly,* ser. 3, 56 (1999): 175–77. See also Schenck, *History of Ionia and Montcalm Counties,* 236; and Martha Munsell Grainger, "Memories: Grave and Gay," ed. Alexis A. Praus and Ruth Howard, *Michigan History* 38 (1954): 123.

31. Robbins, *Our Landed Heritage,* 30–33; Rohrbough, *Land Office Business,* 138–41. Arthur H. Cole, "Cyclical and Sectional Variations in the Sale of Public Lands, 1816–1860," in *The Public Lands: Studies in the History of the Public Domain,* ed. Vernon Carstensen (Madison: University of Wisconsin Press, 1963), 246.

32. Paul W. Gates, "The Role of the Land Speculator in Western Development," in *The Public Lands: Studies in the History of the Public Domain,* ed. Vernon Carstensen (Madison: University of Wisconsin Press, 1963), 360–63; Reginald Horsman, "Changing Images of the Public Domain: Historians and the Shaping of Midwest Frontiers," in *This Land Is Ours: The Acquisition and Disposition of the Public Domain* (Indianapolis: Indiana Historical Society, 1978), 66.

33. Allen G. Bogue, "Land Credit for Northern Farmers, 1789–1940," *Agricultural History* 50 (1976): 68–100.

34. If a speculator had perfect knowledge of the inflation rate of a particular tract, he might "sit and wait" until the land's worth became known generally and make a profit at the end of an extended period, or promote the land's value in order to convince the public of this fact much earlier. In the last case the speculator might make a faster, but somewhat smaller, profit. See Atack and Bateman, *To Their Own Soil,* 122–24; Allan G. Bogue and Margaret Beattie Bogue, "'Profits' and the Frontier Speculator," in *The Public Lands: Studies in the History of the Public Domain,* ed. Vernon Carstensen (Madison: University of Wisconsin Press, 1963), 387–89; and Haeger, *Investment Frontier,* 75. Michigan settlers were clearly aware of the risk of long-term speculation on unimproved lands. One contemporary writer carefully calculated the costs entailed in holding a hypothetical land for a period of twenty years in order to demonstrate that these expenses would substantially exceed any profits likely to be realized by its sale. "The moral of this is," he wrote, "that as a rule it is unsafe to buy lands for speculation, and hold them for a rise; and that the only safe way to hold lands is to improve them" ("Junior," in *Traverse City Herald,* 9 April 1874).

35. Atack and Bateman, *To Their Own Soil,* 125–26.

36. Taylor, *Transportation Revolution,* 335; Rohrbough, *Land Office Business,* 134–35.

37. North, *Economic Growth of the United States,* 70; Taylor, *Transportation Revolution,* 339–40; Rohrbough, *Land Office Business,* 221–22.

38. Elizabeth M. Chandler to Jane Howell, 11 May 1832/EMCP/Box 1/MHC; Thomas Chandler to Uncle, 14 September 1835/EMCP/Box 1/MHC. Similarly, Harriet Martineau, traveling in Wayne County in 1836, noted that a settler's eighty-acre tract had increased in value tenfold in three years. That same year, John M. Gordon, searching for western Michigan lands in which to invest, found that improved Goguac Prairie lands, bought at government prices four years earlier, could not be purchased at under $25 an acre. See Martineau, "Travels in and around Michigan," 53; Gordon and May, "Michigan Land Rush," 277; and William Forbes to Friends, 10 April 1835/MHC. In New Buffalo, on the Lake Michigan shoreline in Berrien County, a local merchant remarked cheerfully that, "Such lands we paid $150 for last spring, cannot be bought short of $350, . . . and there has been some land sold for $20 per acre lying half a mile out of the village which was purchased last spring of Uncle Sam." See Jacob Gerrish to Moses Chamberlain, 31 January 1836/CFP/MSUAHC; and Hoffman, *Winter in the West,* 1:121.

39. Jonathan Wood to Moses Chamberlain, 24 January 1836/CFP/MSUAHC; Chase, *Life-Line of the Lone One,* 58. As early as 1832, N. M. Thomas of Kalamazoo noted that property values had advanced, "far beyond anything of the kind I have ever before witnessed," and lamented, "had I . . . known at the time that property was going to increase so rapidly in value as the event has proved, by obtaining a small capital and making a judicious selection I might have materially bettered my condition by this time" (N. M. Thomas to Jesse Thomas, 9 March 1832/NTP/Box 1/MHC).

See also George C. Bates, "By-Gones of Detroit," *MPHC* 22 (1893): 380. Caroline Kirkland, who with her husband purchased land near Pinckney in Livingston County in 1835, witnessed the transfer of tracts from hand to hand to everyone's profit except the individual who held it when the price would no longer advance. To illustrate this procedure she offered the tale of "a gentleman" who attempted to buy two town lots in Pinckney,

> "at five thousand dollars each." As this price was rather beyond the price which the owner had thought to fix to his ordinary lots, he felt exceedingly obliged, and somewhat at a loss to account for the proposition, til his friend whispered, "and you shall have in payment a lot at New-New York at a thousand: and we have not sold one at that, I can assure you."
>
> The obliged party chanced to meet the agent for New-New York about a year after, and inquired the fortunes of the new emporium, the number of inhabitants, &c. "There's nobody there," said he, "but those we hire to come." (*A New Home*, 49–51)

40. Taylor, *Transportation Revolution*, 341.

41. Edward Pessen, *Jacksonian America: Society, Personality, and Politics* (Urbana: University of Illinois Press, 1985), 139–40; MAL/L/1838:24.

42. Caroline Kirkland commented extensively on this theme in *A New Home*, 191. See also Feller, *Public Lands in Jacksonian Politics*, 184; and *Adrian Daily Times and Expositor*, 31 March 1877.

43. This argument is presented by Arthur M. Schlesinger Jr. in *The Age of Jackson*, abridged (New York: Mentor Books, 1945), 70, and by Feller in *Public Lands in Jacksonian Politics*, 185.

44. Taylor, *Transportation Revolution*, 341–43.

45. J. Seymour to Sidney S. Alcott, 12 October 1838/AFC/MSUAHC. Two years later, Seymour's lands remained unsold. "I am *very desirous* to sell of my lands & get them . . . out of the way of taxes & hope you can clear them off soon," he wrote his agent, "I hope you can find time & purchasers to *take all my lands* for cash or credit." A year later he admitted in resignation, "I assure you it would give me great pleasure to hold onto the lands with a reasonable prospect of getting a fair profit, but I have given up all expectation of that and mean now to sell at about cost" (J. Seymour to Sidney S. Alcott, 30 January 1840, 3 April 1841/AFC/MSUAHC).

46. *Monroe Advocate*, 18 November 1841.

47. Taylor, *Transportation Revolution*, 346; Pessen, *Jacksonian America*, 146; Fuller, *Economic and Social Beginnings*, 69.

48. Henry S. Sanford, Journal, 19 August 1844/HSSP/Box 3/GSML.

49. "History of Hillsdale, Michigan,"/HWP/MSUAHC.

50. Taylor, *Transportation Revolution*, 346; Parkins, *Historical Geography of Detroit*, 188. *North Star*, 15 August 1844. *Michigan Telegraph*, 1 January 1846. Cole, "Cyclical and Sectional Variations," 242.

51. Gates, "Role of the Land Speculator," 350–52; Bogue and Bogue, "'Profits' and the Frontier Speculator," 389–90; Horsman, "Changing Images of the Public Domain," 74–75.

52. *Michigan Statesman*, 20 August 1836; "The City of Ionia," 473; *Kalamazoo Gazette*, 24 March 1838; Leeson, *History of Macomb County*, 274.

53. Alvah Brainard, *A Pioneer History of the Township of Grand Blanc, Genesee County, Michigan* (Flint, Mich.: Globe Power Presses, 1878), 45; Leeson, *History of Macomb County*, 274–75.

54. Kirkland, *A New Home*, 49; Wood, *Wilderness and the Rose*, 113–14; Bates, "By-Gones of Detroit," 379.

55. Gordon and May, "Michigan Land Rush," 140–41, 146–47, 281; *Michigan Statesman*, 11January 1836; *Niles Daily Star*, 14 November 1899.

56. *Detroit Gazette*, 30 August 1825; *Western Emigrant*, 9 December 1829; Albert Baxter, "Some Fragments of Beginnings in the Grand River Valley," *MPHC* 17 (1890): 328.

57. J. Seymour to Sidney S. Alcott, 12 December 1836/AFC/MSUAHC.

58. Haeger, *Investment Frontier,* 77, 81–82, 110. For further information on the lives and careers of these individuals, see Jack Kilfoil, *C. C. Trowbridge: Detroit Banker and Michigan Land Speculator, 1820–1845* (New York: Arno Press, 1979); John Shirigian, *Lucius Lyon: His Place in Michigan History,* Ph.D. dissertation, University of Michigan (Ann Arbor, Mich.: University Microfilms, 1969); Fuller, *Michigan,* 1:145, 2:496; and Dunbar, *Michigan,* 221, 250, 277.

59. Bernard C. Peters, "The Fever Period of Land Speculation in Kalamazoo County: 1835–1837," *Michigan Academician* 8 (1976): 296–97, 299; C. Parker to F. L. Parker, January 1848/FLPP/Box 1/MHC; Barber, "Beginnings in Eaton County," 353, 360.

60. Bernard C. Peters, "Early Town-Site Speculation in Kalamazoo County," *Michigan History* 56 (1972): 214.

61. Gordon and May, "Michigan Land Rush," 448–49; *Detroit Gazette,* 26 February 1819; Peters, "Town-Site Speculation in Kalamazoo County," 202–3; Wade, *Urban Frontier,* 30.

62. C. A. Lamb, "Incidents in Pioneer Life in Clinton County," *MPHC* 1 (1877): 151; Franklin Ellis, *History of Shiawassee and Clinton Counties, Michigan* (Philadelphia: D. W. Ensign, 1880), 363.

63. The rival locations lay on Comstock Creek in Comstock Township and on Portage Creek in Portage Township. See Peters, "Town-Site Speculation in Kalamazoo County," 205–7, 214; Willis F. Dunbar, *Kalamazoo and How It Grew* (Kalamazoo: Western Michigan University, 1959), 40–41; and Durant, *History of Kalamazoo County,* 210–16.

64. Charles C. Trowbridge, "Detroit in 1819," *MPHC* 4 (1883): 473; Bates, "By-Gones of Detroit," 379–80.

65. Wood, *Wilderness and the Rose,* 91–98; Ellis, *History of Shiawassee and Clinton Counties,* 343.

66. Enos Goodrich, "Locating the State Capital at Lansing," *MPHC* 8 (1886): 126.

67. Cochrane, *Development of American Agriculture,* 55; Bogue and Bogue, "'Profits' and the Frontier Speculator," 388.

68. Ruth Evans to Jane Howell, 24 September 1835/EMCP/Box 1/MHC.

69. Everett, *Memorials,* 36; Albert Baxter, "First 'Yankee' Family at Grand Rapids," *MPHC* 29 (1899–1900): 504; Lucy Ball, "Early Days in Grand Rapids," *MPHC* 39 (1912): 95; "The City of Ionia," 470; Ephraim S. Williams, "A Trip on April Fool's Day," *MPHC* 14 (1889): 540; idem, "Personal Reminiscences," 256–57; *Acorn,* 15 February 1905; A. D. P. Van Buren, "First Settlement of Sturgis Prairie," *MPHC* 18 (1891): 518–19; *Clinton County Republican,* 18 September 1899.

70. Ellis, *History of Shiawassee and Clinton Counties,* 406, 409, 499; *Clinton County Republican,* 6 November 1902; Longyear, "Settlement of Clinton County," 362.

71. *Clinton County Republican,* 28 September 1899; Ellis, *History of Shiawassee and Clinton Counties,* 517; Orin Baker to William J. Russell, 6 January 1841/HHCP/Box 1/MHC.

72. Everett, *Memorials,* 10–11.

73. Elizabeth Chandler to Jane Howell, 24 April 1833/EMCP/Box 1/MHC.

74. Betsey Landon to Thomas Cranson, 2 May 1836, in *Stray Leaves from Pioneer days,* comp. Mrs. Hermon Landon Brown (Parma, Mich.: Parma News Printers, [1920]), 24–28; Melancthon Bagg to John L. Powell, 25 March 1835/PFP/MSUAHC; *Portrait and Biographical Album of Hillsdale County,* 425.

75. Sylvanus Bachelder to James Bachelder, 15 February 1859, in Bachelder, *Bachelder Family Letters,* 21.; Pierce, *History of Calhoun County,* 132; Schenck, *History of Ionia and Montcalm Counties,* 426.

76. E. Lakin Brown, "Autobiographical Notes, edited by A. Ada Brown," *MPHC* 30 (1905): 464.

77. Peters, "Town-Site Speculation in Kalamazoo County," 207; B. O. Williams, "First Settlement of Shiawassee County," *MPHC* 2 (1880): 484–86; W. B. Lincoln, "First Settlement of Ionia County," *MPHC* 1 (1877): 193; "The City of Ionia," 470–73.

78. Squatting may be viewed as a means of political action traditionally employed by subordinate social groups to resist or ameliorate conditions imposed upon them. It has been carried out successfully by

groups as diverse as those occupying the peripheral "hardscrabble" regions of Europe in the seventeenth century, urban migrants in present-day Latin America, and frontier immigrants to many colonial regions. See Jordan and Kaups, *American Backwoods Frontier,* 33–34, 52, 69; Hernando de Soto, *The Other Path: The Invisible Revolution in the Third World* (New York: Harper & Row, 1989), 7–10; Allen, *Bush and Backwoods,* 112; A. L. Burt, "If Turner Had Looked to Canada, Australia, and New Zealand When He Wrote about the West," in *The Frontier in Perspective,* ed. Walker D. Wyman and Clifton B. Kroeber (Madison: University of Wisconsin Press, 1957), 72–74; Bowman, *Pioneer Fringe,* 21, 252, 299, 310; and Feller, *Public Lands in Jacksonian Politics,* 16.

79. Henretta, *Evolution of American Society,* 120–121; Rohrbough, *Land Office Business,* 3–4.

80. T. Lynn Smith, *The Sociology of Rural Life* (New York: Harper & Brothers, 1940), 248–50; Paul W. Gates, *History of Public Land Law Development* (Washington, D.C.: Government Printing Office, 1968), 66.

81. Rohrbough, *Land Office Business,* 94, 203; Hibbard, *History of the Public Land Policies,* 145–47, 150; Feller, *Public Lands in Jacksonian Politics,* 16.

82. Hibbard, *History of the Public Land Policies,* 151; SLUS/1799/1:728–29; Burke, *Ohio Lands,* 17–18; The American Inhabitants of the Illinois to Gov. St. Clair, 23 May 1790/TPUS/NWT/2:252; Raymond Hammes, ed., "Squatters in Territorial Illinois," *Illinois Libraries* 59 (1977): 320–21; SLUS/1820/3:566.

83. Hibbard, *History of the Public Land Policies,* 152; SLUS/1830/4:420–21; John M. Moore to Sec. of State, 12 October 1830/TPUS/MT/12:207; Petition to Congress by Inhabitants of the Territory and of Indiana, 12 November 1831/TPUS/MT/12:384. In 1832 Congress passed two acts to extend the filing period for preemptions and adjust claims, and the following year extended the residence period to 1832. The Preemption Act of 1834 extended the filing period until 1836 and the residence period to 1833. After a two-year hiatus, acts passed in 1838 and 1840 extended both periods for eligibility and filing and introduced provisions to protect special-purpose lands, such as those reserved for schools, salt springs, or universities, from settler encroachment. See SLUS/1832/4:603; SLUS/1832/4:503; SLUS/1833/4:663–64; SLUS/1834/4:678; SLUS/1838/5:251–52; and SLUS/1840/5:382.

84. SLUS/1841/5:453–54; Robbins, *Our Landed Heritage,* 91.

85. *Michigan Sentinel,* 14 October 1826; Thaddeus Smith to Elizabeth Smith, 14 June 1829/SBSFC/WMUARHC; Abraham Edwards, "A Sketch of Pioneer Life," *MPHC* 3 (1881): 151.

86. *Semi-Weekly Free Press,* 7 May 1837; *Democratic Free Press,* 11 July 1838; *Kalamazoo Gazette,* 29 October 1838; *Michigan Sentinel,* 2 October 1830; *Detroit Journal and Michigan Advertiser,* 5 January 1831; *Democratic Free Press,* 27 July 1836.

87. See, for example, *Portrait and Biographical Album of Kalamazoo, Allegan, and Van Buren Counties,* 557, 747, 1060; Everett, *Memorials,* 127; *Grand River Times,* 12 March 1856; Schenck, *History of Ionia and Montcalm Counties,* 292.

88. Gordon and May, "Michigan Land Rush," 458.

89. Everett, *Memorials,* 171–72, 210–11, 413; Fuller, *Economic and Social Beginnings,* 431; Baxter, "Beginnings in the Grand River Valley," 327–28; S. D. Bingham, *Early History of Michigan, with Biographies of State Officers, Members of Congress, Judges and Legislators* (Lansing, Mich.: Thorp & Godfrey, 1888), 559.

90. MAL/R/1838/9:284–86; *Democratic Free Press,* 18 April 1838.

91. Gates, *Farmer's Age,* 88–89.

92. Davenport, *Timberland Times,* 39–40.

93. Henry S. Sanford, Journal, 15 August 1844/HSSP/Box 3/GSML.

94. Hibbard, *History of the Public Land Policies,* 198; *Kalamazoo Gazette,* 27 December 1838. This phrase was taken from the "Constitution of the Squatters' Union, in Lake County, Indiana, 1837," quoted in Wayne

D. Rasmussen, *Agriculture in the United States: A Documentary History* (New York: Random House, 1975), 1:348.

95. Gordon and May, "Michigan Land Rush," 463–64.

96. Everett, *Memorials*, 32.

97. Sanford C. Cox observed this behavior at Crawfordsville, Indiana, on 24 December 1824, as described in Rasmussen, *Agriculture in the United States*, 1:462. The Chicago incident was reported in James Platt Clapham, Diary, 1836/DWC/WMUARHC. See Everett, *Memorials*, 128, for the Ionia events.

98. *Detroit Journal and Michigan Advertiser*, 5 January 1831; Delegate Biddle to Elijah Haywood, 14 February 1831; Robert Clark to William Lytle, 17 October 1830/TPUS/MT/12: 209; Elijah Haywood to Moses Rice and others, 28 July 1832/TPUS/MT/12:512.

99. In the prairie region along the St. Joseph River, for example, preemptors were reported to have taken "all the choice spots of prairie," a practice the editor felt was certain to discourage immigration to that region (*Detroit Journal and Michigan Advertiser*, 24 November 1830). Settlement dispersal as a general effect of preemption in the United States was noted by Hildegard Binder Johnson, *Order Upon the Land: The U. S. Rectangular Land Survey and the Upper Mississippi Country* (New York: Oxford University Press, 1976), 74.

CHAPTER 7

1. Thompson, "Pioneer Colonization," 9–10; W. H. Hutt, "Immigration under 'Economic Freedom,'" in *Economic Issues in Immigration*, with an introduction by Arnold Plant (London: Institute of Economic Affairs, 1970), 20–21.

2. *Grand River Times*, 18 April 1837.

3. D. L. Porter to W. P. Porter, 1 May 1830/DLPP/CHL.

4. Lanman, *History of Michigan: Civil and Topographical*, 296–97.

5. Charles Butler to Eliza Butler, 11 July 1833, quoted in Haeger, *Investment Frontier*, 66; *Portrait and Biographical Album of Kalamazoo, Allegan, and Van Buren Counties*, 489; Polly Ely to Herman and Betsey Landon, 27 October 1835, in Brown, *Stray Leaves*, 11–12.

6. James Selkirk, Recollections/MJC/WMUARHC.

7. James Platt Clapham, Diary, 19 June 1836/DWC/WMUARHC.

8. Henretta, *Evolution of American Society*, 120–21, 200–201. Frederick Jackson Turner saw population pressure resulting from limited land resources as a powerful motive for emigration, and this inspired his view of western lands as a "safety valve" for growth. See Morris C. Taber, "New England Influence in South Central Michigan." *Michigan History* 45 (1961): 306. Timothy W. Hunt, of Onondaga County, New York, recalled clearly that a lower cost of production for market was the principal motivation for his move to Michigan. See *History of Washtenaw County*, 443.

9. *Detroit Courier*, 15 September 1831.

10. *Detroit Gazette*, 7 January 1820, 6 February 1824, 8 December 1830; *Western Emigrant*, 12 November 1829; Brainard, *Pioneer History*, 5.

11. Stewart, "Early Settlement of Ann Arbor," 443; McCormick, "Early Life in the Saginaw Valley," 367. The attraction of western lands to eastern farmers with limited means was frequently mentioned in contemporary accounts of both travelers and pioneer residents of Lower Michigan. For example, see Henry Chamberlain to Amos Chamberlain, 18 March 1845/CFP/MSUAHC; Sylvanus Bachelder to James Bachelder, December 1846, in Bachelder, *Bachelder Family Letters*, 8–9; Bela Hubbard, Notebooks, 10 May 1839/BHP/Box 1/MHC; Marion Palmer Greene, "Reflections in the River Raisin," *Michigan History*

33 (1949): 52; M. Shoemaker, of Jackson, in *History of Jackson County,* 209; and Joseph Lindsey, of Allegan County, and Nehemiah Elwell, of Kalamazoo County, in *Portrait and Biographical Album of Kalamazoo, Allegan, and Van Buren Counties,* 286, 950.

12. Kirkland, *American Economic Life,* 145; Wolf, *Europe and the People without History,* 364; Marcus Lee Hansen, *The Atlantic Migration, 1607–1860 A History of the Continuing Settlement of the United States* (Cambridge, Mass.: Harvard University Press, 1940), 67–68, 89, 220–22, 244, 286; Gottfried Pfeifer, "The Quality of Peasant Living in Central Europe," in *Man's Role in Changing the Face of the Earth,* ed. William L. Thomas Jr. (Chicago: University of Chicago Press, 1956), 266; Maldwyn A. Jones, "The Background to Emigration from Great Britain in the Nineteenth Century," *Perspectives in American History* 7 (1973): 3–92; Henry S. Lucas, *Netherlanders in America* (Ann Arbor: University of Michigan Press, 1955; reprint, Grand Rapids, Mich.: Williams B. Eerdmans, 1989), 53–58; Letter in the *Christian Intelligencer,* 26 November 1846, in *Dutch Immigrant Memoirs and Related Writings,* ed. Henry B. Lucas (Assen, Netherlands: Van Gorcum, 1955), 25.

13. Henry Bradshaw Fearon, *Sketches of America: A Narrative of a Journey of Five Thousand Miles through the Eastern and Western States of America* (London: Longman, Hurst, Rees, Orme, and Brown, 1818; reprint, New York: Benjamin Blom, 1969), 49; W. Faux, *Memorable Days in America: Being a Journal of a Tour of the United States* (London: W. Simpkin and R. Marshall, 1823), reprint in *Early Western Travels, 1748–1846,* ed. Reuben Gold Thwaites (Cleveland: A. H. Clark Co., 1904–5), 11:302–3.

14. Karl Neidhard, "Karl Neidhard's 'Reise Nach Michigan,'" trans. Frank X. Braun and ed. Robert Boneway Brown, *Michigan History* 35 (1951): 59–60; Smith, *Settler's New Home,* 17; William E. Van Vugt, "Running from Ruin?" *Journal of Economic History* 48 (1988): 426–27.

15. Social structure is basic to the integration of human societies. It provides a framework within which the relationships among people are carried out, and defines the roles individuals within a group assume during the course of their activities. Social structure may be defined as a basic model of social action that tends to remain unchanged over time, in contrast to social organization, which constitutes a society's current working arrangements. See Raymond Firth, "Social Organization and Social Change," *Journal of the Royal Anthropological Institute* 84 (1954): 10. Social structure is more than just a summation of all social relations. It is also an interrelated system within which social relations operate. See Claude Levi-Strauss, *Structural Anthropology,* trans. Claire Jacobson and Brooke Grundfestt Schoepf (New York: Doubleday, 1967), 270–71. There are many bases for social structure, particularly in complex industrialized societies where social relations are based on a variety of criteria. Its forms are a result of cultural influences and reflect the nature of a group's adaptations. Thus, the social structure of an industrial state represents social relations adjusted to a large-scale, complexly organized economy. Institutions, which may be seen as fixed modes of behavior within a society, also vary with the nature of its social structure. In the emerging industrial society of antebellum America, a variety of institutions were linked to its organization. In addition to those based on kinship, institutions were associated with religion, politics, occupation, class, trade, and other sets of activities integral to the working of these complex societies. See A. L. Kroeber, *Anthropology: Culture, Patterns, and Processes* (New York: Harcourt, Brace & World, 1963), 10; Abram Kardiner, *The Individual and His Society: The Psychodynamics of Primitive Social Organization* (New York: Columbia University Press, 1939), 484; and Victor Barnouw, *Culture and Personality* (Homewood, Ill.: Dorsey Press, 1963), 107.

   For an introduction to the function of kinship as an institution, see Robert H. Lowie, *Social Organization* (New York: Rinehart, 1948), 59–60; Kingsley Davis and W. Lloyd Warner, "Structural Analysis of Kinship," *American Anthropologist* 30 (1937): 291–92; and Burton Pasternak, *Introduction to Kinship and Social Organization* (Englewood Cliffs, N.J.: Prentice-Hall, 1976). Kinship and community in British colonial America are discussed in Henretta, *Evolution of American Society,* 23–25; Stuart A.

Queen and Robert W. Habenstein, *The Family in Various Cultures* (Philadelphia: J. B. Lippincott, 1967), 245; John Demos, *A Little Commonwealth: Family Life in Plymouth Colony* (New York: Oxford University Press, 1970), 181–88; David Rothman, "A Note on the Study of the Colonial Family," *William and Mary Quarterly*, 3d ser., no. 23 (1966): 27–34; and Philip J. Greven, Jr., "Family Structure in Seventeenth-Century Andover, Massachusetts," *William and Mary Quarterly*, 3d ser., no. 23 (1966): 234–56.

16. The literature of the American frontier is replete with examples of individual pioneer families seeking to acquire the resources unavailable in their place of origin. Because the rootlessness of such individualism stressed the breakdown of earlier kin-based systems, scholars often ignored the value of kinship as an adaptive institution to frontier conditions in the West. Frederick Jackson Turner believed that the individualism produced by this experience was a central contribution of the frontier experience to the American character and elaborated this point throughout his, "Significance of the Frontier" (see esp. 221–22, 223, 226). Statements on the role of individualism and its effect on regional character in the West and Upland South appear in Turner, *Frontier in American History*, 107, 165, who also emphasized its influence on American ideals in ibid., 306. More recent studies of American communities, however, have presented a much different picture of the role of kinship, and have stressed its importance in maintaining the social and economic fabric. See, for example, Demos, *A Little Commonwealth*, 177–78; and Robert C. Kenzer, *Kinship and Neighborhood in a Southern Community: Orange County, North Carolina, 1849–1881* (Knoxville: University of Tennessee Press, 1987), 20–22.

      Separation from kin group members was a trial that had long-lasting effects on emigrants as well as those they left behind. Those who suffered the trauma of parting often compared loss resulting from migration to death and underwent long-term grieving for their absent kin. Such separation created a paradox, in that it did not exclude the possibility of eventual reunion, and thus discouraged acceptance of the condition as final. The ambivalence arising from this situation actually prolonged the grieving process for many and made it more difficult for them to restructure their social networks to replace those now absent. Recent studies of pioneer literature have emphasized the effect of loss on both parties involved in migration. For a discussion of the impact of separation on the lives of colonists and those left behind, see Paul C. Rosenblatt, *Bitter, Bitter Tears: Nineteenth-Century Diarists and Twentieth-Century Grief Theories* (Minneapolis: University of Minnesota Press, 1983), 79–87.

17. Bonnie Loyd, Arlene Rengert, and Janice Monk, "Women and Agricultural Landscapes," in *Women and Spatial Change: Learning Resources for Social Science Courses*, ed. Arlene Rengert and Janice Monk (Dubuque, Iowa: Kendall/Hunt, 1982), 1–2; Linda France Stine, "Social Differentiation Down on the Farm," in *Exploring Gender through Archaeology: Selected Papers from the 1991 Boone Conference*, ed. Cheryl Classen, Monographs in World Archaeology, no. 11 (Madison, Wis.: Prehistory Press, 1992), 106; Kirkland, *A New Home*, 102; Annette Kolodny, *The Land Before Her: Fantasy and Experience of the American Frontier, 1630–1860* (Chapel Hill: University of North Carolina Press, 1984), 93–96.

18. For a discussion of the role of kin groups in New England settlement, see Virginia DeJohn Anderson, "Migrants and Motives: Religion and the Settlement of New England, 1630–1640," *New England Quarterly* 58 (1985): 347–48; and David Hackett Fischer, *Albion's Seed: Four British Folkways in America* (New York: Oxford University Press, 1989), 25–26. The cosmopolitan nature of New England settlement is addressed in Richard Archer, "New England Mosaic: A Demographic Analysis for the Seventeenth Century," *William and Mary Quarterly*, 3d ser., no. 47 (1990): 487. A discussion of the role of kinship in agricultural emigration generally is found in Robert E. Bieder, "Kinship as a Factor in Migration," *Journal of Marriage and the Family* 35 (1973): 434. Its importance in colonization in the antebellum North is addressed by Don Harrison Doyle, *The Social Order of a Frontier Community: Jacksonville, Illinois, 1825–1870* (Urbana: University of Illinois Press, 1978), 116 and Jack E. Eblen, "An Analysis of Nineteenth-Century Frontier Populations," *Demography* 2 (1965): 412–13. A similar role in southern

expansion is noted in John Mack Faragher, *Sugar Creek: Life on the Illinois Prairie* (New Haven, Conn.: Yale University Press, 1986), 57–58; Kenzer, *Kinship and Neighborhood*, 24; and Claire Fuller Martin, "Together in Heart: Southern Frontier Families in Southwestern Oklahoma Territory" (master's thesis, Michigan State University, 1986), 27–28. See also Blois, *Gazetteer*, 160; Barber, "Recollections and Lessons," 183.

19. Enos Goodrich, "Pioneer Sketch of Moses Goodrich and His Trip to Michigan in February, 1836, with His Brother Levi," *MPHC* 17 (1890): 480–82; Brainard, *Pioneer History*, 5.

20. Sylvanus and Mary Bachelder to James Bachelder, 10 December 1846; Sylvanus Bachelder to James Bachelder, 15 February 1859, in Bachelder, *Bachelder Family Letters*, 2, 8–9; N. M. Thomas to Jesse Thomas, 8 August 1831/NTP/Box 1/MHC.

21. Robert A. East, "Puritanism and New England Settlement," *New England Quarterly* 17 (1944): 255–57; Page Smith, *As a City Upon a Hill: The Town in American History* (New York: Alfred A. Knopf, 1966), 42–46; William G. McLoughlin, *Revivals, Awakenings, and Reform: An Essay on Religion and Social Change in America, 1607–1977* (Chicago: University of Chicago Press, 1978), 100–5; Alice Felt Tyler, *Freedom's Ferment: Phases of American Social History from the Colonial Period to the Outbreak of the Civil War* (New York: Harper & Brothers, 1962), 25–29; William Warren Sweet, *Revivalism in America* (New York: Abingdon Press, 1944), 117–18.

22. Hansen, *Atlantic Migration*, 136–38, 140–41; Lucas, *Netherlanders in America*, 50–53, 58–59.

23. HED /1848/19:22–23. Not all foreigners were welcomed in the United States. Increased Catholic immigration from Ireland, for example, precipitated a backlash by Protestant "nativists" who feared competition for jobs in the hard economic times of the late 1830s and early 1840s. Urban capitalist interests seeking to combat working-class solidarity promoted nativism as a means to exploit interethnic rivalry. Nativism became an increasingly important factor in antebellum American immigration policy. See Charles Sellers, *The Market Revolution: Jacksonian America, 1815–1846* (New York: Oxford University Press, 1991), 389–91.

24. Hansen, *Atlantic Migration*, 262–63.

25. Wittke, *History of Canada*, 104–11. American support for the rebellion undoubtedly encouraged Canadian immigration. Many saw the uprising as a sign of imperial dissolution, likened it to the American Revolution, and advocated intervention to insure its success. See Gordon Stewart, *The American Response to Canada since 1776* (East Lansing: Michigan State University Press, 1992), 42–45. Active participation by Americans in a number of border incidents strained relations between Britain and the United States. One of these occurred in December 1838 when a group of Americans gathered illegally in Detroit for an attack on nearby Windsor. Although the rebels were easily driven off by the defending force, the incident and events surrounding it became a focus for American sympathy and indignation. The "Battle of Windsor" was featured prominently in Orlando Willcox's *Shoepac Recollections*, 331–53, in which the protagonist expressed popular contemporary views of the struggle as a noble but futile sacrifice in opposition to tyranny.

26. *Democratic Free Press*, 11 July 1838.

27. R. S. Longley, "Emigration and the Crisis of 1837 in Upper Canada," *Canadian Historical Review* 17 (1936): 34–35; *Maumee* [Ohio] *Express*, quoted in *Democratic Free Press*, 21 February 1838; *Cleveland Advertiser*, quoted in *Democratic Free Press*, 13 June 1838; Everett, *Memorials*, 25; *Portrait and Biographical Album of Kalamazoo, Allegan, and Van Buren Counties*, 310; Wittke, *History of Canada*, 127–31; Dunbar, *Michigan*, 290. Canadians constituted 25 percent of Michigan's foreign immigrants in 1850 and increased to over 30 percent by 1870. At this time they constituted the largest group of foreign-born people entering the state and outnumbered other foreign immigrant groups after this time as well. See Charles Frank Kovacik, "A Geographical Analysis of the Foreign-Born in Huron, Sanilac, and St. Clair

Counties of Michigan, with Particular Reference to Canadians: 1850–1880," Ph.D. diss., Michigan State University (Ann Arbor, Mich.: University Microfilms, 1970), 75–77, table 6.

28. Booker T. Washington, *The Story of the Negro: The Rise of the Race from Slavery* (New York: Doubleday, Page, 1909; reprint, New York: Peter Smith, 1940), 1:193; George K. Hesslink *Black Neighbors: Negroes in a Rural Northern Community* (Indianapolis: Bobbs-Merrill, 1968), 37–38; Howard Holman Bell, *A Survey of the Negro Convention Movement, 1830–1861* (New York: Arno Press and the New York Times, 1969), 91–92.

29. The western expansion of cotton production and the growing opposition to slavery in the northern states resulted in the division of the West into "free" and "slave" regions. Tensions between opponents and supporters of the system led to the Missouri Compromise of 1820, an act that prohibited slavery in the territories north of 36∞ 30' latitude. By the 1820s, black emigration from slave states and territories had become an increasingly popular alternative to remaining in the United States. Schemes involved removal to African colonies, such as Liberia, or to Haiti, the British West Indies, Central America, California, or Canada. Canada, although seen by many supporters of the emigration movement as a temporary refuge on the way to more suitable locations, became a major area of resettlement by the 1830s. Because of its proximity to the United States, Canada remained a major destination for fugitives throughout the antebellum period. See Bell, *Negro Convention Movement,* 124–233; David Brion Davis, *The Problem of Slavery in Western Culture* (Ithaca, N.Y.: Cornell University Press, 1966), 163–64, 269–73; idem, *The Problem of Slavery in the Age of Revolution, 1770–1823* (Ithaca, N.Y.: Cornell University Press, 1975), 35, 342; and Robert William Fogel and Stanley L. Engerman, *Time on the Cross: The Economics of American Negro Slavery* (Boston: Little, Brown, 1974), 37.

30. E. Franklin Frazier, *The Negro in the United States* (New York: Macmillan, 1949), 96; George P. Rawick, *From Sunup to Sundown: The Making of the Black Community* (Westport, Conn.: Greenwood Publishing Co., 1972), 110–11; Hesslink, *Black Neighbors,* 32–33.

31. The concept of "community" links people and a locale, with an emphasis on social relations. As a basic unit of integration and transmission, its organization rather than its form is the key to recognizing its boundaries. See Conrad M. Arensburg, "The Community as Object and Sample," *American Anthropologist* 63 (1961): 248. An understanding of the complex nature of rural communities arose from the work of rural sociologists and historians who investigated the nature of social and economic integration in dispersed agricultural societies and its role in their formation. See, for example, John Mack Faragher, "Open-Country Community: Sugar Creek Illinois, 1820–1850," in *The Countryside in the Age of Capitalist Transformation: Essays in the Social History of Rural America,* ed. Steven Hahn and Jonathan Prude (Chapel Hill: University of North Carolina Press, 1985), 236–37, 245–47; Thompson, *Pioneer Colonization,* 8–9; C. J. Galpin, *The Social Anatomy of an Agricultural Community,* AES Research Bulletin no. 34 (Madison: University of Wisconsin, 1915); Lowry Nelson, *Rural Sociology* (New York: American Book Company, 1952), 72–77; Llewellyn MacGarr, *The Rural Community* (New York: Macmillan, 1923), 74–91; and G. J. Lewis, "Rural Communities," in *Progress in Rural Geography,* ed. Michael Pacione (London: Croom Helm, 1983), 149.

The modern concept of frontier communities contrasts with the emphasis many earlier historians of the American frontier gave to the role of individualism. Indeed, many assumed that individualism was the dominant feature of pioneer life and that conditions there were antithetical to the formation of integrating institutions. Frederick Jackson Turner argued, for example, that the process of frontier settlement was destructive of communal and corporate links and that the dispersed pattern it produced prevented the formation of traditional ties characteristic of older settled areas. See Turner, "Significance of the Frontier," 223.

32. Smith, *City upon a Hill,* 11, 17–21; Timothy Dwight, *Travels,* 2:334; Susan E. Gray, *The Yankee West: Community Life on the Michigan Frontier* (Chapel Hill: University of North Carolina Press, 1996), 26.

33. Kirkland, *American Economic Life*, 147; Blois, *Gazetteer*, 158; Andrew D. Perejda, "Sources and Dispersal of Michigan's Population," *Michigan History* 32 (1948): 355–56; Mathews, *Expansion of New England*, 226–27; Taber, "New England Influence," 305–6; Gray, *Yankee West*, 141.

34. Atack and Bateman, *To Their Own Soil*, 77–78; Blois, *Gazetteer*, 158.

35. Sarah Allen to J. A. Barney, 31 March 1839/SBSFC/WMUARHC; Sylvanus and Mary Bachelder to James Bachelder, 10 December 1846, in Bachelder, *Bachelder Family Letters*, 9; Lafever, "Early Day Life in Michigan," 672.

36. Israel Parsons to Edward Parsons, 28 July 1835/PaFP/MSUAHC; *Michigan Sentinel*, 20 March 1830; *Elsie Sun*, 8 January 1885.

37. Walter A. Terpenning, "Village and Open Country Communities in Michigan," *Michigan History* 16 (1932): 387.

38. Peter Wallace DeForth, "The Spatial Evolution of the German-American Culture Region in Clinton and Ionia Counties, Michigan" (master's thesis, Michigan State University, 1970), 39–48.

39. John Andrew Russell, *The Germanic Influence in the Making of Michigan* (Detroit: University of Detroit Press, 1915), 76–88; Warren Washburn Florer, *Early Michigan Settlements*, vol. 1, *Washtenaw, Westphalia, Frankenmuth, Detroit, 1848* (Ann Arbor, Mich.: By the author, 1941), 12–15.

40. Ruth Evans to Jane Howell, 9 September 1833/EMCP/Box 1/MHC; Arthur Raymond Kooker, "The Antislavery Movement in Michigan, 1796–1840: A Study of Humanitarianism on the American Frontier," Ph.D. diss., University of Michigan (Ann Arbor, Mich: University Microfilms, 1941), 93–97, 144; Ann Burton and Conrad Burton, *Michigan Quakers: Abstracts of Fifteen Meetings of the Society of Friends, 1831–1960* (Decatur, Mich.: Glyndwr Resources, 1989), 1; Dunbar, *Michigan*, 232, 356.

41. Carter G. Woodson, *A Century of Negro Migration* (Washington, D.C.: Association for the Study of Negro Life and History, 1918), 28; Bell, *Negro Convention Movement*, 91–93; Hesslink, *Black Neighbors*, 41–42, 51; Alfred Mathews, *History of Cass County, Michigan* (Chicago: Waterman, Watkins and Co., 1882), 386; Harold B. Fields, "Free Negroes in Cass County before the Civil War," *Michigan History* 44 (1960): 381–82; James O. Wheeler and Stanley D. Brunn, "An Agricultural Ghetto: Negroes in Cass County, Michigan, 1845–1968," *Geographical Review* 59 (1969): 319.

42. Wheeler and Brunn, "Agricultural Ghetto," 323; Fields, "Negroes in Cass County," 380–83; Hesslink, *Black Neighbors*, 50; Anna-Lisa Cox, "A Pocket of Freedom: Blacks in Covert, Michigan, in the Nineteenth Century," *Michigan Historical Review* 21, no. 1 (1995): 3–4.

43. Sonya Salamon, "Ethnic Origin as Explanation for Local Land Ownership Patterns," *Research in Rural Sociology and Development* 1 (1984): 175–76; Goodrich, "Pioneer Sketch," 480–82; Brainard, *Pioneer History*, 14–17.

44. Stack, *The McCleers and the Birneys*, 76–77; Thomas Wright, Diary, 23 September 1837/TWD/MSUAHC. Kinship also formed the basis for long-term partnerships in frontier farming. These usually involved siblings or other immediate family members. If, however, close relatives were not available, more distant relatives were sometimes included in such arrangements. See Gray, *Yankee West*, 103–10.

45. Stack, *The McCleers and the Birneys*, 162, 221.

46. Elizabeth Chandler to Jane Howell, 5 May 1833/EMCP/Box 1/MHC. John Mack Faragher, *Sugar Creek*, 57, found a similar pattern in the arrival of kin groups in central Illinois.

47. Henry S. Sanford, Journal, 19 August 1844/HSSP/Box 3/GSML.

48. Kinship systems define the relationships between people based on descent or consanguinity; however, they often extend beyond the biological ties to facilitate linkages between other members of a society. See Lowie, *Social Organization*, 57. The needs of a society often influence the extent and composition of kin networks. On the Michigan frontier, the absence of social ties led to the creation of fictive kin networks to facilitate mutual assistance. These sometimes included important community members who assumed

a paternalistic relationship with other immigrants, who applied the term "uncle" to individuals instrumental in the success of newcomers. New Buffalo country merchant Jacob Gerrish, for example, helped establish the Chamberlains and other families, who, in turn, referred to him as "uncle" in recognition of his social role in this frontier community. See Henry Chamberlain, "Early Country Store at New Buffalo," in *The Acorn*, 6 January 1915. See also Faragher, "Open-Country Community," 250–51. The economic advantages of kinship varied considerably on the frontier, especially when distance separated family members. When groups that migrated together did not settle adjacent to one another, the extended family often provided little more than emotional support for its dispersed members. See Martin, "Together in the Heart," 30.

49. N. Gordon Thomas, *The Millennial Impulse in Michigan, 1830–1860: The Second Coming in the Third New England* (Lewiston, N.Y.: Edwin Mellen Press, 1989), 5–6, 17–18; Winthrop S. Hudson, *American Protestantism* (Chicago: University of Chicago Press, 1961), 97–99; Sweet, *Revivalism*, 128–29. The activities of these denominations are discussed in John Comin and Harold F. Fredsell, *History of the Presbyterian Church in Michigan* (Ann Arbor, Mich.: Ann Arbor Press, 1950); Colin Brummitt Goodykoontz, *Home Missions on the American Frontier* (Caldwell, Idaho: Caxton Printers, 1939), 146–62, 167–73; Elijah H. Pilcher, *Protestantism in Michigan: Being a Special History of the Methodist Episcopal Church* (Detroit: R. D. S. Tylor, 1878), 108–9; Margaret Burnham MacMillan, *The Methodist Church in Michigan* (Grand Rapids, Mich.: Michigan Area Methodist Historical Society, 1967); and Supply Chase, "Early History of the Baptist Church in Michigan," *MPHC* 1 (1877): 466–68.

50. Samuel Newbury to Milton Badger, 18 September 1845, in Maurice F. Cole, comp., *Voices from the Wilderness* (Ann Arbor, Mich.: Edwards Brothers, 1961), 186; J. N. Parsons to Messrs. Badger and Hall, 28 January 1840, in ibid., 212; Pilcher, *Protestantism in Michigan*, 290–91. For a discussion of the role of churches as integrative institutions in a contemporary frontier community in Illinois, see Faragher, *Sugar Creek*, 160–64. The cohesive role of evangelical religion during the settlement period was also noted by Martin, "Together in the Heart," 34.

51. Doyle, *Social Order of a Frontier Community*, 168–69. For a discussion of the role of evangelical churches in the rural community on Gull Prairie in eastern Kalamazoo County, see Gray, *Yankee West*, 120–24.

52. In at least one instance disagreement among members of a Quaker meeting over the subject of abolition prompted those dissenting to affiliate with another meeting. This decision required many to remove to another part of Michigan. See Burton and Burton, *Michigan Quakers*, 1; Ruth Evans to Jane Howell, 9 September 1833/EMCP/Box 1/MHC.

53. *Detroit Gazette*, 31 May 1822.

54. *Democratic Free Press*, 25 September 1833.

55. With regard to the role of deprivation in the adjustment of contemporary colonists, anthropologist Stephen I. Thompson observed that those whose levels of expectation were realized most completely made the most successful colonists. He employed the concept of "relative deprivation" to contend further that because colonists from the lowest socioeconomic level were least deprived by the demands of initial settlement, they made the easiest adjustment to the frontier. See Thompson, *Pioneer Colonization*, 18–19. See also Casagrande, Thompson, and Young, "Colonization," 316–17. The concept of "relative deprivation" was introduced by Samuel A. Stouffer et al., *The American Soldier: Adjustment during Army Life* (Princeton, N.J.: Princeton University Press, 1949) and is discussed further in Robert Merton, *Social Theory and Social Structure* (Glencoe, Calif.: Free Press, 1957), 227–50.

56. Kirkland, *A New Home*, 229–31. Similar observations were made by Michigan pioneer Cornelia Stone to Maria L Zeh, 7 August 1850/LSCC/SAM.

57. James C. Malin, "The Turnover of Farm Population in Kansas," *Kansas Historical Quarterly* 4 (1935): 351–52.

58. Riley, *Puddleford Papers,* 320.

59. Comparative studies of pioneer persistence have shown that during the initial years of settlement, colonists' perceptions of success were based on a comparison of their present home with a number of potential new ones. See Cyrus P. Bradley, "Journal of Cyrus P. Bradley, with an Introductory Note by George H. Twiss," *Ohio Archaeological and Historical Society Publications* 15 (1906): 254. Persistence rates in nineteenth-century agricultural frontier communities reflect this trend. In Sugar Creek, Illinois, less than 30 percent of the original settlers remained at the end of the first decade of settlement. See Faragher, *Sugar Creek,* 50. Low initial persistence occurred elsewhere as well, as exemplified by a rate of 29 percent in Trempealeau County, Wisconsin (Merle Curti, *The Making of an American Community: A Case Study of Democracy in a Frontier County* [Stanford, Calif.: Stanford University Press, 1959], 68); just under 40 percent in Jacksonville, Illinois (Doyle, *Social Order of a Frontier Community,* 96); between 10 and 50 percent in Grant County Wisconsin (Peter J. Coleman, "Restless Grant County: Americans on the Move," in *The Old Northwest: Studies in Regional History, 1787–1910,* ed. Harry N. Scheiber [Lincoln: University of Nebraska Press, 1969], 284–85); 44 percent in Wapello County, Iowa (Mildred Thorne, "A Population Study of an Iowa County in 1850," *Iowa Journal of History* 57 [1959]: 316–20); and between 24 and 42 percent in eastern Kansas (Malin, "Turnover of Farm Population," 365–69). See also Kirkland, *A New Home,* 36.

60. Kirkland, *A New Home,* 175.

61. D. L. Porter to W. P. Porter, 29 December 1829/DLPP/CHL. Such deprecating characterizations of failed farmers correctly described the situation in which many immigrants found themselves; however, such images failed to recognize the temporary nature of failure. Most contemporary observations were made at one point in the colonist's career and extrapolated to construct a portrait of a perpetually unsuccessful group. By ignoring the eventual triumph of many failed agriculturists, they overlooked the fact that not all who moved on were doomed to repeat this experience indefinitely.

62. Theodore E. Potter, "A Boy's Story of Pioneer Life in Michigan," *MPHC* 35 (1907): 393–96; P. S. Richards, "Eighty Years in Michigan," *MPHC* 38 (1912): 365–69; *Portrait and Biographical Album of Branch County, Michigan* (Chicago: Chapman Bros., 1888), 193.

63. These results are based on an investigation of agricultural persistence in Trempealeau County, Wisconsin, in which Merle Curti examined the importance of the pioneer's age, ownership of land, and size of holding with regard to persistence. John Mack Faragher's examination of the rural Sugar Creek community in Illinois supported Curti's conclusions regarding the role of land ownership in persistence and stressed the advantages of longer-term residence in establishing social and economic ties. See Curti, *Making of an American Community,* 65–77, 141–43; Faragher, "Open-Country Community," 248–51.

64. Charles F. Heller and F. Stanley Moore, "Continuity in Rural Land Ownership: Western Kalamazoo County, Michigan, 1830–1861," *Michigan History* 56 (1972): 240–46.

65. Faragher, "Open-Country Community," 252.

66. The varieties of covenanted communities are discussed in Smith, *City upon a Hill,* 18–21.

67. Blois, *Gazetteer,* 160–61.

68. Other covenanted communities of shared interest also helped colonize Lower Michigan. In 1829, for example, a Detroit newspaper reported that during the previous year several "Michigan Companies" had been organized in western New York alone. See *Detroit Gazette,* 24 December 1829. One such community was the Kalamazoo Emigration Society, which settled at Gull Prairie in 1832. For a detailed discussion of its organization, see Gray, *Yankee West,* 18–20. The most complete account of Vermontville is Barber, "Vermontville Colony," 203–9.

69. Samuel W. Durant, *History of Ingham and Eaton Counties, Michigan* (Philadelphia: D. W. Ensign & Co., 1880), 516–18; Barber, "Vermontville Colony," 205–10. Barber's account suggests that a substantial

amount of land was actually purchased by individuals in addition to the original tract. If so, the extent of the colony would have been larger than first projected.

70. S. J. Church to Corresponding Secretary of the American Home Missionary Society, 28 September, 1838, in Cole, *Voices from the Wilderness*, 59–60; Barber, "Vermontville Colony," 219–24, 244–45.

71. S. B. Daboll, *Past and Present of Clinton County* (Chicago: S. J. Clarke, 1906), 476, 497; Bronson, "Pioneer History," 329–33; Ellis, *History of Shiawassee and Clinton Counties*, 426.

72. Bela Hubbard, Notebook, 26 August 1840/BHP/Box 1//MHC; Ellis, *History of Shiawassee and Clinton Counties*, 425.

73. Wolcott B. Williams, *A History of Olivet College, 1844–1900* (Olivet, Mich.: [Olivet College], 1901), 56–57.

74. Taber, "New England Influence," 310, 319–23; Oramel Hosford, "Early History of Olivet College," *MPHC* 3 (1881): 411.

75. For a discussion of the role of religion as an integrating factor among territorial groups, see Lowie, *Social Organization*, 179.

76. DeForth, "German-American Culture Region," 43; Ellis, *History of Shiawassee and Clinton Counties*, 533; Daboll, *Past and Present*, 491.

77. DeForth, "German-American Culture Region," 20, 26, 95–96; Ellis, *History of Shiawassee and Clinton Counties*, 534; Thomas L. Norris, "Acculturation in a German Catholic Community" (master's thesis, Michigan State University, 1950), 6, 69; Florer, *Early Michigan Settlements*, 9; Theodore Hengesbach, "Westphalia's History," in *Clinton County Republican*, 31 July 1902.

78. DeForth, "German-American Culture Region," 37–39; *St. Mary's Centennial: Westphalia, Michigan, 1836–1936* (Westphalia, Mich.: n.p., 1936), 110–11; Walter D. Kamphoefner, *The Westfalians: From Germany to Missouri* (Princeton, N.J.: Princeton University Press, 1987), 13; Kathleen Neils Conzen, "Peasant Pioneers: Generational Succession among German Farmers in Frontier Minnesota," in *The Countryside in the Age of Capitalist Transformation: Essays in the Social History of Rural America*, ed. Steven Hahn and Jonathan Prude (Chapel Hill: University of North Carolina Press, 1985), 264; DeForth, "German-American Culture Region," 167; Terry G. Jordan, *German Seed in Texas Soil: Immigrant Farmers in Nineteenth-Century Texas* (Austin: University of Texas Press, 1966), 36–37. The notion of the family farm as a sacred trust has remained a central component among farmers of German descent in the American Midwest. Within the context of a multigenerational family, land is closely linked to family members' identity, and continued ownership by the kin group is seen as both an obligation and an assurance of family security. See Sonya Salamon, "Ethnic Determinants of Farm Community Character" (paper presented at the Annual Meeting of the American Anthropological Association, Washington, D.C., 1985), 32; idem, *Prairie Patrimony: Family, Farming, and Community in the Midwest* (Chapel Hill: University of North Carolina Press, 1992), 101–2; and Conzen, "Peasant Pioneers," 265–66, 282.

79. Two examples from Westphalia illustrate the role of partible inheritance practices in the expansion of the colony. The first involves John Fedewa, who emigrated with his family from Germany in 1841. Upon his marriage to Anna Schaffer, the daughter of another German family, in 1848, he acquired a 40-acre tract from the family estate. To this he subsequently added other lands until the household possessed more than half a section.

Together with his two sons, John J. and Mathias, Fedewa cleared the forested land, a communal effort that both sons later recalled "with mingled feelings." The sons worked the family lands until they reached their mid-twenties, at which time each was married and received 80 acres from his father. Both subsequently added to their holdings and each possessed a 110-acre farm in 1891. At least some of their lands were purchased from their parents. Upon their surviving parent's death, they each received equal shares of a portion of the remaining parental estate.

The Droste family followed a similar pattern. Its head, Theodore Droste, emigrated from Germany with his wife and family in 1840 and purchased 40 acres in Westphalia. He subsequently enlarged the property through the purchase of adjacent tracts to form a substantial estate. Droste and his six sons cleared the family farm and worked it until they married, whereupon each son received a share of 80 acres. One son, Anthony, enlarged his farm to 120 acres within four years.

Although sale and division subsequently altered the estates amassed by both the Fedewas and the Drostes, the families remained as permanent residents of Westphalia. As recently as 1985, a portion of each of these original estates remained in the hands of a direct descendent of the family's founder. See Carolyn B. Lewis, "Imperfect or Identical Images? An Investigation of the Accuracy of Nineteenth-Century Subscription Property Illustrations of Clinton County, Michigan" (report prepared for the Clinton County Historical Commission, St. Johns, Michigan, 1987), 106, 119–20.

The daughters in the Fedewa and Droste families did not inherit shares of land upon marriage. Rather, they appear to have received cash or other property in lieu of real estate, a pattern observed in other German immigrant communities. All of the Fedewa and Droste men married women who were German immigrants or their descendants. Presumably the inheritances brought by wives provided not only the articles of housekeeping but capital that the new households might use to expand the initial landholdings inherited by the husbands. See *Portrait and Biographical Album of Shiawassee and Clinton Counties*, 630–31, 677, 688, 913–14; and John Fedewa, Will, Clinton County Register of Deeds, Liber 88, p. 342, 22 December 1896.

Only in the 1870s, when the occupation of surrounding lands by outsiders prevented further contiguous settlement, did the geographical segmentation of the German community of Westphalia occur. See DeForth, "German-American Culture Region," 55; Norris, "Acculturation," 43.

80. Howard George Johnson, "The Franconian Colonies of the Saginaw Valley, Michigan: A Study in Historical Geography," Ph.D. diss., Michigan State University (Ann Arbor, Mich.: University Microfilms, 1972), 23–24; Florer, *Early Michigan Settlements*, 14–16; Herman F. Zehnder, *Teach My People the Truth! The Story of Frankenmuth, Michigan* (Bay City, Mich.: By the author, 1970), 18–22.

81. The region of Bavaria from which the colonists came was known historically as Franken, after the Franks who had traditionally occupied the area. Because of the cultural unity of the immigrants, this term would be incorporated in the names of all of the settlements established by Bavarian Lutherans in this region of Michigan. See Johnson, *Franconian Colonies*, 14, 38–43.

82. The "Community Regulations for the Community of Frankenmuth" are reproduced in Zehnder, *Teach My People the Truth*, 216–18. See also Florer, *Early Michigan Settlements*, 23–24; and Johnson, *Franconian Colonies*, 55–58, 67, 77, 141.

83. The growth and integration of the Franconian colonies was assisted by the construction of roads intended to link the principal settlements and provide an outlet to markets. In 1849 the Michigan Legislature passed an act authorizing the construction of a road connecting the southernmost settlements of Frankenmuth and Frankentrost with the river port of Saginaw. This road passed northward from Saginaw through Frankenlust and Lower Saginaw, near the mouth of the Saginaw River. See MAL/L/1849/198:241–42; Johnson, *Franconian Colonies*, 42–43, 86, 96–97, 100, 104.

84. Conzen, "Peasant Pioneers," 282; Johnson, *Franconian Colonies*, 104–5.

85. Florer, *Early Michigan Settlements*, 27; MAL/R/1849/7:364; MAL/R/1850/26:21. Edward H. Thompson of Flint was an auspicious choice for this task, and his knowledge of the Franconian colony and its potential for immigration induced him to target promotional literature at German audiences. See William L. Jenks, "Michigan Immigration," *Michigan History* 28 (1944): 75–77; Russell, *Germanic Influence*, 66–68; Johnson, *Franconian Colonies*, 84.

86. The Secession, or Afscheiding, movement developed in opposition to a reorganization of the Netherlands Hervormde Kerk (Reformed Church) instituted by King Willem I in 1816. Viewed by many as an unwarranted move to centralize authority within the church, the new regulations immediately created divisions among the clergy. Attempts at organizing separate churches began in the 1820s; however, formal secession did not occur until the fall of 1834, when a number of church councils severed their ties with the state church. See Jacob Van Hinte, *Netherlanders in America: A Study of Emigration and Settlement in the Nineteenth and Twentieth Centuries in the United States of America*, trans. Adriaan de Wit (Grand Rapids, Mich.: Baker Book House, 1985), 88–93; Bertus Harry Wabeke, *Dutch Emigration to North America, 1624–1860: A Short History* (New York: Netherlands Information Bureau, 1944), 19–20; Lucas, *Netherlanders in America*, 50–54.

87. Henry S. Lucas, "The Beginnings of Dutch Immigration to Western Michigan, 1846," *Michigan History* 6 (1922): 655, 669–74, includes a translation of the document's text and discusses its implications for settlement. See also idem, *Netherlanders in America*, 59; and Aleida J. Pieters, *A Dutch Settlement in Michigan* (Grand Rapids, Mich.: Reformed Press, 1923), 65.

88. Albert Hyma, *Albertus C. Van Raalte and His Dutch Settlements in the United States* (Grand Rapids, Mich.: William B. Eerdmans, 1947), 99–100, 146–52; Van Hinte, *Netherlanders in America*, 132–33; Lucas, *Netherlanders in America*, 80–86; Gordon W. Kirk Jr., *The Promise of American Life: Social Mobility in a Nineteenth-Century Immigrant Community, Holland, Michigan, 1847–1894* (Philadelphia: American Philosophical Society, 1978), 21; Everett, *Memorials*, 481.

89. Van Raalte served as pastor of the First Reformed Church in Holland and president of the Classis of Holland, the ecclesiastical organization of the Dutch immigrant Reformed churches in the colony. In 1850, he led these churches into union with the Reformed Church in America. See Van Hiinte, *Netherlanders in America*, 254–55. Van Raalte's role in the administration of the colony is discussed in Elton J. Bruins, "Albertus Christiaan Van Raalte: Funding His Vision of a Christian Colony" (paper presented at the 8th Biennial Conference of the Association for the Advancement of Dutch American Studies, Holland, Michigan, 19 September 1991), 3–9. These meetings, called *volksvergaderingen,* were organized as an adaptive response to the absence of adequate integrating institutions in the colony. See Lucas, *Netherlanders in America*, 97–98, 104.

90. Van Raalte's affiliation with the Reformed Church of America led to dissention among Dutch immigrants in western Michigan over doctrinal issues and practices. Their division resulted in a secession of dissenters in 1857 to form the Christian Reformed Church. Although divided, Reformed churches continued to play a central role in individual communities throughout the Holland Colony and other areas of Dutch settlement in western Michigan. See Lucas, *Netherlanders in America*, 511–14.

91. In 1849 a visiting church representative reported that five of the six Dutch settlements had erected churches, and they were served by four ministers. An early account of the organization of church congregations and activities in the colony is found in Isaac N. Wyckoff, "An Official Report on the Dutch Kolonie in Michigan, 1849," in Lucas, *Dutch Immigrant Memoirs*, 453–56. See also Anna Kremer Keppel, *The Immigration and Early History of the People of Zeeland, Ottawa County, Michigan, in 1847* (Zeeland, Mich.: Zeeland Record Press, [1925]), 43; and Everett, *Memorials*, 481. The text of the Zeeland covenant is reproduced in Henry S. Lucas, "A Document Relating to the Founding of Zeeland, Michigan, in 1847," *Michigan History* 12 (1928): 99–107. See also Lucas, *Netherlanders in America*, 110, 148–49.

The geographical concentration of Dutch settlers was well known to contemporary observers such as Henry Griffin, in *Detroit Free Press*, 17 July 1848; and Kirk, *Promise of American Life*, 23. The creation and maintenance of common cultural forms within the region of Dutch colonization has been linked to the nature of Reformed Dutch ideology. The degree to which it stressed maintaining integrity through

separation from the outside world was seen as particularly relevant to the creation of a region possessing distinctive characteristics, many of which have persisted into the late twentieth century. See Elaine
M. Bjorklund, "Ideology and Culture Exemplified in Southwestern Michigan," *Annals of the Association
of American Geographers* 54 (1964): 227–41.

92. Lucas, *Netherlanders in America,* 256; Frans Van Driele, "Frans Van Driele's First Experiences," in Lucas,
Dutch Immigrant Memoirs, 338. The success of Dutch immigrants in employing this strategy has been
linked to prevailing ideological tenets that stressed the strength of the family and the avoidance of idle-
ness through continually productive activity. These notions encouraged outside employment by farmers
during the slack season as well as by other family members not necessary for regular farming operations.
See Bjorklund, "Ideology and Culture," 239; and Conzen, "Peasant Pioneers," 263.

93. Lucas, *Netherlanders in America,* 271, 273–75, 279–80; James Stanford Bradshaw, "Grand Rapids
Furniture Beginnings," *Michigan History* 52 (1968): 290–91.

94. Lucas, *Netherlanders in America,* 260–65; MAL/L/1848/32:24–26.

95. For discussions of millenarian movements in America, see Arthur Eugene Bestor, *Backwoods Utopias, the
Sectarian and Owenite Phases of Communitarian Socialism in America: 1663–1829* (Philadelphia:
University of Pennsylvania Press, 1950), 3–4; John Humphrey Noyes, *History of American Socialisms*
(Philadelphia: J. B. Lippincott, 1870; reprint, New York: Hillary House Publishers, 1961), 24–26; and
Maren Lockwood, "The Experimental Utopia in America," in *Utopias and Utopian Thought,* ed. Frank E.
Manuel (Boston: Beacon Press, 1965), 186, and Donald E. Pitzer, "Collectivism, Community, and
Commitment: America's Religious Communal Utopias from the Shakers to Jamestown," in Utopia, ed
Peter Alexander and Roger Gill (LaSalle, Ill.: Open Court Pub. Co., 1984), 119. Brian J. L. Berry has
attributed the rise of these movements to larger economic cycles and has concluded that their occurrence
corresponds to periods of deflationary economic depression during which depressed prices and collaps-
ing asset values result in widespread despair. See *America's Utopian Experiments: Communal Havens from
Long-Wave Crises* (Hanover, N.H.: University Press of New England, 1992), 1–2, 11–12, 18–26. In addition to modifying their own behavior, many millenarian groups promoted social reforms, such as abolition and temperance, in antebellum America. See Hudson, *American Protestantism,* 96–99; William
Warren Sweet, *The Story of Religion in America* (New York: Harper & Bros., 1930), chap. 15; and idem,
Religion and the Development of American Culture, 1765–1840 (New York: Charles Scribner's Sons, 1952),
305–11.

96. Because it lay outside Lower Michigan and did not constitute part of agricultural colonization there, a
third communitarian settlement is not included in this discussion. A Mormon colony on Beaver Island
in northern Lake Michigan was organized in 1848 by a Wisconsin sect under the leadership of James J.
Strang. It endured for eight years, but collapsed soon after the assassination of its powerful and contro-
versial leader whose activities had aroused the enmity of neighboring fishermen and other northern
Michigan residents. Mobs attacked the colonists and forced them to abandon their settlement. See
Dunbar, *Michigan,* 354–55. For further discussion of this colony, see Milo M. Quaife, *The Kingdom of St.
James* (New Haven, Conn.: Yale University Press, 1930). See also Thomas, *Millennial Impulse,* 34–35.

97. Berry, *America's Utopian Experiments,* 85–88.

98. The Alphadelphia colony is discussed in N. Gordon Thomas, "The Alphadelphia Experiment," *Michigan
History* 55 (1971): 206–7, 212–13; idem, *Millennial Impulse,* 37–38; Bestor, *Backwoods Utopias,* 238–39;
Noyes, *American Socialisms,* 389–91, 394–96; A. D. P. Van Buren, "The Alphadelphia Association," *MPHC*
5 (1884): 409–12; and Larry B. Massie, "Communists in Kalamazoo," in *The Romance of Michigan's Past,*
ed. Larry B. Massie (Allegan Forest, Mich.: Priscilla Press, 1991), 77–90.

99. The German Methodist Church also established Michigan congregations at Detroit, Ann Arbor, and Bay
City. Baur was aware of successful communitarian experiments, including the Harmony Society at

Economy, Pennsylvania, the German Zoar community in Ohio, and Brook Farm in Massachusetts. See Carl Wittke, "Ora et Labora: A German Methodist Utopia," *Ohio Historical Quarterly* 67 (1958): 132–35; Account of Walter Baur, grandson of Emil Baur, in *Bay City Times,* 27 June 1971; and Pilcher, *Protestantism in Michigan,* 235, 330, 418.

100. LeRoy Barnett, "Michigan Land Grants to German Organizations," *Michigan Surveyor* 19, no. 6 (1984): 17–18; Wittke, "Ora et Labora," 136, 138–40; Walter Baur in *Bay City Times,* 27 June 1971; Account of Gottlieb Ahr, shoemaker at Ora et Labora, in *Tri-State Trader,* 1 September 1979. Walter Baur recalled that his father returned to the abandoned colony lands and settled on a farm that remained in the family's possession at least as late as 1971. See *Bay City Times,* 27 June 1971.

101. The few attempts at communal economic endeavors usually resulted in failure when costs exceeded returns. Several such ventures took place at Holland in the early years of settlement. The best known were the "Colony Store" and the "Colonial Ship," both sponsored by the colony's organizers to promote trade. Neither generated a sufficient volume of activity to support its operation, and each failed within a year of its creation. See Lucas, *Netherlanders in America,* 100.

CHAPTER 8

1. *History of Jackson County,* 222–23.
2. Joseph Busby, "Recollections of Pioneer Life in Michigan," *MPHC* 9 (1886): 125; Schenck, *History of Ionia and Montcalm Counties,* 30; William Forbes to Friends, 10 April 1835/MHC.
3. Edwin D. Smith, "Pioneer Days in Kalamazoo and Van Buren," *MPHC* 14 (1889): 276; Julia Belle Towner, "My Mother's Girlhood," *MPHC* 35 (1907): 183.
4. ASP/IA/2/1822/187; Lanman, *History of Michigan, Civil and Topographical,* 310; Blois, *Gazetteer,* 155; Ruth Hoppin, "Personal Recollections of Pioneer Days," *MPHC* 38 (1912): 412; Schenck, *History of Ionia and Montcalm Counties,* 30; *Portrait and Biographical Album of Kalamazoo, Allegan, and Van Buren Counties,* 200.
5. George W. Lawton, "Historical Sketch of Van Buren County," *MPHC* 3 (1881): 633.
6. Gray, "Limits and Possibilities," 86; Brainard, *Pioneer History,* 42; *History of Jackson County,* 213; Mrs. A. M. Hayes, "Reminiscences of Pioneer Days in Hastings," *MPHC* 26 (1894–95): 238; Towner, "My Mother's Girlhood," 183; Harvey Haynes, "Sketches of the Early History of Branch County," *MPHC* 6 (1883): 216; Michael Shoemaker, "Historical Sketch of the City of Jackson, Mich.," *MPHC* 2 (1880): 287.
7. HPSP/MHC.
8. D. L. Porter to W. P. Porter, 2 May 1830/DLPP/CHL.
9. Clifton, *Pokagons,* 69–71.
10. Mary M. Hoyt, "Recollections of Pioneer Life in Michigan and the Founding of Yankee Springs, *MPHC* 30 (1905): 298; Kirkland, *A New Home,* 129; Foote, "Early Days of Eaton County," 383; Jacob Gerrish, Diary, 1837–41/JGP/MSUAHC.
11. Goodenough Townsend, "Early History of the Township of Davison," *MPHC* 22 (1893): 548; Albert Miller, "Pioneer Sketches," *MPHC* 7 (1886): 234–35; Jesse Turner, "Reminiscences of Kalamazoo," *MPHC* 18 (1891): 573.
12. Bela Hubbard, "The Early Colonization of Detroit," *MPHC* 1 (1877): 352–53; Lanman, *History of Michigan, Civil and Topographical,* 318–19; Fuller, *Economic and Social Beginnings,* 111.
13. ASP/PL/1/1804/97.
14. Christiancy, "Early History of the City and County of Monroe," 373; ASP/PL/1/1804/97; Hubbard, "Early Colonization of Detroit," 353; Fuller, *Economic and Social Beginnings,* 108.

15. *Detroit Gazette,* 30 January 1819.

16. Henry S. Sanford, Journal, 12 August 1844/HSSP/GSML/Box 3. Similar examples of French "indolence" appeared often in pioneer reminiscences of the late nineteenth century. See, for example, Bela Hubbard, "Early Colonization of Detroit," 352. Although Sanford's secondhand statement is a contemporary account, it may be no more reliable than the others.

17. ASP/ PL/1/1804/97; Hubbard, "Early Colonization of Detroit," 352, 359; Fuller, *Economic and Social Beginnings,* 109.

18. Keeney, "Salmon Keeney's Visit to Michigan," 442–43.

19. *Detroit Gazette,* 19 September 1817, 7 November 1817; J. C. Holmes, "The Early History of Horticulture in Michigan," *MPHC* 10 (1888): 70; Miller, *New States and Territories,* 24.

20. ASP/PL/1/1804/97; *Detroit Gazette,* 19 September 1817, 30 July 1819.

21. Christiancy, "Early History of the City and County of Monroe," 373; *Detroit Gazette,* 22 January 1819.

22. *Detroit Gazette,* 19 September 1817.

23. Lanman, *History of Michigan, Civil and Topographical,* 319; Gov. Cass to Sec. of War, 31 May 1816/TPUS/MT/10:642–43.

24. Dunbar, *Michigan,* 74.

25. J. B. LaRowe, "Address of J. B. LaRowe," *Livingston Republican,* 17 July 1879; Shoemaker, "Sketch of the City of Jackson," 285–86.

26. Sylvanus Bachelder to James Bachelder, 10 December 1846, in *Bachelder Family Letters,* 8–9; Henry Parker Smith, *Reminiscences*/HPSP/MHC; Jacob Gerrish, Diary, 1837–38/JGP/MSUAHC.

27. *History of Jackson County,* 223.

28. Henry Parker Smith described hunting as "the chief occupation of the times" by settlers on Prairie Ronde when they were not engaged in agricultural tasks. See *Reminiscences*/HPSP/MHC.

29. Richard O. Cummings, *The American and His Food* (Chicago: University of Chicago Press, 1940), 236; Atack and Bateman, *To Their Own Soil,* 209.

30. *Portrait and Biographical Album of Genesee, Lapeer, and Tuscola Counties, Michigan* (Chicago: Chapman Bros., 1892), 423. Farm-making was particularly devastating to species occupying relatively limited habitats. Continuous hunting, especially during nesting and breeding seasons, reduced the numbers of many species. The prevalence of uncontrolled hunting in Michigan eventually led to the extinction of such frontier staples as the passenger pigeon and the wild turkey, as well as the decimation of deer populations. Although the patchwork landscape of fields, croplands, orchards, pastures, hayfields, and woodlots created by farm-making contributed to species reduction by eliminating habitats, it also expanded habitats ideal for the proliferation of such species as squirrels, quail, rabbits, and foxes. See James B. Trefethen, "Wildlife Regulation and Restoration," in *Origins of American Conservation,* ed. Henry Clepper (New York: Ronald Press, 1966), 20–21; William T. Hornaday, *Our Vanishing Wildlife: Its Extermination and Preservation* (New York: New York Zoological Society, 1913), 43; and Michigan Writers' Project, *Michigan: A Guide to the Wolverine State* (New York: Oxford University Press, 1941), 83.

31. L. D. Watkins, "Settlement and Natural History of Manchester and Vicinity," *MPHC* 22 (1893): 265; *Emigrant's Guide,* 168; McMath, "Willow Run Settlement," 491; Dunbar, *Michigan,* 310–11; Blois, *Gazetteer,* 55–57.

32. Watkins, "Settlement and Natural History of Manchester," 265; Elizabeth Chandler to Jane Howell, 18 April 1831/EMCP/Box 1/MHC; Jacob Gerrish, Diary, 1837–38/JGP/MSUAHC; Life of William Fulton/SHFP/MSUAHC; Blois, *Gazetteer,* 36; Brainard, *Pioneer History,* 35; McMath, "Willow Run Settlement," 491; Bub Able, "'The Sunny Side,' as Bub Able Saw It in Pioneer Life," *St. Johns News,* 12 July 1900; Davenport, *Timberland Times,* 21–22.

33. Elizabeth Chamberlain to Mellen Chamberlain, 25 September 1847/CFP/MSUAHC.

34. Able, "The Sunny Side"; Elizabeth Chamberlain to Hale E. Crosby, 4 February 1844/CFP/MSUAHC; Bela Hubbard, Notebooks, 10 September 1847/BHP/MHC; *Clinton Independent,* 6 September 1883.

35. Blois, *Gazetteer,* 35; Davenport, *Timberland Times,* 20–21; Able, "The Sunny Side"; Riley, *Puddleford Papers,* 47–52.

36. Margaret B. Holman and Kathryn C. Egan, "Processing Maple Sap with Prehistoric Techniques," *Journal of Ethnobiology* 5 (1985): 69–70; Johnson, *Michigan Fur Trade,* 99; *Detroit Gazette,* 20 November 1818, 30 August 1825; Warden, *Statistical, Political, and Historical Account,* 1:659; Bidwell and Falconer, *Agriculture in the Northern United States,* 505. Accounts of sugar exports may be found in Shipping Manifests, 1825–29/ETBC/SAM.

37. Davenport, *Timberland Times,* 22; Elizabeth Chandler to Jane Howell, 30 August 1832/EMCP/Box 1/MHC. Henry Sanford described the process of maple sugar making as it was conducted in western Kalamazoo County:

> A rough cabin of sticks and bark is made, places erected for the pans and fires. Wooden troughs for the sap are made. Slashes are cut in the trees, and a little beneath a gouging chisel makes a place for the insertion of a stick with a groove in it, on which the sap runs and so falls into the trough below. The sap each day is emptied into their receivers and thence fed into the pans as required . . . These pans have a large surface exposed to the fire, the sap not being more than six inches deep and as fast as [it is] evaporated it is supplied with more from the receiver till it becomes syrup when it is cooked. Thus in one camp will a ton of sugar and two or three barrels of molasses & vinegar ea. be made in one season. (Journal, 15 August 1844/HSSP/Box 3/GSML)

"The most useful tree to the first settlers was the sugar maple," wrote Edward Barber. "In every township maple sugar was much made for home consumption and for sale." The sap vinegar was used primarily for pickling and was consumed at home. See Barber, "Beginnings in Eaton County," 344; Potter, "A Boy's Story," 409; Nowlin, *Bark-Covered House,* 38; McMath, "Willow Run Settlement," 491; Elizabeth Chandler to Jane Howell, 15 April 1831/EMCP/Box 1/MHC; and Henry Sanford, Journal, 15 August 1844/HSSP/Box 3/GSML.

38. Potter, "A Boy's Story," 406, illustrated this complicated process by tracing the course taken by potash made by an Eaton County family who cleared their farm in 1847. It began with their

> gathering the ashes to turn into "blacksalts" by a neighbor who had an ashery and worked them up on shares. The blacksalts were sold to merchants in Charlotte, who had them made into potash, then drawn to Marshall and shipped to Buffalo, where they were made into saleratus, ready to be shipped back to the merchants who sold to the same families who had cut the timber and burned the logs that made the ashes they had raked up to make the blacksalts that made the saleratus that raised the pancakes.

39. Barber, "Beginnings in Eaton County," 34; Foote, "Early Days of Eaton County," 394. Henry Sanford also noted that the size and poor quality of the trees found in the oak openings in western Michigan rendered them good for nothing "but rails or ashes" (Journal, 14 August 1844/HSSP/Box 3/GSML). See also *Detroit Gazette,* 12 July 1822; Jacob Gerrish to Moses Chamberlain, 13 June 1843/CFP/MSUAHC; and Albert Baxter, *History of the City of Grand Rapids, Michigan* (New York: Munsell, 1891), 491.

40. Everett, *Memorials,* 245, 376, 419, 508; Fuller, *Economic and Social Beginnings,* 36, 277; Fox, *History of Saginaw County,* 25, 30. Unlucky pioneers, such as Joseph English of Kent County, turned to shingle making to help rebuild fortunes lost in land speculation. See Edwin Thayer, "Agriculture of Ottawa County," *MPHC* 9 (1886): 263.

41. John P. Powell to Joseph Powell, 22 March 1846/PFP/MSUAHC.

42. A. C. Glidden, "Pioneer Farming," *MPHC* 18 (1891): 419.

43. George W. Thayer, "From Vermont to Lake Superior in 1845," *MPHC* 30 (1905): 553.

44. Betsey Landon to Thomas Cranson, 2 May 1836, in Brown, *Stray Leaves,* 25; *History of Jackson County,* 183.

45. Davenport, *Timberland Times,* 52–54; Hoskins, *Notes upon the Western Country,* 24. Albert Miller of Saginaw stated that "it was customary for settlers to fell the timber and pile the brush neatly and burn it in the spring, and plant and raise their first crop of corn among the logs." See "Incidents in the Early History of the Saginaw Valley," *MPHC* 13 (1888): 355. See also Henry Chamberlain to Mellen Chamberlain, 14 November 1845/CFP/MSUAHC;

46. *History of Jackson County,* 223; Elizabeth Chandler to Jane Howell, 13 December 1832/EMCP/Box 1/MHC; Letter from A. Henry, in *Michigan Farmer* 1851, 42.

47. Thaddeus Smith to Elizabeth Smith, 14 June 1829/SBSFC/WMUARHC; Davenport, *Timberland Times,* 42; Peck, *New Guide for Emigrants,* 117, 118.

   For a discussion of the distinction between the different types of log architecture associated with early frontier settlement in the trans-Appalachian United States, see Terry G. Jordan and Matti Kaups, *The American Backwoods Frontier,* 175–77. They argue that the cruder characteristics of initial construction represent a diffusion of Savo-Karelian architecture. Its adaptiveness to woodland habitats encouraged its adoption by settlers in forested environments and led to the widespread diffusion of this form of log building. Log houses were erected as soon as possible; however, because of the greater amount of work involved in their construction, they were often not finished immediately. An early settler in Lenawee County wrote, "It is the prevailing custom here not to finish their houses for two or three years, that more important business may be attended to, such as breaking up, ploughing, dragging, . . . fencing, etc." (Ruth Evans to Jane Howell, 22 October 1832/EMCP/Box 1/MHC). Some log houses survived as dwellings long after the close of the frontier. A log house in Boston Township, for example, remained the lifelong home of early Ionia County resident James M. Talent, who preferred the familiarity of the early structure to the convenience of a new one. See Everett, *Memorials,* 103–4.

48. Elizabeth Chandler to Jane Howell, 2 August 1831; Ruth Evans to Jane Howell, 22 October 1831; Elizabeth Chandler to Jane Howell, 24 April 1833/EMCP/Box 1/MHC; Everett, *Memorials,* 199.

49. Shoemaker, "Sketch of the City of Jackson," 285.

50. Hardeman, *Shucks, Shocks, and Hominy Blocks,* 54–55; *History of Jackson County,* 183; Northrup, "First Trip to Michigan," 70; Henry Parker Smith, *Reminiscences*/HPSP/MHC; Potter, "A Boy's Story," 397.

51. Samp mills, employing a hollow stump as a mortar and an overhanging pestle attached to a pole or tree, were used to pound corn into smaller particles. See Hardeman, *Shucks, Shocks, and Hominy Blocks,* 126–27; Alvin C. Osborn, "Recollections of an Early Settler," *Hudson Gazette,* 20 February 1874; *History of Washtenaw County,* 453–54; Weller, *Yesterday,* 19; M. A. Leeson, *History of Kent County, Michigan* (Chicago: Chas. C. Chapman, 1881), 238; and R. C. Crawford, "Reminiscences of Pioneer Life in Michigan," *MPHC* 4 (1883): 42.

52. In the woodlands of Nankin Township of Wayne County, Melvin D. Osband recalled that the initial crop of corn planted by his family produced a "growth of corn stalks . . . larger than any I have seen since." Elizabeth Chandler of Lenawee County remarked that their first crop was better than she anticipated. See Osband, "Pioneers and Pioneer Life in Nankin," 446; Elizabeth Chandler to Jane Howell, 2 August 1831/EMCP/Box 1/MHC. See also Hardeman, *Shucks, Shocks, and Hominy Blocks,* 28; McMath, "Willow Run Settlement," 486–87; and Miller, "Pioneer Sketches," 236–37.

53. Henry Chamberlain, for example, delayed planting wheat on his Berrien County farm for a year after his arrival in order to clear an adequate area. Planning his work systematically, he planted spring crops while continuing to clear additional land. Following the corn harvest, he seeded all his cleared land in wheat, which Chamberlain harvested the next spring. Jesse Osborn and Thomas Chandler, both of whom set-

tled near Tecumseh, followed a similar pattern. Each delayed planting wheat on his Lenawee County farm until his second year of residence. See Henry Chamberlain to Mellen Chamberlain, 29 October 1844/CFP/MSUAHC; Osborn, "Recollections," *Hudson Gazette,* 20 February 1874; and Ruth Evans to Jane Howell, 8 September 1831/EMCP/Box 1/MHC.

54. Blois, *Gazetteer,* 24–25; Mrs. S. L. Withey [Marion Louise Hinsdill], "Personal Recollections of Early Days in Kent County," *MPHC* 39 (1915): 346; Pierce, *History of Calhoun County,* 171; Samuel Prescott, "Early Settlers in the Town of Blackman," *MPHC* 7 (1886): 464.

55. James and E. P. Crampton, the second family to settle in Bridgewater Township in Washtenaw County, pounded out the dried seeds to make whole-grain cereal, eaten with milk. Others, like the parents of Jacob Cornell, ground the wheat in coffee mills and bolted it through crepe to produce flour. See L. D. Watkins, "Settlement of the Township of Bridgewater and Vicinity, Washtenaw County," *MPHC* 28 (1897–98): 569; *History of Jackson County,* 213; and Pierce, *History of Calhoun County,* 171.

56. Crawford, "Reminiscences of Pioneer Life," 42.

57. Leeson, *History of Kent County,* 238.

58. Daboll, *Past and Present,* 240. Arriving in Superior Township of Washtenaw County in the summer of 1826, P. S. Richards' family "could only get a little of the wood chopped off to get some seeds in the ground. They . . . would plant their potatoes and sow some turnips where the brush was burned, . . . those turnips . . . were monstrous, and the potatoes were not far behind them" (Richards, "Eighty Years in Michigan," 366). Potatoes were also among the first crops planted by Henry Parker Smith in Kalamazoo County and Thomas Chandler near Tecumseh. See Henry Parker Smith, *Reminiscences*/HPSP/MHC; Elizabeth Chandler to Jane Howell, 2 August 1831/EMCP/Box 1/MHC; and Ruth Evans to Jane Howell, 8 September 1831/EMCP/Box 1/MHC; Osband, "Pioneers and Pioneer Life in Nankin," 446; Weller, *Yesterday,* 19; Ruth Evans to Jane Howell, 8 September 1831/EMCP/Box 1/MHC.

59. Capitalism is a mode of production characterized by a severing of the direct links between labor and the means of production so that the control of production passes into the hands of those having the wealth to acquire it. This permits the latter to deny access to such means, in effect restricting the producers' rights to subsistence. In order to gain access to the means of production, labor must bargain with the owners, selling their labor in exchange for the wages necessary to sustain themselves. Dividing labor from those who control production creates and maintains separate social classes and makes the value of labor a commodity subject to fluctuation with the costs of production. Because production costs reflect both its efficiency and the degree of competition for markets, the value of labor varies considerably. Changes in either of these variables can affect both wages and degree of employment. Labor becomes a distinct class possessing little or no role in guiding the economy, and its welfare remains subject to the actions of others. Owners of the means of production can appropriate the surplus generated by labor as profits, which might be increased by raising labor's output through improvements in technology and organization. These improvements require additional investment, the costs of which necessitate further accumulation of wealth. Competition for markets also encourages production efficiency by bringing increased sales and greater profits to the capitalist who outproduces and undersells competitors. See Wolf, *Europe and the People without History,* 75–78; Pessen, *Jacksonian America,* 78, 102–3.

In simple commodity production the household remains the unit of production, but must sell its surplus in an external market in order to acquire most of what it consumes. Both owners and laborers are part of the household, and the quantity of labor available for production remains fixed. The redistribution of surplus among household members takes precedence over the maximization of profit. The surplus remains the property of the household unit, and as long as all members of the group remain part of it, the surplus can be invested in farm expansion and improvements. When it becomes necessary or desirable for the household to divide, a portion of the surplus is transferred through wage labor to household members seeking to set up farms of their own. The redistribution of surplus to create new units of production is central in the reproduction of simple commodity production. See Harriet Friedmann, "World Market, State, and Family Farm: Social Bases of Household Production in the Era of Wage Labor," *Comparative Studies in Society and History* 20 (1978): 559–62; and idem, "Simple Commodity Production and Wage Labour in the American Plains," *Journal of Peasant Studies* 6 (1979): 96.

60. For a discussion of the role of the household mode of production as a defining feature of the early American economy, see Michael Merrill, "Cash Is Good to Eat: Self-Sufficiency and Exchange in the Rural Economy of the United States," *Radical History Review* 19 (1977): 52–54. A discussion of this form of exchange as a widespread adaptation in colonial North America, especially the Northeast, appeared in James A. Henretta, "Families and Farms: *Mentalite* in Pre-Industrial America," *William and Mary Quarterly,* 3d ser., no. 35 (1978): 15–16 and idem, "The Transition to Capitalism in America," in *The Origins of American Capitalism: Collected Essays* (Boston: Northeastern University Press, 1991), 263–64. Gerald M. Sider, *Culture and Class in Anthropology and History: A Newfoundland Illustration* (Paris: Cambridge University Press, 1986), 109–10, emphasized the significance of property rights in forming the distinctive social relations associated with class societies in economically peripheral areas. He also demonstrated the manner in which changes in these relations shaped the historical development of one such community.

61. Sider, *Culture and Class,* 22–23, 56. This form of exchange is also known as "truck" and is found in isolated economies in which the supply of cash is limited and direct exchanges of goods and services predominate.

62. Michael Merrill, "So What's Wrong with the 'Household Mode of Production,'" *Radical History Review* 22 (1979–80): 144. See also Carole Shammas, "How Self-Sufficient Was Early America?" *Journal of Interdisciplinary History* 13 (1982): 263.

63. Bidwell and Falconer, *Agriculture in the Northern United States,* 165. An emphasis on subsistence was necessary to alleviate deficiencies arising from frontier isolation and did not preclude specialized production for exchange within a wider community whose members wished for more than mere survival. The presence of such production eliminated the existence of a solely subsistence economy, yet the circumstances under which it took place influenced both its scope and the manner of exchange. See James T. Lemon, "Household Consumption in Eighteenth-Century America and Its Relationship to Production and Trade: The Situation Among Farmers in Southeastern Pennsylvania," *Agricultural History* 41 (1967): 68–69; Danhof, *Change in Agriculture,* 13; and Andrew Hill Clark, "Suggestions for the Geographical Study of Agricultural Change in the United States, 1790–1840," *Agricultural History* 46 (1972): 165. Allan Kulikoff applied the term "communal self-sufficiency" to economic systems characterized by local or exchange on the Eastern Seaboard and later in frontier areas. See "Households and Markets: Toward a New Synthesis of American Agrarian History," *William and Mary Quarterly,* 3d ser., no. 50 (1993): 353.

64. Elton B. Hill, "Farm Management," *Michigan History* 22 (1938): 312; Shammas, "How Self-Sufficient Was Early America?" 252–53.

65. Taylor, *Transportation Revolution,* 21–22; SLUS/1802/2:179–80; SLUS/1825/4:135; William F. Gephart, *Transportation and Industrial Development in the Middle West,* Columbia University, Studies in History, Economics, and Public Law, no. 89 (New York: Longmans, Green, 1909), 130.

66. Pilcher, "Forty Years Ago," 83–84.

67. The form of transportation networks in frontier regions is discussed in Taaffe, Morrill, and Gould, "Transport Expansion," 506. See also Caroline MacGill, *History of Transportation in the United States before 1860,* prepared under the direction of Henry Balthasar Meyer (Washington, D.C.: Carnegie Institute, 1917; reprint, New York: Peter Smith, 1948), 26–27; Edwards, "Sketch of Pioneer Life," 149; A.

D. P. Van Buren, "Settlement of Branch County," *MPHC* 18 (1891): 611; and William H. Cross, "Early Michigan," *MPHC* 10 (1886): 55.

68. Bates, "By-Gones of Detroit," 348.

69. Memorial to Congress from the Legislative Council, 21 January 1833/TPUS/MT/12:567–68; Enoch Chase, "Coldwater in 1831," *MPHC* 7 (1886): 346–47; Proceedings of Detroit Meeting, Memorial by Citizens of the Territory, 28 October 1831/TPUS/MT/12:367–68; Cross, "Early Michigan, 55.

70. Martineau, "Travels in and around Michigan," 52–56; Petition to Congress by Inhabitants of the Territory, 18 January 1836/TPUS/MT/12:1098; Gordan and May, "Michigan Land Rush," 433; George Taylor, "First Visit to Michigan," *MPHC* 6 (1883): 15. Enos Goodrich considered that he was among "a favored set of passengers" on an 1834 trip, "for we did not have to travel on foot and carry a rail to pry the stage out of the mire" ("Across Michigan Territory Sixty Years Ago," *MPHC* 26 [1894–95]: 229).

71. Taylor, *Transportation Revolution,* 15–17; *Detroit Gazette,* 24 May 1825; Van Buren, "Settlement of Branch County," 610–11; Bates, "By-Gones of Detroit," 348; Taylor, "First Visit to Michigan," 15; Petition to Congress by Residents of Lenawee County, January 1830/TPUS/MT/12:120.

72. *Detroit Gazette,* 9 April 1824.

73. *Detroit Gazette,* 8 May 1818, 24 July 1818, and 14 June 1822. The high cost of transportation was noted early and remained a significant economic factor decades later. See the *Livingston Courier,* 1 March 1843.

74. Shoemaker, "Sketch of the City of Jackson," 285–86; Haynes, "Early History of Branch County," 219; Crisfield Johnson, *History of Allegan and Barry Counties* (Philadelphia: D. W. Ensign, 1880), 47; *Portrait and Biographical Album of Lenawee County, Michigan* (Chicago: Chapman Bros., 1888), 798. O'Shea Wilder met a Jackson County man named Thompson transporting a load of corn and wheat to mill. Wilder's informant claimed that he had "Come fifty miles through the woods where a team had never before passed, & now has thirty miles to carry [it] to have it ground" (Diary, 21 November 1831/MHC). Upon his arrival home, an exasperated Hart declared that he "was rejoiced to learn that the family had not starved ("N. H. Hart, "Pioneer Sketches," *MPHC* 3 [1881]: 551).

75. David L. Porter to W. P. Porter, 1 November 1829/DLPP/CHL. An early pioneer in southwestern Michigan recalled a similar dependence by residents on the provisions trade. Referring to the general structure of trade, he wrote, "Markets were not of much importance, as they had few products to sell; necessarily few to buy," emphasizing that, "the main reliance for marketing produce was to new settlers." See A. B. Copley, "Early Settlement in Southwestern Michigan," *MPHC* 5 (1884): 150; *Democratic Free Press,* 30 December 1835; and Lanman, *History of Michigan, Civil and Topographical,* 256.

76. Elizabeth Chandler to Jane Howell, 2 September 1833/EMCP/Box 1/MHC. Statistics from Michigan's earliest census in 1837 support this observation (Blois, *Gazetteer,* 390). See also *Emigrant,* 25 May 1831; Benjamin Fay to Simon Fay, 31 March 1839/FFC/MSUAHC; Ruth Evans to Jane Howell, 15 February 1831/EMCP/Box 1/MHC; Edward Parsons, Diaries, 8 July 1835/PaFP/MSUAHC; Jacob Gerrish to Moses Chamberlain, 6 January 1837/CFP/MSUAHC; and Jonathan A. Gale to Moses Chamberlain, 18 April 1837/CFP/MSUAHC.

77. *Detroit Gazette,* 22 January 1819. Immigrant accounts often echoed the words of Lucy B. Jones, who wrote, "All stock and all provisions [are] very high and very scarce. There is not enough raised to supply the emigrants and many suffer for want of food" (Lucy B. Jones to Frederick Hall, 19 May 1835/HFL/MSUAHC). On the other hand, accounts in both Crawford, "Reminiscences of Pioneer Life," 49, and *Detroit Gazette,* 16 April 1829, reveal the effects of overproduction by pioneer producers.

78. Martin L. Daniels to Isaac Arnold, 19 March 1837/MHC; Anson W. Halbert to Harrison Halbert, 20 March 1843/HFP/SAM; Jacob Gerrish to Moses Chamberlain, 6 June 1837/CFP/MSUAHC.

79. Evans, *Pedestrious Tour,* 95–96. Even as late as 1821, the editor of the *Detroit Gazette* chided Michigan farmers because they failed "to produce a surplus in this territory, . . . and still permit the people of Ohio

to sell in our market thousands of barrels of vegetable and animal food." *Detroit Gazette,* 11 May 1821.

80. David L. Porter to W. P. Porter, 20 March 1831/DLPP/CHL.

81. C.B. Stebbins, "Sketch of My Life," 58/SFP/MSUAHC; Everett, *Memorials,* 42; *Democratic Free Press,* 29 June 1836.

82. Caroline Kirkland, *Forest Life* (New York: C. S. Francis, 1842), 2:73–79; Hardeman, *Shucks, Shocks, and Hominy Blocks,* 154; Sam B. Hilliard, "Pork in the Ante-bellum South: The Geography of Self-Sufficiency," *Annals of the Association of American Geographers* 59 (1969): 471–80; idem, *Hog Meat and Hoecake: Food Supply in the Old South, 1840–1860* (Carbondale: Southern Illinois University Press, 1972), 108–9, 131; Gates, *Farmer's Age,* 219.

83. *Genesee Farmer* 1833, 316; *History of Jackson County,* 193–94; *Semi-Weekly Free Press,* 9 May 1837.

84. Evans, *Pedestrious Tour,* 188; William Clark, "Livingston County Pioneers," *MPHC* 1 (1877): 253.

85. William Thompson, *A Tradesman's Travels in the United States and Canada, in the Years 1840, 41, and 42* (Edinburgh: Oliver & Boyd, 1842), 88; *History of Jackson County,* 171.

86. Van Buren, "First Settlement of Sturgis Prairie," 520; Everett, *Memorials,* 483–84.

87. *Michigan Farmer,* 1845, 154–55.

88. Gray, "Limits and Possibilities," 80. The lower mean rates of return characteristic of Michigan were similar to those of other frontier areas in the Old Northwest, which exhibited rates well below those found in the Northeast or South. See Atack and Bateman, *To Their Own Soil,* 260–62.

89. Compared to investment in manufacturing and other contemporary economic ventures, farming yielded a relatively low rate of return. See Theodore Saloutos, "The Agricultural Problem and Nineteenth-Century Industrialism," *Agricultural History* 22 (1948): 156. For discussions of economies characterized by communal self-sufficiency, see Allan Kulikoff, *The Agrarian Origins of American Capitalism* (Charlottesville: University Press of Virginia, 1992), chap. 2; idem, "Households and Markets," 351–53; and Christopher Clark, *The Roots of American Capitalism: Western Massachusetts, 1780–1860* (Ithaca, N.Y.: Cornell University Press, 1990), 84–87. For discussions of the security offered by farming, see Atack and Bateman, *To Their Own Soil,* 264–65; Fred Bateman and Thomas Weiss, *A Deplorable Scarcity* (Chapel Hill: University of North Carolina Press, 1981), 156; and Danhof, *Change in Agriculture,* 104; as well as contemporary sources, Lanman, *History of Michigan, Civil and Topographical,* 321; and *Michigan Farmer,* 1845, 155.

90. Henry Chamberlain to Mellen Chamberlain, 8 May 1847/CFP/MSUAHC; *Portrait and Biographical Album of Lenawee County,* 910.

91. Caroline Kirkland referred to wheat as "a currency that never depreciates." This did not mean that wheat became a token of value that served as money in the sense that it was the basis for calculating the value of all other items. Exchange based on the use of a consumption good as a least common denominator of value is referred to as "money barter." Such value tokens lack the portability, divisibility, and durability of money, which restricts their use in commercial exchange and limits their role as a medium of accumulation and investment. Although a scarcity of cash reduced its use on the Michigan frontier, the employment of cash values to achieve equivalencies anticipated the use of a more flexible medium of exchange and allowed farmers, merchants, and others to make the transition to a capitalist economy. See Kirkland, *A New Home,* 194; George Dalton, "Primitive Money," *American Anthropologist* 67 (1965): 47, 59–60; and Melville J. Herskovitts, *Man and His Works: The Science of Cultural Anthropology* (New York: Alfred A. Knopf, 1948), 277–79.

92. Bela Hubbard, Notebook, 27 October 1850/BHP/Box 3/MHC; *Democratic Expounder and Calhoun County Democrat,* 8 September 1842; Jonathan Searles to Zelotes B. Searles, 20 December 1840/JSP/CHL.

93. *Three Oaks Press,* 21 April 1899.

94. Brainard, *Pioneer History,* 57; Edward Parsons, Diary, 30 August–1 September 1842/PaFP/MSUAHC.

95. *Acorn*, 1 March 1917; Elizabeth Chandler to Jane Howell, 24 April 1833/EMCP/Box 1/MHC.

96. Elizabeth Chandler to Jane Howell, 24 April 1833/EMCP/Box 1/MHC.

97. Kirkland, "Paradise of the Poor," 185; Elizabeth Chandler to Jane Howell, 15 April 1831/EMCP/Box 1/MHC.

98. Van Buren, "Pioneer Annals," 254; Thomas Wright, Diary, 16 January 1832/TWD/MSUAHC; Kirkland, *A New Home*, 291.

99. Brainard, *Pioneer History*, 62; Sylvester Cochrane to the Sec. of the American Home Missionary Society, 3 March 1840, in Cole, *Voices from the Wilderness*, 62. The American Home Missionary Society was formed in 1826 as a cooperative venture of the Congregational, Presbyterial, and Reformed churches. Its principal aim was to encourage the founding of churches and schools in the western territories then undergoing settlement. See Dunbar, *Michigan*, 231; Stebbins, "Sketch of My Life," 71/SFP/MSUAHC; Moses Chamberlain to Mellen Chamberlain, 28 June 1846/CFP/MSUAHC.

100. James Lanman noted that "The purchase of lands and the importation of foreign goods drained the population of their means; the amount raised and the market for products were not sufficient to equalize the balance of trade." See *History of Michigan, Civil and Topographical*, 321; *History of Jackson County*, 222; Everett, *Memorials*, 483.

101. Everett, *Memorials*, 27.

102. Sarah Gains to Joshua Fay, 27 February 1832/JFFC/CHL.

103. Stuart Bruchey, "The Business Economy of Marketing Change, 1790–1840: A Study of Sources of Efficiency," *Agricultural History* 46 (1972): 222; John G. Clark, *The Grain Trade in the Old Northwest* (Urbana: University of Illinois Press, 1966), 41–43; William Cronon, *Nature's Metropolis: Chicago and the Great West* (New York: W. W. Norton, 1991), 61–62.

CHAPTER 9

1. Suitable areas for settlement were determined by overlaying multiple criterion layers within the ArcView Spatial Analyst Geographic Information System (GIS). The Spatial Analyst software provides an environment in which criteria, in the form of Raster GIS layers, can be overlaid or combined based on their relative suitability. Prior to combining, the values on each criterion layer are standardized according to a common evaluation scale such as zero to ten. In such a scenario, pixels with a value of zero do not meet the criteria, while values of ten fully meet the criteria. After standardization, the criterion layers can be added together utilizing the overlay technique within ArcView Spatial Analyst. Regions on the final output with the highest values were deemed the most suitable for settlement. Criteria consisted of the following: (1) distance to reserve lands occupied by Indians perceived as "friendly," (2) Distance to reserves of Indians perceived to be unfriendly, (3) distance to roads, and (4) distance to areas with land cover perceived favorable to agriculture. Land cover types were taken from Comer et al., *Michigan's Presettlement Vegetation*. All criteria were assumed to have equal weight in the final outcome. This process was repeated for six intervals during the period from 1818 to 1836 to produce a sequential picture of settlement spread in Michigan.

GIS has been employed extensively by archaeologists to model historic landscapes. See, for example, R. J. Hasenstab and B. Resnick, "GIS in Historical Predictive Modelling: The Fort Drum Project," in *Interpreting Space: GIS and Archaeology*, ed. K. M. S. Allen, S. W. Green, and E. B. W. Zubrow (New York: Taylor and Francis, 1990), 284–306; and I. Williams, F. W. Limp, and F. L. Briuer, "Using Geographic Information Systems and Exploratory Data Analysis for Archaeological Site Classification and Analysis," in *Interpreting Space*, ed. K. M. S. Allen, S. W. Green, and E. B. W. Zubrow, 239–73. For a description of

IDRISI, see, R. J. Eastman, *IDRISI: Version 4.1* (Worcester, Mass.: Clark University Graduate School of Geography, 1993). For a description of ArcView Spatial Analyst, see T. Ormsby and J. Alvi, *Extending ArcView GIS: With Network Analyst, Spatial Analyst, and 3D Analyst* (Redlands, Calif.: Environmental Systems Research, 1999).

2. Roads shown in figure 9.3 are based on John Farmer, *Map of the Surveyed Part of the Territory of Michigan,* col. map 49 x 54 cm., scale 1:506,880 (Utica, N.Y.: V. Balch and S. Stiles, 1826).

3. Roads shown in figure 9.4 are based on John Farmer, *Map of the Surveyed Part of the Territory of Michigan,* col. map 53 x 78 cm., scale 1:500,000 (Utica, N.Y.: V. Balch and S. Stiles, 1830).

4. Roads shown in figure 9.5 are based on John Farmer, *An Improved Edition of a Map of the Surveyed Part of the Territory of Michigan,* col. map 53 x 78 cm., scale 1:500,000 (New York: J. H. Colton, 1836) and H. S. Tanner, *A New Map of Michigan, with Its Canals, Roads, & Distances,* col. map 51 x 38 cm., scale 1:1,900,800 (Philadelphia: H. S. Tanner, 1836).

5. Roads shown in figure 9.6 are based on John Farmer, *Map of the Surveyed Part of Michigan,* col. map 53 x 78 cm., scale 1:500,000 (New York: J. H. Colton, 1840) and J. Calvin Smith, *Guide through Ohio, Michigan, Indiana, Illinois, Missouri, & Iowa,* col. map 57 x 68 cm., scale 1:1,584,000 (New York: J. H. Colton, 1840).

6. LeRoy Barnett has recently mapped the patterning of initial land sales throughout Michigan. See "Michigan's First Land Sales," 44–46. The order of land purchases clearly reveals the selective purchase of tracts in southern Michigan as well as a later acquisition of lands in the lower Saginaw Valley, the Thumb, and the area north of the Grand River. Large portions of this region were purchased for resale, especially during the mid-1830s boom period, and the patterning of their sales may not always reflect occupance. Because these data also do not measure actual settlement, they cannot be used to estimate its density.

7. For a description of frontier post offices in Michigan and a discussion of the roles they played in this region, see Ralph R. Tingley, "Postal Service in Michigan Territory," *Michigan History* 35 (1951): 447–60. Early residents of Shiawassee County, for example, recalled how the inconvenience of retrieving mail from the nearest post office at Holly in Oakland County produced an immediate demand for the creation of a more centrally located mail facility and led to the establishment of a post office at Byron. See Ellis, *History of Shiawassee and Clinton Counties,* 204; Everett, *Memorials,* 448. The use of post office opening dates as an indicator of frontier expansion has been successfully employed to trace settlement growth in Florida and Montana. See Morton D. Winsberg, "The Advance of Florida's Frontier as Determined from Post Office Openings," *Florida Historical Quarterly* 72 (1993): 189–99; and John A. Alwin, "Post Office Locations and the Historical Geographer: A Montana Example," *Professional Geographer* 26 (1974): 183–86.

8. Brief summaries of population growth in antebellum Michigan appear in George J. Miller, "Some Geographic Influences in the Settlement of Michigan and in the Distribution of Its Population," *American Geographical Society Bulletin* 45 (1913): 321–48; and Rolland H. Maybee, "Population Growth and Distribution in Lower Michigan: 1810–1840," *Michigan Academy of Science and Letters, Papers* 31 (1945): 253–66. The former includes small-scale distribution maps for 1810, 1830, 1850, and 1860, showing the estimated number of persons per square mile.

The development of counties in Michigan and the difficulties involved in discerning the formation of unorganized counties are discussed in William H. Hathaway, "County Organization in Michigan," *Michigan History* 2 (1918): 574–77. The formation of counties in Lower Michigan after the War of 1812 occurred as follows: In 1822 Wayne, Monroe, Macomb. Oakland, and St. Clair were organized and the boundaries of Lapeer were laid off by proclamation (MEA/1822/MTL 1:330–36). The boundaries of Washtenaw, Ingham, Eaton, Barry, Jackson, Calhoun, Kalamazoo, Van Buren, Hillsdale, Branch, St.

Joseph, Cass, and Berrien were established seven years later by legislative act (MTL/2/1829:335–37). Those of Clinton, Ionia, Kent, Allegan, Ottawa, Gratiot, Montcalm, Oceana, Saginaw, Midland, and Isabella were provided for in 1831, and Genesee was set off four years later (MTL/3/1831:871–73; MTL/3/1835:1416–17). Finally, Oceana's boundaries were redefined and those of Newaygo, Mecosta, Tuscola, Sanilac, and Huron were established in 1840 (MAL/L/1840/119:196–200).

9. Baxter, *History of the City of Grand Rapids,* 175–76.

10. These maps are based on information contained in, David M. Ellis, *Michigan Postal History: The Post Offices, 1805–1986* (Oak Grove, Ore.: The Depot, 1993). This book includes full listings of all Michigan post offices together with their locations and dates of operation. These detailed references permitted lists to be compiled of only those post offices open during the reference period selected. On the basis of these lists, complete maps of all post offices were constructed for the periods used in this study.

11. Shoreline expansion followed American immigration after the war, resulting in the expansion of Monroe, neighboring Frenchtown, and the River Raisin. See *Michigan Sentinel,* 16 August 1834; Evans, *Pedestrious Tour,* 109; *Detroit Gazette,* 2 August 1822. Farther north, Samuel Brown noted that, "From the River Rouge to Lake St. Clair, . . . the country resembles the suburbs of a large town" (*Western Gazetteer,* 166). The establishment of Mt. Clemens as the seat of Macomb County spurred population growth there (see *Detroit Gazette,* 10 July 1818), and Detroit became a magnet for settlement expansion immediately inland from the Detroit River (See Darby, *Tour,* 195).

    Along the St. Clair River, timber-cutting and milling, together with a shipbuilding industry, developed before 1820. See Kovacik, *Geographical Analysis,* 47–48. The specialized nature of these activities confined the occupation to the river edge, where "settlements continue[d] for a considerable part of the way on the American shore" (Henry R. Schoolcraft, *Narrative Journal of Travels from Detroit Northwest through the Great Chain of American Lakes to the Sources of the Mississippi River in the Year 1820* [Albany, N.Y.: E. & E. Hosford, 1821; reprint, Ann Arbor, Mich.: University Microfilms, 1966], 79, 81). The American military presence on the upper lakes was represented by Fort Gratiot, constructed in 1814 at the head of the St. Clair River. See Francis Paul Prucha, *A Guide to the Military Posts of the United States, 1789–1895* (Madison: State Historical Society of Wisconsin, 1964), xxxi.

12. John Farmer, *The Emigrant's Guide; or Pocket Gazetteer of the Surveyed Part of Michigan* (Albany, N.Y.: B. D. Packard, 1830), 22; John M. Norton, "A Picture of Memory—Settlement of Oakland County," *MPHC* 22 (1893): 407.

13. Van Buren, "Settlement of Branch County," 611; idem, "Pioneer Annals," 257; idem, "First Settlement of Sturgis Prairie," 519; Brown, "Autobiographical Notes," 452; Mrs. E. M. S. Stewart, "Sketch of the First Settlement of Pontiac, as Given by Mr. Orisson Allen to Mrs. E. M. Sheldon Stewart in 1850," *MPHC* 6 (1883): 385.

14. As late as the early 1840s, the Rev. Elijah Pilcher found northern Ingham County devoid of settlement. See Pilcher, "Forty Years Ago," 83. The removal of the state government, however, transformed the area almost overnight. The presence of the new capital was an immediate stimulus to settlement and rapidly changed the distribution of settlement in this portion of the area of colonization. See Levi Bishop, "Recollections," *MPHC* 1 (1877): 515–16; Anonymous Journal, 30 June 1848/CHL.

15. Gov. Lewis Cass proposed that central roads would encourage the movement of immigrants into Michigan's interior, "insure a safe and predictable communication . . . with the country," and permit for the movement of troops in the event of war with British Canada or hostile Indians. See Memoir, HR/1826/42; Petition to Congress by Inhabitants of the Territory, 7 October 1825/TPUS/MT/11:706–7; Memorial from Martin Davis and Inhabitants of Washtenaw County, 7 December 1831/TPUS/MT/11:395–96; Memorial to Congress by Inhabitants of the Territory, 20 January 1832/TPUS/MT/12:419–20.

Commissioners charged with laying out the central roads stressed the advantages of employing the routes of earlier trails for the course of the proposed roads. The Chicago Road followed the Sauk Trail through the southern counties (Report of James M'Closkey to James Barbour, Sec. of War, 2 November 1825, HD/1826/68), while the "Old Washtenaw Trail" or "Potawatomi Trail," leading into the Kalamazoo drainage, provided a route for the Territorial Road (Little, "Fifty Years Ago," 510; Watkins, "Township of Bridgewater," 568; MTL/1831/3:888). The road to Saginaw followed the "Saginaw Indian Trail" (Williams, "Life of Oliver Williams," 38–39; *Detroit Gazette,* 26 February 1819; Drake, "History of Oakland County," 568; Fox, *History of Saginaw County,* 34; Petition to Congress by Inhabitants of the Territory, 7 October 1825/TPUS/MT/11:706–7), and the Grand River Road, branching westward from the Saginaw Indian Trail at Pontiac, relied heavily on Indian trails to define its route (Pike, "Clinton County History," *Clinton County Republican,* 6 November 1902; Pilcher, "Forty Years Ago," 83; Bronson, "Pioneer History of Calhoun County," 326, Carl E. Pray, "An Historic Michigan Road," *Michigan History* 11 (1927): 329). The routes of Indian trails shown were taken from original survey maps compiled by the General Land Office (GLO), available in digitized form in P. J. Comer et al., *Michigan's Native Landscape, as interpreted from the General Land Office Surveys, 1816–1856* (Lansing: Michigan Department of Natural Resources/Nature Conservancy, Michigan Natural Resources Inventory, 1995).

16. Henry Little, of Jackson County, stated that, "Between Ann Arbor and Kalamazoo county (as then called), the log-cabins of the pioneers were located only upon the Indian trail" ("Fifty Years Ago," 510). The Reverend Pilcher was aware of the presence of Indian trails and incorporated one in his travels between Marshall and Coldwater. See "Forty Years Ago," 83–84, 88. Henry A. Goodyear, described them as "merely trails cleared from timber and underbrush the width of the track, [following] the best grounds for a road, no matter how crooked or how varied from a direct course" ("Sketch of Barry County," *MPHC* 1 [1877]: 116).

17. The production of immigrant and travelers' maps of Michigan began in the mid-1820s. A map published posthumously by Philu Judd in 1825 represented the earliest accurate plat of the territory as a whole. In 1826, John Farmer of Detroit printed the first of a series of finely detailed Michigan maps that were reissued frequently in updated form. See Barnett, "Milestones in Michigan Mapping: Early Settlement," 40–42; idem, "Milestones in Michigan Mapping: Modern Waymarks," *Michigan History* 63 (November/December 1979): 31–32. Farmer's high-quality maps are employed as the primary source of route and settlement data in this study.

18. SLUS/1801/2:125–27; SLUS/1810/2:579–89; SLUS/1820/3:577–81; SLUS/1823/3:763–68; Postal Route Advertisement, 10 June 1823/TPUS/MT/11:367–68; Bates, "By-Gones of Detroit," 377; Memorial to Congress by Inhabitants of the Territory, 4 December 1828/TPUS/MT/11:1221. Fox (*History of Saginaw County,* 36) reported that the entire length of the "Saginaw Turnpike" was completed as a vehicular road in 1841. See also Mileage of Post Routes, January 1824/TPUS/MT/11:505; Carey & Lea, *Michigan Territory, Geographical, Statistical, and Historical Map of Michigan Territory,* col. map 57 x 45 cm., scale 1:1,900,800 (Philadelphia: Carey & Lea, 1822); Philu E. Judd, *Map of Michigan with Part of the Adjoining States,* col. map 53 x 78 cm., scale 1:732,600 (Detroit: Philu Judd, 1825); John Farmer, *Map of the Surveyed Part of the Territory of Michigan,* col. map 49 x 54 cm., scale 1:506,880 (Utica, N.Y.: V. Balch and S. Stiles, 1826). Early routes have also be taken from *Portrait and Biographical Album of Oakland County, Michigan* (Chicago: Chapman Bros., 1891), 602; *Portrait and Biographical Album of Lenawee County,* 1103; and John J. Adam, "Early History of Lenawee County," *MPHC* 2 (1880): 371.

19. John Farmer, "Plat and Field Notes of a Territorial Road from Monroe to Detroit," ms. map 37 x 217 cm., var. scales (1828), SAM; idem, *An Improved Map of the Surveyed Part of the Territory of Michigan,* col. map 56 x 80 cm., scale 1:506,880 (New York: V. Balch and S. Stiles, 1831); S. Allen, "Plat and Field Notes of the Territorial Road Laid Out and Surveyed from Port Lawrence in the County of Monroe through

Blissfield and Logan and through the Village of Adrian in the County of Lenawee to the Chicago Road," ms. map 38 x 32 cm., no scale (1828), SAM; Calvin P. Webster, "Territorial Road in Oakland and Wayne Counties," ms. map on 2 sheets, 102 x 37 cm., scale 1:63,360 (1828), SAM; "Detroit to Clinton River in Wayne and Macomb Counties," Ms. map in 2 parts, 68 x 33 cm., scale 1:2,640 (1828), SAM; Orange Risdon, "Plat and Field Notes of a Territorial Road, Leading from Pontiac in the County of Oakland to Adrian in the County of Lenawee," ms. col. map 25 x 182 cm., no scale (1828), SAM; Gideon Gates to Delegate Biddle, 22 January 1831/TPUS/MT/12:242–45; "Postal Route Advertisement," 18 June 1827/TPUS/MT/11:1087–88; "Postal Route Advertisement," 23 June, 1829/TPUS/MT/12: 52; SLUS/1828/4:315–20; Edwards, "Sketch of Pioneer Life," 150; T. G. Turner, *Gazetteer of the St. Joseph Valley, Michigan and Indiana* (Chicago: Hazlitt and Reed, 1867; reprint, Grand Rapids, Mich.: Black Letter Press, 1978), 22; *Portrait and Biographical Album of St. Joseph County, Michigan* (Chicago: Chapman Bros., 1889), 442; Shoemaker, "Sketch of the City of Jackson," 285–86; Van Buren, "First Settlement of Sturgis Prairie," 519; Hawley Gerrells, "Hawley Gerrells in 1828," *MPHC* 5 (1884): 79.

20. Farmer, *Map of the Surveyed Part of the Territory of Michigan* (1836); Tanner, *New Map of Michigan* (1836); J. H. Young, *Map of Ohio and the Settled Parts of Michigan, 1830,* col. map 47 x 33 cm., scale 1:267,200 (Philadelphia: A. Finley, 1833); J. F. Stratton, "Territorial Road from Wayne County, 2_ Miles from Detroit on the Chicago Road, to Mouth of St. Joseph River, Map and Field Notes," ms. map 20 x 36 cm., scale 1:23,760 (1830), SAM; John T. Durand, "Washtenaw Territorial Road from Jacksonburgh West to St. Joseph River and Beyond to Intersection of Chicago Road on White Pigeon Prairie, Plat and Field Notes," ms. map 192 x 25 cm., no scale (1834), SAM; Nathan Hubble, "Monroe to Ypsilanti, Plat and Field Notes," ms. map on 2 sheets, 32 x 22 cm. and 32 x 38 cm., no scale (1829), SAM; Hiram Willmuth, "Dearborn to Lyndon Highway," ms. map on 4 sheets, 19 x 30 cm., no scale (1831), SAM; A. E. Hathon, "Dearbornville to Flat Rock Highway," ms. map 43 x 22 cm., scale 1:63,360 (1835), SAM; Orange Risdon, "Plat and Field Notes of a Road Leading from Monroe, in the County of Monroe, Up the Saline River by the Salt Springs, the Village of Dexter, the Portage of Grand and Huron Rivers, to the Principal Meridian," ms. col. map 25 x 201 cm., no scale (1828), SAM; Ephraim Calkin, "Plat and Field Notes of the Survey of a Territorial Road from Rochester to the County Seat of Lapeer," ms. map 38 x 32 cm., no scale (1832), SAM; L. E. Nathon, "Territorial Road from Point du Chene to Fort Gratiot Turnpike," ms. map 34 x 84 cm., scale 1:31,680 (1834), SAM; John Woolman, "Plat and Field Notes of the Territorial Road Commencing in the Line Between Section No. 19 & 30 in Township 6 South of Range Number 6 West, and in the Center of the Seat of the County of Branch, . . . to the East End of Broadway Street at the Town of St. Joseph at the Mouth of the St. Joseph," ms. map 39 x 63 cm., scale 1:198,000 (1834), SAM; Petition to Richard M. Johnson from the Citizens of Washington, Shelby, and Ray in Macomb County, 3 January 1831/TPUS/MT/12:243–44; Petition to Congress by Citizens of St. Joseph, Cass, and Berrien Counties, 5 September 1831/TPUS/MT/12:349; Petition to Congress by Inhabitants of St. Joseph County, 5 January 1834/TPUS/MT/12:687; Memorial to Congress by the Legislative Council, 30 January 1834/ TPUS/MT/12:721; "Postal Route Advertisement," 20 June 1831/TPUS/MT/12:298–300; "Postal Route Advertisement," 25 June 1832/TPUS/MT/12:496; "Postal Route Advertisement," 2 July 1835/TPUS/MT/12:949–55; SLUS/1836/5:90–107; Johnson, *History of Allegan and Barry Counties,* 470; *Portrait and Biographical Album of Lenawee County,* 769; Shoemaker, "Sketch of the City of Jackson," 292; *Tecumseh Herald,* 3 April 1884; Frost, "Early Railroads of Southern Michigan," 499; Brown, "Autobiographical Notes," 462; A. M. Beardsley, "Reminiscences and Scenes of Backwoods and Pioneer Life," *MPHC* 28 (1897–98): 140; Leeson, *History of Kent County,* 218; A. D. P. Van Buren, "Some Beginnings in Kalamazoo," *MPHC* 18 (1891): 606; *History of Jackson County,* 203;; James H. Lawrence, "Pioneer Recollections," *MPHC* 18 (1891): 360; Gordon and May, "Michigan Land Rush," 471–72; LaRowe, "Address of J. B. LaRowe," *Livingston Republican,* 17 July 1879; Agnes Pike, "Clinton Co. History,

Interesting Reminiscences Read Before the DeWitt Grange," *Clinton County Republican*, 6 November 1902; Pilcher, "Forty Years Ago," 83; Williams, "First Settlement of Shiawassee County," 481; Prudence Tower, "The Journey of Ionia's First Settlers," *MPHC* 28 (1897–98): 146; Shout, "First Settlement at Owosso," 345; Everett, *Memorials*, 16; Graydon Meints, "Michigan Railroad Construction, 1835–1875" (Ann Arbor: Transportation Library, University of Michigan, 1981, typewritten), 2.

21. The importance of transportation linkages with Indiana settlements for residents of southwestern Michigan has been emphasized in regional histories such as Robert Burgh, *The Region of Three Oaks* (Three Oaks, Mich.: Edward K. Warren Foundation, 1939), 76. The railroad was the Erie and Kalamazoo. See Graydon Meints, *Michigan Railroads and Railroad Companies* (East Lansing: Michigan State University Press, 1992), 2; Mrs. Frank P. Dodge, "Marking Terminus of Erie & Kalamazoo Railroad," *MPHC* 38 (1912): 493.

22. Farmer, *Map of the Surveyed Part of Michigan* (1840); David H. Burr, *Map of Michigan and Part of Wisconsin Territory, Exhibiting the Post Offices, Post Roads, Canals, Railroads, &c.*, col. map 94 x 63 cm., scale 1:635,000 (Washington, D.C.: John Arrowsmith, 1839); Jehiel Saxton, "Adamsville to Cassopolis State Road in Cass County," ms. map 40 x 32 cm., scale 1:38,016 (1838), SAM; John Meachum, "Battle Creek and Hastings State Road in Calhoun and Barry Counties," ms. map on 3 sheets, 43 x 33 cm., scale 1:31,380 (1838), SAM; James B. Tompkins, "Survey of a State Road from Coldwater Village, Branch County, to Battle Creek Village, Calhoun County," ms. map 54 x 42 cm., scale 1:31,680 (1836), SAM; idem, "Map of a Road from Union City to Battle Creek, Being a Continuation of a State Road from Coldwater Village," ms. map on 2 sheets, 54 x 22 cm., scale 1:31, 680 (1836), SAM; Ira Tillotson, "Plat of a State Road from Marshall to the County Seat of Barry," ms. map 34 x 110 cm., scale 1:15,840 (1837), SAM; A. H. Delamatter, "Plat of a Road Commencing at the Junction of the La Plaisance Bay Road and the Chicago Turnpike and Terminating at the Village of Marshall in Calhoun County," ms. map 91 x 41 cm., scale 1:79,200 (1836), SAM; Joseph B. Cook, "Territorial Road in Calhoun, Kalamazoo, and Van Buren Counties," ms. map 64 x 20 cm., scale 1:65,000 (1835), SAM; Anthony M. Kry, "Plat and Field Notes of Re-Survey of the Territorial Road Leading from Vistula to the Line of the State of Indiana," ms. map 23 x 177 cm., scale 1:63,360 (1834), SAM; S. Allen, "Plat and Field Notes of a Territorial Road Laid Out and Established from Vistula in the County of Monroe via the Forks of Ottawa Creek in the Townships Nine South to the Line of Indiana," ms. map 20 x 185 cm., scale 1:63,360 (1833), SAM; "Saginaw County, T 10, 11, 12, 13N; R 1, 2, 3, 4, 5, 6E," ms. map 48 x 51 cm., scale 1: 26,720 [1840], SAM; "Van Buren County, T 1, 2, 3, 4, 5S; R 13, 14, 15, 16, 17W," ms. map 55 x 40 cm., scale 1:126,720 [1840], SAM; Hiram Barritt, "Plat and Field Notes on a Road from Farmington to Byron," ms. map 20 x 30 cm., scale 1:126,720 (1838), SAM; John Southard, "Plat and Field Notes of a Territorial Road from the Village of Pontiac West to the Grand River Road Near the Site of Livingston County," ms. map 16 x 10 cm., no scale (1834), SAM; Samuel Marrs, "Plat and Field Notes of a Territorial Road Laid Out from the Village of Niles in the County of Berrien, M. T. to the Mouth of the Gallien River in Said County," ms. map 18 x 72 cm., scale 1:6,600 (1834), SAM; John Farnsworth, "Dexter and Grand River State Road in Washtenaw, Livingston, and Ingham Counties," ms. map on 2 sheets, 20 x 91 cm., scale 1:33,000 (1837), SAM; idem, "A Plat of a Part of a State Road from Dexter Village in the County of Washtenaw to the Mouth of the Maple River in the County of Ionia at the Village of Lyon," ms. map 31 x 144 cm., scale 1:19,800 (1837), SAM; "Post Roads, Indiana, Michigan," SLUS/1838/5:271–82; Jacob Gerrish to Moses Chamberlain, 6 January 1837/CFP/MSUAHC; "Maps of Roads in Barry County," in Bela Hubbard, Journal, August–September 1840/BHP/Box 1/MHC; *Democratic Free Press*, 10 May 1837; Franklin Ellis, *History of Berrien and Van Buren Counties, Michigan* (Philadelphia: D. W. Ensign, 1880), 345, 400; Barber, "Vermontville Colony," 210, 217; M. J. Niles, "Old Times in Clinton County," *MPHC* 14 (1889): 623; George H. White, "Yankee Lewis' Famous Hostelry in the Wilderness," *MPHC* 26 (1894–95): 303, 305;

Everett, *Memorials*, 15–16, 20, 37; Gordon and May, "Michigan Land Rush," 450; Lafever, "Early Day Life in Michigan," 672–73; Silas Beebe, "A Trip from Utica, New York to Ingham County, Michigan," *MPHC* 1 (1877): 190; Meints, "Michigan Railroad Construction," 2–5. Fuller, *Economic and Social Beginnings*, 322–23, 416–17; Blois, *Gazetteer*, 96; SLUS/1836/5:90–107; *Monroe Times*, 17 November 1836.

23. In the years immediately preceding 1840, railroad construction in southern lower Michigan expanded from the single line of the Erie & Kalamazoo to include the construction of the Central and the Detroit & Pontiac that linked the entrepôt with settlement in Oakland and Washtenaw counties. The Palmyra & Jacksonburg extended the Erie & Kalamazoo into northern Lenawee County in 1838, and the subsequent construction of the Raisin River & Lake Erie and Southern railroads provided direct access to the port of Monroe. See Meints, "Michigan Railroad Construction," 2–5.

24. John Farmer, *Map of the State of Michigan and the Surrounding Country, Exhibiting the Sections and the Latest Surveys*, col. map 82 x 61 cm., scale 1:800,000 (Detroit: John Farmer, 1844); Douglass Houghton, *Map of Jackson County*, col. map 64 x 53 cm., scale 1:126,720 (Washington, D.C.: W. J. Stone, [1842]); idem, *Map of Calhoun County*, col. map 62 x 47 cm., scale 1:126,720 (Washington, D.C.: W. J. Stone, [1842]); idem, *Map of Lenawee County*, col. map 48 x 53 cm., scale 1:126,720 (Washington, D.C.: W. J. Stone, [1842]); idem, *Map of Washtenaw County*, col. map 53 x 63 cm., scale 1:126,720 (Washington, D.C.: W. J. Stone, [1842]); idem, *Map of Wayne County*, col. map 51 x 47 cm., scale 1:126,720 (Cincinnati: Doolittle and Munson, [1842]); Bela Hubbard, *The Western Counties of Michigan*, Map 71 x 84 cm., scale 1:253,440 (New York: Miller's Lith., 1846); M. C. Keith, "Plat and Field Notes of State Road from Galien in St. Joseph County to Kalamazoo in Kalamazoo County," ms. map 33 x 41 cm., no scale (1837), SAM; James Pond, "Plat and Field Notes of a State Road from the County Seat of Calhoun County to the County Seat of Branch and thence Southerly in the Direction of Fort Wayne to the Indiana State Line," ms. map 20 x 88 cm., scale 1:79,200 (1839), SAM; idem, "Plat and Field Notes of State Road Laid Out and Established from the County Seat of Branch County Eastwardly, Intersecting the Chicago Road at or Near the Eastern Extremity of Coldwater Prairie," ms. map 19 x 30 cm., scale 1:63,360 (1839), SAM; Lemuel Sowle, "Plat and Field Notes of State Road and Adjacent Country from Indiana State Line to the Prairie, Terminating Easterly from the Village of Coldwater in Branch County, Michigan," ms. map 32 x 20 cm., no scale (1837), SAM; David Clark, "A Traverse and Survey of a State Road Commencing on a State Road Leading from Jonesville in Hillsdale County to Marshall in Calhoun County," ms. map 55 x 32 cm., no scale (1839–40), SAM; "Post Roads," SLUS/1842/5:568–75; "Post Roads," SLUS/1845/5:778–87; Bela Hubbard, Notebooks, 30 July 1842/BHP/Box 1/MHC; *Three Oaks Press*, 27 January 1893; Carr, "Settlement of Williamstown," 451; Lafever, "Early Day Life in Michigan," 675; White, "Yankee Lewis' Famous Hostelry," 306; Perrine, "Townships in Calhoun County," 211; *Portrait and Biographical Album of Barry and Eaton Counties*, 352; Beebe, "Trip from Utica," 192; Meints, "Michigan Railroad Construction," 6; Lafever, "Early Day Life in Michigan," 675; Carr, "Settlement of Williamstown," 451.

25. During the first half of the decade, three of Michigan's principal railroads extended their lines. The most dramatic growth occurred on the Central, which laid tracks from its Ann Arbor terminus as far west as Jackson in 1841, reached Marshall two years later, and opened service to Battle Creek in 1845. The less well funded Southern extended its tracks from Adrian to Hillsdale during 1843. In the same year, the privately funded Detroit & Pontiac completed its line between Birmingham and Pontiac and began service between its namesake cities. See Meints, "Michigan Railroad Construction," 6; Paul Trap, "The Detroit & Pontiac Railroad," *Railroad History* 168 (1993): 35.

26. This classification of frontier settlements reflects the widely held assumption that the position of each within a functional hierarchy is related to both the number and diversity of its activities, or services, and the degree of access it maintains over the area served. See David Grove, "The Function and Future of

Urban Centres," in *Man, Settlement, and Urbanism,* ed. Peter J. Ucko, Ruth Tringham, and G. W. Dimbleby (London: Gerald Duckworth and Co., 1972), 560–61; and Michael E. Eliot Hurst, ed., *Transportation Geography* (New York: McGraw-Hill, 1974), 54–55.

27. Casagrande, Thompson, and Young ("Colonization," 311–16) recognized these general settlement types and defined their characteristics. The nature of their functions and the resulting hierarchy are also discussed in Lewis, *American Frontier,* 23, 181–82, 201–2, 210.

28. The terms "node" and "link" are commonly used by geographers in analyzing the form and efficiency of transport networks and the discerning the roles of settlements in them. See, for example, Knowles and Wareing, *Economic and Social Geography,* 117.

29. Pontiac, on the Saginaw Road, was settled as early as 1818 and grew rapidly because of its ideal location for waterpower. The location of at least two mills by the early 1820s, Pontiac attracted a variety of artisans. See Mrs. E. M. S. Stewart, "Sketch of the First Settlement of Pontiac, as given by Mr. Orisson Allent to Mrs. E. M. Sheldon Stewart in 1850," *MPHC* 6 (1883): 384; *Detroit Gazette,* 2 February 1821; Hervey Parke, "Reminiscences," *MPHC* 3 (1881): 574; Ephraim S. Williams, "Detroit Three Score Years Ago," *MPHC* 10 (1886): 85; and Lamb, "Incidents in Pioneer Life," 149. Several interior points with multiple road links lay north of Detroit. Set apart from the central overland network, none were nucleated settlements. See *History of Washtenaw County,* 434; Gerrells, "Hawley Gerrells in 1828," 77; and Leeson, *History of Macomb County,* 247.

Founded in 1826 at a salt springs on the Huron River, Ypsilanti's proximity to the central road network, together with the natural advantages of its location, encouraged its development as a regional milling center. See Ezra D. Lay, "Condensed Early History, Or Beginnings of the Several Towns in Washtenaw County," *MPHC* 17 (1890): 460; Wing, "History of Monroe," 320; Richards, "Eighty Years in Michigan," 366; L. D. Norris, "History of Washtenaw County," *MPHC* 1 (1877): 330; and John Geddes, "Ypsilanti Township—Its Settlement, Etc.," *MPHC* 4 (1883): 403.

Ann Arbor grew rapidly from a collection of a half dozen log huts in 1824 to include mills, boarding houses, inns, commercial structures, manufactories, and the public buildings associated with a county seat. It served as the principal settlement in the central interior. See *History of Washtenaw County,* 433; Stewart, "Early Settlement of Ann Arbor," 444; Sessions, "Ann Arbor," 334; and Norris, "History of Washtenaw County," 329.

Saline and Tecumseh lay on the Chicago Road. Although the former remained a small settlement, Tecumseh's links with Monroe and Detroit and location on the Raisin River permitted the rapid growth of milling, and it contained a number of houses and a tavern two years after its founding in 1824. See A. L. Millard, "Historical Sketch of Lenawee County," *MPHC* 1 (1877): 227–28; Cross, "Early Michigan," 54; Turner, *Gazetteer of the St. Joseph Valley,* 22; and Gerrells, "Hawley Gerrells in 1828," 78.

30. Mt. Clemens lay near the mouth of the Clinton River, a navigable stream affording advantages as a mill seat. Established as the seat of justice for Macomb County, Mt. Clemens was a focal point for both political and economic activities for the surrounding region. See John Stockton, "Account of the Early Settlement of Mt. Clemens, as Given to Mrs. E. M. Sheldon Stewart in 1850," *MPHC* 6 (1883): 357; and *Detroit Gazette,* 10 July 1818.

Monroe grew slowly, but by the early 1820s had become a regional milling center and a lake port of growing importance. It soon attracted numerous other commercial retailing and manufacturing activities, as well as the political institutions associated with its role as a county seat. Monroe experienced rapid expansion in 1826 as a central place in the southern interior. See *Michigan Sentinel,* 2 April 1826, 16 August 1834; *Detroit Gazette,* 2 August 1822; and Keeney, "Salmon Keeney's Visit to Michigan," 444.

Situated on the periphery of expansion, the St. Clair River settlements were largely devoted to specialized activities such as shipbuilding, fishing, and the production of forest products and included the military garrison at Fort Gratiot. See Fox, *History of Saginaw County,* 33–34; Prucha, *Military Posts of the United States,* xxxi; Stewart, "Recollections of Aura P. Stewart," 347, 350; O. Poppleton, "History of Fort Gratiot," *MPHC* 18 (1891): 667–76; and Mrs. E. M. Sheldon, "St. Clair River Settlement, Account Given to Mrs. E. M. Sheldon in 1852 by Mrs. Dr. H. Chamberlain of St. Clair," *MPHC* 4 (1883): 356.

31. Pontiac possessed at least fourteen mills as well as other industries. A contemporary resident recalled, "by 1830 . . . Pontiac was . . . a center of trade for all of the region lying north and northwest of it as far as the Saginaws." Ann Arbor contained eighteen mills, various small manufactories, and a dozen mercantile establishments, and maintained a direct link to the mills at the emerging nucleated settlement at Dexter. See Norton, "Settlement of Oakland County," 407; and Farmer, *Emigrant's Guide,* 12.

   Despite its increasingly central position in the road network of the interior, Ypsilanti remained a "small hamlet" well into the 1830s. Saline grew as a nucleated settlement during this time and became the focus of regional trade. See Shoemaker, "Sketch of the City of Jackson," 285; Goodrich, "Michigan Territory Sixty Years Ago," 229; *Michigan Sentinel,* 20 March 1830; and William Richards to Herman Richards, 2 March 1833/MHC.

   Both Tecumseh and Adrian grew rapidly, and they were roughly equal in size. Although Tecumseh possessed the county offices and direct ties with the port of Monroe, Adrian's links with Toledo prevented Tecumseh from dominating regional trade to the same extent as the other interior frontier towns. See Farmer, *Emigrant's Guide,* 25; Elizabeth Chandler to Jane Howell, 15 April 1831, 2 September 1833/EMCP/Box 1/MHC; Thaddeus Smith to Elizabeth Smith, 14 June 1829/SBSFC/WMUARHC; and *Michigan Sentinel,* 20 March 1830.

32. Monroe's extraordinary growth led one contemporary source to describe it as the "second village in Michigan"; however, another lamented that its influence was limited by the number and quality of roads. See *Michigan Sentinel,* 20 March 1830; Farmer, *Emigrant's Guide,* 11. Mt. Clemens's growth as a commercial center and the expansion of its connections into the St. Clair River settlements insured its continued importance as a frontier town. See Farmer, Emigrant's Guide, 12–14, 16–17; and O. C. Thompson, "Observations and Experiences in Michigan Forty Years Ago," *MPHC* 1 (1877): 396. Although these nucleated settlements lacked the multiple functions of the frontier towns, they possessed industrial and commercial facilities and played a growing role in the regional distribution of goods and services. See *Oakland Chronicle,* 11 June 1830.

33. Founded in 1829, Jackson soon contained a mill, a hotel, a tavern, and at least one store. Despite its growth as a nucleated settlement, a contemporary could still describe Jackson as "an apology for a village." Jonesville also remained a small village in 1830. See Stewart, "Early Settlement of Ann Arbor," 446; Shoemaker, "Sketch of the City of Jackson," 285; Brown, "Autobiographical Notes," 451; Little, "Fifty Years Ago," 510; Thompson, "Observations and Experiences," 397; and Reland Tinkham to Foster Tinkham, 23 August 1831/MHC. By the closing years of the decade Niles had emerged as a small nucleated settlement with one store. See Winslow, "Early History of Berrien County," 122; and Edwards, "Sketch of Pioneer Life," 150. St. Joseph was composed of only a few stores and warehouses erected in anticipation of growing inland river trade. Edwardsburg consisted of a cluster of structures on Beardsley's Prairie. See *Detroit Gazette,* 30 October 1828; Farmer, *Emigrant's Guide,* 19–20; Reland Tinkham to Foster Tinkham, 23 August 1831/MHC; Edwards, "Sketch of Pioneer Life," 150; and Van Buren, "Settlement of Branch County," 611.

34. A village of six thousand, Pontiac dominated the regional economy of an increasingly more densely populated area and was described by contemporary observers as "a thriving and busy village, of great expectations, and no small pretensions," although it had yet to lose its "rather hard name." See *Western Traveller's Pocket Directory,* 65; and Bradley, "Journal of Cyrus P. Bradley," 257–58. The quotes are from Supply Chase, "A Pioneer Minister," *MPHC* 5 (1884): 53; Hubbard, *Memorials,* 67; and Tower, "Ionia's First Settlers," 146.

35. Plymouth and Rochester maintained direct connections with Pontiac. The former was particularly well situated to serve as a stop for the increasing numbers of western immigrants, and became a boomtown in the mid-1830s. See H. M. Utley, "Plymouth, the First Settlement—Reminiscences of the Early History of the Place—Incidents and Anecdotes," *MPHC* 1 (1877): 446. See also Gordon and May, "Michigan Land Rush," 258. The earlier settlements included Romeo, Auburn, Utica, Troy, Royal Oak, Franklin, Dearborn, and Schwarzburg. See Osband, "Pioneers and Pioneer Life in Nankin," 448; Hoffman, *Winter in the West,* 1:123–25; *Western Traveller's Pocket Directory,* 59; Martineau, "Travels in and around Michigan," 53–54; Gordon and May, "Michigan Land Rush," 259; Chase, "A Pioneer Minister," 53; Bradley, "Journal," 257; and Miller, "Early History of the Saginaw Valley," 356. Described by contemporary observers as a rapidly growing trading and manufacturing center surrounded by an increasingly more densely populated hinterland, Ann Arbor contained the court offices for Washtenaw County and would soon be designated the site of the University of Michigan. See *Western Traveller's Pocket Directory,* 62; Hoffman, *Winter in the West,* 1:132; Gordon and May, "Michigan Land Rush," 264–65; Lanman, *History of Michigan, Civil and Topographical,* 289; and Lay, "Towns in Washtenaw County," 461.

36. Adrian developed rapidly in the early 1830s as a result of the completion of the Erie & Kalamazoo Railroad in 1835, which made it the western terminus of the only rail line emanating from a Lake Erie port. As it emerged as the dominant commercial center in the southern interior, political agitation soon brought the county offices here and insured its status as a regional frontier town. See Joshua C. Goodrich, Diary, 20, 21, 30 May 1835/EHC/WMUARHC; Dodge, "Terminus of Erie and Kalamazoo Railroad," 494; Meints, "Michigan Railroad Construction," 2; Adam, "Early History of Lenawee County," 364; Fuller, *Economic and Social Beginnings,* 236–37; Lanman, *History of Michigan, Civil and Topographical,* 285; H. A. Rose, "Then and Now," *Clinton County Republican,* 5 July 1900; and Reland Tinkham to Foster Tinkham, 23 August 1831/MHC.

    Mt. Clemens's industrial base included milling, glass-making, shipbuilding, and the production of forest products, and its merchants carried on an expanding trade with Detroit and the interior. Its growth was limited by the realities of a limited agricultural base, restricted transportation, and the handicap of a regional economy. See *Macomb Statesman,* 22 September 1837; and Chase, "Pioneer Minister," 53–54.

    Monroe remained a center of trade and milling and expanded manufacturing, retailing, and wholesaling activities during the boom of the early 1830s. Contemporary descriptions of Monroe attributed its growth to its location relative to the lake and interior routes. See *Monroe Times,* 11 August 1836; Hoffman, *Winter in the West,* 1:107–9; Christiancy, "Early History of the City and County of Monroe," 367; and *Michigan Sentinel,* 16 August 1834.

37. Linked to the port and river settlements in Michigan and Indiana, Niles expanded as a regional commercial and transportation center. "It was the most important business point we had found after leaving Detroit," commented an 1834 visitor. Although not a political center, Niles became a focus of social and religious institutions that promoted its role as a frontier town at this time. See Bishop, "Recollections," 125; *Niles Gazette and Advertiser,* 9 January 1836; Hoffman, *Winter in the West,* 1:190; Martineau, "Travels in and around Michigan," 58, 66–67; Shirreff, *Tour through North America,* 225; *Western Traveller's Pocket Directory,* 73; Goodrich, "Michigan Territory Sixty Years Ago," 230. Rev. James Selkirk, Recollections, MJC/WMUARHC; and *Niles Gazette and Michigan Advertiser,* 10 October 1835, 5 March 1836.

    Established in 1830, White Pigeon remained a small settlement, yet possessed several mills, retail establishments, public houses, and manufactories. The presence of the land office added to the diversity of its activities. See Fuller, *Economic and Social Beginnings,* 272–73. Descriptions of the settlement appear in N. M. Thomas, "Reminiscences," *Michigan Pioneer and* 28 (1897–98): 533; Reland Tinkham to Foster

Tinkham, 23 August 1831/MHC; Alfred L. Driggs, "Early Days in Michigan," *MPHC* 10 (1886): 58; Hoffman, *Winter in the West*, 1:218–19; Goodrich, "Michigan Territory Sixty Years Ago," 230; *Detroit Journal and Michigan Advertiser*, 27 November 1833; and *Michigan Statesman and St. Joseph Chronicle*, 9 August 1834. The significance of White Pigeon's location for the western land office is addressed by Fuller, Economic and Social Beginnings, 272–73.

Jonesville lay in a region largely bypassed by immigration and was the only substantial node lying between the western settlements and those of Lenawee County. One contemporary visitor noted that Jonesville "is called a village—One Mr. Jones Esqr. lives there himself and not only keeps the stage house, but has a barn & corn house too . . . & a pig sty" (Reland Tinkham to Foster Tinkham, 23 August 1831/MHC). Despite its status as a county seat, it emerged as a nucleated settlement only in the mid-1830s. See Mrs. M. W. Clapp, "The Long Ago," *MPHC* 4 (1883): 513; and Fuller, *Economic and Social Beginnings*, 283.

38. From its beginnings as a sawmill site in 1830, Marshall had grown rapidly into a moderate village by mid-decade. In 1836 this milling and retailing center had a wide regional market and was an important dispersion point for immigration in western Michigan. It became a center for missionary activity by several Protestant denominations, and was headquarters of the Presbyterian Home Missionary Society. See Gordon and May, "Michigan Land Rush," 275; Brown, "Autobiographical Notes," 452; Driggs, "Early Days in Michigan," 58; Thompson, "Observations and Experiences," 398; Charles Dickey, "Early Settlement of Calhoun County," *MPHC* 1 (1877): 131; Bishop, "Recollections," 512; Van Buren, "Pioneer Annals," 247; Fuller, *Economic and Social Beginnings*, 340–42; Pilcher, *Protestantism in Michigan*, 292–93; and Daniel R. Campbell, "Village and the World: The Shaping of Culture in Marshall, Michigan" Ph.D. diss., Michigan State University (Ann Arbor, Mich.: University Microfilms, 1986).

Kalamazoo also developed around a mill site and became a regional commercial center with extensive road connections in western Michigan. This immigration center attracted a number of social and religious activities and was the site of the county court. See Driggs, "Early Days in Michigan," 58; Thompson, "Observations and Experiences," 398–99; Van Buren, "Beginnings in Kalamazoo," 605; Edwards, "Sketch of Pioneer Life," 150; Mary V. Gibbs, "Glimpses of Early Michigan Life in and around Kalamazoo," *Magazine of American History* 24 (1890): 459–60; Joshua C. Goodrich, Diary, 27 May 1835/EHC/WMUARHC; *Michigan Statesman*, 4 June 1836; and Fuller, *Economic and Social Beginnings*, 344–45. For the early history of Battle Creek, see A. D. P. Van Buren, "The First Settlers in the Township of Battle Creek," *MPHC* 5 (1884): 292; and Fuller, *Economic and Social Beginnings*, 348.

Jackson's connections were particularly important in promoting the occupation of sparsely settled areas in southern Jackson and eastern Washtenaw Counties. Described as a small village, Jackson possessed potential for growth as the region developed. Despite its status as a county seat, this nucleated settlement had begun to expand commercially only by the mid–1830s. See Little, "Fifty Years Ago," 510; Thompson, "Observations and Experiences," 397; Pilcher, "Forty Years Ago," 81; Joshua C. Goodrich, Diary, 28 May 1835/EHC/WMUARHC; Van Buren, "Pioneer Annals," 246–47; Gordon and May, "Michigan Land Rush," 268–70; Watkins, "Settlement and Natural History of Manchester," 263; and Foote, "Early Days of Eaton County," 388.

Paw Paw consisted of several mill sites situated where the Territorial Road crossed the Paw Paw River. See Brown, "Autobiographical Notes," 459; Lawton, "Historical Sketch of Van Buren County," 630; and Fuller, *Economic and Social Beginnings*, 334–35.

39. The settlements between the Chicago and Territorial Roads emerged as centers of milling and retail activity, but in spite of their commercial significance, and the designation of Cassopolis as a county seat, all remained semi-nucleated settlements. See Hoffman, *Winter in the West*, 1:215; Brown, "Autobiographical Notes," 457–58; Fuller, *Economic and Social Beginnings*, 275, 289; Calvin H. Starr,

"Some of the Beginnings of St. Joseph County," *MPHC* 18 (1891): 514–15; and Perrine, "Townships in Calhoun County," 232. With the exception of Otsego, all those north of the Territorial Road were semi-nucleated settlements with impermanent commercial roles. See Fuller, *Economic and Social Beginnings,* 334; and Bela Hubbard, Notebook, 31 August 1840/BHP/Box 1/MHC.

Situated at the site of Whitmore Knaggs's trading post, Byron developed as a regional milling center but remained a semi-nucleated settlement in 1836. See Lucius E. Gould, "Four Papers on the Early History of Shiawassee County," *MPHC* 32 (1902): 251; Hubbard, *Memorials,* 71; and Fuller, *Economic and Social Beginnings,* 385. Saginaw grew slowly in spite of being designated a county seat. By mid-decade, despite heavy promotion, only eleven buildings existed there. See *Oakland Chronicle,* 10 December 1830; Azuhah L. Jewett, "Pioneer Life in 1830," *MPHC* 6 (1883): 429; "Miller, "Pioneer Sketches," 239–40; and idem, "Early History of the Saginaw Valley," 352. Both Flint and Ionia remained small settlements in 1836, but each expanded rapidly as its region was settled. See Brainard, "Pioneer History," 15–16; McCormick, "Early Life in the Saginaw Valley," 365; and "City of Ionia," 471–73. Lapeer, also a county seat, contained a mill and several residences. See *Democratic Free Press,* 31 May 1832.

40. Pontiac's commercial activities continued to expand, and it was known as "a pretty, business-like place" with a "bustling character." The Detroit & Pontiac Railroad extended its tracks to a point ten miles distant in 1840. See Hubbard, *Memorials,* 67; Mitchell, *View of the United States,* 86. One contemporary source described Mt. Clemens as "a picturesque village." See Lanman, *History of Michigan, Civil and Topographical,* 284. The principal nucleated settlements were Rochester, Romeo, and Utica. A number of villages grew up in southern Oakland County. These nucleated settlements included Northville, Auburn, Troy, Birmingham, Royal Oak, and Franklin. See *Western Traveller's Pocket Directory,* 65; Blois, *Gazetteer,* 285, 343, 269–70; Hoffman, *Winter in the West,* 1:123–25; Lanman, *History of Michigan, Civil and Topographical,* 283.

41. The completion of the Central Railroad to Ann Arbor insured the frontier town's continued importance to trade and western immigration. It grew rapidly and was soon twice the size of its nearest rival. Ann Arbor's role as a center of commerce, manufacturing, finance, and religious and educational activities prompted contemporary observers to compare it to eastern settlements of the time. See Lanman, *History of Michigan, Civil and Topographical,* 289; Swan, *Trip to Michigan in 1841,* 18; and Blois, *Gazetteer,* 248–49.

Ypsilanti grew as a commercial and manufacturing settlement, maintaining a number of road connections. Dexter became a gateway to sparsely settled portions of Ingham and Eaton counties and the middle Grand Valley. See Lanman, *History of Michigan, Civil and Topographical,* 289–90; Blois, *Gazetteer,* 281, 357; and Beebe, "Trip from Utica," 190–91.

Adrian was lined by rail to two ports with the completion of the Southern Railroad to Monroe in 1840. Reached only by a branch line, Tecumseh remained peripheral to the flow of rail traffic. Contemporary views of Adrian are contained in Winifred Lovering Holman, ed., "Diary of Rev. James Hamner Francis," *Ohio Archaeological and Historical Quarterly* 51 (1942): 49; Bela Hubbard, Notebook, 15 June 1839/BHP/Box 1/MHC; and Blois, *Gazetteer,* 246, 372. The influence of railroad construction and other factors are discussed in Adam, "Early History of Lenawee County," 364 and Raymond LaBounty Puffer, "The Michigan Agricultural Frontier: Southeastern Region, 1820–1860," Ph.D. diss., University of New Mexico (Ann Arbor, Mich.: University Microfilms, 1976), 373–79. New settlements included Manchester, Hudson, Petersburg, Blissfield, Palmyra, Dundee, Flat Rock, and Clinton, only the last four of which were nucleated settlements. See Stebbins, "Sketch of My Life," 56–57/SFP/MSUAHC; Blois, *Gazetteer,* 317; 302, 256–57, 337, 265; and Puffer, *Michigan Agricultural Frontier,* 190–99, 358–61. Monroe was also linked directly with the Lake Erie ports of Gibraltar, Brest, and Harve. See Lanman, *History of Michigan, Civil and Topographical,* 284; and Blois, *Gazetteer,* 327–28.

42. Jonesville's extensive road network linked older eastern settlements with settlements in developing regions to the north and west and the settlement lay at the junction of important cross-peninsular mail routes. Despite its role as Hillsdale County's only milling center, it remained a small nucleated settlement. See Clapp, "The Long Ago,"513; Blois, *Gazetteer*, 305; Crisfield Johnson, *History of Hillsdale County, Michigan* (Philadelphia: Everts and Abbot, 1879), 39; and Fuller, *Economic and Social Beginnings*, 285–86. Coldwater grew rapidly as a milling and commercial center in neighboring Branch County. Despite having lost its land office and the county seat, White Pigeon remained a viable commercial center with important road links with the north. See Blois, *Gazetteer*, 266, 381; *Kalamazoo Gazette*, 17 March 1838; and Fuller, *Economic and Social Beginnings*, 292.

The county seat of Jackson grew remarkably as a milling, retailing, and manufacturing center and as the site of the new state prison. It also possessed links to a growing network of emerging frontier settlements. See *History of Jackson County*, 216, 238; Blois, *Gazetteer*, 304–5; *Jackson Sentinel*, 19 June 1839; and Richard Arthur Santer, "A Historical Geography of Jackson, Michigan: A Study on the Changing Character of an American City 1829–1969," Ph.D. diss., Michigan State University (Ann Arbor, Mich.: University Microfilms, 1970), 75–76. Both Marshall and Kalamazoo expanded as processing, manufacturing, and other commercial activities expanded. Both maintained political functions as county seats, and Kalamazoo's acquired the western land office. Marshall's economic success was reflected in its imposing architecture, said to rival the finest forms of the east. See *Democratic Free Press*, 8 August 1838; Blois, *Gazetteer*, 319–20, 306–7; Mitchell, *View of the United States*, 86; Swan, *Trip to Michigan*, 20; Lanman, *History of Michigan, Civil and Topographical*, 287, 289; and *Kalamazoo Gazette*, 15 April 1837, 4 August 1838. The development of substantial commercial and residential architecture at Marshall is treated in Mabel Cooper Skjelver, *Nineteenth-Century Homes of Marshall, Michigan* (Marshall, Mich.: Marshall Historical Society, 1971), chaps. 1 and 2. The nucleated settlements of Battle Creek and Comstock remained small manufacturing and commercial centers with populations less the half those of the neighboring frontier towns. See Blois, *Gazetteer*, 251. A millsite on the river of the same name, Paw Paw's connections linked the Kalamazoo River settlements with southwestern Michigan and the developing region to the north. See ibid., 338; and Fuller, *Economic and Social Beginnings*, 334.

43. Niles was well situated to take advantage of the expanding St. Joseph River trade. It was also linked to the Indiana settlements of LaPorte and South Bend and was known widely as the central place of business for southwestern Michigan. Berrien Springs's central location made it the center of the overland network on the lower St. Joseph. Niles's reputation as a wide-open place of business was noted especially by visiting missionaries. See Holman, "Diary of Rev. James-Hamner Francis," 50. One wrote that Niles "has been notorious even at the *West*, for wickedness. The stores were all open on the Sabbath & that was the great business day" (J. N. Parsons to Milton Badger, 28 January 1840, in Cole, *Voices from the Wilderness*, 211). See also Lanman, *History of Michigan, Civil and Topographical*, 288; and Blois, *Gazetteer*, 332–33. For other Berrien County settlements, see Blois, *Gazetteer*, 255, 331; Lanman, *History of Michigan, Civil and Topographical*, 288; Ellis, *History of Berrien and Van Buren Counties*, 272–25, 316; and Fuller, *Economic and Social Beginnings*, 275–78.

Cassopolis lay at the center of an extensive network extending from Niles and the Berrien County settlements east along the Chicago Road and north to Paw Paw, as well as to those lying between Kalamazoo and White Pigeon. An important destination was Schoolcraft, a small junction from which roads radiated in all directions. These roads provided links to navigable water on the upper St. Joseph at Three Rivers and nucleated settlements at Constantine and Centreville. See Blois, *Gazetteer*, 241, 261, 262, 267, 360; and Fuller, *Economic and Social Beginnings*, 282.

Schoolcraft also provided a connection with Union City, a semi-nucleated milling settlement located at the head of navigation on the St. Joseph midway between the two central roads. Its situation accommodated links to major settlements in the central portion of the state. In addition to Marshall and Jonesville, Union City was connected with settlements in southern Calhoun and Jackson Counties. Although few of these became nucleated settlements, Homer and Concord had developed road networks that integrated the settlements of the region and tied them to those farther east. See Blois, *Gazetteer,* 267, 301, 376. Some of these small settlements played extensive economic roles in the frontier economy. Brooklyn, or Swainsville, in southeastern Jackson County was reported to have drawn farmers from Hillsdale, Calhoun, Eaton, Jackson, and portions of Lenawee Counties during the late 1830s. See "Brooklyn and Vicinity, the Village—Its Population and Business—Early Settlement— Interesting Incidents of Pioneer Life—the Farming Interest, etc," *MPHC,* 4 (1883): 273.

44. Allegan expanded rapidly as a lumbering center on the lower Kalamazoo River and its early commercial and industrial development encouraged the placement of the Allegan County seat there. Its diversified activities allowed it to take on the role of frontier town by the late 1830s. Allegan and its satellites at the mouth of the Kalamazoo provided an important economic framework that supported later farming settlement on the Western Shore. See Lanman, *History of Michigan, Civil and Topographical,* 290; Blois, *Gazetteer,* 212, 247, 331; and Johnson, *History of Allegan and Barry Counties,* 325, 327.

In sparsely settled Barry County, Marshall entrepreneurs promoted Hastings as a mill settlement. This semi-nucleated settlement maintained close ties to the south, but by 1840 it had developed extensive links between the Grand and Kalamazoo River settlements. In 1840, Hastings consisted of about six houses and a saw and grist mill. Other semi-nucleated settlements included Middleville; Yankee Springs, a way stop for travelers; and Geloster, on Gull Prairie. See Hayes, "Pioneer Days in Hastings," 237; Fuller, *Economic and Social Beginnings,* 352–53, 456; Goodyear, "Sketch of Barry County," 114–15; Bela Hubbard, Notebook, 31 August 1840/BHP/Box 1/MHC; Hoyt, "Founding of Yankee Springs," 292; and Blois, *Gazetteer,* 289.

Between Marshall and Ionia lay Bellevue, a nucleated settlement with several sawmills on Battle Creek. Its manufacturing and commercial activities, and the placement there of the county offices until 1840, allowed it to assume the role of a frontier town. Vermontville was the focal point of the dispersed covenanted community in western Eaton County. See Blois, *Gazetteer,* 253–54; Van Buren, "Township of Battle Creek," 292; Foote, "Early Days of Eaton County," 386; Barber, "Vermontville Colony," 226; and idem, "Recollections and Lessons," 191. The road on which Bellevue and Vermontville were situated was purported to be an earlier Indian trail between the Grand and Kalamazoo drainages. See Everett, *Memorials,* 20.

45. The phenomenal economic growth of Grand Rapids promoted its development as a diversified commercial and manufacturing, and the opening of the river to navigation led to its becoming a center for the expanding lumber trade. As a focus of religious and social activities, this county seat became the frontier town for western Michigan. See Everett, *Memorials,* 12–13; Lanman, *History of Michigan, Civil and Topographical,* 291; Blois, *Gazetteer,* 292–94; *Grand River Times,* 18 April 1837; *Calhoun County Patriot,* 1 June 1838; Hoyt, "Founding of Yankee Springs," 294. Blois, *Gazetteer,* 245, 291–92, 295–96; Everett, *Memorials,* 37; Fuller, *Economic and Social Beginnings,* 431; and Baxter, *History of the City of Grand Rapids,* 798.

Ionia was small village with a number of mills and at least one factory. See Everett, *Memorials,* 37; Gordon and May, "Michigan Land Rush," 477; Blois, *Gazetteer,* 303–4, 315–16; Chapin, *Reference Gazetteer of the United States,* 137; and Longyear, "Settlement of Clinton County," 363. Lyons and Portland, located where the Maple and Looking Glass Rivers, respectively, joined the Grand, were centers of commercial activity. Bela Hubbard found the level of commercial activity at Lyons to have been greatly curtailed by the Panic of 1837. "It is in all respects a village of '36," he wrote, "there are no means for sustaining a town here at present" (Notebook, 27 August 1840/BHP/Box 1/MHC). DeWitt was a semi-nucleated settlement on the Looking Glass River and an important link to the covenanted communities in Clinton County. See Chapin, *Reference Gazetteer of the United States*, 82; and Bela Hubbard, Notebook, 26 August 1840/BHP/Box 1/MHC.

46. Howell experienced rapid growth after 1836, acquiring a number of commercial activities as well as the Livingston County offices. See Franklin Ellis, *History of Livingston County, Michigan* (Philadelphia: Everts & Abbott, 1880), 141–45. Other settlements in Livingston and neighboring Ingham County remained small, semi-nucleated entities. Roads linking Howell and Dexter with the Thornapple Valley passed through Pinckney, Unadilla, Stockbridge (Pekin), Mason, and Charlotte. Despite the construction of the southern Grand River Road, the upper Grand drainage remained sparsely populated in 1840. See Lanman, *History of Michigan, Civil and Topographical*, 290; Clark, "Livingston County Pioneers," 255; Blois, *Gazetteer*, 254, 302, 320, 375; J. B. LaRowe, "Address of J. B. LaRowe," *Livingston Republican*, 17 July 1879; and Beebe, "A Trip from Utica," 190–92.

    Corunna was designated a county seat and linked western settlements with those in Oakland County. It also lay on the route connecting Howell with Saginaw. Other semi-nucleated settlements appeared at Shiawasseetown, Owosso, Fenton, Argentine, and Milford. See Bela Hubbard, Notebook, 22 August 1840/BHP/Box 1/MHC; Hubbard, *Memorials*, 68, 71–72; Blois, *Gazetteer*, 260, 268–69, 336, 361–62; and Crawford, "Reminiscences of Pioneer Life," 48.

    Flint's location on the Saginaw Road was enhanced by recent links westward to the Shiawassee County settlements and eastward to Lapeer. Flint grew rapidly in the late 1830s and became the county seat as well as the site of United States land office for the Saginaw District. Abundant waterpower permitted the development of milling and manufacturing activities and Flint became the commercial center and frontier town for the upper Saginaw region. See Blois, *Gazetteer*, 287, 310; and Fuller, *Economic and Social Beginnings*, 382–83.

    Saginaw expanded rapidly as a milling center, regional commercial center, and port. It became the county seat, acquired a United States customs office, and took on the role of a frontier town. See Miller, "Pioneer Sketches," 240; E. L. Wentz, "Recollections of the Saginaw Valley Fifty-Two Years Ago," *MPHC* 17 (1890): 440–42; Hubbard, *Memorials*, 75–76; and Blois, *Gazetteer*, 355. Three semi-nucleated settlements, Carrolton, Lower Saginaw, and Portsmouth, were settled in anticipation of expanding regional trade, but stagnated in the economic depression of the late 1830s. See Blois, *Gazetteer*, 315; Hubbard, *Memorials*, 84–85; and Fox, *History of Saginaw County*, 59–60, 65.

47. Monroe's growth as a commercial and manufacturing center made it the largest agricultural market in southeastern Michigan. The construction of a new ship canal facilitated ship traffic and made Monroe the principal port of entry for southern Michigan, northern Illinois, and Indiana. An increasing number of immigrants completed at least part of their overland journey by rail. See Lanman, *Summer in the Wilderness*, 174, and Mitchell, *View of the United States*, 86. Semi-nucleated settlements at Oakville and Petersburg linked the shoreline and the interior.

    The arrival of the Southern Railroad in 1843 permitted Hillsdale to eclipse its rival Jonesville in importance. Although a regional marketing center, the slowness of settlement farther south prevented the development of an extensive trading network, and Hillsdale failed to become a frontier town. See "History of Hillsdale, Michigan," HWP/MSUAHC; *Michigan Farmer*, 1849, 259, 280; and Meints. "Michigan Railroad Construction," 6.

    In spite of their positions in the regional economy of southwestern Michigan, the growth of secondary centers was limited. Some became nucleated settlements with often highly variable levels of activity, but others, such as Mottville, remained semi-nucleated mill settlements. Henry Sanford referred to Cassopolis as "one of those places that won't improve" (Journal, 17 August 1844/HSSP/Box 3/GSML). In St. Joseph County, mills were the foci of communities at Three Rivers and Constantine. See Silliman,

"Overland to Michigan," 431. Novelist H. H. Riley described Constantine as "a very miscellaneous-look-ing place," in which "the houses, and cabins, and sheds, and pig-sties, had been sown up and down the gorge, as their owners sowed wheat" (*Puddleford Papers,* 10). The nucleated settlements of Buchanan and New Buffalo remained important nodes in the regional transportation system, as did Berrien Springs, the county seat. See Lanman, *Summer in the Wilderness,* 174; Swan, *Trip to Michigan,* 103; Henry S. Sanford, Journal, 17 August 1844/HSSP/Box 3/GSML; Mitchell, *View of the United States,* 86; and Holley, *Picturesque Tourist,* 193.

48. Contemporary observers frequently mentioned Ann Arbor's development as a cultural center. Lanman (*Summer in the Wilderness,* 174) referred to it as "the New Haven of Michigan," and added that it "pos-sesses many attractions in the way of intelligent people, picturesque scenery, and handsome buildings." Important nucleated settlements included Ypsilanti, Saline, Dexter, Manchester, and Plymouth, whose connections provided access to the immediate area and adjacent frontier towns.

　　　One visitor described Jackson as "a considerable place." Jackson's route network also linked it to the nucleated settlements of Grass Lake, Napoleon, and Albion, as well as to semi-nucleated settlements at Brooklyn (Swainsville), Leslie, Spring Arbor, Concord, and Springport, that Lansing B. Swan character-ized as "small villages in the woods" (*Trip to Michigan,* 18–19). Several of these acquired specialized edu-cational roles. Spring Arbor became the site of Michigan Central College, predecessor of Hillsdale College, in 1844, and Michigan Union College, forerunner of Adrian College, was established at Leoni, near Grass Lake, the following year. The Wesleyan Seminary, later to become Albion College, opened its doors in Albion in 1842. See Dunbar, *Michigan,* 343–44.

　　　Marshall's links with Union City and Homer in the south tied it to settlements between the Chicago and Territorial Roads and roads through Bellevue, Charlotte, and Hastings made it a gateway to the Thornapple Valley and the lower Grand. See Mitchell, *View of the United States,* 86; Swan, *Trip to Michigan,* 20; Pierce, *History of Calhoun County,* 52, 55; Holley, *Picturesque Tourist,* 190; and Meints, "Michigan Railroad Construction," 6. Marshall's role as a contender for the state capital is discussed in Goodrich, "Locating the State Capital," 124–25. See also "The City of Battle Creek—Its Early History, Growth, and Present Condition," *MPHC* 3 (1881): 349; and Meints, "Michigan Railroad Construction," 6.

49. The Kalamazoo road network provided links to settlements on the lower Grand as well as those along the Territorial Road in Van Buren County and connections with Schoolcraft to the south, giving Kalamazoo connections with a number of smaller settlements along the St. Joseph River. Paw Paw pos-sessed a direct connection with the extensive road network in southwestern Michigan. See Bela Hubbard, Notebooks, 6, 9 August 1842/BHP/Box 1/MHC; Thayer, "Agriculture of Ottawa County," 553; Everett, *Memorials,* 516; George Torrey, "A Glimpse of Kalamazoo in 1846," *MPHC* 18 (1891): 590–91; Ellis, *History of Allegan and Barry Counties,* 149, 166, 368, 490, 514; Henry S. Sanford, Journal, 14 August 1844/HSSP/Box 3/GSML; Meints, "Michigan Railroad Construction," 6; and Durant, *History of Kalamazoo County,* 227–30.

50. Everett, *Memorials,* 377–84; Baxter, *History of the City of Grand Rapids,* 655–56. Lumber companies acquired large landholdings in the pinelands of northern Kent, Muskegon, Newaygo, and Montcalm Counties and erected mills along principal rivers. Although access to these isolated settlements was pri-marily by river, overland routes also tied several of the larger settlements to those on the lower Grand. See Rolland H. Maybee, "Michigan's White Pine Era, 1840–1900," *Michigan History* 42 (1959): 396–98; Danford, "Social and Economic Effects of Lumbering," 347–48; and Schenck, *History of Ionia and Montcalm Counties,* 468.

　　　Grand Haven's business was devoted largely to lumber milling and forwarding and it possessed important overland ties to settlements along the shoreline as well as the interior. Lying at the confluence of a number of roads leading into the southern interior, Ada emerged as a nucleated settlement. See Everett, *Memorials,* 39–40, 171–72, 212, 375; and Baxter, *History of the City of Grand Rapids,* 799. Ionia grew as it acquired a variety of retail, manufacturing, milling, and storage establishments. Nearby Lyons and Portland remained small, nucleated settlements, yet to develop substantial industries. See Everett, *Memorials,* 74, 88. In 1843, Portland contained a mill and carding machine, several stores and small manufactories, and a hotel and tavern. See Schenck, *History of Ionia and Montcalm Counties,* 238, 242, 321–24.

Semi-nucleated settlements linked to Mason included Eaton Rapids, Rio Grand (at the future site of Lansing), Hamilton (Okemos), and DeWitt. See Fuller, *Economic and Social Beginnings,* 458–459; James I. Rogers to Elias and Abigail Rogers, 19 December 1847/JRL/MSUAHC; and Ellis, *History of Shiawassee and Clinton Counties,* 406–7.

Howell grew during the early 1840s, as its manufacturing and commercial enterprises increased to include milling and machinery manufacture and a variety of retail merchants. Now a county seat, it became a center for the administrative, educational, and religious, activities typical of frontier towns. See Ellis, *History of Livingston County,* 147–78; and R. C. Crawford, "Fifty-Two Years of Itinerant Life in the Michigan Conference of the M. E. Church," *MPHC* 22 (1893): 269.

Connected to the south through the semi-nucleated settlements of Unadilla and Hamburg, Howell's northern network was linked to Byron, Shiawasseetown, and Corunna, and small settlements in southern Genesee County, such as Fenton, or Dibbleville, situated on the northern Grand River Road. See Franklin Ellis, *History of Genesee County, Michigan* (Philadelphia: Everts and Abbott, 1879), 204–5, 207, 230–32; and idem, *History of Livingston County,* 286–87, 274–75, 316. In the mid-1840s, Owosso, Corunna, Shiawasseetown, and Byron were still the only "important" settlements in Shiawassee County. See Crawford, "Itinerant Life," 269; and Ellis, *History of Shiawassee and Clinton Counties,* 151, 167–68, 204–5.

51. By 1845 the growing number of milling and manufacturing businesses and expanding retail trade made Flint "a flourishing place of business" (Lovira Hart to Lyman Abbey, 1845/LHL/MHC). Its road network provided direct links with Grand Blanc, Davisonville, and Lapeer and supported expansion in the Flint drainage and in the lower Thumb region. See Ellis, *History of Genesee County,* 132–36, 245, 257; Pilcher, *Protestantism in Michigan,* 348; and Bela Hubbard, Notebook, 1840/BHP/Box 1/MHC.

Spurred by agricultural immigration and an increased volume of lumber milling, Saginaw experienced rapid growth by the mid-1840s. Although still relatively small, its regional road network linked settlements along the river and Midland, to the northwest, with those in neighboring counties. See *History of Saginaw County,* 605–6; and Fox, *History of Saginaw County,* 36, 59–60, 65.

52. All of the statistics employed in this analysis have been taken from Blois's *Gazetteer,* with additional numerical information supplied by the following sources: Rev. James Selkirk, Recollections, MJC/WMUARHC; *Niles Gazette and Advertiser,* 5 March 1836; *Kalamazoo Gazette,* 15 April 1837; *Jackson Sentinel,* 19 June 1839; "The City of Ionia," 471–73; McCormick, "Early Life in the Saginaw Valley," 367; Wentz, "Saginaw Valley," 440; *Macomb Statesman,* 22 September 1837; and Chase, "Pioneer Minister," 53–54.

53. Government and administrative activities include county offices, as well as federal facilities such as customs offices, arsenals, and district land offices. Because of their ubiquitous presence throughout the area of colonization, post offices were not included among these centralizing activities.

54. A central place model portrays a region as an isotropic surface on which the horizontal arrangement of settlements is seen to reflect a region's vertical structure. In such a model, settlements are centrally located within hexagonal-shaped trade areas placed within a regular lattice. If we assume that centers of a higher order are more widely spaced than lower-order places, and that the latter 'nest' within the trade

areas of higher-order settlements, then the arrangement of the hexagons should indicate the nature of the arrangement between the two levels of centers. The model employed here is essentially that proposed by W. Christaller, *Central Places in Southern Germany,* trans. C. W. Baskin (Englewood Cliffs, N.J.: Prentice-Hall, 1966).

Regions where trade is centered on internal markets are organized around the marketing principle and are characterized by a pattern in which each center serves three markets at the next-lower level. These markets include its own and a third of those found in each of the six surrounding lower-order settlements located at the points of the hexagon. Such a relationship is expressed in a K-value, in this case K-3, and may be portrayed by a lattice in which each lower-ranking center is located at the midpoint between three higher-level centers. See Berry, *Geography of Market Centers,* 68–72; and Garner, "Models of Urban Geography," 315–22.

55. A detailed account of Comstock's early history and an explanation of its early decline appear in Durant, *History of Kalamazoo County,* 388–89. See also, Fuller, *Economic and Social Beginnings,* 349–50. For Constantine's rivalry with nearby Centreville, see Blois, *Gazetteer,* 262, 267–68.

56. Lying on the upper Maumee River, Fort Wayne developed as an important shipping and collection point for agricultural produce in western Indiana. Strategically placed along the state's extensive canal system, Fort Wayne dominated trade in northern Indiana. See E. Chamberlain, *1850 Indiana Gazetteer, or Topographical Directory of the State of Indiana* (Indianapolis: By the author, 1850; reprint, Knightstown, Ind.: Bookmark, 1977), 387; and Ronald E. Shaw, *Canals for a Nation: The Canal Era in the United States, 1790–1860* (Lexington: University Press of Kentucky, 1990), 142. Toledo's role as a port was enhanced by the construction of the Wabash & Erie and Miami & Erie Canals, which made it the terminus for freight and passenger traffic in Indiana and Ohio, as well as by the completion of the Erie and Kalamazoo Railway into southern Michigan. See Ronald E. Shaw, *Canals for a Nation: The Canal Era in the United States, 1790–1860* (Lexington: University of Kentucky Press, 1990), 142, 153. Originally Michigan's southernmost port, Toledo continued to play an important role in the state's development after it became part of Ohio in 1837.

57. Although reliable census data for municipalities in antebellum Michigan are rare, Blois's *Gazetteer* provided estimated figures for a number of Michigan frontier towns in 1838:

Adrian	1,200
Ann Arbor	2,000
Flint	300 families
Grand Rapids	1,000
Marshall	1,000
Monroe	2,795 (includes entire township)
Niles	1,200
Pontiac	1,000
Saginaw	400

Modern rural sociologists would classify all but one of these as small villages. Monroe satisfies the criterion for a town, and only Detroit, with a population of 9,278, could be ranked as a city. See Nelson, *Rural Sociology,* 87. Agriculturists are usually a major component of village populations, even in areas of isolated farm settlement. See ibid., 54–56. In contrast, agriculturists comprised a minimal part of frontier settlements. Only later, as regional populations and specialization and trade grew, did their presence increase. In some areas, notably New England, this change created the perception that agricultural villages were the initial form of settlement. See Handsman, "Early Capitalism," 3. See also Kenneth E. Lewis, *Camden: A Frontier Town in Eighteenth-Century South Carolina,* University of South Carolina, Institute of Archaeology and Anthropology, Anthropological Studies 2 (Columbia: University of South Carolina, 1976), 100–1.

58. Casagrande, Thompson, and Young ("Colonization," 313) suggest that the irregular occurrence of political, social, and economic services in nucleated settlements distinguished them from frontier towns. See also Blois, *Gazetteer*, 251, 254, 320, 333, 369, 372, 383; and Fuller, *Economic and Social Beginnings*, 297–98.

59. Reland Tinkham to Foster Tinkham, 23 August 1831/MHC; Hayes, "Pioneer Days in Hastings," 237; Hoyt, "Founding of Yankee Springs," 292; Bela Hubbard, Notebooks, BHP/Box 1/MHC. The composition and function of Michigan's seminucleated settlements follows closely the characteristics attributed to them in Casagrande, Thompson, and Young, "Colonization," 313.

CHAPTER 10

1. The desire to enter commercial production was expressed in the writings of many contemporary pioneers. For example, Johnson Montgomery of Eaton County recalled that in 1836, "The people had made improvements, and were raising a surplus [but had] no . . . market." The editor of a southwestern Michigan newspaper reported, "The interior of the state is beginning to feel the want of facilities for conveying the superabundant produce to a nearby cash market." Henry Chamberlain, of New Buffalo, expressed similar frustrations in a letter to his son nearly a decade later, claiming that residents of Michigan and neighboring states could "produce double the amount [of wheat] the next year and continue in that ratio for years to come. All we ask is a market at a fair price and we can supply the world." See Johnson Montgomery, "Pioneer History of the Settlement of Eaton County," *MPHC* 22 (1893): 520; *White Pigeon Gazette*, quoted in the *Detroit Free Press*, 1 August 1838; Henry Chamberlain to Mellen Chamberlain, 8 May 1847/CFP/MSUAHC. See also Russell, *Long, Deep Furrow*, 367–69, 373–82; Gates, *Farmer's Age*, 164; and Taylor, *Transportation Revolution*.

2. Lew Allen Chase, "Michigan's Share in the Establishment of Improved Transportation between the East and the West," *MPHC* 38 (1912): 591; Gephart, *Transportation and Industrial Development*, 57–68.

3. Ross M. Robertson *History of the American Economy* (New York: Harcourt, Brace & World, 1955), 125; MacGill, *History of Transportation*, 3–4; Douglas E. Clanin, "Internal Improvements in National Politics, 1816–1830," in *Transportation in the Early Nation* (Indianapolis: Indiana Historical Society, 1982), 44; Taylor, *Transportation Revolution*, 20–21, 24; John F. Stover, "Canals and Turnpikes: America's Early-Nineteenth-Century Transportation Network," in *An Emerging Independent American Economy, 1815–1875*, ed. Joseph R. Frese and Jacob Judd (Tarrytown, N.Y.: Sleepy Hollow Press and Rockefeller Archive Center, 1980), 69–71.

4. Taylor, *Transportation Revolution*, 22–23; Holman, "Diary," 41–50. As early as 1820 the *Detroit Gazette* advised travelers on the most advantageous connections between Buffalo and Boston and New York. See *Detroit Gazette*, 23 June 1820, 20 August 1828.

5. MacGill, *History of Transportation*, 16–17; D. W. Meinig, *Continental America, 1800–1867*, vol. 2 of *The Shaping of America: A Geographic Perspective on 500 Years of History*, vol. 2: (New Haven, Conn.: Yale University Press, 1993), 224–30. Contemporary observers such as Thomas Cooley of Adrian recalled, "Through the Black Swamp of Ohio the stream of emigrant wagons was continuous." See Melish, *Information and Advice to Emigrants*, 100; Thomas M. Cooley, "Address on Laying the Cornerstone of the New Courthouse for Lenawee County at Adrian, June 28, 1884," *MPHC* 7 (1886): 526; D. L. Porter to W. P. Porter, 12 June 1831/DLPP/CHL; and *Detroit Gazette*, 21 January 1826. Despite the inconvenience of cold and snow, Orasmus Lamb's family was able to complete an 1835 trip to Michigan via the southern

route in only seventeen days (see *Adrian Daily Times and Expositor,* 12 March 1877). Moses and Levi Goodrich followed the northern route in the winter of 1834, moving their belongings by ox team and sled overland to Windsor and then by ferry across the river to Detroit. The trip from Buffalo was reputed to have taken only nine days (see Goodrich, "Pioneer Sketch," 482–85). Two years earlier, Chandler M. Church and his family consumed a month following the same route from Monroe County, New York to Calhoun County, Michigan (see Pierce, *History of Calhoun County* [Philadelphia: L. H. Everts, 1877], 145). Moving family livestock overland required planning and coordination as well as the necessary manpower to manage this task. Harriet Munro Longyear's family, which moved to Michigan in 1836, was large enough to travel in two groups so that the livestock could be driven by land across Ohio, while heavy household goods were shipped by boat (see Longyear, "Settlement of Clinton County," 361). Several contemporary sources mention the use of this short lake passage to avoid passing through the Black Swamp (see *Western Traveller's Pocket Directory,* 6; Chloe Clark, Diary, 1836/MHC). Among the southern immigrants was the family of James and Elizabeth Allen of Augusta County, Virginia. Traveling overland in the fall of 1824, they followed the Kanawa River to Charleston, Virginia, and then turned northward toward the Ohio Valley, passing through Gallipolis, Ohio, on their way to Sandusky. From this port they proceeded to Detroit by boat. See Kit Lane, *John Allen: Michigan's Pioneer Promoter* (Douglas, Mich.: Pavilion Press, 1988), 33–40. This estimate is attributed to an unnamed Charleston, Virginia newspaper, quoted in the *Detroit Gazette,* 3 December 1829. See also Fuller, *Economic and Social Beginnings,* 301.

6. *Michigan Farmer,* 1847, 168.

7. Discussions of the inadequacies in the frontier road networks may be found in Van Buren, "Pioneer Annals," 239; *Lake Huron Observer,* 30 December 1844; *Detroit Journal and Michigan Advertiser,* 4 January 1832, 13 June 1832; *Democratic Free Press and Michigan Intelligencer,* 12 April 1832; *Michigan Telegraph,* 2 February 1848; and Williams, "First Settlement of Shiawassee County," 486–87.

8. See MTL/1832/3:934; Petition to Congress by Inhabitants of the Territory, 4 February 1834/TPUS/MT/12:725; Memorial to Congress by Inhabitants of Southern Michigan, 26 December 1834/TPUS/MT/12:831; Petition to Congress by Inhabitants of the St. Joseph Country, 1 April 1834/TPUS/MT/12:766; Baxter, "Beginnings in the Grand River Valley," 329; White, "Yankee Lewis' Famous Hostelry," 306; *Western Traveller's Pocket Directory,* 84; Carr, "Settlement of Williamstown," 448; and Foote, "Early Days of Eaton County," 385.

9. For a discussion of the impact of canals in Europe and Great Britain, see Roger Pilkington, "Canals: Inland Waterways outside Great Britain," in *A History of Technology,* vol. 4, *The Industrial Revolution, c. 1750 to c. 1850,* ed. Charles Singer, E. J. Holmyard, A. R. Hall, and Trevor I. Williams (New York: Oxford University Press, 1958), 548–62; and Charles Hadfield, "Canals: Inland Waterways of the British Isles," in *A History of Technology,* vol. 4, *The Industrial Revolution, c. 1750 to c. 1850,* ed. Charles Singer, E. J. Holmyard, A. R. Hall, and Trevor I. Williams (New York: Oxford University Press, 1958), 563–73.

    South Carolina initiated perhaps the most ambitious early river navigation program by constructing a series of canals designed to provide access to the port of Charleston from a large portion of the state's interior, and its success was not lost on those seeking to extend trade elsewhere in the United States. See MacGill, *History of Transportation,* 276–78; and F. A. Porcher, *The History of the Santee Canal* (Charleston: South Carolina Historical Society, 1903), 1–11. This period also saw efforts along the Atlantic Seaboard. Among these were the extensive Middlesex Canal, intended to redirect the Merrimack River trade to Boston; the Dismal Swamp Canal, linking Norfolk, Virginia, with Albemarle Sound; and smaller projects in Pennsylvania, Virginia, and New York. See Shaw, *Canals for a Nation,* 3–4; and Albion, *Rise of New York Port,* 78.

10. The building of a trans-Appalachian canal had long been frustrated by the inability to surmount the difficulties presented by this topographic barrier; however, the navigability of the Hudson River provided a

feasible path into the interior. Reaching inland, it allowed access to the Mohawk valley and the relatively level lands beyond, which presented a path toward the Lake Erie port of Buffalo. Such a route allowed direct and unimpeded passage from the Atlantic Ocean to the Old Northwest, opening the region bordering the Great Lakes to commercial shipping. See MacGill, *History of Transportation,* 161; and Stover, "Canals and Turnpikes," 84.

11. The enormous cost of the Erie Canal's construction, without the prospect of an immediate return on investment, discouraged private capital. Qualms over the constitutionality of the central government's participation in public transportation also precluded the use of federal funds. See MacGill, *History of Transportation,* 170–80; Clanin, "Internal Improvements," 35; Albion, *Rise of New York Port,* 82–83; Harvey W. Segal, "Canals and Economic Development," in *Canals and American Economic Development,* ed. Carter Goodrich (New York: Columbia University Press, 1961), 221–23; H. Jerome Cranmer, "Canal Investment, 1815–1860," in *Trends in the American Economy in the Nineteenth Century,* vol. 24, *Studies in Income and Wealth* (New York: National Bureau of Economic Research, 1960), 557–58; and Shaw, *Canals for a Nation,* 35. For a discussion of western canal construction and its impact on settlement and economic development, see Harry N. Scheiber, *Ohio Canal Era: A Case Study of Government and the Economy, 1820–1861* (Athens: Ohio University Press, 1969), chaps. 8 and 9; and Paul Fatout, *Indiana Canals* (West Lafayette, Ind.: Purdue University Press, 1972).

12. *Detroit Gazette,* 17 May 1825; *Michigan Sentinel,* 10 June 1825.

13. The Miami and Erie Canal opened much of the western Ohio interior, while the Ohio and Erie Canal provided access to the eastern portion of that state and the newly completed canal system of Pennsylvania. Further west, the Wabash and Erie Canal followed a circuitous path across western Ohio and northern Indiana, a route beset by both political and engineering difficulties. Finally, the Illinois and Michigan Canal created a navigable waterway that eventually opened a portion of northern Illinois to Lake Michigan and the Mississippi drainage via the Illinois River. For a discussion of these canals, see Ronald E. Shaw, "The Canal Era in the Old Northwest," in *Transportation in the Early Nation* (Indianapolis: Indiana Historical Society, 1982), 90–93; idem, *Canals for a Nation,* 127–37; Ralph D. Gray, "The Canal Era in Indiana," in *Transportation in the Early Nation* (Indianapolis: Indiana Historical Society, 1982), 128; Taylor, *Transportation Revolution,* 45–48; Cranmer, "Canal Investment, 557–58; John Bell Rae, "Federal Land Grants in Aid of Canals," *Journal of Economic Research* 4 (1944): 169–75; and Hannah Emily Keith, "An Historical Sketch of Internal Improvements in Michigan, 1836–1846," *Publications of the Michigan Political Science Association* 4 (1902): 12–13, 36–38. For a discussion of the movement for internal improvements in America, see Robert James Parks, *Democracy's Railroads: Public Enterprise in Jacksonian Michigan* (Port Washington, N.Y.: Kennikat Press, 1972), chap. 1.

14. Keith, "Internal Improvements," 36–39.

15. Chase, "Improved Transportation," 593–94; Blois, *Gazetteer,* 294, 306, 368.

16. James Cooke Mills, *Our Inland Seas: Their Shipping and Commerce for Three Centuries* (Chicago: A. C. McClurg, 1910; reprint, Cleveland, Ohio: Freshwater Press, 1976), 106; C. Colton, *Tour of the American Lakes and Among the Indians of the North-West Territory, in 1830: Disclosing the Character and Prospects of the Indian Race* (London: Frederick Westley and A. H. Davis, 1833), 1:22; *Semi-Weekly Free Press,* 3 March 1837; *Lake Huron Observer,* 14 July 1845; Blois, *Gazetteer,* 105–6; and Hatcher, *Lake Erie,* chaps. 12 and 13, discuss in detail the growth of the shipping industry during this period.

17. Taylor, *Transportation Revolution,* 56–57; Mills, *Our Inland Seas,* 89–90, 107; Melish, *Information and Advice to Emigrants,* 102; *Detroit Gazette,* 21 May 1819, 23 June 1820; *Weekly Recorder,* "The Michigan Territory," 6 March 1818, 248.

18. Mills, *Our Inland Seas,* 114–15; *Democratic Free Press and Michigan Intelligencer,* 19 May 1831; *Detroit Gazette,* 29 May 1829; *Democratic Free Press and Michigan Intelligencer,* 4 May 1836.

19. *Michigan Statesman,* 30 May 1835; Shaw, *Canals for a Nation,* 45; Parkins, *Historical Geography of Detroit,* 180; Chase, "Improved Transportation," 589–90; SED/1850/48.

20. *Detroit Gazette,* 9 April 1819, 23 June 1820; Trowbridge, "Detroit, Past and Present," 383.

21. *Detroit Journal and Michigan Advertiser,* 29 June 1831; Petition to Congress by Owners and Masters of Great Lakes Vessels, 1 November 1834/TPUS/MT/12:812; Hoffman, *Winter in the West,* 1:331; Quaife, *Lake Michigan,* 151; Shirreff, *Tour through North America,* 216; Goodrich, "Michigan Territory Sixty Years Ago," 232–34; Wellington Williams, *Appleton's Railroad and Steamboat Companion, being a Travellers' Guide through New England and the Middle States, with Routes in the Southern and Western States, and also in Canada* (New York: D. Appleton & Co., 1847), 183; Delegate Wing to House Committee on Commerce, 7 January 1828/TPUS/MT/11:1141–42.

22. See Quaife, *Lake Michigan,* 254; and Eichenlaub, *Weather and Climate,* 286–87. Lake Michigan's reputation was well known to early settlers along its shores. A resident of New Buffalo warned a correspondent that "Lake Michigan is no humbug. . . . Sometimes it is as placid and harmless as an infant on its mother's breast, sometimes as turbulent & terrific as the raging ocean" (Hale E. Crosby to Mellen Chamberlain, 19 May 1845/CFP/MSUAHC). John Gordon noted the perception that lake travel was "very perilous." "I am told," he wrote, "that it is a case of constant occurrence for a vessel to put out of harbor just before a storm & never to appear again by the slightest trace" (Gordon and May, "Michigan Land Rush," 433).

23. See Schoolcraft, *Narrative Journal of Travels,* 51; Blois, *Gazetteer,* 102–3; Brown, *Western Gazetteer,* 167–68; Darby, *Tour,* 195; Evans, *Pedestrious Tour,* 116; Samuel Zug, "Detroit in 1815–16," *MPHC* 1 (1877): 496–500. For comments and statistics on Detroit's growth, see *Detroit Gazette,* 29 January 1819, 2 January 1824; and *Democratic Free Press,* 3 July 1835, 30 December 1835.

24. See *Detroit Gazette,* 12 July 1822; and *Michigan Sentinel,* 28 October 1825, 25 November 1825. Between 1826 and 1839 Congress appropriated $109,803 for work on Monroe Harbor and its approaches. See E. B. Brown, "Early Recollections of the Village of Tecumseh," *MPHC* 2 (1880): 388. Legislation pertaining to Monroe harbor improvements is found in SLUS/1835/4:752; SLUS/1836/5:67–69; MAL/R/1841/13:212; and HD/1844/210. See also Delegate Wing to the House Committee on Commerce, 7 January 1828/TPUS/MT/11:1142; *Michigan Sentinel,* 4 September 1830, 6 June 1836; Joshua C. Goodrich, Diary, 17 May 1835/EHC/WMUARHC; Blois, *Gazetteer,* 328; Wentz, "Saginaw Valley," 440; Elizabeth Chandler to Jane Howell, 15 April 1831/EMCP/Box 1/MHC; and Christiancy, "Early History of the City and County of Monroe," 369–70.

25. *Macomb Statesman,* 12 September 1837; Tanner, *American Traveller,* 34; Blois, *Gazetteer,* 287–88, 329, 346; Mitchell, *Michigan Traveler's Guide,* 68; *Lake Huron Observer,* 21 June 1844.

26. *Detroit Gazette,* 19 July 1825; Lanman, *History of Michigan, Civil and Topgraphical,* 292; *Democratic Free Press,* 28 July 1837; Busby, "Pioneer Life," 125; George W. Sears, "Michigan in 1845," *Michigan History* 15 (1931): 634. W. R. McCormick, "Pioneer Life in the Saginaw Valley," *MPHC* 3 (1881): 603; Fox, *History of Saginaw County,* 31, 34–35; Sarah J. Frost to Mrs. William Thompson Jr., 4 July 1853; *Portrait and Biographical Album of Midland County, Michigan* (Chicago: Chapman Bros., 1884), 379; Hubbard, *Memorials,* 83.

27. Bessie Louise Pierce, *A History of Chicago,* vol. 1, *The Beginning of a City, 1673–1848* (New York: Alfred A. Knopf, 1937), 76; Blois, *Gazetteer,* 55. The same observation appeared three years later in a western Michigan newspaper, whose editor concluded that, "From the Manitou islands to Chicago, almost the entire length of the lake, there is not a harbor in which a vessel could find refuge from impending destruction" (*Democratic Expounder and Calhoun County Democrat,* 19 February 1841). See also Williams, "Internal Commerce of the West," 36.

28. Shirreff, *Tour Through North America,* 226.

29. Hoffman, *Winter in the West,* 1:204.

30. Cronon, *Nature's Metropolis,* 52. Hoffman, *Winter in the West,* 1:276; Pierce, *History of Chicago,* 79.

31. An 1832 source described the port of St. Joseph as "the principal commercial depot for the North west part of Indiana and South west part of Michigan, embracing a tract of country extending more than one hundred miles, . . ." (*Democratic Free Press and Michigan Intelligencer,* 19 July 1832). Flatboats and keelboats regularly traveled inland as far as Mottville in St. Joseph County, and steamboats were in service on the river's lower reaches. The editor of the *Niles Intelligencer* perceived that

   > The whole St. Joseph country is benefitted by the navigation of the river. Thru this channel they receive their imports, and export their surplus produce. Merchandise to supply the wants of thirty thousand inhabitants is now brought into the interior upon it from Lake Michigan, and the surplus produce of nearly two hundred miles of the most fertile lands of the west, find a market through its channel. . . .
   > (quoted in the *Democratic Free Press,* 14 November 1838)

   Contemporary accounts of river trade appeared in *Niles Intelligencer,* quoted in the *Detroit Free Press* on 14 November 1848; Morgan, "Township of Pine Plains," 294; and Brown, "Autobiographical Notes," 450. For a discussion of the role of river improvements in the development of trade on the St. Joseph in the 1830s and 1840s, see LeRoy Barnett, "Early Improvements of the St. Joseph River," *Inland Seas* 46 (1990): 307–17.

32. For references to the lake trade, see Reland Tinkham to Foster Tinkham, 23 August 1831/MHC; *Niles Gazette and Advertiser,* 5 March 1836; and *Democratic Free Press,* 3 June 1835, 10 October 1838. The *Niles Gazette and Advertiser,* 19 March 1836, predicted that "With improved navigation, . . . lake boats . . . might load at our wharves and discharge their cargoes at Buffalo," and *Democratic Free Press,* 8 May 1833. With regard to harbor improvements, see, Petition to Congress by Inhabitants of the St. Joseph Country, December 1834/TPUS/MT/12:839; HD/1835/20; *Niles Gazette and Advertiser,* 21 November 1835; HD/1844/210; Clark, *Grain Trade,"* 83; and Barnett, "Early Improvements," 316–17.

33. Blois, *Gazetteer,* 331; Jacob Gerrish, Diary, 22 July 1837/JGP/MSUAHC; Jacob Gerrish to Moses Chamberlain, 14 June 1843/CFP/MSUAHC; Everett, *Memorials,* 465–66, 529; MAL/L/1848/32; *Michigan Farmer,* 1849, 354; *Grand River Times,* 21 July 1852. Although river shipping declined generally in the face of railroad competition during the 1840s, the movement of lumber continued on the lower Kalamazoo. See Donald C. Henderson, "Notes on Saugatuck," *MPHC,* 305; Morgan, "Township of Pine Plains," 293–94; and Warner, "Early History of Michigan," 290–91.

34. Henry Griffin, "Commerce and Ship Building of Ottawa County," *MPHC* 9 (1886): 282–85; Everett, *Memorials,* 420–21, 451–52, 527–28; Blois, *Gazetteer,* 291; Lutheria Stoner Crandell, Statement, n.d./LSCC/SAM; Donald W. Linebaugh, "Nineteenth-Century Settlement Patterning in the Grand River Valley, Ottawa County, Michigan" (master's thesis, College of William and Mary, 1982), 86; Thomas D. Gilbert, "Development of Western Michigan," *MPHC* 17 (1890): 321; *Grand River Times,* 21 May 1856; Susan Olsen Haswell and Arnold R. Alanen, *A Garden Apart: An Agricultural and Settlement History of Michigan's Sleeping Bear Dunes National Lakeshore Region* (Omaha, Neb. and Lansing, Mich.: Midwest Regional Office, National Park Service and State Historic Preservation Office, Michigan Bureau of History, 1994), 28–29, 34–35.

35. Topography limited the routes of canals. Although canal locks could accommodate variations in elevation, rapid ascents and descents presented great difficulties that required elaborate and expensive means to overcome. The nature of the soils, the adequacy of a reliable water supply, the susceptibility of the route to flooding, and other factors further affected their placement and success. Climate also limited the use of canals as a mode of intra-regional trade, because subfreezing temperatures in northern latitudes prevented their use for up to five months out of the year. See Taylor, *Transportation Revolution,* 79; Shaw, "Canal Era," 90–92; idem, *Canals for a Nation,* 69–71, 127–32; MacGill, *History of Transportation,* 287;

Cronon, *Nature's Metropolis,* 74; John F. Stover, "Iron Roads in the Old Northwest: Railroads and the Growing Nation," in *Transportation and the Early Nation* (Indianapolis: Indiana Historical Society, 1982), 150; and idem, *American Railroads* (Chicago: University of Chicago Press, 1961), 10.

36. See Alfred D. Chandler, *The Railroads: The Nation's First Big Business* (New York: Harcourt, Brace & World, 1965), 8, 23; and Stover, "Iron Roads," 150–51. Railroads initiated the use of standardized time, based on astronomical measurement and employed on a regional basis, in the 1850s. Promoted by the railroads, standard time became increasingly important to the integration of the American economy. It was adopted on a national scale, with the recognition of four time zones, in 1883. For a discussion of this process and the perceptual changes about time associated with it, see Michael O'Malley, *Keeping Watch: A History of American Time* (New York: Viking, 1990), chap. 3. The railroads' impact on the scheduling of activities on a regional and national scale is also examined in Stover, *American Railroads,* 157–58; and Cronon, *Nature's Metropolis,* 77–78.

37. See Paul H. Cootner, "The Economic Impact of the Railroad Innovation," in *The Railroad and the Space Program: An Exploration in Historical Analogy,* ed. Bruce Mazlish (Cambridge, Mass.: M.I.T. Press, 1965), 125; Taylor, *Transportation Revolution,* 75–78; George Rogers Taylor and Irene D. Neu, *The American Railroad Network, 1861–1890* (Cambridge, Mass.: Harvard University Press, 1956), 4–5; and MacGill, *History of Transportation,* 312. For discussions of the development of railroad track and roadbed in the first half of the nineteenth century, see John H. White Jr., "Tracks and Timber," *Industrial Archaeology* 2 (1976): 36–40, 42–44; C. Hamilton Ellis, "The Development of Railway Engineering," in *A History of Technology,* vol. 5, *The Late Nineteenth Century, c. 1850 to c. 1900,* ed. Charles Singer, E. J. Holmyard, A. R. Hall, and Trevor I. Williams (New York: Oxford University Press, 1958), 323–24; Emory R. Johnson, *American Railway Transportation* (New York: D. Appleton, 1903), 37; Albright G. Zimmerman, "Iron for American Railroads," *Canal History and Technology Proceedings* 5 (1986): 64–75; J. L. Ringwalt, *Development of Transportation Systems in the United States* (Philadelphia: By the author, 1888), 83–86; and Stover, *American Railroads,* 21–24. For a detailed contemporary description and discussion of track employed on the early Michigan railroads, see Franz Anton Ritter von Gerstner, *Die Innern Communicationen der Vereinigten Staaten von Nordamerica,* vol. 2 (Vienna: L. Förster artistische Anstalt, 1843), 17–19, 21–23, 31–34, 34–35, 36–37, 39–42, 42, 46, Pl. XVIII.

     Despite improvements in track construction, the parochial orientation of American railroads resulted in the use of a multiplicity of track gauges. This prevented the exchange of cars among railroads and effectively curtailed the development of a integrated long-distance rail transport system. Michigan, Wisconsin, and Iowa railroads adopted the "standard" gauge of 4 feet, 8_ inches that was common in much of New England and in the system connecting New York with Lake Erie; however, a variety of gauges were employed in the intervening states of Ohio and Pennsylvania, largely by railroads attempting to monopolize regional transportation. Only in 1856 did the extension of the New York system along the southern shore of Lake Erie provide a standard-gauge link between East and West. The continued presence of multiple gauges inhibited the development of an effective regional railroad network until the 1860s. For a discussion of the track gauge problem and its implications, see MacGill, *History of Transportation,* 313–14; Taylor, *Transportation Revolution,* 80–82; Stover, *American Railroads,* 21–24; Taylor and Neu, *American Railroad Network,* 24–37; and Alvin F. Harlow, *The Road of the Century: The Story of the New York Central* (New York: Creative Age Press, 1947), 267–74.

     The 1830s and 1840s also witnessed a number of improvements in railroad motive power. The most comprehensive treatment of antebellum locomotives is found in John H. White Jr., *A History of the American Locomotive, Its Development: 1830–1880* (New York: Dover Publications, 1968), esp. chaps. 3, 8, and 9. See also Ellis, "Railway Engineering," 322–23; Stover, *American Railroads,* 25; Alfred W. Bruce, *The Steam Locomotive in America: Its Development in the Twentieth Century* (New York: Bonanza Books,

1952), 28–29, 36, 144, 199, 231, 247–49, 257–58, 266–69, 282–85; and Ringwalt, *Transportation Systems,* 99–100.

John H. White Jr., *The American Railroad Freight Car: From the Wood Car Era to the Coming of Steel* (Baltimore: Johns Hopkins University Press, 1993), esp. chap. 2, offers a detailed history of the development of early freight cars. Briefer discussions are found in Ringwalt, *Transportation Systems,* 100–2, 208; and M. N. Forney, "American Locomotives and Cars," *Scribner's Magazine* 4 (1888): 192–93. For discussions of passenger car development, see Ellis, "Railway Engineering," 342–43; Forney, "American Locomotives and Cars," 193; Harlow, *Road of the Century,* 258; and Horace Porter, "Railway Passenger Travel," *Scribner's Magazine* 4 (1888): 296–304.

In the imagination of antebellum Americans, steam constituted a powerful force, the limitations of which had not yet begun to be realized. A force that could permit the triumph of machines over nature might be expected to be capable of freeing humanity of other traditional physical restraints. The symbolic power of steam far exceeded the actual extent of its application in the 1830s. For a discussion of the development of railroads as a cultural symbol, and its affect on traditional perceptions of landscape, see Leo Marx, "The Impact of the Railroad on the American Imagination, as a Possible Comparison for the Space Impact," in *The Railroad and the Space Program: An Exploration in Historical Analogy,* ed. Bruce Mazlish (Cambridge, Mass.: MIT Press, 1965), 207–15. See also James A. Ward, *Railroads and the Character of America, 1820–1887* (Knoxville: University of Tennessee Press, 1986), 5–6; MacGill, *History of Transportation,* 317–18; and Taylor, *Transportation Revolution,* 102.

38. *Michigan Whig,* 8 January 1835.

39. *Democratic Free Press,* 10 October 1838; *Democratic Expounder and Calhoun County Democrat,* 24 February 1842; Cronon, *Nature's Metropolis,* 67–70.

40. Parks, *Democracy's Railroads,* 43–52.

41. Millard, "Historical Sketch of Lenawee County," 232.

42. Sherman Stevens, "Continuation of Early Days in Genesee County," *MPHC* 7 (1886): 397–98; Dodge, "Terminus of Erie and Kalamazoo Railroad," 492.

43. Parks, *Democracy's Railroads,* 86.

44. Willis F. Dunbar, *All Aboard! A History of Railroads in Michigan* (Grand Rapids, Mich.: William B. Eerdmans, 1969), 69; Parks, *Democracy's Railroads,* 180, 328, 334. So notorious was the Southern that one western Michigan resident went so far as to warn his immigrating spouse to avoid the railroad altogether in her journey across Michigan (Fabius Miles to Mrs. F. Miles, 23 August 1844/MHC). See also Keith, "Internal Improvements," 37–38.

45. Upon the state's divestiture of its railroads in 1846, the Central was reincorporated as the Michigan Central Rail Road Company and the Southern as the Michigan Southern Railroad Company. The Detroit and Milwaukee Railway Company was authorized by legislative act in 1855. See Michigan Railroad Commission, *Aids, Gifts, Grants and Donations to Railroads, including Outline of Development and Successions in Titles to Railroads in Michigan,* by Edmund A. Calkins (Lansing, Mich.: Wynkoop Hallenbeck Crawford Co., 1919), 96–97, 98–99; Dunbar, *All Aboard!,* 62, 70, 77–78; and *Grand River Times,* 6 January 1852.

46. MacGill, *History of Transportation,* 299, 305.

47. Dunbar, *All Aboard!,* 64–65; MAL/L/1855/82:153–79; Edmund A. Calkins, "Railroads of Michigan since 1850," *Michigan History* 13 (1929): 7–8; Meints, *Michigan Railroads,* 6–7. The most recent and comprehensive historical treatment of Michigan railroad companies is Meints, *Michigan Railroads.* An older but very useful source of detailed statistical information on aid and land grants to Michigan railroads, together with an outline of corporate development, succession of titles, and dates of lines placed in operation, is Michigan Railroad Commission, *Aids, Gifts, Grants, and Donations.*

48. Parkins, *Historical Geography of Detroit,* 273–74.

49. *Grand River Times,* 6 January 1852.

50. Dunbar, *All Aboard!,* 70; Meints, *Michigan Railroads,* 5; Michigan Railroad Commission, *Aids, Gifts, Grants, and Donations,* 100–101.

51. James F. Joy, "Railroad History of Michigan," *MPHC* 22 (1893): 303–4; Meints, *Michigan Railroads,* 5; Michigan Railroad Commission, *Aids, Gifts, Grants, and Donations,* 96–97.

52. Meints, *Michigan Railroads,* 6.

53. Stover, "Iron Roads," 151.

CHAPTER 11

1. *Michigan Farmer,* 1850:68; Hardeman, *Shucks, Shocks, and Hominy Blocks,* 152–53.

2. Samuel R. Aldrich and Earl R. Leng, *Modern Corn Production* (Cincinnati: The Farm Quarterly, 1965), 17–18; U.S. Census Office, *Agriculture of the United States, 1860,* 1; Blois, *Gazetteer,* 37. Observers traveling across the state reported good and abundant crops in all settled parts of the Lower Peninsula. See Harris Seymour to John C. V. Seymour, 9 August 1834/HSC/SAM; Shirreff, *Tour through North America,* 219; Keeney, "Salmon Keeney's Visit to Michigan," 441; Bela Hubbard, Notebook, 10 May 1839, 22 August, 4 September 1840/BHP/Box 1/MHC; *Democratic Free Press and Michigan Intelligencer,* 14 July 1831; Nowlin, *Bark-Covered House,* 185; Obadiah Rogers, Diary, July 1831/ORN/MHC; Elizabeth Chandler to Jane Howell, 27 March 1832/EMCP/Box 1/MHC; William Forbes to Friends, 10 April 1835/MHC; John Searles to Zelotes B. Searles, 29 September 1840/JSP/CHL; Gordon and May, "Michigan Land Rush," 277; and Fox, *History of Saginaw County,* 19.

The hardiness and reliability of corn made it a popular crop in frontier Michigan. Grown in large quantities, corn production consistently exceeded that of wheat and farmers often elected to devote at least as much land to this adaptable crop as they did to wheat. See *Michigan Statesman and St. Joseph Chronicle,* 13 September 1834; Wealthy A. Searles to Zelotes B. Searles, 30 November 1841/JSP/CHL. A Washtenaw County settler reported that he kept only six and one-half acres in wheat, as compared to thirty in corn on his Webster Township farm (C. Dibble to Horace Dibble, 27 February 1840/MHC). In Berrien County, Moses Chamberlain devoted eight acres to wheat and nine to corn (Moses Chamberlain to Mellen Chamberlain, 28 June 1846/CFP/MSUAHC). Nelson and Caroline Russell planted equal amounts of land in each crop on their farm near Bronson in Branch County (Nelson and Caroline Russell to Jonathan Parkhurst, 18 June 1846/CFL/WMUARHC).

3. Gates, *Farmer's Age,* 169; *St. Johns News,* 12 July 1900; Goddard, *Where to Emigrate,* 320; Lanman, *History of Michigan, Civil and Topographical,* 322; Gordon and May, "Michigan Land Rush," 276; U.S Commissioner of Patents, *Report, 1850, Agriculture,* 309, 331, 410, 421; U.S. Commissioner of Patents, *Report, 1851, Agriculture,* 410. Occasionally Michigan farmers reported yields as great as eighty bushels per acre. See *Report, 1851, Agriculture,* 405, 407, 413; Niles, "Old Times in Clinton County," 622–23.

4. *Michigan Farmer,* 1850:68, 113; U.S. Census Office, *Agriculture of the United States, 1860,* cxlix; Bidwell and Falconer, *Agriculture in the Northern United States,* 245, 382; Thomas Wright, Diary, May 1835, January 1836, February 1836/TWD/MSUAHC; Jeremiah D. Williams, "History of the Town of Webster," *MPH C* 13 (1888): 548; Sanford Howard, "Culture of Broom Corn and the Manufacture of Brooms," in U.S. Commissioner of Patents, *Report, 1849, Agriculture* (Washington, D.C.: Office of Printers to the Senate, 1850), 462–63.

5. The driving of cattle and hogs had a long history in colonial British America and provided one of the earliest sources of income for settlers west of the Appalachians. From the early years of the nineteenth century,

drovers moved cattle eastward from Ohio, and the practice spread westward with the expansion of settlement. Cattle raising spread into the openings of west-central Ohio and then onto the prairies of western Indiana and central Illinois. All remained centers of cattle production until after mid-century, when this industry was supplanted by agriculture. The cattle ranges of the Old Northwest supplied stock to adjacent corn-feeding regions, which, in turn, shipped cattle to eastern markets. See Paul C. Henlein, "Early Cattle Ranges of the Ohio Valley," *Agricultural History* 35 (1961): 150–53; Terry G. Jordan, *North American Cattle Ranching Frontiers: Origins, Diffusion, and Differentiation* (Albuquerque: University of New Mexico Press, 1993), 199–200; *Portrait and Biographical Album of Hillsdale County,* 813; *Portrait and Biographical Album of Lenawee County,* 378, 931; *Portrait and Biographical Album of Genesee, Lapeer, and Tuscola Counties,* 249; *Genesee Farmer,* 1833: 316; and Jacob Gerrish to Moses Chamberlain, 16 February 1843/CFP/MSUAHC.

6. See U.S. Census Office, *Agriculture of the United States, 1860,* cxxxv; Barber, "Recollections and Lessons," 216. Henry Sanford found hogs, "through the openings & woods everywhere," during his travels in southwestern Michigan (Journal, 17 August 1844/HSSP/Box 3/GSML). See also Jacob Gerrish to Moses Chamberlain, 16 February 1843/CFP/MSUAHC; *Michigan Farmer,* 1850:68.

7. Hardeman, *Shucks, Shocks, and Hominy Blocks,* 159–61; W. J. Rorabaugh, *The Alcoholic Republic: An American Tradition* (New York: Oxford University Press, 1979), chap. 1, app. 5; Fearon, *Sketches of America,* 29.

8. See John F. Hinman, "My First Journey to Michigan, with Other Reminiscences," *MPHC* 14 (1889): 564. The functions of alcohol consumption were addressed specifically by a resident of Prairie Ronde a decade later. "Whiskey was the only luxury," he recalled, "Everyone drank it to keep out cold, heat, pain of every kind, as an antidote against ague and as a kind of sociability" (Henry Parker Smith, Reminiscences/HPSP/MHC).

9. Leeson, *History of Macomb County,* 291–92.

10. The provision of whiskey was expected when entertaining guests or at "shindigs," as well as at raisings, log rollings, harvest work, corn huskings, and hog killing. See Copley, "Early Settlement of Southwestern Michigan," 150; R. C. Crawford, "Reminiscences of Pioneer Life in Michigan," 44; Williams, "History of the Town of Webster," 555; and Wood, *Wilderness and the Rose,* 70. Although some observers, such as Caroline Kirkland, attributed an increased accident rate to the use of alcohol, the general perception was that whiskey assisted rather than hindered the heavy labor, which was accomplished without the aid of mechanical assistance. See Kirkland, *A New Home,* 67; Leeson, *History of Macomb County,* 292; Potter, "A Boy's Story," 404; and *Tecumseh Herald,* 14 July 1881. Several Farmers commented that harvest workers benefited from "a little stuff," especially when mowing in wet ground. See Harris Seymour to John C. W. Seymour, 19 August 1834/HSC/SAM; and Nowlin, *Bark-Covered House,* 52.

11. MCC /1814/MTL/1:199–201; MCC /1816/MTL/I:195; MLCLB /1822/MTL/1:195; James Platt Clapham, Diary, 1836/DWC/WMUARHC. One Macomb County resident recalled that liquor was so widely available in Michigan that many residents used it as the principal ingredient for pickling. See Leeson, *History of Macomb County,* 252. See also Barnett, "Early Improvements," 312–14; Shipping Manifest, 2 July 1828/ETBC/SAM; And Hoppin, "Personal Recollections," 411.

12. Bissell, "Early Settlement of Mt. Clemens," 454, 467; Mitchell, "History of St. Clair County," 413. In 1854, Michigan's greatest liquor production occurred in Kalamazoo, Calhoun, St. Joseph, and Macomb Counties (Michigan, *Census of Michigan, 1854.* Pioneer accounts mention distilleries in Coldwater, in Branch County; in Ceresco, in Calhoun County; and in an unnamed location in northern St. Joseph County. See Haynes, "Early History of Branch County," 287; Barber, "Recollections and Lessons," 188; and Hoppin, "Personal Recollections," 411.

13. See Rorabaugh, *Alcoholic Republic,* 29, 76–79. This author estimates (table A1.1) that per capita distilled spirits consumption of the total American population rose from 2.0 gallons in 1710 to 3.8 gallons by the

close of the century. Consumption continued to increase over the next three decades, reaching a high of 5.2 gallons by 1830, after which it began to taper off markedly. For purposes of comparison, the per capita consumption in the 1970s was 1.8 gallons. See Clark, *History of Manufactures,* 1:480; and Thomas Senior Berry, *Western Prices before 1861: A Study of the Cincinnati Market* (Cambridge, Mass.: Harvard University Press, 1943), 182–83.

14. G. Thomann, *American Beer: Glimpses of Its History and Description of Its Manufacture* (New York: United States Brewers' Association, 1909), 64–65. In Rorabaugh, *Alcoholic Republic,* Table A1.1 reveals that per capita beer consumption tripled between 1840 and 1860, and this amount doubled again over the next two decades. Between 1835 and 1855 per capita distilled spirits consumption fell by half, and it had decreased to modern levels by 1880. Absolute alcohol consumption per capita from all sources declined steadily between 1835 and 1850, from a high of 3.9 gallons to 1.0 gallon at mid-century. See also Berry, *Western Prices,* 207–8.

15. Temperance sentiments appeared in the writings of many contemporary observers, who shared Caroline Kirkland's contention that whiskey lay at the root of failure and misfortune. See Kirkland, *A New Home,* 13, 67. Although the rabble-rousing of "hot abolitionists and temperance men" infuriated some, many rejoiced at their success in passing prohibition ordinances in Detroit and other Michigan cities in the 1840s. See Corodon B. Parker to Franklin L. Parker, 6 March 1842/FLPP/Box 1/MHC; and Myron Tupper to Edward Merrill, 10 April 1846/HHCP/Box 1/MHC. For a discussion of the development of the temperance movement in antebellum Detroit, see Silas Farmer, *History of Detroit and Wayne County and Early Michigan* (New York: Munsell, 1890; reprint, Detroit: Gale Research, 1969), 838–41; *Detroit Gazette,* 13 August 1820; *Democratic Free Press and Michigan Intelligencer,* 10 October 1831; *Michigan Emigrant,* 23 December 1834; and Rorabaugh, *Alcoholic Republic,* 233, 239, tables A1.2, A2.3.

16. Rorabaugh, *Alcoholic Republic,* 84–85; Berry, *Western Prices,* 185–89, 208; and U.S. Census Office, *Agriculture of the United States, 1860,* cxlviii-cli, tables E, G.

17. Blois, *Gazetteer,* 18; Gates, *Farmer's Age,* 157. For a discussion of the histories of food crops in the United States up to this time, see U.S. Commissioner of Patents, *Report, 1853, Agriculture,* 96–176. See also Melish, *Statistical Account,* 34; Evans, *Pedestrious Tour,* 78; and O. Wilder to the *Genesee Farmer,* 1833:316. Frontier observers reported varying but generally high yields throughout the region. For example, wheat yields of twenty-five to forty bushels per acre were said to have been raised on the prairies of southwestern Michigan; thirty-two bushels per acre in Clinton County; twelve to thirty bushels per acre on the oak openings; twenty bushels per acre in Macomb County; and over twenty-five bushels per acre on land in Ingham County. Farmers in Kalamazoo, Washtenaw, and Oakland Counties who had worked their lands for a number of years all reported that their yields did not normally exceed twenty bushels per acre. See *Detroit Journal and Michigan Advertiser,* 13 April 1831; Bronson, "Pioneer History of Clinton County," 327; Lanman, *History of Michigan, Civil and Topographical,* 323; Bela Hubbard, Notebook, 1843/BHP/Box 1/MHC; Jonathan Shearer, "Wheat in New York and Michigan," *MPHC* 4 (1883): 82–83; U.S. Commissioner of Patents, *Report, 1850, Agriculture,* 309, 330, 421; idem, *Report, 1851,* 404–5.

18. Atack and Bateman, *To Their Own Soil,* 171–80; Williams, "Internal Commerce of the West," 29–30; *Democratic Free Press,* 1 August 1838; *Democratic Expounder and Calhoun County Democrat,* 23 July 1841; Bidwell and Falconer, *Agriculture in the Northern United States,* 263; *Michigan Farmer,* 1850:66.

19. *Michigan Farmer,* 1849:259.

20. Scott, *Missionary Tour,* 191–92.

21. *Jonesville Expositor,* 4 March 1841; *Michigan Farmer,* 1850:244; U.S. Department of Agriculture, *Report of the Commissioner of Agriculture for the Year 1871* (Washington, D.C.: Government Printing Office, 1872), 134. Michigan farmers generally preferred these four types to others, but also reported success with bald, bearded, Mediterranean, Siberian, Indiana, Soules, and Hutchenson varieties. See U.S.

Commissioner of Patents, *Report, 1850, Agriculture,* 309, 331, 411, 421; U.S. Commissioner of Patents, *Report, 1851, Agriculture,* 404.

22. Bidwell and Falconer, *Agriculture in the Northern United States,* 93. Nowlin, *Bark-Covered House,* 185; *Michigan Statesman and St. Joseph Chronicle,* 13 September 1834.

23. Bidwell and Falconer, *Agriculture in the Northern United States,* 238–39; Townsend Glover, "Insects Injurious and Beneficial to Vegetation," in U.S. Commissioner of Patents, *Report, 1854, Agriculture,* 59–89; *Democratic Free Press and Michigan Intelligencer,* 8 November 1832; Bela Hubbard, Notebook, 15 June 1839, 22 June 1839/BHP/Box 1/MHC; *Kalamazoo Gazette,* 13 June 1840; *Lake Huron Observer,* 14 June 1844; Beal, "Pioneer Life in Southern Michigan," 243.

24. Gates, *Farmer's Age,* 163. Contemporary discussions of preventive strategies appeared in Glover, "Insects," 73–74, 76, and Michigan State Agricultural Society, *Transactions of the Michigan State Agricultural Society for 1856,* vol. 8 (Lansing, Mich.: Hosmer & Kerr, 1857), 452–53.

25. *Michigan Farmer,* 1849:217, 1850:47, 66.

26. Cornelia Stoner to Maria L. Zeh, 7 August 1850/LSCC/SAM; Williams, "Town of Webster," 548; Bidwell and Falconer, *History of Agriculture,* 357; U.S. Commissioner of Patents, *Report, 1850, Agriculture,* 309, 411. The Farmers' Brewery of Detroit offered Michigan farmers cash for barley delivered to its brewery. See *Democratic Free Press and Michigan Intelligencer,* 6 October 1831. The role of barley in brewing is discussed in U.S. Census Office, *Census of Agriculture, 1860,* lxviii; and U.S. Commissioner of Patents, *Report, 1851, Agriculture,* 413.

27. Blois, *Gazetteer,* 26–27; Swan, *Trip to Michigan,* 19; Bela Hubbard, Notebook, 6 August 1842/BHP/Box 1/MHC; Gates, *Farmer's Age,* 255; Bidwell and Falconer, *Agriculture in the Northern United States,* 371–72.

28. Bidwell and Falconer, *History of Agriculture,* 374; William Richards to Herman Richards, 2 March 1833/MHC; Thomas Chandler to Jane Howell, 10 October 1830/EMCP/Box 1/MHC; *Monroe Advocate,* 18 February 1841; Melish, *Statistical Account,* 34; Evans, *Pedestrious Tour,* 78; Warden, *Statistical, Political, and Historical Account,* 3:78; Hoyt, "Founding of Yankee Springs," 297.

29. Gates, *Farmer's Age,* 265–66, 268; Michigan State Agricultural Society, *Transactions of the Michigan State Agricultural Society for 1856,* 153; Bidwell and Falconer, *Agriculture in the Northern United States,* 378; U.S. Census Office, *Agriculture of the United States, 1860,* lxxx; Goddard, *Where to Emigrate,* 319.

30. U.S. Census Office, *Agriculture of the United States, 1860,* lx, lxv, lxxiii; U.S. Commissioner of Patents, *Report, 1851,* Agriculture, 413; Bidwell and Falconer, *Agriculture in the Northern United States,* 241; Gates, *Farmer's Age,* 173;.

31. Evans, *Pedestrious Tour,* 78; Warden, *Statistical, Political, and Historical Account,* 3:78; Blois, *Gazetteer,* 37. For biographical information on John Chapman and a discussion of his role in agricultural promotion, see Newell Dwight Hillis, *The Quest for John Chapman: The Story of a Forgotten Hero* (New York: Grosset & Dunlop, 1904) and Harlan Hatcher and Leslie Marshall, *Johnny Appleseed: A Voice in the Wilderness* (Patterson, N.J.: Swendenborg Press, 1945).

32. *Detroit Gazette,* 30 October 1827; Blois, *Gazetteer,* 37; Sarah Allen to J. A. Barney, 31 March 1839//SBSFC/WMUARHC; James I. Rogers to Elias and Abigail Rogers, 19 December 1847/JRL/MSUAHC.

33. *History of Jackson County,* 222; Leeson, *History of Kent County,* 445–46; Michigan State Horticultural Society, *Seventeenth Annual Report of the Secretary of the State Horticultural Society of Michigan, 1887* (Lansing, Mich.: W. S. George, 1887), 314; Henry Whitney to John W. Strong, 21 September 1846/JFFC/CHL.

34. Gates, *Farmer's Age,* 257–58; *Michigan Farmer,* 1849:307, 1850:55, 1851:214, 313. By 1856, fifty-seven varieties of apples were reported to have been grown successfully in Michigan. See U.S. Commissioner of Patents, *Report, 1856, Agriculture,* 376–77.

35. Blois, *Gazetteer*, 37; *Detroit Gazette*, 24 July 1828; *Michigan Farmer*, 1849:363, 1851:214; Beal, "Pioneer Life in Southern Michigan," 239; Elizabeth Chandler to Jane Howell, 11 November 1833/EMCP/Box 1/MHC; Henry S. Sanford, Journal, 14 August 1844/HSSP/Box 3/GSML; Louisa M. McOmber to Nathan Jackson, 26 July 1845/DMP/WMUARHC.

36. Michigan State Horticultural Society, *Seventeenth Annual Report*, 313–14; Henry S. Clubb, "The Fruit Regions of Michigan," *Twelfth Annual Report of the Secretary of the Michigan State Board of Agriculture for the Year 1873* (Lansing, Mich.: W. S. George, 1875), 50–51; Hazel M. Ketcham, "Fruit Growing in Michigan," *Journal of Geography* 16 (1917): 91–95; Veatch, *Agricultural Land Classification*, 47; A. C. Hubbard, "Orchards and Fruits of Michigan," in U.S. Commissioner of Patents, *Report, 1849, Agriculture* (Washington, D.C.: Office of Printers to the Senate, 1850), 281; Sarah Allen to J. A. Barney, 31 March 1839/SBSFC/WMUARHC; Dunbar, *Michigan*, 578.

37. Starr, "Beginnings of St. Joseph County," 515; *Michigan Farmer*, 1850: 240; Michigan, *Census of Michigan, 1854*; idem, *Census of Michigan, 1864*; James E. Landing, "Peppermint and Spearmint in the United States," *Journal of Geography* 67 (1968): 550; idem, *American Essence: A History of the Peppermint and Spearmint Industry in the United States* (Kalamazoo, Mich.: Kalamazoo Public Museum, 1969). Contemporary sources attributed the success of Michigan peppermint growers to the fertility of prairies soils, which they believed obviated the need for annual replanting. See DeWitt C. van Slyck, "Cultivation of Peppermint," in U.S. Commissioner of Patents, *Report, 1849, Agriculture* (Washington, D.C.: Office of Printers to the Senate, 1850), 390.

38. Encouragement for silk production is found in a Memorial to Congress by Inhabitants of Washtenaw County, 21 February 1832/TPUS/MT/12:445; and *Monroe Gazette*, 14 August 1838. Advertisements appeared in the *Monroe Gazette* (28 October 1837), and *Western Statesman* (2 April 1840). The experience of Michigan residents is described in Elizabeth Chandler to Jane Howell, 4 April 1832/EMCP/Box 1/MHC; Sarah Allen to J. A. Barney, 31 March 1839/SBSFC/WMUARHC; and Leeson, *History of Kent County*, 444. See also U.S. Census Office, *Agriculture of the United States, 1840*; idem, *Agriculture of the United States, 1850*; and Gates, *Farmer's Age*, 303–4, 306.

39. Sidney Glazer, "Early Sugar Beet Industry in Michigan," *Michigan History* 28 (1944): 406–7, 409–14; *Democratic Free Press*, 29 January 1836, 16 May 1838; U.S. Census Office, *Agriculture of the United States, 1860*, ci–cvii; *Kalamazoo Gazette*, 28 July 1838; Bidwell and Falconer, *History of Agriculture*, 382; MAL/L/1838/32:101–2; *Democratic Free Press*, 1 August 1838; Bela Hubbard, Notebook, 10 September 1839, 11 September 1839/BHP/Box 1/MHC; R. C. Kedzie, "Domestic Supply of Sugar for Michigan," *MPHC* 29 (1899–1900): 204; F. A. Stilgenbauer, "The Michigan Sugar Beet Industry," *Economic Geography* 3 (1927): 486.

40. Gates, *Farmer's Age*, 239–40, 243, 245–46; Bidwell and Falconer, *Agriculture in the Northern United States*, 228–29, 422, 427–30; Atack and Bateman, *To Their Own Soil*, 152–53, 156–60. An early Shorthorn-native cross, called the Cream Pot, gained popularity, and Holsteins, Ayrshires, and cattle from the Channel Islands were introduced in the 1820s. See Danhof, *Change in Agriculture*, 172–75.

41. Parke, "Reminiscences," 576; George David, "Diary of George David [Extracts], a Trip from London to Chicago in 1833," *Michigan History* 18 (1934): 57–58; Henry S. Sanford, Journal, 30 August 1844/HSSP/Box 3/GSML; *Michigan Farmer*, 1850:47. Other contemporary farmers reported that while cheese and butter were produced to some extent in Michigan, dairying was not engaged in extensively, in spite of its potential. See U.S. Commissioner of Patents, *Report, 1850, Agriculture* 309, 411; U.S. Commissioner of Patents, *Report, 1851, Agriculture*, 407, 410.

42. *Michigan Farmer*, 1848:37; 1849:106; Beal, "Pioneer Life in Southern Michigan," 244; Henry S. Sanford, Journal, 17 August 1844/HSSP/Box 3/ GSML; Leland W. Lamb, "History of Dairying in Michigan," *Michigan History* 24 (1940): 416, 419–20; Elizabeth Chandler to Jane Howell, 30 August 1832/EMCP/Box 1/MHC; M.

43. U.S. Census Office, *Agriculture of the United States in 1860*, lxxxv; Michigan State Agricultural Society, *Transactions of the Michigan State Agricultural Society for 1856*, 125. The counties with the highest butter and cheese production were, in order of importance, Oakland, Lenawee, Hillsdale, Washtenaw, Wayne, Macomb, and St. Clair (Michigan, *Census of Michigan, 1864*). See also Lamb, "History of Dairying," 421; and Richard H. Sewell, "Michigan Farmers and the Civil War," *Michigan History* 44 (1960): 369.

44. Bidwell and Falconer, *Agriculture in the Northern United States*, 221, 223, 406–7; Gates, *Farmer's Age*, 224, 226; Russell, *Long, Deep Furrow*, 352, 354; Danhof, *Change in Agriculture*, 165.

45. *Detroit Journal and Michigan Advertiser*, 11 May 1831; Arthur Bronson to Lucius Lyon, 22 October 1833/LACC/SAM.

46. Pierce, *History of Calhoun County*, 15–16; Bela Hubbard, Notebook, December 1841/BHP/Box 1/MHC; *Democratic Expounder and Calhoun County Democrat*, 24 February 1842; Bela Hubbard, Notebook, 6 August 1842/BHP/Box 1/MHC.

47. *Michigan Farmer*, 1850:52–53; U.S. Commissioner of Patents, *Report, 1850, Agriculture*, 330–31, 422; Edward Mason, "On the Breeding and Management of Sheep," in Michigan State Agricultural Society, *Transactions of the Michigan State Agricultural Society for 1856* 8 (1857): 161, 169, 192; U.S. Commissioner of Patents, *Report, 1851, Agriculture*, 405, 410; Pierce, *History of Calhoun County*, 15–16; *Portrait and Biographical Album of Oakland County*, 525.

48. T. C. Peters, "Sheep, Wool, and Wool Depots," in U.S. Commissioner of Patents, *Report, 1849, Agriculture* (Washington, D.C.: Office of Printers to the Senate, 1850), 252. *History of Calhoun County*, 72. Information on the Washtenaw County wool markets appeared originally in the *Ann Arbor Argus* and was quoted by the *Lake Huron Observer* on 23 June 1845. See also Peters, "Sheep, Wool, and Wool Depots," 253.

49. Asa Shrouds to Luther Landon, 15 March 1845, in Brown, *Stray Leaves*, 56–57.

50. Williams, "Internal Commerce of the West," 31; *Michigan Farmer*, 1849:124, 1850:66; U.S. Census Office, *Agriculture of the United States, 1860*, lxxxviii; Sewell, "Michigan Farmers," 369.

51. *Michigan Farmer*, 1850:292, 66–67; Williams, "Internal Commerce of the West," 31.

52. Gates, *Farmer's Age*, 295; Danhof, *Change in Agriculture*, 50–51; James T. Lemon, *The Best Poor Man's Country: A Geographical Study of Early Southeastern Pennsylvania* (Baltimore: Johns Hopkins University Press, 1972), 183.

53. G. E. Fussell, "Agriculture: Techniques of Farming," in *A History of Technology*, vol. 4: *The Industrial Revolution, ca. 1750 to ca. 1850*, ed. Charles Singer, E. J. Holmyard, A. R. Hall, and Trevor I. Williams (New York: Oxford University Press, 1958), 13–14.

54. Ibid., 18–21, 25–28.

55. Particularly influential was the work of German scientist Justus Leibig, whose experiments in soil chemistry attracted American scientists such as Eben Norton Horsford, John A. Porter, Samuel W. Johnson, and John Pitkin Norton to study in Germany and Great Britain. See Danhof, *Change in Agriculture*, 53; Bidwell and Falconer, *Agriculture in the Northern United States*, 318–20; Cochrane, *Development of American Agriculture*, 244; Lewis Cecil Gray, *History of Agriculture in the Southern United States to 1860* (Washington, D.C.: Carnegie Institute of Washington, 1933; reprint, Gloucester, Mass.: Peter Smith, 1958), 805; U.S. Census Office, *Agriculture of the United States, 1860*, xxxix–xl, liii–lv; Daniel Lee, "The Study of Soils," in U.S. Commissioner of Patents, *Report, 1850, Agriculture* (Washington, D.C.: Printers to the House of Representatives, 1850), esp. 58–71; Thomas G. Clemson, "Fertilizers," in U.S. Commissioner of Patents, *Report, 1859, Agriculture* (Washington, D.C.: George W. Bowman, 1860), 136–78.

56. Rodney H. True, "The Early Development of Agricultural Societies in the United States," *Annual Review of the American Historical Association for the Year 1920* (Washington, D.C.: Government Printing Office, 1925): 297–304; Gates, *Farmer's Age*, 316–20; Bidwell and Falconer, *Agriculture in the Northern United States*, 318.

57. Crops introduced as a result of federal involvement include the Chili potato, alfalfa, the Lima bean, new varieties of cotton, Turkish flint wheat, sorghum, tea and tung trees from Japan, the Chinese yam, the earth almond, the Persian walnut, the cork oak, meadow fescue, trefoil, alsike, Guinea grass, the opium poppy, the vanilla plant, camphor, cinchona, the date palm, pistache, sesame, the asafetida plant, dyer's madder, and the deodar tree. See Gates, *Farmer's Age,* 299–301; Sam Burgess, ed., *The National Program for Conservation of Germ Plasm,* North Central, Northeastern, Southern, and Western State Agricultural Experiment Stations and Agricultural Research Service, U. S. Department of Agriculture (Athens: University of Georgia, 1971), 10. For a discussion of the role of the Patent Office in the promotion of imported plants, see Gladys L. Baker, Wayne D. Rasmussen, Vivian Wiser, and Jane M. Porter, *A Century of Service: The First 100 Years of the United States Department of Agriculture* (Washington, D.C.: Department of Agriculture, 1963), 4–7.

58. Gates, *Farmer's Age,* 338–44.

59. Ibid., 314–15; Cochrane, *Development of American Agriculture,* 240–42.

60. U.S. Census Office, *Agriculture of the United States,* 1840–60; Baker et al., *Century of Service,* 10–14; Gates, *Farmer's Age,* 335–37. See also U.S. Commissioner of Patents, *Reports, 1837–60, Agriculture.*

61. The editor of the *Detroit Gazette,* 31 October 1826, believed that agricultural societies were instrumental to encouraging the cultivation of fruit, improving livestock, promoting more efficient methods of farming, and introducing "the most approved seed of the various grains, grasses and vegetables" (*Detroit Journal and Michigan Advertiser,* 19 September 1832). See also *Genesee Farmer,* 1833:25; *Semi-Weekly Free Press,* 2 May 1837; *Democratic Free Press,* 13 December 1837, 26 May 1838.

62. Legislation authorized counties to raise amounts up to $100 for premiums and provided state matching funds of up to $400 for state society premiums (MAL/L/1844/24:23–24; MAL/L/1849/197:240–41). The Michigan State Agricultural Society was incorporated by law in 1849 (MAL/L/1849/180:225–26).

63. U.S. Commissioner of Patents, *Report, 1858, Agriculture,* 147–52; *Monroe Advocate,* 11 November 1841.

64. *Michigan Farmer,* 1849:306.

65. *Democratic Free Press,* 13 December 1837; *Monroe Gazette,* 3 April 1838; Dunbar, *Michigan,* 324; *Michigan Farmer,* 1848:221.

66. The appropriation for Michigan Agricultural College included twenty-two sections of salt spring lands, and later additional swamplands. See MAL/L/1855/130:279–82; MAL/L/1858/31:169–73; SLUS/1862/130:503–5; Madison Kuhn, *Michigan State University: The First Hundred Years* (East Lansing: Michigan State University Press, 1955), 62–65, 71–73; MAL/L/1861 /188:307–16; W. J. Beal, *History of the Michigan Agricultural College and Biographical Sketches of Trustees and Professors* (East Lansing: Michigan Agricultural College, 1915), 50–51; Michigan, State Board of Agriculture, *Second Annual Report of the Secretary of the State Board of Agriculture* (Lansing, Mich.: John A. Kerr, 1863; Fuller, *Michigan,* 1:378; and Dunbar, *Michigan,* 342–43.

67. *Michigan Farmer,* 1848:221; 1849:117, 233, 266. Drain legislation appeared in two early legislative acts, MAL/L/1839/80:153–55; and MAL/L/1847/104:164–67. For use of the subsoil plow, see Henry S. Sanford, Journal, 14 August 1844/HSSP/Box 3/GSML; *Michigan Farmer,* 1849:115, 233; and Michigan State Agricultural Society, *Transactions of the Michigan State Agricultural Society for 1856,* 565. For a contemporary discussion of the types of drains employed in antebellum Michigan, see S. B. Noble, "Thorough Draining," in Michigan State Agricultural Society, *Transactions of the Michigan State Agricultural Society for 1856,* 261–73.

68. U.S. Census Office, *Agriculture of the United States, 1860,* xxxvi–liv.

69. *Michigan Emigrant,* 16 March 1832.

70. Some innovative agriculturists, such as Mr. Starkweather of Ypsilanti, attributed the use of "a thorough system of rotation of crops," together with the rotation with clover and the addition of plaster (another

source of nitrogen) to their success in restoring recently drained farmlands. See *Michigan Farmer,* 1850:65–66; 1853:278; Goddard, *Where to Emigrate,* 321; and Michigan State Agricultural Society, *Transactions of the Michigan State Agricultural Society for 1856,* 587.

71. Bidwell and Falconer, *Agriculture in the Northern United States,* 204–5; Cochrane, *Development of American Agriculture,* 189–90; H. W. Quaintance, *The Influence of Farm Machinery on Production and Labor* Publications of the American Economic Association, 3d ser., 5, no. 4 (New York: Macmillan, 1904), 19–28.

72. Dolores Greenberg, "Energy Flow in a Changing Economy," in *An Emerging Independent American Economy, 1815–1875,* ed. Joseph R. Frese and Jacob Judd (Tarrytown, N.Y.: Sleepy Hollow Press and Rockefeller Archive Center, 1980), 50–51. So important did these technological innovations become that a Genesee County farmer commented that he had "heard farmers say, in the middle of New York, that without the improvements made during the last fifteen years in agricultural improvements, saving labor and time, they could not have cultivated their farms with any profit" (Michigan State Agricultural Society, *Transactions of the Michigan State Agricultural Society for 1856,* 462).

73. Danhof, *Change in Agriculture,* 182.

74. Michael Partridge, *Farm Tools through the Ages* (Boston: Promontory Press, 1972), 38. Bela Hubbard noted that the French plows of the Eastern Shore were large wheeled devices, well suited for shallow plowing ("Early Colonization of Detroit," 353). See also Henry Parker Smith, Reminiscences of a Young Pioneer/HPSP/MHC; Copley, "Early Settlement," 150; Beal, "Pioneer Life in Southern Michigan," 243; R. Douglas Hurt, *American Farm Tools, from Hand-Power to Steam-Power* (Manhattan, Kans.: Sunflower University Press, 1985), 8; and Bidwell and Falconer, *Agriculture in the Northern United States,* 208–9.

75. Hurt, *American Farm Tools,* 15–17. The plows appear among "Farm Implements, Machinery, &c. Exhibited at the Annual Fair of the Michigan State Agricultural Society" in the years 1850 and 1852, Michigan State Agricultural Society Records/MSUAHC.

76. Hurt, *American Farm Tools,* 12. A Mr. Blanchard, visiting from New York, was astonished to observe that in St. Joseph County, "they have a plow there seven feet long, two feet wide, and they have seven or eight yoke of cattle on [it]" (Israel Parsons to Edward Parsons, 28 July 1835/PaFP/MSUAHC). See also *Michigan Farmer,* 1851:243. The subsoil plow is discussed in Partridge, *Farm Tools,* 30–31; U.S. Census Office, *Agriculture of the United States, 1860,* xviii; and *DeBow's Review* 4 (1848): 80, in Rasmussen, *Agriculture in the United States,* 1:764–65. In a survey of farmers in Oakland County, for example, the *Michigan Farmer* received favorable comments from many who found subsoil plows useful in improving the quality of wet and stony soils there (*Michigan Farmer,* 1846:80), and *Michigan Farmer,* 1849:168, mention the paring plow.

77. Hurt, *American Farm Tools,* 21; Danhof, *Change in Agriculture,* 201; *DeBow's Review* 4 (1848): 132, in Rasmussen, *Agriculture in the United States,* 1:766; *Michigan Farmer,* 1849:349.

78. Hurt, *American Farm Tools,* 25–27; Danhof, *Change in Agriculture,* 208. Grain drills were displayed at both county fairs and the State Agricultural Society Fair as early as 1849 (*Michigan Farmer,* 1849:306; Michigan State Agricultural Society Records/MSUAHC). The use of grain drills on Michigan prairies is discussed in the *Michigan Farmer,* 1850:229, 244. See also Goddard, *Where to Emigrate,* 321.

79. Hardeman, *Shucks, Shocks, and Hominy Blocks,* 74–75; Danhof, *Change in Agriculture,* 215-16; Hurt, *American Farm Tools,* 11, 30–32; Thaddeus Smith to Elizabeth Smith, 14 June 1829/SBSFC/WMUARHC; Hoffman, *Winter in the West,* 1:221; *The Kalamazoo Telegraph,* 16 January 1849, reported the use of corn planters in Michigan before 1850, and the State Agricultural Society exhibited both corn planters and corn drills at its annual fair in 1852. See Michigan State Agricultural Society Records/MSUAHC.

80. Farmers in New York and the middle Atlantic states employed the cradle scythe, a cutting tool modified to catch and deposit cut grain in a pile. The sickle, on the other hand, was the reaping tool of choice in

New England. See Partridge, *Farm Tools,* 134–36; Hurt, *American Farm Tools,* 40–41. Williams, "Town of Webster," 555; Beal, "Pioneer Life," 244; Copley, "Early Settlement," 151; Potter, "Boy's Story," 409; Jacob Gerrish, Diary, 12 July–2 August 1838/JGP/MSUAHC; and *Kalamazoo Telegraph,* 16 June 1849. Michigan farmers used cradle scythes throughout the antebellum period, and they were promoted at agricultural fairs alongside the latest harvesting machinery. See *Three Oaks Press,* 28 April 1899; *Michigan Farmer,* 1849:306; and "Farm Implements, Machinery, &c. Exhibited at the Annual Fairs," 1849, 1850, Michigan State Agricultural Society Records/MSUAHC.

81. The Bell reaper did not fail because of its design. Although it operated successfully in trials, the indifferent quality of its manufacture by many makers who took advantage of its unpatented design and the opposition of farm workers who feared the loss of jobs prevented the machine's adoption in Britain. See Olga Beaumont and J. W. Y. Higgs, "Agriculture: Farm Implements," in *A History of Technology,* vol. 4, *The Industrial Revolution, c. 1750 to c. 1850,* ed. Charles Singer, E. J. Holmyard, A. R. Hall, and Trevor I. Williams (New York: Oxford University Press, 1958), 7; Partridge, *Farm Tools,* 128; Danhof, *Change in Agriculture,* 229–32; and Hurt, *American Farm Tools,* 44–49.

82. Gates, *Farmer's Age,* 287; Danhof, *Change in Agriculture,* 243; *American Agriculturist,* 1844:238; Starr, "Beginnings of St. Joseph County," 515. The observation regarding the popularity of McCormick reapers in southwestern Michigan is from the *Michigan Farmer,* 1850:226.

83. Prices for new reapers ranged from $115 to $150 apiece, the equivalent of over a quarter section of land if purchased from the government. See Danhof, *Change in Agriculture,* 233–34; Cronon, *Nature's Metropolis,* 315; and *Michigan Farmer,* 1850:226. Estimates based on recent research indicate that less than 9 percent of all northern farmers in 1860 would have found individual ownership of harvesters profitable on the basis of cost savings. See Atack and Bateman, *To Their Own Soil,* 195–99; and Alan L. Olmstead, "The Mechanization of Reaping and Mowing in America," *Journal of Economic History* 35 (1975): 337–38. The rapid adoption of mechanical harvesters throughout the Old Northwest hastened the commercialization of agriculture in the region. A discussion of the impact of this technological change in central Illinois appears in Faragher, *Sugar Creek,* 202.

84. Bidwell and Falconer, *Agriculture in the Northern United States,* 212–13; Atack and Bateman, *To Their Own Soil,* 199; Sewell, "Michigan Farmers," 354–55. Mowers were first included among machinery exhibited by the State Agricultural Society Fair in 1852 (Michigan State Agricultural Society Records/MSUAHC).

85. Bidwell and Falconer, *Agriculture in the Northern United States,* 214; Hurt, *American Farm Tools,* 85; *Detroit Gazette,* 2 April 1819; *Michigan Farmer,* 1853:278; Leeson, *History of Kent County,* 922. Horse rakes were displayed at the State Fair in 1852. Unfortunately the records of the machinery exhibited are torn, so that the manufacturers are missing (Michigan State Agricultural Society Records/MSUAHC).

86. Hurt, *American Farm Tools,* 68–69; *Detroit Gazette,* 23 July 1818. Pioneer accounts of fanning mill use appear in Osband, "Pioneers and Pioneer Life in Nankin," 441; *Emigrant,* 5 October 1831; Pierce, *History of Calhoun County,* 16; *Western Statesman,* 13 February 1840, 6 August 1840; and Baxter, *History of the City of Grand Rapids,* 459.

87. J. Sanford Rikoon, *Threshing in the Midwest, 1820–1940: A Study of Traditional Culture and Technological Change* (Bloomington: Indiana University Press, 1988); Bidwell and Falconer, *Agriculture in the Northern United States,* 215–16; Hurt, *American Farm Tools,* 69–74; Gates, *Farmer's Age,* 288. Pioneer farmers recalled threshing with the flail or by trampling and winnowing by hand, but all abandoned these methods as soon as possible. See Brainard, *Pioneer History,* 58–59; Osband, "Pioneers and Pioneer Life in Nankin," 441; Starr, "Beginnings of St. Joseph County," 515; J. B. La Rowe, "Address of J. B. La Rowe," *Livingston Republican,* 17 July 1879; S. B. McCracken, "Fifty Years Ago and Now," *MPHC* 14 (1889): 610; and Pierce, *History of Calhoun County,* 16.

The introduction and use of threshers in southwestern Michigan is discussed in *Detroit Courier,* 9 June 1831; Shirreff, *Tour through North America,* 219; Starr, "Beginnings of St. Joseph County," 515; Henry S. Sanford, Journal, 14 August 1844/HSSP/Box 3/GSML; Pierce, *History of Calhoun County,* 16; and *Kalamazoo Telegraph,* 16 June 1849. By this time several Michigan factories manufactured horse-powers to operate larger machines, and exhibited combines at the State Fair in 1849 and 1850 (Michigan State Agricultural Society Records/MSUAHC). See *Jonesville Expositor,* 5 November 1840; *Michigan Farmer,* 1853:301, 1854:12; and Baxter, *History of the City of Grand Rapids,* 459.

88. Farmers with large landholdings anticipated that the savings provided by the use of these machines would more than pay for their cost. H. Hoffman, for example, calculated that on his Grand Blanc Township farm, a small thresher paid for itself in two years. See Jacob Gerrish, Diary, 13 August 1850/JGP/MSUAHC; *Michigan Farmer,* 1853:265; and Thomas Wright, Diary, 1834/TWD/MSUAHC.

89. Davenport, *Timberland Times,* 220; Kirkland, "Paradise of the Poor," 185.

90. Edward Parsons, Diary, 1834/PaFP/MSUAHC; Harriet Friedmann, "Household Production and the National Economy: Concepts for the Analysis of Agrarian Formations," *Journal of Peasant Studies* 7 (1980): 162.

91. Weller, *Yesterday,* 16–17.

92. Davenport, *Timberland Times,* 220–21.

93. Developed in the 1840s, hay forks were exhibited at the Michigan State Fair in 1850. Fodder choppers and grain mills appeared at the same time, and manufacturers produced them by 1854. See Michigan State Agricultural Society Records/MSUAHC; Hurt, *American Farm Tools,* 65, 98; *Michigan Farmer,* 1854:155; and Hardeman, *Shucks, Shocks, and Hominy Blocks,* 121–22.

94. Hurt, *American Farm Tools,* 77–78. In 1842, Bela Hubbard described a combine on Prairie Ronde as having "look of a moving steamboat" as it ambled across a large wheat field. Observing the Moore-Hascall combine at work on Schoolcraft Prairie two years later, Henry Sanford confided in his journal that "it would astonish a Yankee farmer to see how expeditiously [its work] was done." See Bela Hubbard, Notebook, 15 August 1842/BHP/Box 1/MHC; Henry S. Sanford, Journal, 14 August 1844/HSSP/Box 3/GSML. In spite of widespread support in Michigan, including legislative resolutions seeking the extension of its developers' patents, the Moore-Hascall combine did not achieve success until employed on the extensive bonanza farms of California in 1854. See MAL/R/1849/32:361–62; SMD/1849/6; Lou Allen Chase, "Hiram Moore and the Invention of the Harvester," *Michigan History* 13 (1929): 503; F. Hal Higgins, "The Moore-Hascall Centennial Approaches," *Michigan History* 14 (1930): 424–25; and Hurt, *American Farm Tools,* 79–80.

95. R. J. Forbes, "Power to 1850," in *A History of Technology,* vol. 4: *The Industrial Revolution, c. 1750 to c. 1850,* ed. Charles Singer, E. J. Holmyard, A. R. Hall, and Trevor I. Williams (New York: Oxford University Press, 1958), 151–52. The low gradient of shoreline streams provided insufficient waterpower and encouraged the use of windmills on the Eastern Shore. One purportedly existed until the closing years of the nineteenth century. Adapted to conditions encountered only in this narrow geographical region, windmills were not employed elsewhere in Michigan. See Parkins, *Historical Geography of Detroit,* 288; and Richard Bennett and John Elton, *History of Corn Milling,* vol. 2, *Watermills and Windmills* (New York: Burt Franklin, 1898), 294–95. The relative efficiency of waterwheels is discussed in A. Stowers, "Watermills, c. 1500–c. 1850," in *A History of Technology,* vol. 4, *The Industrial Revolution, c. 1750 to c. 1850,* ed. Charles Singer, E. J. Holmyard, A. R. Hall, and Trevor I. Williams (New York: Oxford University Press, 1958), 202–5; Martha Zimiles and Murray Zimiles, *Early American Mills* (New York: Bramhall House, 1973), 11–15; John Storck and Walter Dorwin Teague, *Flour for Man's Bread* (London: Oxford University Press, 1952), 113–14; J. Allen, "Hydraulic Engineering," in *A History of Technology,* vol. 5, *The Late Nineteenth Century, c. 1850 to c. 1900,* ed. Charles Singer, E. J. Holmyard, A. R. Hall, and Trevor I.

Williams (New York: Oxford University Press, 1958), 528–30; Forbes, "Power to 1850," 156; and Clark, *History of Manufactures,* 409–10.

96. Blois, *Gazetteer,* 109; *Detroit Gazette,* 13 November 1818; Fuller, *Economic and Social Beginnings,* 24–25.

97. Zimiles and Zimiles, *Early American Mills,* 94–95, 97–104; *Detroit Gazette,* 11 May 1821; *Detroit Journal and Michigan Advertiser,* 11 May 1831; *Democratic Expounder and Calhoun County Democrat,* 24 February 1842, 24 March 1842; Rufus Grosman to Pierpont Smith, 20 August 1829/PSC/MSUAHC; Blois, *Gazetteer,* 344.

98. Clark, *History of Manufactures,* 409; Isaac Lippincott, *A History of Manufactures in the Ohio Valley to the Year 1860* (New York: Arno Press, 1973), 160–61.

99. Corporations built sawmills at the mouths of large rivers because they were central locations to which logs cut over a wide area could be floated on tributary streams. Because such sites usually lacked conditions suitable for hydraulic power, steam engines were the only choice for saw milling on this scale. Steam sawmills appeared as early as 1832 in western Michigan, and within five years operated at the mouths of the Grand, St. Joseph, and Muskegon Rivers. A steam-driven sawmill was erected on the slow-moving Saginaw River as early as 1835, and within two years the St. Clair River settlements of Port Huron, Palmer, Newport, Algonac, and Mt. Clemens all had steam sawmills. See Fuller, *Economic and Social Beginnings,* 308–9, 438; Everett, *Memorials,* 432; Blois, *Gazetteer,* 317, 329, 332, 337, 346; and George W. Hotchkiss, *History of the Lumber and Forest Industry of the Northwest* (Chicago: By the author, 1898), 666.

100. William T. Langhorne Jr., "Mill-Based Settlement Patterns in Schoharie County, New York: A Regional Study," *Historical Archaeology* 10 (1976): 78–79; *Weekly Recorder,* 1818:248; *Detroit Journal and Michigan Advertiser,* 13 July 1831; *Niles Gazette and Advertiser,* 5 March 1836.

101. Contemporary observer Anson Brown attributed the success of Ann Arbor, for example, to its central role in milling and trade" (*Detroit Journal and Michigan Advertiser,* 13 July 1831). See also Blois, *Gazetteer,* 390, 245–383; Hart, "Pioneer Sketches," 551; and M. A. Leeson, *History of Saginaw County, Michigan* (Chicago: Charles C. Chapman, 1881), 233.

102. The increasing profitability of lumbering justified the cost of employing new railroad technology in the 1850s, and one steam-powered logging railroad was in operation on Grand River in Ottawa County by 1857. See Danford, "Social and Economic Effects of Lumbering," 347; and Carl J. Bajema, "The First Logging Railroads in the Great Lakes Region," *Forest & Conservation History* 35 (April 1991): 78–80. Harvesting of timber on government-owned land flourished in forested areas throughout Lower Michigan. Although many saw its perpetrators as "land pirates and timber stealers," farmers, who perceived the forest as an impediment to settlement, often saw illegal timbering as beneficial to farm-making. See Ephraim S. Williams, "Incidents of Early Days in Michigan," *MPHC* 9 (1886): 171; Robert Clark to George Graham, 26 February 1824/TPUS/MT/11:526–27; Jonathan Kearsley to Gov. Lewis Cass, 3 December 1825/TPUS/MT/11:817; Henry Waldron, "History of Hillsdale County"/HWP/MSUAHC; Lucius Lyon to William Lytle, 27 January 1831/TPUS/MT/12:249; and Henry S. Sanford, Journal, 5 August 1844/HSSP/Box 3/GSML.

103. Villages such as Saugatuck, near the mouth of the Kalamazoo River, grew up around lumber mills and remained largely dependent on them during the early period of settlement. See Hotchkiss, *Lumber and Forest Industry,* 168, 244, 246, 261, 285, 323, 324; Everett, *Memorials,* 413–14; Henderson, "Notes on Saugatuck," 302; Nina Daugherty, "Incidents of Early Days in Allegan County," *MPHC* 38 (1912): 157; Foote, "Early Days of Eaton County," 394; Fuller, *Economic and Social Beginnings,* 398–99; C. L. Parker to F. L. Parker, June 1848/FLPP/Box 1/MHC; *Lake Huron Observer,* 10 May 1844; and *History of Saginaw County,* 382–83; Leeson, *History of Saginaw County,* 383; Fox, *History of Saginaw County,* 25; and Maybee, "Michigan's White Pine Era," 430.

CHAPTER 12

1. Nettels, *Emergence of a National Economy,* 31–32; Kirkland, *American Economic Life,* 240–41; Bray Hammond, *Banks and Politics in America, from the Revolution to the Civil War* (Princeton, N.J.: Princeton University Press, 1957), 88.

2. Taylor, *Transportation Revolution,* 305–7; Hammond, *Banks and Politics,* 284–85. For a discussion of the bank's role in regulating the national banking system, and particularly as a central bank, see Peter Temin, *The Jacksonian Economy* (New York: W. W. Norton, 1969), chap. 3.

3. The traditional role of banks in short-term credit transactions was enhanced by the wealth of readily disposable commodities in the early United States. Bank notes, supported by such goods pledged to them, were acceptable as money for the purchase or sale of products. See Hammond, *Banks and Politics,* 672–73; and Kirkland, *American Economic Life,* 243–44.

4. Pessen, *Jacksonian America,* 139–41; Taylor, *Transportation Revolution,* 312.

5. Haeger, *Investment Frontier,* 7.

6. Taylor, *Transportation Revolution,* 316; Hammond, *Banking and Politics,* 572–74; Blois, *Gazetteer,* 403–5.

7. Haeger, *Investment Frontier,* 18–19.

8. Ibid., 142–43.

9. These included the Farmers' and Mechanics' Bank of Detroit, the Michigan State Bank, and the Erie and Kalamazoo Railroad Bank. See Farmer, *History of Detroit,* 859–64; Haeger, *Investment Frontier,* 228; Blois, *Gazetteer,* 403; and Floyd Russell Dain, *Every House a Frontier: Detroit's Economic Progress, 1815–1825* (Detroit: Wayne State University Press, 1956), 109–10.

10. Lane, *John Allen,* 55, 77.

11. The United States adopted a bimetallic standard to determine the relative value of its gold and silver coins. This system, overseen by the federal mint, worked well after 1834, when the ratio of gold to silver maintained equivalent values for coins of both metals; however, the drop in gold prices following the 1849 discoveries in California increased the value of silver as bullion and led to an acute shortage of silver coinage. To remedy the situation, Congress passed the Subsidiary Coinage Act of 1853, reducing the silver content of coins to again make them more valuable as money. See Taylor, *Transportation Revolution,* 328–29.

12. John A. Gale to Moses Chamberlain, 3 May 1838/CFP/MSUAHC.

13. *Jeffersonian, and Oakland, Lapeer, and Shiawassee Advertiser,* 16 August 1839.

14. Thomas W. Stockton to Henry Waldron, 28 January 1840/HWP/MSUAHC; Elizabeth Dibble to Augustus Dibble, 14 April 1841/DFC/WMUARHC.

15. *Kalamazoo Gazette,* 2 September 1837; Gordon and May, "Michigan Land Rush," 449–50; Hoyt, "Founding of Yankee Springs," 294–95; Baxter, *History of the City of Grand Rapids,* 29–30. The use of cash by aboriginal peoples in the regional frontier economy in southern Michigan is discussed in greater detail in chapter 8.

16. Taylor, *Transportation Revolution,* 326; *Jonesville Expositor,* 18 November 1841; *Monroe Gazette,* 24 July 1838.

17. *Jonesville Expositor,* 2 December 1841.

18. *History of Saginaw County,* 188; Farmer, *History of Detroit,* 847; Dain, *Every House a Frontier,* 101; Baxter, *History of the City of Grand Rapids,* 670–71.

19. *Monroe Times,* 25 August 1836; *Monroe Advocate,* 13 May 1841; Baxter, *History of the City of Grand Rapids,* 673.

20. Jeremiah Wilkins to Moses Chamberlain, 25 January 1836/CFP/MSUAHC; Moses Chamberlain to Mellen Chamberlain, 31 January 1847/CFP/MSUAHC; Baxter, *History of the City of Grand Rapids,* 672–73; Dunbar, *Michigan,* 387–88; Taylor, *Transportation Revolution,* 314.

21. *Monroe Times,* 18 November 1836; *Kalamazoo Gazette,* 17 March 1838. "I will not hesitate to say," Downing remarked of his discovery, "that there was a solid bank in the vicinity, which was never known to fail. The fluctuating panics of the Wall Street brokers, or the wild cat currency of the speculators never had any effect on its deposits" (*Adrian Daily Times and Expositor,* 13 March 1877). Somewhat less successful, perhaps, was a counterfeiting operation witnessed by Methodist itinerant S. C. Woodard in 1843. The arrest of its operators quickly put an end to what the Rev. Woodard described as "the first manufactory ever started in Clinton County" (S. C. Woodard, "Reminiscences of the Early Itinerancy," *MPHC* 14 [1889]: 557–58).

22. The adoption of a National Banking System in 1862 protected the note issues of chartered banks by requiring deposit of securities with a public agency. This effectively ended the discounting of notes. A year later, the National Bank Act of 1863 recognized the principle that the supervision of banking as a monetary function was the responsibility of the federal government. The act created a system of banks with national charters, which issued a federal currency that was secured by government bonds and deposits. See Taylor, *Transportation Revolution,* 314–15; and Hammond, *Banks and Politics,* 573, 724–25.

23. Temin, *Jacksonian Economy,* 32–34.

24. Danhof, *Change in Agriculture,* 29; Cronon, *Nature's Metropolis,* 319; *Portrait and Biographical Album of Lenawee County,* 431; *Michigan Farmer,* 1849:259; *Monroe Times,* 15 September 1836; Allen O. Whittlesey to Jonas Allen, 11 January 1844/SBSFC/WMUARHC.

25. Smith & Co.'s advertisement, typical of many, proclaimed, "10,000 bushels of wheat wanted; for which cash will be paid at the Jonesville store" (*Jonesville Expositor,* 23 December 1841). See also William Allcott to Sidney S. Allcott, 8 February 1842/AFC/MSUAHC. The New York creditors of St. Joseph merchant Jonas Allen made the importance of the timing of transactions clear when they requested that he

> purchase all that you can at the mill and draw on us, in such sums as suits, at 4 months for the account. We prefer that you should draw at 4 months or so as to have the drafts fall late in May or in June so as to give us an opportunity to meet the paper, and we doubt not that you can negociate [*sic*] the drafts on us in that way as well as if drawn in shorter time. (Allen O. Whittlesey to Jonas Allen, 11 January 1844/SBSFC/WMUARHC)

26. William Allcott to Sidney S. Allcott, 11 November 1839/AFC/MSUAHC.

27. Cronon, *Nature's Metropolis,* 320; *Michigan Farmer,* 1849:259. In a letter admonishing his brother to finalize grain contracts as early as possible to avoid high prices in a rising market, William Allcott wrote, "You had better do no flouring than to lose money" (William Allcott to Sidney S. Allcott, 12 March 1840/AFC/MSUAHC).

28. Jacob Gerrish to Moses Chamberlain, 13 June 1843/CFP/MSUAHC.

29. Cronon, *Nature's Metropolis,* 319; Danhof, *Change in Agriculture,* 29; Jacob Gerrish to Moses Chamberlain, 31 January 1836/CFP/MSUAHC.

30. Cronon, *Nature's Metropolis,* 321.

31. *Acorn,* 6 January 1916; Joseph Allen to Jonas Allen, 2 October 1845/SBSFC/WMUARHC.

32. *Monroe Times,* 15 September 1836; Jacob Gerrish, Diary, various dates, 1837/JGP/MSUAHC.

33. Joseph M. Griswold, "Some Reminiscences of Early Times in Brooklyn, Jackson County, Michigan," *MPHC* 26 (1894–95): 258–59.

34. Wood, *Wilderness and the Rose,* 103; P. D. Hudson to Charles Dibble, 12 September 1842 and Charles Dibble to Augustus Dibble, 2 July 1845/DFC/WMUARHC.

35. Danhof, *Change in Agriculture,* 30; Clark, *Grain Trade,* 43; Scheiber, *Ohio Canal Era,* 252. *Detroit Gazette,* 4 February 1825 and 6 August 1829; *Michigan Sentinel,* 13 January 1835; Parkins, *Historical*

Geography of Detroit, 289; *Democratic Free Press,* 14 October 1835; Moses Chamberlain to Mellen Chamberlain, 6 July 1844/CFP/MSUAHC.

36. SR/1874/307.

37. William Allcott, for example, provided careful instructions for his brother, a merchant in Michigan, on the best way to make arrangements for the storage of their grain and its subsequent shipment eastward. See William Allcott to Sidney S. Allcott, 17 April 1840/AFC/MSUAHC.

38. Cronon, *Nature's Metropolis,* 108.

39. The importance of the Erie & Kalamazoo railroad as a feeder line to the West was recognized by contemporary observers, one of whom wrote that

> We understand that this mammoth work is to . . . enable the proprietors to forward merchandize [sic] destined for the west, upon it to its termination. Several merchants upon the St. Joseph and elsewhere have determined to forward their goods through the medium of this route, and cart them from thence, in lieu of sending them, as usual, by way of the lakes and up the St. Joseph. (*Toledo Gazette,* quoted in *Monroe Times,* 29 September 1836)

See also Dunbar, *All Aboard!,* 19–22; Haeger, *Investment Frontier,* 116–17; and Frost, "Early Railroads of Southern Michigan," 500–501.

40. The acquisition of the Erie & Kalamazoo, and another line linking Adrian and Monroe, gave the Michigan Southern direct access to two Lake Erie ports as outlets for its western traffic. In 1855, the railroad gained a connection with the entrepôt by leasing the newly constructed Detroit, Monroe, & Toledo. The company's investors attempted to further secure the railroad's eastern trade through their purchase in 1849 of a Lake Erie shipping line linking the Michigan ports and Toledo with Buffalo. See Dunbar, *All Aboard!,* 68–70.

    The terms of sale of the Michigan Central stipulated that the purchasers not only complete the line from Kalamazoo to Lake Michigan in three years, but also re-lay the entire route with heavy T-rails. Essentially this meant that the entire structure had to be rebuilt from the ground up. Although an expensive undertaking, the improvements on the Michigan Central would eventually repay its investors by providing a more substantial line that would further reduce shipping time, a factor that would become increasingly important in the export trade. See Harlow, *Road of the Century,* 219–21; Dunbar, *All Aboard!,* 59–60, 62; Meints, *Michigan Railroads,* 4; and Parks, *Democracy's Railroads,* 224–25. For a discussion of the role of New England capitalists in the acquisition, management, and extension of the Michigan Central, see Arthur M. Johnson and Barry E. Supple, *Boston Capitalists and Western Railroads: A Study in Nineteenth-Century Railroad Investment Process* (Cambridge, Mass.: Harvard University Press, 1967), 88–114.

41. Meints, *Michigan Railroads,* 6; Paul Trap, "Foreign Railroads in Michigan, 1857–1893," *Journal of the Old Northwest* 13 (1986): 374–75.

42. Ibid., 327; Lewis Atherton, *The Frontier Merchant in Mid-America* (Columbia: University of Missouri Press, 1970), 70.

43. Cronon, *Nature's Metropolis,* 326; Clark, *Grain Trade,* 77. John Hicks's understanding of the advantages of the railroad for shipping grain is indicated not only by the removal of his business to a strategic location, but also by the fact that he actually transported the first railroad car of grain from St. Johns. See Ellis, *History of Shiawassee and Clinton Counties,* 378. The absence of rail communications, on the other hand, spelled disaster for prospective merchants who established their businesses in unfavorable locations. Sidney Alcott saw his hopes for a quick return on his investment in Eaton County dashed when an anticipated railroad failed to materialize. See Charles Dibble to Augustus Dibble, 6 August 1846/DFC/WMUARHC; William Allcott to Sidney S. Allcott, 7 August 1840/AFC/MSUAHC.

44. Thomas D. Odle, "The American Grain Trade on the Great Lakes, 1825–1873," *Inland Seas* 9 (1953): 167–68; *Michigan Farmer,* 1850:259.

45. Guy A. Lee, "The Historical Significance of the Chicago Grain Elevator System," *Agricultural History* 11 (1937): 23–25; Clark, *History of Manufactures,* 409–10; Cronon, *Nature's Metropolis,* 111; Clark, *Grain Trade,* 122; Hatcher, *Lake Erie,* 228–29; Odle, "American Grain Trade," 8 (1952): 190–91; Farmer, *History of Detroit,* 891.

46. Cronon, *Nature's Metropolis,* 114.

47. Odle, "American Grain Trade," 9 (1953): 166; Farmer, *History of Detroit,* 785–86. Shippers recognized the need to establish flour grades for purposes of trade even before the organization of the Detroit Board of Trade in 1847. Following the lead of eastern flour producers, Michigan's legislature enacted a system of three grades in 1830, superfine, fine, and middling. See MTL/1830/3:853–54; Albion, *Rise of New York Port,* 81–82.

48. Lee, "Chicago Grain Elevator System," 24.

49. Richard B. DuBoff, "The Telegraph and the Structure of Markets in the United States, 1845–1890," *Research in Economic History* 8 (1983): 255–57; John Langdale, "Impact of the Telegraph on the Buffalo Agricultural Commodity Market: 1846–1848," *Professional Geographer* 31 (1979): 166.

50. Cronon, *Nature's Metropolis,* 123; DuBoff, "Telegraph and the Structure of Markets," 269–70; Farmer, *History of Detroit,* 790.

51. Farmer, *History of Detroit,* 883–84; Dunbar, *Michigan,* 321; MAL/L/1847/4:45; MAL/L/1850/290:350–51; MAL/L/1850/293:353–55; MAL/L/1850/327:414–15.

52. A Kalamazoo County history chronicled the changing face of rural Michigan during the transition to commercial agriculture in the 1850s:

> The remaining forest were rapidly falling before the settler's axe, thousands of fertile acres were yearly uncovered to the sun and smiling orchards took the place of gloomy elms and towering oaks. The decade from 1850 to 1860 witnessed the full change from log houses to framed ones. Outside of the villages, few framed houses were erected before 1840. From 1840 to 1850 a small number had taken the place of their rude predecessors, and between 1850 and 1860 a majority of the settlers were able to enjoy the luxury of framed, brick or stone houses. . . . Changes from inconvenience to convenience were to be seen everywhere in the county, and prosperity was the order of the day. (David Fisher and Frank Little, eds., *Compendium of History and Biography of Kalamazoo County, Mich.* [Chicago: A. W. Bowen, 1906], 61)

53. Smith, *Settler's New Home,* 92.

54. Davis, "Transportation and American Settlement Patterns," 174; Clark, *Grain Trade,* 240–41. A similar pattern has emerged from comparative studies of colonial regions. These studies have observed that the development of efficient interior networks in a frontier region creates new links between settlements, which concentrates traffic at particular interior nodes. These centers form the basis for a restructured trade and communications network and become foci for economic activity as the regional economy shifts toward export production. See Taaffe, Morrill, and Gould, "Transport Expansion," 505, 511–12.

CHAPTER 13

1. The advance of the two railroads following their reorganization added 118.8 miles to Michigan's rail system. Both lines reached Chicago before the middle of 1852 and established eastern connections over routes north and south of Lake Erie the following year. Construction and mileage figures are from Meints, "Michigan Railroad Construction," 6–8; and idem, *Michigan Railroads,* 5. Information regarding

the placement of lines in operation may also be found in Michigan Railroad Commission, *Aids, Gifts, Grants, and Donations,* passim; and Dunbar, *All Aboard!,* 73–75.

2. Meints, "Michigan Railroad Construction," 9.

3. The Detroit & Milwaukee Railroad was formed in 1850 from the bankrupt Detroit and Pontiac and the Oakland and Ottawa, a two-year-old company chartered to construct a nothern line to Lake Michigan. As capital became available, the railroad advanced rapidly westward from Pontiac. By the fall of 1855 it had been opened as far as Fenton, in southern Genesee County, and its line reached Owosso the following year. The failure of the Detroit & Milwaukee to generate substantial long-distance revenues was certainly disappointing to its owners, Canada's Great Western Railroad; however, the latter's losses were offset by its ability to acquire western traffic through its connection with the Michigan Central at Detroit. See Dunbar, *All Aboard!,* 75–76; Meints, *Michigan Railroads,* 6; idem, "Michigan Railroad Construction," 10–11; and Michigan Railroad Commission, *Aids, Gifts, Grants, and Donations,* 34–35.

4. Dunbar, *All Aboard!,* 92; Meints, "Michigan Railroad Construction," 10; Michigan Railroad Commission, *Aids, Gifts, Grants, and Donations,* 88–89, 100–1.

5. The cooperative agreement between Michigan's largest railroads resulted from expenses incurred in their furious competition for traffic out of Chicago, together with the impact of the Panic of 1857. Forced to consolidate their resources, the railroads adopted a formula by which to divide business derived from western trade. See Dunbar, *All Aboard!,* 69, 92, 96–97; Meints, *Michigan Railroads,* 6–7; idem, "Michigan Railroad Construction," 10–11; and Michigan Railroad Commission, *Aids, Gifts, Grants, and Donations,* 34–35, 100–1.

6. Although plank roads could not match the speed and volume of freight carried by rail, they were better suited for short-distance movement. Comparing the two modes of transportation, plank road proponent Robert Owen wrote,

> Each has its appropriate sphere; the railway as a great leading thoroughfare, terminating in cities and connecting distant sections of the country; the plank road to afford communication between smaller towns and villages, to form neighborhood and crossroads, often at right angles to a railroad line, supplemental to it, and terminating at its stations. (Robert Dale Owen, *Brief Treatise on the Construction and Management of Plank Roads* [New Albany, N.Y.: Kent & Norman, 1850], 17)

The cost of building and maintaining plank roads was also estimated to be less than that of repairing macadamized roads. According to one authority, these combined costs over a seven- to eight-year period averaged $3,106 per mile for the former, while those of the latter totaled $4,540. See W. Kingsford, *History, Structure, and Statistics of Plank Roads in the United States and Canada* (Philadelphia: A. Hart, 1851), 10, 16.

7. Approximately 170 plank road charters were granted by the Michigan state legislature between 1837 and 1860. The greatest number were issued between 1848 and 1851, when several acts were passed combining the charters of multiple plank road companies. For a listing of these companies, see Michigan, Board of State Tax Commissioners, *Michigan Railroad Appraisal, 1900, Plank Road and River Improvements,* by Mortimer E. Cooley, 9:145–54, *Michigan Historical Collection,* 1900. Legislation pertaining to the construction of particular plank roads in Michigan is also summarized in this work. Charters for individual companies were contained in the following acts: Detroit to Port Huron, MAL/L/1844/46:54–63; Detroit to Birmingham, MAL/L/1844/74:103–9; Detroit and Grand River, MAL/L/1844/91:146–52; Marshall to Union City, MAL/L/1846/101:127–33; Corunna to Northampton, MAL/L/1846/102:133–41; Adrian and Coldwater, MAL/L/1847/73:89–96; Hillsdale and Coldwater, MAL/L/1847/83:114–20; Marshall and Bellevue, MAL/L/1847/97:149–51; Portland and Shiawassee, MAL/L/1847/109:175–81; Pontiac and Corunna, MAL/L/1847/110:181–88; Detroit and Saline, MAL/L/1848/100:110–11; Grand River,

MAL/L/1848/235:366–67; Hillsdale and Indiana, MAL/L/1848/183:243–44; Monroe and Erie, MAL/L/1848/236:367–68; Jackson and Michigan, MAL/L/1848/238:368–69; Brest and Ypsilanti, MAL/L/1848/239:369–70; Pontiac and Lapeer, MAL/L/1848/240:370–71; Dexter and Michigan, MAL/L/1848/241:372; Genesee County, MAL/L/1848/242:373; Michigan and Mason, MAL/L/1848/243:374; Clinton and Bad River, MAL/L/1848/244:375; Detroit and Utica, MAL/L/1848/245:376; Indiana and Adrian, MAL/L/1848/246:377; Lapeer and Pontiac, MAL/L/1848/247:378; Tecumseh and Jackson, MAL/L/1848/248:379; Romeo and Lapeer, MAL/L/1848/249:380; Battle Creek and Union City, MAL/L/1848/250:381; Detroit and Erie, MAL/L/1848/251:382–83; Portland and Michigan, MAL/L/1848/252:383–84; Mt. Clemens and Sterling, MAL/L/1848/253:384–85; Owosso and Bad River, MAL/L/1848/254:384–85; Detroit and Birmingham, MAL/L/1848/255:386–87; Ann Arbor and Monroe, MAL/L/1848/256:387–88; Mt. Clemens and Romeo, MAL/L/1848/257:388–89; Rochester and Royal Oak, MAL/L/1848/258:389–90; Paw Paw, MAL/L/1848/259:390–91; Monroe and Saline, MAL/L/1848/260:391–92; Kalamazoo and Black Lake, MAL/L/1848/261:393–94; Michigan and DeWitt, MAL/L/1848/262:394–95; Ann Arbor and Michigan, MAL/L/1848/264:396–97; Brooklyn and Rome, MAL/L/1848/265:397–98; Detroit and Howell, MAL/L/1848/266:398–400; Eaton Rapids, MAL/L/1848/267:400–401; Battle Creek and Michigan, MAL/L/1848/268:401–2; Battle Creek and Gull Prairie, MAL/L/1848/269:402–3; Detroit and Mt. Clemens, MAL/L/1848/270:403–4; Flint and Fentonville, MAL/L/1848/271:404–5; New Baltimore and Romeo, MAL/L/1848/272:405–6; Adrian and Union City, MAL/L/1848/278:412; Adrian and Jackson, MAL/L/1848/279:413; Adrian and Bean Creek, MAL/L/1848/280:414–15; Adrian and White Pigeon, MAL/L/1848/281:415–16; New Buffalo and Laporte, MAL/L/1849/32:24–25; Lapeer and Port Huron, MAL/L/1849/98:99–100; Monroe and Newport, MAL/L/1849/113:110; Battle Creek and Dry Prairie, MAL/L/1849/115:113–15; Niles and Mottville, MAL/L/1849/119:117–18; Decatur, Lawrence, and Breedsville, MAL/L/1849/120:118–19; Tecumseh and Dundee, MAL/L/1849/121:199–120; Pontiac and Waterford, MAL/L/1849/123:120–21; Ray and Almont, MAL/L/1849/125:127–28; Trenton and Ypsilanti, MAL/L/1849/126:128–29; Monroe and Belleville, MAL/L/1849/134:138–39; Battle Creek and Hastings, MAL/L/1849/146:170–71; Galesburgh and Grand Rapids, MAL/L/1849/182:226–27; Frederick and Utica, MAL/L/1849/207:256–57; Flat Rock, MAL/L/1849/220:294–95; St. Clair, MAL/L/1849/236:315–16; Monroe and Dearborn, MAL/L/1850/30:26–27; Marshall and Bellevue, MAL/L/1850/37:34–35; Utica and Almont, MAL/L/1850/51:43–44; Ypsilanti and Fentonville, MAL/L/1850/56:47–48; Plymouth, MAL/L/1850/57:49–50; Saginaw and Genesee, MAL/L/1850/72:58–59; Royal Oak and Hastings, MAL/L/1850/75:61–62; Romeo and Canandagua, MAL/L/1850/82:69–70; Niles and State Line, MAL/L/1850/84:70–71; Breedsville and South Haven, MAL/L/1850/87:73–74; Paw Paw and Lawrence, MAL/L/1850/89:75–76; Mason and Jackson, MAL/L/1850/90:76–77; Romeo, MAL/L/1850/93:79–80; Grand Haven and Black River, MAL/L/1850/94:80–81; Gibraltar and Flat Rock, MAL/L/1850/102:87–88; Grand Rapids and Plainfield, MAL/L/1850/103:88–89; Hastings and Yankee Springs, MAL/L/1850/105:90–91; Detroit and Newport, MAL/L/1850/106:91–92; Marshall and Ionia, MAL/L/1850/109:93–94; Paw Paw and Schoolcraft, MAL/L/1850/110:95; Centreville and Kalamazoo, MAL/L/1850/113:98–99; Albion and Homer, MAL/L/1850/114:100–101; Portland and Lansing, MAL/L/1850/117:102–3; Plymouth and Dearborn, MAL/L/1850/124:107–8; Fentonville and Milford, MAL/L/1850/127:111–12; Erin Township and Mt. Clemens, MAL/L/1850/128:112–13; Grand River, MAL/L/1850/131:116; Lansing and Howell, MAL/L/1850/132:117–18; Kalamazoo and Gull Prairie, MAL/L/1850/133:118–19; Kalamazoo and Grand Rapids, MAL/L/1850/138:122–23; Paw Paw and Allegan, MAL/L/1850/140:130–31; Union City and Fremont, MAL/L/1850/141:131–32; Cassopolis and Dowagiac, MAL/L/1850/142:133–34; Royal Oak and Rochester, MAL/L/1850/147:137–38; Howell and Byron, MAL/L/1850/148:138–39; Decatur and St. Joseph's, MAL/L/1850/150:142–43; Lawrence and St. Joseph,

MAL/L/1850/152:144–46; Detroit and Lake St. Clair, MAL/L/1850/155:143–44; Clinton and Mooreville, MAL/L/1850/163:158–59; Battle Creek and Gull Prairie, MAL/L/1850/192:192–93; Homer and Jonesville, MAL/L/1850/217:218–19; Ypsilanti and Mooreville, MAL/L/1850/229:233–34; Kalamazoo and Breedsville, MAL/L/1850/234:238–39; Walker and Vergennes, MAL/L/1850/236:240–41; Mt. Clemens and Lenox, MAL/L/1850/315:390–91; Homer and Union City, MAL/L/1848/322:402–3. Plank roads are discussed further in Dunbar, *Michigan*, 319–20; idem, *All Aboard!*, 64–65; Fuller, *Michigan Centennial History*, 342; MacGill, *History of Transportation*, 300–304; and Taylor, *Transportation Revolution*, 30–31.

8. The Grand River Plank Road anticipated the construction of the Detroit and Milwaukee Railroad and is likely to have helped facilitate the development of commercial agricultural production in this region prior to the arrival of more efficient long-distance transportation. Afterward, it served as an important feeder route. See Fuller, *Michigan*, 342; Baxter, *History of the City of Grand Rapids*, 525–26; and Everett, *Memorials*, 392.

9. North, *Economic Growth of the United States*, 212; Dunbar, *All Aboard!*, 65.

10. Tingley, "Postal Service in Michigan," 456–57. Railroads were declared post routes by SLUS/1838/5:271–83. Although the advent of direct mail order merchandise would not come until the 1870s, the railroad already provided a technology that permitted the mails to become an integral part of mid-nineteenth-century trade in the United States. The railroads' role in promoting western settlement has long been recognized; however, of equal, if not greater, importance was that which they played in integrating the economies of settled areas in the West. See Cronon, *Nature's Metropolis*, 332–33.

11. This map is based on the routes of post roads in southern Lower Michigan that were authorized under the following federal legislation:

SLUS/1801/2:125–27	Cincinnati to Detroit, in Northwest Territory
SLUS/1804/2:275–77	Cleveland to Detroit, in Michigan
SLUS/1810/2:579–89	Ft. Miami, by Frenchtown, to Detroit
SLUS/1820/3:577–81	Detroit, by Pontiac, to Mt. Clemens
SLUS/1823/3:763–68	Detroit, by Pontiac, to Ft. Saginaw
SLUS/1827/4:221–26	Stony Creek to Ft. Gratiot
SLUS/1828/4:315–20	Monroe to Tecumseh
	Detroit to Ft. Gratiot
	Maumee, Ohio, to Pontiac
	Detroit to Ann Arbor
SLUS/1832/4:534–49	Tecumseh, by Niles, to Chicago
	Detroit to Tecumseh
	Monguagon to Ypsilanti
	Pontiac to Saginaw
	Ypsilanti to mouth of St. Joseph River
	Niles to Saranac
	Mouth of St. Joseph to White Pigeon
	Bloomfield to South Pekin
	Monroe to Ypsilanti
SLUS/1836/5:90–107	Elkhart, Ind., to Bronson
	Lima P.O., Ind., to Prairie River P.O.
	White Pigeon to Pulaski, Ind.
	Marshall to Coldwater
	Elkhart, Ind., to Cassopolis

                              Niles to New Buffalo
                              Battle Creek to Charlotte
                              Detroit to Lapeer
                              Saline to Grass Lake
                              St. Clair to Grand Blanc
                              Detroit to Ft. Gratiot
                              Pontiac to Ionia
                              Toledo to Adrian
                              Ypsilanti to Pontiac
                              Adrian to Ionia
                              Manhattan to Adrian
                              Marshall to Coldwater
                              Mt. Clemens to Lapeer
                              Plymouth to Dexter
                              Monroe to Tecumseh
                              Toledo to Adrian
                              Maumee, Ohio, to Jonesville
                              Saline to London
                              Detroit to Utica
                              Detroit to Kent, Kent Co.
                              Clinton to Kent, Kent Co.
                              Coldwater to St. Joseph
                              Kalamazoo to Kalamazoo, Allegan Co.
                              Battle Creek to Kent, Kent Co.
                              Ann Arbor to Pontiac
                              Battle Creek to Schoolcraft
                              Bellevue to Middle Village
                              Ft. Defiance, Ohio, to Adrian
                              Michigan City, Ind., to Grand Haven
                              Schoolcraft to Geloster
                              Saginaw to mouth of Saginaw River
                              Grand River rapids to Grand Haven
                              Kalamazoo to mouth of South Black River
                              Northfield to Howell
                              New Buffalo to LaPorte, Ind.
                              Adrian to Coldwater
                              Marshall to White Pigeon
                              Kalamazoo to Kent
SLUS/1838/5:271–83   Ft. Wayne, Ind., to Branch Courthouse
                              Battle Creek to Hastings
                              Whitmanville to Lafayette
                              Belvidere to Mt. Clemens
                              Detroit to Southfield
                              Marshall to Hastings
                              Paxton to Owosso
                              Grandville to Port Sheldon

Flint to Lapeer
Cassopolis to Keelersville
Monroe to Ypsilanti
Flat Rock to Gibralter
Lapeer to Grand Blanc
Ingham to Jefferson
Saranac to Ionia
Springville to Marshall
Battle Creek to Coldwater
Bellevue to Ionia
Jackson to Gamblesville
Geloster to Allegan
Jonesville to Evansport, Ohio
Ingham to mouth of North Black River
Van Buren Co. seat to mouth of South Black River
Monroe to Adrian
Adrian to Springville
Marshall to Ingham

SLUS/1842/5:568–75 Lafayette, Ohio, to Hillsdale
Middleville to Allegan
Grand Rapids to Middleville
Charlotte to Hastings
Bellevue to Grand River City
Owosso to Lyons
Quincy to Brockville, Ind.
Saginaw City to Lower Saginaw
Blissfield to Fairfield P.O.
Kalamazoo to Lima, Ind.
Grand Rapids to Kalamazoo
Lakeville to Groveland
Battle Creek to Hastings
Belvedere to Detroit
Marshall to Girard Branch P.O.
Logansport to White Pigeon
Mason to Jackson

SLUS/1845/5:778–87 Maumee, Ohio, to Jonesville
Grand Rapids to Paw Paw
Ionia to Grand Rapids
Corunna to Northampton
Pontiac to Orion
Pontiac to Lapeer
Port Huron to Lexington
Mt. Clemens to Romeo
Grand Rapids to Grand Haven
Grand Rapids to Muskegon Mills
Grand Rapids to Lincoln's Mills

Lincoln's Mills to Ionia
Ionia to Marshall
Ionia to Yankee Springs
Grand Haven to mouth of Muskegon River
Muskegon to Muskegon Mills
Mt. Clemens to Romeo
SLUS/1847/9:188–202   Owosso to Lyons
SLUS/1848/9:306–20   Pomona, Ohio, to Coldwater
Lansing to Allegan
Battle Creek to Lansing
Marshall to Lansing
Hastings to Lansing
Hillsdale to Montpelier, Ohio
Kalamazoo to Lima, Ohio
Brooklyn to Grass Lake
Dexter to Howell
Dexter to Lansing
Paw Paw to Itsego
Allegan to Grand Haven
Brighton to Fentonville
Lansing to Byron
Howell to Ingham
Bronson to Noble Twp., Branch Co.
Ada to Greenville
SLUS/1850/9:473–96   Lafayette, Ind., to Niles
Quincy to Algansee
Wayne to Brownstown
Flint to Corunna
Mt. Clemens to Algonac
DeWitt to Du Plain
Lyons to Greenville
Grand Rapids to Muskegon
Hastings to Flat River
Lansing to Odessa
Lapeer to Pontiac
Tecumseh to Ypsilanti
Rochester to Romeo
Grand Rapids to Lyons
Dexter to Lansing
Lakeville to Almond
Grand Blanc to Kensington
Cedar to Antrim
Green Oak to Brighton
Paw Paw to Black River
Grand Rapids to Ionia
DeWitt to Maple

	Jackson to Mason
	Lawrence to mouth of Kalamazoo River
SLUS/1851/9:637–45	Romeo to Port Huron
	Grand Rapids to Grand Haven
SLUS/1852/10:134–35	Orangeville Mills to Yankee Springs
	Kalamazoo to Newark
	Otsego to Grand Rapids
	Saugatuck to South Haven
	Quincy to Homer
	Lapeer to Pine Run
	Corunna to Saginaw
	Adrian to Jackson
	Columbus to Almonte
	Detroit to Lansing
	Grand Rapids to Holland
SLUS/1853/10:253	Manchester to Chelsea
	Manchester to Grass Lake
	Bronson's Prairie to Orland, Ind.
SLUS/1855/10:710	Whitneyville to Grand Rapids
	Albion to Charlotte
	Greenville to Muskegon Rapids
	Fentonville to Flint
SLUS/1856/11:130–31	Okemos to Du Plain
	Gardner's Corners to Maple Rapids
	Allegan to Grand Rapids
	Otsego to Paw Paw
	Newaygo to White River
	Laphamville to Croton
	Corunna to Lansing
	Owosso to Lyons
	Owosso to Lansing
	Flint to Corunna
	Corunna to Howell
	St. Johns to St. Louis to seat of Isabella Co.
	St. Louis to Hampton
	Midland to Saginaw
	East Saginaw to Hampton
	Vassar to Auchville
	Vassar to Port Sanilac
	Bridgeport to Corunna
	Fentonville to Ann Arbor
	Lapeer to Lexington
	Almont to North Branch
	Greenville to Muskegon Rapids
	Greenville to Gratiot Center
	Hillsdale to Angola, Ind.

SLUS/1857/11:235	Port Huron to Memphis
	Mason to Eaton Rapids
	Ionia to Fallassburgh
	Ionia to Leonard
	Constantine to Cassopolis
	Ionia to Vermontville
	Boston to Greenville
	Ionia to center of Isabella Co.
	Ionia to Matherton
SLUS/1858/11:352	Corunna to Fowlerville
	Mickleville to Du Plain
	Brooklyn to Napoleon
	Lapeer to Vassar
	Adamsville to White Pigeon
	St. Johns to LaFayette
	Ithaca to St. Charles
	Ithaca to Midland
	St. Johns to Ithaca
	Jackson to Pulaski
	Midland to Albany
	Pewamo to Matherton
	Pewamo to Portland
	Chesaning to St. Charles

These and additional post routes are found in Postal Route Advertisements, 10 June 1823/TPUS/MT/11:367–68; 18 June 1827/TPUS/MT/11:1087–88; 23 June 1829/TPUS/MT/12:52; 20 June 1831/TPUS/MT/12:298–300; 25 June 1832/TPUS/MT/12:495–96; 2 July 1835/TPUS/MT/12:948–55; Mileage of Post Routes, January 1824/TPUS/MT/11:505; and *Monroe Times,* 17 November 1836.

 Overland routes outside the agricultural region covered extremely long distances and their configuration lacked the branching characteristic of agricultural trade networks in southern Lower Michigan. By the close of the 1850s, mail routes to the northern portion of Michigan's Western Shore extended along the shoreline northward from Muskegon to Whitehall, Ludington, Manistee, Sleeping Bear Point, and Traverse City. Overland routes connected the Traverse Bay settlements with those of the Grand Valley via Big Rapids and Cadillac. All of these routes, however, appear to have consisted of "Indian trails," over which mail service was "irregular and uncertain." Regular service accompanied the opening of a stage route at the close of the decade and the arrival of railroads in the 1870s. See S. E. Wait and W. S. Anderson, comps., *Old Settlers: Together with the Personal Reminiscences of Members of the Old Settlers of the Grand Traverse Region. A Historical and Chronological Record* (Traverse City, Mich.: By the compilers, 1918; reprint, Grand Rapids, Mich.: Black Letter Press, 1978), 14–16, 63; and Haswell and Alansen, *A Garden Apart,* 34–35.

12. As trade expanded in the 1860s, increased freight revenues offset the cost of branch line development in these areas and direct rail service rapidly reached all parts of southern lower Michigan. A discussion of the factors involved in the rapid growth of Michigan's rail network may be found in Dunbar, *All Aboard!,* 107–14 and chapter 10 of the present work. By 1869 the mileage of Michigan railroads was nearly three times that of 1855. Nearly all of this increase derived from the construction of lines connecting the major transpeninsular routes and extending the network into the northern portion of the settled agricultural

area. See Meints, "Michigan Railroad Construction," 9–14; and Michigan Railway Commission, *Aids, Gifts, Grants, and Donations,* 30–119 passim.

The routes included the Amboy, Lansing, & Traverse Bay, completed to Lansing in 1861, to Jackson in 1866, to Midland and Bay City in 1867, and to Clare in 1870. The Flint & Pere Marquette, completed between Saginaw and Flint in 1862 and extended to the Detroit & Milwaukee line at Holly the following year. The Kalamazoo, Allegan & Grand Rapids linked its namesake settlements in 1869 and the Michigan Air Line began its penetration of the eastern Thumb in the same year, which also witnessed the completion of the Peninsular, Lansing & Ionia that linked the capitol respectively with Battle Creek and Ionia. The latter was extended as far north as Greenville, in Montcalm County, the following year. Finally, in 1870 the Western Shore was made accessible through the construction of the Chicago & Michigan Lake Shore from New Buffalo and St. Joseph; the opening of a shoreline route from the Kalamazoo, Allegan & Grand Rapids station at Allegan as far north as Muskegon by the Michigan Lake Shore; and the completion of the Kalamazoo & South Haven linking these two points. In the same period other lines were constructed to link the Michigan Central and Michigan Southern lines and provide additional access to Indiana. See Meints, "Michigan Railroad Construction," 12–16.

13. Taaffe, Morrill, and Gould, "Transport Expansion," 511–15, associated this change with the expansion of road traffic over railroads in modern colonial areas, a phenomenon resulting in large part from the flexibility and cost-effectiveness of motorized transport and paved roads. In mid-nineteenth-century America, however, railroads would have represented a similar advantage over contemporary forms of overland transport, and their configuration should be useful in revealing similar information regarding settlement pattering.

14. Settlement names and locations are based on John Farmer, *Map of the Surveyed Part of Michigan,* col. map 71 x 96 cm., scale indeterminable (New York: J. H. Colton, 1855); and John Farmer, J. H. Colton, and Joseph Hutchins, *Colton's Sectional Map of Michigan,* col. Map 59 x 84 cm., scale 1:500,000 (New York: J. H. Colton, 1860).

15. Even before the completion of the three trans-peninsular rail lines, Detroit had become the market for southern Lower Michigan. In 1849, two-thirds of the state's exports and three-fourths of its imports passed through the entrepôt. The effect of trade on manufacturing is evidenced in the remarkable increase in the amount of capital invested in Wayne County industries between 1840 and 1860 and the value of their products. During this period the amount invested rose from a quarter of a million to over four million dollars, and the value of the products of these industries trebled during the decade from 1850 to 1860. Both of these figures would quadruple again in the following decade in response to continued increases in the volume and efficiency of Detroit's trade. See Parkins, *Historical Geography of Detroit,* 273–74; U.S. Census Office, *Population of the United States, 1840* (Washington, D.C.: Thomas Allen, 1841), 333; idem, *Population of the United States, 1850* (Washington, D.C.: A. O. P. Nicholson, 1854), 259; idem, *Manufactures of the United States, 1860* (Washington, D.C.: Government Printing Office, 1865), 273; and Farmer, *History of Detroit,* 802.

16. Henry Waldron, "History of Hillsdale, Michigan"/HWP/MSUAHC.

17. The U.S. Census of 1850 has been referred to as the first of the "modern" censuses because of the introduction of improved reporting and recording techniques, which were expanded in later years. The employment of multiple schedules, printed instructions, and other innovations designed to systematize the information collected accounted for a greater degree of accuracy and reliability which set these censuses apart from those of earlier years. For a discussion of these innovations and their effects, see Carmen R. Delle Donne, *Federal Census Schedules, 1850–80: Primary Sources for Historical Research,* National Archives and Records Service, General Services Administration, Reference Information Paper no. 67 (Washington, D.C.: Government Printing Office, 1973), 1–3.

Moderate coverage of Michigan settlement populations appeared in the 1850 federal census, which provided statistics for twenty municipalities. The populations of six were included in the Michigan census four years later. In 1860, the federal census included the populations of seventy separate settlements, and those of twenty settlements were reported in the 1864 state census. The 1860 census is particularly useful for this study because it represents comprehensive statistics that were compiled in the later part of the transition period. Census figures used here have been taken from U.S. Census Office, *Population of the United States, 1850*, 887–96; idem, *Population of the United States, 1860*, 237–47; Michigan, *Census, 1854*; idem, *Statistics of the State of Michigan, Compiled from the Census of 1860* (Lansing, Mich.: John A. Kerr, 1861); idem, *Census, 1864*; and those summarized in Donald B. Dodd and Wynelle S. Dodd, *Historical Statistics of the United States, 1790–1970*, vol. 2, *The Midwest* (University, Ala.: University of Alabama Press, 1976), 18. The scope of the Michigan censuses for this period is discussed in, U.S. Census Bureau, *State Censuses: An Annotated Bibliography of Censuses of Population Taken after the Year 1790 by States and Territories of the United States*, prepared by Henry J. Dubester (Washington, D.C.: Government Printing Office, 1948), 29–33.

18. The second gazetteer dealing solely with Michigan was published in 1856, eighteen years after the initial work by John Blois. It is H. Huntington Lee & James Sutherland, *State of Michigan, Gazetteer and Business Directory for 1856–7* (Detroit: By the authors, 1856). Gazetteers were published subsequently with increasing frequency; three others represent roughly the same period as that covered by the census records. They are: George W. Hawes, *George W. Hawes' Michigan State Gazetteer and Business Directory for 1860* (Detroit: F. Raymond, 1859; idem, *George W. Hawes' Michigan State Gazetteer and Shipper's Guide and Business Directory for 1865* (Indianapolis: By the author, 1864); and Charles F. Clark, *Michigan State Gazetteer and Business Directory for 1863–4* (Detroit: By the author, 1863). The 1856 gazetteer was not used in this comparison for two reasons. First, the number of settlements included in the 1856 gazetteer totaled 79, while those reported in 1859, 1863, and 1864 were 131, 161, and 172, respectively. Second, the relative sizes of settlement populations in the last three gazetteers contrast markedly with those in the 1856 volume, and absolute population figures listed in the later works often fall below the sometimes strikingly high entries reported in the earlier publication. These discrepancies imply that the earlier figures are unreliable.

19. The fifth group's modal population of 300 and mean of 423 indicate that nearly all of the settlements were substantially larger than were most frontier communities. Although population figures for the earlier period are scarce, Blois's figures for 1838 reveal that, apart from Detroit, only a few of Michigan's frontier towns, such as Marshall, Adrian, and Pontiac, had populations of around 1,000, while others, such as Saginaw, were home to as few as 400 people. Nucleated and semi-nucleated settlements were apparently much smaller. Berrien Springs, for example, had a population of only 100. See Blois, *Gazetteer*, 246, 249, 254, 320, 328, 344, 355. The county seats were Mason, Charlotte, and Lapeer.

In the second-largest population group, Lansing was developing rapidly as a center of inland transportation and communications and became accessible by rail in the early 1860s. Lying in the Lower Saginaw Valley, Bay City was also beyond the limits of the rail net, but possessed important water transportation links that facilitated its growth in an increasingly export-oriented economy. Monroe was an established eastern lake port, the importance of which grew in the post-frontier economy, and Niles retained access to trade on the lower St. Joseph River.

20. Although Saginaw and East Saginaw remained separate corporate entities in 1860, their placement on opposite sides of the river and concurrent development as industrial centers invites their combination as a urban entity. Their combined population of around 9,500 places them among Michigan's largest settlements and implies a substantial economic role. The development of East Saginaw and its relationship to its neighbor are discussed in Fox, *History of Saginaw*, 44–48, *History of Saginaw County*, 500–1.

21. Ionia, Mt. Clemens, and Owosso, for example, all appear to have been important foci of transportation, yet contained relatively small populations.

22. Functional index classification was developed by Wayne K. D. Davies, "Centrality and the Central Place Hierarchy," *Urban Studies* 4 (1967): 61–79, and has been employed successfully in studies of hierarchical groupings of central places in contemporary North America. Two examples of particular relevance to the Midwest are John W. Marshall, *The Location of Service Towns: An Approach to the Analysis of Central Place Systems* (Toronto: University of Toronto Press, Research Publications, 1969) and Fatemeh Beforooz, "The Role of Rural Development and Farmers' Preferences in Changing the Viability and Spatial Distributions of Central Villages," Ph.D. diss., Michigan State University (Ann Arbor, Mich.: University Microfilms International, 1985). For a discussion of the theoretical basis of functional index classification, see David J. Bennison, "The Measurement of Settlement Centrality," *Professional Geographer* 30 (1978): 371–76. Functional index classification involves several steps. First a locational coefficient is calculated for each activity category. The coefficients are derived by dividing one hundred by the total number of examples of activities within that category found in all settlements. Locational coefficients are then used to calculate centrality values for each activity category in every settlement. Centrality values are computed by multiplying the number of activities in the category by the appropriate coefficient to determine four centrality values for each settlement. Summing each settlement's values results in its functional index number (see appendix 3). These numbers are the values used to compare the roles of settlements in the closing years of the frontier period and determine their rankings in the regional hierarchy.

The relationships between the levels of centers in the hierarchy and the variables of total population served, population of center, number of business establishments, and the amount of traffic generated are major variables examined in Central Place Theory, a direction of inquiry aimed at discovering order in the size, ranking, and distribution of settlements in space. Assumptions derived from Central Place models regarding the interdependence of these variables will be useful in ranking Michigan settlements during this period of economic transition. A discussion of Central Place Theory and its implications may be found in Berry, *Geography of Market Centers,* 34–38, 59–75. Hawes, *Michigan State Gazetteer, 1860,* provided the principal source for the Michigan statistical information, which included comprehensive listings of businesses for nearly all settlements it surveyed. Data for those lacking lists of businesses were obtained from Clark, *Michigan State Gazetteer.* A comparison of numbers of businesses in settlements included in both gazetteers implies that increases during this period had not been substantial enough to preclude the use of the later information to supplement that obtained for 1860.

23. The four classes derived from the range of functional index values for Michigan settlements were initially based on a visual interpretation of the curve of the distribution of these values. Breaks in the curve, representing boundaries between classes, were defined further using the nested means classification. This method is designed to create classes based on the characteristics of the data set involved. It allowed us to separate ordered data (in this case the range of functional index numbers) so as to maximize the between-class differences while minimizing within-class differences. In this method, the mathematical mean of the attribute values was calculated and a class break placed there, separating the data into two classes. The data were further classified by calculating the means of the values within these two categories and inserting class breaks at those two points. This created four classes, the limits of which are shown below. For a discussion of nested means classification, see Robert M. Edsall, "Data Classification II," National Center for Geographic Information and Analysis (NCGIA) GIS Core Curriculum for Tecnical Programs, Unit 47: On-Screen Visualization. <http://www.ncgia.ucsb.edu/education/curricula/cctp/units/unit47/html/mas_class.html>.

Class Number	Up Limit	Low Limit
1	.5495453	.08
2	1.355326	.5495453
3	4.520894	1.355326
4	62.97	4.520894

CHAPTER 14

1. The resulting nesting pattern is one in which each central place serves the equivalent of four markets at the next lower level. These markets include its own and a half of those found in each of the six surrounding lower-order settlements located midway between the apexes of the hexagons. This is referred to as a K-4 network and is based on Christaller's model, discussed in Berry, *Geography of Market Centers,* 65, and Garner, "Models of Urban Geography," 308–9.

2. The city's commercial growth is reflected in a nearly sixfold increase in the duties on goods passing through the Detroit customs house between 1850 and 1860. The importance of the role of wholesaling was not lost on the editor of the *Michigan Farmer* (1853:17), who was quick to emphasize its expansion as evidence of Detroit's national prominence. In an article written following his return from an extended visit to Chicago, he wrote that in Detroit,

> the life and prosperity and thrift, were everywhere visible. Above all, we were surprised at the amount of wholesaling done here, . . . And this is but a single instance, out of many others, which may be cited as proof of the astonishing progress of business among us, and of the hitherto unprecedented prosperity of our city.

Contemporary sources also remarked on the rapid growth of Detroit's domestic and foreign commerce. See, for example, Goddard, *Where to Emigrate,* 317. Detroit's foreign trade is discussed in Farmer, *History of Detroit,* 773.

Detroit's geographical location at the center of rail and water transportation networks that permitted access to natural resources originating within and outside of the region, as well as to national markets, facilitated its industrial expansion. Products of its industries included smelted copper and items of copper and brass; sawed lumber; machinery and steam engines; bar iron; leather; flour and meal; malt liquor; pig iron; furs; soap and candles; printed materials; boots and shoes; saws and agricultural implements; carriages, wagons, and carts; marble and stone; and cigars. See U.S. Census Office, *Manufactures of the United States, 1860,* 272–73; Hawes, *Michigan State Gazetteer, 1860;* Parkins, *Historical Geography of Detroit,* 291–93; and Farmer, *History of Detroit,* 802–3.

3. A contemporary observer noted, "Pontiac is the center of business, and draws considerable trade from Lapeer, Genesee, and Livingston counties" (*Michigan Farmer,* 1853:30). The high state of cultivation of Ann Arbor's immediate hinterland contributed measurably to its wealth and the city's "steady, healthful" growth (*Michigan Farmer,* 1854:169). A correspondent described Adrian as "the second city in the state [behind Detroit] for wealth, enterprise and business" (*Michigan Farmer,* 1854:135). For descriptions of late antebellum Ann Arbor and Adrian, see *History of Washtenaw County,* 879–80, 941–46; William A. Whitney and Richard I. Bonner, *History and Biographical Record of Lenawee County, Michigan* (Adrian, Mich.: W. Stearns, 1879–80); and Puffer, *Michigan Agricultural Frontier,* 381–82.

4. *Michigan Farmer,* 1853:302. A later author noted the role of waterpower in Ypsilanti's growth and future industrial expansion:

> The great part in which a system of hydraulics plays in the progress of a city cannot be doubted. . . . To realize the high hopes for the city, which its position and natural resources would lead one to build up, factories must be built up, manufactories encouraged, and the 10,000 horsepower of the Huron utilized. . . . When one takes a survey of the field, which Ypsilanti opens to the manufacturer, . . . one stands astonished to think of all that could be done. (*History of Washtenaw County,* 1142)

5. Tecumseh's later history was linked to its role as a rail center. Access to transportation encouraged "the flourishing business of the village, and all through the years of its existence it has been a place of considerable importance and a very popular trading point, sustained by an excellent farming country." See Richard Illenden Bonner, *Memoirs of Lenawee County, Michigan* (Madison, Wisc.: Western Historical Society, 1909), 232; and Puffer, *Michigan Agricultural Frontier,* 381–82.

6. Leeson, *History of Macomb County,* 620–21; *Michigan Farmer,* 1853:365.

7. *Michigan Farmer,* 1853:299.

8. *Michigan Farmer,* 1849:258–59; William J. Chandler, "The Antebellum Grain Trade in Monroe, Michigan," (master's thesis, Wayne State University, 1999), 34–37.

9. *Michigan Farmer,* 1854:135; Hawes, *Michigan State Gazetteer,* 1860: 208; Archie M. Turrell, "Some Place Names of Hillsdale County," *Michigan History* 6 (1922): 579–80. *History of Washtenaw County,* 1325–27.

10. *History of Washtenaw County,* 832.

11. Crisfield Johnson, *History of Branch County, Michigan,* (Philadelphia: Evarts & Abbott, 1879), 115–16, 146–47; *Michigan Farmer,* 1854:11.

12. *History of Jackson County,* 745; Santer, *Historical Geography of Jackson,* 101–5; *Michigan Farmer,* 1854:9–10, 124.

13. Hawes, *Michigan State Gazetteer,* 1860:208; *Michigan Telegraph,* 3 February 1849; *Michigan Farmer,* 1849:259, 280; 1854:135.

14. *History of Calhoun County,* 105–6; Washington Gardner, *History of Calhoun County, Michigan* (Chicago: Lewis Pub. Co., 1913), 420–21, 447–49; *Michigan Farmer,* 1854:9.

15. Marshall's decline became evident during the 1860s as the state's transportation infrastructure expanded. Looking back on this recent development, the editor of Marshall's newspaper clearly linked it to the town's failure to improve its connections and maintain the extent of its trade:

> The territory for which we were the commercial center for a distance of 30 miles on the north and 18 to 20 miles on the south and southwest, has been . . . circumscribed in its limits to at most, not more than an average of 6 miles in each direction, and all this . . . solely from the fact that we failed to seize upon and improve the great advantages that lay within our reach, and supinely permitted our neighbors to snatch them from us. . . . (*Marshall Statesman,* 9 May 1878)

Marshall's secondary role was also reflected in contemporary gazetteers, which, while never disparaging, always described it in somewhat less complimentary terms than its larger neighbor. One noted, for example, that, "Although not particularly noted as a manufacturing or commercial place, it enjoys a considerable trade, and is regarded as an excellent market for produce." On the other hand, "The educational, mercantile and manufacturing facilities of Battle Creek" were seen as "possessing such a character as to present a strong inducement to men of capital . . . [and] conspire to render the city one of the most desirable locations in interior Michigan." See Clark, *Michigan State Gazetteer,* 191, 393; Hawes, *Michigan State Gazetteer,* 1860: 35–36, 239; and *Michigan Farmer,* 1853:214.

16. Dunbar, *Kalamazoo and How It Grew,* 72–76; Durant, *History of Kalamazoo County,* 257–62; *Michigan Farmer,* 1849:156; 1850:338; 1854:164–65; 1855:203.

17. Durant, *History of Kalamazoo County,* 377–78; Fisher and Little, *History and Biography of Kalamazoo County,* 81.

18. Fort Wayne's importance grew after 1860 as railroads passing through northern Indiana formed trunk lines connecting Chicago and the Mississippi Valley with the East. The completion of a rail line linking Sturgis with Kalamazoo and Fort Wayne in 1870 emphasized the important role of this secondary settlement in the trade of western Michigan. See Meints, "Michigan Railroad Construction," 15; Chamberlain, *1850 Indiana Gazetteer,* 388; *Bailey's Gazetteer and Directory of the Lines of Railway Extending from Cincinnati to Northern Michigan* (Sandusky, Ohio: Western Publishing, 1871); Dunbar, *Michigan,* 433; and Cronon, *Nature's Metropolis,* 90.

19. Perrine, "Townships in Calhoun County," 212.

20. Although Constantine had been the more important settlement during the frontier period, Three Rivers's rapid industrial growth made it the larger settlement in 1860. See Blois, *Gazetteer,* 267–68, 373–74; *Michigan Farmer,* 1850:240; Clark, *Michigan State Gazetteer,* 488; *History of St. Joseph County, Michigan* (Philadelphia: L. H. Everts , 1877), 141; and Turner, *Gazetteer of the St. Joseph Valley,* 27–28, 165. For a description of early Puddleford, see Riley, *Puddleford Papers,* 9–10.

21. Chamberlain, *1850 Indiana Gazetteer,* 228, 286, 388; Turner, *Gazetteer of the St. Joseph Valley,* 59–62; *Bailey's Gazetteer; Michigan Farmer,* 1854:12.

22. Hawes, *Michigan State Gazetteer,* 1860: 253; Clark, *Michigan State Gazetteer,* 208, 419; Turner, *Gazetteer of the St. Joseph Valley,* 78; *Michigan Farmer,* 1853:213.

23. Contemporaries described Decatur as "a great trading town and . . . an important grain purchasing point." Within five years of its founding in 1848, the village contained seventy-five buildings. See Lawton, "Van Buren County," 663; Ellis, *History of Berrien and Van Buren Counties,* 442–43; and Mae R. Schoetzow, *A Brief History of Cass County* (Marcellus, Mich.: Cass County Federation of Women's Clubs, 1935), 68–70.

24. Turner, *Gazetteer of the St. Joseph Valley,* 80; Clark, *Grain Trade,* 83. As late as 1846, Mitchell (*View of the United States,* 86) referred to St Joseph as "the most important town on the east shore of Lake Michigan."

25. The town's location and its links to the emerging commercial transportation network encouraged the tiny community of Bradley to participate in long-distance trade. One of its businessmen, Joseph E. Harding became "the first merchant in Wayland Township who bought goods directly from New York City" (Johnson, *History of Allegan and Barry Counties,* 362–64, 373).

26. Everett, *Memorials,* 392–93, 402–3; Baxter, *History of the City of Grand Rapids,* 39–43; *Michigan Farmer,* 1854:53–54; Bradshaw, "Grand Rapids Furniture Beginnings," 289–91.

27. Everett, *Memorials,* 420–21; Mills, *Our Inland Seas,* 124.

28. Although not important as commercial arteries, overland routes to the northern Lower Peninsula offered a viable alternative to water travel. By the late 1850s, a shoreline road allowed access to Oceana and Mason Counties, and a wagon road connected Grand Rapids with Grand Traverse Bay. See *Grand River Times,* 12 March 1856; and J. R. Smith, "Grand Traverse Country," *Grand River Times,* 21 May 1856.

29. Bela Hubbard, Notebook, 31 August 1840/BHP/Box 3/MHC; Johnson, *History of Allegan and Barry Counties,* 368, 373–80.

30. Schenck, *History of Ionia and Montcalm Counties,* 147, 154; *Michigan Farmer,* 1854:134. Traveler J. A. Baldwin commented that Ionia, "does not exhibit the spirit of advancement manifested by the village of Lyons," which he felt "destined by nature and enterprise to become a commercial mart for a large scope of surrounding country" (J. A. Baldwin, "Grand River Valley," *Grand River Times,* 14 May 1856).

31. *Michigan Farmer,* 1854:134; Lee and Sutherland, *Gazetteer and Business Directory,* 143; Goddard, *Where to Emigrate,* 317; Stebbins, "Sketch of My Life," 107/SFP/MSUAHC.

32. *Michigan Farmer,* 1854:134.

33. Ellis, *History of Shiawassee and Clinton Counties,* 144–48, 151–52; Gould, "Early History of Shiawassee County," 294.

34. Ellis, *History of Genesee County,* 132–37; Hawes, *Michigan State Gazetteer,* 1860; *Michigan Farmer,* 1853:302–3.

35. Contemporary observers attributed Howell's relative economic position as an export center to "the expense of transportation to market" (Elisha H. Smith, *The History of Howell, Michigan* [Lansing, Mich.: John A. Kerr, 1868; reprint, Howell: Livingston County Historical Society, n.d.], 61–62).

36. Ellis, *History of Genesee County,* 209, 222.

37. Samuel W. Durant, *History of Oakland County, Michigan* (Philadelphia: L. H. Everts, 1877).

38. Ellis, *History of Genesee County,* 374.

39. Fox, *History of Saginaw County,* 25–26, 26–37, 45–47. By 1860 Saginaw entrepreneurs had begun commercial salt production through the evaporation of brine by artificial sources of heat. Cheap fuel generated as by-products of lumbering permitted the rapid growth of this industry. See Charles W. Cook, "The Influence of the Lumber Industry upon the Salt Industry in Michigan," *Journal of Geography* 15 (1916): 118, 123.

40. Mitchell, "History of St. Clair County," 414–15; *Michigan Farmer,* 1853:363.

41. Leeson, *History of Macomb County,* 626–27; *Michigan Farmer,* 1853:365.

42. Mitchell, "History of St. Clair County," 414; *Michigan Farmer,* 1853:362.

43. Schenck, *History of Ionia and Montcalm Counties,* 374.

44. Long-distance trade also played an important role in the business of St. Johns merchants. Merchants shipped wheat directly to Detroit, and staves were manufactured for the European market. St. Johns's position attracted additional capital instrumental to the growth of its businesses. Robert M. Steel, for example, invested profits derived from diverse businesses to establish a factory the products of which were destined for a national market. See Ellis, *History of Shiawassee and Clinton Counties,* 366–67, 374–75.

45. Fox, *History of Saginaw County,* 26, 59–60.

46. *Michigan Farmer,* 1853:218–19, 364; *History of Lapeer County, Michigan* (Chicago: H. R. Page, 1884), 65; Kovacik, *Geographical Analysis,* 53.

47. *Michigan Farmer,* 1853:364; *History of Lapeer County,* 38.

CHAPTER 15

1. These strategies were especially important given the need to increase production for the European market while concurrently facing a decrease in available labor due to military service in the Civil War. The 1860s did not witness the introduction of new agricultural machines, but rather the refinement and improvement of earlier types to increase their capacity and reliability. The rate of machinery investment by American farmers more than doubled during the Civil War years. See Fred Shannon, *The Farmer's Last Frontier: Agriculture, 1860–1897,* vol. 5, *The Economic History of the United States* (New York: Holt, Rinehart and Winston, 1945; reprint, New York: Harper & Row, 1968), 126–27; Sewell, "Michigan Farmers," 354–55, 360–71; Joseph J. Marks, ed., *Effects of the Civil War on Farming in Michigan* (Lansing: Michigan Civil War Centennial Observance Commission, 1965), 6–7, 15–18; Cochrane, *Development of American Agriculture,* 196; Marvin W. Towne and Wayne D. Rasmussen, "Gross Farm Product and Gross Investment in the Nineteenth Century," in *Trends in the American Economy in the Nineteenth Century,* vol. 24: *Studies in Income and Wealth* (New York: National Bureau of Economic Research, 1960), 261; and Lamb, "History of Dairying," 421–23.

2. See Hammond, *Banks and Politics,* 725–27; Michael P. Conzen, "Capital Flows and the Developing Urban Hierarchy: State Bank Capital in Wisconsin, 1854–1895," *Economic Geography* 51 (1975): 319–38 and Allan R. Pred, *Urban Growth and the Circulation of Information: The United States System of Cities, 1790–1840* (Cambridge, Mass.: Harvard University Press, 1973), 202. Linkages between banks usually involved the smaller bank maintaining an account at a certain level at the larger city bank. In return, the larger bank provided services such as clearing out-of-town checks, making large loans, investment and management advice, safe keeping of securities, bank wire services, collections, referral of new customers, sharing of credit information, international banking services, and personnel recruitment and training. See Gerald C. Fischer, *American Banking Structure* (New York: Columbia University Press, 1968), 110–13. A comparative analyses of bank linkages and a discussion of Detroit's role in national banking can be found in Michael P. Conzen, "The Maturing Urban System in the United States, 1840–1910," *Annals of the Association of American Geographers* 67 (1977): 93–107. For the history of bank development in these Michigan cities, see Farmer, *History of Detroit,* 866–73; Dunbar, *Kalamazoo and How It Grew,* 94, 102, 120–21; Baxter, *History of the City of Grand Rapids,* 674–690; and *History of Saginaw County,* 643–45.

3. The changing access requirements involved in frontier and post-frontier economic growth are discussed in Edward K. Muller, "Selective Urban Growth in the Middle Ohio Valley, 1800–1860," *Geographical Review* 66 (1976): 179–81; and Pred, *Urban Growth,* 189–94, 200–201.

4. Farmer, *History of Detroit,* 802–24, 854; Fuller, *Michigan,* 534–39; Dunbar, *Michigan,* 465–82; Parkins, *Historical Geography of Detroit,* 271–72, 295–311; Baxter, *History of the City of Grand Rapids,* 537.

5. Fuller, "Settlement of Southern Michigan," 540; Dunbar, *Michigan,* 482.

Bibliography

Manuscript Collections

Allcott Family Correspondence (AFC), 1835–50, Michigan State University Archives and Historical Collections, East Lansing.

Alphadelphia Papers (AP), 1843–48, Michigan Historical Collections, University of Michigan, Ann Arbor.

Bela Hubbard Papers (BHP), 1837–93, Michigan Historical Collections, University of Michigan, Ann Arbor.

Clover Flanders Letters (CFL), 1839–71, 1921, Western Michigan University Archives and Regional History Collection, Kalamazoo, Michigan.

Chamberlain Family Papers (CFP), 1795–1911, Michigan State University Archives and Historical Collections, East Lansing.

Dibble Family Correspondence (DFC), 1824–65, Western Michigan University Archives and Regional History Collection, Kalamazoo, Michigan.

David L. Porter Papers (DLPP), 1829–32, Clark Historical Library, Central Michigan University, Mt. Pleasant, Michigan.

Denison-McOmber Papers (DMP), 1809–76, Western Michigan University Archives and Regional History Collection, Kalamazoo, Michigan.

Dorothy Waage Collection (DWC), 1836, Western Michigan University Archives and Regional History Collection, Kalamazoo, Michigan.

Mr. and Mrs. Emor Hice Collection (EHC), 1835–47, Western Michigan University Archives and Regional History Collection, Kalamazoo, Michigan.

Elizabeth Margaret Chandler Papers (EMCP), 1807–35, Michigan Historical Collections, University of Michigan, Ann Arbor.

Edwin T. Brown Collection (ETBC), 1803–1949, State Archives of Michigan, Michigan Bureau of History, Lansing.

Fay Family Correspondence (FFC), 1832–75, Michigan State University Archives and Historical Collections, East Lansing.

Franklin Leonidas Parker Papers (FLPP), 1820–94, Correspondence, 1816–1911, Michigan Historical Collections, University of Michigan, Ann Arbor.

George Nelson Smith Papers (GNSP), 1835–79, Library of Congress Microfilm Edition. Copy at Michigan State University Archives and Historical Collections, East Lansing.

Hall Family Letters (HFL), 1805–78, HWFP, Michigan State University Archives and Historical Collections, East Lansing.

Halbert Family Papers (HFP), 1839–1919, State Archives of Michigan, Michigan Bureau of History, Lansing.

Henry Howland Crapo Papers (HHCP), 1830–1920, Box 1, Correspondence, 1836–55, Michigan Historical Collections, University of Michigan, Ann Arbor.

Hannah Hinckley Letters (HHL), 1838–46, Clark Historical Library, Central Michigan University, Mt. Pleasant, Michigan.

Henry Parker Smith Papers (HPSP), 1823–44, Michigan Historical Collections, University of Michigan, Ann Arbor.

Harris Seymour Correspondence (HSC), 1831–34, State Archives of Michigan, Michigan Bureau of History, Lansing.

Henry Shelton Sanford Papers (HSSP), 1844, Box 3, General Sanford Memorial Library, Sanford, Florida.

Henry Waldron Papers (HWP), 1832–81, Michigan State University Archives and Historical Collections, East Lansing.

Joshua C. Goodrich Diary (JCGD), 1835–47, EHC, Western Michigan University Archives and Regional History Collection, Kalamazoo, Michigan.

Jane Comstock Letter (JCL), 1845, Michigan State University Archives and Historical Collections, East Lansing.

Joshua Fay Family Correspondence (JFFC), 1823–46, Clark Historical Library, Central Michigan University, Mt. Pleasant, Michigan.

Jacob Gerrish Papers (JGP), 1836–67, Michigan State University Archives and Historical Collections, East Lansing. James Rogers Letter (JRL), 1847, Michigan State University Archives and Historical Collections, East Lansing.

James Rogers Letter (JRL), 1847, Michigan State University Archives and Historical Collections, East Lansing.

Jonathan Searles Papers (JSP), 1812–1920, Clark Historical Library, Central Michigan University, Mt. Pleasant, Michigan.

Kenny Family Papers (KFP), 1828–1943, Michigan Historical Collections, University of Michigan, Ann Arbor.

L. A. Chase Collection (LACC), 1830–40, State Archives of Michigan, Michigan Bureau of History, Lansing.

Lovira Hart Letters (LHL), 1837–53, Michigan Historical Collections, University of Michigan, Ann Arbor.

Lutheria Stoner Crandell Collection (LSCC), 1843–56, State Archives of Michigan, Michigan Bureau of History, Lansing.

Michigan, Department of Natural Resources, vol. 27, Internal Improvement Land Certificates, (MDNRIILC), 1843–79, State Archives of Michigan, Michigan Bureau of History, Lansing.

Mildred Jones Collection (MJC), 1839–77, Western Michigan University Archives and Regional History Collection, Kalamazoo, Michigan.

Mrs. M. L. Sanford Letters (MLSL), 1858–1859, 1871, Clark Historical Library, Central Michigan University, Mt. Pleasant, Michigan.

Michigan, Records of the Executive Office (MREOCAONMS), 1810–1910, Correspondence, Affairs Outside, National, Michigan Senators, Box 5, 1839–43, State Archives of Michigan, Michigan Bureau of History, Lansing.

Michigan, State Agricultural Society Records (MSASR), 1849–50, Michigan State University Archives and Historical Collections, East Lansing.

N. M. Thomas Account Book (NMTAB), 1837–73, Michigan State University Archives and Historical Collections, East Lansing.

Nathan Thomas Papers (NTP), 1818–89, Michigan Historical Collections, University of Michigan, Ann Arbor.

O'Shea Wilder Diary (OWD), 1831, Michigan Historical Collections, University of Michigan, Ann Arbor.

Obadiah Rogers Notebook (ORN), 1831–59, Michigan Historical Collections, University of Michigan, Ann Arbor.

Parsons Family Papers (PaFP), 1827–48, Michigan State University Archives and Historical Collections, East Lansing.

Powell Family Papers (PFP), 1803–87, Michigan State University Archives and Historical Collection, East Lansing.

Pierpont Smith Correspondence (PSC), 1829–42, Michigan State University Archives and Historical Collections, East Lansing.

Stanley-Barney-Smith Family Correspondence (SBSFC), 1829–71, Western Michigan University Archives and Regional History Collection, Kalamazoo, Michigan.

Stebbins Family Papers (SFP), Michigan State University Archives and Historical Collections, East Lansing.

Samuel H. Fulton Papers (SHFP), Michigan State University Archives and Historical Collections, East Lansing.

Thomas Andrews Letters (TAL), 1833, 1836, Clark Historical Library, Central Michigan University, Mt. Pleasant, Michigan.

Thomas Wright Diary (TWD), 1831–41, Michigan State University Archives and Historical Collections, East Lansing.

ARTICLES AND BOOKS

Abernathy, Thomas Perkins. "The Southern Frontier, an Interpretation." In *The Frontier in Perspective,* edited by Walker D. Wyman and Clifton B. Kroeber, 129–42. Madison: University of Wisconsin Press, 1957.

Ackerknecht, Erwin H. "Diseases in the Middle West." In *Essays in the History of Medicine in Honor of David J. Davis, M.D., Ph.D,* 168–181. Chicago: University of Illinois Press for the Davis Lecture Committee, 1965.

Adam, John J. "Early History of Lenawee County." *Michigan Pioneer and Historical Collections* 2 (1880): 357–87.

Adams, Henry. *The United States in 1800*. Ithaca, N.Y.: Cornell University Press, 1955.

Albion, Robert Greenhalgh. *The Rise of New York Port (1815–1860)*. New York: Charles Scribner's Sons, 1939.

Aldrich, Samuel R., and Earl R. Leng. *Modern Corn Production*. Cincinnati: Farm Quarterly, 1965.

Allen, H. C. *Bush and Backwoods: A Comparison of the Frontier in Australia and the United States*. East Lansing: Michigan State University Press, 1959.

Allen, J. "Hydraulic Engineering." In *A History of Technology*, vol. 5, *The Late Nineteenth Century, c. 1850 to c. 1900*, edited by Charles Singer, E. J. Holmyard, A. R. Hall, and Trevor I. Williams, 522–51. New York: Oxford University Press, 1958.

Allen, Robert S. "His Majesty's Indian Allies: Native Peoples, the British Crown and the War of 1812." *Michigan Historical Review* 14 (1988): 1–24.

Alward, Dennis E., and Charles S. Pierce, comp. *Index to the Local and Special; Acts of the State of Michigan, 1803–1927*. Lansing, Mich.: Robert Smith Co., 1928.

Alwin, John A. "Post Office Locations and the Historical Geographer: A Montana Example," *Professional Geographer* 26 (1974): 183–86.

American Agriculturist, 1843–45.

American Railroad Journal, 1853.

American State Papers, Indian Affairs (ASP/IA). *Operations of the Factory System*. Vol. 2, no. 187. 17th Cong., 1st sess., 1822. Washington, D.C.: Gales and Seaton, 1834.

American State Papers, Military Affairs (ASP/MA). *Report of the Survey, Estimate, and Drawing of a Military Road from Saginaw to Mackinac, Michigan*. Vol. 7, no. 793. 25th Cong., 2d sess., 1838. Washington, D.C.: Gales and Seaton, 1861.

American State Papers, Miscellaneous (ASP/M). *Roads and Canals*. Vol. 1, no. 250. 10th Cong., 1st sess., 1808. Washington, D.C.: Gales and Seaton, 1832.

———. *Provision for Making the Roads Designated by the Treaty of Brownstown*. Vol. 2, no. 298. 12th Cong., 1st sess., 1812. Washington, D.C. Gales and Seaton, 1834.

———. *Roads Contemplated by the Treaty of Brownstown*. Vol. 2, no. 491. 16th Cong., 1st sess., 1820. Washington, D.C.: Gales and Seaton, 1934.

American State Papers, Public Lands (ASP/PL). *Description of the Lands and Settlers in the Vicinity of Detroit*. Vol. 1, no. 97. 8th Cong., 1st sess., 1804. Washington, D.C.: Gales and Seaton, 1832.

———. *Land Titles in Michigan Territory*. Vol. 1, no. 112. 9th Cong., 1st sess., 1805. Washington, D.C.: Gales and Seaton, 1832.

———. *Land Titles in Michigan Territory*. Vol. 1, no. 126. 9th Cong., 1st sess., 1806. Washington, D.C.: Gales and Seaton, 1832.

———. *Military Bounty Lands*. Vol. 3, no. 238. 14th Cong., 1st sess., 1816. Washington, D.C.: Gales and Seaton, 1834.

————. *Remonstrance of Sundry Inhabitants of Michigan against Graduating the Price of the Public Lands, &c.* Vol. 5, no. 675. 20th Cong., 1st sess., 1828. Washington, D.C.: Gales and Seaton, 1860.

————. *Operation of the General Land Office and the Several Land Offices during 1834, and the First, Second, and Third Quarters of 1835.* Vol. 8, no. 1339. 24th Cong., 1st sess., 1835. Washington, D.C.: Gales and Seaton, 1861.

————. *Statement of the Quantity of Land Secured by Claimants under the Pre-Emption Laws.* Vol. 8, no. 1525. 24th Cong., 1st sess., 1836. Washington, D.C.: Gales and Seaton, 1861.

————. *Operations of the General Land Office during the Year 1836.* Vol. 8, no. 1546. 24th Cong., 2d sess., 1836. Washington, D.C.: Gales and Seaton, 1861.

Anderson, Virginia DeJohn. "Migrants and Motives: Religion and the Settlement of New England, 1630–1640." *New England Quarterly* 58 (1985): 339–83.

Archer, Richard. "New England Mosaic: A Demographic Analysis for the Seventeenth Century." *William and Mary Quarterly,* 3d ser., no. 47 (1990): 477–502.

Arensberg, Conrad M. "The Community as Object and Sample." *American Anthropologist* 63 (1961): 241–64.

Arensberg, Conrad, and Solon T. Kimball. *Culture and Community.* New York: Harcourt, Brace and World, 1965.

Armour, David A. *The Merchants of Albany, New York, 1686–1760.* New York: Garland, 1986.

Atack, Jeremy, and Fred Bateman. *To Their Own Soil: Agriculture in the Antebellum North.* Ames: Iowa State University Press, 1987.

Atherton, Lewis. *The Frontier Merchant in Mid-America.* Columbia: University of Missouri Press, 1970.

Atkinson's Casket. "Views of the West, Michigan." 5 (1833): 223–24.

Bachelder, Glen L., comp. *Bachelder Family Letters, 1835–1935.* East Lansing, Mich.: By the compiler, 1989.

Bailey's Gazetteer and Directory of the Lines of Railway Extending from Cincinnati to Northern Michigan. Sandusky, Ohio: Western Publishing Co., 1871.

Bajema, Carl J. "The First Logging Railroads in the Great Lakes Region." *Forest & Conservation History* 35 (April 1991): 76–82.

Baker, Gladys L., Wayne D. Rasmussen, Vivian Wiser, and Jane M. Porter. *A Century of Service The First 100 Years of the United States Department of Agriculture.* Washington, D.C.: U. S. Department of Agriculture, 1963.

Bald, F. Clever. *Detroit's First American Decade, 1796–1805.* Ann Arbor: University of Michigan Press, 1948.

Baldwin, Robert E. "Patterns of Development in Newly Settled Regions." *Manchester School of Social and Economic Studies* 24 (1956): 161–79.

Ball, John. "Physical Geography of Kent County." *Michigan Pioneer and Historical Collections* 1 (1877): 214–17.

Ball, Lucy. "Early Days in Grand Rapids." *Michigan Pioneer and Historical Collections* 39 (1912): 92–104.

Barber, Edward W. "The Vermontville Colony: Its Genesis and History, with Personal Sketches of the Colonists." *Michigan Pioneer and Historical Collections* 28 (1897–98): 197–265.

———. "Beginnings in Eaton County: Its Earliest Settlements and Settlers." *Michigan Pioneer and Historical Collections* 29 (1899–1900): 337–97.

———. "Recollections and Lessons of Pioneer Boyhood." *Michigan Pioneer and Historical Collections* 31 (1902): 178–227.

Barnett, LeRoy. "Milestones in Michigan Mapping: Early Settlement." *Michigan History* 63 (September/October 1979): 34–43.

———. "Milestones in Michigan Mapping: Modern Waymarks." *Michigan History* 63 (November/December 1979): 29–38.

———. "Michigan Land Grants to German Organizations." *Michigan Surveyor* 19, no. 6 (1984): 15–19.

———. "State Building Lands: Giving Michigan Grounds for Complaint." *Michigan Surveyor* 22, no. 6 (1987): 10, 12.

———. "Internal Improvement Lands: A Down-to-Earth Solution for Developing Michigan Transportation." *Michigan Surveyor* 25, no. 5 (1990): 10–12.

———. "Early Improvements of the St. Joseph River." *Inland Seas* 46 (1990): 307–17.

———. "Mapping Michigan's First Land Sales," *Michigan Out-of-Doors* 53, no. 2 (February 1999): 44–47.

Barnett, LeRoy, comp. *Checklist of Printed Maps of the Middle West to 1900.* Vol. 5, *Michigan,* gen. ed. Robert W. Karrow. Boston: G. K. Hall, 1981.

Barnouw, Victor. *Culture and Personality.* Homewood, Ill.: Dorsey Press, 1963.

Bartlett, Richard A. *The New Country: A Social History of the American Frontier, 1776–1890.* New York: Oxford University Press, 1974.

Bateman, Fred, and Thomas Weiss. *A Deplorable Scarcity.* Chapel Hill: University of North Carolina Press, 1981.

Bates, George C. "By-Gones of Detroit." *Michigan Pioneer and Historical Collections* 22 (1893): 305–404.

Baxter, Albert. "Some Fragments of Beginnings in the Grand River Valley." *Michigan Pioneer and Historical Collections* 17 (1890): 325–31.

———. *History of the City of Grand Rapids, Michigan.* New York: Munsell, 1891.

———. "First 'Yankee' Family at Grand Rapids." *Michigan Pioneer and Historical Collections* 29 (1899–1900): 503–5.

Beal, W. J. "Pioneer Life in Southern Michigan in the Thirties." *Michigan Pioneer and Historical Collections* 32 (1902): 236–46.

———. *History of the Michigan Agricultural College and Biographical Sketches of Trustees and Professors.* East Lansing, Mich.: Michigan Agricultural College, 1915.

Beardsley, A. M. "Reminiscences and Scenes of Backwoods and Pioneer Life." *Michigan Pioneer and Historical Collections* 28 (1897–98): 137–41.

Beaumont, Olga, and J. W. Y. Higgs. "Agriculture: Farm Implements." In *A History of Technology,* vol. 4, *The Industrial Revolution, c. 1750 to c. 1850,* edited by Charles Singer, E.

J. Holmyard, A. R. Hall, and Trevor I. Williams, 1–12. New York: Oxford University Press, 1958.

Beebe, Silas. "A Trip from Utica, New York to Ingham County, Michigan." *Michigan Pioneer and Historical Collections* 1 (1877): 187–92.

Beforooz, Fatemeh. "The Role of Rural Development and Farmer's Preferences in Changing the Viability and Spatial Distributions of Central Villages." Ph.D. dissertation, Michigan State University. Ann Arbor, Mich.: University Microfilms International, 1985.

Bell, Howard Holman. *A Survey of the Negro Convention Movement, 1830–1861.* New York: Arno Press and the New York Times, 1969.

Benevolo, Leonardo. *The Origins of Modern Town Planning.* Cambridge, Mass.: M.I.T. Press, 1971.

Bennett, Richard, and John Elton. *History of Corn Milling,* vol. 2, *Watermills and Windmills.* New York: Burt Franklin, 1898.

Bennison, David J. "The Measurement of Settlement Centrality." *Professional Geographer* 30 (1978): 371–76.

Berry, Brian J. L. *Geography of Market Centers and Retail Distribution.* Englewood Cliffs, N.J.: Prentice-Hall, 1967.

———. *America's Utopian Experiments: Communal Havens from Long-Wave Crises.* Hanover, N.H.: University Press of New England, 1992.

Berry, Thomas Senior. *Western Prices before 1861: A Study of the Cincinnati Market.* Cambridge, Mass.: Harvard University Press, 1943.

Bestor, Arthur Eugene. *Backwoods Utopias, the Sectarian and Owenite Phases of Communitarian Socialism in America: 1663–1829.* Philadelphia: University of Pennsylvania Press, 1950.

Biddle, John. "Discourse Delivered Before the Historical Society of Michigan." In *Historical and Scientific Sketches of Michigan,* 149–75. Detroit: Stephen Wells and George L. Whitney, 1834.

Bidwell, Percy Wells, and John I. Falconer. *History of Agriculture in the Northern United States, 1620–1860.* Washington, D.C.: Carnegie Institution of Washington, 1925. Reprint, New York: Peter Smith, 1941.

Bieder, Robert E. "Kinship as a Factor in Migration." *Journal of Marriage and the Family* 35 (1973): 429–39.

Billington, Ray Allen. *Westward Expansion: A History of the American Frontier.* New York: Macmillan, 1967.

———. *Land of Savagery, Land of Promise: The European Image of the American Frontier in the Nineteenth Century.* New York: W. W. Norton, 1981.

Bingham, S. D. *Early History of Michigan, with Biographies of State Officers, Members of Congress, Judges and Legislators.* Lansing, Mich.: Thorp and Godfrey, 1888.

Birch, Brian. "British Evaluations of the Forest Openings and Prairie Edges of the North-Central States, 1800–1850." In *The Frontier, Comparative Studies,* vol. 2, edited by William W. Savage and Stephen I. Thompson, 167–92. Norman: University of Oklahoma Press, 1979.

Bishop, Levi. "Recollections." *Michigan Pioneer and Historical Collections* 1 (1877): 125–26.

Bissell, H. N. "The Early Settlement of Mt. Clemens and Vicinity." *Michigan Pioneer and Historical Collections* 5 (1884): 450–69.

Bjorklund, Elaine M. "Ideology and Culture Exemplified in Southwestern Michigan." *Annals of the Association of American Geographers* 54 (1964): 227–41.

Bloget, Lorin. *Climatology of the United States, and the Temperate Latitudes of the North American Continent.* Philadelphia: J. P. Lippincott, 1857.

Blois, John T. *1838 Gazetteer of the State of Michigan.* Detroit: Sydney L. Rood,1838. Reprint, Knightstown, Ind.: Bookmark, 1979.

Bogue, Allan G. "Land Credit for Northern Farmers, 1789–1940." *Agricultural History* 50 (1976): 68–100.

Bogue, Allan G., and Margaret Beattie Bogue. "'Profits' and the Frontier Speculator." In *The Public Lands: Studies in the History of the Public Domain,* edited by Vernon Carstensen, 369–394. Madison: University of Wisconsin Press, 1963.

Bonner, Richard Illenden. *Memoirs of Lenawee County, Michigan.* Madison, Wisc.: Western Historical Society, 1909.

Bowman, Isaiah. *The Pioneer Fringe.* American Geographical Society, Special Publication no. 13, New York , 1931.

Bradley, Cyrus P. "Journal of Cyrus P. Bradley, with an Introductory Note by George H. Twiss." *Ohio Archaeological and Historical Society Publications* 15 (1906): 207–70.

Bradshaw, James Stanford. "Grand Rapids Furniture Beginnings." *Michigan History* 52 (1968): 279–98.

Brainard, Alvah. *A Pioneer History of the Township of Grand Blanc, Genesee County, Michigan.* Flint, Mich.: Globe Power Presses, 1878.

Braudel, Fernand. *The Mediterranean and the Mediterranean World in the Age of Philip II.* 2 vols. Translated by Sian Reynolds. New York: Harper & Row, 1966.

———. *The Structures of Everyday Life.* Vol. 1 of *Civilization and Capitalism, 15th–18th Century.* Translated by Sian Reynolds. New York: Harper and Row, 1981.

———. *The Perspective of the World.* Vol. 3 of *Civilization and Capitalism, 15th–18th century.* Translated by Sian Reynolds. New York: Harper and Row, 1984.

———. *History and Environment.* Vol. 1 of *The Identity of France.* Translated by Sian Reynolds. New York: Harper and Row, 1988.

Brewer, Lawrence G., Thomas W. Hodler, and Henry A. Raup. "Presettlement Vegetation of Southwestern Michigan." *Michigan Botanist* 23 (1984): 153–56.

Bridenbaugh, Carl. *Vexed and Troubled Englishmen, 1590–1642.* New York: Oxford University Press, 1968.

Bronson, William. "Pioneer History of Clinton County." *Michigan Pioneer and Historical Collections* 5 (1884): 325–33.

"Brooklyn and Vicinity, the Village—Its Population and Business—Early Settlement— Interesting Incidents of Pioneer Life—The Farming Interest, etc." *Michigan Pioneer and Historical Collections* 4 (1883): 271–75.

Brown, E. B. "Early Recollections of the Village of Tecumseh." *Michigan Pioneer and Historical Collection* 2 (1880): 387–90.

Brown, E. Lakin. "Autobiographical Notes, edited by A. Ada Brown." *Michigan Pioneer and Historical Collections* 30 (1905): 424–94.

Brown, Mrs. Hermon Landon, comp. *Stray Leaves from Pioneer Days.* Parma, Mich.: Parma News Printers, [1920].

Brown, Samuel. *The Western Gazetteer; or Emigrant's Directory, Containing a Geographical Description of the Western States and Territories.* Auburn, N.Y.: H. C. Southwick, 1817.

Bruce, Alfred W. *The Steam Locomotive in America: Its Development in the Twentieth Century.* New York: Bonanza Books, 1952.

Bruchey, Stuart. "The Business Economy of Marketing Change, 1790–1840: A Study of Sources of Efficiency." *Agricultural History* 46 (1972): 211–26.

Bruins, Elton J. "Albertus Christiaan Van Raalte: Funding His Vision of a Christian Colony." Paper presented at the 8th Biennial Conference of the Association for the Advancement of Dutch American Studies, Holland, Mich., 19 September 1991.

Buckler, Billy D. "Why Does Michigan's Meridian-Baseline Have Two Initial Points?" In *Special Instructions to Deputy Surveyors in Michigan, 1808–1854,* 376–77. Lansing, Mich.: Michigan Museum of Surveying, 1990.

Burgess, Sam, ed. *The National Program for Conservation of Germ Plasm.* North Central, Northeastern, Southern, and Western State Agricultural Experiment Stations and Agricultural Research Service, U.S. Department of Agriculture. Athens: University of Georgia, 1971.

Burgh, Robert. *The Region of Three Oaks.* Three Oaks, Mich.: Edward K. Warren Foundation, 1939.

Burke, Thomas Aquinas. *Ohio Lands: A Short History.* Columbus: Ohio Auditor of State, 1987.

Burt, A. L. "If Turner Had Looked at Canada, Australia, and New Zealand When He Wrote about the West." In *The Frontier in Perspective,* edited by Walker D. Wyman and Clifton B. Kroeber, 59–77. Madison: University of Wisconsin Press, 1957.

Burton, Ann, and Conrad Burton. *Michigan Quakers: Abstracts of Fifteen Meetings of the Society of Friends, 1831–1960.* Decatur, Mich.: Glyndwr Resources, 1989.

Busby, Joseph. "Recollections of Pioneer Life in Michigan." *Michigan Pioneer and Historical Collections* 9 (1886): 118–28.

Butler, Albert F. "Rediscovering Michigan's Prairies." *Michigan History* 31 (1947): 267–86; 32 (1948): 15–36; 33 (1948): 117–30, 220–31.

Calkins, Edmund A. "Old Trails of Central Michigan." *Michigan History* 12 (1928): 327–49.

———. "Railroads of Michigan since 1850." *Michigan History* 13 (1929): 5–25.

Callahan, Colleen M., and William K. Hutchenson. "Antebellum Interregional Trade in Agricultural Goods: Preliminary Results." *Journal of Economic History* 40 (1980): 25–31.

Callender, Charles. "Great Lakes-Riverine Sociopolitical Organization." In *Handbook of North American Indians,* vol. 15, *Northeast,* edited by Bruce G. Trigger, 610–21. Washington, D.C.: Smithsonian Institution, 1978.

————. "Miami." In *Handbook of North American Indians,* vol. 15, *Northeast,* edited by Bruce
    G. Trigger, 681–89. Washington, D.C.: Smithsonian Institution, 1978.
Campbell, Daniel R. "Prosperity and Power: The Success and Failure of Potawatomi Leadership
    in Michigan." *Michigan Archaeologist* 30 (1984): 125–36.
————. "Village and the World: The Shaping of Culture in Marshall, Michigan." Ph.D. diss.,
    Michigan State University (Ann Arbor, Mich.: University Microfilms, 1986).
Cannon, George H. "History of the Township of Shelby, Macomb County, Michigan." *Michigan
    Pioneer and Historical Collections* 17 (1890): 419–29.
Carr, William M. "Settlement of Williamstown—Pioneer Life." *Michigan Pioneer and Historical
    Collections* 18 (1891): 448–53.
Carrington, C. E. *The British Overseas,* part 1, *Making of the Empire.* Cambridge: Cambridge
    University Press, 1968.
Carson, H. H. "Village Trails and Mounds in Michigan." *American Antiquarian* 9 (July 1887):
    237–38.
Carter, Everett. *The American Idea: The Literary Response to American Optimism.* Chapel Hill:
    University of North Carolina Press, 1977.
Carwardine, Richard J. *Evangelicals and Politics in Antebellum America.* New Haven, Conn.: Yale
    University Press, 1993.
Casagrande, Joseph B., Stephen I. Thompson, and Philip D. Young. "Colonization as a Research
    Frontier: The Ecuadorian Case." In *Process and Pattern in Culture: Essays in Honor of Julian
    H. Steward,* edited by Robert A. Manners, 281–325. Chicago: Aldine, 1964.
Cassedy, James H. *Medicine and American Growth, 1800–1860.* Madison: University of
    Wisconsin Press, 1986.
Chamberlain, E. *1850 Indiana Gazetteer, or Topographical Directory of the State of Indiana.*
    Indianapolis: By the author, 1850. Reprint, Knightstown, Ind.: Bookmark, 1977.
Chamberlain, Henry. "A Michigan Octogenarian." *Michigan Pioneer and Historical Collections*
    35 (1907): 662–69.
Champion, Timothy C. Introduction. to *Centre and Periphery: Comparative Studies in
    Archaeology,* edited by Timothy C. Champion, 1–21. London: Unwin Hyman, 1989.
Chandler, Alfred D. *The Railroads: The Nation's First Big Business.* New York: Harcourt, Brace
    and World, 1965.
Chandler, William J. "The Antebellum Grain Trade in Monroe, Michigan." Master's thesis,
    Wayne State University, Detroit, Michigan, 1999.
Chapin, William. *A Complete Reference Gazetteer of the United States of North America.* New
    York: W. Chapin and J. B. Taylor, 1839.
Charbonneau, Hubert. *The First French Canadians: Pioneers in the St. Lawrence Valley.*
    Translated by Paola Colozzo. Newark: University of Delaware Press, 1993.
Chase, Enoch. "Coldwater in 1831." *Michigan Pioneer and Historical Collections* 7 (1886):
    346–48.
Chase, Lew Allen. "Michigan's Share in the Establishment of Improved Transportation between
    the East and the West." *Michigan Pioneer and Historical Collections* 38 (1912): 588–609.

————. *Rural Michigan.* New York: Macmillan, 1922.

————. "Hiram Moore and the Invention of the Harvester." *Michigan History* 13 (1929): 501–5.

Chase, Supply. "Early History of the Baptist Church in Michigan." *Michigan Pioneer and Historical Collections* 1 (1877): 466–68.

————. "A Pioneer Minister." *Michigan Pioneer and Historical Collections* 5 (1884): 52–60.

Chase, Warren. *The Life-Line of the Lone One; Or Autobiography of the World's Child.* Boston: Bela Marsh, 1857.

Choquette, Leslie. *Frenchmen into Peasants: Modernity and Tradition in the Peopling of French Canada.* Harvard Historical Studies, vol. 123. Cambridge, Mass.: Harvard University Press, 1997.

Christaller, W. *Central Places in Southern Germany.* Translated by C. W. Baskin. Englewood Cliffs, N.J.: Prentice-Hall, 1966.

Christiancy, I. P. "Recollections of the Early History of the City and County of Monroe." *Michigan Pioneer and Historical Collections* 6 (1883): 361–73.

"The City of Battle Creek—Its Early History, Growth, and Present Condition." *Michigan Pioneer and Historical Collections* 3 (1881): 347–67.

City of Grand Rapids and Kent County, Michigan, Up to Date, Containing Biographical Sketches of Prominent and Representative Citizens. Logansport, Ind.: Bowen, 1900.

"The City of Ionia. Its First Settlement and Early History." *Michigan Pioneer and Historical Collections* 3 (1881): 470–90.

Clanin, Douglas E. "Internal Improvements in National Politics, 1816–1830." In *Transportation and the Early Nation,* 30–60. Indianapolis: Indiana Historical Society, 1982.

Clapp, Mrs. M. W. "The Long Ago." *Michigan Pioneer and Historical Collections* 4 (1883): 512–14.

Clark, Andrew Hill. "Suggestions for the Geographical Study of Agricultural Change in the United States, 1790–1840." *Agricultural History* 46 (1972): 155–72.

Clark, Charles F. *Michigan State Gazetteer and Business Directory for 1863–4.* Detroit: By the author, 1863.

Clark, Christopher. *The Roots of American Capitalism: Western Massachusetts, 1780–1860.* Ithaca, N.Y.: Cornell University Press, 1990.

Clark, George. "Recollections." *Michigan Pioneer and Historical Collections* 1 (1877): 501–7.

Clark, John G. *The Grain Trade in the Old Northwest.* Urbana: University of Illinois Press, 1966.

Clark, Victor. *History of Manufactures in the United States,* vol. 1, *1607–1860.* Washington, D.C.: Carnegie Institute, 1929. Reprint, New York: Peter Smith, 1949.

Clark, William. "Livingston County Pioneers." *Michigan Pioneer and Historical Collections* 1 (1877): 252–58.

Cleland, Charles E. *Rites of Conquest: The History and Culture of Michigan's Native Americans.* Ann Arbor: University of Michigan Press, 1992.

Clemson, Thomas G. "Feritlizers," in U.S. Commissioner of Patents, *Report, 1859, Agriculture,* 136–78. Washington, D.C.: George W. Bowman, 1860.

Clifton, James A. *The Prairie People: Continuity and Change in Potawatomi Indian Culture, 1665–1965.* Lawrence: Regents Press of Kansas, 1977.

———. *The Pokagons, 1683–1983: Catholic Potawatomi Indians of the St. Joseph Valley.* Lanham, Md.: University Press of America, 1984.

Clinton County, Michigan, Office of the Register of Deeds. John Fedewa, Will, Liber 88, p. 342, 22 December 1896, St. Johns, Mich.

Clubb, Henry S. "The Fruit Regions of Michigan." *Twelfth Annual Report of the Secretary of the Michigan State Board of Agriculture for the Year 1873,* 49–106. Lansing: W. S. George, 1875.

Cochrane, Willard W. *The Development of American Agriculture: An Historical Analysis.* Minneapolis: University of Minnesota Press, 1979.

Coffinberry, S. C. "Incidents Connected with the First Settlement of Nottawa-Sippi Prairie in St. Joseph County." *Michigan Pioneer and Historical Collections* 2 (1880): 489–501.

Cole, Arthur H. "Cyclical and Sectional Variations in the Sale of Public Lands, 1816–1860." In *The Public Lands: Studies in the History of the Public Domain,* edited by Vernon Carstensen, 229–51. Madison: University of Wisconsin Press, 1963.

Cole, J. L. "J. L. Cole's Journal of a Pedestrian Tour from Detroit to Sagana River in 1822." *Michigan Pioneer and Historical Collections* 2 (1880): 470–75.

Cole, Maurice F., comp. *Voices from the Wilderness.* Ann Arbor, Mich.: Edwards Brothers, 1961.

Coleman, Peter J. "Restless Grant County: Americans on the Move." In *The Old Northwest: Studies in Regional History, 1787–1910,* edited by Harry N. Scheiber, 279–87. Lincoln: University of Nebraska Press, 1969.

Colton, C. *Tour of the American Lakes, and Among the Indians of the North-West Territory, in 1830: Disclosing the Character and Prospects of the Indian Race,* 2 vols. London: Frederick Westley and A. H. Davis, 1833.

Comer, P. J., D. A. Albert, H. A. Wells, B. L. Hart, J. B. Raab, D. L. Price, D. M. Kashian, R. A. Comer, and D. W. Schuen. *Michigan's Native Landscape, as Interpreted from the General Land Office Surveys, 1816–1856.* Lansing: Michigan Department of Natural Resources/Nature Conservancy, Michigan Natural Resources Features Inventory, 1995.

Comer, P. J., D. A. Albert, H. A. Wells, B. L. Hart, J. B. Raab, D. L. Price, D. M. Kashian, R. A. Comer, and D. W. Schuen (map interpretation); T. R. Leibfried, M. B. Austin, C. J. DeLain, L. Prange-Gregory, L. J. Scrimger, and J. G. Spitzley (digital map production). *Michigan's Presettlement Vegetation, as Interpreted from the General Land Office Surveys, 1816–1856.* Lansing: Michigan Department of Natural Resources/Nature Conservancy, Michigan Natural Features Inventory, 1995.

Comin, John, and Harold F. Fredsell. *History of the Presbyterian Church in Michigan.* Ann Arbor, Mich.: Ann Arbor Press, 1950.

Conzen, Kathleen Neils. "Peasant Pioneers: Generational Succession among German Farmers in Frontier Minnesota." In *The Countryside in the Age of Capitalist Transformation: Essays in the Social History of Rural America,* edited by Steven Hahn and Jonathan Prude, 259–92. Chapel Hill: University of North Carolina Press, 1985.

Conzen, Michael P. "Local Migration Systems in Nineteenth-Century Iowa." *Geographical Review* 64 (1974): 339–61.

———. "Capital Flows and the Developing Urban Hierarchy: State Bank Capital in Wisconsin, 1854–1895." *Economic Geography* 51 (1975): 319–38.

———. "The Maturing Urban System in the United States, 1840–1910." *Annals of the Association of American Geographers* 67 (1977): 88–108.

Cook, Charles W. "The Influence of the Lumber Industry upon the Salt Industry in Michigan." *Journal of Geography* 15 (1916): 117–25.

Cooley, Thomas M. "Address on Laying the Cornerstone of the New Courthouse for Lenawee County at Adrian, June 28, 1884." *Michigan Pioneer and Historical Collections* 7 (1886): 521–34.

Cooper, James Fenimore. *The Oak-Openings; or the Bee Hunter.* New York: Hurd and Houghton, 1848.

Coornaert, E. L. J. "European Economic Institutions and the New World: The Chartered Companies." In *The Cambridge Economic History of Europe,* vol. 4, *The Economy of Expanding Europe in the Sixteenth and Seventeenth Centuries,* edited by E. E. Rich and C. H. Wilson, 223–75. Cambridge: Cambridge University Press, 1967.

Cootner, Paul H. "The Economic Impact of the Railroad Innovation." In *The Railroad and the Space Program: An Exploration in Historical Analogy,* edited by Bruce Mazlish, 107–26. Cambridge, Mass.: M.I.T. Press, 1965.

Copley, A. B. "Early Settlement of Southwestern Michigan." *Michigan Pioneer and Historical Collections* 5 (1884): 144–51.

"Copy of a Letter from a Gentleman in the Michigan Territory to His Friend in Connecticut, Dated Oct. 1, 1823." *Michigan Pioneer and Historical Collections* 7 (1886): 74–75.

Cornell, Stephen. "The Transformation of Tribe: Organization and Self-Concept in Native American Ethnicities." *Ethnic and Racial Studies* 11 (1988): 27–47.

Cox, Anna-Lisa. "A Pocket of Freedom: Blacks in Covert, Michigan, in the Nineteenth Century." *Michigan Historical Review* 21, no. 1 (1995): 1–18.

Cranmer, H. Jerome. "Canal Investment, 1815–1860." In *Trends in the American Economy in the Nineteenth Century,* Vol. 24: *Studies in Income and Wealth,* 547–70. New York: National Bureau of Economic Research, 1960.

Crawford, R. C. "Reminiscences of Pioneer Life in Michigan." *Michigan Pioneer and Historical Collections* 4 (1883): 41–53.

———. "Fifty-Two Years of Itinerant Life in the Michigan Conference of the M. E. Church." *Michigan Pioneer and Historical Collections* 22 (1893): 266–81.

———. "Reminiscences of Seventy Years in Michigan." *Michigan Pioneer and Historical Collections* 26 (1894–95): 585–93.

Cronon, William. *Nature's Metropolis: Chicago and the Great West.* New York: W. W. Norton, 1991.

Cross, William H. "Early Michigan." *Michigan Pioneer and Historical Collections* 10 (1886): 54–57.

Cummings, Richard O. *The American and His Food.* Chicago: University of Chicago Press, 1940.

Curti, Merle. *The Making of an American Community: A Case Study of Democracy in a Frontier County.* Stanford, Calif.: Stanford University Press, 1959.

Curtis, B. F. "Buildings of Ottawa County, Past, Present, and Future." *Michigan Pioneer and Historical Collections* 9 (1886): 292–95.

Daboll, S. B. *Past and Present of Clinton County.* Chicago: S. J. Clarke, 1906.

Dain, Floyd Russell. *Every House a Frontier: Detroit's Economic Progress, 1815–1825.* Detroit: Wayne State University Press, 1956.

Dalton, George. "Primitive Money." *American Anthropologist* 67 (1965): 44–66.

Danford, Ormond S. "The Social and Economic Effects of Lumbering on Michigan, 1835–1890." *Michigan History* 26 (1942): 346–59.

Danhof, Clarence H. "Farm-Making Costs and the 'Safety Valve': 1850–60." *Journal of Political Economy* 49 (1941): 317–59.

———. *Change in Agriculture: The Northern United States, 1820–1870.* Cambridge, Mass.: Harvard University Press, 1969.

Darby, William. *A Tour from the City of New York, to Detroit, in the Michigan Territory, Made Between the 2d of May and the 22d of September, 1818.* New York: By the author, 1819. Reprint, Chicago: Quadrangle Books, 1962.

Daugherty, Nina. "Incidents of Early Days in Allegan County." *Michigan Pioneer and Historical Collections* 38 (1912): 156–63.

Davenport, Eugene. *Timberland Times.* Urbana: University of Illinois Press, 1950.

David, George. "Diary of George David [Extracts], a Trip from London to Chicago in 1833." *Michigan History* 18 (1934): 53–66.

Davies, Wayne K. D. "Centrality and the Central Place Hierarchy." *Urban Studies* 4 (1967): 61–79.

Davis, Charles M. "The Hydrographic Regions of Michigan." *Papers of the Michigan Academy of Science, Arts, and Letters* 16 (1932): 221–15.

Davis, David Brion. *The Problem of Slavery in Western Culture.* Ithaca, N.Y.: Cornell University Press, 1966.

———. *The Problem of Slavery in the Age of Revolution, 1770–1823.* Ithaca, N.Y.: Cornell University Press, 1975.

Davis, John. "Transportation and American Settlement Patterns." In *The American Environment: Perceptions and Policies,* edited by J. Wreford Watson and Timothy O'Riordan, 169–82. London: John Wiley & Sons, 1976.

Davis, Kingsley, and W. Lloyd Warner. "Structural Analysis of Kinship." *American Anthropologist* 39 (1937): 291–313.

Dawson, C. A. "The Social Structure of a Pioneer Area as Illustrated by the Peace River District." In *Pioneer Settlement: Comparative Studies by Twenty-Six Authors,* edited by W. R. G. Joerg, 37–49. New York: American Geographical Society, 1932.

————. *The Settlement of the Peace River Country: A Study of a Pioneer Area.* Canadian *Frontiers of Settlement,* vol. 6, edited by W. A. Mackintosh and W. L. G. Joerg. Toronto: Macmillan, 1934.

Day, John E. "Sketches and Incidents Concerning the Settlement of Macomb County." *Michigan Pioneer and Historical Collections* 4 (1881): 307–15.

DeForth, Peter Wallace. "The Spatial Evolution of the German-American Culture Region in Clinton and Ionia Counties, Michigan." Master's thesis, Department of Geography, Michigan State University, 1970.

Delle Donne, Carmen R. *Federal Census Schedules, 1850–80: Primary Sources for Historical Research.* National Archives and Records Service, General Services Administration, Reference Information Paper, no. 67. Washington, D.C.: Government Printing Office, 1973.

Demos, John. *A Little Commonwealth: Family Life in Plymouth Colony.* New York: Oxford University Press, 1970.

de Soto, Hernando. *The Other Path: The Invisible Revolution in the Third World.* New York: Harper & Row, 1989.

de Tocqueville, Alexis. *Democracy in America.* Vol. 2. Edited by Phillips Bradley. New York: Vintage Books, 1954.

Diamond, Sigmund. "An Experiment in 'Feudalism': French Canada in the Seventeenth Century." In *Essays on American Colonial History,* edited by Paul Goodman, 49–66. New York: Holt, Rinehart and Winston, 1967.

Dice, Lee R. "A Preliminary Classification of the Major Terrestrial Ecologic Communities of Michigan, Exclusive of Isle Royale." *Papers of the Michigan Academy of Science, Arts, and Letters* 16 (1932): 217–39.

————. *The Biotic Provinces of North America.* Ann Arbor: University of Michigan Press, 1943.

Dickey, Charles. "Early Settlement of Calhoun County." *Michigan Pioneer and Historical Collections* 1 (1877): 129–32.

Dodd, Donald B., and Wynelle S. Dodd. *Historical Statistics of the United States, 1790–1970,* vol. 2, *The Midwest.* University: University of Alabama Press, 1976.

Dodge, Mrs. Frank P. "Marking Terminus of Erie and Kalamazoo Railroad." *Michigan Pioneer and Historical Collections* 38 (1912): 491–98.

Dorr, John A., Jr., and Donald F. Eschman. *Geology of Michigan.* Ann Arbor: University of Michigan Press, 1988.

Doyle, Don Harrison. *The Social Order of a Frontier Community: Jacksonville, Illinois, 1825–70.* Urbana: University of Illinois Press, 1978.

Drake, Thomas J. "History of Oakland County." *Michigan Pioneer and Historical Collections* 4 (1883): 559–72.

Driggs, Alfred L. "Early Days in Michigan." *Michigan Pioneer and Historical Collections* 10 (1886): 57–60.

DuBoff, Richard B. "The Telegraph and the Structure of Markets in the United States, 1845–1890." *Research in Economic History* 8 (1983): 253–77.

Duffield, D. Bethune. "The Underdeveloped Regions and Resources of the State of Michigan, with Some Practical Suggestions in Reference to Their Early Occupancy and Development." In *Three Lectures Delivered before the Michigan State Agricultural Society, at Its Annual Meeting at Lansing, January 17, 1865*, 3–37. Lansing, Mich.: John A. Kerr, 1865.

Dunbar, Willis F. *Kalamazoo and How It Grew*. Kalamazoo: Western Michigan University, 1959.

———. "Frontiersmanship in Michigan." *Michigan History* 50 (1966): 97–110.

———. *All Aboard! A History of Railroads in Michigan*. Grand Rapids, Mich.: William B. Eerdmans, 1969.

———. *Michigan: A History of the Wolverine State*, revised ed. by George S. May. Grand Rapids, Mich.: William B. Eerdmans, 1980.

Duncan, James, and Nancy Duncan. "(Re)Reading the Landscape," *Environment and Planning D: Society and Space* 6 (1988): 117–26.

Durant, Samuel W. *History of Ingham and Eaton Counties, Michigan*. Philadelphia: Evarts and Abbot, 1880.

———. *History of Kalamazoo County, Michigan*. Philadelphia: Evarts and Abbot, 1880.

———. *History of Oakland County, Michigan*. S. H. Evert & Co., Philadelphia, 1877.

Durham, Philip, and Everett L. Jones, ed. *The Frontier in American Literature*. New York: Odyssey Press, 1969.

Dwight, Timothy. *Travels; in New England and New York*. 4 vols. New Haven, Conn.: T. Dwight, 1822.

Earle, Carville. "Regional Economic Development West of the Appalachians, 1815–1860." In *North America, the Historical Geography of a Changing Continent*, edited by Robert D. Mitchell and Paul Groves, 172–97. Totowa, N.J.: Rowman and Littlefield, 1987.

Earle, Carville, and Ronald Hoffman. "Staple Crops and Urban Development in the Eighteenth-Century South." *Perspectives in American History* 10 (1976): 7–80.

"Early History of Olivet College." *Michigan Pioneer and Historical Collections* 3 (1881): 408–12.

East, Robert A. "Puritanism and New England Settlement." *New England Quarterly* 17 (1944): 255–64.

Eastman, R. J. *IDRISI: Version 4.1*. Worcester, Mass.: Clark University Graduate School of Geography, 1993.

Eblen, Jack E. "An Analysis of Nineteenth-Century Frontier Populations." *Demography* 2 (1965): 399–413.

Eccles, W. J. *The Canadian Frontier, 1534–1760*. New York: Holt, Rinehart and Winston, 1969.

Edmunds, R. David, and Joseph L. Peyser. *The Fox Wars: The Mesquakie Challenge to New France*. Norman: University of Oklahoma Press, 1993.

Edsall, Robert M. "Data Classification II." National Center for Geographic Information and Analysis (NCGIA) GIS Core Curriculum for Technical Programs, Unit 47: On-Screen Visualization.<http://www.ncgia.ucsb.edu/education/curricula/cctp/units/unit47/html/mas_class.html>

Edwards, Abraham. "A Sketch of Pioneer Life." *Michigan Pioneer and Historical Collections* 3 (1881): 148–51.

Eichenlaub, Val L. *Weather and Climate of the Great Lakes Region.* Notre Dame, Ind.: University of Notre Dame Press, 1979.

Ellis, C. Hamilton. "The Development of Railway Engineering." In *A History of Technology,* vol. 5, *The Late Nineteenth Century, c. 1850 to c. 1900,* edited by Charles Singer, E. J. Holmyard, A. R. Hall, and Trevor I. Williams, 322–49. New York: Oxford University Press, 1958.

Ellis, David M. *Michigan Postal History: The Post Offices, 1805–1986.* Oak Grove, Ore.: Depot, 1993.

Ellis, Franklin. *History of Genesee County, Michigan.* Philadelphia: Everts and Abbott, 1879.

———. *History of Allegan and Barry Counties, Michigan.* Philadelphia: D. W. Ensign, 1880.

———. *History of Berrien and Van Buren Counties, Michigan.* Philadelphia: D. W. Ensign, 1880.

———. *History of Livingston County, Michigan.* Philadelphia: Everts and Abbott, 1880.

———. *History of Shiawassee and Clinton Counties, Michigan.* Philadelphia: D. W. Ensign, 1880.

Emery, B. Frank. "Fort Saginaw." *Michigan History* 30 (1946): 476–503.

Emigrant's Guide, or Pocket Geography, of the United States: and from the Eastern to the Western States. Philadelphia: Phillips & Speer, 1818.

Ernst, Joseph A., and H. Roy Merrens. "Camden's Turrets Pierce the Skies!": The Urban Process in the Southern Colonies during the Eighteenth Century. *William and Mary Quarterly,* Ser. 3, 30 (1973): 549–74.

Evans, Estwick. *A Pedestrious Tour of Four Thousand Miles, Through the Western States and Territories, During the Winter and Spring of 1818.* Concord, N.H.: Joseph C. Spear, 1819.

Everett, Franklin. *Memorials of the Grand River Valley.* Chicago: Chicago Legal News Co., 1878. Reprint, Grand Rapids, Mich.: Grand Rapids Historical Society, 1984.

Faragher, John Mack. "Open-Country Community: Sugar Creek Illinois, 1820–1850." In *The Countryside in the Age of Capitalist Transformation: Essays in the Social History of Rural America,* edited by Steven Hahn and Jonathan Prude, 233–58. Chapel Hill: University of North Carolina Press, 1985.

———. *Sugar Creek: Life on the Illinois Prairie.* New Haven, Conn.: Yale University Press, 1986.

Farmer, John. *The Emigrant's Guide; or Pocket Gazetteer of the Surveyed Part of Michigan.* Albany: B. D. Packard, 1830.

Farmer, Silas. *History of Detroit and Wayne County and Early Michigan.* New York: Munsell, 1890. Reprint, Detroit: Gale Research Co., 1969.

Fatout, Paul. *Indiana Canals.* West Lafayette, Ind.: Purdue University Press, 1972.

Faust, E. C. "Clinical and Public Health Aspects of Malaria in the United States from an Historical Perspective." *American Journal of Tropical Medicine* 25 (1945): 185–201.

Faux, W. *Memorable Days in America; Being a Journal of a Tour of the United States.* London: W. Simpkin and R. Marshall, 1823. Reprinted in *Early Western Travels, 1748–1846,* vol. 11, edited by Reuben Gold Thwaites. Cleveland: A. H. Clark Co., 1904–5.

Fearon, Henry Bradshaw. *Sketches of America: A Narrative of a Journey of Five Thousand Miles through the Eastern and Western States of America.* London: Longman, Hurst, Rees, Orme, and Brown, 1818. Reprint, New York: Benjamin Blom, 1969.

Feest, Johanna, and Christian F. Feest. "Ottawa." In *Handbook of North American Indians,* vol. 15, *Northeast,* edited by Bruce G. Trigger, 772–86. Washington, D.C.: Smithsonian Institution, 1978.

Feller, Daniel. *The Public Lands in Jacksonian Politics.* Madison: University of Wisconsin Press, 1984.

Ferrell, David. "Settlement along the Detroit Frontier, 1760–1796." *Michigan History* 52 (1968): 89–107.

Field, Arthur. "Road Patterns of the Southern Peninsula of Michigan." *Papers of the Michigan Academy of Science, Arts, and Letters* 14 (1930): 305–28.

Fields, Harold B. "Free Negroes in Cass County before the Civil War." *Michigan History* 44 (1960): 375–83.

Firth, Raymond. "Social Organization and Social Change." *Journal of the Royal Anthropological Institute* 84 (1954): 1–20.

Fischer, David Hackett. *Albion's Seed: Four British Folkways in America.* New York: Oxford University Press, 1989.

Fischer, Gerald C. *American Banking Structure.* New York: Columbia University Press, 1968.

Fisher, David, and Frank Little, eds., *Compendium of History and Biography of Kalamazoo County, Mich.* Chicago: A. W. Bowen, 1906.

Fisher, Marvin. *Workshops in the Wilderness: The European Response to American Industrialization, 1830–1860.* New York: Oxford University Press, 1967.

Fishlow, Albert. "Antebellum Interregional Trade Reconsidered." *American Economic Review* 54 (1961): 354–64.

Fleckenstein, Michael, and Richard W. Pippen. "A Prairie Grove in Southwest Michigan." *Michigan Botanist* 16 (1977): 147–58.

Flinn, M. W. *An Economic and Social History of Britain, 1066–1939.* New York: Macmillan, 1965.

Florer, Warren Washburn. *Early Michigan Settlements.* Vol. 1, *Washtenaw, Westphalia, Frankenmuth, Detroit, 1848.* Ann Arbor, Mich.: By the author, 1941.

Fogel, Robert William, and Stanley L. Engerman. *Time on the Cross: The Economics of American Negro Slavery.* Boston: Little, Brown, 1974.

Foote, Edward A. "Historical Sketch of the Early Days of Eaton County." *Michigan Pioneer and Historical Collections* 4 (1883): 379–407.

Forbes, R. J. "Power to 1850." In *A History of Technology,* vol. 4, *The Industrial Revolution, c. 1750 to c. 1850,* edited by Charles Singer, E. J. Holmyard, A. R. Hall, and Trevor I. Williams, 148–67. New York: Oxford University Press, 1958.

Ford, Henry A. "The Old Moravian Mission at Mt. Clemens." *Michigan Pioneer and Historical Collections* 10 (1886): 107–19.

Forney, M. N. "American Locomotives and Cars." *Scribner's Magazine* 4 (1888): 174–99.

Foster-Carter, Aidan. "The Modes of Production Controversy." *New Left Review* 107 (1978): 47–78.

Fox, Edward Whiting. *History in Geographic Perspective: The Other France.* New York: W. W. Norton & Co., 1971.

Fox, Truman B. *History of Saginaw County, from the Year 1819 Down to the Present Time.* East Saginaw, Mich.: Enterprise Print, 1858. Reprint, Mount Pleasant, Mich.: Central Michigan University Press, n.d.

Fraizer, E. Franklin. *The Negro in the United States.* New York: Macmillan, 1949.

Friedmann, Harriet. "World Market, State, and Family Farm: Social Bases of Household Production in the Era of Wage Labor." *Comparative Studies in Society and History* 20 (1978): 545–86.

———. "Simple Commodity Production and Wage Labour in the American Plains." *Journal of Peasant Studies* 6 (1979): 71–100.

———. "Household Production and the National Economy: Concepts for the Analysis of Agrarian Formations." *Journal of Peasant Studies* 7 (1980): 158–84.

Frost, Clarence. "The Early Railroads of Southern Michigan." *Michigan Pioneer and Historical Collections* 38 (1912): 498–501.

Fuller, George N. "An Introduction to the Settlement of Southern Michigan from 1815 to 1835." *Michigan Pioneer and Historical Collections* 38 (1912): 538–79.

———. *Economic and Social Beginnings of Michigan: A Study of the Settlement of the Lower Peninsula during the Territorial Period, 1805–1837.* Lansing, Mich.: Wynkoop Hallenbeck Crawford, 1916.

———. *Michigan: A Centennial History of the State and Its People.* 5 vols. Chicago: Lewis Publishing Co., 1939.

Fussell, G. E. "Agriculture: Techniques of Farming." In *A History of Technology,* vol. 4, *The Industrial Revolution, ca. 1750 to ca. 1850,* edited by Charles Singer, E. J. Holmyard, A. R. Hall, and Trevor I. Williams, 13–43. New York: Oxford University Press, 1958.

Galpin, C. J. *The Social Anatomy of an Agricultural Community.* AES Research Bulletin no. 34. Madison: University of Wisconsin, 1915.

Gardner, Washington. *History of Calhoun County, Michigan.* Chicago: Lewis Publishing, 1913.

Garner, B. J. "Models of Urban Geography and Settlement Location." In *Models in Geography,* edited by Richard J. Chorley and Peter Haggett, 303–60. London: Methuen, 1967.

Gates, Paul W. *The Farmer's Age: Agriculture, 1815–1860.* Vol. 3, *The Economic History of the United States.* New York: Holt, Rinehart and Winston, 1960.

———. "The Role of the Land Speculator in Western Development." In *The Public Lands: Studies in the History of the Public Domain,* edited by Vernon Carstensen, 349–67. Madison: University of Wisconsin Press, 1963.

———. *History of Public Land Law Development.* Washington, D.C.: Government Printing Office, 1968.

———. *Frontier Landlords and Pioneer Tenants.* Ithaca, N.Y.: Cornell University Press, 1973.

Geddes, John. "Ypsilanti Township—Its Settlement, Etc." *Michigan Pioneer and Historical Collections* 4 (1883): 401–4.

Genesee Farmer, 1833–49.

Gephart, William F. *Transportation and Industrial Development in the Middle West.* Columbia University, Studies in History, Economics, and Public Law, no. 89. New York: Longmans, Green, 1909.

Gerrells, Hawley. "Hawley Gerrells in 1828." *Michigan Pioneer and Historical Collections* 5 (1884): 76–79.

Gibbs, Mary V. "Glimpses of Early Michigan Life in and around Kalamazoo." *Magazine of American History* 24 (1890): 457–64.

Gilbert, Thomas D. "Development of Western Michigan." *Michigan Pioneer and Historical Collections* 17 (1890): 319–25.

Gilman, Carolyn. *Where Two Worlds Meet: The Great Lakes Fur Trade.* Minnesota Historical Society, Museum Exhibit Series no. 2. St. Paul: Minnesota Historical Society, 1982.

Gilpin, Alec R. *The Territory of Michigan, 1805–1837.* East Lansing: Michigan State University Press, 1970.

Glazer, Sidney. "Early Sugar Beet Industry in Michigan." *Michigan History* 28 (1944): 405–14.

Glidden, A. C. "Pioneer Farming." *Michigan Pioneer and Historical Collections* 18 (1891): 418–422.

Glover, Townsend. "Insects Injurious and Beneficial to Vegetation." *Report, 1854, Agriculture,* 58–89. Washington, D.C.: A. P. O. Nicholson, 1855.

Goddard, Frederick B. *Where to Emigrate, and Why.* New York: Frederick P. Goddard, 1869.

Goddard, Ives. "Mascouten." In *Handbook of North American Indians,* vol. 15, *Northeast,* edited by Bruce G. Trigger, 668–72,. Washington, D.C.: Smithsonian Institution, 1978.

Goodrich, Enos. "Locating the State Capitol at Lansing." *Michigan Pioneer and Historical Collections* 8 (1886): 121–30.

———. "Pioneer Sketch of Moses Goodrich and His Trip to Michigan in February, 1836, with His Brother Levi." *Michigan Pioneer and Historical Collections* 17 (1890): 480–90.

———. "Across Michigan Territory Sixty Years Ago." *Michigan Pioneer and Historical Collections* 26 (1894–95): 228–35.

Goodyear, Henry A. "Sketch of Barry County." *Michigan Pioneer and Historical Collections* 1 (1877): 112–17.

Goodykoontz, Colin Brummitt. *Home Missions on the American Frontier.* Caldwell, Idaho: Caxton Printers, 1939.

Gordon, Douglas H., and George S. May, eds., "The Michigan Land Rush in 1836, Michigan Journal, 1836, John M. Gordon." *Michigan History* 43 (1959): 1–42, 129–49, 257–93, 433–78.

Gouger, Lina. "Montreal et le peuplement de Détroit, 1701–1765." *Proceedings of the Eighteenth Meeting of the French Colonial Historical Society, Montreal, May 1992,* edited by James Pritchard, 46–58. Cleveland: French Colonial Historical Society, 1994.

Gould, J. D. *Economic Growth in History, Survey and Analysis.* London: Methuen, 1972.

Gould, Lucius E. "Four Papers on the Early History of Shiawassee County." *Michigan Pioneer and Historical Collections* 32 (1902): 247–304.

Grainger, Martha Munsell. "Memories: Grave and Gay." Edited by Alexis A. Praus and Ruth Howard. *Michigan History* 38 (1954): 116–40.

Gray, H. Peter. *A Generalized Theory of International Trade.* New York: Holmes and Meier, 1976.

Gray, Lewis Cecil. *History of Agriculture in the Southern United States to 1860.* Washington, D.C.: Carnegie Institute of Washington, 1933, Reprint, Gloucester, Mass.: Peter Smith, 1958.

Gray, Ralph D. "The Canal Era in Indiana." In *Transportation in the Early Nation.* Indianapolis: Indiana Historical Society, 1982.

Gray, Susan E. "Limits and Possibilities: White-Indian Relations in Western Michigan in the Era of Removal." *Michigan Historical Review* 20, no. 2 (1994): 71–91.

———. *The Yankee West: Community Life on the Michigan Frontier.* Chapel Hill: University of North Carolina Press, 1996.

Greenberg, Dolores. "Energy Flow in a Changing Economy." In *An Emerging Independent American Economy, 1815–1875,* edited by Joseph R. Frese and Jacob Judd, 29–58. Tarrytown, N.Y.: Sleepy Hollow Press and Rockefeller Archive Center, 1980.

Greene, Marion Palmer. "Reflections in the River Raisin." *Michigan History* 33 (1949): 47–64, 232–39.

Greenman, Emerson F. "The Indians of Michigan," Michigan History 45 (1961): 1–53.

Greven, Philip J., Jr. "Family Structure in Seventeenth-Century Andover, Massachusetts." *William and Mary Quarterly,* 3d ser., no. 23 (1966): 234–56.

Griffin, Henry. "Commerce and Ship Building of Ottawa County." *Michigan Pioneer and Historical Collections* 9 (1886): 280–86.

Griswold, Joseph M. "Some Reminiscences of Early Times in Brooklyn, Jackson County, Michigan." *Michigan Pioneer and Historical Collections* 26 (1894–95): 256–61.

Grove, David. "The Function and Future of Urban Centres." In *Man, Settlement, and Urbanism,* edited by Peter J. Ucko, Ruth Tringham, and G. W. Dimbleby, 559–65. London: Gerald Duckworth, 1972.

Grove, Jean M. *The Little Ice Age.* London: Methuen, 1988.

Groves, Paul A. "The Northeast and Regional Integration, 1800–1860." In *North America, the Historical Geography of a Changing Continent,* edited by Robert D. Mitchell and Paul Groves, 198–217. Totowa, N.J.: Rowman and Littlefield, 1987.

Gwinn, Florence H. "Huron County from 1800 to 1850." *Michigan Pioneer and Historical Collections* 39 (1915): 353–59.

Hadfield, Charles. "Canals: Inland Waterways of the British Isles." In *A History of Technology,* vol. 4, *The Industrial Revolution, c. 1750 to c. 1850,* edited by Charles Singer, E. J. Holmyard, A. R. Hall, and Trevor I. Williams, 563–73. New York: Oxford University Press, 1958.

Haeger, John Denis. *The Investment Frontier: New York Businessmen and the Development of the Old Northwest.* Albany: State University of New York Press, 1981.

Hall, James. *Statistics of the West, at the Close of the Year 1836.* Cincinnati: J. A. James, 1836.

———. *Notes on the Western States; Containing Descriptive Sketches of Their Soil, Climate, Resources, and Scenery.* Philadelphia: Harrison Hall, 1838.

————. *The West: Its Commerce and Navigation.* New York: H. W. Darby, 1848.

Hallowell, A. Irving. "The Impact of the American Indian on American Culture." *American Anthropologist* 59 (1957): 201–16.

Hamil, Fred C. "Michigan in the War of 1812." *Michigan History* 44 (1960): 257–91.

Hammes, Raymond, ed. "Squatters in Territorial Illinois." *Illinois Libraries* 59 (1977): 319–82.

Hammond, Bray. *Banks and Politics in America, from the Revolution to the Civil War.* Princeton, N.J.: Princeton University Press, 1957.

Handsman, Russell G. "Early Capitalism and the Center Village of Canaan, Connecticut: A Study of Transformations and Separations." *Artifacts* 9 (1981): 1–20.

Hansen, Marcus Lee. *The Atlantic Migration, 1607–1860: A History of the Continuing Settlement of the United States.* Cambridge, Mass.: Harvard University Press, 1940.

Hardeman, Nicholas P. *Shucks, Shocks, and Hominy Blocks: Corn as a Way of Life in Pioneer America.* Baton Rouge: Louisiana State University Press, 1981.

Hardesty, Donald L. "Evolution on the Industrial Frontier." In *The Archaeology of Frontiers and Boundaries,* edited by Stanton W. Green and Stephen M. Perlman, 213–29. Orlando, Fla.: Academic Press, 1985.

Harlow, Alvin F. *The Road of the Century: The Story of the New York Central.* New York: Creative Age Press, 1947.

Harman, Jay R. "Environmental Significance of a Great Lakes Location." In *Michigan: A Geography,* by Lawrence M. Sommers, 71–92. Boulder, Colo.: Westview Press, 1984.

Harrington, Daniel B. "Daniel B. Harrington." *Michigan Pioneer and Historical Collections* 5 (1884): 138–43.

Harrington, M. W. "Notes on the Climate of Detroit." *American Meteorological Journal* 2 (1885): 317–23.

Harris, R. Cole. "The Extension of France into Rural Canada." In *European Settlement and Development in North America: Essays on Geographical Change in Honor and Memory of Andrew Hill Clark,* edited by James R. Gibson, 27–45. Toronto: University of Toronto Press, 1978.

————. *Historical Atlas of Canada.* Vol. 1, *From the Beginning to 1800.* Toronto: University of Toronto Press, 1987.

Hart, John Fraser. *The Look of the Land.* Englewood Cliffs, N.J.: Prentice-Hall, 1975.

Hart, N. H. "Pioneer Sketches." *Michigan Pioneer and Historical Collections* 3 (1881): 548–52.

Hasenstab, R. J. and B. Resnick. "GIS in Historical Predictive Modelling: The Fort Drum Project." In *Interpreting Space: GIS and Archaeology,* edited by K. M. S. Allen, S. W. Green, and E. B. W. Zubrow, 284–306. New York: Taylor and Francis, 1990.

Haswell, Susan Olsen, and Arnold R. Alanen. *A Garden Apart: An Agricultural and Settlement History of Michigan's Sleeping Bear Dunes National Lakeshore Region.* Omaha, Neb. and Lansing, Mich.: Midwest Regional Office, National Park Service and State Historic Preservation Office, Michigan Bureau of History, 1994.

Harlan, Hatcher. *Lake Erie.* Indianapolis: Bobbs-Merrill, 1945.

————. *The Western Reserve: The Story of New Connecticut in Ohio.* Indianapolis: Bobbs-Merrill, 1949.

Hatcher, Harlan, and Leslie Marshall. *Johnny Appleseed: A Voice in the Wilderness.* Patterson, N.J.: Swendenborg Press, 1945.

Hathaway, William H. "County Organization in Michigan." *Michigan History* 2 (1918): 573–629.

Hawes, George W. *George W. Hawes' Michigan State Gazetteer and Business Directory for 1860.* Detroit: F. Raymond, 1859.

————. *George W. Hawes' Michigan State Gazetteer and Shipper's Guide and Business Directory for 1865.* Indianapolis: By the author, 1864.

Hayes, Mrs. A. M. "Reminiscences of Pioneer Days in Hastings." *Michigan Pioneer and Historical Collections* 26 (1894–95): 235–41.

Haynes, Harvey. "Sketches of the Early History of Branch County." *Michigan Pioneer and Historical Collections* 6 (1883): 284–88.

Hazard, Lucy Lockwood. *The Frontier in American Literature.* New York: Frederick Unger, 1927.

Heller, Charles F., and F. Stanley Moore. "Continuity in Rural Land Ownership: Western Kalamazoo County, Michigan, 1830–1861." *Michigan History* 56 (1972): 233–46.

Henderson, Donald C. "Allegan County—Its Rise, Progress, and Growth in Population, with a Brief History of Its Press." *Michigan Historical Collections* 3 (1881): 270–76.

————. "Notes on Saugatuck." *Michigan Pioneer and Historical Collections* 3 (1881): 301–10.

Henlein, Paul. "Early Cattle Ranges of the Ohio Valley." *Agricultural History* 35 (1961): 150–54.

Henretta, James A. *The Evolution of American Society, 1700–1815: An Interdisciplinary Analysis.* Lexington, Mass.: D. C. Heath, 1973.

————. "Families and Farms: *Mentalite* in Pre-Industrial America." *William and Mary Quarterly*, 3d ser., no. 35 (1978): 3–32.

————. "The Transition to Capitalism in America." In *The Origins of American Capitalism: Collected Essays*, 256–94. Boston: Northeastern University Press, 1991.

Herskovitts, Melville J. *Man and His Works: The Science of Cultural Anthropology.* New York: Alfred A. Knopf, 1948.

Hesslink, George K. *Black Neighbors: Negroes in a Rural Northern Community.* Indianapolis: Bobbs-Merrill, 1968.

Hewitt, D. *The American Traveller; or National Directory, Containing an Account of All the Great Post Roads, and Important Cross Roads, in the United States.* Washington, D.C.: Davis and Force, 1825.

Hibbard, Benjamin Horace. *A History of the Public Land Policies.* Madison: University of Wisconsin Press, 1965.

Higgins, F. Hal. "The Moore-Hascall Harvester Centennial Approaches." *Michigan History* 14 (1930): 415–37.

Hill, Elton B. "Farm Management." *Michigan History* 22 (1938): 311–25.

Hill, Elton B., and Russell G. Mawby. *Types of Farming in Michigan.* Agricultural Experiment Station, Special Bulletin no. 206. East Lansing: Michigan State College, 1954.

Hilliard, Sam B. "Pork in the Ante-Bellum South: The Geography of Self-Sufficiency." *Annals of the Association of American Geographers* 59 (1969): 461–80.

———. *Hog Meat and Hoecake: Food Supply in the Old South, 1840–1860.* Carbondale: Southern Illinois University Press, 1972.

———. A Robust New Nation. In *North America, the Historical Geography of a Changing Continent,* edited by Robert D. Mitchell and Paul Groves, 149–71. Totowa, N.J.: Rowman and Littlefield, 1987.

Hillis, Newell Dwight. *The Quest of John Chapman: The Story of a Forgotten Hero.* New York: Grosset and Dunlop, 1904.

Hinman, John F. "My First Journey to Michigan, with Other Reminiscences." *Michigan Pioneer and Historical Collections* 14 (1889): 563–71.

History of Jackson County, Michigan. Chicago: Inter-State Publishing Co., 1881.

History of Lapeer County, Michigan. Chicago: H. R. Page, 1884.

History of Saginaw County, Michigan. Chicago: Chas. C. Chapman, 1881.

History of St. Joseph County, Michigan. Philadelphia: L. H. Everts, 1877.

History of Washtenaw County, Michigan. Chicago: Chas. C. Chapman, 1881.

Hoffman, Charles Fenno. *A Winter in the West.* 2 vols. New York: Harper & Brothers, 1835.

Hofstadter, Richard. *The Progressive Historians: Turner, Beard, Parrington.* New York: Alfred A. Knopf, 1968.

Holbrook, S. H. *The Yankee Exodus: An Account of Migration from New England.* New York: Macmillan, 1950.

Holley, O. L. *The Picturesque Tourist; Being a Guide Through the Northern and Eastern States and Canada.* New York: J. Disturnell, 1844.

Holman, Margaret B., and Kathryn C. Egan. "Processing Maple Sap with Prehistoric Techniques." *Journal of Ethnobiology* 5 (1985): 61–75.

Holman, Winifred Lovering. ed. "Diary of Rev. James-Hanmer Francis." *Ohio Archaeological and Historical Quarterly* 51 (1942): 41–61.

Holmes, J. C. "The Early History of Horticulture in Michigan." *Michigan Pioneer and Historical Collections* 10 (1888): 69–84.

Hoppin, Ruth. "Personal Recollections of Pioneer Days." *Michigan Pioneer and Historical Collections* 38 (1912): 410–16.

Hornaday, William T. *Our Vanishing Wildlife: Its Extermination and Preservation.* New York: New York Zoological Society, 1913.

Horsman, Reginald. "Changing Images of the Public Domain: Historians and the Shaping of Midwest Frontiers." In *This Land Is Ours: the Acquisition and Disposition of the Public Domain,* 60–86. Indianapolis: Indiana Historical Society, 1978.

Horton, Rod W. *Backgrounds of Literary Thought.* New York: Appleton-Century-Crofts, 1952.

Hosford, Oramel. "Early History of Olivet College." *Michigan Pioneer and Historical Collections* 3 (1881): 408–14.

Hoskins, Nathan. *Notes Upon the Western Country, Contained Within the States of Ohio, Indiana, Illinois, and the Territory of Michigan; Taken on a Tour Through that Country in the Summer of 1832.* Greenfield, Mass.: J. P. Fogg, 1833.

Hotchkiss, George W. *History of the Lumber and Forest Industry of the Northwest.* Chicago: By the author, 1898.

Houdek, John T., and Charles F. Heller. "Searching for Nineteenth-Century Farm Tenants: An Evaluation of Methods." *Historical Methods* 19 (1986): 55–61.

Howard, Sanford. "Culture of Broom Corn and the Manufacture of Brooms." In *Report of the Commissioner of Patents for the Year 1849,* part 2, *Agriculture,* 462–63. Washington, D.C.: Office of the Printers to the Senate, 1850.

Hoyt, Joseph B. "The Cold Summer of 1816." *Annals of the Association of American Geographers* 48 (1958): 118–31.

Hoyt, Mary M. "Early Recollections of Pioneer Life in Michigan and the Founding of Yankee Springs." *Michigan Pioneer and Historical Collections* 30 (1905): 289–302.

Hubbard, A. C. "Orchards and Fruits of Michigan." U.S. Commissioner of Patents, *Report, 1849, Agriculture,* 281–83. Washington, D.C.: Office of Printers to the Senate, 1850.

Hubbard, Bela. "The Early Colonization of Detroit." *Michigan Pioneer and Historical Collections* 1 (1877): 347–68.

———. *Memorials of a Half-Century in Michigan and the Lake Region.* New York: G. P. Putnam's Sons, 1888.

Hubbart, Henry Clyde. *The Older Middle West, 1840–1880.* New York: D. Appleton Century, 1936.

Hudgins, Bert. "Evolution of Metropolitan Detroit." *Economic Geography* 21 (1945): 206–20.

———. *Michigan: Geographic Backgrounds in the Development of the Commonwealth.* Detroit: By the author, 1961.

Hudson, John C. "A Locational Theory for Rural Settlement." *Annals of the Association of American Geographers* 59 (1969): 365–81.

Hudson, Winthrop S. *American Protestantism.* Chicago: University of Chicago Press, 1961.

Huggins, Andrew. "History of the Epidemic of 1848 in Shiawassee County." *Michigan Pioneer and Historical Collections* 28 (1897–98): 506–11.

Hunt, George T. *The Wars of the Iroquois: A Study of Intertribal Trade Relations.* Madison: University of Wisconsin Press, 1967.

Hurst, Michael E. Eliot, ed. *Transportation Geography.* New York: McGraw-Hill, 1974.

Hurt, R. Douglas. *American Farm Tools: From Hand-Power to Steam-Power.* Manhattan, Kans.: Sunflower University Press, 1985.

Hutt, W. H. "Immigration Under 'Economic Freedom.'" In *Economic Issues in Immigration,* 17–44. Introduction by Arnold Plant. London: Institute of Economic Affairs, 1970.

Hyma, Albert. *Albertus C. Van Raalte and His Dutch Settlements in the United States.* Grand Rapids, Mich.: William B. Eerdmans, 1947.

Innis, Harold A. *The Fur Trade in Canada: An Introduction to Canadian Economic History.* New Haven, Conn.: Yale University Press, 1962.

Jakle, John A. *Images of the Ohio Valley: A Historical Geography of Travel, 1740–1860.* New York: Oxford University Press, 1977.

Jamison, Knox. "The Survey of the Public Lands in Michigan." *Michigan History* 42 (1958): 197–214.

Jefferson, Thomas. *Notes on the State of Virginia*, edited by W. Peden. Chapel Hill: University of North Carolina Press, 1955.

Jenks, William L. "Michigan Immigration." *Michigan History* 28 (1944): 67–100.

Jewett, Azuhah L. "Pioneer Life in 1830." *Michigan Pioneer and Historical Collections* 6 (1883): 426–30.

Johnson, Arthur M., and Barry E. Supple. *Boston Capitalists and Western Railroads: A Study in Nineteenth-Century Railroad Investment Process.* Cambridge, Mass.: Harvard University Press, 1967.

Johnson, Crisfield. *History of Branch County, Michigan.* Philadelphia: Everts and Abbott, 1879.

———.*History of Allegan and Barry Counties, Michigan.* Philadelphia: D. W. Ensign, 1880.

———. *History of Hillsdale County, Michigan.* Philadelphia: Everts and Abbott, 1879.

Johnson, Emory R. *American Railway Transportation.* New York: D. Appleton, 1903.

Johnson, Hildegard Binder. *Order Upon the Land: The U.S. Rectangular Land Survey and the Upper Mississippi Country.* New York: Oxford University Press, 1976.

Johnson, Howard George. "The Franconian Colonies of the Saginaw Valley, Michigan: A Study in Historical Geography." Ph.D. diss., Michigan State University. Ann Arbor, Mich.: University Microfilms, 1972.

Johnson, Ida Amanda. *The Michigan Fur Trade.* Lansing: Michigan Historical Commission, 1919. Reprint, Grand Rapids, Mich.: Black Letter Press, 1971.

Jones, Maldwyn A. "The Background to Emigration from Great Britain in the Nineteenth Century." *Perspectives in American History* 7 (1973): 3–92.

Jordan, Terry G. *German Seed in Texas Soil: Immigrant Farmers in Nineteenth-Century Texas.* Austin: University of Texas Press, 1966.

———. "Pioneer Evaluation of Vegetation in Frontier Texas." *Southwestern Historical Quarterly* 76 (1973): 233–54.

———. "Antecedents of the Long-Lot in Texas." *Annals of the Association of American Geographers* 64 (1974): 70–86.

———. *North American Cattle Ranching Frontiers: Origins, Diffusion, and Differentiation.* Albuquerque: University of New Mexico Press, 1993.

Jordan, Terry G., and Matti Kaups. *The American Backwoods Frontier: An Ethnic and Ecological Interpretation.* Baltimore: Johns Hopkins University Press, 1989.

Joy, James F. "Railroad History of Michigan." *Michigan Pioneer and Historical Collections* 22 (1893): 292–304.

Kaatz, Martin R. "The Black Swamp: A Study in Historical Geography." *Annals of the Association of American Geographers* 45 (1955): 1–35.

Kamphoefner, Walter D. *The Westfalians: From Germany to Missouri.* Princeton, N.J.: Princeton University Press, 1987.

Kardiner, Abram. *The Individual and His Society: The Psychodynamics of Primitive Social Organization.* New York: Columbia University Press, 1939.

Karpinski, Louis C. *Bibliography of the Printed Maps of Michigan, 1804–1880.* Lansing: Michigan Historical Commission, 1931.

———. "Early Maps of Michigan and the Great Lakes Region." *Michigan History* 27 (1943): 143–55.

———. "Early Michigan Maps: Three Outstanding Peculiarities." *Michigan History* 29 (1945): 506–11.

———. "Michigan and the Great Lakes upon the Map, 1636–1802." *Michigan History* 29 (1945): 287–312.

Katzman, Martin T. "The Brazilian Frontier in Comparative Perspective." *Comparative Studies in Society and History* 17 (1975): 266–85.

Kedzie, R. C. "Soil, Productions, and Climate." In *Michigan and Its Resources,* compiled by Frederick Morely, 59–63. Lansing, Mich.: W. S. George, 1881.

———. "Domestic Supply of Sugar for Michigan." *Michigan Pioneer and Historical Collections* 29 (1899–1900): 201–4.

Keeney, Salmon. "Salmon Keeney's Visit to Michigan in 1827." Edited by Helen Everett. *Michigan History* 40 (1956): 433–46.

Keith, Hannah Emily. "An Historical Sketch of Internal Improvements in Michigan, 1836–1846." *Publications of the Michigan Political Science Association* 4 (1902): 1–48.

Keller, Velera. "An Early Visitor to Michigan." *Michigan History* 12 (1928): 252–66.

Kenoyer, Leslie A. "Forest Distribution in Southwestern Michigan as Interpreted from the Original Land Survey (1826–32)." *Papers of the Michigan Academy of Science, Arts, and Letters* 11 (1934): 107–11.

Kenzer, Robert C. *Kinship and Neighborhood in a Southern Community: Orange County, North Carolina, 1849–1881.* Knoxville: University of Tennessee Press, 1987.

Keppel, Anna Kremer. *The Immigration and Early History of the People of Zeeland, Ottawa County, Michigan, in 1847.* Zeeland, Mich.: Zeeland Record Press, [1925].

Ketcham, Hazel M. "Fruit Growing in Michigan." *Journal of Geography* 16 (1917): 90–96.

Kilfoil, Jack. *C. C. Trowbridge: Detroit Banker and Michigan Land Speculator, 1820–1845.* New York: Arno Press, 1979.

Killebrew, J. B. *Introduction to the Resources of Tennessee.* Nashville, Tenn.: Tavel, Eastman and Howell, 1874. Reprint, Spartanburg, S.C.: Reprint Company, 1974.

Kingsford, W. *History, Structure, and Statistics of Plank Roads in the United States and Canada.* Philadelphia: A. Hart, 1851.

Kirk, Gordon W., Jr. *The Promise of American Life: Social Mobility in a Nineteenth-Century Immigrant Community, Holland, Michigan, 1847–1894.* Philadelphia: American Philosophical Society, 1978.

Kirkland, Caroline Matilda [Mary Clavers]. *A New Home—Who'll Follow? Or Glimpses of Western Life.* New York: C. S. Francis, 1839.

———. *Forest Life.* 2 vols. New York: C. S. Francis, 1842.

Kirkland, Edward C. *A History of American Economic Life.* New York: F. S. Crofts, 1939.

Kirkland, William. "The West, the Paradise of the Poor." *United States Magazine and Democratic Review,* n.s., 15 (1844): 182–90.

Kleinschmidt, Earl E. "Prevailing Diseases and Hygienic Conditions in Early Michigan." *Michigan History* 25 (1941): 57–99.

Knowles, R., and J. Wareing. *Economic and Social Geography.* London: W. H. Allen, 1976.

Knuth, Helen. "Economic and Historical Background for Valuation as of March 28, 1836, of Lands Involved in Ottawa-Chippewa Indians, Indian cases." Testimony Indian Claims Commission, Docket 18E-58, 1958.

Kolodny, Annette. *The Land Before Her: Fantasy and Experience of the American Frontier, 1630–1860.* Chapel Hill: University of North Carolina Press, 1984.

Kooker, Arthur Raymond. "The Antislavery Movement in Michigan, 1796–1840: A Study of Humanitarianism on the American Frontier." Ph.D. diss., University of Michigan. Ann Arbor, Mich.: University Microfilms, 1941.

Kovacik, Charles Frank. "A Geographical Analysis of the Foreign-Born in Huron, Sanilac, and St. Clair Counties of Michigan, with Particular Reference to Canadians: 1850–1880." Ph.D. diss., Michigan State University. Ann Arbor, Mich.: University Microfilms, 1970.

Kristof, Ladis K. D. "The Nature of Frontiers and Boundaries." *Annals of the Association of American Geographers* 49 (1959): 269–82.

Kroeber, A. L. *Anthropology: Culture Patterns and Processes.* New York: Harcourt, Brace & World, 1963.

Kuhn, Madison. *Michigan State University: The First Hundred Years.* East Lansing: Michigan State University Press, 1955.

———. "Tiffin, Morse, and the Reluctant Pioneer." *Michigan History* 50 (1966): 111–38.

Kulikoff, Allan. *The Agrarian Origins of American Capitalism.* Charlottesville: University Press of Virginia, 1992.

———. "Households and Markets: Toward a New Synthesis of American Agrarian History." *William and Mary Quarterly,* 3d ser., no. 50 (1993): 342–55.

Ladurie, Emmanuel Le Roy. *Times of Feast, Times of Famine: A History of Climate since the Year 1000.* Translated by Barbara Bray. Garden City, N.Y.: Doubleday, 1971.

Lafever, Margaret. "Story of Early Day Life in Michigan." *Michigan Pioneer and Historical Collections* 38 (1912): 672–77.

Lamb, C. A. "Incidents in Pioneer Life in Clinton County." *Michigan Pioneer and Historical Collections* 1 (1877): 149–51.

Lamb, Leland W. "History of Dairying in Michigan." *Michigan History* 24 (1940): 409–33.

Landing, James E. "Peppermint and Spearmint in the United States." *Journal of Geography* 67 (1968): 548–53.

———. *American Essence: A History of the Peppermint and Spearmint Industry in the United States.* Kalamazoo, Mich.: Kalamazoo Public Museum, 1969.

Lane, Kit. *John Allen: Michigan's Pioneer Promoter.* Douglas, Mich.: Pavilion Press, 1988.

Langdale, John. "Impact of the Telegraph on the Buffalo Agricultural Commodity Market: 1846–1848." *Professional Geographer* 31 (1979): 165–69.

Langhorne, William T., Jr. "Mill-Based Settlement Patterns in Schoharie County, New York: A Regional Study." *Historical Archaeology* 10 (1976): 73–92.

Lanman, Charles. *A Summer in the Wilderness; Embracing a Canoe Voyage Up the Mississippi and Around Lake Superior.* New York: D. Appleton, 1847.

Lanman, James H. *History of Michigan, Civil and Topographical, in a Compendious Form; With a View of the Surrounding Lakes.* New York: E. French, 1839.

———. *History of Michigan, from Its Earliest Colonization to the Present Time.* New York Harper and Brothers, 1841.

Larkin, Jack. *The Reshaping of Everyday Life, 1790–1840.* New York: Harper and Row, 1988.

Larsen, Curtis E. "A Century of Great Lakes Levels Research: Finished or Just Beginning." In *Retrieving Michigan's Buried Past: The Archaeology of the Great Lakes State,* edited by John R. Halsey, 1–30. Cranbrook Institute of Science, Bulletin no. 64. Bloomfield Hills, Mich.: Cranbrook Institute of Science, 1999.

Lattimore, Owen. *Studies in Frontier History.* London: Oxford University Press, 1962.

Lawrence, James H. "Pioneer Recollections." *Michigan Pioneer and Historical Collections* 18 (1891): 360–73.

Lawton, George W. "Historical Sketch of Van Buren County." *Michigan Pioneer and Historical Collections* 3 (1881): 625–37.

Lay, Ezra D. "Condensed Early History, Or Beginnings of the Several Towns in Washtenaw County." *Michigan Pioneer and Historical Collections* 17(1890): 450–62.

Lee, Daniel. "The Study of Soils," in U.S. Commissioner of Patents, Report, 1850, Agriculture, 58–71. Washington, D.C.: Printers to the House of Representatives, 1850.

Lee, Guy A. "The Historical Significance of the Chicago Grain Elevator System." *Agricultural History* 11 (1937): 16–32.

Lee, H. Huntington, and James Sutherland. *State of Michigan, Gazetteer and Business Directory for 1856–7.* Detroit: By the authors, 1856.

Lee, S. P., and P. Passell. *A New Economic View of American History.* New York: Norton, 1979.

Leeson, M. A. *History of Kent County, Michigan.* Chicago: Chas. C. Chapman, 1881.

———. *History of Saginaw County, Michigan.* Chicago: Chas. C. Chapman, 1881.

———. *History of Macomb County, Michigan.* Chicago: M. A. Leeson, 1882.

Leighly, John. "Some Comments on Contemporary Geographic Method." *Annals of the Association of American Geographers* 27 (1937): 125–41.

Lemon, James T. "Household Consumption in Eighteenth-Century America and Its Relationship to Production and Trade: The Situation among Farmers in Southeastern Pennsylvania." *Agricultural History* 41 (1967): 59–70.

———. *The Best Poor Man's Country: A Geographical Study of Early Southeastern Pennsylvania.* Baltimore: Johns Hopkins University Press, 1972.

Leverett, Frank. *Surface Geology and Agricultural Conditions in Michigan.* Michigan Geological and Biological Survey, Publication no. 25. Lansing, Mich.: Wynkoop Hallenbeck Crawford Co., 1917.

Levi-Strauss, Claude. *Structural Anthropology.* Translated by Claire Jacobson and Brooke Grundfestt Schoepf. New York: Doubleday, 1967.

Lewis, Carolyn B. "Imperfect or Identical Images? An Identification of the Accuracy of Nineteenth-Century Subscription Property Illustrations of Clinton County, Michigan." Report prepared for the Clinton County Historical Commission, St. Johns, Michigan, 1987.

Lewis, Frank D., and M. C. Urquhart. "Growth and the Standard of Living in a Pioneer Economy: Upper Canada, 1826–1851." *William and Mary Quarterly,* 3d ser., no. 56 (1999): 151–81.

Lewis, G. J. "Rural Communities." In *Progress in Rural Geography,* edited by Michael Pacione, 149–72. London: Croom Helm, 1983.

Lewis, Kenneth E. *Camden: A Frontier Town in Eighteenth-Century South Carolina.* University of South Carolina, Institute of Archaeology and Anthropology, Anthropological Studies no. 2. Columbia, South Carolina, 1976.

————. "Sampling the Archaeological Frontier: Regional Models and Component Analysis. In *Research Strategies in Historical Archaeology,* edited by Stanley South, 151–201. New York: Academic Press, 1977.

————. *The American Frontier: An Archaeological Study of Settlement Pattern and Process.* Orlando: Academic Press, 1984.

Lewis, Peirce F. "Axioms for Reading the Landscape: Some Guides to the American Scene." In *The Interpretation of Ordinary Landscapes,* edited by D. W. Meinig, 11–32. New York: Oxford University Press, 1979.

Leyburn, James G. *Frontier Folkways.* New Haven, Conn.: Yale University Press, 1935.

Lincoln, W. B. "First Settlement of Ionia County." *Michigan Pioneer and Historical Collections* 1 (1877): 193–94.

Lindstrom, Diane. "Southern Dependence upon Interregional Grain Supplies: A Review of the Trade Flows, 1840–1860." *Agricultural History* 44 (1970): 101–13.

Linebaugh, Donald W. "Nineteenth-Century Settlement Patterning in the Grand River Valley, Ottawa County, Michigan." Master's thesis, College of William and Mary, 1982.

Lippincott, Isaac. *A History of Manufactures in the Ohio Valley to the Year 1860.* New York: Arno Press, 1973.

Little, Henry. "Fifty Years Ago, Jacksonburg and Jackson County—1829–1879." *Michigan Pioneer and Historical Collections* 4 (1883): 509–12.

Lockwood, Maren. "The Experimental Utopia in America." In *Utopias and Utopian Thought,* edited by Frank E. Manuel, 183–200. Boston: Beacon Press, 1965.

Longley, R. S. "Emigration and the Crisis of 1837 in Upper Canada." *Canadian Historical Review* 17 (1936): 29–40.

Longyear, Harriet Munro. "The Settlement of Clinton County." *Michigan Pioneer and Historical Collections* 39 (1915): 360–64.

Lowenthal, David. "Geography, Experience, and Imagination: Towards a Geographical Epistemology." *Annals of the Association of American Geographers* 51 (1961): 241–60.

Lowie, Robert. *Social Organization.* New York: Rinehart, 1948.

Loyd, Bonnie, Arlene Rengert, and Janice Monk. "Women and Agricultural Landscapes." In *Women and Spatial Change: Learning Resources for Social Science Courses,* edited by Arlene Rengert and Janice Monk, 1–2. Dubuque, Iowa: Kendall/Hunt, 1982.

Lucas, Henry S. "The Beginnings of Dutch Immigration to Western Michigan, 1846." *Michigan History* 6 (1922): 642–74.

————. "A Document Relating to the Founding of Zeeland, Michigan, in 1847." *Michigan History* 12 (1928): 99–107.

————. *Netherlanders in America*. Ann Arbor: University of Michigan Press, 1955. Reprint, Grand Rapids, Mich.: William B. Eerdmans, 1989.

Lucas, Henry S., ed., *Dutch Immigrant Memoirs and Related Writings*. Assen, Netherlands: Van Gorcum, 1955.

Ludlam, David M. *Early American Winters, 1604–1820*. Boston: American Meteorological Society, 1966.

————. *Early American Winters II, 1821–1870*. Boston: American Meteorological Society, 1968.

Lurie, Nancy Oestreich. "Indian Cultural Adjustment to European Civilization." In *Seventeenth-Century America*, edited by James Morton Smith, 33–60. Chapel Hill: University of North Carolina Press, 1959.

Lyster, Henry F. "The State with Reference to Malarious Diseases." In *Michigan and Its Resources*, edited by Frederick Morley, 69–71. Lansing, Mich.: W. S. George, 1881.

MacGarr, Llewellyn. *The Rural Community*. New York: Macmillan, 1923.

MacGill, Caroline. *History of Transportation in the United States before 1860*. Prepared under the direction of Henry Balthasar Meyer. Washington, D.C.: Carnegie Institute, 1917. Reprint, New York: Peter Smith, 1948.

MacLeod, William Christie. *The American Indian Frontier*. New York: Alfred A. Knopf, 1928.

MacMillan, Margaret Burnham. *The Methodist Church in Michigan*. Grand Rapids: Michigan Area Methodist Historical Society, 1967.

Malin, James C. "The Turnover of Farm Population in Kansas." *Kansas Historical Quarterly* 4 (1935): 339–72.

Mandel, Ernest. *Marxist Economic Theory*. 2 vols. New York: Monthly Review Press, 1968.

Marks, Joseph J., ed. *Effects of the Civil War on Farming in Michigan*. Lansing: Michigan Civil War Centennial Observance Commission, 1965.

Marquardt, William H., and Carole L. Crumley. "Theoretical Issues in the Analysis of Spatial Patterning. In *Regional Dynamics, Burgundian Landscapes in Historical Perspective*, edited by Carole L. Crumley and William H. Marquardt, 1–18. San Diego: Academic Press, 1987.

Marshall, John W. *The Location of Service Towns: An Approach to the Analysis of Central Place Systems*. Toronto: University of Toronto Press, Research Publications, 1969.

Martin, Claire Fuller. "Together in the Heart: Southern Frontier Families in Southwestern Oklahoma Territory." Master's thesis, Michigan State University, 1986.

Martineau, Harriet. "Harriet Martineau's Travels in and around Michigan, 1836." *Michigan History* 7 (1923): 49–99.

Marx, Leo. *The Machine in the Garden: Technology and the Pastoral Ideal in America*. London: Oxford University Press, 1964.

————. "The Impact of the Railroad on the American Imagination, as a Possible Comparison for the Space Impact." In *The Railroad and the Space Program: An Exploration in Historical Analogy*, edited by Bruce Mazlish, 207–15. Cambridge, Mass.: MIT Press, 1965.

Mason, Edward. "On the Breeding and Management of Sheep," in Michigan State Agricultural Society, Transactions of the Michigan State Agricultural Society for 1856, 8:155–95. Lansing, Mich.: Hosmer and Kerr, 1857.

Mason, Roger D. *Euro-American Pioneer Settlement Systems in the Central Salt River Valley of Northeast Missouri*. Publications in Archaeology no. 2,. Columbia: American Archaeology Division, University of Missouri-Columbia, 1984.

Masselman, George. *The Cradle of Colonialism*. New Haven, Conn.: Yale University Press, 1963.

Massie, Larry B. *From Frontier Folk to Factory Smoke: Michigan's First Century of Historical Fiction*. Au Train, Mich.: Avery Color Studios, 1987.

———. "Communists in Kalamazoo." In *The Romance of Michigan's Past,* edited by Larry B. Massie, 77–90. Allegan Forest, Mich.: Priscilla Press, 1991.

Mathews, Alfred. *History of Cass County, Michigan*. Chicago: Waterman, Watkins, and Co., 1882.

Mathews, Lois Kimball. *The Expansion of New England: The Spread of New England Settlement and Institutions to the Mississippi River, 1620–1865*. Boston: Houghton Mifflin, 1909.

Maybee, Rolland H. "Population Growth and Distribution in Lower Michigan: 1810–1940." *Michigan Academy of Science and Letters, Papers* 31 (1945): 253–66.

———. "Michigan's White Pine Era, 1840–1900." *Michigan History* 42 (1959): 385–432.

McClurken, James M. "Ottawa Adaptive Strategies to Indian Removal." *Michigan Historical Review* 12 (1986): 29–55.

———."We Wish To Be Civilized: Ottawa-American Political Contests on the Michigan Frontier." Ph.D. diss., Michigan State University. Ann Arbor, Mich.: University Microfilms, 1988.

McCormick, W. R. "Pioneer Life in the Saginaw Valley." *Michigan Pioneer and Historical Collections* 3 (1881): 602–5.

———. "Sketch of Early Life in the Saginaw Valley." *Michigan Pioneer and Historical Collections* 4 (1883): 364–73.

McCracken, S. B. "Fifty Years Ago and Now." *Michigan Pioneer and Historical Collections* 14 (1889): 609–20.

McGee, Melville. "The Early Days of Concord, Jackson County, Michigan." *Michigan Pioneer and Historical Collections* 21 (1892): 418–31.

McLoughlin, William G. *Revivals, Awakenings, and Reform: An Essay on Religion and Social Change in America, 1607–1977*. Chicago: University of Chicago Press, 1978.

McMath, J. M. "The Willow Run Settlement." *Michigan Pioneer and Historical Collections* 14 (1889): 483–95.

Medley, Kimberley E., and Jay R. Harman. "Relationships between the Vegetation Tension Zone and Soils Distribution across Central Lower Michigan." *Michigan Botanist* 26 (1987): 78–87.

Meinig, D. W. "American Wests: Preface to a Geographical Interpretation." *Annals of the Association of American Geographers* 62 (1972): 159–84.

————. "Spatial Models of a Sequence of Transatlantic Interactions." *XXIII International Geographical Congress, International Geography '76,* sec. 9, *Historical Geography,* 30–35. Moscow: n.p., 1976.

————. "The Beholding Eye, Ten Versions of the Same Scene." In *The Interpretation of Ordinary Landscapes,* edited by D. W. Meinig, 33–48. New York: Oxford University Press, 1979.

————. *Atlantic America, 1492–1800.* Vol. 1 of *The Shaping of America: A Geographical Perspective on 500 Years of History.* New Haven, Conn.: Yale University Press, 1986.

————. *Continental America, 1800–1867.* Vol. 2 of *The Shaping of America: A Geographical Perspective on 500 Years of History.* New Haven, Conn.: Yale University Press, 1993.

Meints, Graydon. "Michigan Railroad Construction, 1835–1875." Ann Arbor: Transportation Library, University of Michigan, 1981. Typewritten.

————. *Michigan Railroads and Railroad Companies.* East Lansing: Michigan State University Press, 1992.

Melish, John. *A Statistical Account of the United States, with Topographical Tables of the Counties, Population, etc.* Philadelphia: G. Palmer, 1813.

————. *A Geographical Description of the United States, with the Contiguous British and Spanish Possessions.* Philadelphia: By the author, 1816.

————. *Information and Advice to Emigrants to the United States and from the Eastern to the Western States.* Philadelphia: By the author, 1819.

————. *The Traveller's Directory through the United States; Containing a Description of all the Principal Roads through the United States, with Copious Remarks on the Rivers and Other Objects.* New York: By the author, 1825.

Mellen, Grenville. *A Book of the United States, Exhibiting Its Geography, Divisions, Constitution, and Government . . . and Presenting a View of the Republic Generally, and of the Individual States . . . Together with a Condensed History of the Land . . . [and] a Description of the Principal Cities and Towns; with Statistical Tables.* Hartford, Conn.: H. Frederick Sumner, 1842.

Merrens, H. Roy. "Historical Geography and Early American History." *William and Mary Quarterly,* 3d ser., no. 22 (1965): 529–48.

————. "The Physical Environment of Early America: Image and Image Makers in Colonial South Carolina." *Geographical Review* 59 (1969): 530–56.

————. "Settlement of the Colonial Atlantic Seaboard." In *Pattern and Process: Research in Historical Geography,* edited by Ralph Ehrenberg, 235–43. Washington, D.C.: Howard University Press, 1975.

Merrill, Michael. "Cash Is Good to Eat: Self-Sufficiency and Exchange in the Rural Economy of the United States." *Radical History Review* 19 (1977): 42–71.

————. "So What's Wrong with the 'Household Mode of Production?'" *Radical History Review* 22 (1979–80): 141–46.

Merton, Robert. *Social Theory and Social Structure.* Glencoe, Calif.: Free Press, 1957.

Meyer, David R. "Emergence of the American Manufacturing Belt: An Interpretation." *Journal of Historical Geography* 9 (1983): 145–74.

Michigan. *Census of Michigan, 1854–1864.* Lansing: Various publishers, , 1854–64.

Michigan. *Statistics of the State of Michigan, Compiled from the Census of 1860.* Lansing, Mich.: John A. Kerr, 1861.

Michigan, *Acts of the Legislature, Acts* (MAL/L), 1837–1872. Detroit and Lansing, 1837–.

Michigan, *Acts of the Legislature, Resolutions* (MAL/R), 1837–1860. Detroit and Lansing, 1837–60.

Michigan, *Board of State Tax Commissioners.* "Michigan Railroad Appraisal, 1900, Plank Road and River Improvements," by Mortimer E. Cooley, 9:145–54. Michigan Historical Collection, 1900.

Michigan, *Cass Code* (MCC), 1816. MTL, 1:109–26. Lansing, Mich.: W. S. George, 1871.

Michigan, *Executive Acts* (MEA), 1815–22. MTL, 1:323–36. Lansing, Mich.: W. S. George, 1871.

Michigan, *Laws Compiled by the Legislative Board* (MLCLB), 1824. MTL, 1:233–79. Lansing, Mich.: W. S. George, 1871.

Michigan, Laws Compiled by the Legislative Council (MLCLC), 1825. MTL, 1:283–314. Lansing, Mich.: W. S. George, 1871.

Michigan, State Board of Agriculture (MSBA). *Second Annual Report of the Secretary of the State Board of Agriculture.* Lansing, Mich.: John A. Kerr, 1863.

———. *Twelfth Annual Report of the Secretary of State Board of Agriculture.* Lansing, Mich.: W. S. George, 1875.

Michigan, State Land Office. *Tract Books.* Michigan Historical Collection, 1818–40.

Michigan, Territorial Laws, 1805–35 (MTL). 4 vols. Lansing, Mich.: W. S. George, 1871–84.

Michigan Farmer. 1845–55

Michigan Railroad Commission. *Aids, Gifts, Grants, and Donations to Railroads, Including Outline of Development and Successions in Titles to Railroads in Michigan,* by Edmund A. Calkins. Lansing, Mich.: Wynkoop Hallenbeck Crawford Co., 1919.

Michigan State Agricultural Society. *Transactions of the Michigan State Agricultural Society for 1856.* Vol. 8. Lansing, Mich.: Hosmer and Kerr, 1857.

Michigan State Horticultural Society. *Seventeenth Annual Report of the State Horticultural Society of Michigan, 1887.* Lansing, Mich.: W. S. George, 1887.

Michigan Writers' Project. *Michigan: A Guide to the Wolverine State.* New York: Oxford University Press, 1941.

Mikesell, Marvin W. "Comparative Studies in Frontier History." In *Turner and the Sociology of the Frontier,* edited by Richard Hofstadter and Seymour Martin Lipset, 152–71. New York: Basic Books, 1968.

Millard, A. L. "Historical Sketch of Lenawee County." *Michigan Pioneer and Historical Collections* 1 (1877): 224–37.

Miller, Albert. "Pioneer Sketches." *Michigan Pioneer and Historical Collections* 7 (1886): 229–461.

———. "Incidents in the Early History of the Saginaw Valley." *Michigan Pioneer and Historical Collections* 13 (1888): 351–83.

Miller, Andrew. *New States and Territories, or the Ohio, Indiana, Illinois, Michigan, North-Western, Missouri, Louisiana, Mississippi and Alabama, in Their Real Characters, in 1818.* Keene, N.H.: By the author, 1819.

Miller, George J. "The Establishment of Michigan's Boundaries: A Study in Historical Geography." *American Geographical Society Bulletin* 43 (1911): 339–51.

———. "Some Geographic Influences in the Settlement of Michigan and in the Distribution of Its Population." *American Geographical Society Bulletin* 45 (1913): 321–48.

Mills, James Cooke. *Our Inland Seas: Their Shipping and Commerce for Three Centuries.* Chicago: A. C. McClurg, 1910. Reprint, Cleveland, Ohio: Freshwater Press, 1976.

Mitchell, Robert D. *Commercialism and Frontier: Perspectives on the Early Shenandoah Valley.* Charlottesville: University Press of Virginia, 1977.

———. "The Formation of Early American Culture Regions." In *European Settlement and Development in North America: Essays on Geographical Change in Honor and Memory of Andrew Hill Clark,* edited by James R. Gibson, 66–90. Toronto: University of Toronto Press, 1978.

Mitchell, Samuel Augustus. *Mitchell's Traveler's Guide through the United States, Containing the Principal Cities, Towns, &c. Alphabetically Arranged; Together with the Stage, Steam-Boat, Canal, and Railroad Routes, with the Distances in Miles from Place to Place.* Philadelphia: Thomas Cowperthwait, 1836.

———. *A General View of the United States; Comprising, also, a Description of Each Individual State and Territory in the Union.* Philadelphia: By the author, 1846.

Mitchell, William T. "History of St. Clair County." *Michigan Pioneer and Historical Collections* 6 (1883): 403–16.

Montfort, Margaret Mary. "Ethnic and Tribal Identity among the Saginaw Chippewa of Nineteenth Century Michigan." Master's thesis, Michigan State University, 1990.

Montgomery, Johnson. "Pioneer History of the Settlement of Eaton County." *Michigan Pioneer and Historical Collections* 22 (1893): 518–24.

Morgan, G. A. "Township of Pine Plains—A Historical Sketch." *Michigan Pioneer and Historical Collections* 3 (1881): 293–96.

Morley, Frederick, ed. *Michigan and Its Resources.* Lansing, Mich.: W. S. George, 1881.

Morrison, Samuel Eliot. *The European Discovery of America: The Northern Voyages, A.D. 500–1600.* New York: Oxford University Press, 1971.

Morse, Jedidiah. *The American Gazetteer, Exhibiting, in Alphabetical Order, a Much More Full and Accurate Account, than has been Given, of the State, Provinces, Counties, Cities, Towns, . . . of the American Continent.* Boston: S. Hall, 1797.

———. *American Universal Geography.* Boston: S. Hall, 1805.

Muller, Edward K. "Selective Urban Growth in the Middle Ohio Valley, 1800–1860." *Geographical Review* 66 (1976): 178–99.

Nash, Roderick. *Wilderness and the American Mind.* New Haven, Conn.: Yale University Press, 1967.

Neidhard, Karl. "Karl Neidhard's 'Reise nach Michigan.'" Translated by Frank X. Braun and edited by Robert Boneway Brown. *Michigan History* 35 (1951): 32–84.

Nelson, Lowry. *Rural Sociology.* New York: American Book Company, 1952.

Nettels, Curtis P. *The Emergence of a National Economy.* Vol. 2, *The Economic History of the United States.* New York: Holt, Rinehart and Winston, 1962.

Neumeyer, Elizabeth. "Michigan Indians Battle against Removal." *Michigan History* 55 (1971): 287–88.

Niedringhaus, Thomas E. *A Climatology of Michigan.* Ph.D diss., Michigan State University. Ann Arbor, Mich.: University Microfilms, 1966.

Niles, M. J. "Old Times in Clinton County." *Michigan Pioneer and Historical Collections* 14 (1889): 621–26.

Noble, S. B. "Thorough Draining," in Michigan State Agricultural Society, *Transactions of the Michigan State Agricultural Society for 1856,* 261–73. Lansing, Mich.: Hosmer and Kerr, 1857.

Norris, L. D. "History of Washtenaw County." *Michigan Pioneer and Historical Collections* 1 (1877): 327–33.

Norris, Thomas L. "Acculturation in a German Catholic Community." Master's thesis, Michigan State University, 1950.

North, Douglass C. *The Economic Growth of the United States, 1790–1860.* New York: W. W. Norton, 1966.

Northrup, Enos. "First Trip to Michigan." *Michigan Pioneer and Historical Collections* 5 (1884): 69–70.

Norton, John M. "A Picture of Memory—Settlement of Oakland County." *Michigan Pioneer and Historical Collections* 22 (1893): 404–8.

Norton, Thomas Elliot. *The Fur Trade in Colonial New York, 1686–1776.* Madison: University of Wisconsin Press, 1974.

Nowlin, William. *The Bark-Covered House, or Back in the Woods Again; Being a Graphic and Thrilling Description of Real Pioneer Life in the Wilderness of Michigan.* Detroit: By the author, 1876. Reprint, Chicago: R.R. Donnelley and Sons, 1937.

Noyes, John Humphrey. *History of American Socialisms.* Philadelphia: J. B. Lippincott, 1870. Reprint, New York: Hillary House Publishers, 1961.

Noyes, Thomas L. "Acculturation in a German Catholic Community." Master's thesis, Michigan State University, 1950.

Nutter, David Charles. "Malaria in Michigan." Master's thesis, Michigan State University, 1988.

Odle, Thomas D. "The American Grain Trade on the Great Lakes, 1825–1873." *Inland Seas* 7 (1951): 237–45; 8 (1952): 23–28, 99–104, 177–92, 248–54; 9 (1953): 52–58, 105–9, 162–68, 256–62.

Olmstead, Alan L. "The Mechanization of Reaping and Mowing in America." *Journal of Economic History* 35 (1975): 327–52.

O'Malley, Michael. *Keeping Watch: A History of American Time.* New York: Viking, 1990.

Ormsby, T., and J. Alvi. *Extending ArcView GIS: with Network Analyst, Spatial Analyst, and 3D Analyst.* Redlands, Calif.: Environmental Systems Research, 1999.

Osband, Melvin D. "My Recollections of Pioneers and Pioneer Life in Nankin." *Michigan Pioneer and Historical Collections* 14 (1889): 431–82.

Osborne, William S. *Caroline M. Kirkland.* New York: Twayne, 1972.

Owen, Robert Dale. *Brief Treatise on the Construction and Management of Plank Roads.* New Albany, N.Y.: Kent and Norman, 1850.

Parke, Hervey. "Reminiscences." *Michigan Pioneer and Historical Collections* 3 (1881): 572–90.

Parkins, Almon Ernest. *The Historical Geography of Detroit.* Lansing: Michigan Historical Commission, 1918.

Parks, Robert James. *Democracy's Railroads: Public Enterprise in Jacksonian Michigan.* Port Washington, N.Y.: Kennikat Press, 1972.

Parrington, Vernon Louis. *The Romantic Revolution in America, 1800–1860.* New York: Harcourt, Brace and Company, 1927.

Parry, J. H. *The Age of Reconnaissance.* New York: Mentor Books, 1963.

Partridge, Michael. *Farm Tools through the Ages.* Boston: Promontory Press, 1972.

Pasternak, Burton. *Introduction to Kinship and Social Organization.* Englewood Cliffs, N.J.: Prentice Hall, 1976.

Pawson, Eric. *Transport and Economy: The Turnpike Roads of Eighteenth-Century Britain.* London: Academic Press, 1977.

Paxon, Frederick L. "The Gateways of the Old Northwest." *Michigan Pioneer and Historical Collections* 38 (1912): 139–48.

Paynter, Robert W. *Models of Spatial Inequality: Settlement Patterns in Historical Archaeology.* New York: Academic Press, 1982.

———. "Surplus Flows between Frontiers and Homelands." In *The Archaeology of Frontiers and Boundaries,* edited by Stanton F. Green and Stephen M. Perlman, 163–211. Orlando, Fla.: Academic Press, 1985.

Peck, John Mason. *A New Guide for Emigrants to the West, Containing Sketches of Ohio, Indiana, Illinois, Missouri, Michigan, with the Territories of Wisconsin and Arkansas, and the Adjacent Parts.* Boston: Gould, Kendall and Lincoln, 1837.

Peet, Richard. "Von Thünen and the Dynamics of Agricultural Expansion." *Explorations in Economic History* 8 (1970–71): 181–201.

Perejda, Andrew D. "Sources and Dispersal of Michigan's Population." *Michigan History* 32 (1948): 355–66.

Perrine, W. H. "Notes on the Settlement of Townships in Calhoun County." *Michigan Pioneer and Historical Collections* 2 (1880): 208–62.

Pessen, Edward. *Jacksonian America: Society, Personality, and Politics.* Urbana: University of Illinois Press, 1985.

Peters, Bernard C. *Early American Impressions and Evaluations of the Landscape of Inner Michigan, with Emphasis on Kalamazoo County.* Ph.D diss., Michigan State University, 1962. Ann Arbor, Mich.: University Microfilms, 1969.

————. "Pioneer Evaluation of the Kalamazoo County Landscape." *Michigan Academician* 3 (1970): 15–25.

————. "Early Town-Site Speculation in Kalamazoo County." *Michigan History* 56 (1972): 201–15.

————. "Changing Ideas about the Use of Vegetation as an Indicator of Soil Quality: Example of New York and Michigan." *Journal of Geography* 72 (1973): 18–28.

————. "The Fever Period of Land Speculation in Kalamazoo County: 1835–1837." *Michigan Academician* 8 (1976): 287–301.

Peters, T. C. "Sheep, Wool, and Wool Depots," U.S. Commissioner of Patents, Report, 1849, Agriculture, 251–55. Washington, D.C.: Office of Printers to the Senate, 1850.

Peterson, Jacqueline. "Many Roads to Red River: Métis Genesis in the Great Lakes Region, 1680–1815." In *The New Peoples: Being and Becoming Métis in North America,* edited by Jacqueline Peterson and Jennifer S. H. Brown, 37–71. Winnipeg: University of Manitoba Press, 1985.

Peyser, Joseph L., ed. and trans. *Letters from New France: The Upper Country, 1686–1783.* Urbana: University of Illinois Press, 1992.

Pfeifer, Gottfried. "The Quality of Peasant Living in Central Europe." In *Man's Role in Changing the Face of the Earth,* edited by William L. Thomas Jr., 240–77. Chicago: University of Chicago Press, 1956.

Phelps, H. *Phelps' Traveller's Guide through the United States; Containing Upwards of Seven Hundred Railroad, Canal, and Stage and Steam-Boat Routes, Accompanied by a New Map of the United States.* New York: Ensigns and Thayer, 1848.

Phillips, Paul Chrisler. *The Fur Trade.* 2 vols. Norman: University of Oklahoma Press, 1961.

Pierce, Bessie Louise. *A History of Chicago.* Vol. 1, *The Beginning of a City, 1673–1848.* New York: Alfred A. Knopf, 1937.

Pierce, Henry B. *History of Calhoun County, Michigan.* Philadelphia: L. H. Everts, 1877.

Pieters, Aleida J. *A Dutch Settlement in Michigan.* Grand Rapids, Mich.: Reformed Press, 1923.

Pike, Agnes. Clinton County History, Interesting Reminiscences Read Before the DeWitt Grange. *Clinton County Republican,* 6 November 1902.

Pilcher, Elijah H. *Protestantism in Michigan: Being a Special History of the Methodist Episcopal Church.* Detroit: R.D.S. Tylor, 1878.

————. "Forty Years Ago." *Michigan Pioneer and Historical Collections* 5 (1884): 80–89.

Pilkington, Roger. "Canals: Inland Waterways outside Great Britain." In *A History of Technology,* vol. 4, *The Industrial Revolution, c. 1750–c. 1850,* edited by Charles Singer, E. J. Holmyard, A. R. Hall, and Trevor I. Williams, 548–62. New York: Oxford University Press, 1958.

"Pioneer History of the Settlement of Eaton County, Written by Early Settlers." *Michigan Pioneer and Historical Collections* 22 (1893): 502–26.

Pitzer, Donald E. "Collectivism, Community, and Commitment: America's Religious Communal Utopias from the Shakers to Jamestown," in *Utopias,* edited by Peter Alexander and Roger Gill, 119–35. LaSalle, Ill.: Open Court, 1984.

Poppleton, O. "Why Birmingham Was Not Located on the Jas. R. Cooper Farm." *Michigan Pioneer and Historical Collections* 18 (1891): 662–63.

————. "History of Fort Gratiot." *Michigan Pioneer and Historical Collections* 18: 667–72.

Porcher, F. A. *The History of the Santee Canal.* Charleston: South Carolina Historical Society, 1903.

Porter, Horace. "Railway Passenger Travel." *Scribner's Magazine* 4 (1888): 296–319.

Portrait and Biographical Album of Barry and Eaton Counties, Michigan. Chicago: Chapman Bros., 1891.

Portrait and Biographical Album of Branch County, Michigan. Chicago: Chapman Bros., 1888.

Portrait and Biographical Album of Genesee, Lapeer, and Tuscola Counties, Michigan. Chicago: Chapman Bros., 1892.

Portrait and Biographical Album of Hillsdale County, Michigan. Chicago: Chapman Bros., 1888.

Portrait and Biographical Album of Huron County, Michigan. Chicago: Chapman Bros., 1883.

Portrait and Biographical Album of Kalamazoo, Allegan, and Van Buren Counties, Michigan. Chicago: Chapman Bros., 1892.

Portrait and Biographical Album of Lenawee County, Michigan. Chicago: Chapman Bros., 1888.

Portrait and Biographical Album of Midland County, Michigan. Chicago: Chapman Bros., 1884.

Portrait and Biographical Album of Oakland County, Michigan. Chicago: Chapman Bros., 1891.

Portrait and Biographical Album of St. Joseph County, Michigan. Chicago: Chapman Bros., 1889.

Portrait and Biographical Album of Sanilac County, Michigan. Chicago: Chapman Bros., 1884.

Portrait and Biographical Album of Shiawassee and Clinton Counties, Michigan. Chicago: Chapman Bros., 1891.

Potter, Theodore E. "A Boy's Story of Pioneer Life in Michigan." *Michigan Pioneer and Historical Collections* 35 (1907): 393–412.

Pray, Carl E. "An Historic Michigan Road." *Michigan History* 11 (1927): 325–41.

Pred, Allen R. *Urban Growth and the Circulation of Information: The United States System of Cities, 1790–1840.* Cambridge, Mass.: Harvard University Press, 1973.

Prescott, J. R. V. *The Geography of Frontiers and Boundaries.* Chicago: Aldine, 1965.

Prescott, Samuel. "Early Settlers in the Town of Blackman." *Michigan Pioneer and Historical Collections* 7 (1886): 464.

Price, Edward T. "The Central Courthouse Square in the American County Seat." *Geographical Review* 58 (1968): 29–60.

Prucha, Francis Paul. *A Guide to the Military Posts of the United States, 1789–1895.* Madison: State Historical Society of Wisconsin, 1964.

————.*The Great Father: The United States Government and the American Indians.* 2 vols. Lincoln: University of Nebraska Press, 1984.

Puffer, Raymond LaBounty. "The Michigan Agricultural Frontier: Southeastern Region, 1820–1860." Ph.D. diss., University of New Mexico. Ann Arbor, Mich.: University Microfilms, 1976.

Quaife, Milo M. *The Kingdom of St. James.* New Haven, Conn.: Yale University Press, 1930.

————. *Lake Michigan.* Indianapolis: Bobbs-Merrill, 1944.

Quaintance, H. W. *The Influence of Farm Machinery on Production and Labor.* Publications of the American Economic Association, 3d ser., 5, no. 4. New York: Macmillan, 1904.

Queen, Stuart A., and Robert W. Habenstein. *The Family in Various Cultures*. Philadelphia: J. B. Lippincott, 1967.

Quinn, David Beers. *England and the Discovery of America, 1481–1620*. New York: Alfred A. Knopf, 1974.

Rae, John Bell. "Federal Land Grants in Aid of Canals." *Journal of Economic History* 4 (1944): 167–77.

Rasmussen, Wayne D. "Introduction to U.S. Land Policies, 1783–1840." In *Agriculture in the United States, a Documentary History*, edited by Wayne D. Rasmussen, 273–80. New York: Random House, 1975.

———, ed. *Agriculture in the United States: A Documentary History*. 2 vols. New York: Random House, 1975.

Rawick, George P. *From Sunup to Sundown: The Making of the Black Community*. Westport, Conn.: Greenwood Publishing Co., 1972.

Rees, Peter W. "Origins of Colonial Transportation in Mexico." *Geographical Review* 65 (1975): 323–34.

Reps, John W. *Town Planning in Frontier America*. Columbia: University of Missouri Press, 1980.

Richards, P. S. "Eighty Years in Michigan." *Michigan Pioneer and Historical Collections* 38 (1912): 365–69.

Rikoon, J. Sanford. *Threshing in the Midwest, 1820–1940: A Study of Traditional Culture and Technological Change*. Bloomington: Indiana University Press, 1988.

Riley, H. H. *Puddleford Papers, or, Humors of the West*. New York: Derby and Jackson, 1857.

Ringenberg, William Carey. "The Protestant College on the Michigan Frontier." Ph.D. diss., Michigan State University. Ann Arbor, Mich.: University Microfilms, 1970.

Ringwalt, J. L. *Development of Transportation Systems in the United States*. Philadelphia: By the author, 1888.

Robbins, Roy M. *Our Landed Heritage: The Public Domain, 1776–1970*. Lincoln: University of Nebraska Press, 1976.

Robertson, Ross M. *History of the American Economy*. New York: Harcourt, Brace & World, 1955.

Rogers, E. S. "Southeastern Ojibwa." In *Handbook of North American Indians*, vol. 15, *Northeast*, edited by Bruce G. Trigger, 760–71. Washington, D.C.: Smithsonian Institution, 1978.

Rohrbach, Peter J., and Lowell S. Newman. *American Issue: The U. S. Postage Stamp, 1842–1869*. Washington, D.C.: Smithsonian Institution Press, 1984.

Rohrbough, Malcolm J. *The Land Office Business: The Settlement and Administration of American Public Lands, 1789–1837*. New York: Oxford University Press, 1968.

Rorabaugh, W. J. *The Alcoholic Republic: An American Tradition*. New York: Oxford University Press, 1979.

Rosenblatt, Paul C. *Bitter, Bitter Tears: Nineteenth-Century Diarists and Twentieth-Century Grief Theories*. Minneapolis: University of Minnesota Press, 1983.

Rothenburg, WinifredB. "The Market and Massachusetts Farmers, 1750–1855." *Journal of Economic History* 41 (1981): 283–314.

————. "The Emergence of a Capitalist Market in Rural Massachusetts, 1730–1838." *Journal of Economic History* 45 (1985): 781–807.

Rothman, David. "A Note on the Study of the Colonial Family." *William and Mary Quarterly,* 3d ser., no. 23 (1966): 627–34.

Russell, Howard S. *A Long, Deep Furrow: Three Centuries of Farming in New England.* Hanover, N.H.: University Press of New England, 1976.

Russell, John Andrew. *The Germanic Influence in the Making of Michigan.* Detroit: University of Detroit Press, 1915.

Salamon, Sonya. "Ethnic Origin as Explanation for Local Land Ownership Patterns." *Research in Rural Sociology and Development* 1 (1984): 161–86.

————. "Ethnic Determinants of Farm Community Character." Paper presented at the Annual Meeting of the American Anthropological Association, Washington, D.C., 1985.

————. *Prairie Patrimony: Family, Farming, and Community in the Midwest.* Chapel Hill: University of North Carolina Press, 1992.

Saloutos, Theodore. "The Agricultural Problem and Nineteenth-Century Industrialism." *Agricultural History* 22 (1948): 156–74.

Santer, Richard Arthur. "A Historical Geography of Jackson, Michigan: A Study on the Changing Character of an American City 1829–1969." Ph.D. diss., Michigan State University. Ann Arbor, Mich.: University Microfilms, 1970.

————. *Michigan: Heart of the Great Lakes.* Dubuque, Iowa: Kendall/Hunt, 1977.

Sauer, Carl Ortwin. "Foreword to Historical Geography." In *Land and Life: A Selection from the Writings of Carl Ortwin Sauer,* edited by John Leighly, 351–79. Berkeley: University of California Press, 1963.

————. "The Morphology of Landscape." In *Land and Life: A Selection from the Writings of Carl Ortwin Sauer,* edited by John Leighly, 315–50. Berkeley: University of California Press, 1963.

Savage, William W., Jr., and Stephen I. Thompson. "The Comparative Study of the Frontier: An Introduction." In *The Frontier: Comparative Studies,* edited by William W. Savage Jr. and Stephen I. Thompson, 2:3–24. Norman: University of Oklahoma Press, 1979.

Scheiber, Harry N. *Ohio Canal Era: A Case Study of Government and the Economy, 1820–1861.* Athens: Ohio University Press, 1969.

Schenck, John S. *History of Ionia and Montcalm Counties, Michigan.* Philadelphia: D. W. Ensign, 1881.

Schlesinger, Arthur M., Jr. *The Age of Jackson.* Abridged. New York: Mentor Books, 1945.

Schoetzow, Mae R. *A Brief History of Cass County.* Marcellus, Mich.: Cass County Federation of Women's Clubs, 1935.

Schoolcraft, Henry R. *Narrative Journal of Travels from Detroit Northwest through the Great Chain of American Lakes to the Sources of the Mississippi River in the Year 1820.* Albany, N.Y.: E. and E. Hosford, 1821. Reprint, Ann Arbor, Mich.: University Microfilms, 1966.

————. "Natural History . . . Extracts . . . Taken from a Lecture Delivered before the Detroit Lyceum." In *Historical and Scientific Sketches of Michigan,* 177–91. Detroit: Stephen Well and George L. Whitney, 1834.

————. *History of the Indian Tribes of the United States: Their Present Condition and Prospects, and a Sketch of Their Ancient Status.* Philadelphia: J. B. Lippincott, 1857.

Scott, David. "Early History of Clinton County, Michigan." *Michigan Pioneer and Historical Collections* 17 (1890): 410–13.

Scott, James L. *Journal of a Missionary Tour through Pennsylvania, Ohio, Indiana, Illinois, Iowa, Wiskonsin, and Michigan.* Providence, R.I.: By the author, 1843. Reprint, Ann Arbor, Mich.: University Microfilms, 1966.

Sears, George W. "Michigan in 1845." *Michigan History* 15 (1931): 634–44.

Seeley, Dewey A. "The Climate of Michigan and Its Relation to Agriculture." Master's thesis, Michigan State College, 1917.

Segal, Harvey W. "Canals and Economic Development." In *Canals and American Economic Development,* edited by Carter Goodrich, 216–48. New York: Columbia University Press, 1961.

Sellers, Charles. *The Market Revolution: Jacksonian America, 1815–1846.* New York: Oxford University Press, 1991.

Sessions, J. Q. A. "Ann Arbor—A History of Its Early Settlement." *Michigan Pioneer and Historical Collections* 1 (1877): 333–39.

Sewell, Richard H. "Michigan Farmers and the Civil War." *Michigan History* 44 (1960): 353–74.

Seymour, C. B. "Early Days in Old Washtenaw County." *Michigan Pioneer and Historical Collections* 28 (1897–98): 391–99.

Shammas, Carole. "How Self-Sufficient Was Early America?" *Journal of Interdisciplinary History* 13 (1982): 247–72.

Shannon, Fred. *The Farmer's Last Frontier: Agriculture, 1860–1897.* Vol. 5, *The Economic History of the United States.* New York: Holt, Rinehart and Winston, 1945. Reprint, New York: Harper & Row, 1968.

Shaw, Ronald E. "The Canal Era in the Old Northwest." In *Transportation and the Early Nation,* 89–112. Indianapolis: Indiana Historical Society, 1982.

————. *Canals for a Nation: The Canal Era in the United States, 1790–1860.* Lexington: University of Kentucky Press, 1990.

Shearer, Jonathan. "Wheat in New York and Michigan." *Michigan Pioneer and Historical Collections* 4 (1883): 82–83.

Sheehan, Bernard W. *Seeds of Extinction: Jeffersonian Philanthropy and the American Indian.* New York: W. W. Norton, 1974.

————. "The Northwest Ordinance: An Annotated Text, Article the Third." In *The Northwest Ordinance, 1787: A Bicentennial Handbook,* edited by Robert M. Taylor Jr., 61–65. Indianapolis: Indiana Historical Society, 1987.

Sheldon, Mrs. E. M. "St. Clair River Settlement, Account Given to Mrs. E. M. Sheldon in 1852 by Mrs. Dr. H. Chamberlain of St. Clair." *Michigan Pioneer and Historical Collections* 4 (1883): 355–57.

Shirigian, John. "Lucius Lyon: His Place in Michigan History." Ph.D. diss., University of Michigan. Ann Arbor, Mich.: University Microfilms, 1969.

Shirreff, Patrick. *A Tour through North America; Together with a Comprehensive View of the Canadas and the United States, as Adapted for Agricultural Emigration.* Edinburgh: Oliver and Boyd, 1835.

Shoemaker, Michael. "Historical Sketch of the City of Jackson, Mich." *Michigan Pioneer and Historical Collections* 2 (1880): 272–97.

Shout, Mary E. "Reminiscences of the First Settlement at Owosso." *Michigan Pioneer and Historical Collections* 30 (1905): 344–52.

Sider, Gerald M. *Culture and Class in Anthropology and History: A Newfoundland Illustration.* Paris: Cambridge University Press, 1986.

Silliman, Sue I. "Overland to Michigan in 1846." *Michigan History* 5 (1921): 424–34.

Silverberg, Robert. *Mound Builders of Ancient America: The Archaeology of a Myth.* Greenwich, Conn.: New York Graphic Society, 1968.

Skjelver, Mabel Cooper. *Nineteenth-Century Homes of Marshall, Michigan.* Marshall, Mich.: Marshall Historical Society, 1971.

Sleeper-Smith, Susan. *Native Women and French Men: Rethinking Cultural Encounter in the Western Great Lakes.* Amherst: University of Massachusetts Press, forthcoming.

Slotkin, Richard. *The Fatal Environment: The Myth of the Frontier in the Age of Industrialization, 1800–1890.* New York: HarperCollins, 1985.

Smith, D. C., H. W. Borns, W. R. Baron, and A. E. Bridges. "Climatic Stress and Maine Agriculture, 1785–1885." In *Climate and History, Studies in Past Climates and Their Impact on Man,* edited by T. M. L. Wigley, M. J. Ingram, and G. Farmer, 450–64. Cambridge: Cambridge University Press, 1981.

Smith, Dwight L. "The Land Cession: A Valid Instrument of Transfer of Indian Title." In *This Land Is Ours: The Acquisition and Disposition of the Public Domain,* 87–102. Indianapolis: Indiana Historical Society, 1978.

Smith, Edwin D. "Pioneer Days in Kalamazoo and Van Buren." *Michigan Pioneer and Historical Collections* 14 (1889): 272–80.

Smith, Elisha H. *The History of Howell, Michigan.* Lansing, Mich.: John A. Kerr, 1868. Reprint, Howell, Mich.: Livingston County Historical Society, n.d.

Smith, Henry Nash. *Virgin Land: The American West as Symbol and Myth.* Cambridge, Mass.: Harvard University Press, 1950.

Smith, Page. *As a City upon a Hill: The Town in American History.* New York: Alfred A. Knopf, 1966.

Smith, Sidney. *The Settler's New Home: or the Emigrant's Location, Being a Guide to Emigrants in the Selection of a Settlement, and the Preliminary Details of the Voyage.* London: John Kendrick, 1849.

Smith, T. Lynn. *The Sociology of Rural Life.* New York: Harper and Brothers, 1940.

———. "Brazilian Land Surveys, Land Division, and Land Titles." *Rural Sociology* 9 (1944): 264–70.

Sommers, Lawrence M. "Economy." In *Atlas of Michigan,* edited by Lawrence M. Sommers, 135–70. East Lansing: Michigan State University Press, 1977.

————. *Michigan: A Geography.* Boulder, Colo.: Westview Press, 1984.

Stack, Robert Edward. "The McCleers and the Birneys—Irish Immigrant Families–Into Michigan and the California Gold Fields, 1820–1893." Ph.D. diss., St. Louis University. Ann Arbor, Mich.: University Microfilms, 1972.

Starr, Calvin H. "Some of the Beginnings of St. Joseph County." *Michigan Pioneer and Historical Collections* 18 (1891): 513–17.

Statutes at Large of the United States of America (*SLUS*), Washington, D.C.: Government Printing Office, 1937–.

Stebbins, C. B. "Story of Another Pioneer." *Michigan Pioneer and Historical Collections* 5 (1882): 125–37.

Steffen, Jerome O. "Insular vs. Cosmopolitan Frontiers: A Proposal for Comparative Frontier Studies." In *The American West, New Perspectives, New Dimensions,* edited and with an introduction by Jerome O. Steffen, 94–123. Norman: University of Oklahoma Press, 1979.

————.*Comparative Frontiers: A Proposal for Studying the American West.* Norman: University of Oklahoma Press, 1980.

Stevens, Sherman. "Sketch of Early Pioneer Life." *Michigan Pioneer and Historical Collections* 7 (1886): 93–98.

————. "Continuation of Early Days in Genesee County." *Michigan Pioneer and Historical Collections* 7 (1886): 394–98.

Stevens, Wayne E. "The Michigan Fur Trade." *Michigan History* 29 (1945): 489–505.

Stewart, Aura P. "Recollections of Aura P. Stewart, of St. Clair County, of Things Relating to the Early History of Michigan." *Michigan Pioneer and Historical Collections* 4 (1883): 324–54.

Stewart, Gordon. *The American Response to Canada since 1776.* East Lansing: Michigan State University Press, 1992.

Stewart, Mrs. E. M. S. "Early Settlement of Ann Arbor—Account Given to Mrs. E. M. S. Stewart in 1852 by Mr. Bethuel Farrand, who died in Ann Arbor, July 23, 1852." *Michigan Pioneer and Historical Collections* 6 (1883): 443–46.

————. "Sketch of the First Settlement of Pontiac, as Given by Mr. Orisson Allen to Mrs. E. M. Sheldon Stewart in 1850." *Michigan Pioneer and Historical Collections* 6 (1883): 384–86.

————. "Childhood's Recollections of Detroit." *Michigan Pioneer and Historical Collections* 18 (1891): 458–65.

Stilgenbauer, F. A. "The Michigan Sugar Beet Industry." *Economic Geography* 3 (1927): 486–506.

Stilgoe, John R. *Common Landscape of America, 1580 to 1845.* New Haven, Conn.: Yale University Press, 1982.

Stilwell, Lewis D. "Migration from Vermont, 1776–1860." *Proceedings of the Vermont Historical Society* 5 (1937): 63–245.

Stine, Linda France. "Social Differentiation Down on the Farm." In *Exploring Gender through Archaeology: Selected papers from the 1991 Boone Conference,* Monographs in World Archaeology, no. 11, edited by Cheryl Classen, 103–9. Madison, Wisc.: Prehistory Press, 1992.

St. Mary's Centennial: Westphalia, Michigan, 1836–1936. Westphalia, Mich.: n.p., 1936.

Stockton, John. "Account of the Early Settlement of Mt. Clemens, as Given to Mrs. E. M. Sheldon Stewart in 1850." *Michigan Pioneer and Historical Collections* 6 (1883): 357–59.

Storck, John, and Walter Dorwin Teague. *Flour for Man's Bread*. London: Oxford University Press, 1952.

Stouffer, Samuel A., A. E. Suchman, L. C. DeVinney, S. A. Star, and R. M. Williams Jr. *The American Soldier: Adjustment during Army Life*. Princeton, N.J.: Princeton University Press, 1949.

Stover, John F. *American Railroads*. Chicago: University of Chicago Press, 1961.

———. "Canals and Turnpikes: America's Early-Nineteenth-Century Transportation Network." In *An Emerging Independent American Economy, 1815–1875*, edited by Joseph R. Frese and Jacob Judd, 60–98. Tarrytown, N.Y.: Sleepy Hollow Press and Rockefeller Archive Center, 1980.

———. "Iron Roads in the Old Northwest: Railroads and the Growing Nation." In *Transportation in the Early Nation*, 135–56. Indianapolis: Indiana Historical Society, 1982.

Stowers, A. "Watermills, c. 1500–c. 1850." In *A History of Technology*, vol. 4, *The Industrial Revolution, c. 1750 to c. 1850*, edited by Charles Singer, E. J. Holmyard, A. R. Hall, and Trevor I. Williams, 199–213. New York: Oxford University Press, 1958.

Strickon, Arnold. "The Euro-American Ranching Complex." In *Man, Culture, and Animals, the Role of Animals in Human Ecological Adjustments*, edited by Anthony Leeds and Andrew P. Vayda, 229–58. American Association for the Advancement of Science, Publication 78. Washington, D.C., 1965.

Swan, Lansing B. *Journal of a Trip to Michigan in 1841*. Rochester, N.Y.: George P. Humphrey, 1904.

Sweet, William H. "Brief History of Saginaw County." *Michigan Pioneer and Historical Collections* 28 (1897–98): 481–501.

Sweet, William Warren. *The Story of Religion in America*. New York: Harper and Bros., 1930.

———. *Revivalism in America*. New York: Abingdon Press, 1944.

———. *Religion and the Development of American Culture, 1765–1840*. New York: Charles Scribner's Sons, 1952.

Sweezy, Paul M., and Harry Magdoff. "Capitalism and the Distribution of Income and Wealth." *Monthly Review* 39 (1987): 1–16.

Taaffe, E. J., R. L. Morrill, and P. R. Gould. "Transport Expansion in Underdeveloped Countries: A Comparative Analysis." *Geographical Review* 53 (1963): 503–29.

Taber, Morris C. "New England Influence in South Central Michigan." *Michigan History* 45 (1961): 305–36.

Tanner, H. S. *Memoir on the Recent Surveys, Observations, and Internal Improvements in the United States, with Brief Mention of the New Counties, Towns, Villages, Canals, and Railroads Never Before Delineated*. Philadelphia: By the author, 1829.

———. *The American Traveller: Or Guide through the United States*. Philadelphia: By the author, 1836.

Tanner, Helen Hornbeck. "The Location of Indian Tribes in Southeastern Michigan and Northern Ohio: 1700–1817." In *Indians in Northern Ohio and Southeastern Michigan*, compiled and edited by David Agee Horr, 317–75. New York: Garland Publishing, 1974.

———, ed., *Atlas of Great Lakes Indian History*. Norman: University of Oklahoma Press, 1987.

Taylor, Benjamin F. *Theophilus Trent, Old Times in the Oak Openings*. Chicago: S. C. Griggs, 1887.

Taylor, George. "First Visit to Michigan." *Michigan Pioneer and Historical Collections* 6 (1883): 15–17.

Taylor, George Rogers. *The Transportation Revolution, 1815–1860*. Vol. 4, *The Economic History of the United States*. New York: Rinehart, 1951.

Taylor, George Rogers, and Irene D. Neu. *The American Railroad Network, 1861–1890*. Cambridge, Mass.: Harvard University Press, 1956.

Taylor, K. W. "Some Aspects of Population History." *Canadian Journal of Economics and Political Sciences* 16 (1950): 301–13.

Temin, Peter. *The Jacksonian Economy*. New York: W. W. Norton, 1969.

Terpenning, Walter A. "Village and Open Country Communities in Michigan." *Michigan History* 16 (1932): 384–97.

Territorial Papers of the United States. Vols. 2–3, *The Territory Northwest of the Ohio River, 1787–1803*, (TPUS/NWT), compiled and edited by Clarence Edwin Carter. Washington, D.C.: Government Printing Office, 1934.

Territorial Papers of the United States. Vols. 10–12, *Territory of Michigan, 1805–1837*, (TPUS/MT), compiled and edited by Clarence Edwin Carter. Washington, D.C.: Government Printing Office, 1942–45.

Thayer Edwin. "Agriculture of Ottawa County." *Michigan Pioneer and Historical Collections* 9 (1886): 263.

Thayer, George W. "From Vermont to Lake Superior in 1845." *Michigan Pioneer and Historical Collections* 30 (1905): 549–66.

Thomann, G. *American Beer: Glimpses of Its History and Description of Its Manufacture*. New York: United States Brewers' Association, 1909.

Thomas, N. Gordon. "The Alphadelphia Experiment." *Michigan History* 55 (1971): 205–16.

———. *The Millennial Impulse in Michigan, 1830–1860: The Second Coming in the Third New England*. Lewiston, N.Y.: Edwin Mellen Press, 1989.

Thomas, N. M. "Reminiscences." *Michigan Pioneer and Historical Collections* 28 (1897–98): 533–36.

Thompson, O. C. "Observations and Experiences in Michigan Forty Years Ago." *Michigan Pioneer and Historical Collections* 1 (1877): 395–402.

Thompson, Stephen I. *San Juan Yapacani: A Japanese Pioneer Colony in Eastern Bolivia*. Ph.D diss., University of Illinois. Ann Arbor, Mich.: University Microfilms, 1970.

———. *Pioneer Colonization: A Cross-Cultural View*. Addison-Wesley Modules in Anthropology no. 33. Reading, Mass.: Addison Wesley, 1973.

Thompson, William. *A Tradesman's Travels in the United States and Canada, in the Years 1840, 41, and 42*. Edinburgh: Oliver and Boyd, 1842.

Thomson, E. H. "The City of Flint." *Michigan Pioneer and Historical Collections* 3 (1881): 431–63.

Thorne, Mildred. "A Population Study of an Iowa County in 1850." *Iowa Journal of History* 57 (1959): 305–30.

Tingley, Ralph R. "Postal Service in Michigan Territory." *Michigan History* 35 (1951): 447–60.

Torrey, George. "A Glimpse of Kalamazoo in 1846." *Michigan Pioneer and Historical Collections* 18 (1891): 589–92.

Tower, Prudence. "The Journey of Ionia's First Settlers." *Michigan Pioneer and Historical Collections* 28 (1897–98): 145–48.

Towne, Marvin W., and Wayne D. Rasmussen. "Gross Farm Product and Gross Investment in the Nineteenth Century." In *Trends in the American Economy in the Nineteenth Century*, vol. 24, *Studies in Income and Wealth*, 255–315. New York: National Bureau of Economic Research, 1960.

Towner, Julia Belle. "My Mother's Girlhood." *Michigan Pioneer and Historical Collections* 35 (1907): 180–83.

"Towns in Calhoun County." *Michigan Pioneer and Historical Collections* 2 (1880): 208–62.

Townsend, Goodenough. "Early History of the Township of Davison." *Michigan Pioneer and Historical Collections* 22 (1893): 542–55.

Transeau, Edgar Nelson. "The Prairie Peninsula." *Ecology* 16 (1935): 423–37.

Trap, Paul. "Foreign Railroads in Michigan, 1857–1893." *Journal of the Old Northwest* 13 (1986): 371–98.

———. "The Detroit and Pontiac Railroad." *Railroad History* 168 (1993): 17–50.

Trefethen, James B. "Wildlife Regulation and Restoration." In *Origins of American Conservation*, edited by Henry Clepper, 16–37. New York: Ronald Press, 1966.

Trigger, Bruce G. "The Determination of Settlement Patterns." In *Settlement Archaeology*, edited by K. C. Chang, 53–78. Palo Alto, Calif.: National Press, 1968.

Trowbridge, Charles C. "Detroit, Past and Present." *Michigan Pioneer and Historical Collections* 1 (1877): 371–85.

———. "Detroit in 1819." *Michigan Pioneer and Historical Collections* 4 (1883): 471–79.

True, Rodney H. "The Early Development of Agricultural Societies in the United States." *Annual Report of the American Historical Association for the Year 1920*, 293–306. Washington, D.C.: Government Printing Office, 1925.

Turner, Frederick Jackson. "The Significance of the Frontier in American History." *Annual Report of the American Historical Association for the Year 1893*, 199–227. Washington, D.C.: Government Printing Office, 1893.

———. *The Frontier in American History*. New York: Henry Holt, 1920.

Turner, Jesse. "Reminiscences of Kalamazoo." *Michigan Pioneer and Historical Collections* 18 (1891): 570–88.

Turner, T. G. *Gazetteer of the St. Joseph Valley, Michigan and Indiana*. Chicago: Hazlitt and Reed, 1867. Reprint, Grand Rapids, Mich.: Black Letter Press, 1978.

Turrell, Archie M. "Some Place Names of Hillsdale County," *Michigan History* 6 (1922): 573–82.

Tyler, Alice Felt. *Freedom's Ferment: Phases of American Social History from the Colonial Period to the Outbreak of the Civil War.* New York: Harper and Brothers, 1962.

U.S. Census Bureau. *State Censuses: An Annotated Bibliography of Censuses of Population Taken after the Year 1790 by States and Territories of the United States,* prepared by Henry J. Dubester. Washington, D.C.: Government Printing Office, 1948.

U.S. Census Office. *Agriculture of the United States, 1860.* Washington, D.C.: Various publishers, 1840–60.

———. *Manufactures of the United States, 1860: Compiled from the Original Returns of the Eighth Census.* Washington, D.C.: Government Printing Office, 1865.

———. *Population of the United States.* Washington, D.C.: Various publishers, 1800–60.

U.S. Commissioner of Patents. *Reports, Agriculture.* Washington, D.C.: Various publishers, 1837–60.

U.S. Department of Agriculture. *Report of the Commissioner of Agriculture for the Year 1871.* Washington, D.C.: Government Printing Office, 1872.

U.S. House of Representatives, Documents (HD). *Road—Detroit to Chicago.* 19th Cong., 1st sess. H. Doc. 68. Serial 134, 1826.

———. *Harbor at St. Joseph.* 24th Cong., 1st sess. H. Doc. 20. Serial 287, 1835.

———. *Annual Report, Commissioner, General Land Office.* 26th Cong., 2d sess. H. Doc. 38. Serial 383, 1841.

———. *Annual Report, Commissioner, General Land Office.* 27th Cong., 2d sess. H. Doc. 24. Serial 401, 1842.

———. *Public Lands in the States of Ohio, Indiana, Illinois, Missouri, Alabama, Mississippi, Michigan, Louisiana, and Arkansas.* 28th Cong., 1st sess. H. Doc. 210. Serial 443, 1844.

U.S. House of Representatives, Executive Documents (HED). *Commerce of the Lakes and Western Rivers.* 30th Cong., 1st sess. H. Exec. Doc. 19. Serial 516, 1848.

U.S. House of Representatives, Reports (HR). *Military Road in Michigan.* 19th Cong., 1st sess. H. Rept. 42. Serial 141, 1826.

———. *Ionia Land Office, Michigan.* 27th Cong, 2d sess. H. Rept. 512. Serial 408, 1842.

U.S. Senate, Executive Documents (SED). *Annual Report of the Commissioner of the General Land Office.* 31st Cong., 1st sess. S. Exec. Doc. 1, part 2. Serial 550, 1849.

———. *Report of the Secretary of War in Relation to the Commerce of the Great Lakes.* 31st Cong., 1st sess. E. Exec. Doc. 48. Serial 558, 1850.

U.S. Senate, Miscellaneous Documents (SMD). *Resolutions of the Legislature of Michigan in Relation to Moore and Hascall's Harvesting Machine.* 31st Cong., 1st sess. S. Misc. Doc. 6. Serial 563, 1849.

U.S. Senate, Reports (SR). *Report to Accompany S. 7, a Bill Relative to the Office of Surveyor General for the States of Ohio, Indiana, and Michigan.* 28th Cong., 1st sess. S. Rept. 49. Serial 432, 1844.

———. Report of the Select Committee on Transportation Routes to the Seaboard. 43d Cong., 1st sess., S. Rept. 307, 1874.

U.S. Senate, Resolutions (SRes). *Resolution to the Legislature of Michigan, in Relation to a Reduction in the Price of the Public Lands.* 25th Cong., 2d sess. S. Res. 160. Serial 316, 1838.

Utley, H. M. "Plymouth, the First Settlement—Reminiscences of the Early History of the Place—Incidents and Anecdotes." *Michigan Pioneer and Historical Collections* 1 (1877): 444–48.

Van Buren, A. D. P. "The Alphadelphia Association." *Michigan Pioneer and Historical Collections* 5 (1884): 406–12.

———. "The First Settlers in the Township of Battle Creek." *Michigan Pioneer and Historical Collections* 5 (1884): 272–93.

———. "Pioneer Annals: Containing the History of the Early Settlement of Battle Creek City and Township, with Vivid Sketches of Pioneer Life and Pen Portraits of the Early Settlers." *Michigan Pioneer and Historical Collections* 5 (1884): 237–59.

———. "First Settlement of Sturgis Prairie." *Michigan Pioneer and Historical Collections* 18 (1891): 518–21.

———. "Settlement of Branch County." *Michigan Pioneer and Historical Collections* 18 (1891): 608–12.

———. "Some Beginnings in Kalamazoo." *Michigan Pioneer and Historical Collections* 18 (1891): 605–8.

Van Hinte, Jacob. *Netherlanders in America: A Study of Emigration and Settlement in the Nineteenth and Twentieth Centuries in the United States of America*, translated by Adriaan de Wit. Grand Rapids, Mich.: Baker Book House, 1985.

Van Schelven, G. "Early History of Holland." *Michigan Pioneer and Historical Collections* 26 (1894–95): 569–79.

Van Slyck, DeWitt. "Cultivation of Peppermint." U.S. Commissioner of Patents, Report, 1849, Agriculture, 387–90. Washington, D.C.: Office of Printers to the Senate, 1850.

Van Vugt, William E. "Running from Ruin?" *Journal of Economic History* 48 (1988): 411–28.

Veatch, J. O. "The Dry Prairies of Michigan." *Papers of the Michigan Academy of Science, Arts, and Letters* 8 (1927): 269–78.

———. "Reconstruction of Forest Cover Based on Soil Maps." *Michigan Quarterly Bulletin* 10 (1928): 116–26.

———. *Agricultural Land Classification and Land Types in Michigan*. Agricultural Experiment Station. Special Bulletin no. 231. East Lansing: Michigan State College, 1933.

———. *Soils and Land of Michigan*. East Lansing, Mich.: Michigan State College Press, 1953.

Verlinden, Charles. *The Beginnings of Modern Colonialism: Eleven Essays with an Introduction*. Translated by Yvonne Freccero. Ithaca, N.Y.: Cornell University Press, 1970.

"A Visit with a Lady Who Knew Detroit as a Frontier Post." *Michigan Pioneer and Historical Collections* 14 (1889): 535–39.

von Gerstner, Franz Anton Ritter. *Die Innern Communicationen der Vereinigten Staaten von Nordamerica*, vol. 2. vienna: L. Förrster artistische Anstalt, 1843.

von Thünen, Johann Heinrich. *Isolated State: An English Translation of Der Isolierte Staat*. Translated by Carla M. Wertenberg, editing and introduction by Peter Hall. Oxford: Pergamon Press, 1966.

Wabeke, Bertus Harry. *Dutch Emigration to North America, 1624–1860: A Short History*. New York: Netherlands Information Bureau, 1944.

Wade, Richard C. *The Urban Frontier: Pioneer Life in Early Pittsburgh, Cincinnati, Lexington, Louisville, and St. Louis.* Chicago: University of Chicago Press, 1959.

Wait, S. E., and W. S. Anderson, comps. *Old Settlers: A Historical and Chronological Record, Together with Personal Experiences and Reminiscences of Members of the Old Settlers of the Grand Traverse Region.* Traverse City, Mich.: By the compilers, 1918. Reprint, Grand Rapids, Mich.: Black Letter Press, 1978.

Wallace, Anthony F. C. *The Death and Rebirth of the Seneca.* New York: Alfred A. Knopf, 1970

Wallerstein, Immanuel. *The Modern World System: Capitalist Agriculture and the Origins of the European World Economy in the Sixteenth Century.* New York: Academic Press, 1974.

————. *The Modern World System II: Mercantilism and the Consolidation of the European World Economy.* New York: Academic Press, 1980.

Ward, James A. *Railroads and the Character of America, 1820–1887.* Knoxville: University of Tennessee Press, 1986.

Warden, D. B. *Statistical, Political, and Historical Account of the United States of America; from the Period of Their First Colonization to the Present Day.* 3 vols. Edinburgh: Archibald Constable, 1819.

Warner, William W. "Early History of Michigan." *Michigan Pioneer and Historical Collections* 27 (1896): 289–304.

Washington, Booker T. *The Story of the Negro: The Rise of the Race from Slavery.* 2 vols. New York: Doubleday, Page, 1909. Reprint, New York: Peter Smith, 1940.

Watkins, L. D. "Settlement and Natural History of Manchester and Vicinity." *Michigan Pioneer and Historical Collections* 22 (1893): 262–66.

————. "Settlement of the Township of Bridgewater and Vicinity, Washtenaw County." *Michigan Pioneer and Historical Collections* 28 (1897–98): 568–69.

Webb, Walter Prescott. *The Great Frontier.* Boston: Houghton Mifflin, 1952.

Weigert, Hans W., Henry Brodie, Edward W. Doherty, John R. Fernstrom, Eric Fischer, and Dudley Kirk. *Principles of Political Geography.* New York: Appleton-Century-Croft, 1957.

Weissert, Charles A. "The Indians and the Trading Posts in the Northwest of Barry County, Michigan." *Michigan Pioneer and Historical Collections* 38 (1912): 654–72.

Weller, Charles E. *Yesterday: A Chronicle of Early Life in the West.* Indianapolis: Cornelius Printing Co., 1921.

Wentz, E. L. "Recollections of the Saginaw Valley Fifty-Two Years Ago." *Michigan Pioneer and Historical Collections* 17 (1890): 440–46.

The Western Traveller's Pocket Directory and Stranger's Guide; Exhibiting the Principal Distances on the Canal and Stage Routes in the States of New York and Ohio, in the Territory of Michigan, and the Province of Lower Canada, &c. Schenectady, N.Y.: S. S. Riggs, 1834.

Wheat, Renville. *Maps of Michigan and the Great Lakes, 1545–1845.* Detroit: Detroit Public Library, 1967.

Wheeler, James O., and Stanley D. Brunn. "An Agricultural Ghetto: Negroes in Cass County, Michigan, 1845–1968." *Geographical Review* 59 (1969): 317–29.

White, George H. "Yankee Lewis' Famous Hostelry in the Wilderness." *Michigan Pioneer and Historical Collections* 26 (1894–95): 302–7.

White, John H., Jr. *A History of the American Locomotive, Its Development: 1830–1880*. New York: Dover Publications, 1968.

———. "Tracks and Timber." *Industrial Archaeology* 2 (1976): 35–46.

———. *The American Railroad Freight Car: From the Wood Car Era to the Coming of Steel*. Baltimore: Johns Hopkins University Press, 1993.

White, Lynn, Jr. "The Historical Roots of Our Ecological Crisis." *Science* 155, no. 3767 (1967): 1203–7.

White, Richard. *The Middle Ground: Indians, Empires, and Republics in the Great Lakes Region, 1650–1815*. Cambridge: Cambridge University Press, 1991.

Whiteside, E. P., I. F. Schneider, and R. L. Cook. *Soils of Michigan*. Agricultural Experiment Station, Special Bulletin 402. East Lansing: Michigan State University, 1959.

Whiting, J. L. "Pioneer Sketch Relative to the Military Occupation of the Saginaw Valley, and Other Reminiscences." *Michigan Pioneer and Historical Collections* 2 (1880): 460–62.

Whitney, William A., and Richard I. Bonner. *History and Biographical Record of Lenawee County, Michigan*. Adrian, Mich.: W. Stearns, 1879–1880.

Widder, Keith R. "Mapping the Great Lakes: 1761 Balfour Expedition Maps." *Michigan History* 75 (May/June 1991): 24–31.

Willcox, Orlando B. *Shoepac Recollections: A Way-Side Glimpse of American Life*. New York: Bunce and Brother, Publishers, 1856.

Willey, Gordon R. *Prehistoric Settlement Patterns in the New World*. Smithsonian Institution, Bureau of American Ethnology, Bulletin no. 155. Washington, D.C.: Government Printing Office, 1956.

Willey, Gordon R., and Jeremy A. Sabloff. *A History of American Archaeology*. San Francisco: W. H. Freeman, 1974.

Williams, B. O. "First Settlement of Shiawassee County." *Michigan Pioneer and Historical Collections* 2 (1880): 475–88.

———. "Sketch of the Life of Oliver Williams and Family." *Michigan Pioneer and Historical Collections* 2 (1880): 36–40.

Williams, Ephraim S. "Detroit Three Score Years Ago." *Michigan Pioneer and Historical Collections* 10 (1886): 84–87.

———. "Flint Twenty Years Ago." *Michigan Pioneer and Historical Collections* 10 (1886):121–24.

———. "Incidents of Early Days in Michigan." *Michigan Pioneer and Historical Collections* 9 (1886): 166–72.

———. "Indians and an Indian Trail—a Trip from Pontiac to Grand Blanc and the Saginaws." *Michigan Pioneer and Historical Collections* 10 (1886): 136–42.

———. "Personal Reminiscences." *Michigan Pioneer and Historical Collections* 8 (1886): 233–59.

———. "A Trip on April Fool's Day," *Michigan Pioneer and Historical Collections* 14 (1889): 539–41.

Williams, I., F. W. Limp, and F. L. Briuer. "Using Geographic Information Systems and Exploratory Data Analysis for Archaeological Site Classification and Analysis." In

Interpreting Space: GIS and Archaeology, edited by K. M. S. Allen, S. W. Green, and E. B. W. Zubrow, 239–73. New York: Taylor and Francis, 1990.

Williams, J. R. "Internal Commerce of the West: Its Condition and Wants, as Illustrated by the Commerce of Michigan." *Merchants' Magazine and Commercial Review* 19 (1848): 19–40.

Williams, Jeremiah D. "History of the Town of Webster." *Michigan Pioneer and Historical Collections* 13 (1888): 546–67.

Williams, Stephen. *Fantastic Archaeology: The Wild Side of American Prehistory.* Philadelphia: University of Pennsylvania Press, 1991.

Williams, Wellington. *Appleton's Railroad and Steamboat Companion, being a Travellers' Guide through New England and the Middle States, with Routes in the Southern and Western States, and also in Canada.* New York: D. Appleton, 1847.

Williams, Wolcott B. *A History of Olivet College, 1844–1900.* Olivet, Mich.: [Olivet College], 1901.

Wing, Talcott E. "Continuation of the History of Monroe." *Michigan Pioneer and Historical Collections* 6 (1883): 318–24.

Winsberg, Morton D. "The Advance of Florida's Frontier as Determined from Post Office Openings," *Florida Historical Quarterly* 72 (1993): 189–99.

Winslow, Damon A. "Early History of Berrien County." *Michigan Pioneer and Historical Collections* 1 (1877): 120–25.

Withey, Mrs. S. L. [Marion Louise Hinsdill]. "Personal Recollections and Incidents of the Early Days of Richland and Grand Rapids." *Michigan Pioneer and Historical Collections* 5 (1884): 434–39.

———. "Personal Recollections of Early Days in Kent County." *Michigan Pioneer and Historical Collections* 39 (1915): 345–52.

Wittke, Carl. *A History of Canada.* New York: F. S. Crofts, 1941.

———. "Ora et Labora: A German Methodist Utopia." *Ohio Historical Quarterly* 67 (1958): 129–40.

Wolf, Eric R. *Europe and the People without History.* Berkeley: University of California Press, 1982.

Wood, Jerome James. *The Wilderness and the Rose: A Story of Michigan.* Hudson, Mich.: Wood Book Co., 1890.

Woodard, S. C. "Reminiscences of the Early Itinerancy." *Michigan Pioneer and Historical Collections* 14 (1889): 553–60.

Woodson, Carter G. *A Century of Negro Migration.* Washington, D.C.: Association for the Study of Negro Life and History, 1918.

Wyman, Walker D., and Clifton Kroeber, eds. *The Frontier in Perspective.* Madison: University of Wisconsin Press, 1957.

Zehnder, Herman F. *Teach My People the Truth! The Story of Frankenmuth, Michigan.* Bay City, Mich.: By the author, 1970.

Zimiles, Martha, and Murray Zimiles. *Early American Mills.* New York: Bramhall House, 1973.

Zimmerman, Albright G. "Iron for American Railroads." *Canal History and Technology Proceedings* 5 (1986): 63–108.

Zug, Samuel. "Detroit in 1815–16." *Michigan Pioneer and Historical Collections* 1 (1877): 496–501.

NEWSPAPERS

Acorn (Three Oaks), 1900–1930.

Adrian Daily Times and Expositor, 1877–88.

Bay City Times, 1971

Calhoun County Patriot (Marshall), 1838–40.

Clinton County Republican (St. Johns), 1881–1924.

Clinton Independent (St. Johns), 1883–1903.

Democratic Expounder and Calhoun County Democrat (Marshall), 1841–42.

Democratic Free Press (Detroit), 1832–40.

Democratic Free Press and Michigan Intelligencer (Detroit), 1831–32.

Detroit Courier, 1830–34.

Detroit Free Press, 1837–91.

Detroit Gazette, 1817–30.

Detroit Journal and Michigan Advertiser, 1830–33.

Elsie Sun, 1885–87.

Emigrant (Ann Arbor), 1831–32.

Florida Star (Titusville, Fla.), 1885.

Grand Ledge Independent, 1874–1980.

Grand River Times (Grand Rapids and Grand Haven), 1837, 1851–56.

Hudson Gazette, 1874.

Jackson Michigan State Gazette, 1840–41.

Jackson Sentinel, 1839–40.

Jeffersonian, and Oakland, Lapeer, and Shiawassee Advertiser (Pontiac), 1839–41.

Jonesville Expositor, 1840–43.

Kalamazoo Gazette, 1837–43.

Kalamazoo Telegraph, 1849.

Lake Huron Observer (Port Huron), 1844–45.

Livingston Courier (Brighton and Howell), 1843–46.

Livingston Republican (Howell), 1873–83.

Macomb Statesman (Mt. Clemens), 1837.

Marshall Statesman, 1878.

Michigan Emigrant (Ann Arbor), 1832–34.

Michigan Sentinel (Monroe), 1825–36.

Michigan Statesman (Kalamazoo), 1835–36.

Michigan Statesman and St. Joseph Chronicle (White Pigeon), 1834–35.

Michigan Telegraph (Kalamazoo), 1845–49.

Michigan Whig (Ann Arbor), 1834–35.

Monroe Advocate, 1841–45.

Monroe Gazette, 1837–41.

Monroe Times, 1836–37.

Niles Daily Star, 1887–90.

Niles Gazette and Advertiser, 1835–37.

North Star (Saginaw), 1843–48.

Oakland Chronicle (Pontiac), 1830–31.

Owosso Weekly Press, 1862–99.

Semi-Weekly Free Press (Detroit), 1837–39.

St. Johns News, 1900.

Tecumseh Herald, 1850–98.

Tecumseh News, 1884.

Three Oaks Press, 1891–1900.

Traverse City Herald, 1874.

Tri-State Trader (Knightstown, Ind.), 1979.

Weekly Recorder (Chillicothe, Ohio), 1814–21.

Western Emigrant (Ann Arbor), 1829–30.

Western Statesman (Marshall), 1839–45.

MAPS

Allen, S. "Plat and Field Notes of the Territorial Road Laid Out and Surveyed from Port Lawrence in the County of Monroe through Blissfield and Logan and through the Village of Adrian in the County of Lenawee to the Chicago Road." Ms. map 38 x 32 cm., no scale, 1828. SAM.

———. "Plat and Field Notes of a Territorial Road Laid Out and Established from Vistula in the County of Monroe via the Forks of Ottawa Creek in the Townships Nine South to the Line of Indiana." Ms. map 20 x 185 cm., scale 1:63,360, 1833. SAM.

Barritt, Hiram. "Plat and Field Notes on a Road from Farmington to Byron." Ms. map 20 x 30 cm., scale 1:126,720, 1838. SAM.

Burr, David H. *Map of Michigan and Part of Wisconsin Territory, Exhibiting the Post Offices, Post Roads, Canals, and Railroads, &c.* Col. map 94 x 63 cm., scale 1:635,000. Washington, D. C.: John Arrowsmith, 1839.

Calkin, Ephraim. "Plat and Field Notes of a Survey of a Territorial Road from Rochester to the County Seat of Lapeer." Ms. map 38 x 32 cm., no scale, 1832. SAM.

Carey & Lea. *Michigan Territory, Geographical, Statistical, and Historical Map of Michigan Territory.* Col. map 57 x 45 cm., scale 1:1,900,800. Philadelphia: Carey & Lea, 1822.

Clark, David. "A Traverse and Survey of a State Road Commencing on a State Road Leading from Jonesville in Hillsdale County to Marshall in Calhoun County." Ms. map 55 x 32 cm., no scale, 1839–1840. SAM.

Cook, Joseph B. "Territorial Road in Calhoun, Kalamazoo, and Van Buren Counties." Ms. Map 64 x 20 cm., scale 1:65,000, 1835. SAM.

Delamatter, A. H. "Plat of a Road Commencing at the Junction of the La Plaisance Bay Road and the Chicago Turnpike and Terminating at the Village of Marshall in Calhoun County." Ms. map 91 x 41 cm., scale 1:79,200, 1836. SAM.

"Detroit to Clinton River in Wayne and Macomb Counties." Ms. map on 2 sheets, 68 x 33 cm., scale 1:2,640, 1828. SAM.

Durand, John T. "Washtenaw Territorial Road from Jacksonburgh West to St. Joseph River and Beyond to Intersection of Chicago Road on White Pigeon Prairie, Plat and Field Notes." Ms. map 192 x 25 cm., no scale, 1834. SAM.

Farmer, John. *Map of the Surveyed Part of the Territory of Michigan.* Col. map 49 x 54 cm., scale 1:506,880. Utica, NY: V. Balch & S. Stiles, 1826.

———. "Plat and Field Notes of a Territorial Road from Monroe to Detroit." Ms. map 37 x 217 cm., var. scales, 1828. SAM.

———. *Map of the Surveyed Part of the Territory of Michigan.* Col. map 53 x 78 cm., scale 1:500,000. Utica, NY: V. Balch & S. Stiles, 1830.

———. *An Improved Map of the Surveyed Part of the Territory of Michigan.* Col. map 56 x 80 cm., scale 1:506,880. New York: V. Balch & S. Stiles, 1831.

———. *An Improved Edition of a Map of the Surveyed Part of the Territory of Michigan.* Col. map 53 x 78 cm., scale 1:500,000. New York: J. H. Colton, 1836.

———. *Map of the Surveyed Part of Michigan.* Col. map 53 x 78 cm., scale 1:500,000. New York: J. H. Colton, 1840.

———. *Map of the State of Michigan and the Surrounding Country, Exhibiting the Sections and the Latest Surveys.* Col. map 82 x 61 cm., scale 1:800,000. Detroit: John Farmer, 1844.

———. *Map of the Surveyed Part of Michigan.* Col. Map 71 x 96 cm., scale indeterminable. New York: J. H. Colton, 1855.

Farmer, John, J. H. Colton, and Joseph Hutchins. *Colton's Sectional Map of Michigan.* Col map 59 x 84 cm., scale 1:500,000. New York: J. H. Colton, 1865.

Farnsworth, John. "Dexter and Grand River State Road in Washtenaw, Livingston, and Ingham Counties." Ms. map on 2 sheets, 20 x 91 cm., scale 1:33,000, 1837. SAM.

———. "A Plat of a Part of State Road from Dexter Village in the County of Washtenaw to the Mouth of the Maple River in the County of Ionia at the Village of Lyon." Ms. map 31 x 144 cm., scale 1:19,800, 1837. SAM.

Gibson, Edmond O. *Indian Sites in Kent County Michigan.* Map 85 x 50 cm., scale 1:97,477. Grand Rapids, Mich.: By the author, 1956.

Hathon, A. E. "Dearbornville to Flat Rock Highway." Ms. map 43 x 22 cm., scale 1:63,360, 1835. SAM.

Houghton, Douglass. *Map of Calhoun County.* Col. map 62 x 47 cm., scale 1:126,720. Washington, D. C.: W. J. Stone, [1842].

————. *Map of Jackson County.* Col. map 64 x 53 cm., scale 1:126,720. Washington, D, C.: W. J. Stone, [1842].

————. *Map of Lenawee County.* Col. map 48 x 53 cm., scale 1:126,720. Washington, D. C.: W. J. Stone, [1842].

————. *Map of Washtenaw County.* Col. map 53 x 63 cm., scale 1:126,720. Washington, D. C.: W. J. Stone, [1842].

————. *Map of Wayne County.* Col. map 51 x 47 cm., scale 1:126,720. Cincinnati: Doolittle & Munson, [1842].

Hubbard, Bela. *The Western Counties of Michigan.* Map 71 x 84 cm., scale 1:253,440. New York: Miller's Lith., 1846.

Hubble, Nathan. "Monroe to Ypsilanti, Plat and Field Notes." Ms. map on 2 sheets, 32 x 22 cm. and 32 x 38 cm., no scale, 1829. SAM.

Judd, Philu E. *Map of Michigan with Part of the Adjoining States.* Col. map 53 x 78 cm., scale 1:732,600. Detroit: Philu Judd, 1825.

Keith, M. C. "Plat and Field Notes of State Road from Galien in St. Joseph County to Kalamazoo in Kalamazoo County." Ms. map 33 x 41 cm., no scale, 1837. SAM.

Kry, Anthony M. "Plat and Field Notes of Re-Survey of the Territorial Road Leading from Vistula to the Line of the State of Indiana." Ms. map 23 x 177 cm., scale 1:63,360, 1834. SAM.

Marrs, Samuel. "Plat and Field Notes of a Territorial Road Laid Out from the Village of Niles in the County of Berrien, M. T. to the Mouth of the Gallien River in Said County." Ms. map 18 x 72 cm., scale 1:6,600, 1834. SAM.

Meachum, John. "Battle Creek and Hastings State Road in Calhoun and Barry Counties." Ms. map on 3 sheets, 43 x 33 cm., scale 1:31,380, 1838. SAM.

"Michigan Map with Census Figures for 1840, 1845, and 1850." Ms. col. map 178 x 178 cm., no scale, n.d. SAM.

Nathon, L. E. "Territorial Road from Point du Chene to Fort Gratiot Turnpike." Ms. map 34 x 84 cm., scale 1:31,680, 1834. SAM.

Pond, James. "Plat and Field Notes of a State Road from the County Seat of Calhoun County to the County Seat of Branch and thence Southerly in the Direction of Fort Wayne to the Indiana State Line." Ms. map 20 x 88 cm., scale 1:79,200, 1837. SAM.

————. "Plat and Field Notes of State Road Laid Out and Established from the County Seat of Branch County Eastwardly, Intersecting the Chicago Road at or Near the Eastern Extremity of Coldwater Prairie." Ms. map 19 x 30 cm., scale 1:63,360, 1839. SAM.

Risdon, Orange. "Plat and Field Notes of a Road Leading from Monroe, in the County of Monroe, Up the Saline River by the Salt Springs, the Village of Dexter, the Portage of Grand and Huron Rivers, to the Principal Meridian." Ms. col. map 25 x 201 cm., no scale, 1828. SAM.

———. "Plat and Field Notes of a Territorial Road, Leading from Pontiac in the County of Oakland to Adrian in the County of Lenawee." Ms. col. map 25 x 182 cm., no scale, 1828. SAM.

"Saginaw County, T 10, 11, 12, 13N; R1, 2, 3, 4, 5, 6E." Ms. map 48 x 51 cm., scale 1:26,720, [1840]. SAM.

Saxton, Jehiel. "Adamsville to Cassopolis State Road in Cass County." Ms. map 40 x 32 cm., scale 1:38,016, 1838. SAM.

Smith, J. Calvin. *Guide through Ohio, Michigan, Indiana, Illinois, Missouri, & Iowa.* Col. map 57 x 68 cm., scale 1:1,584,000. New York: J. H. Colton, 1840.

Southard, John. "Plat and Field Notes of a Territorial Road from the Village of Pontiac West to the Grand River Road Near the Site of Livingston County." Ms. map 16 x 10 cm., no scale, 1834. SAM.

Sowle, Lemuel. "Plat and Field Notes of State Road and Adjacent Country from Indian State Line to the Prairie, Terminating Easterly from the Village of Coldwater in Branch County, Michigan." Ms. map 32 x 20 cm., no scale, 1837. SAM.

Stratton, J. F. "Territorial Road from Wayne County, 2 1/2 Miles from Detroit on the Chicago Road, to Mouth of St. Joseph River, Map and Field Notes." Ms. map 20 x 36 cm., scale 1:23,760, 1830. SAM.

Tanner, H. S. *A New Map of Michigan, with Its Canals, Roads, & Distances.* Col. map 51 x 38 cm., scale 1:1,900,800. Philadelphia: H. S. Tanner, 1836.

Tillotson, Ira. "Plat of a State Road from Marshall to the County Seat of Barry." Ms. Map 34 x 110 cm., scale 1:15,840, 1837. SAM.

Tompkins, James B. "Map of a Road from Union City to Battle Creek, Being a Continuation of a State Road from Coldwater Village." Ms. map on 2 sheets, 54 x 22 cm., scale 1:31,680, 1836. SAM.

———. "Survey of a State Road from Coldwater Village, Branch County, to Battle Creek Village, Calhoun County." Ms. map 54 x 42 cm., scale 1:31,680, 1836. SAM.

Trygg, J. W. M. *Composite Map of United States Land Surveyors' Original Plats and Field Notes, Michigan Series.* Col. map on 13 sheets, 56 x 43 cm., scale 1:253,440. Ely, Minn.: By the author, 1964.

"Van Buren County, T1, 2, 3, 4, 5S; R13, 14, 15, 16, 17W." Ms. map 55 x 40 cm., scale 1:126,720, [1840]. SAM.

Veatch, J. O. *Presettlement Forest in Michigan.* Map on 2 sheets, 79 x 55 cm. and 56 x 79 cm., scale 1:500,000. East Lansing: Department of Resource Development, Michigan State University, 1959.

Webster, Calvin P. "Territorial Road in Oakland and Wayne Counties." Ms. map on 2 sheets, 102 x 37 cm., scale 1:63,360, 1828. SAM.

Willmuth, Hiram. "Dearborn to Lyndon Highway." Ms. map on 4 sheets, 19 x 30 cm., no scale, 1831. SAM.

Woolman, John. "Plat and Field Notes of the Territorial Road Commencing in the Line Between Section No. 19 & 30 in Township 6 South of Range Number 6 West, and in the Center of the Seat of the County of Branch, . . . to the East End of Broadway Street at the

Town of St. Joseph at the Mouth of the St. Joseph." Ms. map 39 x 63 cm., scale 1:198,000, 1834. SAM.

Young, J. H. *Map of Ohio and the Settled Parts of Michigan, 1830.* Col. map 47 x 33 cm., scale 1:267,200. Philadelphia: A. Finley, 1833.

Index